Wow! 1001 Homemade Mushroom Recipes

(Wow! 1001 Homemade Mushroom Recipes - Volume 1)

Mary Grace

Copyright: Published in the United States by Mary Grace/ © MARY GRACE

Published on October, 13 2020

All rights reserved. No part of this publication may be reproduced, stored in retrieval system, copied in any form or by any means, electronic, mechanical, photocopying, recording or otherwise transmitted without written permission from the publisher. Please do not participate in or encourage piracy of this material in any way. You must not circulate this book in any format. MARY GRACE does not control or direct users' actions and is not responsible for the information or content shared, harm and/or actions of the book readers.

In accordance with the U.S. Copyright Act of 1976, the scanning, uploading and electronic sharing of any part of this book without the permission of the publisher constitute unlawful piracy and theft of the author's intellectual property. If you would like to use material from the book (other than just simply for reviewing the book), prior permission must be obtained by contacting the author at author@pennsylvaniarecipes.com

Thank you for your support of the author's rights.

Content

CHAPTER 1: OYSTER MUSHROOM RECIPES 16

1. Asian Chicken And Corn Soup 16
2. Cream Of Wild Mushroom Soup 16
3. Creamy Coconut Carbonara (Without Milk!) 17
4. Fried Polenta Squares With Creamy Mushroom Ragu 18
5. Marty's Ginger Pad Thai 18
6. Oyster Mushroom Pasta 19
7. Pesto And Prawn Lasagna 20
8. Pork With Apples And Mushrooms 21
9. Slow Cooker 5 Mushroom Barley Soup 21
10. South Dakota Wild Mushroom Dip 22
11. Spinach And Red Chard Quiche 22
12. Sundubu Jjigae (Uncurdled Tofu Stew) 23
13. Trio Of Mushroom Soup (Cream Of Mushroom Soup) 24
14. Warm Mushroom Salad 24

CHAPTER 2: MUSHROOM SANDWICH RECIPES 25

15. Asian Burgers 25
16. Bacon Avocado Quesadillas 25
17. Bacon Blue Cheese Stuffed Burgers 26
18. Bacon Blue Cheese Stuffed Burgers For Two 26
19. Barbecued Mushroom Turkey Burgers 27
20. Beef Stroganoff Melt 28
21. Beef Stroganoff Sandwiches 28
22. Blues Burgers 29
23. Burgers Cacciatore 29
24. Cheesy Chicken Subs 30
25. Chicken Cheddar Wraps 30
26. Chicken Veggie Pockets 31
27. Chili Beef Quesadillas 31
28. Contest Winning Grilled Roast Beef Sandwiches 32
29. Creamy Eggplant & Mushroom Monte Cristo 32
30. Eggplant Muffuletta 33
31. Eggplant Portobello Sandwich Loaf 34
32. English Muffin Egg Sandwiches 34
33. Feta Mushroom Burgers 35
34. Freezer Veggie Burgers 35
35. Fresh Veggie Pockets 36
36. Garlic Roast Beef Sandwiches 36
37. Green Onion Burgers 37
38. Grilled Beef Tenderloin Sandwiches 37
39. Grilled Blue Cheese Sandwiches 38
40. Grilled Burgers With Horseradish Sauce .. 39
41. Grilled Cheese Supreme 39
42. Grilled Deli Sandwiches 40
43. Grilled Havarti & Mushrooms 40
44. Grilled Italian Turkey Burgers 41
45. Grilled Portobello Burgers 41
46. Grilled Portobello Sandwiches 42
47. Grilled Steak And Portobello Stacks 42
48. Grilled Veggie Wraps 43
49. Ham & Cheese Sandwich Loaf 44
50. Hearty Sausage Stromboli 44
51. Italian Chicken Pockets 45
52. Italian Meat Stromboli 45
53. MLT 46
54. Mahogany Glazed Mushroom Burgers 47
55. Makeover Philly Steak And Cheese Stromboli 47
56. Meatless Calzones 48
57. Mediterranean Salad Sandwiches 48
58. Mini Chicken Salad Croissants 49
59. Molasses Steak Sandwiches 50
60. Moo Shu Mushroom Wraps 50
61. Mushroom & Swiss Turkey Burgers 51
62. Mushroom Burger Stromboli 51
63. Mushroom Burgers 52
64. Mushroom Cheese Stromboli 53
65. Mushroom Pastrami Hoagies 53
66. Mushroom Pear Melts 54
67. Mushroom Pizza Burgers 54
68. Mushroom Swiss Burgers 55
69. Mushroom Stuffed Cheeseburgers 55
70. My Favorite Burger 56
71. My Favorite Burger For 2 56
72. Open Faced Chicken Sandwiches 57
73. Open Faced Mushroom Crostini 57
74. Open Faced Portobello Sandwiches 58
75. Paul Bunyan Burgers 58
76. Pepperoni Pizza Burgers 59
77. Philly Cheese Fakes 59

78. Pizza Joes 60
79. Pizza Wraps 60
80. Portobello Burgers 61
81. Portobello Burgers With Pear Walnut Mayonnaise 61
82. Portobello Melts 62
83. Portobello Mushroom Burgers 63
84. Portobello Pizza Burgers 63
85. Portobello Pockets 64
86. Portobello Roast Beef Hoagies 64
87. Roasted Veggie Wraps 65
88. Saucy Portobello Pitas 65
89. Sausage 'n' Spinach Pockets 66
90. Sausage Cheese Snacks 67
91. Sausage Egg Subs 67
92. Smoked Gouda Veggie Melt 67
93. Spinach Egg Croissants 68
94. Spinach Meatball Subs 68
95. Spinach Mushroom Beef Patties 69
96. Steak House Burgers 69
97. Stuffed Barbecue Burgers 70
98. Stuffed Burgers On Portobellos 71
99. Stuffed Pizza Burgers 71
100. Stuffed Pork Burgers 72
101. Supreme Pizza Burgers 72
102. Switchman Sandwiches 73
103. Teriyaki Veggie Wraps 73
104. Texas Sized Beef Sandwiches 74
105. Triple Pepper Steak Sandwiches 74
106. Turkey Burgers With Blueberry BBQ Sauce 75
107. Turkey Divan Croissants 76
108. Turkey Florentine Sandwiches 76
109. Turkey Sandwich 77
110. Vegetarian Calzones 77
111. Vegetarian Reubens 78
112. Veggie Bean Burgers 78
113. Veggie Brown Rice Wraps 79
114. Veggie Cheese Sandwiches 80
115. Veggie Delights 80
116. Veggie Tuna Melts 81
117. Wild Rice Burgers 81
118. Zucchini Pizza Loaves 82

CHAPTER 3: MUSHROOM SOUP RECIPES 82

119. "Bring An Ingredient" Soup 82
120. Asian Chicken Noodle Soup 83
121. Beef And Bean Chili 83
122. Best Chicken Noodle Soup 84
123. Brie Mushroom Soup 85
124. Broccoli Barley Soup 85
125. Cheeseburger Paradise Soup 86
126. Contest Winning Pizza Soup 86
127. Crab Bisque 87
128. Cream Of Mushroom Soup 87
129. Creamy Bacon Mushroom Soup 88
130. Creamy Garlic & Mushroom Soup 88
131. Creamy Garlic & Mushroom Soup With Pastry Caps 89
132. DIY Ramen Soup 90
133. Deluxe Chili Con Carne 90
134. Elegant Mushroom Soup 91
135. Gnocchi Chicken Minestrone 91
136. Golden State Mushroom Soup 92
137. Healthy Clam Chowder 92
138. Herbed Fish Soup 93
139. Italian Chicken Chili 94
140. Italian Chicken Sausage Soup 94
141. Italian Chili 95
142. Leek Soup With Brie Toasts 95
143. Lentil Barley Soup 96
144. Lighter Mushroom Barley Soup 97
145. Marjoram Mushroom Soup 97
146. Marvelous Mushroom Soup 98
147. Meat And Potato Soup 98
148. Morel Mushroom Soup 99
149. Mushroom Onion Barley Soup 99
150. Mushroom Potato Soup 99
151. Mushroom Spinach Barley Soup 100
152. Mushroom Veggie Barley Soup 101
153. Mushroom Veggie Chowder 101
154. Mushroom And Potato Chowder 102
155. Onion Soup With Sausage 102
156. Pea Soup With Mushroom Cream Sauce 103
157. Pizza Soup With Garlic Toast Croutons 103
158. Quick Cream Of Mushroom Soup 104
159. Rosemary Mushroom Soup 104
160. Sauerkraut Sausage Soup 105
161. Savory Mushroom Barley Soup 105
162. Tomato Mushroom Soup 106
163. Tomato Spinach Soup 106
164. Turkey Barley Soup 107
165. Vegetable Chicken Barley Soup 108

166. Wild Rice Turkey Soup 108
167. Wild Rice And Mushroom Soup 109
168. Zesty Corn Chowder 109
169. Zippy Chicken Mushroom Soup 110

CHAPTER 4: MUSHROOM STEW RECIPES 110

170. Artichoke Beef Stew 111
171. Beef & Mushroom Braised Stew 111
172. Beef Bourguignon 112
173. Beef Stew For Two 113
174. Beef Stew With Ghoulish Mashed Potatoes 114
175. Beef Stew With Vegetables 114
176. Beef And Barley Stew 115
177. Beef And Lamb Stew 115
178. Burgundy Beef Stew 116
179. Calendula Paella 117
180. Candlelight Stew 118
181. Chicken Mushroom Stew 118
182. Contest Winning Gone All Day Stew 119
183. Easy Burgundy Stew 119
184. Flavorful Beef Stew 120
185. Garlic Mushroom French Beef Stew 120
186. Gone All Day Stew 121
187. Hearty Beef & Sweet Potato Stew 122
188. Herbed Beef Stew 122
189. Holiday Beef Bourguignon 123
190. Homemade Italian Stew 124
191. Irish Beef Stew 124
192. Mainly Mushroom Beef Carbonnade 125
193. Mushroom Burger Stew 126
194. Mushroom Onion Beef Stew 126
195. Northwoods Beef Stew 127
196. Orange Barley Chicken 127
197. Pork Tenderloin Stew 128
198. Pork And Pasta Stew 128
199. Pork And Winter Squash Stew 129
200. Portobello Beef Burgundy 130
201. Presto Beef Stew 130
202. Quick Mushroom Stew 131
203. Quicker Mushroom Beef Stew 131
204. Sausage And Mushroom Stew 132
205. Savory Braised Chicken With Vegetables 132
206. Savory Pork Stew 133
207. Simple Chicken Stew 133
208. Slow Cook Beef Stew 134
209. Slow Cooker Beef Burgandy Stew 134
210. Slow Cooked Vegetable Beef Stew 135
211. Slow Simmered Burgundy Beef Stew 136
212. Stew With Confetti Dumplings 136
213. Tangy Beef And Vegetable Stew 137
214. Winter Beef Stew 138

CHAPTER 5: MUSHROOM SIDE DISH RECIPES 138

215. Artichoke Spinach Casserole 138
216. Asparagus Mushroom Casserole 139
217. Asparagus Stir Fry 140
218. Asparagus And Mushrooms In Lemon Thyme Butter 140
219. Bacon 'n' Veggie Pasta 140
220. Broccoli Noodle Side Dish 141
221. Broccoli Mushroom Medley 142
222. Brown Rice Veggie Stir Fry 142
223. Bundle Of Veggies 143
224. Cheesy Bacon Ranch Potato Stuffing 143
225. Cheesy Cauliflower With Peas 144
226. Cheesy Pasta Pea Bake 144
227. Cherry & Fontina Stuffed Portobellos ... 145
228. Citrus Veggie Stir Fry 145
229. Colorful Grilled Veggies 146
230. Contest Winning Grilled Mushrooms 146
231. Contest Winning Mushroom Wild Rice . 147
232. Creamy Mushroom Potato Bake 147
233. Far North Wild Rice Casserole 148
234. Five Veggie Stir Fry 148
235. Flavorful Rice Dressing 149
236. French Peas 150
237. Fresh Green Beans With Mushrooms 150
238. Garden Saute 150
239. Garlic Buttered Green Beans 151
240. Green Beans With Mushrooms 151
241. Grill Bread 152
242. Grilled Dijon Summer Squash 152
243. Grilled Mushroom Kabobs 153
244. Grilled Vegetable Medley 153
245. Harvest Vegetables 154
246. Hawaiian Kabobs 154
247. Heavenly Onion Casserole 155
248. Italian Mushrooms 155
249. Italian Veggie Skillet 156
250. Kasha Varnishkes 156
251. Lentil White Bean Pilaf 157

252. Makeover Sausage Pecan Stuffing 157
253. Mixed Veggies 158
254. Mushroom Barley Bake 158
255. Mushroom Cornbread Dressing 159
256. Mushroom Pea Casserole 160
257. Mushroom And Rice Pilaf 160
258. Northwoods Wild Rice 160
259. Orange Vegetable Kabobs 161
260. Orange Scented Leeks & Mushrooms 162
261. Peas With Mushrooms 162
262. Roasted Green Vegetable Medley 163
263. Roasted Veggie Orzo 163
264. Saucy Mushrooms 164
265. Sausage And Mushroom Corn Bread Dressing 164
266. Sausage And Rice Casserole Side Dish ... 165
267. Sauteed Garlic Mushrooms 165
268. Savory Green Bean Casserole 166
269. Scalloped Tomatoes 166
270. Shiitake & Butternut Risotto 167
271. Slow Cooker Mushroom Rice Pilaf 167
272. Spaghetti Squash Casserole Bake 168
273. Spaghetti Squash With Sweet Peppers ... 169
274. Special Herb Dressing 169
275. Spectacular Spaghetti Squash 170
276. Spinach Artichoke Pie 170
277. Spinach Rice Casserole 171
278. Summer Vegetable Medley 171
279. Summer's Bounty Soup 172
280. Sweet Peas And Mushrooms 172
281. Three Rice Pilaf 173
282. Thyme Roasted Vegetables 173
283. Tomato Sesame Pasta Toss 174
284. Unstuffing Side Dish 174
285. Vegetable Kabobs 175
286. Vegetable Kabobs With Rice 175
287. Vegetable Wild Rice Stuffing 176
288. Vegetarian Cabbage Rolls 176
289. White Beans With Rigatoni 177
290. Wild Rice Medley 178
291. Wild Rice Mushroom Casserole 178
292. Wild Rice Pancakes 179
293. Zesty Rice 'N' Bean Casserole 179
294. Zucchini Mushroom Bake 180

CHAPTER 6: VEGETARIAN MUSHROOM RECIPES 180

295. All Veggie Lasagna 180
296. Amber's Sourdough Stuffing 181
297. Artichoke Blue Cheese Fettuccine 182
298. Asparagus Mushroom Salad 182
299. Asparagus Soup 183
300. Balsamic Mushroom Bread Pudding 183
301. Basil Garden Salad 184
302. Black Bean Veggie Enchiladas 184
303. Broccoli Veggie Pasta Primavera 185
304. Cheese Trio Artichoke & Spinach Dip ... 185
305. Cheesy Bread 186
306. Chili Lime Mushroom Tacos 186
307. Contest Winning Garden Harvest Chili . 187
308. Creamy Eggs & Mushrooms Au Gratin . 187
309. Creamy Pasta With Florets 188
310. Diploma Appetizers 189
311. Easy Marinated Mushrooms 189
312. Favorite Marvelous Mushroom Soup 190
313. Foolproof Mushrooms 190
314. Fresh Broccoli Salad 191
315. Fresh Veggie Pizza 191
316. Garden Focaccia 192
317. Garlic Mushroom Appetizer 192
318. Gnocchi Alfredo 193
319. Goat Cheese Mushrooms 193
320. Green Bean Quiche 194
321. Grilled Mediterranean Eggplant & Tomato Salad 194
322. Grilled Vegetable Orzo Salad 195
323. Grilled Veggies With Caper Butter 196
324. Hearty Portobello Linguine 196
325. Herbed Portobello Pasta 197
326. Homemade Marinated Vegetables 197
327. Italian Salad Bowl 198
328. Italian Spaghetti Squash 198
329. Italian Style Pizzas 199
330. Makeover Meatless Lasagna 199
331. Manchester Stew 200
332. Marinated Garden Platter 200
333. Marinated Mushrooms & Artichokes 201
334. Marinated Vegetables 201
335. Mixed Mushroom Tartlets 202
336. Mushroom & Leek Strudel 203
337. Mushroom & Peas Rice Pilaf 203
338. Mushroom Bisque 204
339. Mushroom Brunch Toast 204
340. Mushroom Cheesecake Appetizers 205

341. Mushroom Marsala With Barley 205
342. Mushroom Spinach Dip 206
343. Mushroom Spinach Omelet 206
344. Mushroom Turnovers 207
345. Mushroom And Spinach Saute 207
346. Mushroom, Walnut & Thyme Cheesecake 208
347. Nutty Stuffed Mushrooms 208
348. Onion Stuffed Portobellos 209
349. Overnight Baked Eggs Bruschetta 210
350. Pepper Salad 210
351. Peppered Portobello Penne 211
352. Pickled Mushrooms 211
353. Portobello Bruschetta With Rosemary Aioli 212
354. Portobello Gouda Grilled Sandwiches 213
355. Quick Italian Salad 213
356. Rainbow Quiche 213
357. Refried Bean Tostadas 214
358. Salad With Vinaigrette Dressing 215
359. Satisfying Cremini Barley 215
360. Savory Marinated Mushroom Salad 216
361. Spinach Dip Stuffed Mushrooms 216
362. Stuffed Asiago Basil Mushrooms 217
363. Summer Salad With Lemon Vinaigrette .. 217
364. Swiss Mushroom Loaf 218
365. Tuscan Portobello Stew 218
366. Ultimate Breakfast Burritos 219
367. Vegetable Quiche 219
368. Vegetable Salad 220
369. Vegetable Stuffed Portobellos 220
370. Vegetarian Black Bean Pasta 221
371. Vegetarian Egg Strata 221
372. Very Veggie Frittata 222
373. Whole Wheat Veggie Pizza 223
374. Wild Rice And Squash Pilaf 223
375. Zucchini Harvest Salad 224

CHAPTER 7: AWESOME MUSHROOM RECIPES 224

376. 10 Minute Mushroom Carbonara 225
377. A Simple Seafood Bisque 225
378. Absolutely Fabulous Portobello Mushroom Tortellini 225
379. Alice Chicken 226
380. Allison's Trout 226
381. Angela's Alfredo Ham 227

382. Antipasto Skewers 227
383. Asian Noodle Bowl With Sausage And Kale 228
384. Asian Veggie Packets 228
385. Asian Style Watercress Soup 229
386. Asparagus Portobello Pasta 229
387. Asparagus And Morel Risotto 230
388. Asparagus And Mushroom Casserole 230
389. Asparagus Spinach Artichoke Casserole 231
390. Aunty Pasto's Seafood Lasagna 232
391. BBQ Teriyaki Pork Kabobs 232
392. Babushka's Slow Cooker Root Vegetable And Chicken Stew 233
393. Baby Bok Choy And Shiitake Stir Fry 234
394. Bacon Wrapped Delights 234
395. Bacon Wrapped Stuffed Mushrooms 235
396. Bacon And Cheddar Stuffed Mushrooms 235
397. Bacon, Brussels Sprouts, And Mushroom Linguine 236
398. Bacon Wrapped Venison Tenderloin With Garlic Cream Sauce 236
399. Baked Asparagus With Portobello Mushrooms And Thyme 237
400. Baked Brie And Mushroom Sourdough Appetizer 237
401. Baked Chicken On Rice 238
402. Baked Eggs, Grandma Style 238
403. Baked Mushrooms With Thyme And White Wine 239
404. Baked Potato With Mushrooms 239
405. Baked Rice And Vegetables In Broth 240
406. Baked Spaghetti From Borden® Cheese 240
407. Balsamic Chicken Salad 241
408. Balsamic Mushrooms 241
409. Banh Mi Style Vietnamese Baguette 242
410. Barilla® Spicy Sriracha Pasta Bowl 243
411. Barley Bake 243
412. Barley Chicken Casserole 244
413. Barley, Lentil And Mushroom Soup 244
414. Basil Mushrooms In Cream Sauce 245
415. Bavarian Chanterelle Mushrooms With Bacon 245
416. Beef Stroganoff For Instant Pot® 246
417. Beef Sukiyaki 246
418. Beefy Mushroom Barley Soup 247
419. Belle And Chron's Spinach And Mushroom

Quiche 247
420. Beth's Portobello Mushroom Burgers 248
421. Better Slow Cooker Robust Chicken 248
422. Black Olive, Mushroom, And Sausage Stuffing 249
423. Blue Cheese Stuffed Mushrooms With Grilled Onions 249
424. Bow Tie Tuna Florentine 250
425. Bow Tie Pasta With Sausage, Peas, And Mushrooms 250
426. Braised Tofu 251
427. Bratwurst Pot Pie 251
428. Brazilian Chicken Stroganoff 252
429. Brazilian Stroganoff 253
430. Brie And Mushroom Phyllo Puffs 253
431. Broccoli And Carrot Lasagna 254
432. Broken Pasta With Mushroom, Onion, And Crispy SPAM® 254
433. Buffalo Cheesy Chicken Lasagna 255
434. Busted Up Veggie Omelet 256
435. Busy Day Chicken Rice Casserole 256
436. Cajun Crab Stuffed Mushrooms 257
437. California Grilled Pizza 257
438. California Melt 258
439. Cally's Omelet 258
440. Cauliflower "Risotto" With Porcini Mushrooms And Peas 258
441. Champinones A La Sevillana (Seville Style Mushrooms) 259
442. Chanterelle Mushroom And Bacon Tartlets 259
443. Chanterelle Shazam 260
444. Chanterelle And Caramelized Onion Bruschetta 260
445. Cheese Stuffed Mushroom Appetizer 261
446. Cheesy Chicken Bundles 262
447. Cheesy Chicken Tetrazzini 262
448. Cheesy Grits Mexicano 263
449. Cheesy Hash Brown Cups 264
450. Cheesy Mashed Potato Stuffed Mushrooms 264
451. Cheesy Spinach Chicken Rolls 264
452. Chef John's Bigos (Polish Hunter's Stew) 265
453. Chef John's Chicken Cacciatore 266
454. Chef John's Chicken Marsala 267
455. Chef John's Chicken Riggies 267

456. Chef John's Chicken A La King 268
457. Chef John's Classic Beef Stroganoff 269
458. Chef John's Mushroom Gravy 269
459. Chef John's Truffled Potato Gratin 270
460. Chicago Style Pan Pizza 271
461. Chicken And Artichoke Penne With A White Sauce 271
462. Chicken Breasts Stuffed With Perfection 272
463. Chicken Breasts Supreme 272
464. Chicken Casserole Del Sol 273
465. Chicken Diane Style 274
466. Chicken Divan 274
467. Chicken Hekka 275
468. Chicken Livers With Gorgonzola Polenta 275
469. Chicken Marsala Florentine 276
470. Chicken Marsala Meatballs 276
471. Chicken Marsala With Portobello Mushrooms 277
472. Chicken Pasta Shannon Style 278
473. Chicken Riggies I 278
474. Chicken Supreme II 279
475. Chicken Supreme IV 279
476. Chicken Susan 280
477. Chicken Tetrazzini 280
478. Chicken Tetrazzini For A Crowd 281
479. Chicken Thigh Fricassee With Mushrooms And Rosemary 281
480. Chicken Thighs With Mushroom Leek Sauce 282
481. Chicken Valdostano 282
482. Chicken Wild Rice Soup I 283
483. Chicken With Mushrooms 284
484. Chicken With Portobello Mushrooms And Artichokes 284
485. Chicken A La Can Can 285
486. Chicken A La King III 285
487. Chicken A La Queen 285
488. Chicken And Bacon Fajitas 286
489. Chicken And Bowtie Pasta With Asiago Cream Sauce 287
490. Chicken And Herbs In White Wine 287
491. Chicken And Mushroom Chowder 288
492. Chicken And Mushroom Crepes 289
493. Chicken And Portobello Rollups 289
494. Chicken And Spinach Alfredo Lasagna .. 290
495. Chicken And Wild Rice Casserole 291

496. Chicken With Mushrooms, Prosciutto, And Cream Sauce 291
497. Chicken With Red Grapes And Mushrooms 292
498. Chicken, Cheese, And Biscuits 292
499. Chicken, Fennel And Mushroom Soup .. 293
500. Chicken, Sweet Potato, And Mushroom Stew 293
501. Chicken Stuffed Mushrooms 294
502. Chicken Stuffed Shells With Sherry Sauce 295
503. Chinese Chicken Rice Salad 296
504. Chinese Clay Pot Chicken Rice 296
505. Chinese Ham Stew 297
506. Chipotle Burgers With Avocado Salsa 297
507. Chunky Broccoli Cheese Soup 298
508. Cindy's Beef Tips 298
509. Classic Meatloaf 299
510. Company Liver With Onions 300
511. Coq Au Vin Alla Italiana 300
512. Corey's Steak, Cheese, And Mushroom Subs 301
513. Corn And Porcini Mushroom Cornbread Dressing 301
514. Crab Stuffed Mushrooms II 302
515. Crab And Lobster Stuffed Mushrooms .. 302
516. Crab And Mushroom Enchiladas 303
517. Crab Stuffed Filet Mignon With Whiskey Peppercorn Sauce 303
518. Crab Stuffed Mushrooms 304
519. Crabby Cliff's Mushroom Puffs 305
520. Crazy Good Stuffing And Baked Chops. 305
521. Cream Cheese Chicken 306
522. Cream Of Mushroom Chicken 307
523. Creamy Chicken Marsala Fettuccine 307
524. Creamy Chicken And Mushroom Tart With Nabisco® Chicken In A Biscuit Cracker Crust.308
525. Creamy Drunken Mushroom Pork Chops 309
526. Creamy Morel Mushroom Grits 309
527. Creamy Mushroom Pasta 310
528. Creamy Mushroom Risotto 310
529. Creamy Mushroom Soup 311
530. Creamy Shrimp Pasta With Mushrooms.311
531. Creamy Slow Cooker Beef Stroganoff 312
532. Creamy Spinach & Mushroom Risotto ... 313
533. Creamy Spinach Tortellini 313

534. Creamy Spinach And Zucchini Soup 313
535. Creme Fraiche Chicken 314
536. Crispy Tofu And Bacon Wraps 315
537. Crock Pot® Mushrooms 315
538. Crustless Spinach, Mushroom, And Tomato Quiche (Keto) 315
539. Cubed Steak And Wild Rice 316
540. Curried Celery Apple Soup With Shiitake 316
541. Deer Soup With Cream Of Mushroom And Celery 317
542. Delicious Potato Salad Bake 318
543. Deviled Chicken Breasts 318
544. Diane's Chicken Dish 319
545. Earth, Sea And Fire Salmon 319
546. Easier Chicken Marsala 320
547. Easy Baked Cheese And Vegetable Twist 320
548. Easy Barbeque Chicken And Red Potatoes 321
549. Easy Beef Stroganoff In The Slow Cooker 321
550. Easy Chanterelle Mushrooms In Cream Sauce 322
551. Easy Chicken Casserole 322
552. Easy Chicken With Mushrooms And Zucchini In Cream Sauce 322
553. Easy Lentil Feta Wraps 323
554. Easy Mushroom Rice 323
555. Easy Salmon 324
556. Easy Slow Cooker Stroganoff 324
557. Easy Spaghetti With Tomato Sauce 325
558. Easy Turkey Tetrazzini 325
559. Easy Vegetarian Pasta 326
560. Easy Vegetarian Stroganoff 326
561. Egg Foo Yung II 326
562. Egg Foo Yung For Two 327
563. Eggplant Mixed Grill 328
564. Eggplant Zucchini Pasta Bake With Mushrooms 328
565. Eggs Over Toast 329
566. Enoki Protein Egg Bakes 329
567. Essanaye's Sesame Beef Stir Fry 330
568. Farro With Wild Mushrooms 331
569. Fast And Easy Ricotta Cheese Pizza With Mushrooms, Broccoli, And Chicken 331
570. Fettuccine And Zoodles Topped With

Chicken Sausage, Asparagus, And Mushrooms 332
571. Fettuccine In Creamy Mushroom And Sage Sauce 333
572. Fireball Mushrooms.....................333
573. Flaky Crescent Mushroom Turnovers.....334
574. Flank Steak With Mushroom Sauce.........334
575. Flat Iron Steak And Spinach Salad............335
576. Foil Pack Mushrooms 335
577. Frank's Famous Spaghetti Sauce 336
578. French Onion Casserole 336
579. French Onion Chicken....................337
580. Fried Tilapia With Oyster Mushrooms ...337
581. Garbanzo Stir Fry.............................338
582. Garden Tomato Soup.....................338
583. Garlic Chicken Marinara 339
584. Garlic Herb Cheese Stuffed Mushrooms 339
585. Garlic Mushroom Burgers....................340
586. Garlic Mushroom Pasta 340
587. Garlic Pork Tenderloin With Mushroom Gravy 341
588. Garlic Wine Chicken......................341
589. Garlicky Ham, Mushroom, And Spinach Frittata 342
590. Glenda's Mandarin Orange Salad 342
591. Gluten Free Elbows With Mixed Mushrooms And Italian Sausage Soup............343
592. Gluten Free Penne With Cajun Chicken.343
593. Gnocchi And Peppers In Balsamic Sauce 344
594. Golden Lasagna 344
595. Goldy's Special Salad 345
596. Gourmet Cream Of Wild Mushroom Soup 345
597. Grandma Sylvia's Brisket 346
598. Grandma's Pork Chops In Mushroom Gravy 346
599. Grandpa's Beef, Mushroom, And Barley Soup 347
600. Great Grilled Smoky Vegetables With Avocado And Goat Cheese Crumbles 348
601. Greek Pasta 348
602. Greek Pita Pockets....................349
603. Green Bean Casserole My Way 349
604. Green Bean And Portobello Mushroom Casserole 350
605. Green Olive Chicken II 350
606. Grilled Beef Sirloin & Farmer's Market Skewers 351
607. Grilled Chicken And Portobello Lasagna Rollups 351
608. Grilled Kansas City Smothered BBQ Chicken....................352
609. Grilled Mushroom Sandwich With Citrus Mayo 353
610. Grilled Mushroom Swiss Burgers............353
611. Grilled Steak And Vegetable Salad From Publix®..................... 354
612. Grilled Stuffed Duckling 355
613. Ground Beef Stroganoff Casserole 355
614. Grown Up Macaroni And Cheese............356
615. Grzybki Marynowane (Pickled Wild Mushrooms).....................357
616. Guay Diaw Lawd (Pork Belly, Chicken Wing, And Noodle Stew) 357
617. Gumbo Style Chicken Creole 358
618. Ham Mushroom Barley Soup................359
619. Ham, Garden Vegetable And Spring Mix Salad With Swiss Cheese 359
620. Hawaiian Shrimp 360
621. Hazelnut Mushroom Pilaf....................360
622. Healthy Mince Pies.................361
623. Hearty Meat Sauce....................361
624. Hearty Vegetable Lasagna 361
625. Hemp Seed Soup 362
626. Homemade Chicken A La King 363
627. Honey Curried Chicken...................363
628. Honey Roasted Potatoes And Mushrooms 364
629. Hunter Style Chicken 364
630. Imitation Hamburger Gravy....................365
631. Individual Grilled Veggie Pizzas............365
632. Individual Mushroom Tortilla Pizza 366
633. Instant Pot® Easy Chicken Marsala 366
634. Instant Pot® Goulash 367
635. Instant Pot® Shredded Flank Steak........367
636. Italian Meat And Spinach Pie 368
637. Italian Sausage Delight!.........................369
638. Jagerschnitzel....................369
639. Jan's Peppered Pork Chops With Mushrooms And Herb Sherry Sauce 370
640. Japanese Beef Rolls 371
641. Japanese Onion Soup....................371
642. Japanese Style Grilled Mushrooms...........372

643. Jeff's Bordelaise Sauce 372
644. Jen's One Pan Penne With Mushrooms And Arugula 373
645. Jerk Chicken Pizza 373
646. Jet Tila's Tom Yum Goong Soup 374
647. Jim's Beer Battered Portobello Mushrooms 375
648. Joe's Homemade Mushroom Soup 375
649. Kale And Mushroom Vegan "Quiche" 375
650. Kansas Quail 376
651. Kelly's Slow Cooker Beef, Mushroom, And Barley Soup 376
652. Keto Buffalo Cauliflower Chorizo "Mac" N Cheese 377
653. Keto Omelet With Zucchini And Chanterelle Mushrooms 377
654. Killer Chicken With Mushroom, Asparagus, And Red Bell Pepper 378
655. Kobe Beef And Oyster Mushroom Meatballs 379
656. Korean Beef Short Rib Stew (Galbi Jjim) 379
657. Korean Kalbi Jjim (Braised Beef Short Ribs) 380
658. Korean Short Ribs (Kalbi Jjim) 381
659. Kung Pao Tofu Stir Fry 381
660. LaDonna's Spaghetti With Sauce 382
661. Leftover Ham And Bacon Hash 383
662. Leftover Roast Beef Hash 383
663. Lemony Grilled Vegetable Kabobs 384
664. Leslie's Broccoli, Wild Rice, And Mushroom Stuffing 384
665. Less Butter Steak Diane 385
666. Linguine With Clam Sauce And Baby Portobello Mushrooms 385
667. Linguine With Clams 386
668. Linguine With Clams And Porcini Mushrooms 386
669. Linguine With Portobello Mushrooms 387
670. Loaded Sweet Potato Lasagna 387
671. Loaded Vegetarian Quiche 388
672. Lobster Salad With Red Devil Dressing ..389
673. Low 'N Slow Mushroom Barley Soup 389
674. Low Calorie Vegan Chili 390
675. Low Carb, Gluten Free Black Bean And Lentil Burgers 390
676. Lyn's Chicken 391

677. Magic Chicken 391
678. Mahi Mahi With Onions And Mushrooms 392
679. Mahi And Mushrooms 392
680. Make Ahead Marsala Turkey Gravy 393
681. Make Ahead Turkey Gravy With Porcini Mushrooms And Marsala Wine 394
682. Mandarin Chicken Skillet 395
683. Manicotti Italian Casserole 395
684. Marcel's Spicy Slow Cooker Chicken Thighs 396
685. Marinated Chanterelle Mushroom Canapes 396
686. Marinated Mushrooms 397
687. Marinated Mushrooms II 397
688. Marinated Mushrooms For Antipasto 398
689. Marinated Mushrooms With Blue Cheese 398
690. Marinated Mushrooms With Red Bell Peppers 399
691. Mediterranean Vegetable Stew 399
692. Melt In Your Mouth Meat Loaf 400
693. Microwave Steamed Mushroom Rice 400
694. Mike's Mushroom Bread 401
695. Minnesota Pork Chops 401
696. Miso Soup With Shiitake Mushrooms 402
697. Mom's Chicken Cacciatore 402
698. Mom's Sweet Spaghetti Sauce 403
699. Mozzarella Chicken Marsala 403
700. Mozzarella Mushroom Chicken 404
701. Muenster Chicken And Mushrooms 404
702. Mushroom Artichoke Sandwich 405
703. Mushroom Bagna Cauda 405
704. Mushroom Barley Soup 405
705. Mushroom Bok Choy Soup 406
706. Mushroom Bouchees 406
707. Mushroom Bundles 407
708. Mushroom Cap Chorizo Burger 407
709. Mushroom Cheese Puffs 408
710. Mushroom Chicken Piccata 408
711. Mushroom Chicken Tetrazzini 409
712. Mushroom Chile Relleno Casserole 409
713. Mushroom Cream Sauce With Shallots ..410
714. Mushroom Curry With Galangal 411
715. Mushroom Gravy/Sauce 411
716. Mushroom Kabobs 411
717. Mushroom Lentil Barley Stew 412

718. Mushroom Mint Pasta Salad 412
719. Mushroom Moong Dal Dosas 413
720. Mushroom Rice Turnovers 414
721. Mushroom Salad II 414
722. Mushroom Slow Cooker Roast Beef 415
723. Mushroom Soup Without Cream 415
724. Mushroom Spinach Soup 415
725. Mushroom Stuffing 416
726. Mushroom Stuffing Balls 416
727. Mushroom Toast Cups 417
728. Mushroom And Artichoke Soup 417
729. Mushroom And Asparagus Casserole 418
730. Mushroom And Bacon Green Beans 419
731. Mushroom And Chorizo Stuffed Pork Tenderloin 419
732. Mushroom And Mascarpone Ravioli 420
733. Mushroom And Sausage Rice Pilaf 420
734. Mushroom And Swiss Burger Meatloaf .. 421
735. Mushroom And Swiss Chicken 421
736. Mushroom And Tomato Bruschetta 422
737. Mushroom And Walnut Stuffed Cornish Hens 422
738. Mushroom, Cheese, And Haddock Bake 423
739. Mushroom, Kale, And Bok Choy Ramen 424
740. Mushroom, Leek, Chicken Sausage And Tortellini Soup 424
741. Mushroom, Leek, And Sausage Pot Pie .. 425
742. Mushroom, Spinach And Cheese Torta .. 426
743. Mushroom Walnut Loaf (Garden Loaf) . 426
744. Mushrooms And Peas Rice 427
745. Mushrooms And Spinach Italian Style 427
746. Mushrooms In White Wine Sauce 428
747. Mushrooms With A Soy Sauce Glaze 428
748. Nayza's Mushroom Fiesta Cups 429
749. Neptune's Favor 429
750. Night Before Scrambled Eggs 430
751. Nikki's Pork Chops With A Mushroom Cream Sauce Over White Jasmine Rice 431
752. No Noodle Zucchini Lasagna 431
753. No Peek Beef Stew 432
754. Noodles Marmaduke 433
755. Nutmeg Mushrooms 433
756. Onion And Mushroom Scrambled Eggs 433
757. Opa George's Wild Rice 434
758. Orzo Delicioso 434
759. Outstanding Chicken Dinner 435
760. Owen's Chicken Rice 435
761. Oxtail Soup I 436
762. Oyster And Mushroom Stuffing 437
763. PHILLY Slow Cooker Beef Stroganoff . 437
764. Paleo Chicken Marsala 438
765. Pan Fried Fingerling Potatoes With Wild Mushroom Sauce 438
766. Pan Roasted Halibut With Clamshell Mushrooms And Lemon Butter Sauce 439
767. Pan Seared Cod, Broccoli, And Mushrooms With Creamy Alfredo Sauce 439
768. Parchment Cooked Fish With Morels, Spring Garlic, And Thyme 440
769. Pasta Salad I 441
770. Pasta Shells With Portobello Mushrooms And Asparagus In Boursin Sauce 442
771. Pasta With Sugar Snap Peas, Parmesan And Mushrooms 442
772. Pasta And Fresh Cilantro Crunchy Stuff 443
773. Pasta With Clam Sauce 443
774. Pasta With Tomato Sauce, Sausage, And Mushrooms 444
775. Pasta, Chicken And Artichokes 444
776. Pastachutta 445
777. Pastrami Chicken Bake 445
778. Penne With Asparagus And Mushrooms 446
779. Penne With Pancetta And Mushrooms .. 446
780. Pita Bread Tofu Sandwiches 447
781. Pita Pizza 447
782. Plantain Veggie Burgers 448
783. Porcini Mushroom Pasta 448
784. Porcini Mushroom Soup 449
785. Porcini Braised Boar With Artichoke And Fennel 449
786. Pork Chop Casserole I 450
787. Pork Chop And Potato Casserole 451
788. Pork Chops In Mushroom Gravy 451
789. Pork Chops With Garden Rice 452
790. Pork Chops With Italian Sausage 452
791. Pork Chops With Mushrooms And Grape Tomatoes 453
792. Pork Stroganoff 453
793. Portabella Mushroom Dressing 454
794. Portobello Artichoke Soup 454
795. Portobello Bellybuttons 455
796. Portobello Burgers With Goat Cheese ... 455
797. Portobello Mushroom Appetizer 456

798. Portobello Mushroom Caps And Veggies 456
799. Portobello Mushroom Pasta With Basil..457
800. Portobello Mushroom Stroganoff............457
801. Portobello Pesto Egg Omelette................458
802. Portobello Pot Pie......................................458
803. Portobello Stacks.......................................459
804. Portobello Stuffed Mushroom Burger 459
805. Portobello, Eggplant, And Roasted Red Pepper Panini...460
806. Potato Casserole...461
807. Potato Ginger Soup....................................461
808. Potsticker Salad..461
809. Prime Rib With Au Jus..............................462
810. Pumpkin Lasagna......................................463
811. Pumpkin Ravioli With Crispy Margherita® Prosciutto..463
812. Purple Yam Pancakes................................464
813. Quiche Au Chou Romanesco (Romanesco And Mushroom Quiche)..............................465
814. Quick Chick...465
815. Quick Ground Beef Stroganoff.................466
816. Quick Mushroom Ceviche........................466
817. Quick And Easy Greek Spaghetti.............467
818. Quinoa Chard Pilaf...................................467
819. Quinoa Mushroom 'Risotto'.....................468
820. Rabbit Loin Cigars....................................468
821. Rachel's Turkey Loaf.................................469
822. Ravioli Soup...469
823. Refreshing Salad With Grilled Oyster Mushrooms..470
824. Restaurant Style Shoyu Miso Ramen.......470
825. Rice So Nice...471
826. Rich Viennese Potato Soup......................472
827. Risotto Ai Funghi Porcini In Pentola A Pressione (Porcini Mushroom Risotto)......472
828. Roast Beef Tenderloin................................473
829. Roasted Eggplant And Mushrooms..........474
830. Roasted Mushroom And Sunchoke Bisque 474
831. Roasted Portobello, Red Pepper, And Arugula Salad For One................................475
832. Roasted Vegetables With Walnuts, Basil And Balsamic Vinaigrette.............................476
833. Roasted Wild Mushrooms And Potatoes 476
834. Rolled Flank Steak....................................477
835. Romantic Chicken With Artichokes And Mushrooms..478
836. Rosemary Chicken Stew...........................478
837. Russian Mushroom Salad.........................479
838. Salisbury Steak Slow Cooker Style...........479
839. Salmon With Green Fettuccine................480
840. Sauceless Garden Lasagna........................480
841. Saucy Chicken Cordon Bleu.....................481
842. Sauerkraut Pierogi Filling.........................482
843. Sausage Mushroom Pizza.........................482
844. Sausage Mushroom Quiche.....................483
845. Sausage Stuffed Mushrooms....................483
846. Sausage And Kale Soup............................484
847. Sausage And Mushroom Mini Pizzas......484
848. Sausage And Mushroom Stuffing............485
849. Sauteed Mushrooms.................................486
850. Sauteed Sugar Snap Peas With Mushrooms 486
851. Savory Crab Stuffed Mushrooms.............486
852. Savory French Crepes...............................487
853. Scim's Fettucine Alfredo With Shrimp...488
854. Scrumptious Salisbury Steak In Mushroom Gravy...488
855. Seafood Lasagna II....................................489
856. Sensational Sirloin Kabobs......................489
857. Sensational Steak Sandwich.....................490
858. Sesame Cabbage And Mushrooms..........491
859. Sherry Chicken And Mushrooms............491
860. Shiitake Angel Hair Pasta.........................492
861. Shiitake Mushroom, Sun Dried Tomato Pesto, And Shrimp Pasta...............................492
862. Shiitake Scallopine...................................493
863. Shredded Roast Spaghetti Sauce..............493
864. Shrimp & Scallop Stroganoff...................494
865. Shrimp Cognac And Baked Cheese Grits 494
866. Shrimp Piccata...495
867. Shrimp Stuffed Mushrooms.....................496
868. Shrimp Tetrazzini......................................496
869. Shrimp And Mushroom Linguini With Creamy Cheese Herb Sauce.........................497
870. Simple Hot And Sour Soup.....................497
871. Simply Marinated Mushrooms................498
872. Sirloin Tips And Mushrooms...................498
873. Slovak Sauerkraut Christmas Soup..........499
874. Slow Cooked Beef Stew............................500
875. Slow Cooked Goose..................................500
876. Slow Cooker Chicken Cacciatore............501

877. Slow Cooker Chicken Creole 501
878. Slow Cooker Chicken And Mushroom Stew 501
879. Slow Cooker Chicken With Mushroom Wine Sauce 502
880. Slow Cooker Pork With Mushrooms And Barley 503
881. Slow Cooker Stuffing 503
882. Smothered Pork Chops With Bourbon And Mushrooms 504
883. Snapper In Black Sauce 504
884. So Divine Stuffed Mushrooms 505
885. So Shiitake Wontons 505
886. Sour Cream Mushroom Chicken 506
887. Southern Fried Cabbage With Bacon, Mushrooms, And Onions 506
888. Southern Style Fried Mushrooms 507
889. Spaghetti With Broccoli And Mushrooms 507
890. Spaghetti With Tomato And Sausage Sauce 508
891. Special Vegan Chili 508
892. Spicy Basil Chicken 509
893. Spicy Harissa Chicken Kebabs 509
894. Spicy Italian Sausage Blended Burger 510
895. Spicy Korean Chicken And Ramen Noodle Packets 511
896. Spinach Mushroom Omelet 511
897. Spinach Mushroom Quiche 512
898. Spinach Mushroom And Ricotta Fettuccine 512
899. Spinach Salad With Curry Vinaigrette 513
900. Spinach And Mushroom Casserole 513
901. Spinach And Mushroom Frittata 514
902. Spinach And Mushroom Quesadillas 514
903. Spinach And Mushroom Quiche With Shiitake Mushrooms 515
904. Spinach And Mushroom Salad 515
905. Spinach, Turkey, And Mushroom Lasagna 516
906. Steak N Gravy 517
907. Steak Salad (Ranen Salad) 517
908. Steak Tips With Mushroom Sauce 518
909. Steak And Ale Pie With Mushrooms 518
910. Steak And Kidney Pie With Bacon And Mushrooms 519
911. Strip Steak With Red Wine Cream Sauce 520
912. Stroganoff Casserole 520
913. Stroganoff Casserole With A Twist 521
914. Stuffed Chicken With Margherita® Capicola 522
915. Stuffed Cod Wrapped In Bacon 522
916. Stuffed Mega 'Shrooms 523
917. Stuffed Morel Mushrooms 523
918. Stuffed Mushrooms I 524
919. Stuffed Mushrooms II 524
920. Stuffed Mushrooms With Sour Cream ... 524
921. Stuffed Mushrooms With Spinach 525
922. Stuffed Mushrooms, Leeks, White Beans And Pecans 526
923. Stuffed Pork Loin 526
924. Stuffed Pork Tenderloin 527
925. Stuffed Red Peppers With Quinoa, Mushrooms, And Turkey 528
926. Stuffing Recipe 528
927. Suki's Spinach And Feta Pasta 529
928. Summer Lamb Kabobs 529
929. Summer Vegetarian Chili 530
930. Sunday Brunch Bake 530
931. Super Easy Slow Cooker Chicken 531
932. Suz's Vegetable Manicotti 531
933. Swedish Chanterelle Mushroom Pate 532
934. Sweet Maple Pork Chops 533
935. Sweet Potato And Mushroom Croquettes 533
936. Sweet And Sour Tofu Veggies 534
937. Swiss Steak Quick And Easy 535
938. Tarte Flambee 535
939. Tava Or Turkish Stew 536
940. Teresa's Hearty Chicken Cacciatore 536
941. Terrific Turkey Tetrazzini 537
942. Thai Hot And Sour Soup 538
943. Thai Noodles 538
944. Thai Shrimp Curry With A Kick 539
945. Thai Stuffed Tofu 539
946. The Best Seafood Stuffed Mushrooms ... 540
947. The Mushroom Steak Stuff 541
948. The Very Best Spaghetti Sauce 541
949. Three Pepper Pilaf 542
950. Tofu Egg Noodles In Coconut Sauce 542
951. Tofu Mushroom Ramen Soup 543
952. Tofu With Ground Pork Stir Fry 544
953. Tom Yum Koong Soup 544
954. True Italian Porcini Mushroom Risotto . 545

955. Turkey Mushroom Tetrazzini 545
956. Turkey Tetrazzini 546
957. Turkey A La King 547
958. Twenty Minute Chicken 547
959. Uszka Do Barszczu (Mushroom Dumplings For Borscht) 547
960. Vareniky 548
961. Veal Chop With Portabello Mushrooms 549
962. Veal Forestiere 549
963. Veal Meat Loaf 550
964. Veal Or Chicken Marsala 550
965. Vegan Lettuce Wraps 551
966. Vegan Mushroom Bolognese 551
967. Vegan Mushroom Ceviche 552
968. Vegan Pasta With Spinach, Mushrooms, And Garlic 553
969. Vegan Shepherd's Pie 553
970. Vegan Spaghetti 554
971. Vegan Stir Fry Noodles 554
972. Vegan Stroganoff 555
973. Vegan Stuffing 555
974. Vegan Tacos With Mushrooms And Tomatillos 556
975. Vegan Tofu Quiche 557
976. Vegan Tofu Spinach Lasagna 557
977. Vegan Vegetable Double Tortilla Pizza .. 558
978. Vegetable Cashew Saute 558
979. Vegetable Lo Mein Delight 559
980. Vegetable Medley II 559
981. Vegetable Stuffed Cannelloni 560
982. Vegetable And Tofu Stir Fry 560
983. Vegetarian Sloppy Joe 561
984. Veggie Quinoa Burgers 562
985. Veggie Tacos 562
986. Veneto Chicken 563
987. Vietnamese Kabocha Squash Soup 563
988. West Coast Cod And Shrimp 564
989. White Pizza With Porcinis 564
990. White Wine Almond Chicken 565
991. White Wine And Mushroom Sauce 566
992. Wild Mushroom Balls 566
993. Wild Mushroom Sauce 567
994. Wild Mushroom Stuffing 568
995. Wild Rice Pilaf 568
996. Ziti With Italian Sausage 569
997. Zucchilattas 569
998. Zucchini Boats With Ground Turkey 570
999. Zucchini Saute 570
1000. Zucchini And Mushroom Salad With Ricotta Salata 571
1001. Zucchini With Chickpea And Mushroom Stuffing 571

INDEX 573
CONCLUSION 580

Chapter 1: Oyster Mushroom Recipes

***

1. Asian Chicken And Corn Soup

Serving: 6 | Prep: 25mins | Cook: 30mins | Ready in:

Ingredients

- 1 tablespoon vegetable oil
- 10 button mushrooms, sliced thin
- 10 small oyster mushrooms, sliced thin
- 1 (3 ounce) package enoki mushrooms, roots removed
- 1/4 cup chopped onion
- 1/4 cup chopped celery
- 1/4 cup chopped green bell pepper
- 1/4 cup chopped carrot
- 3 cloves garlic, smashed
- salt and pepper to taste
- 2 (14.5 ounce) cans chicken broth
- 1 (15 ounce) can cream-style corn
- 1 (5 ounce) can chunk white chicken (such as Swanson®), drained
- 1 tablespoon rice wine vinegar
- 2 teaspoons Chinese five-spice powder
- 1 tablespoon cornstarch
- 1/2 cup cold milk
- 15 leaves fresh Thai basil, chopped

Direction

- In a big pot, heat the vegetable oil on medium-high heat, then mix in the enoki mushrooms, oyster mushrooms and button mushrooms and cook and stir until it turns a bit brown. Add the garlic, carrot, green bell pepper, celery and onion, then sprinkle pepper and salt to season. Let it cook and stir for 3-4 minutes, then stir in the five-spice powder, rice wine vinegar, chicken, cream style corn and chicken broth, then boil. Put cover and lower the heat to medium-low. Let it simmer for around 20 minutes. In a small bowl, mix cornstarch with the milk and stir it into the soup. Mix until the soup becomes thick. Put chopped basil on top of each serving to garnish.

Nutrition Information

- Calories: 168 calories;
- Sodium: 371
- Total Carbohydrate: 23.2
- Cholesterol: 16
- Protein: 9.7
- Total Fat: 5.3

2. Cream Of Wild Mushroom Soup

Serving: 6 | Prep: 40mins | Cook: 30mins | Ready in:

Ingredients

- 5 cups vegetable broth
- 1/2 cup butter, divided
- 1 carrot, cut into matchstick-size pieces
- 1/2 white onion, cut into matchstick-size pieces
- 1/2 leek, cut into matchstick-size pieces
- 2 stalks celery, cut into matchstick-size pieces
- 1 clove garlic, minced
- 2 small yellow squash, cut into matchstick-size pieces
- 2 small zucchini, cut into matchstick-size pieces
- 2 ounces shiitake mushrooms, thinly sliced
- 2 ounces chanterelle mushrooms, thinly sliced
- 2 ounces oyster mushroom caps, coarsely chopped
- 2 white button mushrooms, thinly sliced

- 1 portobello mushroom, quartered and thinly sliced
- 1/4 cup all-purpose flour
- 2 1/2 cups heavy whipping cream
- 1 pinch cayenne pepper
- 1 pinch salt and ground black pepper to taste
- 1 bunch chives, chopped

Direction

- Allow vegetable broth in a large pot to simmer over medium heat.
- Place a large saucepan on low heat; melt 1/4 cup of butter. Raise heat to medium. Add in carrot; cook while stirring for 3-5 minutes, till the carrot starts to soften. Include in garlic, celery, leek and onion; cook while stirring for around 5 minutes, till the onion turns translucent. Add in zucchini and yellow squash; keep cooking for 2 minutes.
- Transfer the carrot mixture into the vegetable broth. Keep the broth simmering over low heat.
- In the saucepan, melt the remaining 1/4 cup of butter. Cook while stirring in Portobello mushroom, button mushrooms, oyster mushrooms and chanterelle mushrooms for around 5 minutes, till the mushrooms start to soften. Sprinkle flour over, keep stirring for 2-3 minutes, till a paste forms.
- Combine the mushroom and flour mixture into the vegetable broth. Transfer in heavy cream; simmer for around 8 minutes, till heated through. Taste with pepper, salt and cayenne. Use chives for garnish.

Nutrition Information

- Calories: 571 calories;
- Sodium: 589
- Total Carbohydrate: 20.4
- Cholesterol: 177
- Protein: 6.6
- Total Fat: 53

3. Creamy Coconut Carbonara (Without Milk!)

Serving: 2 | Prep: 20mins | Cook: 20mins | Ready in:

Ingredients

- 4 ounces fettuccine pasta
- 1 tablespoon vegetable oil
- 2 onions, coarsely chopped, or to taste
- 1 tablespoon minced garlic
- 1 cup coconut milk, divided
- 1/2 cup fresh oyster mushrooms, diced small
- 1/3 cup thinly sliced red bell pepper
- 1/3 cup thinly sliced green bell pepper
- salt and ground black pepper to taste
- 2 spring onions, sliced, or more to taste
- 1 tablespoon chopped fresh basil

Direction

- Put big pot of lightly salted water on rolling boil. Mix fettuccine in and boil again. Cook on medium heat for 8 minutest till tender yet firm to bite; drain.
- Heat oil in big saucepan on high heat. Add garlic and onion; cook for 2-4 minutes till slightly browned, constantly mixing. Add green and red bell pepper, oyster mushrooms and 1/2 cup coconut milk. Mix and cook for 3-5 minutes till just tender.
- Mix leftover 1/2 cup coconut milk and fettuccine into saucepan; season with pepper and salt. Mix basil and spring onions in. Cook for 2-3 minutes longer till sauce coats fettuccine and is creamy, uncovered.

Nutrition Information

- Calories: 601 calories;
- Total Fat: 32.6
- Sodium: 112
- Total Carbohydrate: 70.4
- Cholesterol: 0
- Protein: 13.7

4. Fried Polenta Squares With Creamy Mushroom Ragu

Serving: 4 | Prep: 2hours30mins | Cook: 1hours15mins | Ready in:

Ingredients

- 4 cups water
- 1 cup polenta
- 1/2 cup finely grated Parmesan cheese
- 3/4 teaspoon kosher salt, divided
- 2 tablespoons olive oil
- 1 small yellow onion, diced
- 3 cloves garlic, minced
- 1 pound mixed wild mushrooms (like shiitake, oyster, chanterelle, hen of the woods), cleaned and sliced
- 1 pound cremini mushrooms, cleaned and sliced
- 1 tablespoon minced fresh thyme
- 2 tablespoons all-purpose flour
- 1/2 cup dry white wine
- 1/4 cup heavy cream
- 1 teaspoon sugar
- 1 squeeze fresh lemon juice
- 1/2 cup chopped flat-leaf parsley
- 1 sheet Reynolds Wrap® Aluminum Foil

Direction

- Bring to a boil 4 cups of water. Whisk in the polenta. As the polenta starts to thicken, lessen heat to a simmer and cook for 45 minutes until thickened and creamy, avoid sticking by stirring occasionally. Stir in Parmesan and a quarter teaspoon of salt. Mix until melted and cheese is no longer visible. Take away from heat.
- Line a baking dish of 8x11 inch with Reynolds Wrap(R) Aluminum Foil and pour into the baking dish the polenta carefully, smooth it to an even thickness by using a spatula, about 3/4 inch. Refrigerate covered for two hours at least and up to 2 days until set.
- Make your ragu while the polenta chills. In a large heavy skillet, heat the olive oil over medium heat until shimmering. Add the garlic and onion and sauté for about 5 minutes until fragrant and translucent. Prevent browning by stirring often. Add thyme and mushrooms, cook over medium-high heat till the liquid flows out from the mushrooms. Add a half teaspoon of salt and continue to cook for another 5 minutes till they are starting to softened more.
- Add flour, stirring for about 1 minute until it is no longer visible. Add in sugar, cream and wine, and allow the mixture to simmer. Adjust salt to taste if wished. Simmer for about 15 minutes until creamy and thick and the mushrooms are nicely coated. Finish with a half cup minced parsley and a squeeze of fresh lemon juice. Set aside and cover to keep warm.
- Slice your polenta into squares – any size you want. Wipe down your skillet, use nonstick cooking spray to coat, and heat it over medium-high. In the pan, fry the squares until warmed through and golden brown. Top with warm mushroom ragu for serving.

Nutrition Information

- Calories: 448 calories;
- Sodium: 949
- Total Carbohydrate: 46.9
- Cholesterol: 33
- Protein: 19
- Total Fat: 19

5. Marty's Ginger Pad Thai

Serving: 4 | Prep: 45mins | Cook: 44mins | Ready in:

Ingredients

- 1 (8 ounce) package rice noodles (rice vermicelli)
- 2 cups chicken stock

- 1 cup water
- 2 stalks lemongrass, chopped
- 1 cup peanuts
- 1/2 cup coconut powder
- 1 pound boneless chicken breast, sliced
- 1/4 cup oyster sauce
- 2 tablespoons fish sauce
- 2 tablespoons dark soy sauce
- 2 teaspoons salt
- 2 teaspoons ground black pepper
- 2 teaspoons peanut oil, divided
- 1/2 cup chopped ginger
- 1 small Spanish onion, chopped
- 2 jalapeno peppers, seeded and chopped
- 4 cloves garlic, chopped
- 1 habanero pepper, seeded and chopped, or more to taste
- 1 large carrot, cut into matchsticks
- 1 large yellow bell pepper, sliced
- 1 small green bell pepper, sliced
- 4 small radishes, sliced
- 1 large king oyster mushroom, sliced
- 2 tablespoons red curry paste
- 1 teaspoon curry powder, or more to taste
- 1/4 cup white wine
- 1/4 wedge lime, juiced
- 5 sprigs cilantro leaves, chopped

Direction

- In a big pot, put noodles and use lukewarm water to cover. Let submerge for half an hour till softened. Boil; cook for 3 minutes till noodles are tender yet still firm to the bite, mixing from time to time. Drain and put back to the pot.
- In a small saucepan, mix together lemongrass, a cup water and chicken stock. Boil; allow to simmer for 5 minutes till broth is aromatic. Filter out lemongrass and throw.
- Using a mortar and pestle, pound peanuts. In a big skillet or wok, toast for 2 to 3 minutes over medium heat till aromatic. Move to a bowl.
- In the wok, toast coconut for 2 to 3 minutes till aromatic and golden brown, mixing frequently. Move to a bowl.
- In a big bowl, put chicken. Cover with pepper, salt, soy sauce, fish sauce and oyster sauce.
- In the wok over medium-high heat, heat a teaspoon peanut oil. Put in ginger and chicken mixture; cook and mix for 2 minutes each side till chicken is browned. Take out of the wok.
- In the wok over medium-high heat, heat leftover 1 teaspoon peanut oil. Put in habanero pepper, garlic, jalapeno peppers and onion; sauté for 2 minutes till aromatic. Put in radishes, green bell pepper, yellow bell pepper and carrot; cook and mix for a minute. Mix in curry powder, red curry paste and mushroom for 1 to 2 minutes till well-incorporated.
- Put white wine and broth into the wok. Cook for 5 minutes till reduced. Mix in all the coconut and half of the toasted peanuts; allow to simmer for 2 minutes. Put in chicken; keep on simmering for 5 minutes till sauce has reduced to about 1 1/2 cup and chicken is not pink in the middle anymore.
- In the pot, put sauce and chicken atop noodles; put leftover peanuts. Mix for 2 to 3 minutes over low heat till well-incorporated. Add lime juice and jazz up with cilantro.

Nutrition Information

- Calories: 740 calories;
- Total Fat: 31.6
- Sodium: 2942
- Total Carbohydrate: 77.3
- Cholesterol: 59
- Protein: 37.8

6. Oyster Mushroom Pasta

Serving: 4 | Prep: 15mins | Cook: 30mins | Ready in:

Ingredients

- 1 (16 ounce) package linguine pasta
- 1/2 cup butter
- 1 pound oyster mushrooms, chopped

- 1/3 cup chopped fresh parsley
- salt and ground black pepper to taste
- 2/3 cup heavy whipping cream
- 4 green onions, chopped
- 1/4 cup Parmesan cheese

Direction

- Boil a big pot of lightly salted water. Cook linguine at a boil for 11 minutes till tender yet firm to chew; drain. Put in a serving bowl.
- Melt butter in a big skillet on medium heat. Add mushrooms; mix and cook for 5 minutes till lightly browned and tender. Mix in black pepper, salt and parsley; cook for 1 minute till flavors merge. Add heavy cream; gently boil. Cook for 5 minutes till sauce slightly thickens.
- Put sauce on pasta in the serving bowl; toss to mix. Add Parmesan cheese and green onions; toss till mixed.

Nutrition Information

- Calories: 819 calories;
- Sodium: 325
- Total Carbohydrate: 91.6
- Cholesterol: 120
- Protein: 22.1
- Total Fat: 42.2

7. Pesto And Prawn Lasagna

Serving: 6 | Prep: 20mins | Cook: 2hours6mins | Ready in:

Ingredients

- 2 cups fresh basil leaves
- 1 cup reduced fat cream of mushroom soup
- 1 tablespoon grated Parmesan cheese
- 1 teaspoon olive oil
- 1/4 teaspoon garlic powder
- 1 pinch salt and ground black pepper to taste
- 2 cups fresh spinach
- 6 sun-dried tomatoes, chopped
- 2 tablespoons butter
- 1 cup reduced fat cottage cheese
- olive oil cooking spray
- 1 cup chopped oyster mushrooms
- 1/2 cup chopped white mushrooms
- 9 dry lasagna noodles, uncooked
- 3 cups frozen king prawns
- 1/2 cup fresh mozzarella cheese, torn into pieces

Direction

- Mix together pepper, salt, garlic powder, olive oil, Parmesan cheese, cream of mushroom soup and basil. Using an immersion blender, puree till smooth.
- In a big microwave-safe bowl, mix together butter, sun-dried tomatoes and spinach. Microwave for 1 to 2 minutes till spinach wilts. Stir in pepper, salt and cottage cheese.
- Preheat an oven to 175 °C or 350 °F.
- On high heat, heat a big skillet. Coat in cooking spray. Put in white mushrooms and oyster mushrooms; cook and mix for 5 to 8 minutes till tender.
- Spread approximately 3 tablespoons of basil puree on the bottom of a square 8-inch baking pan. Spread 3 lasagna noodles over. Spread half of the spinach mixture evenly on top of noodles. Set half of the prawns over. Put 3 lasagna noodles to cover. Top with half of basil puree and put mushroom mixture on top to cover. Put the leftover 3 lasagna noodles to cover the top.
- Top the leftover prawns and spinach mixture evenly over lasagna noodles. On top, put the rest of basil puree. Scatter mozzarella cheese over. Cover using aluminum foil.
- In prepped oven, bake for approximately 90 minutes till sauce bubbles and noodles are tender. Take off aluminum foil and keep baking for about 30 minutes till mozzarella browns.

Nutrition Information

- Calories: 395 calories;
- Total Fat: 10.8
- Sodium: 1110
- Total Carbohydrate: 48.8
- Cholesterol: 121
- Protein: 28.6

8. Pork With Apples And Mushrooms

Serving: 4 | Prep: 15mins | Cook: 25mins | Ready in:

Ingredients

- 1 pound boneless pork tenderloin, cut into 1/2-inch thick slices
- 1/2 teaspoon dried thyme, crushed
- 1/4 teaspoon ground black pepper
- 1 tablespoon canola oil
- 1 large onion, cut in half and sliced
- 8 ounces assorted sliced mushrooms (baby bellas, shiitake, and oyster)
- 1 medium apple, sliced
- 1 (10.5 ounce) can Campbell's® Healthy Request® Condensed Cream of Mushroom Soup
- 2 tablespoons balsamic vinegar
- 3/4 cup Swanson® Natural Goodness® Chicken Broth
- 2 cups hot cooked instant brown rice

Direction

- Season pork with black pepper and thyme.
- In a nonstick 12 inch skillet, heat oil over medium-high heat, and add the pork, then cook until both sides are brown. Take out of the skillet.
- Cook onion and mushrooms in the same skillet, occasionally stirring, for 5 minutes. Stir in the apple and cook until crisp-tender, about 5 minutes. Stir in broth, vinegar, and soup, then boil. Place the pork back into the skillet and bring down heat to low. Cook while covered for 5 minutes until the pork is cooked through. Serve sauce and pork with rice.

Nutrition Information

- Calories: 376 calories;
- Total Fat: 11.1
- Sodium: 463
- Total Carbohydrate: 40.1
- Cholesterol: 66
- Protein: 27.4

9. Slow Cooker 5 Mushroom Barley Soup

Serving: 6 | Prep: 20mins | Cook: 8hours | Ready in:

Ingredients

- 3 cups water
- 1 cup barley
- 4 cups beef broth
- 1 cup milk
- 2 tablespoons olive oil
- 1 cup diced onion
- 1/2 cup diced celery
- 1/2 cup diced carrot
- 1 tablespoon finely chopped garlic
- 1 (6 ounce) package sliced white mushrooms
- 1/2 cup chopped brown beech mushrooms
- 1/2 cup chopped oyster mushrooms
- 1/4 cup dried shiitake mushrooms
- 1/4 cup dried black mushrooms, broken into small pieces
- 1 (10.75 ounce) can condensed cream of mushroom soup (optional)
- 1/2 teaspoon salt
- 1/2 teaspoon ground mixed peppercorns

Direction

- Set the heat to high, and use a slow cooker to heat some water. Pour the barley, milk, beef broth, olive oil, celery, onion, garlic, carrot,

white mushrooms, brown beech mushrooms, shiitake mushrooms, black mushrooms, oyster mushrooms, cream of mushroom soup, salt, and ground mixed peppercorns into the slow cooker.
- Set it to high. Put on the cover and let it cook for an hour.
- Use a slotted spoon to take the shiitake mushrooms and cut them into 1/2-inch pieces. Adjust the heat to Low and let it cook for another 7 hours.

Nutrition Information

- Calories: 271 calories;
- Cholesterol: 3
- Protein: 10.3
- Total Fat: 9.6
- Sodium: 1092
- Total Carbohydrate: 38.5

10. South Dakota Wild Mushroom Dip

Serving: 12 | Prep: 5mins | Cook: 20mins | Ready in:

Ingredients

- 1 tablespoon butter
- 1 cup sliced mushrooms, such as oyster, portobello or shiitake
- 1/4 cup chopped onion
- 1/2 cup milk
- 1/2 cup water
- 1 (.87 ounce) package McCormick® Brown Gravy Mix
- 1 cup shredded Monterey Jack cheese, divided

Direction

- Set the oven to 350°F. In a large skillet, melt butter over medium-high heat. Add onion and mushrooms, stir and cook until softened.
- In a small bowl, stir Gravy Mix, water and milk. Mix into mushroom mixture. Cook over medium heat until the gravy comes to a boil, stirring often. Lower heat to simmer. Mix in 3/4 cup cheese. Simmer for 1-2 minutes or until the gravy slightly thickens and cheese is melted.
- Spoon the mixture into 1-quart baking dish. Sprinkle the remaining 1/4 cup cheese on top.
- Bake in the oven until cheese is melted, 5-10 minutes. Serve with crusty bread, fries or onion rings.

Nutrition Information

- Calories: 59 calories;
- Total Fat: 4.2
- Sodium: 180
- Total Carbohydrate: 2.3
- Cholesterol: 12
- Protein: 2.9

11. Spinach And Red Chard Quiche

Serving: 5 | Prep: 20mins | Cook: 50mins | Ready in:

Ingredients

- 1 (9 inch) unbaked 9 inch pie crust
- 1/2 pound spinach, rinsed and chopped
- 1/2 pound red Swiss chard, rinsed and chopped
- 1 tablespoon vegetable oil
- 1 onion, diced
- 3 cloves garlic, minced
- 1/4 teaspoon curry powder
- 1 teaspoon dried parsley
- 1/2 teaspoon salt
- 1/2 teaspoon ground black pepper
- 8 small oyster mushrooms, chopped
- 2 teaspoons capers
- 1 (12 ounce) package firm tofu, cubed
- 1/4 cup skim milk
- 1/4 teaspoon ground nutmeg

- 1 pinch ground cinnamon
- 1 pinch ground cardamom
- 1/2 cup grated Parmesan cheese
- 1/2 cup shredded Cheddar cheese

Direction

- Preheat the oven to 175°C or 350°Fahrenheit.
- Bake the pie crust until light brown. In the meantime, put the Swiss chard and spinach in a steamer set over an inch of boiling water; cover. Cook lightly for about 5mins.
- On medium heat, heat oil in a big pan; sauté garlic and onions. Add chard and spinach once the onions turn transparent. Mix in pepper, curry powder, salt and parsley. Sauté until the chard and spinach reduce; put in capers and mushrooms. Mix then take off from heat.
- Process Parmesan cheese, tofu, cardamom, milk, cinnamon and nutmeg together in a food processor or blender until creamy and smooth; add on top of the veggies then stir well. Move the mixture over the pie crust.
- Bake for 20mins in the 350°Fahrenheit preheated oven. Take the quiche out of the oven then add Cheddar cheese on top. Bake for another 10mins until the cheese turns light brown.

Nutrition Information

- Calories: 442 calories;
- Total Fat: 27.7
- Sodium: 816
- Total Carbohydrate: 28.7
- Cholesterol: 21
- Protein: 23.5

12. Sundubu Jjigae (Uncurdled Tofu Stew)

Serving: 2 | Prep: 15mins | Cook: 13mins | Ready in:

Ingredients

- 7 ounces littleneck clams, in shell
- 2 (4 inch) pieces dashi kombu (dried kelp)
- 1 1/3 cups water
- 1 (3 ounce) package enoki mushrooms
- 1 tablespoon olive oil
- 1 tablespoon chili powder
- 1 teaspoon minced garlic
- 1 (14 ounce) package tofu
- 5 small oyster mushrooms, stemmed, or to taste
- 1/2 teaspoon soy sauce
- 1/4 teaspoon salt
- 1 spring onion, sliced on the diagonal
- 3 dashes ground black pepper
- 1 dash sesame oil

Direction

- Cover clams with lightly salted water in a bowl. Place kelp with 1 1/3 cups of water in another bowl. Allow kelp and clams to steep for half an hour. Drain, saving only the kelp soaking water.
- Trim 1 1/2 inches of roots from the bottom of enoki mushrooms; discard. Rinse mushrooms.
- Heat olive oil, garlic and chili powder over medium heat in a pot. Stir in tofu, kelp soaking water and clams. Bring mixture to a boil. Add salt, soy sauce, oyster mushrooms and enoki mushrooms; return to a boil. Add sesame oil, black pepper and spring onion. Cook for 3 to 6 minutes longer until flavors are intensified.

Nutrition Information

- Calories: 345 calories;
- Protein: 31.9
- Total Fat: 18.6
- Sodium: 520
- Total Carbohydrate: 16.7
- Cholesterol: 34

13. Trio Of Mushroom Soup (Cream Of Mushroom Soup)

Serving: 8 | Prep: 20mins | Cook: 36mins | Ready in:

Ingredients

- 1/2 cup unsalted butter, divided
- 3 tablespoons olive oil
- 1/4 cup diced white onion
- 8 ounces portobello mushrooms, stemmed and sliced
- 8 ounces baby bella mushrooms, sliced
- 8 ounces oyster mushrooms, sliced
- 1 1/2 teaspoons dried tarragon
- 3 (16 ounce) cans chicken broth
- 1 large baking potato, peeled and diced into small cubes
- 2 tablespoons fresh thyme
- 1 1/2 teaspoons dried oregano
- 1/2 cup heavy whipping cream (optional)
- salt and ground black pepper to taste

Direction

- Place a large pot on medium heat; heat oil and 1/4 cup of butter for 1-2 minutes, till the butter melts. Add in onion; cook while stirring for around 5 minutes, till soft. Include in tarragon, oyster mushrooms, baby bella mushrooms, Portobello mushrooms and the remaining 1/4 cup of butter; cook while stirring for 5-7 minutes, till tender.
- Mix in oregano, thyme, potato and chicken broth. Allow to boil; keep simmering for 15-20 minutes, till the potato turns tender.
- Take away from the heat; using an immersion blender, purée until smooth.
- Turn the soup back to heat; continue simmering for around 5 minutes, till heated through. Mix in heavy cream. Taste with pepper and salt.

Nutrition Information

- Calories: 260 calories;
- Sodium: 863
- Total Carbohydrate: 10.9
- Cholesterol: 55
- Protein: 4.3
- Total Fat: 22.8

14. Warm Mushroom Salad

Serving: 4 | Prep: 15mins | Cook: 10mins | Ready in:

Ingredients

- 1 tablespoon olive oil
- 1 1/2 cups sliced fresh mushrooms
- 1 clove garlic, chopped (optional)
- 2 1/2 tablespoons olive oil
- 2 1/2 tablespoons balsamic vinegar
- salt and pepper to taste
- 1 (10 ounce) package baby greens mix

Direction

- Over medium heat, heat 1 tbsp. of olive oil in a pan. Put in mushrooms, and cook while stirring until tender. Keep on cooking until the juices from the mushrooms have decreased to roughly two tbsps. Mix in the pepper, salt, balsamic vinegar and the leftover olive oil until equally blended. Turn the heat off, and let the mushrooms rest in the pan till just warm but not hot anymore – or else the greens will be overly wilted.
- Transfer the baby greens to a serving bowl, and put the warm mushroom mixture on top of them. Blend by tossing, and serve right away.

Nutrition Information

- Calories: 130 calories;
- Total Fat: 12.1
- Sodium: 24
- Total Carbohydrate: 4.9
- Cholesterol: 0
- Protein: 2.2

Chapter 2: Mushroom Sandwich Recipes

***

15. Asian Burgers

Serving: 8 servings. | Prep: 20mins | Cook: 10mins | Ready in:

Ingredients

- 2 tablespoons soy sauce
- 1 tablespoon sesame oil
- 1 can (8 ounces) sliced water chestnuts, drained and chopped
- 1 cup bean sprouts
- 1/2 cup finely chopped fresh mushrooms
- 1 celery rib, finely chopped
- 4 green onions, finely chopped
- 1 teaspoon pepper
- 1/2 teaspoon salt
- 2 pounds ground beef
- 4 teaspoons canola oil
- 1/2 cup mayonnaise
- 1 tablespoon prepared wasabi
- 8 sesame seed hamburger buns, split
- 3 cups shredded Chinese or napa cabbage

Direction

- Mix the first 9 ingredients together in a big bowl; break and mix the beef in the mixture. Form the mixture into 8 patties.
- On medium heat, cook burgers in 2 big large pans with oil for 5-6mins per side until an inserted thermometer registers 160 degrees F.
- In the meantime, mix wasabi and mayonnaise together; slather on buns. Serve burgers with cabbage on buns.

Nutrition Information

- Calories: 508 calories
- Fiber: 3g fiber)
- Total Carbohydrate: 29g carbohydrate (5g sugars
- Cholesterol: 75mg cholesterol
- Protein: 27g protein.
- Total Fat: 31g fat (8g saturated fat)
- Sodium: 787mg sodium

16. Bacon Avocado Quesadillas

Serving: 2-4 servings. | Prep: 20mins | Cook: 0mins | Ready in:

Ingredients

- 8 bacon strips, diced
- 1/2 pound fresh mushrooms, sliced
- 1 to 2 tablespoons butter, softened
- 4 flour tortillas (8 inches)
- 2 cups shredded Colby-Monterey Jack cheese
- 1 medium tomato, chopped
- 1 ripe avocado, peeled and sliced
- Sour cream and salsa, optional

Direction

- Cook bacon in a big skillet on moderate heat until crispy. Transfer to paper towels. Drain, saving 1 tbsp. of drippings. Sauté mushrooms in drippings.
- Spread over 1 side of each tortilla with butter. Put 2 tortillas on a skillet or griddle with buttered side facing down. Put avocado, tomato, cheese, mushrooms and bacon on top. Use leftover tortillas to cover with buttered side facing up.

- Cook on low heat until golden brown, about 1 to 2 minutes. Turn and cook until cheese melts, about 1 to 2 minutes. Slice into wedges then serve together with salsa and sour cream if you want.

Nutrition Information

- Calories: 722 calories
- Sodium: 960mg sodium
- Fiber: 3g fiber)
- Total Carbohydrate: 34g carbohydrate (2g sugars
- Cholesterol: 88mg cholesterol
- Protein: 23g protein.
- Total Fat: 56g fat (25g saturated fat)

17. Bacon Blue Cheese Stuffed Burgers

Serving: 4 servings. | Prep: 30mins | Cook: 10mins | Ready in:

Ingredients

- 1-1/2 pounds lean ground beef (90% lean)
- 3 ounces cream cheese, softened
- 1/3 cup crumbled blue cheese
- 1/3 cup bacon bits
- 1/2 teaspoon salt
- 1/2 teaspoon garlic powder
- 1/4 teaspoon pepper
- 1 pound sliced fresh mushrooms
- 1 tablespoon olive oil
- 1 tablespoon water
- 1 tablespoon Dijon mustard
- 4 whole wheat hamburger buns, split
- 1/4 cup mayonnaise
- 4 romaine leaves
- 1 medium tomato, sliced

Direction

- Form beef into 8 thin patties. Mix bacon bits, blue cheese, and cream cheese together; on the center of 4 patties, spoon the mixture. Use remaining patties to top and firmly press edges for sealing. Mix pepper, garlic powder, and salt together; dredge over patties.
- Cover and grill burgers over medium heat or broil 4 inches from the heat for 5-7 minutes per side till juices are clear and a thermometer reads 160 degrees.
- In the meantime, sauté mushrooms with oil in a large skillet till softened. Stir mustard and water in.
- Place burgers on buns with mushroom mixture, tomato, romaine, and mayonnaise for serving.

Nutrition Information

- Calories: 701 calories
- Cholesterol: 149mg cholesterol
- Protein: 48g protein.
- Total Fat: 43g fat (15g saturated fat)
- Sodium: 1280mg sodium
- Fiber: 5g fiber)
- Total Carbohydrate: 31g carbohydrate (7g sugars

18. Bacon Blue Cheese Stuffed Burgers For Two

Serving: 2 servings. | Prep: 30mins | Cook: 10mins | Ready in:

Ingredients

- 3/4 pound lean ground beef (90% lean)
- 4-1/2 teaspoons cream cheese, softened
- 3 tablespoons crumbled blue cheese
- 3 tablespoons bacon bits
- 1/4 teaspoon salt
- 1/4 teaspoon garlic powder
- 1/8 teaspoon pepper
- 1/2 pound sliced fresh mushrooms

- 1-1/2 teaspoons olive oil
- 1-1/2 teaspoons water
- 1-1/2 teaspoons Dijon mustard
- 2 whole wheat hamburger buns, split
- 2 tablespoons mayonnaise
- 2 romaine leaves
- 4 tomato slices

Direction

- Form the beef into 4 thin patties. Mix bacon bits, blue cheese, and cream cheese together; scoop in the middle of 2 patties then place the remaining patties on top. Firmly press the sides together to seal. Mix pepper, garlic powder, and salt together; spread all over the patties.
- On medium heat, grill burgers without cover or broil four inches from heat for 5-7mins per side until the juices are clear and a thermometer registers 160 degrees F.
- In the meantime, sauté mushrooms in a big pan with oil until tender. Mix in mustard and water.
- Place burgers on buns; add the mushroom mixture, mayonnaise, tomato, and romaine.

Nutrition Information

- Calories: 675 calories
- Fiber: 5g fiber)
- Total Carbohydrate: 31g carbohydrate (7g sugars
- Cholesterol: 140mg cholesterol
- Protein: 48g protein.
- Total Fat: 40g fat (13g saturated fat)
- Sodium: 1308mg sodium

19. Barbecued Mushroom Turkey Burgers

Serving: 4 servings. | Prep: 25mins | Cook: 20mins | Ready in:

Ingredients

- 3/4 cup chopped sweet onion
- 2 teaspoons butter
- 1 cup sliced fresh mushrooms
- 1 medium carrot, grated
- 1/4 cup dry red wine or chicken broth
- 1/2 teaspoon salt
- 1/4 teaspoon pepper
- 1 pound lean ground turkey
- 1/2 cup barbecue sauce, divided
- 4 hamburger buns, split
- 4 Bibb lettuce leaves
- 4 slices tomato

Direction

- Sauté the onion in butter in a big nonstick frying pan for 3 minutes, then add carrot and mushrooms. Let it cook and stir for 3 minutes, then add the pepper, salt and wine. Let it simmer until the liquid evaporates or for 2-3 minutes.
- Move to a big bowl and let it cool a bit. Crumble the turkey on top of the mixture and stir well, then form it into 4 patties. Put cover and let it chill for a minimum of one hour.
- Use cooking oil to moisten a paper towel using long-handled tongs and coat the grill rack lightly. Grill the patties on medium heat, without cover, or let it broil for 8 to 10 minutes per side, placed 4 inches from the heat source or until the juices run clear and a thermometer registers 165 degrees, brushing from time to time, with 1/4 cup barbecue sauce. Serve with leftover barbecue sauce, tomato and lettuce on buns.

Nutrition Information

- Calories: 371 calories
- Total Fat: 14g fat (4g saturated fat)
- Sodium: 926mg sodium
- Fiber: 3g fiber)
- Total Carbohydrate: 32g carbohydrate (11g sugars
- Cholesterol: 95mg cholesterol

- Protein: 25g protein. Diabetic Exchanges: 3 lean meat
- Total Fat: 37g fat (22g saturated fat)
- Sodium: 899mg sodium
- Fiber: 3g fiber)
- Total Carbohydrate: 38g carbohydrate (7g sugars

20. Beef Stroganoff Melt

Serving: 8 servings. | Prep: 15mins | Cook: 15mins | Ready in:

Ingredients

- 2 pounds ground beef
- 1 cup sliced fresh mushrooms
- 1 medium onion, chopped
- 1 teaspoon salt
- 1/2 teaspoon garlic powder
- 1/2 teaspoon pepper
- 2 cups (16 ounces) sour cream
- 1 loaf (1 pound) unsliced French bread
- 3 tablespoons butter, softened
- 3 cups shredded Swiss cheese
- 1 medium green pepper, thinly sliced
- 2 medium tomatoes, thinly sliced

Direction

- Cook onion, mushrooms and beef together in a big skillet on moderate heat until beef is not pink anymore, then drain. Stir in beef mixture with pepper, garlic powder and salt. Take away from the heat and stir in sour cream. Halve the French bread lengthways and arrange on a grease-free baking sheet. Smear butter on cut halves. Put the meat mixture as well as 1/2 of the cheese on top.
- Top with tomatoes and green pepper then use leftover cheese to sprinkle over top. Bake at 375 degrees until cheese melts, about 15 minutes.

Nutrition Information

- Calories: 665 calories
- Cholesterol: 144mg cholesterol
- Protein: 40g protein.

21. Beef Stroganoff Sandwiches

Serving: 6 servings. | Prep: 15mins | Cook: 10mins | Ready in:

Ingredients

- 1 pound ground beef
- 1 cup sliced fresh mushrooms
- 1 small green pepper, finely chopped
- 1 small onion, finely chopped
- 1 envelope ranch dip mix
- 3/4 cup sour cream
- 1 loaf (about 8 ounces) French bread
- 2 cups shredded part-skim mozzarella cheese

Direction

- Set up the broiler to preheat. Cook together onion, pepper, mushrooms and beef in a big skillet on moderately-high heat until beef is not pink anymore, about 8-10 minutes while breaking up into crumbles, then drain. Stir in sour cream and dip mix.
- Halve the French bread horizontally and arrange them on a baking sheet with cut-side facing up. Broil bread halves 3 to 4 inches away from the heat source until toasted slightly, about 1 to 2 minutes. Take out of the broiler.
- Scoop over bread with the beef mixture and sprinkle cheese over top. Broil for 1 to 2 more minutes, until cheese brown slightly. Cut each into 3 pieces to serve.

Nutrition Information

- Calories:
- Protein:

- Total Fat:
- Sodium:
- Fiber:
- Total Carbohydrate:
- Cholesterol:

22. Blues Burgers

Serving: 4 servings. | Prep: 10mins | Cook: 20mins | Ready in:

Ingredients

- 1/2 pound sliced fresh mushrooms
- 2 tablespoons butter
- 1-1/2 pounds lean ground beef (90% lean)
- 1/2 teaspoon ground cumin
- 1/2 teaspoon paprika
- 1/4 teaspoon salt
- 1/4 teaspoon chili powder
- 1/4 teaspoon pepper
- Pinch cayenne pepper
- 2 ounces crumbled blue cheese
- 2/3 cup barbecue sauce
- 4 onion rolls or hamburger buns, split

Direction

- In butter, sauté mushrooms in a skillet until tender, about 2 to 3 minutes. Put aside; keep warm.
- Mix seasonings and beef together in a bowl just until combined. Form into 8 thin patties. Sprinkle blue cheese on top of half of the patties, and top with the rest of patties; seal edges by pressing firmly.
- Grill over medium-hot heat without a cover, about 3 minutes per side. Brush some of barbecue sauce on the surface. Grill until juices run clear, about 10 to 12 more minutes, turning and basting from time to time. Drain mushrooms. Place burgers on rolls and put mushrooms on top to serve.

Nutrition Information

- Calories: 552 calories
- Total Fat: 26g fat (13g saturated fat)
- Sodium: 1128mg sodium
- Fiber: 2g fiber)
- Total Carbohydrate: 34g carbohydrate (8g sugars
- Cholesterol: 109mg cholesterol
- Protein: 43g protein.

23. Burgers Cacciatore

Serving: 4 servings. | Prep: 20mins | Cook: 20mins | Ready in:

Ingredients

- 5 large portobello mushrooms (4 to 4-1/2 inches)
- 3/4 teaspoon salt, divided
- 1 small onion, finely chopped
- 1/2 cup chopped sweet red pepper
- 1/3 cup shredded part-skim mozzarella cheese
- 3 tablespoons tomato paste
- 3 tablespoons minced fresh parsley
- 1 tablespoon Worcestershire sauce
- 2 garlic cloves, minced
- 1/4 teaspoon pepper
- 1 pound lean ground turkey
- 2 cups chopped fresh arugula or baby spinach
- 4 slices part-skim mozzarella cheese
- 2 plum tomatoes, sliced
- 2 slices red onion, separated into rings

Direction

- Take out the stems from the mushrooms and put aside. On a broiler pan coated with cooking spray, put 4 mushroom caps, then sprinkle 1/4 tsp of salt on top.
- Let it broil for 4-6 minutes per side, placed 4 inches from the heat source or until it becomes soft, then keep it warm.

- Chop the leftover mushroom cap and mushroom stems finely, then put it in a big bowl. Add leftover salt, pepper, garlic, Worcestershire sauce, parsley, tomato paste, shredded cheese, red pepper and chopped onion, then crumble the turkey on top of the mixture and stir well.
- Form it into 4 patties and let it broil for 5 to 7 minutes per side, placed 4 inches from the heat source or until the juices run clear and a thermometer registers 165 degrees.
- On each mushroom cap, put 1/2 cup of arugula. Put a slice of cheese and turkey patty on top, then let it broil until the cheese melts or for one minute. Put slices of onion and tomato on top.

Nutrition Information

- Calories: 347 calories
- Sodium: 809mg sodium
- Fiber: 4g fiber)
- Total Carbohydrate: 16g carbohydrate (7g sugars
- Cholesterol: 110mg cholesterol
- Protein: 34g protein.
- Total Fat: 16g fat (7g saturated fat)

24. Cheesy Chicken Subs

Serving: 4 servings. | Prep: 25mins | Cook: 0mins | Ready in:

Ingredients

- 12 ounces boneless skinless chicken breasts, cut into strips
- 1 envelope Parmesan Italian or Caesar salad dressing mix
- 1 cup sliced fresh mushrooms
- 1/2 cup sliced red onion
- 1/4 cup olive oil
- 4 submarine buns, split and toasted
- 4 slices Swiss cheese

Direction

- Arrange chicken in a large bowl, and scatter salad dressing mix over. Sauté onion and mushrooms in oil in a large skillet for 3 minutes. Put in chicken; sauté until chicken is no longer pink, or for 6 minutes.
- Scoop chicken mixture over bun bottoms, then place cheese over. Broil 4 inches from the heat source until cheese is melted, or for 4 minutes. Place back top buns over to finish.

Nutrition Information

- Calories: 709 calories
- Sodium: 1478mg sodium
- Fiber: 4g fiber)
- Total Carbohydrate: 72g carbohydrate (8g sugars
- Cholesterol: 72mg cholesterol
- Protein: 35g protein.
- Total Fat: 29g fat (9g saturated fat)

25. Chicken Cheddar Wraps

Serving: 12 wraps. | Prep: 15mins | Cook: 0mins | Ready in:

Ingredients

- 1 cup sour cream
- 1 cup chunky salsa
- 2 tablespoons mayonnaise
- 4 cups cubed cooked chicken
- 2 cups shredded cheddar cheese
- 1 cup thinly sliced fresh mushrooms
- 2 cups shredded lettuce
- 1 cup guacamole, optional
- 12 flour tortillas (6 inches), room temperature
- Tomato wedges and additional guacamole, optional

Direction

- Mix mayonnaise, salsa, and sour cream together in a big bowl. Mix in mushrooms, cheese, and chicken.
- Split guacamole and lettuce among tortillas if you want. Put about 1/2 cup of chicken mixture on each tortilla. Wrap the sides over the stuffing. Use more guacamole and tomato to garnish if you want.

Nutrition Information

- Calories: 271 calories
- Protein: 18g protein. Diabetic Exchanges: 2 starch
- Total Fat: 6g fat (0 saturated fat)
- Sodium: 537mg sodium
- Fiber: 2g fiber)
- Total Carbohydrate: 35g carbohydrate (0 sugars
- Cholesterol: 34mg cholesterol

26. Chicken Veggie Pockets

Serving: 2 servings. | Prep: 15mins | Cook: 15mins | Ready in:

Ingredients

- 3 ounces cream cheese, softened
- 1 tablespoon whole milk
- 1/4 to 1/2 teaspoon Italian seasoning
- 1/4 teaspoon salt
- 1/8 teaspoon pepper
- 1 cup cubed cooked chicken
- 2 small fresh mushrooms, sliced
- 1/4 cup frozen corn, thawed and patted dry
- 3 tablespoons frozen cut green beans, thawed and patted dry
- 1 tube (4 ounces) refrigerated crescent rolls

Direction

- Beat milk and cream cheese in a small bowl until combined. Stir in pepper, salt and Italian seasoning then blend well together. Stir in green beans, corn, mushrooms and chicken. Unroll crescent roll dough and divide into 2 rectangles, sealing perforations. Put on one side of each rectangle with 1/2 of the filling and fold in half, sealing edges. The pockets will become full. Put pockets on a grease-free baking sheet and bake at 375 degrees until golden brown, about 15 to 20 minutes.

Nutrition Information

- Calories: 534 calories
- Total Carbohydrate: 29g carbohydrate (6g sugars
- Cholesterol: 110mg cholesterol
- Protein: 29g protein.
- Total Fat: 33g fat (14g saturated fat)
- Sodium: 945mg sodium
- Fiber: 1g fiber)

27. Chili Beef Quesadillas

Serving: 4 servings. | Prep: 30mins | Cook: 10mins | Ready in:

Ingredients

- 3/4 pound lean ground beef (90% lean)
- 1 medium onion, chopped
- 3/4 cup finely chopped fresh mushrooms
- 1 medium zucchini, shredded
- 1 medium carrot, shredded
- 2 garlic cloves, minced
- 2 teaspoons chili powder
- 1/4 teaspoon salt
- 1/4 teaspoon hot pepper sauce
- 2 medium tomatoes, seeded and chopped
- 1/4 cup minced fresh cilantro
- 4 whole wheat tortillas (8 inches), warmed
- Cooking spray
- 1/2 cup shredded part-skim mozzarella cheese

Direction

- Cook the onion and beef in a big nonstick frying pan over medium heat, until meat is no longer pink; drain. Take out and keep warm. Cook and stir the pepper sauce, salt, chili powder, garlic, carrot, zucchini and mushrooms using the same frying pan, until the vegetables become soft. Mix in the beef mixture, cilantro and tomatoes.
- Use cooking spray to spritz one side of each tortilla, then put in a 15x10x1-inch baking pan coated with cooking spray, plain side facing up. Over half of each tortilla, spread the beef mixture and sprinkle with cheese. Fold the tortillas over the filling.
- Bake for 5 minutes at 400 degrees then turn them over gently. Continue to bake for 5-6 minutes more until the cheese melts, then slice into wedges.

Nutrition Information

- Calories: 353 calories
- Total Fat: 12g fat (4g saturated fat)
- Sodium: 475mg sodium
- Fiber: 5g fiber)
- Total Carbohydrate: 33g carbohydrate (7g sugars
- Cholesterol: 50mg cholesterol
- Protein: 26g protein. Diabetic Exchanges: 3 lean meat

28. Contest Winning Grilled Roast Beef Sandwiches

Serving: 4 servings. | Prep: 15mins | Cook: 15mins | Ready in:

Ingredients

- 1 medium onion, sliced
- 1 medium green pepper, sliced
- 1/2 pound fresh mushrooms, sliced
- 2 to 3 garlic cloves, minced
- 2 tablespoons canola oil
- 1/4 teaspoon salt
- 1/8 teaspoon pepper
- 8 slices sourdough bread
- 16 slices Colby-Monterey Jack or Swiss cheese, divided
- 8 slices deli roast beef
- 1/2 cup butter, softened
- Garlic salt, optional

Direction

- Sauté together garlic, mushrooms, green pepper and onion in a big skillet with oil until soft, then sprinkle pepper and salt on top. Layer on 4 bread slices with 2 cheese slices, 2 beef slices and 1/4 of the vegetable mixture. Put leftover cheese followed by bread on top.
- Coat the outside of bread with butter and sprinkle garlic salt on top if you want. Toast sandwiches on a big skillet or hot griddle until golden brown, about 3 to 4 minutes per side.

Nutrition Information

- Calories: 825 calories
- Sodium: 1540mg sodium
- Fiber: 4g fiber)
- Total Carbohydrate: 46g carbohydrate (5g sugars
- Cholesterol: 151mg cholesterol
- Protein: 33g protein.
- Total Fat: 60g fat (32g saturated fat)

29. Creamy Eggplant & Mushroom Monte Cristo

Serving: 4 servings. | Prep: 15mins | Cook: 15mins | Ready in:

Ingredients

- 5 tablespoons olive oil, divided
- 6 slices eggplant (1/2 inch thick), halved

- 2-1/2 cups sliced fresh shiitake or baby portobello mushrooms (about 6 ounces)
- 1 large garlic clove, minced
- 1/2 teaspoon salt
- 1/4 teaspoon pepper
- 2 large eggs
- 2 tablespoons 2% milk
- 1/2 cup garlic-herb spreadable cheese (about 3 ounces)
- 8 slices wide-loaf white bread

Direction

- Heat 1 tbsp. of oil in a big nonstick frying pan over medium heat, then add eggplant. Cook for 2-3 minutes per side or until it turns light brown and tender. Take it out of the pan.
- Heat 2 tbsp. of oil in the same pan over medium heat, then add mushrooms. Cook and stir for 2 to 3 minutes or until they become soft. Add pepper, salt and garlic and cook for 1 minute more. Take them out of the pan and wipe the frying pan to clean.
- Whisk the milk and eggs in a shallow bowl until combined. Spread 1 tbsp. of herb cheese on top of each bread slice. Layer eggplant and mushrooms on 4 slices, then put the leftover bread on top.
- Heat 1 tbsp. of oil in the same pan over medium heat. Dunk both sides of the sandwiches in the egg mixture gently; allow each side to submerge for 5 seconds. In a frying pan, put 2 sandwiches and toast for 2 to 3 minutes per side or until they turn golden brown in color. Redo the process with the leftover sandwiches and oil.

Nutrition Information

- Calories: 573 calories
- Protein: 15g protein.
- Total Fat: 36g fat (13g saturated fat)
- Sodium: 939mg sodium
- Fiber: 6g fiber)
- Total Carbohydrate: 52g carbohydrate (9g sugars
- Cholesterol: 129mg cholesterol

30. Eggplant Muffuletta

Serving: 18 servings. | Prep: 35mins | Cook: 5mins | Ready in:

Ingredients

- 1 jar (8 ounces) roasted sweet red peppers, drained
- 1 cup pimiento-stuffed olives
- 1 cup pitted ripe olives
- 1 cup giardiniera
- 3/4 cup olive oil, divided
- 1/4 cup packed fresh parsley sprigs
- 3 tablespoons white wine vinegar
- 4 garlic cloves, halved
- 1-1/2 teaspoons salt, divided
- 1/2 teaspoon pepper, divided
- 1 pound sliced fresh mushrooms
- 1 large onion, thinly sliced
- 2 tablespoons butter
- 1 cup all-purpose flour
- 1 medium eggplant, cut into nine slices
- 3 loaves (10 ounces each) focaccia bread
- 2 large tomatoes, sliced
- 9 slices provolone cheese
- 9 slices part-skim mozzarella cheese

Direction

- Mix together the 1/4 tsp. pepper, 1 tsp. salt, garlic, vinegar, parsley, 1/4 cup oil, giardiniera, olives and red peppers in a food processor. Put a cover and process until combined, then put aside.
- Sauté the onion and mushrooms in 1/4 cup oil and butter in a big frying pan. Take it out and keep it warm.
- Mix together the leftover pepper and salt and flour in a big resealable plastic bag, then add the eggplant, a few slices at a time, then jiggle to coat. Cook the eggplant in the leftover oil for 2 to 3 minutes per side in the same frying pan or until it turns golden brown.

- Halve each loaf of focaccia. Spread the reserved olive mixture on top of each focaccia bottom, then top with eggplant, mushroom mixture, tomatoes and cheeses.
- Place it on a baking tray. Let it broil for 2 to 4 minutes, placed 2 to 3 inches from the heat source or until the cheese melts. Place back the focaccia tops, then slice each loaf into 6 wedges.

Nutrition Information

- Calories: 372 calories
- Protein: 12g protein.
- Total Fat: 20g fat (6g saturated fat)
- Sodium: 881mg sodium
- Fiber: 3g fiber)
- Total Carbohydrate: 39g carbohydrate (5g sugars
- Cholesterol: 18mg cholesterol

31. Eggplant Portobello Sandwich Loaf

Serving: 4 servings. | Prep: 25mins | Cook: 20mins | Ready in:

Ingredients

- 1 loaf (1 pound) Italian bread
- 1/2 cup olive oil
- 2 teaspoons minced garlic
- 1 teaspoon Italian seasoning
- 1/2 teaspoon salt
- 1/4 teaspoon pepper
- 1 large eggplant (1 pound), cut into 1/2-inch slices
- 1 package (6 ounces) sliced portobello mushrooms
- 1 cup marinara sauce
- 2 tablespoons minced fresh basil
- 4 ounces smoked fresh mozzarella cheese, cut into 1/4-inch slices

Direction

- Halve the bread lengthwise. Hollow out the bottom and top gently and leave a 1/2-inch shell, then put aside. Mix together the pepper, salt, Italian seasoning, garlic and oil in a small bowl, then brush it on top of the mushrooms and eggplant.
- Let it grill for 3-5 minutes per side on medium heat with cover or until the vegetables become soft.
- On the bottom of the bread, spread 1/2 of the marinara sauce, then put mushrooms and eggplant on top. Spread with the leftover sauce and put cheese and basil on top. Place back the bread top.
- Wrap the loaf in a big piece of heavy-duty foil, approximately 28-inch x 18-inch; tightly seal. Let it grill for 4 to 5 minutes per side on medium heat with a cover.

Nutrition Information

- Calories: 632 calories
- Cholesterol: 22mg cholesterol
- Protein: 16g protein.
- Total Fat: 36g fat (8g saturated fat)
- Sodium: 949mg sodium
- Fiber: 7g fiber)
- Total Carbohydrate: 60g carbohydrate (11g sugars

32. English Muffin Egg Sandwiches

Serving: 8 servings. | Prep: 15mins | Cook: 10mins | Ready in:

Ingredients

- 1/2 pound sliced fresh mushrooms
- 1 small sweet red pepper, chopped
- 1 small sweet onion, chopped
- 1/2 teaspoon garlic salt
- 1/4 teaspoon pepper

- 1/4 teaspoon crushed red pepper flakes, optional
- 7 large eggs, lightly beaten
- 8 whole wheat English muffins, split and toasted
- 4 ounces reduced-fat cream cheese

Direction

- Over medium-high heat, put a big nonstick skillet. Put in seasonings, onion, red pepper and mushrooms; cook and mix for 5-7 minutes or until mushrooms are soft. Take out from pan.
- Clean up the skillet and grease with cooking spray; put skillet over medium heat. Put in eggs; cook and mix just until eggs thickened and no liquid egg remains. Put in vegetables; heat thoroughly, gently mix.
- Spread cream cheese on muffin bottoms; garnish with egg mixture. Replace tops.

Nutrition Information

- Calories: 244 calories
- Fiber: 5g fiber)
- Total Carbohydrate: 30g carbohydrate (7g sugars
- Cholesterol: 173mg cholesterol
- Protein: 14g protein. Diabetic Exchanges: 2 starch
- Total Fat: 9g fat (4g saturated fat)
- Sodium: 425mg sodium

33. Feta Mushroom Burgers

Serving: 6 servings. | Prep: 15mins | Cook: 10mins | Ready in:

Ingredients

- 1 pound lean ground beef (90% lean)
- 3 Italian turkey sausage links (4 ounces each), casings removed
- 2 teaspoons Worcestershire sauce
- 1/2 teaspoon garlic powder
- 2 tablespoons balsamic vinegar
- 1 tablespoon olive oil
- 6 large portobello mushrooms, stems removed
- 1 large onion, cut into 1/2-inch slices
- 6 tablespoons crumbled feta or blue cheese
- 6 whole wheat hamburger buns or sourdough rolls, split
- 10 fresh basil leaves, thinly sliced

Direction

- Mix the first 4 ingredients thoroughly but lightly; form into 6 half-inch thick patties. Combine oil and vinegar; slather over the mushrooms.
- Place the onion, mushrooms, and burgers on a greased grill rack. On medium heat, grill for 4-6mins on each side, covered, until the onion and mushrooms are tender and an inserted thermometer in the burger registers 165 degrees F.
- Scoop cheese in the mushroom caps until full; grill for 1-2mins, covered, until the cheese melts. With the cut-side down, grill buns for 30-60secs until toasted. Serve burgers with onion, basil, and mushrooms on buns.

Nutrition Information

- Calories: 371 calories
- Fiber: 5g fiber)
- Total Carbohydrate: 31g carbohydrate (8g sugars
- Cholesterol: 72mg cholesterol
- Protein: 28g protein. Diabetic Exchanges: 4 lean meat
- Total Fat: 15g fat (5g saturated fat)
- Sodium: 590mg sodium

34. Freezer Veggie Burgers

Serving: 6 servings. | Prep: 25mins | Cook: 30mins | Ready in:

Ingredients

- 1 can (16 ounces) kidney beans, rinsed and drained
- 1/2 cup old-fashioned oats
- 2 tablespoons ketchup
- 1/2 cup finely chopped fresh mushrooms
- 1 medium onion, finely chopped
- 1 medium carrot, shredded
- 1 small sweet red pepper, finely chopped
- 2 garlic cloves, minced
- 1/2 teaspoon salt
- 1/8 teaspoon white pepper
- 6 hamburger buns, split
- 6 lettuce leaves
- 6 slices tomato

Direction

- In a food processor, put the ketchup, oats and beans. Put on a cover and pulse until combined. Move to a small bowl and mix in the seasonings, garlic and vegetables. Form the mixture into six 3-inch patties, then use plastic wrap to wrap each then freeze.
- Using frozen burgers: Take the wrap away from the burgers and put them on a baking tray coated with cooking spray. Bake for 30 minutes at 350° until heated through, flipping once. Serve with tomato and lettuce on buns.

Nutrition Information

- Calories: 241 calories
- Protein: 11g protein. Diabetic Exchanges: 2-1/2 starch
- Total Fat: 3g fat (1g saturated fat)
- Sodium: 601mg sodium
- Fiber: 7g fiber)
- Total Carbohydrate: 45g carbohydrate (8g sugars
- Cholesterol: 0 cholesterol

35. Fresh Veggie Pockets

Serving: 4 servings. | Prep: 15mins | Cook: 0mins | Ready in:

Ingredients

- 1 carton (8 ounces) spreadable cream cheese
- 1/4 cup sunflower kernels
- 1 teaspoon seasoned salt or salt-free seasoning blend
- 4 whole wheat pita breads (6 inches), halved
- 1 medium tomato, thinly sliced
- 1 medium cucumber, thinly sliced
- 1 cup sliced fresh mushrooms
- 1 ripe avocado, peeled and sliced

Direction

- Mix together seasoned salt, sunflower kernels and cream cheese in a big bowl, then spread on the inside of each pita half with 2 tbsp. of the mixture. Layer with avocado, mushrooms, cucumber and tomato.

Nutrition Information

- Calories: 434 calories
- Fiber: 8g fiber)
- Total Carbohydrate: 48g carbohydrate (6g sugars
- Cholesterol: 37mg cholesterol
- Protein: 14g protein.
- Total Fat: 23g fat (9g saturated fat)
- Sodium: 571mg sodium

36. Garlic Roast Beef Sandwiches

Serving: 6 servings. | Prep: 20mins | Cook: 5mins | Ready in:

Ingredients

- 1 loaf (10 ounces) frozen garlic bread
- 1/2 pound sliced fresh mushrooms

- 2/3 cup sliced onion
- 4 teaspoons butter
- 1 teaspoon minced garlic
- 1 teaspoon Worcestershire sauce
- 1 pound shaved deli roast beef
- 6 slices Colby cheese

Direction

- Follow directions on package to bake garlic bread. In the meantime, sauté onion and mushrooms with butter in a big skillet until soft. Put in garlic; continue to cook for another minute. Stir in Worcestershire sauce.
- On each half of garlic bread, layer with roast beef then mushroom mixture and cheese. Put back in oven; bake for about 3-5 minutes or until cheese melts and bread is heated through.

Nutrition Information

- Calories: 395 calories
- Sodium: 913mg sodium
- Fiber: 2g fiber)
- Total Carbohydrate: 24g carbohydrate (3g sugars
- Cholesterol: 81mg cholesterol
- Protein: 28g protein.
- Total Fat: 22g fat (10g saturated fat)

37. Green Onion Burgers

Serving: 12 servings. | Prep: 20mins | Cook: 15mins | Ready in:

Ingredients

- 1/4 cup soy sauce
- 2 tablespoons beef broth
- 1/4 pound fresh mushrooms, finely chopped
- 3/4 cup chopped water chestnuts
- 1/2 cup chopped green onions
- 2 tablespoons minced fresh gingerroot
- 1 tablespoon cornstarch
- 1/4 teaspoon cayenne pepper
- 2 pounds lean ground beef (90% lean)
- 12 hamburger buns, split

Direction

- Mix the first 8 ingredients together in a large bowl. Crumble beef and add into the mixture; combine well. Form into 12 patties. Cover and grill over medium heat or broil 4 inches from the heat till not pink anymore, about 6-9 minutes per side. Place onto buns and serve.

Nutrition Information

- Calories: 252 calories
- Sodium: 609mg sodium
- Fiber: 2g fiber)
- Total Carbohydrate: 24g carbohydrate (4g sugars
- Cholesterol: 37mg cholesterol
- Protein: 19g protein.
- Total Fat: 8g fat (3g saturated fat)

38. Grilled Beef Tenderloin Sandwiches

Serving: 4 servings. | Prep: 15mins | Cook: 01hours10mins | Ready in:

Ingredients

- 1 tablespoon brown sugar
- 2 garlic cloves, minced
- 1/2 teaspoon coarsely ground pepper
- 1/4 teaspoon salt
- 1 beef tenderloin roast (1 pound)
- 1 whole garlic bulb
- 1/2 teaspoon canola oil
- 1/4 cup fat-free mayonnaise
- 1/4 cup plain yogurt
- ONION TOPPING:
- 1 tablespoon olive oil

- 1 large sweet onion, thinly sliced
- 1/2 pound sliced fresh mushrooms
- 2 tablespoons balsamic vinegar
- 1-1/2 teaspoons sugar
- 1/8 teaspoon salt
- 1/8 teaspoon pepper
- 4 slices French bread (3/4 inch thick)
- 1 cup fresh arugula

Direction

- Mix together the initial 4 ingredients, then massage it over the meat. Let it chill in the fridge for 2 hours. Take off the papery outer skin from the garlic; avoid peeling or separating the cloves. Slice off the top of the garlic, then brush it with oil.
- Use heavy duty foil to wrap the bulb and let it bake for 30-35 minutes at 425 degrees or until it becomes soft. Let it cool for 10 to 15 minutes. In the food processor, squeeze the garlic, then add yogurt and mayonnaise. Process it until it becomes smooth, then chill.
- Heat the olive oil in a big nonstick frying pan and sauté the onion for 5 minutes. Lower the heat then cook and stir until the onion turns golden or for 10 to 12 minutes. Add mushrooms then cook and stir until it becomes soft. Add the next 4 ingredients and let it cook until reduced a bit. Use cooking oil to moisten the paper towel using a long-handled tongs and coat the grill rack lightly. Let the beef grill on medium heat with a cover, or let it broil for 5 to 6 minutes per side, placed 4 inches from the heat source or until the meat achieves the preferred doneness; a thermometer should read 170 degrees for well done, 160 degrees for medium, 145 degrees for medium-rare. Allow it to stand for 10 minutes prior to slicing into four pieces.
- Serve warm with onion mixture, arugula and garlic mayonnaise on bread.

Nutrition Information

- Calories: 418 calories
- Total Carbohydrate: 40g carbohydrate (11g sugars
- Cholesterol: 75mg cholesterol
- Protein: 31g protein. Diabetic Exchanges: 3 lean meat
- Total Fat: 15g fat (4g saturated fat)
- Sodium: 702mg sodium
- Fiber: 3g fiber)

39. Grilled Blue Cheese Sandwiches

Serving: 6 servings. | Prep: 30mins | Cook: 0mins | Ready in:

Ingredients

- 1-1/2 cups sliced fresh mushrooms
- 2 tablespoons chopped onion
- 1/2 cup mayonnaise, divided
- 2 cups shredded cheddar cheese
- 1/4 cup crumbled blue cheese
- 1 teaspoon yellow or Dijon mustard
- 1 teaspoon Worcestershire sauce
- 1/4 teaspoon salt
- 1/8 teaspoon cayenne pepper
- 12 slices white or wheat bread
- 2 to 4 tablespoons butter

Direction

- Sauté the onion and mushrooms in 3 tbsp. of mayonnaise in a big frying pan for 5 minutes or until the mushrooms become soft; allow it to cool. Mix together the leftover mayonnaise, mushroom mixture, cayenne, salt, Worcestershire sauce, mustard and cheeses in a big bowl. Spread 1/3 cup on 6 bread slices. Melt 2 to 3 tbsp. of butter in a griddle or big frying pan, then toast the sandwiches until the cheese melts and the bread turns light brown on both sides; add butter if needed.

Nutrition Information

- Calories: 460 calories
- Protein: 14g protein.
- Total Fat: 33g fat (14g saturated fat)
- Sodium: 830mg sodium
- Fiber: 1g fiber)
- Total Carbohydrate: 27g carbohydrate (3g sugars
- Cholesterol: 62mg cholesterol

40. Grilled Burgers With Horseradish Sauce

Serving: 6 servings. | Prep: 20mins | Cook: 10mins | Ready in:

Ingredients

- 1/2 cup reduced-fat sour cream
- 1 tablespoon snipped fresh dill or 1 teaspoon dill weed
- 1 tablespoon finely chopped onion
- 1 tablespoon sweet pickle relish
- 2 teaspoons prepared horseradish
- BURGERS:
- 3/4 cup chopped fresh mushrooms
- 1/4 cup shredded carrot
- 1/4 cup finely chopped onion
- 2 tablespoons minced fresh parsley
- 1 tablespoon Worcestershire sauce
- 1/2 teaspoon salt
- 1/4 teaspoon hot pepper sauce
- 1/8 teaspoon pepper
- 1-1/4 pounds lean ground beef (90% lean)
- 6 whole wheat hamburger buns, split
- 6 lettuce leaves
- 12 tomato slices

Direction

- Mix together horseradish, pickle relish, onion, dill and sour cream in a small bowl; put into refrigerator with a cover. Mix together the first 8 ingredients for burger in another bowl. Add crumbled beef to the mixture and stir well to combine. Form into 6 patties of 1/2 inch thickness.
- Put patties on grill grate over medium-hot heat with a cover until no longer pink, about 3 to 4 minutes per side. Put horseradish sauce, tomato, lettuce and burgers on buns to serve.

Nutrition Information

- Calories: 418 calories
- Sodium: 688mg sodium
- Fiber: 3g fiber)
- Total Carbohydrate: 42g carbohydrate (0 sugars
- Cholesterol: 41mg cholesterol
- Protein: 29g protein. Diabetic Exchanges: 2-1/2 starch
- Total Fat: 15g fat (7g saturated fat)

41. Grilled Cheese Supreme

Serving: 6 servings. | Prep: 15mins | Cook: 5mins | Ready in:

Ingredients

- 12 slices hearty rye bread
- 12 teaspoons mayonnaise
- 18 slices cheddar cheese
- 3 small tomatoes, thinly sliced
- 1-1/2 cups sliced fresh mushrooms
- 6 thin slices sweet onion
- 1 medium ripe avocado, peeled and cut into 12 wedges
- 12 teaspoons butter, softened

Direction

- Spread 1 tsp of mayonnaise on each of the 6 slices of bread, then layer it with a slice of cheese, tomatoes, mushrooms, another slice of cheese, onion, 2 avocado wedges and leftover slice of cheese. Spread leftover mayonnaise on the leftover bread and place it on top.

- Butter the exteriors of the sandwiches. Let it toast for 2-3 minutes per side on a heated griddle or until the cheese melts and the bread turns light brown.

Nutrition Information

- Calories: 674 calories
- Cholesterol: 107mg cholesterol
- Protein: 28g protein.
- Total Fat: 46g fat (23g saturated fat)
- Sodium: 1034mg sodium
- Fiber: 7g fiber)
- Total Carbohydrate: 38g carbohydrate (5g sugars

42. Grilled Deli Sandwiches

Serving: 6 servings. | Prep: 15mins | Cook: 10mins | Ready in:

Ingredients

- 1 medium onion, sliced
- 1 cup sliced fresh mushrooms
- 1 cup julienned green pepper
- 1 cup julienned sweet red pepper
- 2 tablespoons canola oil
- 12 slices sourdough bread
- 1/2 pound each thinly sliced deli ham, smoked turkey and pastrami
- 6 bacon strips, cooked and crumbled
- 6 slices process American cheese
- 6 slices Swiss cheese

Direction

- Sauté together peppers, mushrooms and onion in a big skillet with oil until soft. Layer ham, turkey, pastrami, bacon, vegetables and cheese on top of 6 slices of bread, then place leftover bread on top. Use foil to wrap each sandwich.
- Grill with a cover on moderate heat until heated through, about 4 to 5 minutes per side.

Nutrition Information

- Calories: 548 calories
- Protein: 40g protein.
- Total Fat: 24g fat (11g saturated fat)
- Sodium: 1745mg sodium
- Fiber: 3g fiber)
- Total Carbohydrate: 41g carbohydrate (5g sugars
- Cholesterol: 96mg cholesterol

43. Grilled Havarti & Mushrooms

Serving: 4 servings. | Prep: 10mins | Cook: 10mins | Ready in:

Ingredients

- 12 ounces Havarti cheese with dill, thinly sliced
- 8 slices onion rye or other bakery bread (round loaf)
- 2 medium tomatoes, sliced
- 1 cup sliced fresh mushrooms
- 1/4 cup butter, softened

Direction

- On 4 slices of bread, put half of the cheese then top it with leftover cheese, mushrooms and tomatoes. Spread butter on the exteriors of the sandwiches
- Toast the sandwiches in a big frying pan for 3 to 4 minutes per side on medium heat or until the cheese melts and turns golden brown.

Nutrition Information

- Calories: 653 calories
- Fiber: 6g fiber)
- Total Carbohydrate: 47g carbohydrate (8g sugars
- Cholesterol: 110mg cholesterol

- Protein: 28g protein.
- Total Fat: 40g fat (24g saturated fat)
- Sodium: 1122mg sodium

44. Grilled Italian Turkey Burgers

Serving: 4 servings. | Prep: 10mins | Cook: 15mins | Ready in:

Ingredients

- 1/2 pound sliced baby portobello mushrooms
- 2 cups chopped fresh spinach
- BURGERS:
- 2 egg whites, lightly beaten
- 1/2 cup panko (Japanese) bread crumbs
- 2 tablespoons minced fresh parsley
- 2 tablespoons ketchup
- 1 tablespoon brown sugar
- 1 tablespoon Worcestershire sauce
- 2 teaspoons paprika
- 2 teaspoons prepared pesto
- 1/2 teaspoon garlic powder
- 1 pound lean ground turkey
- 4 slices reduced-fat provolone cheese
- 4 whole wheat hamburger buns, split

Direction

- On medium-high heat, heat a big non-stick pan that is greased with cooking spray. Cook and stir mushrooms in the pan for 3-4mins until tender; put spinach. Cook and stir until it wilts.
- Combine the first 9 ingredients; lightly but thoroughly mix in turkey then form into 4 half-inch thick patties.
- On medium heat, put the burgers on a greased grill rack; grill for 4-6mins on each side, covered until an inserted thermometer registers 165 degrees F.
- Add cheese on top then grill for another 1-2mins, covered, until the cheese melts.
- Serve burgers on buns with the mushroom mixture on top.

Nutrition Information

- Calories: 423 calories
- Protein: 36g protein. Diabetic Exchanges: 4 lean meat
- Total Fat: 16g fat (5g saturated fat)
- Sodium: 663mg sodium
- Fiber: 5g fiber)
- Total Carbohydrate: 37g carbohydrate (11g sugars
- Cholesterol: 88mg cholesterol

45. Grilled Portobello Burgers

Serving: 4 servings. | Prep: 15mins | Cook: 10mins | Ready in:

Ingredients

- 4 large portobello mushrooms (4 to 4-1/2 inches), stems removed
- 6 tablespoons reduced-fat balsamic vinaigrette, divided
- 4 slices red onion
- 1 cup roasted sweet red peppers, drained
- 3 ounces fresh mozzarella cheese, cut into 4 slices
- 4 kaiser rolls, split
- 1/4 cup fat-free mayonnaise

Direction

- Use 4 tbsp. of vinaigrette to brush the mushrooms. Grill the onion and mushrooms for 3 to 4 minutes per side on medium heat with a cover, or until it becomes soft. Top mushrooms with red peppers, onion and cheese, then grill it for 2-3 minutes more with a cover or until the cheese melts. Grill the rolls for 1-2 minutes cut side facing down, or until it becomes toasted.
- Spread mayonnaise on the roll bottoms and drizzle it with the leftover vinaigrette. Put

mushrooms on top then place back the roll tops.

Nutrition Information

- Calories: 329 calories
- Sodium: 860mg sodium
- Fiber: 3g fiber)
- Total Carbohydrate: 42g carbohydrate (8g sugars
- Cholesterol: 19mg cholesterol
- Protein: 12g protein.
- Total Fat: 11g fat (4g saturated fat)

46. Grilled Portobello Sandwiches

Serving: 4 servings. | Prep: 10mins | Cook: 20mins | Ready in:

Ingredients

- 2 tablespoons sesame oil
- 2 tablespoons balsamic vinegar
- 1/4 teaspoon salt
- 1/4 teaspoon pepper
- 4 to 5 portobello mushrooms (about 1 pound), stems removed
- 1 large sweet onion, cut into 1/4-inch slices
- 4 flour tortillas (10 inches)
- 2-1/2 cups (10 ounces each) shredded Monterey Jack cheese
- Salsa and sour cream

Direction

- Mix together the pepper, salt, vinegar and oil in a shallow bowl, then add the onion and mushrooms; flip to coat.
- Use cooking spray to coat a grill rack prior to starting the grill. Grill the onion for 8 to 10 minutes on medium heat or until it turns crisp-tender, flipping frequently. Take it out and put aside. Let the mushrooms grill for 3 to 4 minutes, flipping every minute or until it turns light brown. Take it out and slice it into 1/4-inch pieces.
- On 1/2 of each tortilla, layer the mushroom and onion and sprinkle cheese on top. Fold the tortilla atop the filling and let it grill for 1 to 2 minutes per side or until the cheese melts and turns brown. Serve with sour cream and salsa.

Nutrition Information

- Calories: 583 calories
- Sodium: 928mg sodium
- Fiber: 8g fiber)
- Total Carbohydrate: 40g carbohydrate (5g sugars
- Cholesterol: 63mg cholesterol
- Protein: 26g protein.
- Total Fat: 32g fat (15g saturated fat)

47. Grilled Steak And Portobello Stacks

Serving: 8 servings. | Prep: 45mins | Cook: 20mins | Ready in:

Ingredients

- 2 tablespoons plus 1/4 cup olive oil, divided
- 1 tablespoon herbes de Provence
- 1 beef tenderloin roast (1-1/4 pounds)
- 4 large portobello mushrooms
- 2 tablespoons balsamic vinegar
- BALSAMIC ONION:
- 1 large onion, halved and thinly sliced
- 4-1/2 teaspoons sugar
- 1/2 teaspoon salt
- 1/2 teaspoon pepper
- 1 tablespoon olive oil
- 2 tablespoons balsamic vinegar
- HORSERADISH SAUCE:
- 1/2 cup sour cream
- 1-1/2 teaspoons prepared horseradish
- 1/4 teaspoon Worcestershire sauce
- SANDWICHES:

- 12 slices white bread
- 1/4 cup butter, melted
- 4 cups spring mix salad greens
- 2 tablespoons red wine vinaigrette
- 3/4 cup julienned roasted sweet red peppers

Direction

- Mix herbes de Provence and 2 tablespoons of oil in small bowl. Massage on tenderloin; put on the cover and chill for 2 hours. In a small bowl, put the mushrooms; toss together with the rest of the oil and the vinegar. Put on the cover and chill till grilling.
- In oil, cook pepper, salt, sugar and onion for 15 to 20 minutes in a big skillet over moderate heat or till golden brown, mixing often. Take off from heat; mix in the vinegar. Reserve.
- Mix the ingredients for sauce in small bowl. Put on the cover and chill till serving.
- Grill mushrooms and tenderloin with cover for 8 to 10 minutes per side, on moderate heat or till meat achieves preferred doneness, a thermometer must register 145° for medium-rare, 160° for medium and 170° for well-done and mushrooms are soft. For 10 minutes, allow the tenderloin to sit.
- In the meantime, brush butter on each side of the bread. Grill for a minute per side on moderate heat or till browned. Toss salad greens together with the vinaigrette. Slice mushrooms and tenderloin into thin pieces.
- Distribute mushrooms between 4 bread slices. Layer with greens, the roasted peppers and one more bread slice. Put beef and onion mixture on top of each. Scatter sauce on top of the rest of bread slices; put on top of beef. Halve every sandwich diagonally.

Nutrition Information

- Calories: 460 calories
- Protein: 21g protein.
- Total Fat: 26g fat (9g saturated fat)
- Sodium: 554mg sodium
- Fiber: 3g fiber)
- Total Carbohydrate: 33g carbohydrate (10g sugars
- Cholesterol: 50mg cholesterol

48. Grilled Veggie Wraps

Serving: 4 servings. | Prep: 15mins | Cook: 15mins | Ready in:

Ingredients

- 2 tablespoons balsamic vinegar
- 1-1/2 teaspoons minced fresh basil
- 1-1/2 teaspoons olive oil
- 1-1/2 teaspoons molasses
- 3/4 teaspoon minced fresh thyme
- 1/8 teaspoon salt
- 1/8 teaspoon pepper
- 1 medium zucchini, cut lengthwise into 1/4-inch slices
- 1 medium sweet red pepper, cut into 1-inch pieces
- 1 medium red onion, cut into 1/2-inch slices
- 4 ounces whole fresh mushrooms, cut into 1/2-inch pieces
- 4 ounces fresh sugar snap peas
- 1/2 cup crumbled feta cheese
- 3 tablespoons reduced-fat cream cheese
- 2 tablespoons grated Parmesan cheese
- 1 tablespoon reduced-fat mayonnaise
- 4 flour tortillas (8 inches)
- 4 romaine leaves

Direction

- Mix together the initial 7 ingredients in a big resealable plastic bag, then add vegetables. Close the bag tightly and flip to coat, then chill in the fridge for 2 hours, flipping once.
- Drain and set aside the marinade. Move the vegetables to a grill basket or wok. Grill for 5 minutes over medium-high heat without a cover, stirring often.
- Reserve 1 tsp of marinade. Flip the vegetables and baste them with the leftover marinade.

Grill until they becomes tender, about 5-8 minutes more, stirring often. In the meantime, mix together the mayonnaise and cheeses in a small bowl, then put aside.
- Use the reserved marinade to brush one side of each tortilla. On a grill, put the tortillas, marinade side facing down, for 1 to 3 minutes or until they become slightly toasted.
- Spread 3 tbsp. of cheese mixture on top of the ungrilled side of each tortilla, then put romaine and 1 cup of grilled vegetables on top, then roll up.

Nutrition Information

- Calories: 332 calories
- Sodium: 632mg sodium
- Fiber: 4g fiber)
- Total Carbohydrate: 39g carbohydrate (9g sugars
- Cholesterol: 26mg cholesterol
- Protein: 13g protein. Diabetic Exchanges: 2 starch
- Total Fat: 14g fat (6g saturated fat)

49. Ham & Cheese Sandwich Loaf

Serving: 8 servings. | Prep: 35mins | Cook: 30mins | Ready in:

Ingredients

- 1 loaf sourdough bread (1 pound)
- 1 cup sliced fresh mushrooms
- 1 medium green pepper, cut into strips
- 1 medium sweet red pepper, cut into strips
- 1 celery rib, sliced
- 3 green onions, sliced
- 2 tablespoons olive oil
- 1/2 cup mayonnaise
- 2 teaspoons Italian seasoning
- 1/2 teaspoon pepper
- 1 pound shaved deli ham
- 1 cup shredded Colby cheese
- 1/2 cup shredded part-skim mozzarella cheese

Direction

- Halve the bread horizontally. Hollow out the top and the bottom halves, leaving a-half-inch shells. Get rid of the removed bread or reserve for future use. In a big skillet, sauté onions, celery, peppers and mushrooms in oil till becoming soft. Take out of the heat; put aside.
- Mix pepper, Italian seasoning and mayonnaise; spread on the bread. On bread bottom, layer vegetable mixture, 1/2 of ham and cheeses. Repeat the layers, lightly press down if necessary. Replace the bread top.
- Wrap it tightly in the heavy-duty foil. Bake at 400 degrees or grill, with a cover, on medium heat till thoroughly heated or for 30 to 35 minutes. Chop into wedges using the serrated knife.

Nutrition Information

- Calories: 437 calories
- Cholesterol: 48mg cholesterol
- Protein: 23g protein.
- Total Fat: 22g fat (6g saturated fat)
- Sodium: 1097mg sodium
- Fiber: 2g fiber)
- Total Carbohydrate: 37g carbohydrate (4g sugars

50. Hearty Sausage Stromboli

Serving: 6 servings. | Prep: 25mins | Cook: 15mins | Ready in:

Ingredients

- 1/2 pound Johnsonville® Ground Mild Italian sausage
- 1/4 pound ground beef
- 1/2 cup chopped onion
- 1/2 cup sliced fresh mushrooms
- 1/4 cup chopped green pepper

- 1/2 cup water
- 1/3 cup tomato paste
- 2 tablespoons grated Parmesan cheese
- 1/2 teaspoon salt
- 1/4 teaspoon dried oregano
- 1/4 teaspoon minced garlic
- 1/8 teaspoon dried rosemary, crushed
- 1 loaf (1 pound) Italian bread
- 6 slices part-skim mozzarella cheese

Direction

- Sauté green pepper, mushrooms, onion, beef and sausage over medium heat in a large skillet until meat is no longer pink; drain. Mix in rosemary, garlic, oregano, salt, Parmesan cheese, tomato paste and water. Bring mixture to a boil. Lower the heat; simmer without a cover until thickened, or for 5 minutes.
- In the meantime, cut top third off the bread loaf; hollow out bread bottom carefully, leaving a shell about 1/2 inch. (Discard the inside part or reserve for later use).
- Place 3 slices of mozzarella cheese over the bottom half; place sausage mixture over, and top with the rest of cheese. Put back the bread top over to cover filling. Wrap the sandwich loaf with aluminum foil.
- Bake for 15 to 20 minutes at 400° or until cheese is melted. Allow to sit for 5 minutes prior to cutting to serve.

Nutrition Information

- Calories: 411 calories
- Total Carbohydrate: 44g carbohydrate (4g sugars
- Cholesterol: 41mg cholesterol
- Protein: 23g protein.
- Total Fat: 16g fat (7g saturated fat)
- Sodium: 1016mg sodium
- Fiber: 3g fiber)

51. Italian Chicken Pockets

Serving: 6 servings. | Prep: 15mins | Cook: 0mins | Ready in:

Ingredients

- 3/4 pound boneless skinless chicken breast, cubed
- 2 tablespoons olive oil
- 1 medium green pepper, chopped
- 1 cup sliced fresh mushrooms
- 1 package (3-1/2 ounces) sliced pepperoni
- 1 cup spaghetti sauce
- 3 pita breads (6 inches), halved and warmed
- Grated Parmesan cheese, optional

Direction

- In a big skillet, cook the chicken on medium heat in the oil till not pink anymore. Put in the mushrooms and green pepper; cook till becoming soft, whisk once in a while. Put in the spaghetti sauce and pepperoni; thoroughly heat.
- Scoop into the pita bread halves. Drizzle with cheese if you want.

Nutrition Information

- Calories: 304 calories
- Sodium: 700mg sodium
- Fiber: 2g fiber)
- Total Carbohydrate: 23g carbohydrate (4g sugars
- Cholesterol: 46mg cholesterol
- Protein: 19g protein.
- Total Fat: 15g fat (4g saturated fat)

52. Italian Meat Stromboli

Serving: 10 servings. | Prep: 25mins | Cook: 25mins | Ready in:

Ingredients

- 1 loaf (1 pound) frozen bread dough, thawed
- 1 can (8 ounces) pizza sauce
- 1/4 teaspoon garlic powder, divided
- 1/4 teaspoon dried oregano, divided
- 8 ounces brick cheese, sliced
- 1 cup shredded part-skim mozzarella cheese
- 1/2 cup chopped green pepper
- 1/4 cup chopped onion
- 1 cup sliced fresh mushrooms
- 1/2 cup shredded Parmesan cheese
- 1 package (3 ounces) sliced pepperoni
- 5 ounces sliced deli ham

Direction

- Add the dough into a greased bowl, flip one time to grease top. Use the plastic wrap to cover and allow it to rise in the warm area, for roughly 60 minutes till becoming double.
- Preheat the oven to 350 degrees. Combine 1/8 tsp. each of the oregano and garlic powder with the pizza sauce.
- Punch the dough down. On a lightly-floured surface, roll the dough out into one 15x10-inch rectangle. Add the rest of ingredients, sauce mixture and brick cheese on top to within 1 inch of edges.
- Roll it up, in the jelly-roll style, begin with a long side. Pinch the seam to seal and tuck the ends underneath; move into a greased baking sheet. Drizzle with the rest of oregano and garlic powder. Bake for 25 to 30 minutes till golden-brown.

Nutrition Information

- Calories: 335 calories
- Total Fat: 16g fat (8g saturated fat)
- Sodium: 871mg sodium
- Fiber: 3g fiber)
- Total Carbohydrate: 27g carbohydrate (4g sugars
- Cholesterol: 46mg cholesterol
- Protein: 19g protein.

53. MLT

Serving: 4 servings. | Prep: 20mins | Cook: 20mins | Ready in:

Ingredients

- 4 large portabello mushrooms
- 2 to 3 tablespoons olive oil
- 1 teaspoon salt-free garlic seasoning blend
- 1/2 cup reduced-fat mayonnaise
- 2 teaspoons minced fresh gingerroot
- 2 cups fresh baby spinach
- 2 small tomatoes, thinly sliced
- 4 Italian herb flatbread wraps, warmed
- Additional salt-free garlic seasoning blend, optional

Direction

- Brush oil on mushrooms and sprinkle seasoning blend on top. To grill the mushrooms, put it on a hot grill for about 10 minutes until it turns deep brown. Flip and grill for additional 6 to 8 minutes until it turns golden brown.
- In the meantime, mix together the ginger and mayonnaise in a small bowl, then spread it on top of the tortillas. Put slices of tomato and spinach on top. Once the mushrooms are done, cut it into thin strips and sprinkle additional seasoning blend on top if preferred. Put the mushrooms on wraps and roll it up tightly.

Nutrition Information

- Calories:
- Sodium:
- Fiber:
- Total Carbohydrate:
- Cholesterol:
- Protein:
- Total Fat:

54. Mahogany Glazed Mushroom Burgers

Serving: 6 servings. | Prep: 30mins | Cook: 10mins | Ready in:

Ingredients

- 1/4 cup maple syrup
- 1/4 cup Kahlua (coffee liqueur)
- 1/4 cup reduced-sodium soy sauce
- 10 ounces sliced baby portobello mushrooms
- 1/2 cup thinly sliced red onion
- 2 tablespoons olive oil
- 1/4 teaspoon kosher salt
- 1/8 teaspoon pepper
- CHEESE SPREAD:
- 1/2 cup Mascarpone cheese
- 1/2 cup crumbled goat cheese
- 1/4 cup minced fresh parsley
- 2 tablespoons minced fresh basil or 2 teaspoons dried basil
- 1/8 teaspoon pepper
- BURGERS:
- 1-1/2 pounds ground beef
- 1 teaspoon kosher salt
- 1/2 teaspoon pepper
- 6 hard rolls, split

Direction

- Mix together soy sauce, Kahlua, and maple syrup in a small saucepan. Heat to a boil. Cook until liquid is decreased by half, about 8 minutes.
- In oil, sauté onion and mushrooms in a big skillet until tender. Put in 1/4 cup of Kahlua mixture, pepper, and salt. Stir and cook until most of liquid is evaporated.
- Mix cheese spread ingredients in a small bowl; cover then put in the fridge until serving.
- Break beef into crumbles and put in a big bowl. Sprinkle pepper and salt on top; combine thoroughly. Form into 6 patties.
- Grill burgers with cover for 6 minutes over medium heat. Turn. Allow to grill until juices run clear and a thermometer registers 160°, about 5-8 more minutes, basting from time to time with the rest of Kahlua mixture. Grill rolls for 1-2 minutes without cover until toasted.
- Use cheese spread to spread rolls, place mushroom mixture and burgers on top. Replace tops.

Nutrition Information

- Calories: 674 calories
- Total Fat: 40g fat (17g saturated fat)
- Sodium: 1238mg sodium
- Fiber: 3g fiber)
- Total Carbohydrate: 45g carbohydrate (12g sugars
- Cholesterol: 128mg cholesterol
- Protein: 32g protein.

55. Makeover Philly Steak And Cheese Stromboli

Serving: 8 servings. | Prep: 30mins | Cook: 25mins | Ready in:

Ingredients

- 2 large green peppers, julienned
- 1/2 pound sliced fresh mushrooms
- 1 large onion, halved and sliced
- 2 tablespoons canola oil
- 1/2 teaspoon garlic powder
- 1/4 teaspoon pepper
- 1 loaf (1 pound) frozen whole wheat bread dough, thawed
- 12 ounces reduced-fat process cheese (Velveeta), sliced
- 1/2 pound shaved deli roast beef, chopped
- 1 large egg white
- 1 teaspoon water
- 1/4 cup shredded part-skim mozzarella cheese

Direction

- Sauté the onion, mushrooms and peppers in oil in a big nonstick frying pan, until it becomes soft. Stir in the pepper and garlic powder, then put aside.
- Use cooking spray to coat a baking tray, then roll the dough into a 15x10-inch rectangle. Over half of the dough, layer half of the sliced cheese, all of roast beef and vegetable mixture lengthwise to within 1/2 inch of the edges. Put leftover slice of cheese on top. Fold the dough over the filling, then seal by pinching the seams and tuck the ends under.
- Mix together the water and egg white, then brush it on top of the dough. Slice slits on top and let it bake for 20 to 25 minutes at 350 degrees or until it turns golden brown. Sprinkle mozzarella cheese on top and let it bake for 5 minutes more or until the cheese melts. Allow it to stand for 10 minutes prior to slicing.

Nutrition Information

- Calories: 331 calories
- Fiber: 5g fiber)
- Total Carbohydrate: 38g carbohydrate (8g sugars
- Cholesterol: 33mg cholesterol
- Protein: 23g protein.
- Total Fat: 12g fat (3g saturated fat)
- Sodium: 1055mg sodium

56. Meatless Calzones

Serving: 2 servings. | Prep: 15mins | Cook: 15mins | Ready in:

Ingredients

- 2 frozen Texas-size white dinner rolls
- 1/2 cup each chopped sweet red pepper, fresh mushrooms and broccoli
- 1 tablespoon chopped green onion
- 1 garlic clove, minced
- 3 teaspoons olive oil, divided
- 1/3 cup shredded part-skim mozzarella cheese
- 2 tablespoons grated Parmesan cheese
- 2 tablespoons crumbled feta cheese
- 1 tablespoon minced fresh parsley
- 4 teaspoons Italian salad dressing

Direction

- Allow rolls to rise doubled according to package directions. At the same time, sauté together garlic, onion, broccoli, mushrooms and red pepper with 2 tsp. of oil until tender-crisp, about 2 to 3 minutes. Mix parsley with cheeses and stir into vegetables.
- Roll each dinner roll into a 7-inch circle on a surface coated lightly with flour, then brush salad dressing to the roll's surface. Scoop onto half of each circle with the vegetable mixture to within 1 inch of edges. Fold dough over filling and seal by pinching edges.
- Put rolls in an ungreased baking sheet and brush with leftover oil. Bake at 350 degrees until turn golden brown, about 15 to 20 minutes.

Nutrition Information

- Calories: 333 calories
- Protein: 15g protein.
- Total Fat: 16g fat (5g saturated fat)
- Sodium: 782mg sodium
- Fiber: 3g fiber)
- Total Carbohydrate: 32g carbohydrate (7g sugars
- Cholesterol: 19mg cholesterol

57. Mediterranean Salad Sandwiches

Serving: 4 servings. | Prep: 15mins | Cook: 15mins | Ready in:

Ingredients

- 2 tablespoons olive oil, divided
- 1 garlic clove, minced
- 1/4 teaspoon salt
- 4 large portobello mushrooms, stems removed
- 2 cups spring mix salad greens
- 1 medium tomato, chopped
- 1/2 cup chopped roasted sweet red peppers
- 1/4 cup crumbled reduced-fat feta cheese
- 2 tablespoons chopped pitted Greek olives
- 1 tablespoon red wine vinegar
- 1/2 teaspoon dried oregano
- 4 slices sourdough bread, toasted and halved

Direction

- Mix together the salt, garlic and 1 tbsp. oil in a small bowl, then brush the mixture on top of the mushrooms.
- Use cooking oil to moisten a paper towel, then coat the grill rack lightly using long-handled tongs. Grill the mushrooms for 6-8 minutes per side over medium heat with a cover until they become soft.
- Mix together the olives, cheese, peppers, tomato and salad greens in a big bowl. Whisk the leftover oil, oregano and vinegar in a small bowl. Pour the mixture on top of the salad mixture, then toss until coated.
- Layer a mushroom and 3/4 cup salad mixture on each of the 4 half slices of toast, then put leftover toast on top.

Nutrition Information

- Calories: 225 calories
- Protein: 8g protein. Diabetic Exchanges: 2 vegetable
- Total Fat: 9g fat (2g saturated fat)
- Sodium: 495mg sodium
- Fiber: 3g fiber)
- Total Carbohydrate: 26g carbohydrate (4g sugars
- Cholesterol: 3mg cholesterol

58. Mini Chicken Salad Croissants

Serving: 20 servings. | Prep: 25mins | Cook: 0mins | Ready in:

Ingredients

- 1/3 cup sour cream
- 1/3 cup mayonnaise
- 4 teaspoons lemon juice
- 1 teaspoon salt
- 1/4 teaspoon pepper
- 4 celery ribs, thinly sliced
- 1 cup chopped fresh mushrooms
- 1/4 cup chopped green pepper
- 1/4 cup chopped sweet red pepper
- 3 cups cubed cooked chicken
- 4 bacon strips, cooked and crumbled
- 1/2 cup chopped pecans, toasted
- 20 miniature croissants, split
- Lettuce leaves

Direction

- Combine the first 5 ingredients in a big bowl; mix in the vegetables. Add chicken; mix to coat. Chill with a cover on for a minimum of 4 hours.
- Mix in pecans and bacon. Use lettuce to line croissants; stuff each with 1/4 cup of the chicken mixture.

Nutrition Information

- Calories: 217 calories
- Protein: 10g protein.
- Total Fat: 14g fat (5g saturated fat)
- Sodium: 403mg sodium
- Fiber: 1g fiber)
- Total Carbohydrate: 14g carbohydrate (1g sugars
- Cholesterol: 41mg cholesterol

59. Molasses Steak Sandwiches

Serving: 4 servings. | Prep: 15mins | Cook: 15mins | Ready in:

Ingredients

- 1/4 cup molasses
- 2 tablespoons brown sugar
- 2 tablespoons olive oil, divided
- 1 tablespoon Dijon mustard
- 4 beef tenderloin steaks (1 inch thick and 4 ounces each)
- 2 large portobello mushrooms, stems removed
- 4 kaiser rolls, split
- 4 slices Swiss cheese

Direction

- Combine mustard, molasses, a tablespoon oil, and brown sugar in a big ziplock bag; put in steaks. Seal and flip the bag to coat steaks with marinade. Let it chill in the refrigerator for 2 hours.
- Drain beef and get rid of the marinade. Slather mushrooms with leftover oil. On medium heat, grill steak for 5-7 minutes per side while covered until it reaches the preferred doneness (an inserted thermometer in the steak should register 170° Fahrenheit for well-done, 160 degrees F for medium done, and 145° Fahrenheit for medium rare). Grill the oiled mushrooms for 8-10 mins while covered until tender, flip mushrooms for time to time. Take the mushroom and steaks out of the grill and set aside for 5 minutes.
- Place the rolls on the grill with its cut-side down. Grill for 2-3 minutes until a bit toasted. Slice steaks and mushrooms; place on toasted roll. Add cheese on top; serve.

Nutrition Information

- Calories:
- Protein:
- Total Fat:
- Sodium:
- Fiber:
- Total Carbohydrate:
- Cholesterol:

60. Moo Shu Mushroom Wraps

Serving: 5 servings. | Prep: 15mins | Cook: 15mins | Ready in:

Ingredients

- 4 teaspoons sesame or canola oil, divided
- 4 large eggs, lightly beaten
- 1/2 pound sliced fresh mushrooms
- 1 package (12 ounces) broccoli coleslaw mix
- 2 garlic cloves, minced
- 2 teaspoons minced fresh gingerroot
- 2 tablespoons rice vinegar
- 2 tablespoons reduced-sodium soy sauce
- 2 teaspoons Sriracha Asian hot chili sauce
- 1 cup fresh bean sprouts
- 1/2 cup hoisin sauce
- 10 flour tortillas (6 inches), warmed
- 6 green onions, sliced

Direction

- Heat 1 tsp. of oil in a big non-stick frying pan on medium heat, then pour in the eggs. Let it cook and stir until no liquid egg remains and the eggs becomes thick. Take it out of the pan.
- Heat the leftover oil in a small frying pan on medium high heat, then add mushrooms. Let it cook and stir until it becomes soft. Add ginger, garlic and coleslaw mix, then cook for 1 to 2 minutes more or until the slaw becomes crisp-tender. Combine the chili sauce, soy sauce and vinegar in a small bowl, then add it to the pan. Mix in the eggs and sprouts, then heat through.
- On each tortilla, spread approximately 2 tsp. of hoisin sauce to within 1/4-inch of the edges. Layer it with 1/2 cup vegetable mixture and around 1 tbsp. of green onion, then roll it up tightly.

Nutrition Information

- Calories: 381 calories
- Protein: 16g protein.
- Total Fat: 15g fat (2g saturated fat)
- Sodium: 1234mg sodium
- Fiber: 4g fiber)
- Total Carbohydrate: 48g carbohydrate (12g sugars
- Cholesterol: 170mg cholesterol

61. Mushroom & Swiss Turkey Burgers

Serving: 2 servings. | Prep: 20mins | Cook: 10mins | Ready in:

Ingredients

- 1-3/4 cups sliced baby portobello mushrooms
- 1 teaspoon olive oil
- 1 garlic clove, minced
- 1/4 teaspoon salt, divided
- 1/8 teaspoon pepper, divided
- 1/4 cup frozen chopped spinach, thawed and squeezed dry
- 2 tablespoons chopped sweet onion
- 1/2 pound lean ground turkey
- 1 slice reduced-fat Swiss cheese, cut in half
- 2 whole wheat hamburger buns, split and toasted
- 2 lettuce leaves
- 2 slices sweet onion
- 2 slices tomato

Direction

- Cook the mushrooms in oil in a small frying pan until they become soft. Add garlic and cook for 1 minute more. Mix in a dash of pepper and 1/8 tsp salt, then take away from the heat; put aside.
- Mix the pepper, leftover salt, chopped onion and spinach together in a small bowl. Crumble the turkey on top of the mixture and stir thoroughly, then form the mixture into 2 patties.
- Cook the patties in a big nonstick frying pan coated with cooking spray for 4 minutes over medium heat. Flip over and cook for 3 minutes more. Put cheese on top of burgers, the cover and cook for 3-6 minutes more or until the cheese melts and a thermometer registers 165 degrees. Serve with reserved mushroom mixture, tomato, onion and lettuce on buns.

Nutrition Information

- Calories: 371 calories
- Cholesterol: 95mg cholesterol
- Protein: 30g protein.
- Total Fat: 16g fat (4g saturated fat)
- Sodium: 645mg sodium
- Fiber: 5g fiber)
- Total Carbohydrate: 30g carbohydrate (6g sugars

62. Mushroom Burger Stromboli

Serving: 2 loaves. | Prep: 30mins | Cook: 30mins | Ready in:

Ingredients

- 1 package (1/4 ounce) active dry yeast
- 2-1/2 cups warm water (110° to 115°)
- 2 tablespoons vegetable oil
- 2 tablespoons salt
- 2 teaspoons sugar
- 7 to 7-1/2 cups all-purpose flour
- 1 pound ground beef
- 1/4 cup chopped onion
- 1 can (10-3/4 ounces) condensed cream of mushroom soup, undiluted
- 1/2 pound fresh mushrooms, chopped
- 1/2 teaspoon onion salt

- 1/2 teaspoon seasoned salt
- 1/8 teaspoon pepper
- 4 cups shredded mozzarella cheese
- Optional toppings: sour cream, jalapeno peppers, hot pepper sauce

Direction

- Dissolve yeast in a bowl of water. Add 2 cups flour, sugar, salt and oil; whisk until smooth. Put in enough of the remaining flour until a soft dough is formed. Transfer dough to a surface dusted with flour; knead for about 6 to 8 minutes until elastic and smooth. Position dough in a lightly oiled bowl, flipping once to grease the top. Allow to rise, covered, for about 60 minutes in a warm area until twice the size.
- In the meantime, cook onion and beef over medium heat in a skillet until meat is no longer pink; drain well, add seasonings, mushrooms and soup; put aside.
- Punch down the dough; split in half. Roll each dough half into 15x10-inch rectangle on a surface dusted with flour. Remove dough to a lightly oiled baking sheet. Scoop the beef mixture down half of the rectangle lengthwise to within 1 inch of edges. Fold the dough over the filling. Pinch the edges for sealing. Cut 4 diagonal slits on top of each loaf. Allow to rise, covered, for 45 minutes until dough is twice the size.
- Bake for 30 to 35 minutes at 350° or until golden brown. Slice loaves into slices. Serve warm with your favorite toppings.

Nutrition Information

- Calories: 721 calories
- Fiber: 4g fiber)
- Total Carbohydrate: 91g carbohydrate (4g sugars
- Cholesterol: 73mg cholesterol
- Protein: 34g protein.
- Total Fat: 24g fat (11g saturated fat)
- Sodium: 2496mg sodium

63. Mushroom Burgers

Serving: 6 | Prep: 20mins | Cook: 10mins | Ready in:

Ingredients

- 1 pound fresh mushrooms, sliced
- 1 large onion, minced
- 2 slices white bread, finely diced
- 2 tablespoons oyster sauce
- 1 egg
- salt to taste
- ground black pepper to taste

Direction

- Coat a big skillet with cooking spray and put on moderate heat. Put in onions and mushrooms, then cook and stir about 4 minutes just until mushrooms start to draw out their juices. Stir in oyster sauce and bread cubes, then cook and stir for a minute. Take mixture out of the pan and set aside to cool. Wipe pan clean.
- Beat egg and combine into the mushroom mixture, then season with pepper and salt, to taste.
- Coat cooking spray to the skillet and put on moderate heat. Scoop the mixture into skillet in 6 equal quantity. Brown one side then flip over and brown the rest side. Serve.

Nutrition Information

- Calories: 61 calories;
- Total Carbohydrate: 9.2
- Cholesterol: 31
- Protein: 4.3
- Total Fat: 1.4
- Sodium: 110

64. Mushroom Cheese Stromboli

Serving: 36 slices. | Prep: 20mins | Cook: 30mins | Ready in:

Ingredients

- 1/4 pound fresh mushrooms, sliced
- 1 tablespoon butter
- 1 loaf (1 pound) frozen bread dough, thawed
- 3 ounces thinly sliced pepperoni
- 6 ounces thinly sliced mozzarella cheese
- 1/4 pound thinly sliced Provolone cheese
- 1 cup grated Parmesan cheese
- 1/3 cup spaghetti sauce
- 1 tablespoon dried parsley flakes
- 1/2 teaspoon dried oregano
- 1 egg yolk
- 1/2 teaspoon water
- Additional Parmesan cheese, optional

Direction

- In a skillet, sauté the mushrooms in butter till becoming soft; put aside. On a lightly-floured board, roll the dough out into one 30x8-inch rectangle; chop into two 15x8-inch pieces.
- On the long side of each of the pieces, layer the pepperoni, the cheeses, the mushrooms, the spaghetti sauce, parsley and oregano. Fold over the dough and pinch it to seal. Mix the water and egg; brush on the edges and ends of the dough. Use a sharp knife, slice 5 small steam vents in each roll's top.
- Add onto the greased baking sheets. Drizzle with the Parmesan if you want. Bake at 350 degrees till turning golden-brown or for 27 to 30 minutes. Cut and serve them warm.

Nutrition Information

- Calories: 176 calories
- Sodium: 431mg sodium
- Fiber: 1g fiber)
- Total Carbohydrate: 14g carbohydrate (2g sugars
- Cholesterol: 33mg cholesterol
- Protein: 9g protein.
- Total Fat: 9g fat (5g saturated fat)

65. Mushroom Pastrami Hoagies

Serving: 6 servings. | Prep: 15mins | Cook: 10mins | Ready in:

Ingredients

- 3 tablespoons butter
- 1 pound sliced fresh mushrooms
- 1 large onion, halved and sliced
- 2 medium sweet red peppers, julienned
- 2 garlic cloves, minced
- 1/4 teaspoon salt
- 1/4 teaspoon pepper
- 6 hoagie buns, split
- 1-1/2 pounds sliced deli pastrami
- 12 slices provolone cheese

Direction

- Preheat the broiler. In a 6-quart stockpot, heat the butter on medium heat. Put in the peppers, onion and mushrooms; cook and whisk till becoming soft or for 5 to 7 minutes. Put in the garlic; cook for 60 seconds more. Drain the vegetable mixture; whisk in the pepper and salt.
- Arrange the buns onto a baking sheet. Layer the bun bottoms with the vegetable and pastrami mixture; add the cheese on top. Broil at 4 to 5 inches away from the heat source till the bun tops become toasted and the cheese melts or for 1 to 2 minutes.

Nutrition Information

- Calories: 572 calories
- Cholesterol: 110mg cholesterol
- Protein: 43g protein.
- Total Fat: 26g fat (14g saturated fat)
- Sodium: 1787mg sodium

- Fiber: 3g fiber)
- Total Carbohydrate: 43g carbohydrate (9g sugars

66. Mushroom Pear Melts

Serving: 4 servings. | Prep: 15mins | Cook: 10mins | Ready in:

Ingredients

- 2 tablespoons butter
- 4 cups sliced fresh shiitake or baby portobello mushrooms (about 10 ounces)
- 1/2 teaspoon salt
- 1/4 teaspoon pepper
- 8 slices whole wheat bread, toasted
- 2 large ripe Bosc pears, thinly sliced
- 8 slices provolone cheese

Direction

- Set the broiler to preheat. Heat the butter in a big frying pan on medium-high heat, then add mushrooms. Let it cook and stir for 5 to 7 minutes or until it becomes soft. Stir in pepper and salt.
- Put the toasts on a rack of a broiler pan, then put mushrooms on top. Layer it with pears and cheese. Let it broil for 2 to 3 minutes, placed 3-4 inches from the heat source or until the cheese turns light brown.

Nutrition Information

- Calories: 421 calories
- Sodium: 883mg sodium
- Fiber: 9g fiber)
- Total Carbohydrate: 46g carbohydrate (15g sugars
- Cholesterol: 45mg cholesterol
- Protein: 19g protein.
- Total Fat: 20g fat (11g saturated fat)

67. Mushroom Pizza Burgers

Serving: 6 servings. | Prep: 15mins | Cook: 15mins | Ready in:

Ingredients

- 1/2 cup sliced fresh mushrooms
- 1/4 cup chopped onion
- 1 garlic clove, minced
- 1/2 teaspoon dried oregano
- 1 cup crushed tomatoes, undrained
- BURGERS:
- 1-1/2 cups finely chopped fresh mushrooms
- 1/3 cup minced fresh basil
- 1 egg white, lightly beaten
- 2 tablespoons grated Parmesan cheese
- 2 tablespoons dry bread crumbs
- 1/2 teaspoon salt
- 1/8 teaspoon pepper
- 1 pound lean ground beef (90% lean)
- 6 slices part-skim mozzarella cheese (3 ounces)
- 6 hamburger buns, split and toasted

Direction

- Sauté the onion and mushrooms for 3 minutes in a small frying pan that is coated with cooking spray. Add oregano and garlic and let it cook for another 1 minute. Mix in tomatoes and let it cook for 5 minutes on medium-low heat without cover, stirring from time to time. Put aside and keep it warm.
- Mix together the pepper, salt, breadcrumbs, Parmesan cheese, egg white, basil and mushrooms in a big bowl. Crumble the beef on top of the mixture and stir well. Form it into 6 patties.
- Grill the patties on a grill rack that's lightly oiled on medium-hot heat with cover, or let it broil for 4-5 minutes per side, placed 4-inches from the heat source or until the meat juices run clear and a thermometer registers 160 degrees. Put tomato sauce and cheese on top of the patties, then serve it on buns.

Nutrition Information

- Calories: 333 calories
- Protein: 25g protein. Diabetic Exchanges: 3 lean meat
- Total Fat: 12g fat (5g saturated fat)
- Sodium: 757mg sodium
- Fiber: 3g fiber)
- Total Carbohydrate: 28g carbohydrate (0 sugars
- Cholesterol: 36mg cholesterol

68. Mushroom Swiss Burgers

Serving: 6 servings. | Prep: 5mins | Cook: 25mins | Ready in:

Ingredients

- 1-1/2 pounds ground beef
- 1 pound sliced fresh mushrooms
- 1 can (10-3/4 ounces) condensed cream of mushroom soup, undiluted
- 1 cup water
- 6 slices Swiss cheese
- 6 hamburger buns, split

Direction

- Form beef into 6 patties. On medium-high heat, cook patties for 5-7mins per side in a big pan until the juices are clear and an inserted thermometer registers 160 degrees F. Drain burgers on paper towels; save 2tbsp of the drippings. Cook and stir mushrooms in the drippings until they are tender.
- In the meantime, mix water and soup together in a microwaveable bowl; cover. On high, microwave the mixture for 2 1/2-3 1/2mins until completely heated.
- Place the patties back in the pan; mix in soup mixture then boil. Lower heat, let it simmer for 3mins without cover.
- Place a cheese slice on top of each patty. Take off heat then cover. Let it rest until the cheese melts. Serve burgers on buns with mushrooms on top.

Nutrition Information

- Calories:
- Sodium:
- Fiber:
- Total Carbohydrate:
- Cholesterol:
- Protein:
- Total Fat:

69. Mushroom Stuffed Cheeseburgers

Serving: 8 servings. | Prep: 30mins | Cook: 10mins | Ready in:

Ingredients

- 2 bacon strips, finely chopped
- 2 cups chopped fresh mushrooms
- 1/4 cup chopped onion
- 1/4 cup chopped sweet red pepper
- 1/4 cup chopped green pepper
- 2 pounds lean ground beef (90% lean)
- 2 tablespoons steak sauce
- 1/2 teaspoon seasoned salt
- 4 slices provolone cheese, halved
- 8 kaiser rolls, split

Direction

- Cook bacon in a large skillet over medium heat with occasional stirs until they are crispy. Use a slotted spoon to take them out of the skillet and transfer to paper towels to drain. In bacon drippings, cook and stir peppers, onion and mushrooms to tender. Transfer them to a small bowl with a slotted spoon; let them cool completely. Add bacon and stir.
- Mix together seasoned salt, steak sauce and beef in a large bowl thoroughly yet lightly.

Form into 16 thin patties. Add cheese on top of 8 patties so that the cheese fit with 3/4 inch of edge. Use mushroom mixture to spread. Add the remaining patties on top; enclose the filling by pressing the edges.
- Broil the burgers 4 inches from heat or put burgers on grill grate over medium-high heat without a cover until a thermometer reaches 160 degrees, about 5 to 6 minutes per side. Put onto rolls to serve.

Nutrition Information

- Calories: 418 calories
- Fiber: 2g fiber)
- Total Carbohydrate: 33g carbohydrate (2g sugars
- Cholesterol: 82mg cholesterol
- Protein: 31g protein.
- Total Fat: 17g fat (7g saturated fat)
- Sodium: 653mg sodium

70. My Favorite Burger

Serving: 4 servings. | Prep: 25mins | Cook: 15mins | Ready in:

Ingredients

- 1/4 cup grated onion
- 1/2 teaspoon garlic powder
- 1/4 teaspoon salt
- 1/4 teaspoon pepper
- 1 pound lean ground beef (90% lean)
- 1 cup sliced fresh mushrooms
- 1/2 cup sliced sweet onion
- 4 kaiser rolls, split
- 4 ounces fat-free cream cheese
- 2 bacon strips, cooked and crumbled

Direction

- Mix together the pepper, salt, garlic powder and onion in a big bowl. Crumble the beef on top of the mixture and stir thoroughly, then form into 4 patties.
- Oil the grill rack lightly. Grill patties over medium heat with a cover or broil 4 inches from the heat source for 4-6 minutes per side, until a thermometer registers 160 degrees.
- In the meantime, cook and stir the onion and mushrooms in a small frying pan coated with cooking spray over medium heat until the onion turns golden brown. Grill the rolls until lightly toasted, about 1-2 minutes.
- Spread cream cheese on rolls, then put burgers and mushroom mixture on top and sprinkle with bacon.

Nutrition Information

- Calories: 410 calories
- Protein: 33g protein.
- Total Fat: 13g fat (5g saturated fat)
- Sodium: 737mg sodium
- Fiber: 2g fiber)
- Total Carbohydrate: 37g carbohydrate (4g sugars
- Cholesterol: 75mg cholesterol

71. My Favorite Burger For 2

Serving: 2 servings. | Prep: 10mins | Cook: 15mins | Ready in:

Ingredients

- 2 tablespoons grated onion
- 1/4 teaspoon garlic powder
- 1/8 teaspoon salt
- 1/8 teaspoon pepper
- 1/2 pound lean ground beef (90% lean)
- 1/2 cup sliced fresh mushrooms
- 1/4 cup sliced sweet onion
- 2 kaiser rolls, split
- 2 ounces fat-free cream cheese
- 1 bacon strips, cooked and crumbled

Direction

- Mix together the pepper, salt, garlic powder and onion in a big bowl. Crumble the beef on top of the mixture and stir well, then form it into 2 patties.
- Grill the patties on a greased grill rack on medium heat with a cover, or let it broil for 4 minutes per side, placed 4-6 inches from the heat source or until a thermometer registers 160 degrees.
- In the meantime, use cooking spray to coat a small frying pan, then cook and stir the onion and mushrooms on medium heat until the onion turns golden brown. Grill the rolls for 1 to 2 minutes or until a bit toasted.
- Spread cream cheese on rolls then top with burgers and mushroom mixture. Sprinkle bacon on top.

Nutrition Information

- Calories: 402 calories
- Fiber: 2g fiber)
- Total Carbohydrate: 36g carbohydrate (3g sugars
- Cholesterol: 75mg cholesterol
- Protein: 33g protein.
- Total Fat: 13g fat (5g saturated fat)
- Sodium: 736mg sodium

72. Open Faced Chicken Sandwiches

Serving: 8 servings. | Prep: 25mins | Cook: 5mins | Ready in:

Ingredients

- 1 pound fresh mushrooms, sliced
- 1 large sweet onion, sliced
- 1 cup fat-free mayonnaise
- 1/2 cup crumbled blue cheese
- 1/4 teaspoon pepper
- 8 slices French bread (1 inch thick)
- 1 pound boneless skinless chicken breasts, grilled and sliced
- 1 cup shredded part-skim mozzarella cheese

Direction

- Slice the bread into eight 1-inch slices, then toast the slices. In the meantime, sauté the onion and mushrooms in a big non-stick frying pan coated with cooking spray, until the onion turns golden brown and becomes soft, about 15-20 minutes, then put aside.
- Mix together the pepper, blue cheese and mayonnaise in a small bowl. On each slice of bread, spread the blue cheese mixture. Put chicken, mushroom mixture and mozzarella cheese on top.
- Broil 4-6 inches from the heat source until the cheese melts, about 3-4 minutes.

Nutrition Information

- Calories: 276 calories
- Total Fat: 8g fat (4g saturated fat)
- Sodium: 618mg sodium
- Fiber: 3g fiber)
- Total Carbohydrate: 23g carbohydrate (0 sugars
- Cholesterol: 66mg cholesterol
- Protein: 27g protein. Diabetic Exchanges: 3 lean meat

73. Open Faced Mushroom Crostini

Serving: 1 serving. | Prep: 5mins | Cook: 15mins | Ready in:

Ingredients

- 2 tablespoons olive oil
- 4 ounces small fresh mushrooms, sliced
- 1/4 teaspoon salt
- Pinch white pepper

- 1 slice multigrain bread
- 1 slice Jarlsberg cheese

Direction

- Heat olive oil in a nonstick frying pan on medium-high heat, then add a single layer of mushrooms. Let it cook for around 5 minutes without mixing or until the mushrooms turn red brown on one side. Add pepper and salt, then turn and cook for 5 minutes more until the other side turns red-brown in color.
- Take the mushrooms out of the pan and pour off any leftover liquid. Place the bread in a pan and heat both sides. With the bread placed in pan, top the slice with cheese and mushrooms, then heat through.

Nutrition Information

- Calories:
- Protein:
- Total Fat:
- Sodium:
- Fiber:
- Total Carbohydrate:
- Cholesterol:

74. Open Faced Portobello Sandwiches

Serving: 2 servings. | Prep: 10mins | Cook: 5mins | Ready in:

Ingredients

- 4 teaspoons prepared pesto
- 2 slices Italian bread (3/4 inch thick), toasted
- 3 oil-packed sun-dried tomatoes, cut into strips
- 2 slices part-skim mozzarella cheese (3/4 ounce each)
- 2 large portobello mushrooms, stems removed

Direction

- Spread the toast with pesto and put tomatoes and cheese on top. On a microwavable plate, put the mushrooms and cover the plate using a paper towel. Microwave for 1 minute on high or until mushrooms become soft.
- Slice the mushrooms into 1/2-inch slices, then put them on the cheese. Cook the sandwiches for 15 to 20 seconds on high until the cheese melts.

Nutrition Information

- Calories: 236 calories
- Total Fat: 11g fat (4g saturated fat)
- Sodium: 382mg sodium
- Fiber: 3g fiber)
- Total Carbohydrate: 22g carbohydrate (2g sugars
- Cholesterol: 15mg cholesterol
- Protein: 12g protein. Diabetic Exchanges: 1 starch

75. Paul Bunyan Burgers

Serving: 3 servings. | Prep: 20mins | Cook: 10mins | Ready in:

Ingredients

- 6 bacon strips, diced
- 1 cup sliced fresh mushrooms
- 3 thin onion slices
- 1 egg, lightly beaten
- 1 tablespoon Worcestershire sauce
- 1/2 teaspoon seasoned salt
- 1/2 teaspoon salt
- 1/2 teaspoon pepper
- 1/2 teaspoon prepared horseradish
- 1 pound ground beef
- 3 slices process American cheese
- 3 hamburger buns, split

Direction

- Cook bacon in a big skillet until crisp. Use a slotted spoon to transfer to paper towels. Sauté onion and mushrooms in the drippings until tender. With a slotted spoon, remove to a big bowl; put in bacon.
- Mix horseradish, pepper, salt, seasoned salt, Worcestershire sauce, and egg together in another bowl; arrange beef on top of mixture and combine well. Form into six patties of 1/4-inch thickness.
- Separate bacon mixture and put onto 3 patties. Place a cheese slice on top; fold in cheese corners. Put the rest of patties over top; seal edges.
- Grill over medium-hot heat without cover, 5-6 minutes per side, until meat juices run clear and the thermometer registers 160°. Place onto buns to serve.

Nutrition Information

- Calories: 797 calories
- Total Fat: 55g fat (22g saturated fat)
- Sodium: 1653mg sodium
- Fiber: 2g fiber)
- Total Carbohydrate: 27g carbohydrate (6g sugars
- Cholesterol: 229mg cholesterol
- Protein: 46g protein.

76. Pepperoni Pizza Burgers

Serving: 6 servings. | Prep: 20mins | Cook: 15mins | Ready in:

Ingredients

- 6 pieces frozen garlic Texas toast
- 1-3/4 pounds ground beef
- 1 cup pizza sauce, divided
- 18 slices pepperoni
- 12 slices part-skim mozzarella cheese, divided
- 1 cup sliced fresh mushrooms
- 2 teaspoons butter
- 6 teaspoons grated Parmesan cheese
- Sliced green pepper and ripe olives, optional

Direction

- Follow package instructions to prepare Texas toast. At the same time, form beef into 12 thin patties.
- Place 1 slice of mozzarella cheese, 3 slices of pepperoni, and 1 tablespoon pizza sauce on top of 6 patties. Top with the rest of patties; firmly press to seal edges.
- Grill over medium heat with a cover until juices run clear and a thermometer shows 160°, about 6 to 8 min. per side. At the same time, sauté mushrooms in butter in a small skillet.
- Place the rest of mozzarella cheese and pizza sauce on top of burgers. Cover; cook until cheese melts, about 3 more minutes. Place burgers on Texas toast; serve with Parmesan cheese, olives, and mushrooms and peppers and olives if wished.

Nutrition Information

- Calories: 689 calories
- Protein: 50g protein.
- Total Fat: 42g fat (18g saturated fat)
- Sodium: 1017mg sodium
- Fiber: 2g fiber)
- Total Carbohydrate: 26g carbohydrate (5g sugars
- Cholesterol: 147mg cholesterol

77. Philly Cheese Fakes

Serving: 4 servings. | Prep: 30mins | Cook: 5mins | Ready in:

Ingredients

- 1/4 cup lemon juice

- 3 garlic cloves, minced
- 1 tablespoon olive oil
- 1/2 teaspoon smoked paprika
- 1/4 teaspoon salt
- 1/4 teaspoon pepper
- 1 pound sliced fresh shiitake mushrooms
- 2 medium green peppers, sliced
- 1 small onion, thinly sliced
- 4 hoagie buns, split
- 4 slices reduced-fat provolone cheese

Direction

- Set the oven to 450 degrees to preheat. Whisk the first 6 ingredients together in a small bowl. Mix together onion, green pepper and mushrooms in a big bowl, then drizzle vegetables with dressing and toss to coat.
- Remove to 2 15-inchx10-inch x1-inch baking pans greased with cooking spray. Bake until tender yet still crispy while stirring one time, about 15 to 20 minutes.
- Split mixture of mushroom among buns and put cheese on top. Broil 3 to 4 inches from heat source until cheese melts, about 2 to 3 minutes. Replace top buns.

Nutrition Information

- Calories: 344 calories
- Fiber: 4g fiber)
- Total Carbohydrate: 47g carbohydrate (9g sugars
- Cholesterol: 10mg cholesterol
- Protein: 17g protein.
- Total Fat: 12g fat (4g saturated fat)
- Sodium: 681mg sodium

78. Pizza Joes

Serving: 6 servings. | Prep: 10mins | Cook: 20mins | Ready in:

Ingredients

- 1 pound lean ground beef (90% lean)
- 1 can (15 ounces) pizza sauce
- 1 teaspoon dried oregano
- 1/2 medium onion
- 1/2 medium green pepper
- 1 ounce sliced pepperoni
- 6 hamburger buns, split
- 1/2 cup shredded mozzarella cheese
- 1/2 cup sliced fresh mushrooms

Direction

- Cook beef in a large skillet over medium heat until no longer pink; drain well; mix in oregano and pizza sauce.
- Combine pepperoni, pepper, and onion in a food processor; put on the lid and process until chopped. Add to beef mixture. Simmer until vegetables are tender, for 20 to 25 minutes. Spread mixture over buns. Top with mushrooms and cheese.

Nutrition Information

- Calories: 320 calories
- Fiber: 3g fiber)
- Total Carbohydrate: 29g carbohydrate (7g sugars
- Cholesterol: 57mg cholesterol
- Protein: 22g protein.
- Total Fat: 12g fat (5g saturated fat)
- Sodium: 594mg sodium

79. Pizza Wraps

Serving: 4 wraps. | Prep: 15mins | Cook: 0mins | Ready in:

Ingredients

- 1 package (8 ounces) sliced pepperoni
- 4 flour tortillas (8 inches), room temperature
- 1/2 cup chopped tomatoes

- 1/4 cup each chopped sweet onion, chopped fresh mushrooms and chopped ripe olives
- 1/4 cup chopped green pepper, optional
- 1 cup shredded part-skim mozzarella cheese

Direction

- Place down off center of each tortilla with pepperoni, then put leftover ingredients on top. Fold sides and bottom tortilla over filling, then roll it up.

Nutrition Information

- Calories: 498 calories
- Sodium: 1428mg sodium
- Fiber: 1g fiber)
- Total Carbohydrate: 29g carbohydrate (2g sugars
- Cholesterol: 64mg cholesterol
- Protein: 22g protein.
- Total Fat: 33g fat (13g saturated fat)

80. Portobello Burgers

Serving: 2 servings. | Prep: 10mins | Cook: 15mins | Ready in:

Ingredients

- 2 tablespoons balsamic vinegar
- 1 tablespoon olive oil
- 3 garlic cloves, minced
- 1-1/2 teaspoons minced fresh basil or 1/2 teaspoon dried basil
- 1-1/2 teaspoons minced fresh oregano or 1/2 teaspoon dried oregano
- Dash salt
- Dash pepper
- 2 large portobello mushrooms, stems removed
- 2 slices reduced-fat provolone cheese
- 2 hamburger buns, split
- 2 lettuce leaves
- 2 slices tomato

Direction

- Mix the first 7 ingredients together in a small bowl. Add mushroom caps; allow to rest for 15 minutes, turning twice. Strain and save marinade for later use.
- Moisten a paper towel with cooking oil and coat the grill rack lightly using long-handled tongs. Cover and grill mushrooms over medium heat or broil 4 inches from the heat till tender, about 6-8 minutes per side, using reserved marinade for basting. During the last 2 minutes of cooking time, use cheese to dredge on top.
- For serving, place onto buns with tomato and lettuce.

Nutrition Information

- Calories: 280 calories
- Protein: 11g protein. Diabetic Exchanges: 2 starch
- Total Fat: 13g fat (3g saturated fat)
- Sodium: 466mg sodium
- Fiber: 3g fiber)
- Total Carbohydrate: 31g carbohydrate (8g sugars
- Cholesterol: 10mg cholesterol

81. Portobello Burgers With Pear Walnut Mayonnaise

Serving: 4 servings. | Prep: 30mins | Cook: 10mins | Ready in:

Ingredients

- 1/4 cup olive oil
- 1/4 cup balsamic vinegar
- 3 garlic cloves, minced
- 1 tablespoon minced fresh thyme or 1 teaspoon dried thyme
- 4 large portobello mushrooms, stems removed
- 1 medium pear, peeled and chopped

- 1 tablespoon olive oil
- 1 tablespoon lemon juice
- 2 tablespoons mayonnaise
- 4-1/2 teaspoons chopped walnuts
- 4 slices onion
- 6 ounces Gorgonzola cheese, thinly sliced
- 4 whole wheat hamburger buns, split
- 2 cups fresh arugula

Direction

- Mix thyme, garlic, vinegar and oil together in a big resealable plastic bag. Insert mushrooms and close the bag up. Layer the mushrooms with the mixture by flipping it around. Leave it in the fridge for up to 2 hours.
- At a moderate heat, heat oil and lemon juice in a small skillet before inserting the pear. Cook until the pears turn tender. Process the pears in a little food processor with the lid on until it is blended then mix in the walnuts and mayonnaise. Keep it in the fridge until ready to serve. After draining the mushrooms, get rid of the marinade. Over medium heat, broil the mushrooms four inches from the heat or grill them with a cover on until they become tender. Leave it cooking for 3 to 4 minutes per side. Layer cheese and onion on top. Continue grilling until the cheese melts, about 2 to 3 minutes. Place them on buns, topped with arugula and mayonnaise mixture. Serve.

Nutrition Information

- Calories: 509 calories
- Sodium: 832mg sodium
- Fiber: 8g fiber)
- Total Carbohydrate: 39g carbohydrate (12g sugars
- Cholesterol: 40mg cholesterol
- Protein: 16g protein.
- Total Fat: 33g fat (12g saturated fat)

82. Portobello Melts

Serving: 2 servings. | Prep: 10mins | Cook: 10mins | Ready in:

Ingredients

- 2 large portobello mushrooms (4 ounces each), stems removed
- 1/4 cup olive oil
- 2 tablespoons balsamic vinegar
- 1/2 teaspoon salt
- 1/2 teaspoon dried basil
- 4 tomato slices
- 2 slices mozzarella cheese
- 2 slices Italian bread (1 inch thick)
- Chopped fresh basil

Direction

- Set a broiler to preheat. In a shallow bowl, put the mushrooms then mix the dried basil, salt, vinegar and oil and brush it onto both sides of the mushrooms. Allow it to stand for 5 minutes, then save the leftover marinade.
- On a greased rack of a broiler pan, put the mushrooms, stem side down. Let it broil for 3 to 4 minutes on each side, placed 4 inches from the heat source until it becomes soft. Put tomato and cheese on top of the stem sides, then broil for approximately 1 minute until the cheese melts.
- On a baking tray, put the bread then brush it with the reserved marinade. Let it broil for 45 to 60 seconds, placed 4 inches from the heat source until it becomes a bit toasted. Put mushrooms on top and sprinkle it with chopped basil.

Nutrition Information

- Calories: 460 calories
- Fiber: 3g fiber)
- Total Carbohydrate: 26g carbohydrate (8g sugars
- Cholesterol: 22mg cholesterol
- Protein: 12g protein.

- Total Fat: 35g fat (7g saturated fat)
- Sodium: 934mg sodium

83. Portobello Mushroom Burgers

Serving: 4 | Prep: 15mins | Cook: 20mins | Ready in:

Ingredients

- 4 portobello mushroom caps
- 1/4 cup balsamic vinegar
- 2 tablespoons olive oil
- 1 teaspoon dried basil
- 1 teaspoon dried oregano
- 1 tablespoon minced garlic
- salt and pepper to taste
- 4 (1 ounce) slices provolone cheese

Direction

- Put mushroom caps in a shallow dish, smooth side up. Whisk pepper, salt, garlic, oregano, basil, oil and vinegar in a small bowl. Put on mushrooms; let stand for 15 minutes, turning twice, at room temperature.
- Preheat a grill to medium high heat.
- Brush oil on grate; put mushrooms on grill. Keep marinade to baste. Grill till tender, 5-8 minutes per side. Frequently brush marinade on. At final 2 minutes of grilling, top with cheese.

Nutrition Information

- Calories: 203 calories;
- Total Fat: 14.6
- Sodium: 259
- Total Carbohydrate: 9.8
- Cholesterol: 20
- Protein: 10.3

84. Portobello Pizza Burgers

Serving: 4 servings. | Prep: 10mins | Cook: 15mins | Ready in:

Ingredients

- 4 large portobello mushrooms (4 to 4-1/2 inches)
- 4 teaspoons plus 1 tablespoon olive oil, divided
- 1-1/2 cups finely chopped plum tomatoes
- 3/4 cup shredded part-skim mozzarella cheese
- 1-1/2 teaspoons Italian seasoning
- 4 hamburger buns, split

Direction

- Start heating broiler. Take the mushrooms and cut off and through away stems. Use a spoon to carefully take off the gills by scraping. Take 4 teaspoons of oil and brush mushroom caps. In a 15x10x1-in. ungreased pan, place mushrooms with stem side facing down. Put pan 4 in. from heat and broil for 5 minutes. In separate bowl, mix remaining oil, tomatoes, Italian seasoning, and cheese. Take the mushrooms out of the broiler and place tomato mixture in caps. Place back in broiler and broil until cheese is melty and mushrooms are tender, 4-6 minutes. Tastes great on buns.

Nutrition Information

- Calories: 284 calories
- Sodium: 314mg sodium
- Fiber: 3g fiber)
- Total Carbohydrate: 29g carbohydrate (7g sugars
- Cholesterol: 12mg cholesterol
- Protein: 12g protein. Diabetic Exchanges: 2 starch
- Total Fat: 13g fat (4g saturated fat)

85. Portobello Pockets

Serving: 8 servings. | Prep: 30mins | Cook: 10mins | Ready in:

Ingredients

- 1/4 cup water
- 3 tablespoons lime juice
- 2 tablespoons canola oil
- 1 tablespoon Italian seasoning
- 1 teaspoon dried minced garlic
- 1/2 teaspoon dried celery flakes
- 1/4 teaspoon salt
- 1/4 teaspoon ground cumin
- 1/4 teaspoon ground nutmeg
- 1/4 teaspoon pepper
- 1/8 teaspoon cayenne pepper
- 1 pound sliced baby portobello mushrooms
- 1 each medium sweet yellow and red pepper, thinly sliced
- 1 medium red onion, thinly sliced
- 2 small zucchini, cut into 1/4-inch slices
- 1 cup shredded reduced-fat Mexican cheese blend
- 8 pita breads (6 inches), cut in half

Direction

- Mix together the initial 11 ingredients in a big resealable bag, then add the zucchini, onion, peppers and mushrooms. Seal the bag and turn to coat and let it chill in the fridge overnight.
- Use cooking spray to coat a big nonstick frying pan, then cook and stir the vegetable mixture for 6 to 8 minutes on medium high heat or until it becomes crisp-tender. Mix in cheese, then cook for 2 to 3 minutes more or until the cheese melts. Use 1/2 cup vegetable cheese mixture to stuff each pita half.

Nutrition Information

- Calories: 272 calories
- Protein: 12g protein. Diabetic Exchanges: 2 starch
- Total Fat: 8g fat (2g saturated fat)
- Sodium: 500mg sodium
- Fiber: 3g fiber)
- Total Carbohydrate: 41g carbohydrate (4g sugars
- Cholesterol: 10mg cholesterol

86. Portobello Roast Beef Hoagies

Serving: 4 servings. | Prep: 10mins | Cook: 5mins | Ready in:

Ingredients

- 4 whole wheat hoagie buns, split
- 4 tablespoons butter, softened, divided
- 1 teaspoon Italian seasoning
- 1/4 teaspoon garlic salt
- 3/4 pound sliced deli roast beef, julienned
- 1/2 pound sliced baby portobello mushrooms
- 1 teaspoon dried rosemary, crushed
- 1/4 teaspoon pepper
- 1/2 pound sliced provolone cheese
- 1/2 cup sour cream
- 1 tablespoon prepared horseradish

Direction

- Use 2 tbsp. of butter to spread over the cut sides of buns, then use garlic salt as well as Italian seasoning to sprinkle over cut sides. Put aside.
- Sauté together pepper, rosemary, mushrooms and beef in a big skillet with leftover butter until mushrooms soften. Scoop the beef mixture on buns and put cheese on top.
- Arrange buns on a baking sheet and broil 2 to 3 inches away from the heat until cheese melts, about 2 to 4 minutes. Mix together horseradish and sour cream in a small bowl, then serve together with sandwiches.

Nutrition Information

- Calories: 722 calories
- Protein: 43g protein.
- Total Fat: 39g fat (22g saturated fat)
- Sodium: 1637mg sodium
- Fiber: 8g fiber)
- Total Carbohydrate: 53g carbohydrate (10g sugars
- Cholesterol: 136mg cholesterol

87. Roasted Veggie Wraps

Serving: 6 servings. | Prep: 15mins | Cook: 25mins | Ready in:

Ingredients

- 1 envelope Parmesan Italian salad dressing mix
- 1/4 cup water
- 1/4 cup red wine vinegar
- 2 tablespoons olive oil
- 1 medium sweet red pepper, sliced
- 1 cup julienned carrots
- 1 cup quartered fresh mushrooms
- 1 cup fresh broccoli florets
- 1 medium onion, sliced and separated into rings
- 1 medium yellow summer squash, sliced
- 6 flour tortillas (8 inches)
- 1-1/2 cups shredded part-skim mozzarella cheese
- Salsa, optional

Direction

- Mix together the oil, vinegar, water and dressing mix in a jar with a lid that's tight-fitting, then shake well. In a big bowl, put the vegetables and drizzle the dressing on top, then toss until coated.
- In two 15x10x1-inch baking pans coated with cooking spray, spread the vegetables. Bake at 425 degrees for 20-25 minutes without a cover until tender, mixing from time to time.
- In the middle of each tortilla, place around 3/4 cup of roasted vegetables, then sprinkle each with 1/4 cup of cheese. Put on a baking tray.
- Broil 4-6 inches from the heat source for 2 minutes, or until the cheese melts. Fold sides and one end of tortilla over the filling then roll it up. If preferred, serve with salsa.

Nutrition Information

- Calories: 299 calories
- Protein: 13g protein. Diabetic Exchanges: 2 vegetable
- Total Fat: 12g fat (4g saturated fat)
- Sodium: 849mg sodium
- Fiber: 2g fiber)
- Total Carbohydrate: 35g carbohydrate (0 sugars
- Cholesterol: 16mg cholesterol

88. Saucy Portobello Pitas

Serving: 4 servings. | Prep: 25mins | Cook: 10mins | Ready in:

Ingredients

- CUCUMBER SAUCE:
- 1 cup (8 ounces) reduced-fat plain yogurt
- 1/2 cup chopped peeled cucumber
- 1/4 to 1/3 cup minced fresh mint
- 1 tablespoon grated lemon peel
- 1 tablespoon lemon juice
- 1 teaspoon garlic powder
- PITAS:
- 4 large portobello mushrooms, stems removed
- 1/2 teaspoon pepper
- 1/4 teaspoon onion powder
- 1/4 teaspoon garlic powder
- 1/4 teaspoon Greek seasoning
- 2 tablespoons canola oil
- 8 pita pocket halves, warmed
- 8 thin slices red onion, separated into rings
- 8 slices tomato

Direction

- Mix together the cucumber sauce ingredients in a small bowl. Put a cover and let it chill in the fridge until ready to serve.
- Sprinkle Greek seasoning, garlic powder, onion powder and pepper on mushrooms. Cook the mushrooms in oil in a big frying pan for 3-5 minutes per side or until it becomes soft.
- Halve the pita breads then line each with tomato and onion slice. Halve the mushrooms then put it in pitas. Serve it with cucumber sauce.

Nutrition Information

- Calories: 303 calories
- Protein: 11g protein. Diabetic Exchanges: 3 starch
- Total Fat: 9g fat (1g saturated fat)
- Sodium: 411mg sodium
- Fiber: 4g fiber)
- Total Carbohydrate: 45g carbohydrate (9g sugars
- Cholesterol: 3mg cholesterol

89. Sausage 'n' Spinach Pockets

Serving: 8 servings. | Prep: 20mins | Cook: 15mins | Ready in:

Ingredients

- 1/2 pound Jones No Sugar Pork Sausage Roll sausage
- 1/3 cup chopped onion
- 1 garlic clove, minced
- 1 cup chopped fresh spinach
- 1/4 cup chopped fresh mushrooms
- 3/4 cup shredded part-skim mozzarella cheese
- 1/2 teaspoon salt
- 1/4 teaspoon pepper
- 2 tablespoons grated Parmesan cheese, optional
- 2 tubes (8 ounces each) refrigerated crescent rolls
- 1 egg
- 1 tablespoon water
- 1 tablespoon cornmeal

Direction

- Cook garlic, onion and sausage over medium heat in a large skillet until meat is no longer pink; drain well. Take off the heat; mix in mushrooms and spinach. Add Parmesan cheese (if using), pepper, salt and mozzarella cheese; stir to combine; put aside.
- Split crescent dough into 8 rectangles; seal perforations and flatten slightly into 5x4 1/2-inch rectangles. Add approximately 1/3 cup sausage mixture to within 2 inches of edges on half of each rectangle. Whisk together water and egg; brush egg wash on dough's edges. Fold the unfilled half over the filling; seal by pressing the edges using a fork. Brush egg wash over tops. Scatter cornmeal all over a lightly oiled baking sheet; arrange pocket on the cornmeal-coated baking sheet.
- Bake for 15 to 20 minutes at 350° or until golden brown.

Nutrition Information

- Calories: 213 calories
- Sodium: 547mg sodium
- Fiber: 0 fiber)
- Total Carbohydrate: 14g carbohydrate (3g sugars
- Cholesterol: 43mg cholesterol
- Protein: 8g protein.
- Total Fat: 14g fat (5g saturated fat)

90. Sausage Cheese Snacks

Serving: 22 slices. | Prep: 20mins | Cook: 20mins | Ready in:

Ingredients

- 1 pound Jones No Sugar Pork Sausage Roll
- 1/2 cup chopped onion
- 1 can (15 ounces) pizza sauce
- 1/2 pound sliced fresh mushrooms
- 1 loaf (16 ounces) French bread, cut into 22 slices
- 1 package (8 ounces) sliced mozzarella cheese, halved

Direction

- Cook onion and sausage over medium heat in a large skillet until sausage is no longer pink; drain well. Mix in mushrooms and pizza sauce.
- Arrange bread slices on a 15x10x1-inch baking pan; top each slice by scooping over 2 tablespoons of sausage mixture. Place a half slice of cheese over sausage mixture on each portion. Bake for 20 to 25 minutes at 350° or until cheese melts.

Nutrition Information

- Calories: 259 calories
- Total Carbohydrate: 26g carbohydrate (3g sugars
- Cholesterol: 32mg cholesterol
- Protein: 13g protein.
- Total Fat: 11g fat (5g saturated fat)
- Sodium: 631mg sodium
- Fiber: 2g fiber)

91. Sausage Egg Subs

Serving: 6 servings. | Prep: 30mins | Cook: 0mins | Ready in:

Ingredients

- 1-1/4 pounds Jones No Sugar Pork Sausage Roll sausage
- 1/4 cup chopped onion
- 12 large eggs, lightly beaten
- 1/2 cup chopped fresh mushrooms
- 1 to 2 tablespoons finely chopped green pepper
- 1 to 2 tablespoons finely chopped sweet red pepper
- 6 submarine sandwich buns (about 6 inches), split

Direction

- Cook onion and sausage in a big skillet over medium heat until there's no pink anymore; let drain. Use a slotted spoon to remove; keep warm.
- Cook while stirring the eggs in the same skillet for 6-7 minutes over medium heat till almost set. Put in the sausage mixture, peppers and mushrooms. Keep cooking till the mixture is evenly heated and the eggs are totally solid. Put on buns and serve.

Nutrition Information

- Calories: 576 calories
- Sodium: 968mg sodium
- Fiber: 2g fiber)
- Total Carbohydrate: 44g carbohydrate (6g sugars
- Cholesterol: 459mg cholesterol
- Protein: 26g protein.
- Total Fat: 32g fat (10g saturated fat)

92. Smoked Gouda Veggie Melt

Serving: 4 servings. | Prep: 10mins | Cook: 15mins | Ready in:

Ingredients

- 1 cup chopped fresh mushrooms
- 1 cup chopped fresh broccoli
- 1 medium sweet red pepper, chopped
- 1 small onion, chopped
- 2 tablespoons olive oil
- 8 slices Italian bread (1/2 inch thick)
- 1/2 cup mayonnaise
- 1 garlic clove, minced
- 1 cup shredded smoked Gouda cheese

Direction

- Set the oven to 425 degrees to preheat. Put in a greased 15"x10"x1" baking pan with onion, pepper, broccoli and mushrooms. Drizzle over with oil and toss to coat well. Roast until softened, about 10 to 12 minutes.
- At the same time, put on a baking sheet with bread slices. Combine garlic and mayonnaise then spread over bread slices.
- With the oven, choose broil setting. Scoop over bread slices with vegetables and sprinkle with cheese. Broil about 3 to 4 inches from the source of heat until cheese is melted, about 2 to 3 minutes.

Nutrition Information

- Calories: 523 calories
- Total Carbohydrate: 35g carbohydrate (5g sugars
- Cholesterol: 34mg cholesterol
- Protein: 14g protein.
- Total Fat: 37g fat (9g saturated fat)
- Sodium: 695mg sodium
- Fiber: 3g fiber)

93. Spinach Egg Croissants

Serving: 8 servings. | Prep: 20mins | Cook: 0mins | Ready in:

Ingredients

- 1 cup sliced fresh mushrooms
- 1 package (10 ounces) fresh spinach, chopped
- 1 small onion, chopped
- 2 to 3 tablespoons canola oil
- 10 eggs, lightly beaten
- 1 cup shredded Monterey Jack cheese
- 8 croissants, split
- 2 cups prepared hollandaise sauce

Direction

- Sauté the onion, spinach and mushrooms in oil in a big frying pan until it becomes soft. Add the eggs and let it cook and stir on medium heat until the eggs are fully set, then mix in the cheese.
- Under the broiler, toast the croissant halves until it turns golden brown in color. Put egg mixture and hollandaise sauce on top.

Nutrition Information

- Calories: 596 calories
- Total Carbohydrate: 34g carbohydrate (4g sugars
- Cholesterol: 364mg cholesterol
- Protein: 19g protein.
- Total Fat: 43g fat (22g saturated fat)
- Sodium: 891mg sodium
- Fiber: 3g fiber)

94. Spinach Meatball Subs

Serving: 6 servings. | Prep: 20mins | Cook: 30mins | Ready in:

Ingredients

- 2 large fresh mushrooms, quartered
- 2 tablespoons Worcestershire sauce
- 6 garlic cloves, minced
- 2 tablespoons Italian seasoning
- 1 teaspoon pepper
- 1/2 teaspoon salt

- 1 package (10 ounces) frozen chopped spinach, thawed and squeezed dry
- 1/4 cup grated Parmesan cheese
- 2 egg whites
- 1 pound lean ground beef (90% lean)
- 1 jar (14 ounces) marinara or spaghetti sauce
- 6 Italian rolls or submarine buns, split
- 6 tablespoons shredded part-skim mozzarella cheese

Direction

- Mix together the initial 6 ingredients in a food processor. Put a cover and process it until combined. Add the Parmesan cheese, spinach and egg whites. Put a cover and process it until combined. Move to a big bowl, then crumble the beef on top of the mixture and stir well.
- Form it into 1 1/2-inch balls, then put the meatballs in a shallow pan on a greased rack and let it bake for 10 to 13 minutes at 400 degrees or until the meat has no hint of pink color; drain.
- In a big saucepan, pour the marinara sauce and add meatballs, then boil. Lower the heat, put a cover and let it simmer for 15 minutes.
- Onto the rolls, spoon the sauce and meatballs, then sprinkle mozzarella cheese on top. Let it broil for 5-8 minutes or until the cheese melts.

Nutrition Information

- Calories: 355 calories
- Total Fat: 9g fat (4g saturated fat)
- Sodium: 769mg sodium
- Fiber: 4g fiber)
- Total Carbohydrate: 40g carbohydrate (7g sugars
- Cholesterol: 53mg cholesterol
- Protein: 27g protein. Diabetic Exchanges: 2 starch

95. Spinach Mushroom Beef Patties

Serving: 8 servings. | Prep: 15mins | Cook: 10mins | Ready in:

Ingredients

- 1 package (10 ounces) frozen chopped spinach, thawed and squeezed dry
- 1 cup shredded part-skim mozzarella cheese
- 1 cup chopped fresh mushrooms
- 1 envelope onion mushroom soup mix
- 2 pounds ground beef

Direction

- Mix together soup mix, mushrooms, cheese and spinach in a large bowl. Add crumbled beef onto the mixture; stir well to combine.
- Form to 8 patties. Put on grill over medium-high heat with cover until the juices run clear and a thermometer inserted into the burgers reaches 160 degrees or for 5 to 7 minutes per side.

Nutrition Information

- Calories: 295 calories
- Cholesterol: 94mg cholesterol
- Protein: 29g protein.
- Total Fat: 18g fat (7g saturated fat)
- Sodium: 368mg sodium
- Fiber: 1g fiber)
- Total Carbohydrate: 4g carbohydrate (1g sugars

96. Steak House Burgers

Serving: 4 servings. | Prep: 25mins | Cook: 10mins | Ready in:

Ingredients

- 5 tablespoons mayonnaise
- 4-1/2 teaspoons prepared horseradish

- 1/4 cup shredded Parmesan cheese
- 3 tablespoons butter, softened, divided
- 1/2 teaspoon garlic powder
- 4 hamburger buns, split
- 1-1/2 pounds ground beef
- 1/4 cup steak sauce
- 4-1/2 teaspoons onion soup mix
- 4 slices Swiss cheese
- 1-1/2 pounds sliced fresh mushrooms
- 2 green onions, chopped
- 1/4 cup French-fried onions
- Sliced tomato and lettuce, optional

Direction

- Mix horseradish and mayonnaise together in a small bowl; refrigerate, covered, till serving time. Mix garlic powder, a tablespoon of butter, and Parmesan cheese together in the second small bowl; use to spread over bun tops. Put aside.
- Mix onion soup mix, steak sauce, and beef together in a large bowl. Form into 4 patties.
- Moisten a paper towel with cooking oil and coat the grill rack lightly using long-handled tongs. Cover and grill burgers over medium heat or broil 4 inches from the heat for 4-5 minutes per side till juices are clear and a thermometer reads 160 degrees.
- Use Swiss cheese to place on top; grill, covered till cheese melts, about 1-2 more minutes. Lay buns on grill, cut-side down, till toasted, about 1-2 minutes.
- In the meantime, sauté green onions and mushrooms with remaining butter in a large skillet till softened. For serving, place burgers on buns; put mushroom mixture, French-fried onions, horseradish sauce and if preferred, lettuce and tomato on top.

Nutrition Information

- Calories: 833 calories
- Total Fat: 55g fat (22g saturated fat)
- Sodium: 1143mg sodium
- Fiber: 4g fiber)
- Total Carbohydrate: 36g carbohydrate (8g sugars
- Cholesterol: 163mg cholesterol
- Protein: 48g protein.

97. Stuffed Barbecue Burgers

Serving: 4 servings. | Prep: 10mins | Cook: 20mins | Ready in:

Ingredients

- 2 pounds ground beef
- 1 cup shredded cheddar or cheese of your choice
- 1/3 cup finely chopped green pepper
- 1/3 cup finely chopped tomato
- 3 fresh mushrooms, finely chopped
- 2 green onions, finely chopped
- 1/2 cup barbecue sauce
- 1 tablespoon sugar
- 4 hamburger buns, split

Direction

- Form beef into 8 patties. Mix together onions, mushrooms, tomato, green pepper, and cheese in a big bowl. Put vegetable mixture on top of half of the patties. Use the rest of patties to cover; seal edges by pressing firmly.
- Grill over medium heat with a cover or broil 4 inches from heat, 3 minutes per side. Brush barbecue sauce over and sprinkle sugar on top. Grill with a cover or broil 5-6 more minutes per side till juices run clear and a thermometer shows 160°, basting from time to time. Place onto buns to serve.

Nutrition Information

- Calories: 714 calories
- Sodium: 777mg sodium
- Fiber: 2g fiber)

- Total Carbohydrate: 32g carbohydrate (11g sugars
- Cholesterol: 180mg cholesterol
- Protein: 56g protein.
- Total Fat: 39g fat (18g saturated fat)

98. Stuffed Burgers On Portobellos

Serving: 4 servings. | Prep: 15mins | Cook: 15mins | Ready in:

Ingredients

- 1 teaspoon Worcestershire sauce
- 1/2 teaspoon salt
- 1/2 teaspoon pepper
- 1-1/3 pounds ground beef
- 1/2 cup shredded cheddar cheese
- 5 bacon strips, cooked and crumbled
- 4 large portobello mushrooms (about 4 inches), stems removed
- 1 tablespoon olive oil
- 4 tomato slices
- 4 lettuce leaves

Direction

- Mix pepper, salt, and Worcestershire sauce together in a big bowl; crumble and mix beef well. From the mixture into 8 thin patties. Mix bacon and cheese together; scoop in the middle of 4 patties then add the remaining patties on top. Seal patties by pressing the edges together firmly.
- On medium heat, grill patties, covered, for 6mins per side until the juices are clear and an inserted thermometer registers 160 degrees F.
- In the meantime, slather oil over the mushroom caps. On medium heat, grill mushrooms, covered, for 3-4mins per side until tender. Arrange mushrooms on serving plates with the round-side down. Add lettuce, tomato, and burger on top of each.

Nutrition Information

- Calories:
- Total Carbohydrate:
- Cholesterol:
- Protein:
- Total Fat:
- Sodium:
- Fiber:

99. Stuffed Pizza Burgers

Serving: 8 servings. | Prep: 30mins | Cook: 10mins | Ready in:

Ingredients

- 2 large eggs, lightly beaten
- 1 medium onion, finely chopped
- 1 medium green pepper, finely chopped
- 1/2 cup crushed cornflakes
- 1/2 cup chopped fresh mushrooms
- 1 tablespoon minced fresh basil or 1 teaspoon dried basil
- 1 tablespoon minced fresh oregano or 1 teaspoon dried oregano
- 2 garlic cloves, minced
- 2 pounds lean ground turkey
- 1 cup pizza sauce, divided
- 1/2 cup finely chopped turkey pepperoni
- 1/2 cup shredded part-skim mozzarella cheese
- 8 hamburger buns, split

Direction

- Mix the first 8 ingredients together in a large bowl. Crumble turkey and add into mixture; combine well. Form into sixteen patties. On the center of every of 8 patties, layer a tablespoon of pizza sauce, then pepperoni, and cheese. Use remaining patties to top and firmly press edges for sealing.
- Grease a grill rack, place burgers on; cover and grill over medium heat or broil 4 inches from the heat for 4-6 minutes per side till juices are

clear and a thermometer reads 165 degrees. For serving, place onto buns and pair with remaining pizza sauce.

Nutrition Information

- Calories: 385 calories
- Protein: 31g protein. Diabetic Exchanges: 4 lean meat
- Total Fat: 14g fat (4g saturated fat)
- Sodium: 613mg sodium
- Fiber: 2g fiber)
- Total Carbohydrate: 32g carbohydrate (6g sugars
- Cholesterol: 155mg cholesterol

100. Stuffed Pork Burgers

Serving: 4 servings. | Prep: 20mins | Cook: 10mins | Ready in:

Ingredients

- 1/2 cup chopped fresh mushrooms
- 1/4 cup sliced green onions
- 1/4 teaspoon garlic powder
- 1 tablespoon butter
- 2 tablespoons Worcestershire sauce
- 1 teaspoon ground mustard
- 1/2 teaspoon salt
- 1/2 teaspoon pepper
- 1-1/2 pounds ground pork
- 4 kaiser rolls, split
- 4 lettuce leaves
- 4 slices red onion
- 8 thin slices tomato
- Prepared mustard

Direction

- Cook the onions, garlic powder, mushrooms in butter on a small skillet until vegetables are soft. Take from heat.
- Mix the mustard, Worcestershire sauce, pepper and salt in a big bowl. Cook pork and crumble on mixture, mix through.
- Form into 8 patties. Scoop mushroom mixture into the middle of 4 patties until it reach half inch from the edges. Put remaining patties on top; press the edges to close.
- Grill without cover over medium heat, 4 to 5 minutes per side or until an instant read thermometer inserted in the meat shows 160°. Serve patties on rolls with onion, lettuce, mustard and tomato.

Nutrition Information

- Calories:
- Protein:
- Total Fat:
- Sodium:
- Fiber:
- Total Carbohydrate:
- Cholesterol:

101. Supreme Pizza Burgers

Serving: 4 servings. | Prep: 20mins | Cook: 10mins | Ready in:

Ingredients

- 1/3 cup each chopped fresh mushrooms, onion and green pepper
- 1/3 cup chopped ripe olives
- 10 slices turkey pepperoni
- 2 tablespoons tomato paste
- 2 teaspoons Italian seasoning
- 1/4 teaspoon garlic powder
- 1/4 teaspoon salt
- 1/4 teaspoon pepper
- 1/3 cup seasoned bread crumbs
- 1 pound lean ground beef (90% lean)
- 4 whole wheat hamburger buns, split
- 4 slices provolone cheese
- 4 tablespoons pizza sauce

- OPTIONAL TOPPINGS:
- Sliced ripe olives, fresh mushrooms and/or green pepper rings

Direction

- Mix together seasonings, tomato paste, pepperoni, olives, and vegetables in a food processor; cover and pulse until just combined. Remove to a big bowl; mix in bread crumbs. Crumble beef into the mixture; combine well. Form into 4 patties.
- Place burgers on a greased grill rack and grill over medium heat with a cover or broil 4 inches from heat, about 5-7 minutes per side, until juices run clear and a thermometer shows 160°.
- Place onto buns along with pizza sauce and cheese; serve. If wished, put in toppings.

Nutrition Information

- Calories: 470 calories
- Fiber: 5g fiber)
- Total Carbohydrate: 35g carbohydrate (7g sugars
- Cholesterol: 94mg cholesterol
- Protein: 36g protein.
- Total Fat: 21g fat (9g saturated fat)
- Sodium: 1019mg sodium

102. Switchman Sandwiches

Serving: 2 sandwiches. | Prep: 15mins | Cook: 10mins | Ready in:

Ingredients

- 4 slices dark rye bread
- 4 teaspoons reduced-fat mayonnaise
- 1/4 pound sliced deli turkey
- 1/4 pound sliced deli ham
- 4 medium fresh mushrooms, sliced
- 1 small tomato, thinly sliced
- 1/2 cup alfalfa sprouts
- 1/2 cup shredded reduced-fat cheddar cheese

Direction

- Put mayonnaise onto the bread slices and spread all over. Layer 2 slices with turkey, ham, mushrooms, tomato, sprouts and cheese. Put remaining bread on top.
- Put into a clean and dry baking sheet. Bake for 10-12 minutes at 350° until the cheese melts.

Nutrition Information

- Calories: 414 calories
- Sodium: 1726mg sodium
- Fiber: 5g fiber)
- Total Carbohydrate: 38g carbohydrate (7g sugars
- Cholesterol: 69mg cholesterol
- Protein: 35g protein.
- Total Fat: 14g fat (5g saturated fat)

103. Teriyaki Veggie Wraps

Serving: 2 servings. | Prep: 10mins | Cook: 10mins | Ready in:

Ingredients

- 1 medium green pepper, thinly sliced
- 1 small onion, thinly sliced
- 2 garlic cloves, minced
- 1 teaspoon olive oil
- 1 cup sliced fresh mushrooms
- 3 tablespoons reduced-sodium teriyaki sauce
- 2 flour tortillas (8 inches), warmed
- 1/4 cup shredded reduced-fat Mexican cheese blend

Direction

- Sauté the garlic, onion and green pepper in oil in a small nonstick frying pan coated with cooking spray for two minutes. Add

mushrooms and cook for 3 minutes more. Mix in the teriyaki sauce and cook and stir for 1 to 2 minutes or until the veggies become soft.
- In the center of each tortilla, place the vegetable mixture, then sprinkle cheese on top. Roll it up tightly.

Nutrition Information

- Calories: 271 calories
- Protein: 12g protein. Diabetic Exchanges: 2 starch
- Total Fat: 9g fat (2g saturated fat)
- Sodium: 833mg sodium
- Fiber: 2g fiber)
- Total Carbohydrate: 40g carbohydrate (9g sugars
- Cholesterol: 10mg cholesterol

104. Texas Sized Beef Sandwiches

Serving: 2 servings. | Prep: 15mins | Cook: 10mins | Ready in:

Ingredients

- 1/2 medium green pepper, thinly sliced
- 1/3 cup thinly sliced onion
- 1/4 cup sliced fresh mushrooms
- 1/4 teaspoon ground cumin
- 1 teaspoon butter
- 2 teaspoons mayonnaise
- 1 teaspoon Dijon mustard
- 1/4 teaspoon prepared horseradish
- 2 slices Texas toast, toasted
- 6 slices deli roast beef or ham (1/2 ounce each)
- 1/2 medium tomato, sliced
- 1/2 cup shredded cheddar cheese

Direction

- Sauté cumin, mushrooms, onion and green pepper in butter in a nonstick skillet until the vegetables become tender.
- Combine horseradish, mustard and mayonnaise in a small bowl, then spread over the toast. Add cheese, tomato, beef and pepper mixture on top.
- Broil for 2 to 3 mins, 4-6 inches from the heat, until cheese melts.

Nutrition Information

- Calories: 280 calories
- Total Fat: 12g fat (7g saturated fat)
- Sodium: 792mg sodium
- Fiber: 2g fiber)
- Total Carbohydrate: 27g carbohydrate (5g sugars
- Cholesterol: 49mg cholesterol
- Protein: 18g protein.

105. Triple Pepper Steak Sandwiches

Serving: 4 servings. | Prep: 40mins | Cook: 5mins | Ready in:

Ingredients

- 2 boneless beef top loin steaks (1 inch thick and 8 ounces each)
- 1/4 teaspoon salt
- 1/8 teaspoon pepper
- 1 large sweet onion, thinly sliced
- 1 cup sliced fresh mushrooms
- 1 poblano pepper, thinly sliced
- 2 tablespoons plus 2 teaspoons butter, divided
- 2 tablespoons chopped onion
- 1 garlic clove, minced
- 1/2 cup heavy whipping cream
- 1 chipotle pepper in adobo sauce, minced
- 1/2 teaspoon ground cumin
- 1/4 teaspoon chicken bouillon granules
- 1 loaf (14 ounces) ciabatta bread

- 4 slices pepper Jack cheese

Direction

- Sprinkle pepper and salt over steaks. Grill over medium heat, covered, or broil 3-4 in. from the heat until meat achieves desired doneness (a thermometer should read 145deg for medium-rare; 160deg for medium; and 170deg for well-done), 7-9 minutes per side. Let steaks stand for 5 minutes before cutting.
- At the same time, sauté sliced onion, poblano pepper, and mushrooms in 2 tablespoons butter in a large skillet until tender. Take off from the heat; add sliced steak and stir.
- Use the remaining butter to sauté with chopped onion in a small saucepan until tender. Add in garlic; cook more for 1 minute. Add the cream, bouillon, chipotle, and cumin into the mixture; cook and stir until thickened.
- Halve ciabatta horizontally, and then slice into four equal portions. Add cheese on bottom bread slices; Arrange steak mixture, remaining bread and chipotle cream sauce on the top. Cook on an indoor grill or panini maker until cheese is melted and bread is browned, about 3-4 minutes.

Nutrition Information

- Calories: 768 calories
- Protein: 43g protein.
- Total Fat: 37g fat (20g saturated fat)
- Sodium: 1013mg sodium
- Fiber: 4g fiber)
- Total Carbohydrate: 71g carbohydrate (9g sugars
- Cholesterol: 145mg cholesterol

106. Turkey Burgers With Blueberry BBQ Sauce

Serving: 4 servings. | Prep: 15mins | Cook: 15mins | Ready in:

Ingredients

- 1/4 cup chopped onion
- 1 garlic clove, minced
- 1 teaspoon olive oil
- 2 cups fresh or frozen blueberries, thawed
- 2 tablespoons brown sugar
- 1 chipotle pepper in adobo sauce, chopped
- 2 tablespoons red wine vinegar
- 1 tablespoon Dijon mustard
- 1 tablespoon Worcestershire sauce
- BURGERS:
- 1 pound lean ground turkey
- 1/2 teaspoon salt
- 1/2 teaspoon pepper
- 1 cup sliced fresh mushrooms
- 4 slices reduced-fat provolone cheese
- 4 whole wheat hamburger buns, split
- 1/2 cup fresh baby spinach

Direction

- Sauté onion in oil in a big frying pan until onions are tender over medium heat. Add in pepper, mustard, brown sugar, Worcestershire sauce, vinegar, and blueberries; cook while stirring for 10 minutes until thickened. Allow to slightly cool. Pour into the food processor. Cover and blend until it becomes smooth.
- Divide turkey to 4 portions and mold into patties. Season the pepper and salt. Prepare a 12-in square heavy-duty foil with double thickness. Put the mushrooms and fold the foil to tightly seal the mushroom.
- Place the mushroom packet and burgers into grill over medium heat. Cover and cook for 5-7 minutes on each sides until burger juices run out clear and meat thermometer inserted at the burgers registers 165°. Add cheese on top of the burgers. Cover and grill for 1 to 2 minutes more, cook until cheese melts.
- Put bun, seam side down into the grill to toast for 1 to 2 minutes. Serve burgers with spinach, blueberry sauce, and mushrooms.

Nutrition Information

- Calories: 433 calories
- Protein: 30g protein. Diabetic Exchanges: 4 lean meat
- Total Fat: 16g fat (5g saturated fat)
- Sodium: 912mg sodium
- Fiber: 6g fiber)
- Total Carbohydrate: 44g carbohydrate (19g sugars
- Cholesterol: 100mg cholesterol

107. Turkey Divan Croissants

Serving: 6 servings. | Prep: 15mins | Cook: 5mins | Ready in:

Ingredients

- 1/3 cup mayonnaise
- 1/4 cup Dijon mustard
- 1-1/2 teaspoons lemon juice
- 1/2 teaspoon dill weed
- 1 pound bunch broccoli, finely chopped
- 1/2 cup chopped onion
- 2 tablespoons butter
- 1 cup sliced fresh mushrooms
- 6 croissant, split
- 6 ounces thinly sliced cooked turkey
- 6 slices Swiss cheese

Direction

- In a small-sized bowl, mix the dill, lemon juice, mustard and mayonnaise; put them aside.
- In a big skillet, sauté the onion and broccoli in butter till becoming soft or for 10 minutes. Put in the mushrooms; cook and whisk till becoming soft.
- Spread the mustard mixture onto the bottom halves of the croissants. Add the broccoli mixture, turkey and cheese on top; replace the tops.
- Add onto a baking sheet. Bake at 350 degrees till the cheese melts and thoroughly heated or for 5 minutes.

Nutrition Information

- Calories: 239 calories
- Total Carbohydrate: 37g carbohydrate (0 sugars
- Cholesterol: 3mg cholesterol
- Protein: 11g protein. Diabetic Exchanges: 2 starch
- Total Fat: 6g fat (0 saturated fat)
- Sodium: 846mg sodium
- Fiber: 3g fiber)

108. Turkey Florentine Sandwiches

Serving: 2 servings. | Prep: 15mins | Cook: 5mins | Ready in:

Ingredients

- 1/2 cup sliced fresh mushrooms
- 2 teaspoons olive oil
- 1 cup fresh baby spinach
- 2 garlic cloves, minced
- 4 ounces sliced deli turkey breast
- 2 slices part-skim mozzarella cheese
- 4 slices whole wheat bread
- Cooking spray

Direction

- Sauté the mushrooms in oil in a small nonstick frying pan, until it becomes soft, then add garlic and spinach and cook for 1 minute more.
- On 2 slices of bread, layer the spinach mixture, turkey and cheese, then put the leftover bread on top. Use cooking spray to spritz the exterior of the sandwiches. Let it cook on an indoor grill or panini maker for 4-5 minutes or until the cheese melts and the bread turns brown.

Nutrition Information

- Calories: 346 calories
- Protein: 27g protein.
- Total Fat: 14g fat (5g saturated fat)
- Sodium: 937mg sodium
- Fiber: 4g fiber)
- Total Carbohydrate: 27g carbohydrate (4g sugars
- Cholesterol: 35mg cholesterol

109. Turkey Sandwich

Serving: 8 servings. | Prep: 25mins | Cook: 5mins | Ready in:

Ingredients

- 1-1/3 cups sliced fresh mushrooms
- 1/2 cup chopped onion
- 1/2 cup finely chopped celery
- 1/3 cup butter, cubed
- 1/4 cup all-purpose flour
- 1-1/2 cups chicken broth
- 1/2 cup milk
- 1 egg, lightly beaten
- 1/2 cup shredded Swiss cheese
- 1/4 teaspoon ground nutmeg
- 1/8 teaspoon white pepper
- 8 slices white bread, toasted
- 8 slices cooked turkey
- 8 bacon strips, cooked and crumbled
- 8 slices tomato
- 1/4 cup shredded Parmesan cheese

Direction

- In a big skillet, sauté celery, onion and mushrooms in butter till soft. Whisk in the flour till blended; slowly pour in milk and broth. Boil; cook and whisk till becoming thick or for 2 minutes.
- Whisk a small amount of the hot filling to the egg; bring all of them back to the pan, whisk continuously. Heat to a gentle boiling; cook and whisk for 2 more minutes. Whisk in pepper, nutmeg and Swiss cheese till the cheese melts. Take out of heat.
- Add the toast onto a baking sheet. Layer with the turkey, cheese sauce, the bacon, the tomatoes and Parmesan cheese. Broil at 3 to 4 inches away from heat source till the cheese melts or for 3 to 4 minutes.

Nutrition Information

- Calories: 378 calories
- Total Fat: 19g fat (9g saturated fat)
- Sodium: 689mg sodium
- Fiber: 1g fiber)
- Total Carbohydrate: 19g carbohydrate (3g sugars
- Cholesterol: 121mg cholesterol
- Protein: 32g protein.

110. Vegetarian Calzones

Serving: 2 servings. | Prep: 15mins | Cook: 20mins | Ready in:

Ingredients

- 1 cup chopped sweet onion
- 1/2 cup chopped sweet red pepper
- 1/4 cup chopped fresh mushrooms
- 2 tablespoons olive oil
- 1/2 cup chopped fresh spinach
- 2 teaspoons each shredded Swiss, mozzarella and Parmesan cheese
- 1 teaspoon minced chives
- 1 teaspoon minced fresh basil or 1/4 teaspoon dried basil
- 1/2 teaspoon minced fresh dill or 1/8 teaspoon dill weed
- Salt and pepper to taste
- 1 egg, separated
- 4 frozen bread dough rolls, thawed
- Fresh dill sprigs, optional

Direction

- Sauté the mushrooms, red pepper and onion in oil in a frying pan until it becomes soft. Take it out of the heat and stir in the egg white, seasonings, cheeses and spinach, then put aside. Roll each ball of dough into a 5-inch round on a lightly floured surface. Spoon 1/4 of the vegetable mixture onto the middle of each round to within 1-inch of the edge. Fold the dough on top of the filling and seal by pinching the edges.
- Put it on a greased baking tray. If preferred, put a fresh dill sprig on each, then beat the egg yolk and brush it over the tops. Let it bake for 18 to 20 minutes at 375 degrees or until it turns golden brown in color.

Nutrition Information

- Calories: 419 calories
- Cholesterol: 111mg cholesterol
- Protein: 14g protein.
- Total Fat: 21g fat (4g saturated fat)
- Sodium: 478mg sodium
- Fiber: 5g fiber)
- Total Carbohydrate: 47g carbohydrate (9g sugars

111. Vegetarian Reubens

Serving: 6 | Prep: 10mins | Cook: 15mins | Ready in:

Ingredients

- 1 pound smoked Cheddar cheese, shredded
- 1 cup thousand island salad dressing, or to taste
- 1 (16 ounce) jar sauerkraut, drained
- 12 slices dark rye bread
- 2 tablespoons butter
- 2 tomatoes, sliced

Direction

- Mix together the sauerkraut and cheese in a big mixing bowl, then add enough dressing to coat and stir thoroughly.
- Put butter on one side of each bread slice. On the unbuttered side of half of the slices of bread, spread a thick layer of the cheese mixture, then put sliced tomato and another bread slice on top.
- Heat a big frying pan to medium-high heat, then fry the sandwiches on both sides until the cheese melts and exterior becomes toasted.

Nutrition Information

- Calories: 710 calories;
- Total Carbohydrate: 46.6
- Cholesterol: 104
- Protein: 25.4
- Total Fat: 48.2
- Sodium: 1903

112. Veggie Bean Burgers

Serving: 8 servings. | Prep: 45mins | Cook: 15mins | Ready in:

Ingredients

- 1/2 cup uncooked long grain brown rice
- 1 cup water
- 2 cans (15 ounces each) black beans, rinsed and drained
- 2 large eggs, lightly beaten
- 2 teaspoons hot pepper sauce
- 3 teaspoons ground cumin
- 3 teaspoons chili powder
- 1-1/2 teaspoons garlic powder
- 3/4 teaspoon salt
- 1-1/2 cups Fiber One bran cereal
- 1 medium green pepper, coarsely chopped
- 1 medium onion, quartered
- 3/4 cup sliced fresh mushrooms
- 6 garlic cloves, minced
- 3/4 cup shredded part-skim mozzarella cheese

- 8 whole wheat hamburger buns, split and warmed
- Lettuce leaves, optional
- Tomato slices, optional
- Sliced onion, optional

Direction

- Let the broiler preheat. Mix together the water and rice in a small saucepan, then boil. Lower the heat and let it simmer for 30 to 40 minutes with a cover, until the rice becomes tender and the liquid has been absorbed.
- Mash the beans in a big bowl until it's nearly smooth. Stir in the seasonings, pepper sauce and eggs. In a food processor, pulse the bran cereal until it turns finely ground, then move to a small bowl. In a food processor, pulse the garlic and vegetables until chopped finely, then add it to the bean mixture. Add the rice and cheese to the food processor and pulse to combine, then add it to the bean mixture. Mix in ground cereal.
- Form the mixture into eight half-inch thick patties, then put it on a greased baking tray lined with foil. Let it broil for 6 to 8 minutes on each side, placed 4-6 inches from the heat source, until it turns brown. Serve it in buns. Put onion, tomato and lettuce on top if preferred.

Nutrition Information

- Calories: 334 calories
- Protein: 16g protein.
- Total Fat: 6g fat (2g saturated fat)
- Sodium: 814mg sodium
- Fiber: 15g fiber)
- Total Carbohydrate: 60g carbohydrate (6g sugars
- Cholesterol: 53mg cholesterol

113. Veggie Brown Rice Wraps

Serving: 6 servings. | Prep: 10mins | Cook: 10mins | Ready in:

Ingredients

- 1 medium sweet red or green pepper, diced
- 1 cup sliced fresh mushrooms
- 1 tablespoon olive oil
- 2 garlic cloves, minced
- 2 cups cooked brown rice
- 1 can (16 ounces) kidney beans, rinsed and drained
- 1 cup frozen corn, thawed
- 1/4 cup chopped green onions
- 1/2 teaspoon ground cumin
- 1/2 teaspoon pepper
- 1/4 teaspoon salt
- 6 flour tortillas (8 inches), room temperature
- 1/2 cup shredded reduced-fat cheddar cheese
- 3/4 cup salsa

Direction

- Sauté the mushrooms and red pepper in oil in a big nonstick frying pan, until it becomes soft, then add garlic. Let it cook for 1 minute more, then add the salt, pepper, cumin, green onions, corn, beans and rice. Let it cook and stir until heated through or for 4-6 minutes.
- Spoon 3/4 cup onto each tortilla, then sprinkle cheese on top and drizzle it with salsa. Over the filling, fold the sides of the tortilla, then serve right away.

Nutrition Information

- Calories: 377 calories
- Sodium: 675mg sodium
- Fiber: 7g fiber)
- Total Carbohydrate: 62g carbohydrate (4g sugars
- Cholesterol: 7mg cholesterol
- Protein: 15g protein.
- Total Fat: 8g fat (2g saturated fat)

114. Veggie Cheese Sandwiches

Serving: 4 servings. | Prep: 10mins | Cook: 15mins | Ready in:

Ingredients

- 1/2 cup sliced onion
- 1/2 cup julienned green pepper
- 2/3 cup chopped tomato
- 1/2 cup sliced fresh mushrooms
- 8 slices Italian bread (1/2 inch thick)
- 4 slices reduced-fat process American cheese product
- 4 teaspoons butter, softened

Direction

- Cook the green pepper and onion in a small nonstick frying pan coated with cooking spray on medium heat for 2 minutes, then add mushrooms and tomato. Let it cook and stir until the vegetables become soft, then drain.
- Over the 4 bread slices, distribute the vegetable mixture, then put the cheese and leftover bread on top. Spread butter on the bottom and top of each sandwich. Toast the sandwiches in a frying pan until both sides turn light brown.

Nutrition Information

- Calories: 168 calories
- Cholesterol: 15mg cholesterol
- Protein: 8g protein. Diabetic Exchanges: 1 starch
- Total Fat: 6g fat (3g saturated fat)
- Sodium: 415mg sodium
- Fiber: 2g fiber)
- Total Carbohydrate: 20g carbohydrate (3g sugars

115. Veggie Delights

Serving: 4 servings. | Prep: 30mins | Cook: 0mins | Ready in:

Ingredients

- 1/2 cup thinly sliced onion rings
- 2 cups sliced fresh mushrooms
- 3 tablespoons butter, divided
- 1/4 teaspoon salt
- 1/4 teaspoon pepper
- 1/4 teaspoon garlic powder
- 1/8 teaspoon onion powder
- 1/8 teaspoon celery seed
- 4 French rolls, split
- 8 thin green pepper rings
- 8 slices Colby-Monterey Jack cheese or cheddar cheese, halved
- 8 thin slices tomato
- 20 thin slices zucchini
- 8 thin sweet red pepper rings
- 1/4 cup sliced pimiento-stuffed olives

Direction

- Sauté the mushrooms and onion rings in 1 tbsp. butter in a frying pan, until it becomes soft. Sprinkle pepper and salt on top, then put aside. Mix together the celery seed, onion powder and garlic powder with the remaining butter, then spread it on top of the cut sides of the rolls. Let it broil for 1 to 2 minutes, placed 4-5 inches from the heat source or until it turns light brown.
- On the bottom of each roll, put around 1/4 cup of the mushroom mixture, then layer it with green pepper rings and 2 slices of cheese. Layer the tomato and slices of zucchini, red pepper rings, olives and leftover cheese on the top halves.
- Let it broil for 3 to 4 minutes, placed 4 inches from the heat source or until the cheese bubbles. Put together the tops and bottoms of the sandwiches.

Nutrition Information

- Calories: 455 calories
- Fiber: 3g fiber)
- Total Carbohydrate: 41g carbohydrate (7g sugars
- Cholesterol: 63mg cholesterol
- Protein: 18g protein.
- Total Fat: 27g fat (14g saturated fat)
- Sodium: 1011mg sodium

116. Veggie Tuna Melts

Serving: 8 servings. | Prep: 10mins | Cook: 10mins | Ready in:

Ingredients

- 2 cans (6 ounces each) light water-packed tuna, drained and flaked
- 3/4 cup chopped sweet red pepper
- 1/2 cup chopped fresh mushrooms
- 1/2 cup shredded reduced-fat cheddar cheese
- 1/4 cup sliced pimiento-stuffed olives
- 4-1/2 teaspoons reduced-fat mayonnaise
- 4 English muffins, split and toasted
- 8 thin slices tomato

Direction

- Mix olives, cheese, mushrooms, red pepper and tuna in a large bowl. Fold in mayonnaise. Spread the mixture over the English muffin halves. Add a tomato slice on top of each half.
- Broil 6 inches from the heat until lightly browned, or about 7-9 minutes. Enjoy immediately.

Nutrition Information

- Calories: 165 calories
- Protein: 14g protein. Diabetic Exchanges: 2 lean meat
- Total Fat: 5g fat (2g saturated fat)
- Sodium: 413mg sodium
- Fiber: 2g fiber)
- Total Carbohydrate: 16g carbohydrate (0 sugars
- Cholesterol: 24mg cholesterol

117. Wild Rice Burgers

Serving: 6 servings. | Prep: 15mins | Cook: 15mins | Ready in:

Ingredients

- 1 cup cooked wild rice
- 1 medium onion, chopped
- 1/4 cup chopped mushrooms
- 1/4 cup chopped green pepper
- Salt and pepper to taste
- 1 pound ground beef
- 6 hamburger buns, split and toasted

Direction

- Mix pepper, rice, salt, onion, green pepper, and mushrooms together in a bowl; mix in crumbled beef thoroughly then form into 6 patties. Broil or grill until the patties are not pink. Serve burgers on buns.

Nutrition Information

- Calories: 311 calories
- Protein: 20g protein.
- Total Fat: 12g fat (4g saturated fat)
- Sodium: 279mg sodium
- Fiber: 2g fiber)
- Total Carbohydrate: 30g carbohydrate (5g sugars
- Cholesterol: 50mg cholesterol

118. Zucchini Pizza Loaves

Serving: 2 loaves (4 servings each). | Prep: 30mins | Cook: 30mins | Ready in:

Ingredients

- 2 medium zucchini, thinly sliced
- 1 medium onion, finely chopped
- 1 cup sliced fresh mushrooms
- 2 teaspoons olive oil
- 2 garlic cloves, minced
- 1 can (8 ounces) no-salt-added tomato sauce
- 1 medium tomato, seeded and chopped
- 1 can (2-1/4 ounces) sliced ripe olives, drained
- 2 teaspoons Italian seasoning
- 2 tubes (11 ounces each) refrigerated crusty French loaf
- 3 slices provolone cheese, chopped
- 1 ounce sliced turkey pepperoni, julienned
- 1 cup shredded part-skim mozzarella cheese

Direction

- Sauté mushrooms, onion, and zucchini in oil in a large skillet until they are tender. Add garlic and cook for 1 more minute. Stir in the Italian seasoning, olives, tomato, and tomato sauce; then retrieve from the heat.
- Beginning with the seam, unroll a loaf of dough. Pat to a 14x12-inch rectangle. Scatter pepperoni and 1/2 of the provolone leaving 1/2 inch border from edges. Scatter 1/2 of the zucchini mixture over; scatter with 1/2 of the mozzarella.
- Beginning at a long side, roll up jelly-roll style; press the seams to seal. Arrange on a baking sheet greased using cooking spray, seam side down. Repeat with the rest of the zucchini mixture, cheeses, pepperoni, and dough.
- Bake at 350 degrees until golden brown, 30-35 minutes. Cut and serve it warm.

Nutrition Information

- Calories: 322 calories
- Protein: 15g protein.
- Total Fat: 10g fat (5g saturated fat)
- Sodium: 801mg sodium
- Fiber: 3g fiber)
- Total Carbohydrate: 42g carbohydrate (8g sugars
- Cholesterol: 20mg cholesterol

Chapter 3: Mushroom Soup Recipes

***

119. "Bring An Ingredient" Soup

Serving: 16-18 servings (4-1/2 quarts). | Prep: 30mins | Cook: 01hours15mins | Ready in:

Ingredients

- 4 cups thinly sliced onions
- 1 garlic clove, minced
- 3 tablespoons butter
- 3 tablespoons all-purpose flour
- 6 cans (14-1/2 ounces each) beef broth
- 2 cups tomato puree
- 1 tablespoon red wine vinegar
- 1 tablespoon Worcestershire sauce
- 1 tablespoon sugar
- 1/2 teaspoon each dried oregano, tarragon, ground cumin, salt and pepper
- 1/4 to 1/2 teaspoon hot pepper sauce
- VEGETABLES: (choose two or three):
- VEGETABLES: (choose two or three):
- 1-1/2 cups each diced green pepper, tomato or carrots
- 2 cups sliced fresh mushrooms

- MEATS: (choose two):
- 3 cups cooked mini meatballs
- 3 cups cubed cooked chicken
- 3 cups diced fully cooked ham
- 1 package (10 ounces) Johnsonville® Fully Cooked Polish Kielbasa Sausage Rope, sliced and browned
- GARNISH: (choose three or four):
- GARNISH: (choose three or four):
- Shredded cheddar cheese, garbanzo beans, sour cream, minced fresh parsley, croutons or popcorn

Direction

- Sauté garlic and onions in butter in a big Dutch oven until soft. Mix in flour and stir thoroughly. Add seasonings, vinegar, puree, and broth, stir thoroughly. Boil it, lower the heat and bring to a simmer for 40 minutes.
- Add 2 or 3 vegetables; bring to a simmer until soft, or for about 30 minutes. Add 2 meats, heat thoroughly. Garnish as you like.

Nutrition Information

- Calories: 135 calories
- Sodium: 505mg sodium
- Fiber: 1g fiber)
- Total Carbohydrate: 8g carbohydrate (4g sugars
- Cholesterol: 38mg cholesterol
- Protein: 12g protein.
- Total Fat: 6g fat (2g saturated fat)

120. Asian Chicken Noodle Soup

Serving: 2 | Prep: 10mins | Cook: 20mins | Ready in:

Ingredients

- 4 ounces dry Chinese noodles
- 1 (14.5 ounce) can chicken broth
- 6 shiitake mushrooms, sliced
- 2 green onions, chopped
- 1 skinless, boneless chicken breast half
- 2 eggs

Direction

- Fill a large pot with water then bring to a boil. Cook noodles in boiling water for 8 to 10 minutes or until al dente. If a chewier texture is desired, pour a cup of cold water in the pot when the water starts to foam. Let it boil again to cook. Drain the noodles then place into two separate bowls.
- In a medium-sized pot, bring chicken broth to boil in a medium saucepan with mushrooms and green onions. Slice the chicken into bite-sized pieces. Add to the boiling broth, then crack eggs into it. Let the chicken cook for about 10 minutes, until the eggs are cooked and the chicken is no longer pink. Once the soup is done, pour into the noodles in bowls. Serve right away.

Nutrition Information

- Calories: 356 calories;
- Total Fat: 7.1
- Sodium: 113
- Total Carbohydrate: 51
- Cholesterol: 220
- Protein: 27.2

121. Beef And Bean Chili

Serving: Makes 6 servings | Prep: | Cook: | Ready in:

Ingredients

- 1 tablespoon olive oil
- 2 large red onions, chopped
- 5 tablespoons chopped jalapeño chilies with seeds
- 8 garlic cloves, chopped

- 2 1/3 pounds ground beef (15% fat)
- 1/4 cup chili powder
- 2 tablespoons ground cumin
- 1 teaspoon sweet paprika
- 1 28-ounce can diced tomatoes in juice
- 2 15 1/4-ounce cans kidney beans, drained
- 1 14-ounce can beef broth
- Sour cream
- Grated cheddar cheese
- Chopped green onions
- Chopped fresh cilantro

Direction

- In a big heavy pot, heat oil over medium-high heat. Add onions, sauté for 6 minutes until turning brown. Add garlic and jalapeños, sauté for 1 minute. Add beef, sauté for 5 minutes until turning brown, crumble using the back of a fork. Add paprika, cumin, and chili powder, and then mix in broth, beans, and tomatoes with juices; boil it. Lower the heat and simmer for 45 minutes until the flavors combine and the chili thickens, whisking sometimes. Remove any fat from the surface of chili. (You can prepare 2 days in advance. Let cool slightly. Chill without a cover until cold, and then cover and keep chilled. Simmer before continuing, whisking sometimes).
- Spoon the chili into bowls. Enjoy, passing bowls of cilantro, green onions, grated cheese, and sour cream individually.

122. Best Chicken Noodle Soup

Serving: 10 servings (2-3/4 quarts). | Prep: 02hours00mins | Cook: 30mins | Ready in:

Ingredients

- 1 tablespoon dried rosemary, crushed
- 2 teaspoons garlic powder
- 2 teaspoons pepper
- 2 teaspoons seasoned salt
- 2 broiler/fryer chickens (3 to 3-1/2 pounds each)
- 5 cups chicken broth
- 2-1/4 cups sliced fresh mushrooms
- 1/2 cup chopped celery
- 1/2 cup sliced carrots
- 1/2 cup chopped onion
- 1/4 teaspoon pepper
- NOODLES:
- 2-1/4 cups all-purpose flour
- 1 teaspoon salt
- 2 eggs
- 1 can (5 ounces) evaporated milk
- 1 tablespoon olive oil

Direction

- Mix the first 4 ingredients together, rub on the chickens. Put in a non-oiled 13x 9-inch baking pan. Put a cover on and bake at 350° until a thermometer reaches 170° - 175° when you insert it in the thickest part of the thigh, or for about 1-1/4 hours. Strain and save the drippings. Remove the fat. Once cool enough to touch, cut the meat off the bones and dispose the bones. Slice the meat into bite-size chunks. Put a cover on and chill the chicken.
- Boil the saved drippings and chicken broth in a soup kettle or Dutch oven. Add pepper, onion, carrots, celery, and mushrooms, bring to a simmer until the vegetables are soft, or for about 30 minutes.
- Mix salt and flour together in a big bowl. Create a well in the middle. Whisk oil, milk, and egg; add to the well. Whisk together, making a dough. Put the dough on a surface scattered with flour, knead 8-10 times. Split into 3 portions. Roll out each portion into 1/8-inch thickness, slice to wanted width.
- Freeze 2 portions to another use. Boil the soup. Add 1 portion of noodles; cook until the noodles are nearly soft, or for about 7-9 minutes. Add chicken, thoroughly heat.

Nutrition Information

- Calories: 330 calories
- Cholesterol: 100mg cholesterol
- Protein: 24g protein.
- Total Fat: 13g fat (4g saturated fat)
- Sodium: 1087mg sodium
- Fiber: 2g fiber)
- Total Carbohydrate: 29g carbohydrate (4g sugars

123. Brie Mushroom Soup

Serving: 4 servings. | Prep: 15mins | Cook: 20mins | Ready in:

Ingredients

- 1/4 cup butter, cubed
- 1 pound sliced fresh mushrooms
- 2 large onions, chopped
- 1 can (14-1/2 ounces) chicken broth
- 1 tablespoon paprika
- 1 tablespoon reduced-sodium soy sauce
- 2 teaspoons dill weed
- 3 tablespoons all-purpose flour
- 1 cup milk
- 4 ounces Brie cheese, rind removed, cubed
- 1/4 cup minced fresh parsley
- 2 teaspoons lemon juice
- 1/2 teaspoon salt
- 1/4 teaspoon pepper

Direction

- Heat butter in a Dutch oven over medium-high heat. Cook and mix onions and mushrooms in melted butter until softened. Mix in dill, soy sauce, paprika, and broth. Bring to a boil. Lower heat; cover and simmer for about 5 minutes.
- Combine milk and flour in a small bowl until no lumps remain. Mix into mushroom mixture. Bring to a boil. Cook, stirring, until thickened, about 1 to 2 minutes. Lower heat; put in the remaining ingredients; cook and mix until cheese melts (do not boil the mixture).

Nutrition Information

- Calories: 328 calories
- Total Carbohydrate: 21g carbohydrate (9g sugars
- Cholesterol: 67mg cholesterol
- Protein: 14g protein.
- Total Fat: 22g fat (14g saturated fat)
- Sodium: 1192mg sodium
- Fiber: 3g fiber)

124. Broccoli Barley Soup

Serving: 8 servings (about 2 quarts). | Prep: 15mins | Cook: 50mins | Ready in:

Ingredients

- 2 medium onions, chopped
- 2 garlic cloves, minced
- 4 ounces sliced fresh mushrooms
- 3 tablespoons butter
- 3 cups chicken broth
- 3 cups vegetable broth
- 3/4 cup uncooked medium pearl barley
- 1/4 to 1/2 teaspoon dried rosemary, crushed
- 1 pound fresh broccoli, cut into florets
- 2 tablespoons cornstarch
- 1/4 cup cold water
- 2 cups half-and-half cream
- Salt and pepper
- Grated Parmesan cheese

Direction

- Sauté the first 3 ingredients in butter in a Dutch oven or large saucepan until tender. Add rosemary, barley, vegetable broths, and chicken. Bring to a boil. Lower heat; simmer, covered until barley is tender, or for 30

minutes. Add broccoli; cook, covered until broccoli softens, or for 10 minutes.
- Combine cold water and cornstarch in a small bowl until no lumps remain; add into the soup. Bring to a boil; cook, stirring until thickened, or for 2 minutes. Lower heat; mix in pepper, salt, and cream (no boiling). Scatter with Parmesan cheese on top.

Nutrition Information

- Calories: 240 calories
- Total Fat: 11g fat (7g saturated fat)
- Sodium: 816mg sodium
- Fiber: 6g fiber)
- Total Carbohydrate: 27g carbohydrate (7g sugars
- Cholesterol: 41mg cholesterol
- Protein: 8g protein.

125. Cheeseburger Paradise Soup

Serving: 14 servings (about 3-1/2 quarts). | Prep: 30mins | Cook: 25mins | Ready in:

Ingredients

- 6 medium potatoes, peeled and cubed
- 1 small carrot, grated
- 1 small onion, chopped
- 1/2 cup chopped green pepper
- 2 tablespoons chopped seeded jalapeno pepper
- 3 cups water
- 2 tablespoons plus 2 teaspoons beef bouillon granules
- 2 garlic cloves, minced
- 1/8 teaspoon pepper
- 2 pounds ground beef
- 1/2 pound sliced fresh mushrooms
- 2 tablespoons butter
- 5 cups 2% milk, divided
- 6 tablespoons all-purpose flour
- 1 package (16 ounces) process cheese (Velveeta), cubed
- Crumbled cooked bacon

Direction

- Bring the first 9 ingredients to a boil in a Dutch oven. Reduce the heat and cover, simmering until potatoes are already tender, or for 10-15 minutes.
- In the meantime, cook the beef in a large skillet with the mushrooms in the butter over a medium heat until the meat is all brown, then drain. Add them to the soup and stir in 4 cups milk, heating through.
- Combine the remaining milk and the flour in a small bowl until smooth. Stir the flour mixture gradually into the soup, then, make it boil. Cook while stirring until the soup is thick, or for 2 minutes. Reduce the heat and stir in the cheese until it melts, then garnish with bacon.

Nutrition Information

- Calories: 370 calories
- Protein: 23g protein.
- Total Fat: 20g fat (10g saturated fat)
- Sodium: 947mg sodium
- Fiber: 1g fiber)
- Total Carbohydrate: 24g carbohydrate (8g sugars
- Cholesterol: 79mg cholesterol

126. Contest Winning Pizza Soup

Serving: 10 servings (about 2-1/2 quarts). | Prep: 5mins | Cook: 40mins | Ready in:

Ingredients

- 2 cans (14-1/2 ounces each) diced tomatoes
- 2 cans (10-3/4 ounces each) condensed tomato soup, undiluted

- 2-1/2 cups water
- 1 package (3-1/2 ounces) sliced pepperoni, quartered
- 1 medium sweet red pepper, chopped
- 1 medium green pepper, chopped
- 1 cup sliced fresh mushrooms
- 2 garlic cloves, minced
- 1/2 teaspoon rubbed sage
- 1/2 teaspoon dried basil
- 1/2 teaspoon dried oregano
- Salt and pepper to taste
- 10 slices French bread, toasted
- 1-1/2 cups shredded part-skim mozzarella cheese

Direction

- Bring water, soup, and tomatoes in a Dutch oven to a boil. Lower heat; simmer, covered for 15 minutes. Mash using a potato masher. Add pepper, salt, oregano, basil, sage, garlic, mushrooms, red and green peppers, and pepperoni. Simmer, covered until vegetables are softened, or for 10 minutes.
- Spoon into oven-safe bowls. Add a slice of bread and cheese over each bowl. Broil 4 inches away from the heat source until cheese melts and starts bubbling.

Nutrition Information

- Calories: 303 calories
- Total Carbohydrate: 42g carbohydrate (6g sugars
- Cholesterol: 18mg cholesterol
- Protein: 13g protein.
- Total Fat: 9g fat (4g saturated fat)
- Sodium: 884mg sodium
- Fiber: 4g fiber)

127. Crab Bisque

Serving: 4 | Prep: 5mins | Cook: 15mins | Ready in:

Ingredients

- 1 (10.75 ounce) can condensed tomato soup
- 1 (10.75 ounce) can condensed cream of mushroom soup
- 1 1/4 cups milk
- 1 1/4 cups imitation crabmeat
- salt to taste
- ground black pepper to taste
- 1 pinch curry powder

Direction

- Mix milk and soups till smooth. Add crabmeat and curry powder, pepper and salt to taste. Heat, don't boil, till steaming; serve.

Nutrition Information

- Calories: 197 calories;
- Total Carbohydrate: 25.5
- Cholesterol: 15
- Protein: 8.4
- Total Fat: 7.4
- Sodium: 1316

128. Cream Of Mushroom Soup

Serving: Makes 8 servings | Prep: | Cook: | Ready in:

Ingredients

- 2 tablespoons (1/4 stick) butter
- 3 leeks, halved, thinly sliced (white and pale green parts only)
- 2 pounds button mushrooms, sliced
- 2 garlic cloves, minced
- 1/4 cup long-grain white rice
- 3 1/4 cups (or more) canned low-salt chicken broth
- 3 1/4 cups canned beef broth
- 1/2 cup whipping cream
- 1/4 cup chopped fresh chives

Direction

- In a heavy large pot, melt butter over medium heat. Sauté leeks in melted butter for about 5 minutes until softened. Raise heat to medium-high. Add mushrooms and sauté for about 10 minutes until tender and dry. Add garlic and sauté 1 minute. Mix in rice. Add 3 1/4 cups chicken broth and beef broth to the pot. Bring to a boil. Turn heat to low, simmer with a cover for about 30 minutes until rice is very tender. Allow to cool a bit. Puree soup in batches in a blender until no lumps remain. Pour the pureed soup back into the pot. Mix in cream. Make the soup thinner by adding more chicken broth if needed. (Soup can be cooked 1 day beforehand. Allow to cool a bit, and chill, covered. Bring to a simmer before serving.)
- Transfer soup into 8 serving bowls. Top with chives and serve.

Nutrition Information

- Calories: 191
- Sodium: 953 mg(40%)
- Fiber: 2 g(7%)
- Total Carbohydrate: 17 g(6%)
- Cholesterol: 24 mg(8%)
- Protein: 12 g(24%)
- Total Fat: 10 g(15%)
- Saturated Fat: 5 g(27%)

129. Creamy Bacon Mushroom Soup

Serving: 8 servings (2 quarts). | Prep: 10mins | Cook: 20mins | Ready in:

Ingredients

- 10 bacon strips, diced
- 1 pound sliced fresh mushrooms
- 1 medium onion, chopped
- 3 garlic cloves, minced
- 1 quart heavy whipping cream
- 1 can (14-1/2 ounces) chicken broth
- 1-1/4 cups shredded Swiss cheese
- 3 tablespoons cornstarch
- 1/2 teaspoon salt
- 1/2 teaspoon pepper
- 3 tablespoons cold water

Direction

- Over medium heat in a big saucepan, cook bacon until turns crispy. Transfer to paper towels with a slotted spoon; drain, keep 2 tablespoons of drippings reserved. Sauté onion and mushrooms in the drippings until soft. Add garlic; cook for another minute. Stir in broth and cream. Stir in cheese gradually until melted.
- Mix water, pepper, salt and cornstarch until smooth in a small bowl. Stir into soup. Cook until boiling; continue stirring and cooking for 2 minutes or until soup is thickened. Top with bacon.

Nutrition Information

- Calories: 592 calories
- Protein: 13g protein.
- Total Fat: 56g fat (33g saturated fat)
- Sodium: 649mg sodium
- Fiber: 1g fiber)
- Total Carbohydrate: 12g carbohydrate (3g sugars
- Cholesterol: 193mg cholesterol

130. Creamy Garlic & Mushroom Soup

Serving: 13 servings (1 cup each). | Prep: 15mins | Cook: 30mins | Ready in:

Ingredients

- 1 pound medium fresh mushrooms, halved

- 1 pound sliced baby portobello mushrooms
- 1/2 pound sliced fresh shiitake mushrooms
- 7 tablespoons butter
- 12 garlic cloves, minced
- 2 green onions, chopped
- 1/2 cup all-purpose flour
- 2 cans (14-1/2 ounces each) chicken broth
- 3-1/3 cups 2% milk
- 1-2/3 cups heavy whipping cream
- 4 teaspoons minced fresh thyme or 1-1/2 teaspoons dried thyme
- 2 teaspoons minced fresh basil or 3/4 teaspoon dried basil
- 1 teaspoon salt
- 1 teaspoon pepper
- Minced fresh parsley

Direction

- In batches, sauté mushrooms in a Dutch oven with butter until soft. Put all back to the pan; add onions and garlic. Sauté for 2 minutes. Add a sprinkling of flour; stir until combined.
- Stir in milk and broth gradually. Cook until boiling; cook and stir until thickened or for 2 minutes. Stir in pepper, salt, basil, thyme and cream; thoroughly heat. Top each serving with a sprinkling of parsley.

Nutrition Information

- Calories: 246 calories
- Total Carbohydrate: 13g carbohydrate (5g sugars
- Cholesterol: 66mg cholesterol
- Protein: 6g protein.
- Total Fat: 20g fat (12g saturated fat)
- Sodium: 539mg sodium
- Fiber: 1g fiber)

131. Creamy Garlic & Mushroom Soup With Pastry Caps

Serving: 12 servings. | Prep: 50mins | Cook: 15mins | Ready in:

Ingredients

- 1 pound medium fresh mushrooms, halved
- 1 pound sliced baby portobello mushrooms
- 1/2 pound sliced fresh shiitake mushrooms
- 7 tablespoons butter
- 12 garlic cloves, minced
- 2 green onions, chopped
- 1/2 cup all-purpose flour
- 2 cans (14-1/2 ounces each) chicken broth
- 3-1/3 cups whole milk
- 1-2/3 cups heavy whipping cream
- 2 tablespoons sherry
- 4 teaspoons minced fresh thyme or 1-1/2 teaspoons dried thyme
- 2 teaspoons minced fresh basil or 3/4 teaspoon dried basil
- 1 teaspoon salt
- 1 teaspoon pepper
- 3 sheets frozen puff pastry, thawed
- 1 egg, beaten
- 1 teaspoon water

Direction

- Sauté mushrooms in batches with butter in a Dutch oven until tender. Put all mushrooms back into the pan; add onions and garlic. Cook and mix for 2 minutes. Dust with flour; mix until combined.
- Slowly mix in milk and broth. Bring to a boil; cook, stirring, until thickened, about 2 minutes. Mix in seasonings, sherry, and cream; cook through.
- Roll out each sheet of puff pastry into a 12-inch square on a work surface thinly coated with flour. Use a 10-oz ramekin as a pattern to cut out 4 circles of pastry 1 inch larger than the diameter of the ramekin from each square.

- Pour the soup into twelve 10-oz. ramekins, about 1 cup in each ramekin. Combine water and egg in a small mixing bowl. Brush egg mixture over the edges of the pastry circles; seal circles to edges of the ramekins. Arrange ramekins on baking sheets. Bake for 12 to 15 minutes at 400° until golden brown.

Nutrition Information

- Calories: 574 calories
- Cholesterol: 89mg cholesterol
- Protein: 12g protein.
- Total Fat: 38g fat (17g saturated fat)
- Sodium: 792mg sodium
- Fiber: 6g fiber)
- Total Carbohydrate: 48g carbohydrate (5g sugars

132. DIY Ramen Soup

Serving: 2 servings. | Prep: 20mins | Cook: 5mins | Ready in:

Ingredients

- 1 package (3 ounces) ramen noodles
- 1 tablespoon reduced-sodium chicken base
- 1 to 2 teaspoons Sriracha Asian hot chili sauce
- 1 teaspoon minced fresh gingerroot
- 1/2 cup shredded carrots
- 1/2 cup shredded cabbage
- 2 radishes, halved and sliced
- 1/2 cup sliced fresh shiitake mushrooms
- 1 cup shredded cooked chicken breast
- 1/4 cup fresh cilantro leaves
- 1 hard-boiled large egg, halved
- 2 lime wedges
- 4 cups boiling water

Direction

- Follow instructions on package to cook ramen; chill.
- In each of two canning jars with 1-qt. wide mouth, split and put ingredients following the order in a layer: ramen noodles, base of chicken, Sriracha, ginger then carrots, cabbage, radishes then mushrooms, chicken, and cilantro. In resealable plastic bags or 4-oz. glass jars, place lime wedge and egg. Pour over cilantro in 1-qt. jars. Keep covered in the refrigerator until serving.
- Remove lime and egg to serve. Into each 1-qt. glass jar, add 2 cups of boiling water; allow to sit until thoroughly warmed or the base of chicken has dissolved. Mix seasonings by stirring. Over soup, squeeze lime juice and top with egg.

Nutrition Information

- Calories: 401 calories
- Total Fat: 14g fat (6g saturated fat)
- Sodium: 1092mg sodium
- Fiber: 2g fiber)
- Total Carbohydrate: 35g carbohydrate (4g sugars
- Cholesterol: 153mg cholesterol
- Protein: 31g protein.

133. Deluxe Chili Con Carne

Serving: 4 servings. | Prep: 10mins | Cook: 01hours25mins | Ready in:

Ingredients

- 1 pound ground beef
- 1 medium green pepper, chopped
- 1 medium onion, chopped
- 1 garlic clove, minced
- 1 can (10-3/4 ounces) condensed tomato soup, undiluted
- 1 can (8 ounces) kidney beans, rinsed and drained
- 4-1/2 teaspoons chili powder
- 1 tablespoon Worcestershire sauce

- 1-1/2 teaspoons salt
- 1 teaspoon pepper
- 1/2 pound fresh mushrooms, halved

Direction

- Cook garlic, onion, green pepper, and beef in a large saucepan over medium heat until beef is no longer pink; drain well. Add pepper, salt, Worcestershire sauce, chili powder, beans, and the soup; bring to a boil. Lower heat; simmer, covered until thickened and bubbly, or for 1 hour. Add mushrooms; simmer, covered for 15 minutes longer.

Nutrition Information

- Calories: 327 calories
- Protein: 28g protein.
- Total Fat: 11g fat (5g saturated fat)
- Sodium: 1575mg sodium
- Fiber: 7g fiber)
- Total Carbohydrate: 31g carbohydrate (11g sugars
- Cholesterol: 56mg cholesterol

134. Elegant Mushroom Soup

Serving: 2-3 servings. | Prep: 5mins | Cook: 5mins | Ready in:

Ingredients

- 1 large onion, chopped
- 1/2 pound fresh mushrooms, sliced
- 2 tablespoons butter
- 2 tablespoons all-purpose flour
- 1/4 teaspoon pepper
- 1/8 teaspoon salt
- 1 cup milk
- 1 cup chicken broth
- 1 tablespoon minced fresh parsley
- Ground nutmeg, optional
- Sour cream

Direction

- Sauté mushrooms and onion in butter for 3 minutes in a large saucepan or until onion is tender. Mix in salt, pepper, and flour; slowly pour in broth and milk. Bring to a boil; cook, stirring until thickened, or for 2 minutes. Add nutmeg, and parsley if desired.
- Top each serving with a dollop of sour cream.

Nutrition Information

- Calories: 180 calories
- Total Fat: 11g fat (6g saturated fat)
- Sodium: 531mg sodium
- Fiber: 2g fiber)
- Total Carbohydrate: 16g carbohydrate (8g sugars
- Cholesterol: 32mg cholesterol
- Protein: 7g protein.

135. Gnocchi Chicken Minestrone

Serving: 8 servings (2-3/4 quarts). | Prep: 30mins | Cook: 30mins | Ready in:

Ingredients

- 1-1/4 pounds chicken tenderloins, cut into 1/2-inch pieces
- 3/4 teaspoon dried oregano
- 1/4 teaspoon salt
- 1/4 teaspoon pepper
- 2 tablespoons olive oil, divided
- 1 each small green, sweet red and yellow peppers, finely chopped
- 1 medium zucchini, finely chopped
- 1 cup chopped fresh baby portobello mushrooms
- 1/3 cup chopped red onion
- 1/3 cup chopped prosciutto or deli ham
- 4 garlic cloves, minced
- 2 cans (14-1/2 ounces each) chicken broth

- 1 can (14-1/2 ounces) Italian diced tomatoes, undrained
- 3/4 cup canned white kidney or cannellini beans, rinsed and drained
- 1/2 cup frozen peas
- 3 tablespoons tomato paste
- 1 package (16 ounces) potato gnocchi
- 1/2 cup shredded Asiago cheese
- 8 fresh basil leaves, thinly sliced

Direction

- Sprinkle pepper, salt, and oregano over the chicken. Sauté the chicken in 1 tablespoon oil in a Dutch oven until the chicken is not pink anymore. Take out of the pan and put aside.
- Cook onion, mushrooms, zucchini, and peppers in the leftover oil in the same pan until soft. Add garlic and prosciutto, cook for another 1 minute. Add chicken, tomato paste, peas, beans, tomatoes, and broth. Boil it. Lower the heat; bring to a simmer without a cover, mixing sometimes, about 20 minutes.
- In the meantime, cook gnocchi following the package's instructions. Strain, mix into the soup. Use basil and cheese to garnish each serving.

Nutrition Information

- Calories: 324 calories
- Protein: 27g protein.
- Total Fat: 8g fat (2g saturated fat)
- Sodium: 1163mg sodium
- Fiber: 4g fiber)
- Total Carbohydrate: 38g carbohydrate (10g sugars
- Cholesterol: 59mg cholesterol

136. Golden State Mushroom Soup

Serving: 4-6 servings. | Prep: 20mins | Cook: 0mins | Ready in:

Ingredients

- 1 pound fresh mushrooms, sliced
- 1 medium onion, chopped
- 1/4 cup butter, cubed
- 1/4 cup all-purpose flour
- 1/2 teaspoon salt
- 1/8 teaspoon pepper
- 1-1/2 cups milk
- 1 can (14-1/2 ounces) chicken broth
- 1 teaspoon chicken bouillon granules
- 1 cup sour cream
- Minced fresh parsley, optional

Direction

- Sauté onion and mushrooms in butter until tender in a large saucepan. Mix in pepper, salt, and flour. Slowly mix in bouillon, broth, and milk; bring to a boil. Cook, stirring until thickened, or for 2 minutes. Lower heat. Mix in sour cream; cook through without boiling. Garnish with parsley if desired.

Nutrition Information

- Calories: 238 calories
- Total Carbohydrate: 14g carbohydrate (7g sugars
- Cholesterol: 55mg cholesterol
- Protein: 7g protein.
- Total Fat: 17g fat (11g saturated fat)
- Sodium: 749mg sodium
- Fiber: 2g fiber)

137. Healthy Clam Chowder

Serving: 10 servings. | Prep: 10mins | Cook: 35mins | Ready in:

Ingredients

- 2 cups sliced fresh mushrooms
- 4 celery ribs with leaves, chopped
- 1 medium onion, chopped

- 2 tablespoons reduced-fat margarine
- 2 cans (10-3/4 ounces each) reduced-fat reduced-sodium condensed cream of mushroom soup, undiluted
- 1 bottle (8 ounces) clam juice
- 1/2 cup white wine or chicken broth
- 6 medium unpeeled red potatoes, cubed
- 1/2 teaspoon salt
- 1/4 teaspoon white pepper
- 3 cans (6-1/2 ounces each) minced clams, undrained

Direction

- Cook celery, mushrooms, and onions in butter in a soup pot or Dutch oven. Mix broth or wine, clam juice, and soup in a bowl; add to the veggie mixture. Mix in salt and pepper, and potatoes. Leave to boil.
- Lower the heat; put on a lid and allow to simmer for 25 minutes. Mix in clams; cover again and return to simmer until the potatoes become tender or for 5 to 15 minutes

Nutrition Information

- Calories: 202 calories
- Sodium: 497mg sodium
- Fiber: 2g fiber)
- Total Carbohydrate: 24g carbohydrate (0 sugars
- Cholesterol: 43mg cholesterol
- Protein: 17g protein. Diabetic Exchanges: 2 lean meat
- Total Fat: 4g fat (1g saturated fat)

138. Herbed Fish Soup

Serving: 7 servings (about 2 quarts). | Prep: 15mins | Cook: 30mins | Ready in:

Ingredients

- 1 pound cod or haddock, cut into 3/4-inch pieces
- 2 bacon strips, diced, optional
- 1 cup chopped carrot
- 1 cup sliced fresh mushrooms
- 1 medium onion, sliced
- 1 garlic clove, minced
- 2 tablespoons canola oil
- 1/2 cup all-purpose flour
- 1/4 teaspoon dried thyme
- 1/4 teaspoon dill weed
- Dash pepper
- 4 cups chicken broth
- 1 bay leaf
- 1-1/2 cups frozen cut green beans

Direction

- Cook bacon in a large saucepan until it's crispy. Transfer to paper towels to drain, discard bacon fat. In the same pan, sauté garlic, onion, mushrooms, and carrots in oil until onion is softened. Mix in pepper, dill, thyme, and flour until no lumps remain. Pour in broth; bring everything in the pan to a boil. Add bay leaf. Lower heat; simmer, covered until mushrooms and carrots are tender, or for 12 to 15 minutes. Add beans and fish. Uncover and simmer until fish easily flakes with fork, or for 5 minutes. Discard bay leaf. Top each serving with bacon.

Nutrition Information

- Calories: 143 calories
- Sodium: 76mg sodium
- Fiber: 0 fiber)
- Total Carbohydrate: 13g carbohydrate (0 sugars
- Cholesterol: 25mg cholesterol
- Protein: 14g protein. Diabetic Exchanges: 1 meat
- Total Fat: 4g fat (0 saturated fat)

139. Italian Chicken Chili

Serving: 8 servings (2-3/4 quarts). | Prep: 20mins | Cook: 06hours45mins | Ready in:

Ingredients

- 1/2 pound Johnsonville® Ground Mild Italian sausage
- 1 teaspoon olive oil
- 1 pound boneless skinless chicken breasts, cut into 1-inch cubes
- 1 can (28 ounces) crushed tomatoes
- 1 can (28 ounces) diced tomatoes, undrained
- 1 can (15 ounces) white kidney or cannellini beans, rinsed and drained
- 2 celery ribs, chopped
- 1 cup chopped onion
- 1 small sweet red pepper, chopped
- 1/2 cup dry red wine or chicken broth
- 2 tablespoons chili powder
- 2 teaspoons dried oregano
- 2 teaspoons minced garlic
- 1 teaspoon dried thyme
- 1 medium zucchini, diced
- 1 cup sliced fresh mushrooms
- 1/4 cup minced fresh parsley
- Shredded Italian cheese blend, optional

Direction

- In oil, cook sausage in a large skillet over medium heat till not pink anymore; drain.
- Put to a 5-qt. slow cooker. Mix in the thyme, garlic, oregano, chili powder, broth or wine, red pepper, onion, celery, beans, tomatoes and chicken. Put cover and cook till chicken is not pink anymore for 6 hours and on low.
- Mix in the mushrooms and zucchini. Put cover and cook on high till vegetables are soft for 45 minutes. Top with parsley. If wished, serve with cheese.

Nutrition Information

- Calories: 243 calories
- Fiber: 8g fiber)
- Total Carbohydrate: 25g carbohydrate (6g sugars
- Cholesterol: 43mg cholesterol
- Protein: 20g protein. Diabetic Exchanges: 2 lean meat
- Total Fat: 7g fat (2g saturated fat)
- Sodium: 516mg sodium

140. Italian Chicken Sausage Soup

Serving: 6 servings (2-1/2 quarts). | Prep: 15mins | Cook: 40mins | Ready in:

Ingredients

- 1 package (12 ounces) fully cooked Italian chicken sausage links, halved lengthwise and sliced
- 1 medium onion, chopped
- 1 tablespoon olive oil
- 3 garlic cloves, minced
- 2 cans (15 ounces each) white kidney or cannellini beans, rinsed and drained
- 2 cans (14-1/2 ounces each) no-salt-added diced tomatoes
- 2 medium zucchini, quartered and sliced
- 1 can (14-1/2 ounces) reduced-sodium chicken broth
- 8 ounces whole fresh mushrooms, quartered
- 1 cup water
- 1/4 cup prepared pesto
- 1/4 cup dry red wine or additional reduced-sodium chicken broth
- 1 tablespoon balsamic vinegar
- 1 teaspoon minced fresh oregano or 1/4 teaspoon dried oregano
- 1/2 teaspoon pepper
- Grated Parmesan cheese

Direction

- Cook sausage and onion in oil in a Dutch oven until it becomes brown in color. Put in garlic and cook for one more minute.

- Mix in the pepper, oregano, vinegar, wine, pesto, water, mushrooms, broth, zucchini, tomatoes and beans. Let it boil. Lower the heat and let it simmer without cover until veggies become tender, about 25-30 minutes. Drizzle with cheese.

Nutrition Information

- Calories: 337 calories
- Sodium: 838mg sodium
- Fiber: 10g fiber)
- Total Carbohydrate: 35g carbohydrate (8g sugars
- Cholesterol: 47mg cholesterol
- Protein: 22g protein. Diabetic Exchanges: 2 lean meat
- Total Fat: 12g fat (3g saturated fat)

141. Italian Chili

Serving: 6 servings. | Prep: 20mins | Cook: 06hours30mins | Ready in:

Ingredients

- 1 pound ground beef
- 1/2 pound Johnsonville® Ground Mild Italian sausage
- 1 can (28 ounces) diced tomatoes
- 1 can (8 ounces) tomato sauce
- 1 cup chopped onion
- 1 cup chopped sweet red pepper
- 1 cup water
- 1/2 cup chopped celery
- 1/4 cup beef broth
- 1 tablespoon chili powder
- 1 tablespoon Italian seasoning
- 1 teaspoon sugar
- 1 teaspoon minced garlic
- 1/2 teaspoon salt
- 1 can (16 ounces) kidney beans, rinsed and drained
- 1 cup sliced fresh mushrooms
- 1 cup diced zucchini
- 3 tablespoons minced fresh parsley
- Shredded part-skim mozzarella cheese, optional

Direction

- Cook sausage and beef together in a big skillet on moderate heat until it is not pink anymore. At the same time, mix together salt, garlic, sugar, Italian seasoning, chili powder, broth, celery, water, red pepper, onion, tomato sauce and tomatoes in a 3-quart slow cooker.
- Drain the beef mixture and put into the slow cooker. Cover and cook on low setting until vegetables are softened, about 6 hours.
- Put in parsley, zucchini, mushrooms and beans. Cover and cook on high setting until vegetables are softened, about a half hour. Top with cheese, if wanted.

Nutrition Information

- Calories: 316 calories
- Total Fat: 12g fat (5g saturated fat)
- Sodium: 947mg sodium
- Fiber: 8g fiber)
- Total Carbohydrate: 28g carbohydrate (10g sugars
- Cholesterol: 52mg cholesterol
- Protein: 25g protein.

142. Leek Soup With Brie Toasts

Serving: 6 servings. | Prep: 15mins | Cook: 25mins | Ready in:

Ingredients

- 6 medium leeks (white portion only), thinly sliced
- 1/2 pound sliced fresh mushrooms
- 1/2 teaspoon dried tarragon

- 1/4 teaspoon white pepper
- 2 tablespoons plus 6 teaspoons butter, softened, divided
- 1 garlic clove, minced
- 7-1/2 teaspoons all-purpose flour
- 4 cups chicken broth
- 1/2 cup heavy whipping cream
- 12 slices French bread or bread of your choice (1/2 inch thick)
- 1 round (8 ounces) Brie cheese, cut into 1/4-inch slices

Direction

- In a Dutch oven, sauté pepper, tarragon, mushrooms, and leeks in 2 tablespoons butter until vegetables are tender, or for 8 to 10 minutes. Stir in garlic for 1 minute longer. Add flour and mix until well combined; slowly pour in cream and broth. Bring to a boil; cook, stirring until thickened, or for 2 minutes.
- Arrange bread slices on an unoiled baking sheet. Broil 3 to 4 inches away from the heat source until golden brown, or for 1 to 2 minutes. Spread 1/2 teaspoon butter on one side of each slice of bread. Add Brie on the buttered side of the toasts.
- Broil 3 to 4 inches away from the heat sources until cheese is melted, or for 1 to 2 minutes. Spoon soup into six 8-ounce serving bowls; serve each bowl with 2 toasts.

Nutrition Information

- Calories: 411 calories
- Total Carbohydrate: 30g carbohydrate (5g sugars
- Cholesterol: 88mg cholesterol
- Protein: 14g protein.
- Total Fat: 27g fat (16g saturated fat)
- Sodium: 1110mg sodium
- Fiber: 3g fiber)

143. Lentil Barley Soup

Serving: 8-10 servings (about 2-1/2 quarts). | Prep: 25mins | Cook: 40mins |Ready in:

Ingredients

- 1 medium onion, chopped
- 1/2 cup chopped green pepper
- 3 garlic cloves, minced
- 1 tablespoon butter
- 1 can (49-1/2 ounces) chicken broth
- 3 medium carrots, chopped
- 1/2 cup dried lentils
- 1-1/2 teaspoons Italian seasoning
- 1 teaspoon salt
- 1/4 teaspoon pepper
- 1 cup cubed cooked chicken or turkey
- 1/2 cup quick-cooking barley
- 2 medium fresh mushrooms, chopped
- 1 can (28 ounces) crushed tomatoes, undrained

Direction

- Sauté garlic, green pepper, and onion in butter in a soup kettle or a Dutch oven until soft. Add pepper, salt, Italian seasoning, lentils, carrots, and broth; boil it. Lower the heat, put a cover on and simmer for 25 minutes.
- Add mushrooms, barley, and chicken; boil again. Lower the heat, put a cover on and simmer until the carrots, barley, and lentils are soft, about 10-15 minutes. Add tomatoes, cook through.

Nutrition Information

- Calories: 155 calories
- Cholesterol: 16mg cholesterol
- Protein: 11g protein.
- Total Fat: 3g fat (1g saturated fat)
- Sodium: 949mg sodium
- Fiber: 7g fiber)
- Total Carbohydrate: 23g carbohydrate (4g sugars

144. Lighter Mushroom Barley Soup

Serving: 10 servings. | Prep: 10mins | Cook: 01hours15mins | Ready in:

Ingredients

- 6 cups sliced fresh mushrooms
- 2 large onions, chopped
- 1 cup chopped celery
- 1 cup chopped carrots
- 5 cups water, divided
- 4 cups cooked medium pearl barley
- 4 cups beef broth
- 4 teaspoons Worcestershire sauce
- 1-1/2 teaspoons salt
- 1 teaspoon dried basil
- 1 teaspoon dried parsley flakes
- 1 teaspoon dill weed
- 1 teaspoon dried oregano
- 1/2 teaspoon salt-free seasoning blend
- 1/2 teaspoon dried thyme
- 1/2 teaspoon garlic powder

Direction

- Combine 1 cup water, carrots, celery, onions, and mushrooms together in a soup kettle or Dutch oven. Cook, stirring, over medium-high heat until veggies soften. Add the rest of the ingredients; bring to a boil. Lower heat; simmer, covered, for 60 minutes.

Nutrition Information

- Calories: 119 calories
- Sodium: 722mg sodium
- Fiber: 4g fiber)
- Total Carbohydrate: 25g carbohydrate (0 sugars
- Cholesterol: 0 cholesterol
- Protein: 4g protein. Diabetic Exchanges: 2 vegetable
- Total Fat: 1g fat (0 saturated fat)

145. Marjoram Mushroom Soup

Serving: 6 servings. | Prep: 30mins | Cook: 0mins | Ready in:

Ingredients

- 1 large potato, peeled and diced
- 1 large leek (white portion only), chopped
- 1 medium onion, diced
- 2 tablespoons canola oil
- 1/2 pound sliced fresh mushrooms
- 4 cups chicken broth or vegetable broth
- 1 tablespoon minced fresh marjoram or 1 teaspoon dried marjoram, divided
- 1 cup sour cream
- 2 tablespoons butter
- Salt and pepper to taste

Direction

- Sauté onion, leek, and potato in oil in a Dutch oven for 4 minutes. Add mushrooms and keep cooking for 2 minutes. Mix in 1/2 marjoram and broth. Simmer, covered, until the potato is softened, about 10 minutes. Allow to cool slightly.
- Puree mixture in a blender in small batches; pour all pureed mixture back to the pan. Stir in butter and sour cream; add pepper and salt to season. Cook until thoroughly heated, but do not bring to boil. Sprinkle with the rest of marjoram just before serving.

Nutrition Information

- Calories: 213 calories
- Total Fat: 16g fat (8g saturated fat)
- Sodium: 685mg sodium
- Fiber: 2g fiber)
- Total Carbohydrate: 13g carbohydrate (5g sugars

- Cholesterol: 37mg cholesterol
- Protein: 5g protein.

146. Marvelous Mushroom Soup

Serving: 9 servings (about 2 quarts). | Prep: 10mins | Cook: 20mins | Ready in:

Ingredients

- 3 medium onions, chopped
- 2 garlic cloves, minced
- 1/4 cup butter
- 2 pounds fresh mushrooms, chopped
- 2 cups heavy whipping cream
- 2 cups beef broth
- 1/2 teaspoon salt
- 1/2 teaspoon pepper
- Grated Parmesan cheese and minced fresh parsley, optional

Direction

- In a large saucepan, sauté garlic and onions in butter over medium-low heat until softened. Turn heat to low; add mushrooms. Cook, stirring occasionally until tender, or for 8 to 10 minutes. Add pepper, salt, broth, and cream; cook, stirring over low heat until thoroughly heated. Sprinkle with parsley and Parmesan cheese if desired.

Nutrition Information

- Calories: 278 calories
- Sodium: 391mg sodium
- Fiber: 2g fiber)
- Total Carbohydrate: 11g carbohydrate (6g sugars
- Cholesterol: 86mg cholesterol
- Protein: 5g protein.
- Total Fat: 25g fat (15g saturated fat)

147. Meat And Potato Soup

Serving: 6 servings (2 quarts). | Prep: 15mins | Cook: 15mins | Ready in:

Ingredients

- 4 cups water
- 3 cups cubed cooked beef chuck roast
- 4 medium red potatoes, cubed
- 4 ounces sliced fresh mushrooms
- 1/2 cup chopped onion
- 1/4 cup ketchup
- 2 teaspoons beef bouillon granules
- 2 teaspoons cider vinegar
- 1 teaspoon brown sugar
- 1 teaspoon Worcestershire sauce
- 1/8 teaspoon ground mustard
- 1 cup coarsely chopped fresh spinach

Direction

- Combine the first 11 ingredients in a Dutch oven. Bring to a boil. Lower heat; simmer, covered, until potatoes are tender, 14 to 18 minutes. Mix in spinach; cook until softened, about 1 to 2 minutes more.

Nutrition Information

- Calories: 210 calories
- Sodium: 431mg sodium
- Fiber: 2g fiber)
- Total Carbohydrate: 18g carbohydrate (4g sugars
- Cholesterol: 49mg cholesterol
- Protein: 17g protein. Diabetic Exchanges: 2 lean meat
- Total Fat: 8g fat (3g saturated fat)

148. Morel Mushroom Soup

Serving: 6 servings. | Prep: 20mins | Cook: 10mins | Ready in:

Ingredients

- 1 pound fresh morel or other mushrooms, sliced
- 2 tablespoons lemon juice
- 1 large onion, chopped
- 3 tablespoons butter
- 2 tablespoons all-purpose flour
- 4 cups milk
- 3 teaspoons chicken bouillon granules
- 1/2 teaspoon dried thyme
- 1/2 teaspoon salt
- 1/8 teaspoon pepper

Direction

- Sprinkle lemon juice over the mushrooms. Sauté onion and the mushrooms in butter in a saucepan until soft. Scatter with flour, whisk thoroughly. Slowly add pepper, salt, thyme, bouillon, and milk. Boil for 2 minutes while mixing. Lower the heat and bring to a simmer for 10-15 minutes.

Nutrition Information

- Calories: 198 calories
- Cholesterol: 38mg cholesterol
- Protein: 9g protein.
- Total Fat: 12g fat (7g saturated fat)
- Sodium: 896mg sodium
- Fiber: 2g fiber)
- Total Carbohydrate: 16g carbohydrate (11g sugars

149. Mushroom Onion Barley Soup

Serving: 7 servings. | Prep: 15mins | Cook: 45mins | Ready in:

Ingredients

- 1 large onion, chopped
- 2 cups sliced fresh mushrooms
- 1 tablespoon olive oil
- 2 garlic cloves, minced
- 7 cups reduced-sodium chicken broth
- 2 cups water
- 1/2 cup medium pearl barley
- 2 tablespoons reduced-sodium soy sauce
- 1 teaspoon dried thyme
- 1/4 teaspoon pepper

Direction

- Sauté mushrooms and onion in a big saucepan with oil until veggies are soft. Put in garlic; cook for 1 more minute.
- Stir in the rest of ingredients. Cook to a boil. Lower heat; simmer for 45-50 minutes with cover off or until barley is soft.

Nutrition Information

- Calories: 101 calories
- Fiber: 3g fiber)
- Total Carbohydrate: 16g carbohydrate (2g sugars
- Cholesterol: 0 cholesterol
- Protein: 6g protein.
- Total Fat: 2g fat (0 saturated fat)
- Sodium: 746mg sodium

150. Mushroom Potato Soup

Serving: 12 servings (3 quarts). | Prep: 15mins | Cook: 25mins | Ready in:

Ingredients

- 2 medium leeks, sliced
- 2 large carrots, sliced
- 6 tablespoons butter, divided
- 6 cups chicken broth
- 5 cups diced peeled potatoes
- 1 tablespoon minced fresh dill
- 1 teaspoon salt
- 1/8 teaspoon pepper
- 1 bay leaf
- 1 pound sliced fresh mushrooms
- 1/4 cup all-purpose flour
- 1 cup heavy whipping cream

Direction

- Sauté carrots and leeks in 3 tablespoons butter in a soup kettle or Dutch oven until tender, or for 5 minutes. Mix in bay leaf, pepper, salt, dill, potatoes, and broth. Bring to a boil. Lower heat; simmer, covered until potatoes are tender, or for 15 to 20 minutes.
- In the meantime, sauté mushrooms in remaining butter in a large skillet until tender, or for 4 to 6 minutes. Throw away bay leaf. Mix in mushroom mixture.
- Combine cream and flour in a small bowl until no lumps remain; slowly add into soup; stir well. Bring the mixture to a boil; cook, stirring until thickened, or for 2 minutes.

Nutrition Information

- Calories:
- Sodium:
- Fiber:
- Total Carbohydrate:
- Cholesterol:
- Protein:
- Total Fat:

---

151. Mushroom Spinach Barley Soup

Serving: 10 servings (about 3 quarts). | Prep: 30mins | Cook: 45mins | Ready in:

Ingredients

- 1 medium leek (white portion only), halved and thinly sliced
- 1 cup chopped celery
- 2 teaspoons olive oil
- 4 garlic cloves, minced
- 3/4 pound sliced fresh mushrooms
- 1-1/2 cups chopped peeled turnips
- 1-1/2 cups chopped carrots
- 4 cans (14-1/2 ounces each) reduced-sodium beef broth or vegetable broth
- 1 can (14-1/2 ounces) diced tomatoes, undrained
- 1 bay leaf
- 1/2 teaspoon salt
- 1/2 teaspoon dried thyme
- 1/4 teaspoon pepper
- 1/4 teaspoon caraway seeds
- 1 cup quick-cooking barley
- 4 cups fresh baby spinach, cut into thin strips

Direction

- With cooking spray, coat a big saucepan, for 2 minutes, cook celery and leek in oil. Add garlic; cook for 1 more minute. Add carrots, turnips and mushrooms; cook for 4-5 minutes additionally or until mushrooms are soft.
- Stir in seasonings, tomatoes and broth. Cook to a boil. Lower heat; simmer with the cover on for 10-15 minutes or until turnips are soft. Add barley; continue to simmer for another 10 minutes. Mix in spinach; cook for additional 5 minutes or until barley and spinach are soft. Discard bay leaf.

Nutrition Information

- Calories: 126 calories
- Total Fat: 2g fat (0 saturated fat)

- Sodium: 517mg sodium
- Fiber: 6g fiber)
- Total Carbohydrate: 23g carbohydrate (5g sugars
- Cholesterol: 3mg cholesterol
- Protein: 6g protein. Diabetic Exchanges: 1 starch

152. Mushroom Veggie Barley Soup

Serving: 11 servings (about 2-3/4 quarts). | Prep: 15mins | Cook: 55mins | Ready in:

Ingredients

- 1 can (49 ounces) reduced-sodium chicken broth
- 2 medium carrots, thinly sliced
- 1 medium onion, chopped
- 2 garlic cloves, minced
- 1/2 teaspoon dried basil
- 1/2 teaspoon dried oregano
- 1/2 teaspoon pepper
- 1-1/2 cups medium pearl barley
- 2 cups reduced-sodium tomato juice
- 1 can (14-1/2 ounces) no-salt-added diced tomatoes, undrained
- 1/2 pound fresh mushrooms, thinly sliced

Direction

- Combine pepper, oregano, basil, garlic, onion, carrots, and broth in a Dutch oven or a soup kettle; bring to a boil. Put in barley. Lower heat; simmer, covered, until barley softens, about 45 to 55 minutes.
- Add the rest of ingredients; cook until mushrooms are tender, 10 to 15 minutes.

Nutrition Information

- Calories: 136 calories
- Fiber: 6g fiber)

- Total Carbohydrate: 29g carbohydrate (5g sugars
- Cholesterol: 0 cholesterol
- Protein: 6g protein. Diabetic Exchanges: 1-1/2 starch
- Total Fat: 0 fat (0 saturated fat)
- Sodium: 359mg sodium

153. Mushroom Veggie Chowder

Serving: 50 servings (12-1/2 quarts). | Prep: 30mins | Cook: 10mins | Ready in:

Ingredients

- 4 pounds fresh mushrooms, sliced
- 4 large onions, chopped
- 1-1/2 cups butter, cubed
- 1-1/2 cups all-purpose flour
- 3 to 4 tablespoons salt
- 2 to 2-1/2 teaspoons pepper
- 3 quarts milk
- 4 cartons (32 ounces each) chicken broth
- 2 packages (24 ounces each) frozen broccoli cuts, thawed
- 3 packages (8 ounces each) frozen corn, thawed
- 8 cups (32 ounces) shredded cheddar cheese

Direction

- Melt butter in three or four soup kettles, then cook the onions and mushrooms until they soften. Mix the flour with salt and pepper, then pour it onto the mushrooms until thoroughly blended. Slowly pour the milk in. Let it cook, stirring occasionally, until it starts to boil. Leave it to cook for another 2 minutes or until it starts to bubble and thicken.
- Mix in the broccoli, corn, and broth. Let it heat thoroughly. Melt in some cheese just before serving.

Nutrition Information

- Calories: 185 calories
- Protein: 8g protein.
- Total Fat: 13g fat (8g saturated fat)
- Sodium: 697mg sodium
- Fiber: 1g fiber)
- Total Carbohydrate: 10g carbohydrate (4g sugars
- Cholesterol: 42mg cholesterol

154. Mushroom And Potato Chowder

Serving: 4-6 servings. | Prep: 20mins | Cook: 50mins | Ready in:

Ingredients

- 1/2 cup chopped onion
- 1/4 cup butter, cubed
- 2 tablespoons all-purpose flour
- 1 teaspoon salt
- 1/2 teaspoon pepper
- 3 cups water
- 1 pound fresh mushrooms, sliced
- 1 cup chopped celery
- 1 cup diced peeled potatoes
- 1/2 cup chopped carrots
- 1 cup half-and-half cream
- 1/4 cup grated Parmesan cheese

Direction

- Sauté the onion in butter in a big pot until it's tender. Mix in the flour, pepper, and salt then stir to form a smooth paste. Pour in the water gradually with constant stirring. Bring this to a boil and continue to cook and stir for another minute. Toss in the mushrooms, potatoes, carrots, and celery. Lower the heat, cover the pot and let it simmer until the vegetables are tender, about 30 minutes. Pour in the cream and the Parmesan cheese then heat the soup through.

Nutrition Information

- Calories: 199 calories
- Protein: 6g protein.
- Total Fat: 13g fat (8g saturated fat)
- Sodium: 578mg sodium
- Fiber: 2g fiber)
- Total Carbohydrate: 15g carbohydrate (5g sugars
- Cholesterol: 43mg cholesterol

155. Onion Soup With Sausage

Serving: 4 servings. | Prep: 20mins | Cook: 0mins | Ready in:

Ingredients

- 1/2 pound pork sausage links, cut into 1/2-inch pieces
- 1 pound sliced fresh mushrooms
- 1 cup sliced onion
- 2 cans (14-1/2 ounces each) beef broth
- 4 slices Italian bread
- 1/2 cup shredded part-skim mozzarella cheese

Direction

- Cook sausage in a big saucepan on medium heat till not pink anymore; drain. Add onion and mushrooms; cook till tender, about 4-6 minutes. Mix broth in; boil. Lower heat; simmer for 4-6 minutes till heated through, uncovered.
- Put soup in 4 2-cup ovenproof bowls. Put a bread slice on top of each. Sprinkle cheese. Broil till cheese melts.

Nutrition Information

- Calories: 378 calories
- Sodium: 1325mg sodium
- Fiber: 3g fiber)

- Total Carbohydrate: 23g carbohydrate (5g sugars
- Cholesterol: 58mg cholesterol
- Protein: 21g protein.
- Total Fat: 23g fat (9g saturated fat)

156. Pea Soup With Mushroom Cream Sauce

Serving: 6 servings. | Prep: 25mins | Cook: 15mins | Ready in:

Ingredients

- 1/2 pound sliced baby portobello mushrooms, divided
- 1 tablespoon butter
- 1/4 cup chopped onion
- 1 garlic clove, minced
- 1/2 cup half-and-half cream
- 3 tablespoons sherry or reduced-sodium chicken broth
- 1 tablespoon minced fresh thyme or 1 teaspoon dried thyme
- 3/4 teaspoon salt, divided
- 5 cups fresh or frozen peas, divided
- 3 cups reduced-sodium chicken broth
- 2 tablespoons lemon juice
- 4-1/2 teaspoons minced fresh basil or 1-1/2 teaspoons dried basil

Direction

- Put aside 3 tablespoons mushrooms to garnish. Sauté the leftover of the mushrooms in butter in a big frying pan until soft.
- Add onion to the frying pan, sauté until soft. Add garlic, cook for another 1 minute. Mix in 1/4 teaspoon of salt, thyme, sherry, and cream. Boil it. Lower the heat; bring to a simmer without a cover for 2 minutes. Let cool slightly. Move to a blender, blend until smooth. Put aside.
- Mix the leftover of the salt, chicken broth, and 4-1/2 cups peas together in a Dutch oven. Boil it. Lower the heat; bring to a simmer without a cover until the peas are soft, or for about 4 minutes. Mix in basil and lemon juice; heat thoroughly. Move to a blender, blend in batches until combined.
- Spoon the soup into serving bowls, put mushroom cream sauce on top. Use the leftover peas and the saved mushroom to garnish.

Nutrition Information

- Calories: 169 calories
- Protein: 10g protein. Diabetic Exchanges: 1-1/2 starch
- Total Fat: 5g fat (3g saturated fat)
- Sodium: 612mg sodium
- Fiber: 7g fiber)
- Total Carbohydrate: 22g carbohydrate (9g sugars
- Cholesterol: 15mg cholesterol

157. Pizza Soup With Garlic Toast Croutons

Serving: 10 servings (about 4 quarts). | Prep: 10mins | Cook: 06hours00mins | Ready in:

Ingredients

- 1 can (28 ounces) diced tomatoes, drained
- 1 can (15 ounces) pizza sauce
- 1 pound boneless skinless chicken breasts, cut into 1-inch pieces
- 1 package (3 ounces) sliced pepperoni, halved
- 1 cup sliced fresh mushrooms
- 1 small onion, chopped
- 1/2 cup chopped green pepper
- 1/4 teaspoon pepper
- 2 cans (14-1/2 ounces each) chicken broth
- 1 package (11-1/4 ounces) frozen garlic Texas toast
- 1 package (10 ounces) frozen chopped spinach, thawed and squeezed dry

- 1 cup shredded part-skim mozzarella cheese

Direction

- Mix first 9 ingredients in a 6-qt. slow cooker. Cook on low, covered, for 6-8 minutes till chicken is tender.
- Croutons: Slice Texas toast to cubes. Bake following package directions. Put spinach into soup then heat through, occasionally mixing. Put warm croutons and cheese on top of servings. Freezing: In freezer containers, freeze cooled soup. Using: in the fridge, partially thaw overnight. In a saucepan, heat through, occasionally mixing. Prep croutons as directed. Put croutons and cheese over soup.

Nutrition Information

- Calories: 292 calories
- Fiber: 4g fiber)
- Total Carbohydrate: 24g carbohydrate (7g sugars
- Cholesterol: 46mg cholesterol
- Protein: 20g protein.
- Total Fat: 13g fat (5g saturated fat)
- Sodium: 1081mg sodium

158. Quick Cream Of Mushroom Soup

Serving: 6 servings. | Prep: 15mins | Cook: 15mins | Ready in:

Ingredients

- 2 tablespoons butter
- 1/2 pound sliced fresh mushrooms
- 1/4 cup chopped onion
- 6 tablespoons all-purpose flour
- 1/2 teaspoon salt
- 1/8 teaspoon pepper
- 2 cans (14-1/2 ounces each) chicken broth
- 1 cup half-and-half cream

Direction

- Over medium-high heat, in a big saucepan, heat butter; sauté onion and mushrooms until soft.
- Mix one can of broth, pepper, salt and flour to make a smooth mixture; stir into mixture of mushroom. Stir in the rest of broth. Cook until boiling; cook and stir for 2 minutes until thickened. Lower heat; stir in cream. Simmer for 15 minutes with the cover off, until flavors are combined, stirring occasionally.

Nutrition Information

- Calories: 136 calories
- Total Fat: 8g fat (5g saturated fat)
- Sodium: 842mg sodium
- Fiber: 1g fiber)
- Total Carbohydrate: 10g carbohydrate (3g sugars
- Cholesterol: 33mg cholesterol
- Protein: 4g protein.

159. Rosemary Mushroom Soup

Serving: 3 servings. | Prep: 15mins | Cook: 0mins | Ready in:

Ingredients

- 1 cup sliced fresh mushrooms
- 2 garlic cloves, minced
- 1/4 cup butter
- 1 can (10-3/4 ounces) condensed cream of mushroom soup, undiluted
- 1 cup half-and-half cream
- 1 tablespoon minced fresh rosemary or 1 teaspoon dried rosemary, crushed
- 1/2 teaspoon paprika
- 2 tablespoons minced chives

Direction

- Sauté garlic and mushrooms in butter in a large saucepan until softened. Mix in paprika, rosemary, cream, and mushroom soup; cook through without boiling. Top with chives.

Nutrition Information

- Calories: 335 calories
- Protein: 5g protein.
- Total Fat: 28g fat (16g saturated fat)
- Sodium: 909mg sodium
- Fiber: 1g fiber)
- Total Carbohydrate: 13g carbohydrate (4g sugars
- Cholesterol: 85mg cholesterol

160. Sauerkraut Sausage Soup

Serving: 10 servings. | Prep: 20mins | Cook: 05hours00mins | Ready in:

Ingredients

- 4 cups chicken broth
- 1 pound smoked Polish sausage, cut into 1/2-inch slices
- 1 can (16 ounces) sauerkraut, rinsed and well drained
- 2 cups sliced fresh mushrooms
- 1-1/2 cups cubed peeled potatoes
- 1 can (10-3/4 ounces) condensed cream of mushroom soup, undiluted
- 1-1/4 cups chopped onions
- 2 large carrots, sliced
- 2 celery ribs, chopped
- 2 tablespoons white vinegar
- 2 teaspoons dill weed
- 1 teaspoon sugar
- 1/4 teaspoon pepper

Direction

- Mix together all ingredients in a 5-qt. slow cooker. Put the cover on and cook on low setting until veggies become tender, about 5-6 hours.

Nutrition Information

- Calories: 222 calories
- Cholesterol: 33mg cholesterol
- Protein: 8g protein.
- Total Fat: 14g fat (5g saturated fat)
- Sodium: 1285mg sodium
- Fiber: 3g fiber)
- Total Carbohydrate: 15g carbohydrate (4g sugars

161. Savory Mushroom Barley Soup

Serving: 10 servings (about 3-1/2 quarts). | Prep: 5mins | Cook: 45mins | Ready in:

Ingredients

- 4 cups water
- 3/4 cup uncooked medium pearl barley
- 4 medium onions, chopped
- 2 celery ribs, chopped
- 1 tablespoon olive oil
- 1-1/2 pounds sliced fresh mushrooms
- 6 cups reduced-sodium beef broth or vegetable broth
- 2 cups sliced carrots
- 1 can (6 ounces) tomato paste
- 1/2 teaspoon salt
- 1/4 teaspoon pepper
- 1/2 cup minced fresh parsley

Direction

- Boil barley and water in a big saucepan. Lower the heat, put a cover on and bring to a simmer until the barley is partly cooked, or for about 30 minutes (do not strain). In the meantime, sauté celery and onions in oil in a Dutch oven or a soup kettle until soft. Add mushrooms,

stir and cook for 5 minutes. Mix in barley mixture, tomato paste, carrots, and broth.
- Boil over medium heat. Lower the heat, put a cover on and bring to a simmer for 30 minutes, whisking continually. Mix in pepper and salt. Scatter with parsley.

Nutrition Information

- Calories: 136 calories
- Cholesterol: 3mg cholesterol
- Protein: 6g protein. Diabetic Exchanges: 2 vegetable
- Total Fat: 2g fat (1g saturated fat)
- Sodium: 416mg sodium
- Fiber: 6g fiber)
- Total Carbohydrate: 26g carbohydrate (0 sugars

162. Tomato Mushroom Soup

Serving: about 12 servings (3 quarts). | Prep: 10mins | Cook: 45mins | Ready in:

Ingredients

- 1 pound sliced fresh mushrooms
- 6 tablespoons butter, divided
- 2 medium onions, finely chopped
- 1 garlic clove, minced
- 2 medium carrots, chopped
- 3 celery ribs, finely chopped
- 3 tablespoons all-purpose flour
- 8 cups beef broth
- 2 medium tomatoes, peeled, seeded and chopped
- 1 can (15 ounces) tomato sauce
- 1 teaspoon salt
- 1/2 teaspoon pepper
- 3 tablespoons minced fresh parsley
- Sour cream, optional

Direction

- In a Dutch oven or large kettle, sauté mushrooms in 4 tablespoons butter until softened. Take the mushrooms out using a slotted spoon; put to one side and keep warm.
- In the same kettle, sauté celery, carrots, garlic, and onions in the remaining butter until softened. Mix in flour until well combined. Add 1/2 of the reserved mushrooms, pepper, salt, tomato sauce, tomatoes, and broth. Simmer, covered, for half an hour.
- Mix in the remaining mushrooms and parsley; simmer without a cover until thoroughly heated, about 5 minutes. Top with sour cream to decorate if desired.

Nutrition Information

- Calories: 111 calories
- Protein: 4g protein.
- Total Fat: 7g fat (4g saturated fat)
- Sodium: 981mg sodium
- Fiber: 2g fiber)
- Total Carbohydrate: 11g carbohydrate (5g sugars
- Cholesterol: 15mg cholesterol

163. Tomato Spinach Soup

Serving: 8-10 servings (2-1/2 quarts). | Prep: 15mins | Cook: 45mins | Ready in:

Ingredients

- 2 large yellow onions, cubed
- 2 tablespoons olive oil
- 1 can (28 ounces) diced tomatoes, undrained
- 1 quart water
- 4 beef bouillon cubes
- 1 cup sliced fresh mushrooms
- 3/4 teaspoon Italian seasoning
- 1/2 teaspoon dried basil
- 1/2 teaspoon salt
- 1/8 teaspoon pepper
- 4 cups loosely packed spinach leaves

- Grated Parmesan or shredded cheddar cheese, optional

Direction

- Over medium heat, sauté onions in a soup kettle or Dutch oven with oil for 10 minutes or until soft. Add the following 8 ingredients; cook to a boil. Lower heat; simmer with the cover on for half an hour. Stir in spinach; simmer until soft or for 3-5 minutes. If you like, top with cheese on each servings.

Nutrition Information

- Calories: 58 calories
- Sodium: 575mg sodium
- Fiber: 2g fiber)
- Total Carbohydrate: 7g carbohydrate (5g sugars
- Cholesterol: 0 cholesterol
- Protein: 2g protein.
- Total Fat: 3g fat (0 saturated fat)

164. Turkey Barley Soup

Serving: 10 | Prep: 20mins | Cook: 3hours15mins | Ready in:

Ingredients

- Stock:
- 2 tablespoons vegetable oil
- 3 pounds turkey bones
- 1 onion, quartered
- 1 stalk celery, coarsely chopped
- 1 carrot, coarsely chopped
- 16 cups water
- 2 sprigs fresh thyme
- Soup:
- 2 1/2 cups water
- 1 cup barley
- 2 tablespoons olive oil
- 1 onion, diced
- 2 carrots, sliced
- 2 stalks celery, sliced
- 2 cloves garlic, minced
- 2 cups chopped cooked turkey
- 1/4 cup chopped fresh parsley
- 2 sprigs fresh thyme, leaves stripped
- 1/4 teaspoon salt
- 1/4 teaspoon ground black pepper
- 1/8 teaspoon cayenne pepper
- 1/2 lemon, juiced

Direction

- In a large stockpot, heat vegetable oil on medium-high heat and add the turkey bones, then cook, occasionally turning, for 10 minutes until it browns. Transfer the bones into a bowl.
- Use the same stockpot to cook, stirring, coarsely chopped carrots, coarsely chopped celery, and quartered onion with hot oil for 2 minutes until fragrant. Place the turkey bones into the stockpot and add sprigs of thyme and 16 cups of water. Allow to boil and skim off the foam. Turn the heat to medium - low and simmer for 2 hours until the liquid reduces to 10 cups. Strain the stock into a big bowl and allow to stand for 15 minutes. Spoon the fat off the top of the stock.
- In a saucepan, boil barley with 2 1/2 cup of water. Cover, turn heat to low, and simmer for 30 - 40 minutes until the barley becomes tender.
- In a large stockpot, heat olive oil on medium-high heat and cook while stirring garlic, sliced celery, sliced carrots, and diced onion for 5 minutes until they are slightly soft. Add in the turkey stock and set to boil.
- Mix cayenne pepper, black pepper, salt, thyme leaves, parsley, barley, and turkey meat into the soup. Turn the heat to medium-low and allow to simmer for 20 minutes. Stir in the lemon juice.

Nutrition Information

- Calories: 262 calories;
- Protein: 13.7

- Total Fat: 14.1
- Sodium: 126
- Total Carbohydrate: 21
- Cholesterol: 38

165. Vegetable Chicken Barley Soup

Serving: 6 servings. | Prep: 20mins | Cook: 45mins | Ready in:

Ingredients

- 1 pound boneless skinless chicken breasts, cut into 3/4-inch pieces
- 2 tablespoons canola oil, divided
- 2 cups chopped leeks (white portion only)
- 1 celery rib, thinly sliced
- 1 carrot, thinly sliced
- 2 cups sliced fresh mushrooms
- 1 garlic clove, minced
- 2 cans (14-1/2 ounces each) reduced-sodium chicken broth
- 2-1/4 cups water
- 1 bay leaf
- 1/2 teaspoon dried thyme
- 1/4 teaspoon salt
- 1/4 teaspoon pepper
- 1/2 cup quick-cooking barley

Direction

- Cook chicken in 1 tablespoon oil in a Dutch oven until it is no longer pink. Take out and put to one side.
- Sauté carrot, celery, and leeks in the same pan in the remaining oil for 4 minutes. Add garlic and mushrooms, sauté for 2 more minutes. Mix in chicken, seasonings, water, and broth. Bring the mixture to a boil. Lower heat; simmer, covered, for 15 minutes.
- Mix in barley and bring the mixture to another boil. Lower heat; simmer, covered, until vegetables and barley are tender, about 10 to 15 minutes. Remove bay leaf.

Nutrition Information

- Calories: 218 calories
- Total Fat: 7g fat (1g saturated fat)
- Sodium: 550mg sodium
- Fiber: 4g fiber)
- Total Carbohydrate: 19g carbohydrate (3g sugars
- Cholesterol: 42mg cholesterol
- Protein: 21g protein. Diabetic Exchanges: 2 lean meat

166. Wild Rice Turkey Soup

Serving: 8 servings (2-3/4 quarts). | Prep: 10mins | Cook: 01hours15mins | Ready in:

Ingredients

- 1 cup uncooked wild rice
- 7 cups chicken broth, divided
- 1/2 pound sliced fresh mushrooms
- 1 medium onion, chopped
- 1 celery rib, chopped
- 1/4 cup butter, cubed
- 1/2 cup all-purpose flour
- 1/2 teaspoon salt
- 1/2 teaspoon ground mustard
- 1/2 teaspoon poultry seasoning
- 1/4 teaspoon pepper
- 4 cups cubed cooked turkey
- 2 cups half-and-half cream

Direction

- Boil rice and 3 cups of broth in a large saucepan. Decrease the heat and simmer while covered until the rice becomes tender, or for 50 - 60 minutes.
- Use a Dutch oven to sauté celery, onion, and mushrooms with butter until tender. Stir in seasonings and flour until combined, then slowly add in the remaining broth. Set to boil,

then cook, stirring, until the soup thickens, or for 2 minutes. Stir in the cooked rice, cream, and turkey, then heat through without boiling.

Nutrition Information

- Calories: 393 calories
- Total Carbohydrate: 30g carbohydrate (5g sugars
- Cholesterol: 103mg cholesterol
- Protein: 28g protein.
- Total Fat: 16g fat (9g saturated fat)
- Sodium: 1130mg sodium
- Fiber: 2g fiber)

167. Wild Rice And Mushroom Soup

Serving: Serves 4 | Prep: | Cook: |Ready in:

Ingredients

- 1 14 1/2-ounce can chicken broth
- 1/2 cup wild rice
- 1 ounce dried shiitake mushrooms
- 1 1/2 cups hot water
- 2 tablespoons butter
- 1 onion, chopped
- 2 garlic cloves, chopped
- 1/4 teaspoon dried rosemary, crumbled
- 1/4 teaspoon dried thyme, crumbled
- 1 8-ounce russet potato, peeled, diced
- 2 cups beef stock or canned beef broth
- 3/4 cup (about) milk
- 2 tablespoons Madeira

Direction

- In a small saucepan, combine rice and chicken broth. Simmer, covered over medium-low heat for about 50 minutes until liquid is absorbed and the rice is tender.
- In the meantime, soak mushrooms for about 20 minutes in 1 1/2 cups hot water until soft.

Drain mushrooms, saving soaking liquid. Discard mushroom stems. Slice mushrooms thinly.
- In a heavy big saucepan, melt 1 tablespoon butter over medium-high heat. Sauté mushrooms in melted butter for about 5 minutes until golden brown and soft. Transfer mushrooms to a small bowl. Melt the remaining 1 tablespoons butter in the same pan. Sauté thyme, rosemary, garlic, and onion for about 10 minutes until onion is really soft. Stir in the reserved mushroom soaking liquid, beef stock, and potato. Simmer, covered for about 15 minutes until the potato is really tender.
- Puree mixture in batches in a blender until no lumps remain. Pour soup back in the saucepan. Mix in Madeira, 3/4 cup milk, mushrooms, and wild rice. Simmer, covered until flavors blend, for 15 minutes. Add pepper and salt to season (soup can be made 1 day beforehand. Chill, covered. Bring soup to a simmer before serving). Make the soup thinner with more milk, if necessary.

Nutrition Information

- Calories: 251
- Cholesterol: 20 mg(7%)
- Protein: 9 g(18%)
- Total Fat: 8 g(12%)
- Saturated Fat: 5 g(23%)
- Sodium: 680 mg(28%)
- Fiber: 3 g(13%)
- Total Carbohydrate: 36 g(12%)

168. Zesty Corn Chowder

Serving: 6-8 servings (2 quarts). | Prep: 10mins | Cook: 15mins |Ready in:

Ingredients

- 1-1/2 cups whole milk

- 1 can (10-3/4 ounces) condensed cream of potato soup, undiluted
- 1 can (10-3/4 ounces) condensed cream of chicken soup, undiluted
- 1 cup chicken broth
- 2 cups cubed cooked chicken
- 1 can (11 ounces) Mexican-style corn, undrained
- 1 can (4 ounces) chopped green chilies
- 1/2 cup sliced fresh mushrooms
- 1-1/2 cups shredded cheddar cheese

Direction

- Mix broth, soups, and milk together in a big saucepan. Add mushrooms, chilies, corn, and chicken. Boil it. Lower the heat, bring to a simmer until thoroughly heated, whisking sometimes. Take away from heat. Mix in cheese until melted.

Nutrition Information

- Calories: 270 calories
- Protein: 19g protein.
- Total Fat: 14g fat (7g saturated fat)
- Sodium: 1148mg sodium
- Fiber: 2g fiber)
- Total Carbohydrate: 18g carbohydrate (5g sugars
- Cholesterol: 66mg cholesterol

169. Zippy Chicken Mushroom Soup

Serving: 11 servings (2-3/4 quarts). | Prep: 15mins | Cook: 25mins | Ready in:

Ingredients

- 1/2 pound fresh mushrooms, chopped
- 1/4 cup each chopped onion, celery and carrot
- 1/4 cup butter, cubed
- 1/2 cup all-purpose flour
- 5-1/2 cups chicken broth
- 1 teaspoon pepper
- 1/2 teaspoon white pepper
- 1/4 teaspoon dried thyme
- Pinch dried tarragon
- 1/2 teaspoon hot pepper sauce
- 3 cups half-and-half cream
- 2-1/2 cups cubed cooked chicken
- 1 tablespoon minced fresh parsley
- 1-1/2 teaspoons lemon juice
- 1/2 teaspoon salt

Direction

- Sauté carrot, celery, onion, and mushrooms in butter in a Dutch oven until soft. Mix in flour until combined. Slowly add seasonings and broth. Boil it. Lower the heat; simmer without a cover for 10 minutes.
- Mix in salt, lemon juice, parsley, chicken, and cream, heat thoroughly without boiling.

Nutrition Information

- Calories:
- Total Fat:
- Sodium:
- Fiber:
- Total Carbohydrate:
- Cholesterol:
- Protein:

Chapter 4: Mushroom Stew Recipes

***

170. Artichoke Beef Stew

Serving: 6-8 servings. | Prep: 25mins | Cook: 07hours30mins | Ready in:

Ingredients

- 1/3 cup all-purpose flour
- 1 teaspoon salt
- 1/2 teaspoon pepper
- 2-1/2 pounds beef stew meat, cut into 1-inch cubes
- 3 tablespoons canola oil
- 1 can (10-1/2 ounces) condensed beef consomme, undiluted
- 2 medium onions, halved and sliced
- 1/2 pound small fresh mushrooms, halved
- 1 cup red wine or beef broth
- 1 garlic clove, minced
- 1/2 teaspoon dill weed
- 2 jars (6-1/2 ounces each) marinated artichoke hearts, drained and chopped
- Hot cooked noodles

Direction

- Mix in a big resealable plastic bag the pepper, salt and flour. Put in beef, only a few pieces at a time, and coat by shaking. Brown beef in oil in a big skillet in batches.
- With a slotted spoon, move to a 3- or 4-qt. slow cooker. Add consomme gradually to the pan, stirring to make browned bits loosen. Stir in dill, garlic, wine, mushrooms and onions. Pour over beef.
- Cook for low with cover on for 7-8 hours or until soft. Add the artichokes and stir; cook for half an hour more or until completely heated. Serve with noodles.

Nutrition Information

- Calories: 355 calories
- Total Carbohydrate: 11g carbohydrate (3g sugars
- Cholesterol: 90mg cholesterol
- Protein: 30g protein.
- Total Fat: 19g fat (5g saturated fat)
- Sodium: 682mg sodium
- Fiber: 1g fiber)

171. Beef & Mushroom Braised Stew

Serving: 6 servings. | Prep: 35mins | Cook: 01hours30mins | Ready in:

Ingredients

- 1 boneless beef chuck roast (2 to 3 pounds), cut into 1-inch cubes
- 1/4 teaspoon salt
- 1/4 teaspoon pepper
- 3 tablespoons olive oil
- 1 pound sliced fresh mushrooms
- 2 medium onions, sliced
- 2 garlic cloves, minced
- 1 carton (32 ounces) beef broth
- 1 cup dry red wine or additional beef broth
- 1/2 cup brandy
- 1 tablespoon tomato paste
- 1/4 teaspoon each dried parsley flakes, rosemary, sage leaves, tarragon and thyme
- 3 tablespoons all-purpose flour
- 3 tablespoons water
- Hot mashed potatoes

Direction

- Turn oven to 325° to preheat. Season beef with pepper and salt. Heat oil in an oven-safe Dutch oven over medium heat; cook beef in batches until browned. Take cooked beef out of the pan.
- Sauté onions and mushrooms in the pan until softened. Add garlic; cook for 1 minute longer. Mix in herbs, tomato paste, brandy, wine, and broth. Add beef back to the pan. Bring everything in the pan to a boil. Cover and bake for 60 minutes. Whisk together water and flour in a small bowl until no lumps remain; slowly mix into stew. Cover and bake for 30 minutes

longer or until beef is tender and stew is thickened. Ladle off fat. Enjoy the stew with mashed potatoes. Freeze option: allow stew to cool and store in freezer containers, partially defrost in the fridge overnight to use. Thoroughly heat the stew in a saucepan; stirring from time to time and add broth, a little at a time or water if desired.

Nutrition Information

- Calories: 395 calories
- Protein: 34g protein.
- Total Fat: 22g fat (7g saturated fat)
- Sodium: 761mg sodium
- Fiber: 2g fiber)
- Total Carbohydrate: 12g carbohydrate (4g sugars
- Cholesterol: 98mg cholesterol

172. Beef Bourguignon

Serving: 6–8 servings | Prep: | Cook: | Ready in:

Ingredients

- One 6-ounce chunk of bacon
- 1 tablespoon of olive oil or cooking oil
- 3 pounds lean stewing beef, cut into 2-inch cubes
- 1 carrot, sliced
- 1 onion, sliced
- 1 teaspoon salt
- 1/4 teaspoon pepper
- 2 tablespoons flour
- 3 cups of a full-bodied young red wine
- 2 to 3 cups brown beef stock or canned boullion
- 1 tablespoon tomato paste
- 2 cloves mashed garlic
- 1/2 teaspoon thyme
- A crumbled bay leaf
- 18 to 24 small white onions, brown-braised in stock
- 1 pound quartered fresh mushrooms sautéed in butter
- 9–10 inch fireproof casserole 3 inches deep

Direction

- Remove rind; cut bacon to lardons, 1 1/2-in. long and 1/4-in. thick sticks. Simmer bacon and rind in 1 1/2-qt. water for 10 minutes. Drain then dry.
- Preheat an oven to 450°.
- Sauté bacon in oil on medium heat to lightly brown for 2-3 minutes. Use slotted spoon to remove to side dish; put aside casserole. Reheat before sautéing beef till fat is nearly smoking.
- In paper towels, dry beef; if it's damp, it won't brown. A few pieces at a time, sauté in hot oil and bacon fat till all sides are browned nicely. Add to bacon.
- Brown sliced veggies in same fat, pouring sautéing fat out.
- Put bacon and beef back in casserole; toss with pepper and salt. Sprinkle on flour, tossing again to lightly coat beef in flour. Put casserole in center of preheated oven, uncovered, for 4 minutes. Toss meat then put back in oven for 4 minutes to cove meat with light crust and brown flour. Remove casserole and put oven to 325°.
- Mix enough bouillon/stock and wine in to barely cover meat. Add bacon rind, herbs, garlic and tomato paste; simmer on top of stove. Cover casserole and put in lower third of the preheated oven. Regulate heat so liquid very slowly simmers for 2 1/2-3 ours. If fork easily pierces meat, it is done.
- Prep mushrooms and onions as beef cooks; put aside till needed.
- Put casserole's contents into sieve set above saucepan when meat is tender.
- Wash casserole out; put bacon and beef back in it. Distribute mushrooms and cooked onions over meat.
- Skim off fat from sauce; simmer for 1-2 minutes, skimming extra fat off while rising. You should get 2 1/2 cups sauce that's thick

enough to lightly coat spoon. Boil down rapidly if too thin, mix a few tbsp. stock in if too thick. For seasoning, carefully taste.
- At this point, you can prep recipe in advance.
- Immediate serving: Cover casserole; simmer, basting veggies and meat with sauce a few times for 2-3 minutes. Serve in its casserole or put stew on platter surrounded by rice/noodles/potatoes then decorate with parsley.
- Later serving: Cover and refrigerate when cold; simmer with cover 15-20 minutes before serving. Very slowly simmer for 10 minutes, basting meat and veggies with sauce occasionally.

Nutrition Information

- Calories: 881
- Saturated Fat: 36 g(178%)
- Sodium: 752 mg(31%)
- Fiber: 4 g(15%)
- Total Carbohydrate: 24 g(8%)
- Cholesterol: 243 mg(81%)
- Protein: 44 g(88%)
- Total Fat: 65 g(99%)

173. Beef Stew For Two

Serving: 2 servings. | Prep: 30mins | Cook: 60mins | Ready in:

Ingredients

- 1-1/2 cups dry red wine or beef broth, divided
- 3 tablespoons lemon juice
- 2 teaspoons reduced-sodium soy sauce
- 2 teaspoons Worcestershire sauce
- 1/2 pound beef stew meat, cut into 1-inch cubes
- 2 teaspoons olive oil
- 1 small onion, chopped
- 3 garlic cloves, minced
- 2-1/2 cups beef broth, divided
- 2 small potatoes, cut into 1-inch cubes
- 2 medium carrots, cut into 1-inch slices
- 1 cup sliced baby portobello mushrooms
- 2 fresh thyme sprigs
- 1/8 teaspoon cayenne pepper
- 2 teaspoons cornstarch

Direction

- Combine Worcestershire sauce, soy sauce, lemon juice, and 1 cup of wine in a big plastic resealable bag, then add the beef. Seal the bag, turning to coat, and refrigerate for 8 hours or overnight.
- Drain and throw out the marinade. Brown the beef with oil in a large saucepan then remove the meat and put aside. Using the same pan, sauté the onion until tender. Add garlic and cook for 1 more minute. Add the remaining wine and 2 cups of beef broth, then return the meat onto the pan.
- Allow the stew to boil. Decrease the heat and simmer, covered, for 30 minutes. Add cayenne, thyme, mushrooms, carrots, and potatoes, then allow to boil. Decrease the heat and simmer while covered until the beef and vegetables are tender, or for about 30 minutes. Throw away the thyme sprigs.
- Combine remaining beef broth and cornstarch in a small bowl until smooth, then stir into the stew gradually and allow to boil. Cook while stirring for 2 minutes or until thick.

Nutrition Information

- Calories: 466 calories
- Sodium: 697mg sodium
- Fiber: 5g fiber)
- Total Carbohydrate: 44g carbohydrate (10g sugars
- Cholesterol: 77mg cholesterol
- Protein: 29g protein.
- Total Fat: 13g fat (4g saturated fat)

174. Beef Stew With Ghoulish Mashed Potatoes

Serving: 6 servings. | Prep: 30mins | Cook: 08hours00mins | Ready in:

Ingredients

- 2 pounds beef stew meat, cut into 1-inch cubes
- 1 pound fresh mushrooms, halved
- 2 cups fresh baby carrots
- 2 medium parsnips, peeled, halved lengthwise and sliced
- 2 medium onions, chopped
- 1-1/2 cups beef broth
- 3 tablespoons tomato paste
- 1 tablespoon Worcestershire sauce
- 2 garlic cloves, minced
- 1/2 teaspoon ground cloves
- 1/4 teaspoon pepper
- 8 medium potatoes (2-1/3 pounds), peeled and cubed
- 2/3 cup sour cream
- 6 tablespoons butter, cubed
- 1 teaspoon salt, divided
- 1 cup frozen peas
- 2 tablespoons all-purpose flour
- 2 tablespoons water

Direction

- Mix first 11 ingredients in a 5-qt. slow cooker. Place cover and set on low; cook until vegetables and beef are tender, 8-9 hours. Thirty minutes before serving, put potatoes in a big pot and add water to cover. Heat to a boil. Cover, decrease heat, and simmer until tender, 15-20 minutes. Drain water from potatoes. Put the potatoes back in the pot and add butter, 1/2 teaspoon salt, and sour cream. Mash potatoes until smooth. Take 12 peas and set to the side for garnishing. Put the rest of the peas in the slow cooker. Set the heat on high. In a different bowl, stir remaining salt, water, and flour until not lumpy. Mix into the stew. Cover and cook until thick, 5 minutes. Between six bowls divide the stew. Put the mashed potatoes in a big resealable plastic bag and in one corner cut a 2-in. hole. Use to pipe ghost figures on top of stew. Use reserved peas to garnish.

Nutrition Information

- Calories:
- Total Fat:
- Sodium:
- Fiber:
- Total Carbohydrate:
- Cholesterol:
- Protein:

175. Beef Stew With Vegetables

Serving: 2 servings. | Prep: 20mins | Cook: 02hours00mins | Ready in:

Ingredients

- 1 tablespoon all-purpose flour
- 1/4 teaspoon salt
- 1/8 teaspoon pepper
- 1/2 pound beef stew meat, cut into 3/4 inch cubes
- 1 tablespoon vegetable oil
- 1/3 cup chopped onion
- 1 garlic clove, minced
- 1-1/4 cups beef broth
- 1/3 cup white wine or additional beef broth
- 1 medium potato, cut into large chunks
- 2 medium carrots, cut into chunks
- 1/4 pound fresh mushrooms, halved
- 1 bay leaf
- 4-1/2 teaspoons quick-cooking tapioca
- 1/2 teaspoon dried thyme

Direction

- Mix pepper, salt and flour in a big resealable plastic bag; put in beef and coat by shaking.

Brown beef in a big saucepan with oil. Add garlic and onion; cook for 2 more minutes while stirring. Stir in broth and wine or more broth, scraping from pan the brown bits. Transfer to a greased 5-cup baking dish. Stir in thyme, tapioca, bay leaf, mushrooms, carrots and potato. Allow to sit for 15 minutes. For 1 hour, bake at 350° with a cover on. Remove cover; bake until veggies and meat are soft, for 1 to 1-1/2 more hours, mixing every half an hour. Discard bay leaf.

Nutrition Information

- Calories: 445 calories
- Protein: 28g protein.
- Total Fat: 16g fat (4g saturated fat)
- Sodium: 887mg sodium
- Fiber: 5g fiber)
- Total Carbohydrate: 42g carbohydrate (9g sugars
- Cholesterol: 70mg cholesterol

176. Beef And Barley Stew

Serving: 6-8 servings. | Prep: 20mins | Cook: 01hours50mins | Ready in:

Ingredients

- 1 pound beef stew meat, cut into 1/2-inch pieces
- 1 tablespoon olive oil
- 2 cups sliced carrots
- 1 cup chopped onion
- 1 cup sliced celery
- 2 to 3 garlic cloves, minced
- 2 cups sliced baby portobello mushrooms
- 1 can (14-1/2 ounces) stewed tomatoes
- 1 cup water
- 1 cup dry red wine
- 1 cup beef broth
- 2 bay leaves
- 1 teaspoon salt
- 3/4 teaspoon dried thyme
- 1/4 teaspoon pepper
- 1/3 cup uncooked medium pearl barley
- 1/4 cup all-purpose flour
- 1/3 cup cold water
- 1 to 2 tablespoons balsamic vinegar
- Minced fresh parsley, optional

Direction

- Cook beef in oil in a Dutch oven until the meat is not pink anymore. Add celery, onion, and carrots; cook for 5 minutes. Add garlic, cook for another 1 minute. Add pepper, thyme, salt, bay leaves, broth, wine, water, stewed tomatoes, and mushrooms.
- Boil it. Lower the heat, put a cover on and bring to a simmer for 1 hour. Add barley, put a cover on and bring to a simmer until the meat and barley are soft, or for about another 45 minutes.
- Mix cold water and flour together until smooth. Slowly mix into the pan. Boil it, stir and cook until thickened, or for about 2 minutes. Take away from heat. Remove the bay leaves. Mix in balsamic vinegar right before eating. Sprinkle parsley over each serving if you want.

Nutrition Information

- Calories: 209 calories
- Protein: 14g protein.
- Total Fat: 6g fat (2g saturated fat)
- Sodium: 541mg sodium
- Fiber: 4g fiber)
- Total Carbohydrate: 21g carbohydrate (7g sugars
- Cholesterol: 35mg cholesterol

177. Beef And Lamb Stew

Serving: 12 servings (3 quarts). | Prep: 50mins | Cook: 08hours30mins | Ready in:

Ingredients

- 1/2 cup dry red wine or beef broth
- 1/2 cup olive oil
- 4 garlic cloves, minced, divided
- 1-1/2 teaspoons salt, divided
- 1-1/2 teaspoons dried thyme, divided
- 1-1/4 teaspoons dried marjoram, divided
- 3/4 teaspoon dried rosemary, crushed, divided
- 3/4 teaspoon pepper, divided
- 1 pound beef stew meat, cut into 1-inch cubes
- 1 pound lamb stew meat, cut into 1-inch cubes
- 10 small red potatoes, halved
- 1/2 pound medium fresh mushrooms, halved
- 2 medium onions, thinly sliced
- 2 cups fresh cauliflowerets
- 1 can (16 ounces) kidney beans, rinsed and drained
- 1-1/2 cups cut fresh green beans
- 3 medium carrots, cut into 1/2-inch slices
- 1 celery rib, thinly sliced
- 1 cup beef broth
- 2 tablespoons minced fresh parsley
- 2 teaspoons sugar
- 3 tablespoons cornstarch
- 1/4 cup cold water
- 6 cups hot cooked brown rice

Direction

- Combine 1/4 teaspoon pepper, 1/2 teaspoon rosemary, 3/4 teaspoon marjoram. 1 teaspoon thyme, 1/2 teaspoon salt, 2 minced garlic cloves, oil, and wine in a large resealable plastic bag; add lamb and beef. Close the bag and shake well to coat; chill for 8 hours.
- Layer celery, carrots, green beans, kidney beans, cauliflower, onions, mushrooms, and potatoes in a 5- or 6-quart slow cooker.
- Drain beef and discard marinade; transfer meat to the slow cooker. Combine pepper, rosemary, marjoram, thyme, salt, remaining garlic, sugar, parsley, and the broth; pour the mixture over the meat.
- Cook, covered on low setting until meat and vegetables are softened, or for 8 to 10 hours.
- Whisk together water and cornstarch until no lumps remain; mix into stew. Cook, covered until thickened, or for 30 minutes longer. Serve warm with rice.

Nutrition Information

- Calories: 377 calories
- Total Carbohydrate: 44g carbohydrate (5g sugars
- Cholesterol: 48mg cholesterol
- Protein: 22g protein. Diabetic Exchanges: 2-1/2 starch
- Total Fat: 12g fat (3g saturated fat)
- Sodium: 499mg sodium
- Fiber: 7g fiber)

178. Burgundy Beef Stew

Serving: 6 servings. | Prep: 25mins | Cook: 08hours00mins | Ready in:

Ingredients

- 1/2 cup all-purpose flour
- 1 pound beef top sirloin steak, cut into 1/2-inch pieces
- 3 turkey bacon strips, diced
- 8 small red potatoes, halved
- 2 medium carrots, cut into 1-inch pieces
- 1 cup sliced fresh mushrooms
- 3/4 cup frozen pearl onions, thawed
- 3 garlic cloves, minced
- 1 bay leaf
- 1 teaspoon dried marjoram
- 1/2 teaspoon salt
- 1/2 teaspoon dried thyme
- 1/4 teaspoon pepper
- 1/2 cup reduced-sodium beef broth
- 1 cup Burgundy wine or additional reduced-sodium beef broth
- 6 cups hot cooked egg noodles

Direction

- In a big resealable plastic bag, put flour. Add beef, several pieces each time, and shake to coat. In a big grease-coated frying pan, brown bacon and beef on all sides in batches.
- In a 5-qt. slow cooker, put bacon and beef. Mix in wine, broth, seasonings, garlic, and vegetables.
- Put a cover on and cook on low until the meat is soft, or for about 8-9 hours. Remove the bay leaf. Thicken the cooking juices if you want. Enjoy with noodles.

Nutrition Information

- Calories: 388 calories
- Sodium: 434mg sodium
- Fiber: 4g fiber)
- Total Carbohydrate: 49g carbohydrate (4g sugars
- Cholesterol: 70mg cholesterol
- Protein: 26g protein. Diabetic Exchanges: 3 starch
- Total Fat: 7g fat (2g saturated fat)

179. Calendula Paella

Serving: 10-12 servings. | Prep: 20mins | Cook: 40mins | Ready in:

Ingredients

- 4 cups chicken broth
- 2-1/2 cups uncooked long grain rice
- 1 cup chopped onion
- 4 garlic cloves, minced, divided
- 1 teaspoon salt
- 1/2 teaspoon ground turmeric
- 1/4 teaspoon pepper
- 1 bay leaf
- 1 large green pepper, julienned
- 3 green onions, sliced
- 1 teaspoon minced parsley
- 1 teaspoon dried thyme
- 1/4 teaspoon hot pepper sauce
- 2 tablespoons olive oil
- 1 cup sliced fresh mushrooms
- 2 medium tomatoes, chopped
- 1 package (10 ounces) frozen peas
- 1/2 pound fresh or frozen uncooked shrimp, peeled and deveined
- 1 pound boneless skinless chicken breasts, thinly sliced
- 2 tablespoons lemon juice
- 1/2 cup calendula petals (about 12 blossoms)

Direction

- Combine bay leaf, pepper, turmeric, salt, half of the garlic, onion, rice and broth in a saucepan. Bring to a boil. Lower the heat and simmer, covered, for 20 minutes or until rice is softened. In the meantime, sauté remaining garlic, hot pepper sauce, thyme, parsley, onions and green pepper in oil for 2 minutes in a skillet. Add mushrooms and continue cooking until green pepper turn crisp-tender. Add peas and tomato; heat through. Throw away bay leaf; add rice mixture to vegetable mixture and place over medium-high heat to keep warm. Combine shrimp and lemon juice in another skillet, cook, stirring, for 2 minutes. Add chicken and cook for about 3 to 5 minutes until chicken loses its pink color and shrimp is completely cooked. Add calendula petals, rice and vegetable mixture; toss until well combined.

Nutrition Information

- Calories:
- Cholesterol:
- Protein:
- Total Fat:
- Sodium:
- Fiber:
- Total Carbohydrate:

180. Candlelight Stew

Serving: 6 servings. | Prep: 10mins | Cook: 02hours00mins |Ready in:

Ingredients

- 2 pounds beef stew meat
- 2 tablespoons olive oil
- Salt and pepper
- 1 can (10-3/4 ounces) condensed cream of mushroom soup, undiluted
- 1 medium carrot, shredded
- 1/3 cup Burgundy wine
- 1/2 pound sliced fresh mushrooms
- 2 tablespoons onion soup mix

Direction

- Cook meat in hot oil until browned; add pepper and salt to season.
- Transfer meat to a 2-quart baking dish. Mix together remaining ingredients; pour over meat. Bake, covered for about 2 hours at 350°, stirring occasionally or until meat is tender. If you want more gravy, add a small amount of beef broth.

Nutrition Information

- Calories:
- Fiber:
- Total Carbohydrate:
- Cholesterol:
- Protein:
- Total Fat:
- Sodium:

181. Chicken Mushroom Stew

Serving: 4 | Prep: 30mins | Cook: 50mins |Ready in:

Ingredients

- 2 tablespoons olive oil
- 2 skinless, boneless chicken breast halves - cut into 1 inch cubes
- 1 tablespoon butter
- 1 leek, halved lengthwise and thinly sliced crosswise
- 1 small onion, diced
- 3 spring onions, finely sliced
- 2 cloves garlic, smashed
- 1 carrot, thickly sliced
- 2 stalks celery, strings peeled, finely diced
- 1 (16 ounce) package fresh mushrooms, quartered
- 1/2 cup white wine
- 2 cups chicken stock
- salt and ground black pepper to taste
- 2 sprigs fresh thyme
- 2 sprigs fresh rosemary
- 2 sprigs fresh tarragon
- 2 sprigs fresh oregano
- 2 sprigs fresh parsley
- 2 bay leaves
- 2 tablespoons all-purpose flour (optional)
- 3 tablespoons water (optional)

Direction

- In a big pot, heat olive oil on medium high heat. Stir and cook chicken for 5 minutes till light brown yet pink inside. Put aside chicken. Lower heat to medium. In same pot, melt butter. Stir and cook onion and leek for 8 minutes till it begins to brown. Mix garlic in. Cook for 1 minute till fragrant. Mix celery and carrot in. Cook veggies for 1-2 minutes more. Mix mushrooms in; cook, mixing often, for 10 minutes till mushrooms release liquid and juice starts to dry up.
- Put white wine in. Scrape pot to melt and loose the bottom brown flavor bits. Mix stock in; simmer. Season with black pepper and salt to taste.
- Tightly knot a short kitchen twine piece around sprigs of bay leaves, parsley, oregano, tarragon, rosemary and thyme to create a neat package. Put herb bouquet into pot.
- Mix chicken pieces in. Cover pot. Very gently simmer for 30 minutes till chicken cooks

through. Don't boil. Whisk water and flour in a small bowl for a thick stew then whisk into simmering sauce; let thicken for 3 minutes. Before serving in bowls, remove herb bundle.

Nutrition Information

- Calories: 261 calories;
- Cholesterol: 41
- Protein: 17.5
- Total Fat: 11.9
- Sodium: 577
- Total Carbohydrate: 17.7

182. Contest Winning Gone All Day Stew

Serving: 8 servings. | Prep: 25mins | Cook: 04hours00mins | Ready in:

Ingredients

- 1/4 cup all-purpose flour
- 1 boneless beef chuck roast (2 pounds), cut into 1-inch cubes
- 2 tablespoons canola oil
- 1 can (10-3/4 ounces) condensed tomato soup, undiluted
- 1 cup water or red wine
- 2 teaspoons beef bouillon granules
- 3 teaspoons Italian seasoning
- 1 bay leaf
- 1/2 teaspoon coarsely ground pepper
- 6 medium onions, quartered
- 4 medium potatoes, cut into 1-1/2-inch pieces
- 3 medium carrots, cut into 1-inch pieces
- 12 large fresh mushrooms
- 1 celery rib, cut into 1-inch pieces
- Hot cooked egg noodles, optional

Direction

- In a big resealable plastic bag, add flour. Put in beef, several pieces at a time, and coat by shaking.
- In batches, brown meat in a big skillet with oil; drain. Move to a 5-qt. slow cooker. Mix the seasonings, bouillon, water and tomato soup in a small bowl; add mixture on top of beef. Add the celery, mushrooms, carrots, potatoes and onions.
- Cook on low with a cover on until meat is soft or for 4-5 hours. Discard bay leaf. If you like, serve with egg noodles.

Nutrition Information

- Calories: 416 calories
- Sodium: 497mg sodium
- Fiber: 6g fiber)
- Total Carbohydrate: 43g carbohydrate (14g sugars
- Cholesterol: 74mg cholesterol
- Protein: 28g protein.
- Total Fat: 15g fat (5g saturated fat)

183. Easy Burgundy Stew

Serving: 7 servings. | Prep: 20mins | Cook: 03hours00mins | Ready in:

Ingredients

- 1 boneless beef chuck roast (2 pounds), cut into 1-inch cubes
- 1 can (14-1/2 ounces) diced tomatoes, undrained
- 1/2 pound sliced fresh mushrooms
- 4 medium carrots, sliced
- 2 medium onions, sliced
- 2 celery ribs, chopped
- 1 cup Burgundy wine or reduced-sodium beef broth
- 1 tablespoon minced fresh thyme or 1 teaspoon dried thyme
- 1/2 teaspoon salt

- 1/2 teaspoon ground mustard
- 1/4 teaspoon pepper
- 3 tablespoons all-purpose flour
- 1 cup water

Direction

- Combine the first 11 ingredients in an oven-safe Dutch oven. Whisk together water and flour until no lumps remain. Slowly mix into stew. Bake, covered, at 325°, stirring every 30 minutes, until meat and vegetables are tender, about 3 hours.

Nutrition Information

- Calories: 287 calories
- Sodium: 332mg sodium
- Fiber: 4g fiber)
- Total Carbohydrate: 15g carbohydrate (7g sugars
- Cholesterol: 84mg cholesterol
- Protein: 28g protein. Diabetic Exchanges: 3 lean meat
- Total Fat: 13g fat (5g saturated fat)

184. Flavorful Beef Stew

Serving: 6 servings. | Prep: 25mins | Cook: 06hours00mins | Ready in:

Ingredients

- 1/2 pound medium fresh mushrooms, quartered
- 2 medium red potatoes, cubed
- 3 medium carrots, sliced
- 1 medium onion, chopped
- 1 celery rib, thinly sliced
- 1/4 cup all-purpose flour
- 1 tablespoon paprika
- 3/4 teaspoon salt
- 1/4 teaspoon pepper
- 1 pound beef stew meat
- 1 can (14-1/2 ounces) beef broth
- 4-1/2 teaspoons reduced-sodium teriyaki sauce
- 2 garlic cloves, minced
- 1 bay leaf

Direction

- Place celery, onion, carrots, potatoes, and mushrooms in a 3-quart slow cooker. Combine pepper, salt, paprika, and flour in a large resealable plastic bag. Add a few pieces of beef at a time and shake until evenly coated. Put into the slow cooker.
- Combine bay leaf, garlic, teriyaki sauce, and the broth; pour the mixture over thee coated beef. Cook, covered on low setting until meat and vegetables are tender, or for 6 to 8 hours. Remove bay leaf.

Nutrition Information

- Calories: 202 calories
- Protein: 19g protein. Diabetic Exchanges: 2 lean meat
- Total Fat: 6g fat (2g saturated fat)
- Sodium: 745mg sodium
- Fiber: 3g fiber)
- Total Carbohydrate: 19g carbohydrate (5g sugars
- Cholesterol: 47mg cholesterol

185. Garlic Mushroom French Beef Stew

Serving: 20 servings (1 cup each). | Prep: 40mins | Cook: 02hours15mins | Ready in:

Ingredients

- 5 pounds beef sirloin tip roast, cut into 1-inch cubes
- 1-1/2 teaspoons salt
- 1/2 teaspoon pepper

- 3 tablespoons olive oil
- 2 large sweet onions, chopped
- 3 medium carrots, sliced
- 5 tablespoons butter, divided
- 6 garlic cloves, minced
- 2 pounds assorted fresh mushrooms, such as portobello, shiitake and/or oyster), sliced
- 4 large Yukon Gold potatoes, cubed
- 1 carton (32 ounces) beef broth
- 1 cup dry red wine or additional beef broth
- 1 tablespoon minced fresh basil or 1 teaspoon dried basil
- 3 tablespoons all-purpose flour
- 1 cup heavy whipping cream
- 2/3 cup crumbled blue cheese

Direction

- With pepper and salt, season the beef. Put oil in stockpot and brown beef in batches. Remove the beef and keep warm. Add 2 tablespoons butter to the same stockpot and sauté carrots and onions for 4 minutes. Mix in the garlic and cook for 2 more minutes. Mix in potatoes, beef, mushrooms, basil, wine, and broth. Heat to boiling. Cover, decrease heat, and gently boil for 1 1/4 hours. Remove cover and simmer until meat is tender, 20-30 minutes. Melt the rest of the butter in a small pan. Mix in flour until not lumpy. Slowly add the cream. Heat to boiling; stir constantly and cook until thick, about 2 minutes. Mix into stockpot with stew and cook until entirely heat. Sprinkle cheese on top.

Nutrition Information

- Calories: 336 calories
- Cholesterol: 100mg cholesterol
- Protein: 27g protein.
- Total Fat: 16g fat (8g saturated fat)
- Sodium: 517mg sodium
- Fiber: 2g fiber)
- Total Carbohydrate: 18g carbohydrate (4g sugars

186. Gone All Day Stew

Serving: 8 servings. | Prep: 25mins | Cook: 04hours00mins | Ready in:

Ingredients

- 1/4 cup all-purpose flour
- 2 pounds boneless beef chuck roast, trimmed and cut into 1-inch cubes
- 2 tablespoons canola oil
- 1 can (10-3/4 ounces) condensed tomato soup, undiluted
- 1 cup water or red wine
- 2 teaspoons beef bouillon granules
- 3 teaspoons Italian seasoning
- 1 bay leaf
- 1/2 teaspoon coarsely ground pepper
- 6 white onions or yellow onions, quartered
- 4 medium potatoes, cut into 1-1/2-inch slices
- 3 medium carrots, cut into 1-inch slices
- 12 large fresh mushrooms
- 1/2 cup sliced celery

Direction

- Put flour in a big resealable plastic bag. Put in beef, a few pieces at a time, and coat by shaking.
- Cook meat in oil in batches in a large skillet until browned; drain well. Transfer cooked meat to a 5-quart slow cooker. Combine seasonings, bouillon, wine or water, and tomato soup; pour the mixture over beef. Add celery, mushrooms, carrots, potatoes, and onions.
- Cook, covered, on low setting until beef is tender, about 4 to 5 hours. Remove bay leaf. Serve along with French bread or noodles.

Nutrition Information

- Calories: 385 calories
- Total Fat: 15g fat (5g saturated fat)
- Sodium: 416mg sodium

- Fiber: 5g fiber)
- Total Carbohydrate: 36g carbohydrate (7g sugars
- Cholesterol: 74mg cholesterol
- Protein: 27g protein.

187. Hearty Beef & Sweet Potato Stew

Serving: 8 servings (2-1/2 quarts). | Prep: 40mins | Cook: 02hours00mins | Ready in:

Ingredients

- 3 tablespoons canola oil, divided
- 1-1/2 pounds boneless beef chuck steak, cut into 1-inch pieces
- 2 medium onions, chopped
- 2 garlic cloves, minced
- 2 cans (14-1/2 ounces each) reduced-sodium beef broth
- 1/3 cup dry red wine or additional reduced-sodium beef broth
- 1 tablespoon minced fresh thyme or 1 teaspoon dried thyme
- 1 tablespoon Worcestershire sauce
- 1 teaspoon salt
- 3/4 teaspoon pepper
- 3 tablespoons cornstarch
- 3 tablespoons cold water
- 1-1/4 pounds sweet potatoes (about 2 medium), cut into 1-inch cubes
- 1 pound baby portobello mushrooms, halved
- 4 medium carrots, cut into 1/2-inch slices
- 2 medium parsnips, cut into 1/2-inch slices
- 1 medium turnip, cut into 3/4-inch cubes

Direction

- Turn oven to 325° to preheat. Heat 2 tablespoons oil in an oven-safe Dutch oven over medium-high heat. Cook beef in batches until browned. Take cooked beef out using a slotted spoon.
- Sauté onions in remaining oil in the pan until softened, or for 2 to 3 minutes. Add garlic, and cook for 1 minute longer. Put in wine and broth, stir to remove browned bits from the pan. Mix in pepper, salt, Worcestershire sauce, and thyme. Pour beef back to the pan; bring to a boil. Cover and bake for 1 hour and 15 minutes.
- Combine cold water and cornstarch together in a small bowl until smooth; slowly mix into stew. Add turnip, parsnips, carrots, mushrooms, and sweet potatoes to the pan. Cover and bake until beef and vegetables are softened, or for 45 minutes to 1 hour longer. Drain cooking juice, if necessary; ladle off fat. Pour cooking juice back in the Dutch oven.

Nutrition Information

- Calories: 354 calories
- Protein: 22g protein. Diabetic Exchanges: 3 lean meat
- Total Fat: 14g fat (4g saturated fat)
- Sodium: 586mg sodium
- Fiber: 6g fiber)
- Total Carbohydrate: 36g carbohydrate (14g sugars
- Cholesterol: 57mg cholesterol

188. Herbed Beef Stew

Serving: 10-12 servings. | Prep: 15mins | Cook: 02hours30mins | Ready in:

Ingredients

- 2 pounds beef stew meat, cut into 1-inch cubes
- 2 tablespoons canola oil
- 3 cups water
- 1 large onion, chopped
- 2 teaspoons pepper
- 1 to 2 teaspoons salt, optional
- 1-1/2 teaspoons garlic powder
- 1 teaspoon rosemary, crushed

- 1 teaspoon dried oregano
- 1 teaspoon dried basil
- 1 teaspoon ground marjoram
- 2 bay leaves
- 1 can (6 ounces) tomato paste
- 2 cups cubed peeled potatoes
- 2 cups sliced carrots
- 1 large green pepper, chopped
- 1 package (9 ounces) frozen cut green beans
- 1 package (10 ounces) frozen corn
- 1/4 pound mushrooms, sliced
- 3 medium tomatoes, chopped

Direction

- Cook meat in oil until browned in a Dutch oven. Add tomato paste, seasonings, onion, and water. Simmer, covered until meat is tender, or for 1 1/2 hours.
- Mix in green pepper, carrots, and potatoes; simmer for 30 minutes. Add more water if needed. Mix in remaining ingredients, simmer with a cover for 20 minutes.

Nutrition Information

- Calories: 223 calories
- Sodium: 83mg sodium
- Fiber: 4g fiber)
- Total Carbohydrate: 21g carbohydrate (7g sugars
- Cholesterol: 47mg cholesterol
- Protein: 18g protein.
- Total Fat: 8g fat (2g saturated fat)

189. Holiday Beef Bourguignon

Serving: 12 servings (3 quarts). | Prep: 40mins | Cook: 02hours30mins | Ready in:

Ingredients

- 2/3 cup all-purpose flour
- 1-1/2 teaspoons salt, divided
- 1 boneless beef chuck roast (about 4 pounds), cut into 1-inch cubes
- 4 tablespoons olive oil, divided
- 2 garlic cloves, minced
- 2-1/2 cups Burgundy wine or beef broth
- 3 cups beef broth
- 1/4 cup minced fresh parsley or 4 teaspoons dried parsley flakes
- 2 bay leaves
- 1 package (14.4 ounces) frozen pearl onions
- 3 bacon strips, chopped
- 8 fresh thyme sprigs
- 2 tablespoons tomato paste
- 1/2 teaspoon pepper
- 3 tablespoons butter
- 1 pound medium fresh mushrooms, stems removed
- Hot cooked egg noodles

Direction

- Preheat oven to 325°. Mix 1 teaspoon salt and flour in a shallow bowl. Put in beef, several pieces at a time, and coat by tossing; shake off excess.
- Over medium heat, heat in an ovenproof Dutch oven 2 tablespoons of oil. In batches, brown beef, adding more oil as required. Use a slotted spoon to take out.
- Add garlic; cook for 1 more minute. Pour in wine, stirring to make browned bits loosen from pan. Stir in the rest of salt, bay leaves, parsley and broth. Put beef back in pan. Cook until boiling. Bake for 2 hours with the cover on.
- In the meantime, over medium-high heat in a big skillet, for 10-12 minutes, cook bacon and onions, stirring occasionally, or until bacon turns crisp.
- Take stew out of oven. Transfer onion mixture with a slotted spoon to stew; stir in pepper, tomato paste and thyme. Put back in oven; bake with a cover until onions and beef are soft or for 30-45 minutes.

- Over medium-high heat in a big skillet, heat butter. Add mushrooms; cook for 6-8 minutes while stirring or until soft.
- Remove from stew the thyme sprigs and bay leaves. Stir in mushrooms. With egg noodles, serve stew.

Nutrition Information

- Calories: 407 calories
- Protein: 33g protein.
- Total Fat: 25g fat (9g saturated fat)
- Sodium: 657mg sodium
- Fiber: 1g fiber)
- Total Carbohydrate: 11g carbohydrate (2g sugars
- Cholesterol: 111mg cholesterol

190. Homemade Italian Stew

Serving: 8 servings. | Prep: 10mins | Cook: 01hours10mins | Ready in:

Ingredients

- 2 pounds turkey Italian sausage links, casings removed
- 1 cup chopped onion
- 3/4 cup chopped green pepper
- 3 garlic cloves, minced
- 1 can (28 ounces) diced tomatoes, undrained
- 1 can (15 ounces) Italian-seasoned tomato sauce
- 1/2 pound fresh mushrooms, sliced
- 1 cup water
- 1/2 cup beef broth
- 1/2 cup dry red wine or beef broth
- 1-1/2 cups cooked spiral pasta
- 1/2 cup shredded reduced-fat mozzarella cheese

Direction

- With cooking spray, coat a big nonstick saucepan, put in the garlic, green pepper, onion and sausage and cook until meat is not pink anymore; drain off. Add wine and broth or more broth, water, mushrooms, tomato sauce, and tomatoes. Boil. Lower heat; simmer with the cover on for 1 hour. Add pasta; heat completely. On top of each serving, add 1 tablespoon cheese.

Nutrition Information

- Calories: 300 calories
- Protein: 25g protein. Diabetic Exchanges: 3 lean meat
- Total Fat: 12g fat (4g saturated fat)
- Sodium: 1237mg sodium
- Fiber: 3g fiber)
- Total Carbohydrate: 22g carbohydrate (0 sugars
- Cholesterol: 65mg cholesterol

191. Irish Beef Stew

Serving: 8 | Prep: 30mins | Cook: 6hours | Ready in:

Ingredients

- 2 tablespoons olive oil
- 3 tablespoons all-purpose flour
- 2 pounds beef chuck, cut into 1 1/2-inch cubes
- 1 pound carrots, peeled and cut into 1-inch chunks
- 6 large potatoes, peeled and cut into large chunks
- 1 white onion, cut into large chunks
- 2 cloves garlic, minced
- 2 cups beef broth
- 1 (6 ounce) can tomato paste
- 1 (12 fluid ounce) can or bottle Irish stout beer (e.g. Guinness®)
- 1 tablespoon cold water
- 1 tablespoon cornstarch

Direction

- In a big skillet over medium heat, heat the oil. Coat beef cubes with flour by tossing, then fry till browned in the hot oil. In a big slow cooker, put the garlic, onion, potatoes and carrots. Put the meat over the vegetables. Stir the tomato paste and beef broth then put into the slow cooker together with the beer.
- Put cover, cook for 6 hours on High or 8 hours on Low. On the last hour prior serving, melt cornstarch in cold water and mix into the broth. Let simmer for a several minutes to thicken on the High setting.

Nutrition Information

- Calories: 597 calories;
- Sodium: 498
- Total Carbohydrate: 62.5
- Cholesterol: 82
- Protein: 27.6
- Total Fat: 26.8

192. Mainly Mushroom Beef Carbonnade

Serving: 6 servings. | Prep: 45mins | Cook: 02hours00mins | Ready in:

Ingredients

- 2 tablespoons plus 1-1/2 teaspoons canola oil, divided
- 1-1/2 pounds beef stew meat, cut into 1-inch cubes
- 3/4 teaspoon salt
- 1/4 teaspoon plus 1/8 teaspoon pepper
- 3 medium onions, chopped
- 1-1/4 pounds portobello mushrooms, stems removed, cut into 3/4-inch dice
- 4 garlic cloves, minced
- 2 tablespoons tomato paste
- 1/2 pound fresh baby carrots
- 1 thick slice day-old rye bread, crumbled (about 1-1/2 cups)
- 3 bay leaves
- 1-1/2 teaspoons dried thyme
- 1 teaspoon beef bouillon granules
- 1 bottle (12 ounces) light beer or beef broth
- 1 cup water
- 1 ounce bittersweet chocolate, grated

Direction

- Turn heat to 325° to preheat. Heat 2 tablespoons oil in an oven-safe Dutch oven over medium-high heat. Season beef with pepper and salt; cook in batches until browned. Take cooked beef out using a slotted spoon. Lower heat to medium. Sauté onions in drippings, stirring frequently for about 8 minutes until dark golden brown. Mix in the remaining oil; add garlic and mushrooms. Sauté until liquid has released and mushrooms start to turn brown. Mix in tomato paste.
- Add bouillon, thyme, bay leaves, bread, and carrots. Pour in water and beer; stirring well to loosen browned bits from the pan. Bring to a boil; add beef back to the pan.
- Cover and bake from 2 hours to 2 hours and 15 minutes until meat is tender. Take the pan out; remove bay leaves. Mix in chocolate until melted.

Nutrition Information

- Calories: 333 calories
- Total Fat: 16g fat (4g saturated fat)
- Sodium: 547mg sodium
- Fiber: 4g fiber)
- Total Carbohydrate: 18g carbohydrate (7g sugars
- Cholesterol: 71mg cholesterol
- Protein: 26g protein.

193. Mushroom Burger Stew

Serving: 6-8 servings. | Prep: 15mins | Cook: 40mins | Ready in:

Ingredients

- 1 pound ground beef
- 1 small onion, chopped
- 4 cups water
- 4 medium potatoes, cubed
- 5 medium carrots, chopped
- 1 can (14-1/2 ounces) stewed tomatoes
- 1 envelope onion soup mix
- Salt and pepper to taste
- 1/2 pound fresh mushrooms, quartered

Direction

- Cook onion and beef in a large saucepan over medium heat until the beef is no longer pink; drain. Add pepper, salt, soup mix, tomatoes, carrots, potatoes, and water; bring to a boil. Lower heat; uncover and simmer until vegetables are tender, 20 to 25 minutes. Put in mushrooms and simmer for 5 more minutes.

Nutrition Information

- Calories:
- Sodium:
- Fiber:
- Total Carbohydrate:
- Cholesterol:
- Protein:
- Total Fat:

194. Mushroom Onion Beef Stew

Serving: 2 servings. | Prep: 15mins | Cook: 01hours30mins | Ready in:

Ingredients

- 3/4 pound beef stew meat, cut into 3/4-inch cubes
- 2 tablespoons canola oil, divided
- 1 garlic clove, minced
- 1/4 cup beef broth
- 1/2 cup red wine or additional beef broth
- 2 thin strips orange peel (about 3 inches x 1/4 inch each)
- 1/4 teaspoon salt
- 1/4 teaspoon dried thyme
- 1/4 pound small fresh mushrooms
- 1 cup frozen pearl onions, thawed
- 1/2 cup frozen peas, thawed
- 2 teaspoons cornstarch
- 2 tablespoons water

Direction

- Brown stew meat in a big saucepan with 1 tablespoon oil. Put in garlic; cook for a minute while stirring. Stir in thyme, salt, orange peel, wine and broth. Cook to a boil. Lower heat; simmer until meat is soft with the cover on or for 1-1/4 to 1-1/2 hours. Discard orange peel.
- Remove mushrooms stems. Cook mushroom stems and caps in a saucepan with the rest of oil until soft. Put in onions; cook until lightly turn browned. Stir into mixture of meat; add peas. Combine water and cornstarch to make a smooth mixture. Stir into stew gradually. Cook to a boil; cook and stir until thickened or for 1-2 minutes.

Nutrition Information

- Calories: 533 calories
- Protein: 38g protein.
- Total Fat: 26g fat (6g saturated fat)
- Sodium: 539mg sodium
- Fiber: 3g fiber)
- Total Carbohydrate: 26g carbohydrate (7g sugars
- Cholesterol: 106mg cholesterol

195. Northwoods Beef Stew

Serving: 11 servings (2-3/4 quarts). | Prep: 30mins | Cook: 08hours00mins | Ready in:

Ingredients

- 3 large carrots, cut into 1-inch pieces
- 3 celery ribs, cut into 1-inch pieces
- 1 large onion, cut into wedges
- 1/4 cup all-purpose flour
- 1/2 teaspoon salt
- 1/4 teaspoon pepper
- 3-1/2 pounds beef stew meat
- 1 can (10-3/4 ounces) condensed tomato soup, undiluted
- 1/2 cup dry red wine or beef broth
- 2 tablespoons quick-cooking tapioca
- 1 tablespoon Italian seasoning
- 1 tablespoon paprika
- 1 tablespoon brown sugar
- 1 tablespoon beef bouillon granules
- 1 tablespoon Worcestershire sauce
- 1/2 pound sliced baby portobello mushrooms
- Hot cooked egg noodles

Direction

- Place onion, celery, and carrots in a 5-quart slow cooker. Combine pepper, salt, and flour in a large resealable plastic bag. Add a few pieces of beef at a time, and shake until coated. Place coated beef over vegetables.
- Combine Worcestershire sauce, bouillon, brown sugar, paprika, Italian seasoning, tapioca, wine, and soup in a small bowl. Pour the mixture over the top.
- Cook, covered, on low setting until beef and vegetables are tender, about 8 to 10 hours, adding mushroom during the last hour. Serve along with noodles.

Nutrition Information

- Calories: 285 calories
- Total Carbohydrate: 15g carbohydrate (6g sugars
- Cholesterol: 90mg cholesterol
- Protein: 30g protein. Diabetic Exchanges: 4 lean meat
- Total Fat: 10g fat (4g saturated fat)
- Sodium: 582mg sodium
- Fiber: 2g fiber)

196. Orange Barley Chicken

Serving: 8 servings. | Prep: 30mins | Cook: 45mins | Ready in:

Ingredients

- 1 cup all-purpose flour
- 1 teaspoon celery salt
- 1/2 teaspoon pepper
- 1 broiler/fryer chicken (3 to 4 pounds), cut up and skin removed
- 2 teaspoons olive oil
- 1 medium onion, thinly sliced
- 1 tablespoon butter
- 3 cups reduced-sodium chicken broth
- 3 cups orange juice
- 2 medium parsnips, peeled and chopped
- 1-1/2 cups medium pearl barley
- 1-1/2 cups sliced fresh mushrooms
- 1-1/2 cups fresh baby carrots
- 2 bay leaves

Direction

- Combine pepper, celery salt and flour in a plastic zip bag. Add few pieces of chicken to bag at a time, shake until well coated.
- Brown chicken in oil in a Dutch oven a batch at a time. Remove and keep warm. Add onion to the same pan and sauté in butter until softened. Add chicken, bay leaves, carrots, mushrooms, barley, parsnips, orange juice and broth. Bring to a boil. Lower the heat and cook, covered, for 45 to 50 minutes or until barley is softened, remember to occasionally flip chicken.

- Remove from the heat; allow to stand for 5 minutes. Throw away bay leaves.

Nutrition Information

- Calories: 386 calories
- Total Fat: 8g fat (2g saturated fat)
- Sodium: 361mg sodium
- Fiber: 8g fiber)
- Total Carbohydrate: 55g carbohydrate (14g sugars
- Cholesterol: 59mg cholesterol
- Protein: 25g protein.

197. Pork Tenderloin Stew

Serving: 8 servings. | Prep: 20mins | Cook: 40mins | Ready in:

Ingredients

- 2 pork tenderloins (1 pound each), cut into 1-inch cubes
- 1 tablespoon olive oil
- 1 medium onion, chopped
- 1 garlic clove, minced
- 1 can (14-1/2 ounces) reduced-sodium chicken broth
- 2 pounds red potatoes, peeled and cubed
- 1 cup sliced fresh carrots
- 1 cup sliced celery
- 1/2 pound sliced fresh mushrooms
- 2 tablespoons cider vinegar
- 2 teaspoons sugar
- 1-1/2 teaspoons dried tarragon
- 1 teaspoon salt
- 2 tablespoons all-purpose flour
- 1/2 cup fat-free milk
- 1/2 cup reduced-fat sour cream

Direction

- In batches over medium heat in a big nonstick skillet, cook pork in oil until not pink anymore; take out and keep warm.
- Sauté onion until tender-crisp in the same pan. Add garlic; cook for 1 more minute. Add salt, tarragon, sugar, vinegar, veggies and broth; cook to a boil. Lower heat; simmer with the cover on for 25-30 minutes or until veggies are soft.
- Mix milk and flour until smooth; stir into vegetable mixture gradually. Cook to a boil; cook, stirring, for 2 minutes or until thickened. Put in pork and thoroughly heat. Lower heat; right prior to serving, stir in sour cream (without boiling).

Nutrition Information

- Calories: 293 calories
- Sodium: 521mg sodium
- Fiber: 3g fiber)
- Total Carbohydrate: 28g carbohydrate (7g sugars
- Cholesterol: 68mg cholesterol
- Protein: 28g protein. Diabetic Exchanges: 3 lean meat
- Total Fat: 7g fat (3g saturated fat)

198. Pork And Pasta Stew

Serving: 6 servings. | Prep: 15mins | Cook: 20mins | Ready in:

Ingredients

- 1 pound lean boneless pork, cut into 1-inch strips
- 1/2 teaspoon lemon-pepper seasoning
- 1 tablespoon olive oil
- 1 medium onion, sliced into thin wedges
- 1 garlic clove, minced
- 1 cup chicken broth
- 3/4 cup salsa
- 1 tablespoon brown sugar

- 3 quarts water
- 1 teaspoon salt, optional
- 1 package (8 ounces) spiral pasta
- 1 cup fresh cut green beans (1-inch pieces)
- 1 cup sliced yellow summer squash
- 1 cup sliced zucchini
- 1 cup sliced fresh mushrooms
- 1 tablespoon cornstarch
- 2 tablespoons cold water

Direction

- Toss the pepper-lemon with the pork; brown them in the oil on medium heat in a skillet. Put in the garlic and onion; sauté till becoming soft. Whisk in brown sugar, salsa and broth; boil. Lower the heat; keep covered and let it simmer till the pork softens or for 15 to 20 minutes.
- At the same time, in a big sauce pan on medium heat, boil the salt (if you want) and water. Put in the beans and pasta; bring back to boiling. Cook, without a cover, for 7 minutes. Put in mushrooms, zucchini and squash. Cook, without covering, till the veggies and pasta soften or for 6 to 7 minutes longer. Drain; put aside and keep them warm.
- Mix the cold water with the cornstarch till becoming smooth; put into pork mixture and stir them well. Boil; boil and whisk for 2 minutes. To serve, arrange the veggies and pasta into a serving dish; add pork mixture atop.

Nutrition Information

- Calories: 318 calories
- Total Fat: 7g fat (2g saturated fat)
- Sodium: 283mg sodium
- Fiber: 4g fiber)
- Total Carbohydrate: 39g carbohydrate (8g sugars
- Cholesterol: 44mg cholesterol
- Protein: 22g protein. Diabetic Exchanges: 2 starch

199. Pork And Winter Squash Stew

Serving: 8 servings. | Prep: 25mins | Cook: 01hours30mins | Ready in:

Ingredients

- 2 pounds lean boneless pork, cut into 1-inch cubes
- 2 tablespoons canola oil, divided
- 2 cups chopped onion
- 2 garlic cloves, minced
- 3 cups sliced fresh mushrooms
- 2-1/2 cups diagonally sliced carrots
- 2 cans (14-1/2 ounces each) Italian stewed tomatoes
- 2 teaspoons dried thyme
- 1/2 teaspoon pepper
- 1-1/2 teaspoon salt, optional
- 4 cups cubed peeled butternut squash
- Hot cooked noodles, optional

Direction

- Brown pork in a saucepan or Dutch oven with 1 tablespoon of oil. Take out from pan and drain. Over medium heat, in the same pan, heat the rest of oil. For 3 minutes, sauté garlic and onion.
- Put pork back to pan. Add the seasonings, tomatoes, carrots and mushrooms; cook to a boil. Lower heat; simmer for 1 hour with the cover on.
- Add squash; simmer with cover off for half an hour or until veggies and meat are soft. If you like, serve with noodles.

Nutrition Information

- Calories: 298 calories
- Protein: 22g protein. Diabetic Exchanges: 2 meat
- Total Fat: 14g fat (0 saturated fat)
- Sodium: 393mg sodium

- Fiber: 0 fiber)
- Total Carbohydrate: 26g carbohydrate (0 sugars
- Cholesterol: 60mg cholesterol

200. Portobello Beef Burgundy

Serving: 6 servings. | Prep: 30mins | Cook: 07hours30mins | Ready in:

Ingredients

- 1/4 cup all-purpose flour
- 1/2 teaspoon salt
- 1/2 teaspoon seasoned salt
- 1-1/2 teaspoons minced fresh thyme or 1/2 teaspoon dried thyme
- 3/4 teaspoon minced fresh marjoram or 1/4 teaspoon dried thyme
- 1/2 teaspoon pepper
- 2 pounds beef sirloin tip steak, cubed
- 2 bacon strips, diced
- 3 tablespoons canola oil
- 1 garlic clove, minced
- 1 cup Burgundy wine or beef broth
- 1 teaspoon beef bouillon granules
- 1 pound sliced baby portobello mushrooms
- Hot cooked noodles, optional

Direction

- Combine the first 6 ingredients in a large resealable plastic bag. Add a few pieces of beef at a time until finish, and shake to coat.
- Cook bacon in a large skillet over medium heat until it's crispy. Transfer to paper towels to drain using a slotted spoon. Cook beef in batches in hot oil until browned in the same skillet, adding garlic to the last batch; cook for 1 to 2 minutes longer. Drain well.
- Transfer to a 4-quart slow cooker. Pour in wine into the skillet, stirring to loosen browned bits from the pan. Add bouillon; bring to a boil. Mix into slow cooker. Mix in bacon. Cook, covered on low setting until meat is tender, or for 7 to 9 hours.
- Mix in mushrooms. Cook, covered on high setting until sauce thickens slightly and mushrooms are tender, or for 30 to 45 minutes longer. Enjoy with noodles if desired.

Nutrition Information

- Calories: 321 calories
- Fiber: 1g fiber)
- Total Carbohydrate: 8g carbohydrate (2g sugars
- Cholesterol: 100mg cholesterol
- Protein: 34g protein.
- Total Fat: 15g fat (3g saturated fat)
- Sodium: 552mg sodium

201. Presto Beef Stew

Serving: 2 servings. | Prep: 10mins | Cook: 20mins | Ready in:

Ingredients

- 2 individually frozen biscuits
- 2 tablespoons butter
- 2 cups sliced fresh mushrooms
- 1 package (17 ounces) refrigerated beef roast au jus
- 1/4 teaspoon pepper
- 2 tablespoons cornstarch
- 1 cup cold water

Direction

- Bake biscuits following the package's instructions.
- In the meantime, melt butter over medium heat in a big saucepan. Add mushrooms, stir and cook until soft. Use two forks to shred beef; add to the pan. Add pepper. Mix water and cornstarch together until smooth; mix into the stew. Boil it, stir and cook until thickened, or for about 1-2 minutes.

- Distribute the stew among 2 bowls; put a biscuit on top each.

Nutrition Information

- Calories: 710 calories
- Total Carbohydrate: 38g carbohydrate (10g sugars
- Cholesterol: 176mg cholesterol
- Protein: 54g protein.
- Total Fat: 40g fat (18g saturated fat)
- Sodium: 1595mg sodium
- Fiber: 2g fiber)

202. Quick Mushroom Stew

Serving: 6-8 servings. | Prep: 10mins | Cook: 02hours30mins | Ready in:

Ingredients

- 1 can (10-3/4 ounces) condensed tomato soup, undiluted
- 1 can (10-3/4 ounces) condensed cream of mushroom soup, undiluted
- 2-1/2 cups water
- 2 pounds beef stew meat, cut into cubes
- 2 bay leaves
- 3 medium potatoes, peeled and cut into 1-inch chunks
- 4 carrots, cut into 1/2-inch slices
- 1 pound medium fresh mushrooms, halved
- 1 tablespoon quick-cooking tapioca

Direction

- Stir water and soups until smooth in a Dutch oven. Add bay leaves and meat. For 1-1/2 hours, bake at 325° with a cover on.
- Stir in tapioca, mushrooms, carrots and potatoes. Bake with a cover until the veggies and meat are soft or for 1 more hour. Prior to serving discard the bay leaves.

Nutrition Information

- Calories: 297 calories
- Protein: 26g protein.
- Total Fat: 10g fat (4g saturated fat)
- Sodium: 552mg sodium
- Fiber: 3g fiber)
- Total Carbohydrate: 26g carbohydrate (7g sugars
- Cholesterol: 72mg cholesterol

203. Quicker Mushroom Beef Stew

Serving: 8 servings. | Prep: 15mins | Cook: 15mins | Ready in:

Ingredients

- 1 pound sliced baby portobello mushrooms
- 1 pound fresh baby carrots, sliced
- 1 large onion, chopped
- 3 tablespoons butter
- 3 garlic cloves, minced
- 1 teaspoon dried rosemary, crushed
- 3 tablespoons all-purpose flour
- 1 teaspoon pepper
- 4 cups water
- 4 teaspoons beef base
- 2 packages (17 ounces each) refrigerated beef tips with gravy
- Hot cooked egg noodles
- Crumbled blue cheese

Direction

- In a Dutch oven, sauté onion, carrots, and mushrooms until soft. Add rosemary and garlic, cook for another 1 minute. Mix in pepper and flour until combined, slowly add water. Mix in the beef base.
- Boil it, stir and cook until thickened, or for about 2 minutes. Add beef tips with gravy, heat thoroughly. Enjoy with cheese and noodles.

Nutrition Information

- Calories: 237 calories
- Protein: 20g protein.
- Total Fat: 11g fat (5g saturated fat)
- Sodium: 1077mg sodium
- Fiber: 3g fiber)
- Total Carbohydrate: 16g carbohydrate (8g sugars
- Cholesterol: 59mg cholesterol

204. Sausage And Mushroom Stew

Serving: 6-8 servings. | Prep: 10mins | Cook: 01hours45mins | Ready in:

Ingredients

- 2 cans (10-3/4 ounces each) condensed cream of mushroom soup, undiluted
- 1-1/2 pounds Johnsonville® Fully Cooked Polish Kielbasa Sausage Rope, cut into 1-inch slices
- 5 medium potatoes, peeled and cut into 1-inch chunks
- 4 medium carrots, peeled and cut into 1-inch pieces
- 3 medium onions, coarsely chopped
- 1 cup fresh green beans, halved
- 3/4 pound fresh mushrooms, halved
- 1/2 medium head cabbage, coarsely chopped

Direction

- Mix the first 7 ingredients in an ovenproof 5-qt. baking dish or Dutch oven. Bake for 1-1/4 hours at 350° with a cover on.
- Remove cover and stir. Put in the cabbage. Put the cover on and bake until veggies are soft or for half an hour more. Stir prior to serving.

Nutrition Information

- Calories:
- Protein:
- Total Fat:
- Sodium:
- Fiber:
- Total Carbohydrate:
- Cholesterol:

205. Savory Braised Chicken With Vegetables

Serving: 6 servings. | Prep: 15mins | Cook: 40mins | Ready in:

Ingredients

- 1/2 cup seasoned bread crumbs
- 6 boneless skinless chicken breast halves (4 ounces each)
- 2 tablespoons olive oil
- 1 can (14-1/2 ounces) beef broth
- 2 tablespoons tomato paste
- 1 teaspoon poultry seasoning
- 1/2 teaspoon salt
- 1/2 teaspoon pepper
- 1 pound fresh baby carrots
- 1 pound sliced fresh mushrooms
- 2 medium zucchini, sliced
- Sliced French bread baguette, optional

Direction

- In a shallow bowl, put in bread crumbs. Coat both sides of chicken breasts with bread crumbs. Shake to remove excess.
- Heat oil on medium heat in a Dutch oven. Add in batches of chicken; for each side, cook for 2-4 minutes or until browned. Take chicken out of the pan.
- In the same pan, place seasonings, tomato paste, and broth; cook on medium-high heat, stir to loosen browned pieces from pan. Add in chicken and vegetables; heat to a boil.

Decrease heat; cover and simmer until vegetables are tender and a thermometer inserted in chicken shows 165°, or for 25-30 minutes. Serve with baguette if desired.

Nutrition Information

- Calories: 247 calories
- Total Carbohydrate: 16g carbohydrate (6g sugars
- Cholesterol: 63mg cholesterol
- Protein: 28g protein. Diabetic Exchanges: 3 lean meat
- Total Fat: 8g fat (1g saturated fat)
- Sodium: 703mg sodium
- Fiber: 3g fiber)

206. Savory Pork Stew

Serving: 8 | Prep: 15mins | Cook: 2hours | Ready in:

Ingredients

- 1 tablespoon extra virgin olive oil
- 2 pounds cubed pork stew meat
- salt to taste
- ground black pepper to taste
- garlic powder to taste
- 2 tablespoons cornstarch, or as needed
- 8 red potatoes
- 1 green bell pepper, chopped
- 1 red bell pepper, chopped
- 1 sweet onion, diced
- 1 (11 ounce) can whole kernel corn
- 1 (14 ounce) can stewed tomatoes
- 1 (10.75 ounce) can cream of mushroom soup
- 1 1/4 cups milk
- 1 (14 ounce) can beef broth
- 1 tablespoon Italian seasoning

Direction

- Heat olive oil over medium heat in a skillet. Season all sides of pork with garlic powder, pepper, and salt, and coat lightly with cornstarch. Transfer pork to the skillet, and cook until browned lightly, but not done. Transfer pork to a slow cooker; add corn, onion, red bell pepper, green bell pepper, and potatoes to the slow cooker.
- Combine Italian seasoning, broth, milk, cream of mushroom soup, and tomatoes in a bowl. Pour the mixture into the slow cooker.
- Cook, covered, on High setting for 60 minutes. Turn heat to low, and keep on cooking for at least 60 minutes.

Nutrition Information

- Calories: 526 calories;
- Cholesterol: 71
- Protein: 30
- Total Fat: 22.5
- Sodium: 707
- Total Carbohydrate: 52.9

207. Simple Chicken Stew

Serving: 2 servings. | Prep: 20mins | Cook: 06hours00mins | Ready in:

Ingredients

- 1 can (10-3/4 ounces) condensed cream of chicken soup, undiluted
- 1 cup water
- 1/2 pound boneless skinless chicken breast, cubed
- 1 large potato, peeled and cubed
- 2 medium carrots, sliced
- 1/2 cup sliced fresh mushrooms
- 1/4 cup chopped onion
- 1 teaspoon chicken bouillon granules
- 1/4 teaspoon poultry seasoning

Direction

- Combine all the ingredients in a 1 1/2 quart slow cooker.
- Cook, covered, on a low setting for 6 - 7 hours or until the vegetables and chicken are tender.

Nutrition Information

- Calories: 427 calories
- Fiber: 6g fiber)
- Total Carbohydrate: 62g carbohydrate (11g sugars
- Cholesterol: 75mg cholesterol
- Protein: 30g protein.
- Total Fat: 6g fat (2g saturated fat)
- Sodium: 834mg sodium

208. Slow Cook Beef Stew

Serving: 6 servings. | Prep: 20mins | Cook: 06hours00mins | Ready in:

Ingredients

- 2 pounds beef top round steak, cut into 1-inch cubes
- 8 medium carrots, cut into 1-inch pieces
- 1 pound small red potatoes, quartered
- 1/2 pound sliced fresh mushrooms
- 1 medium sweet red pepper, chopped
- 1 can (14-1/2 ounces) diced tomatoes, undrained
- 1/4 cup all-purpose flour
- 1 can (6 ounces) tomato paste
- 3/4 cup beef broth
- 1/3 cup dry red wine or additional beef broth
- 1-1/2 teaspoons salt
- 1 teaspoon minced garlic
- 1 teaspoon pepper
- 1/2 teaspoon dried thyme

Direction

- Cook beef in a large skillet until all sides are browned. Combine red pepper, mushrooms, potatoes, and carrots in a 5-quart slow cooker. Add tomatoes on top.
- Combine broth, tomato paste, and flour in a small bowl until no lumps remain. Mix in thyme, pepper, garlic, salt, and wine; transfer into the slow cooker. Top with beef.
- Cook, covered on low setting until beef is tender, or for 6 to 8 hours.

Nutrition Information

- Calories:
- Total Fat:
- Sodium:
- Fiber:
- Total Carbohydrate:
- Cholesterol:
- Protein:

209. Slow Cooker Beef Burgandy Stew

Serving: 11 servings. | Prep: 25mins | Cook: 09hours00mins | Ready in:

Ingredients

- 2-1/4 cups Burgundy wine, divided
- 1/4 cup olive oil
- 1-1/2 teaspoons pepper, divided
- 1 teaspoon salt, divided
- 4 pounds beef stew meat, cut into 1-inch cubes
- 8 bacon strips, chopped
- 1 large onion, chopped
- 1 pound medium fresh mushrooms, halved
- 2 garlic cloves, minced
- 1/4 cup plus 1/3 cup all-purpose flour, divided
- 1 tablespoon tomato paste
- 1 teaspoon dried thyme
- 1 teaspoon dried parsley flakes
- 1/2 cup beef broth
- Hot cooked noodles, optional

Direction

- Combine 1/2 teaspoon salt, 1 teaspoon pepper, oil, and 1 cup of wine in a large resealable plastic bag. Add beef; seal the bag and shake to coat. Chill in the fridge for 8 hours or overnight.
- Cook bacon in a large skillet over medium heat until nearly crispy. Transfer to paper towels to drain using a slotted spoon, saving 2 tablespoons bacon drippings. Sauté onion in drippings until browned. Add garlic and mushrooms, cook for 3 more minutes. Pour bacon and onion mixture in a 4-quart slow cooker.
- Drain off marinade and discard. Add 1/4 cup flour to beef in the bag; coat by tossing. Place coated beef in a slow cooker. Combine salt, pepper, remaining wine, parsley, thyme, and tomato paste in a small bowl. Pour mixture over beef. Cook, covered, on low until beef is tender, 9 to 10 hours.
- Whisk together broth and remaining flour until no lumps remain; slowly mix into beef mixture. Cook, covered, on high until gravy is thick, about 30 minutes. Serve with noodles if desired.

Nutrition Information

- Calories: 353 calories
- Protein: 35g protein.
- Total Fat: 18g fat (6g saturated fat)
- Sodium: 383mg sodium
- Fiber: 1g fiber)
- Total Carbohydrate: 9g carbohydrate (2g sugars
- Cholesterol: 110mg cholesterol

210. Slow Cooked Vegetable Beef Stew

Serving: 7-8 servings. | Prep: 20mins | Cook: 09hours00mins | Ready in:

Ingredients

- 5 medium red potatoes, peeled and cut into 1/2 inch chunks
- 2-1/2 cups sliced fresh mushrooms
- 4 medium carrots, sliced
- 2 celery ribs, thinly sliced
- 3 bacon strips, diced
- 1/4 cup all-purpose flour
- 3/4 teaspoon pepper, divided
- 1/2 teaspoon salt, divided
- 2 pounds beef stew meat, cut into 3/4 inch cubes
- 1 large onion, chopped
- 2 garlic cloves, minced
- 1 tablespoon canola oil
- 1 can (14-1/2 ounces) beef broth
- 1/2 cup dry red wine or additional beef broth
- 1 bay leaf
- 1/8 teaspoon dried thyme
- 1 can (10-3/4 ounces) condensed tomato soup, undiluted
- 1/3 cup water
- 2 tablespoons cornstarch
- 3 tablespoons cold water

Direction

- In a 5-qt. slow cooker, put the first 4 ingredients. Cook bacon in a big frying pan over medium heat until crunchy. Transfer onto paper towels to strain with a slotted spoon. Save the drippings.
- Mix 1/4 teaspoon of salt, 1/4 teaspoon of pepper, and flour together in a big resealable plastic bag. Add meat, several pieces each time, close the bag and shake to coat. Brown garlic, onion, and beef in oil and the drippings.
- Move to the slow cooker. Mix in the leftover pepper and salt, the saved bacon, thyme, bay leaf, extra broth or wine, and broth. Put the lid on and cook on Low until the meat is soft, or for about 8-9 hours. Remove the bay leaf.
- Mix water and soup together, pour in the slow cooker. Put the lid on and cook for 30 minutes on high. Mix cold water and cornstarch together, mix into the slow cooker. Put the lid

on and cook until thickened, or for about 30-40 minutes.

Nutrition Information

- Calories:
- Sodium:
- Fiber:
- Total Carbohydrate:
- Cholesterol:
- Protein:
- Total Fat:

211. Slow Simmered Burgundy Beef Stew

Serving: 4 servings. | Prep: 30mins | Cook: 01hours45mins | Ready in:

Ingredients

- 1-1/2 pounds beef stew meat (1-1/4-inch pieces)
- 3 tablespoons all-purpose flour
- 3/4 teaspoon salt
- 2 to 4 teaspoons canola oil, divided
- 2 teaspoons beef bouillon granules
- 2 teaspoons dried parsley flakes
- 1-1/2 teaspoons Italian seasoning
- 2 cups water
- 1 cup Burgundy wine or beef stock
- 3 medium potatoes (about 1-1/3 pounds), peeled and quartered
- 1 cup fresh mushrooms, halved
- 1 medium onion, cut into eight wedges
- 2 medium carrots, cut into 1-inch pieces
- 2 celery ribs, cut into 1/2-inch pieces
- Additional water, optional

Direction

- Turn oven to 350° to preheat. Combine beef with salt and flour until lightly coated; shake to remove excess. Heat 2 teaspoons oil in an oven-safe Dutch oven over medium heat. Cook beef in batches until browned. Add more oil if necessary. Take browned beef out of the pan.
- Add wine, 2 cups water, herbs, and bouillon to the same pan; bring the mixture to a boil, mixing well to loosen browned bits from the pan. Add beef, and bring the mixture to another boil. Move to oven; cover and bake for 1 hour.
- Mix in vegetables and make it thinner by adding more water if necessary. Bake, covered, for 45 minutes to 1 hour until vegetables and beef are tender.

Nutrition Information

- Calories: 419 calories
- Sodium: 949mg sodium
- Fiber: 4g fiber)
- Total Carbohydrate: 33g carbohydrate (5g sugars
- Cholesterol: 106mg cholesterol
- Protein: 37g protein.
- Total Fat: 15g fat (5g saturated fat)

212. Stew With Confetti Dumplings

Serving: 10-12 servings (about 3 quarts). | Prep: 40mins | Cook: 01hours40mins | Ready in:

Ingredients

- 2 pounds boneless beef chuck roast, cut into 1-inch cubes
- 2 tablespoons vegetable oil
- 1/2 pound fresh mushrooms, halved
- 1 large onion, thinly sliced
- 1 garlic clove, minced
- 2 cans (14-1/2 ounces each) beef broth
- 1 teaspoon Italian seasoning
- 1 teaspoon salt
- 1/4 teaspoon pepper

- 1 bay leaf
- 1/3 cup all-purpose flour
- 1/2 cup water
- 1 package (10 ounces) frozen peas
- DUMPLINGS:
- 1-1/2 cups biscuit/baking mix
- 2 tablespoons diced pimientos, drained
- 1 tablespoon minced chives
- 1/2 cup milk

Direction

- Brown meat in oil in a Dutch oven. Add garlic, onion and mushrooms; cook, stirring occasionally, until onion becomes soft. Stir in bay leaf, pepper, salt, Italian seasoning and broth; cook to a boil. For 1-1/2 hours, simmer with the cover on.
- Discard bay leaf. Combine water and flour to make a smooth mixture; stir into stew. Cook to a boil; for 1 minute, cook and stir. Lower heat. Mix in peas.
- In a bowl, mix chives, pimientos and biscuit mix for dumplings. Stir in milk, just enough to make a soft dough. Onto the simmering stew, drop the mixture by tablespoonfuls. Simmer with the cover on for 10-12 minutes or until the test for dumplings is done (while simmering, do not open lid). Serve immediately.

Nutrition Information

- Calories: 260 calories
- Sodium: 573mg sodium
- Fiber: 2g fiber)
- Total Carbohydrate: 18g carbohydrate (3g sugars
- Cholesterol: 51mg cholesterol
- Protein: 19g protein.
- Total Fat: 12g fat (4g saturated fat)

213. Tangy Beef And Vegetable Stew

Serving: 12-16 servings. | Prep: 25mins | Cook: 05hours45mins | Ready in:

Ingredients

- 6 cups cubed peeled potatoes (1/2-inch pieces)
- 8 medium carrots, cut into 1/2-inch pieces
- 2 medium onions, cubed
- 4 pounds beef stew meat, cut into 1-inch pieces
- 1/3 cup canola oil
- 1/3 cup all-purpose flour
- 4 teaspoons beef bouillon granules
- 3 cups boiling water
- 1/3 cup white vinegar
- 1/3 cup ketchup
- 3 tablespoons prepared horseradish
- 3 tablespoons prepared mustard
- 2 tablespoons sugar
- 2 cups each frozen peas and corn
- 2 cups sliced fresh mushrooms

Direction

- In a 6-quart slow cooker, place onions, carrots, and potatoes. Cook beef with oil in batches until browned; place beef over the vegetables. Scatter with flour.
- Dissolve bouillon in boiling water. Mix in sugar, mustard, horseradish, ketchup, and vinegar; pour over vegetables and beef. Cook, covered, for 5 hours on high setting.
- Add mushrooms, corn, and peas. Cook, covered, on high setting until beef and vegetables are tender, about 45 more minutes.

Nutrition Information

- Calories: 334 calories
- Fiber: 4g fiber)
- Total Carbohydrate: 29g carbohydrate (7g sugars
- Cholesterol: 71mg cholesterol
- Protein: 26g protein.
- Total Fat: 13g fat (4g saturated fat)

- Sodium: 397mg sodium

214. Winter Beef Stew

Serving: 6 servings. | Prep: 40mins | Cook: 02hours30mins | Ready in:

Ingredients

- 1-1/2 pounds boneless beef chuck roast, cut into 1-1/4-inch pieces
- 1 cup chopped onion
- 2 teaspoons canola oil
- 2 garlic cloves, minced
- 1-1/2 pounds small red potatoes, cut into chunks
- 3 medium carrots, cut into 1-inch pieces
- 2 medium onions, quartered
- 1/2 pound fresh mushrooms, halved
- 1 can (14-1/2 ounces) reduced-sodium beef broth
- 1 cup unsweetened apple juice
- 1/4 cup tomato paste
- 1/2 cup minced fresh parsley
- 2 bay leaves
- 1/2 teaspoon salt
- 1/2 teaspoon dried thyme
- 1/2 teaspoon pepper
- 1 bacon strip, cooked and crumbled

Direction

- Cooke chopped onion and meat in oil over medium-high heat in a Dutch oven until all sides are browned. Add garlic; cook for 1 minute longer. Drain well. Add mushrooms, quartered onions, carrots, and potatoes. Stir pepper, thyme, salt, bay leaves, parsley, tomato paste, apple juice, and broth in a small bowl then pour the mixture over meat.
- Bake, covered for 2 hours at 325°. Stir well. Remove cover and bake until desired thickness is reached, or for 30 to 45 minutes longer. Remove bay leaves; top with bacon.

Nutrition Information

- Calories: 364 calories
- Total Fat: 9g fat (3g saturated fat)
- Sodium: 544mg sodium
- Fiber: 6g fiber)
- Total Carbohydrate: 39g carbohydrate (0 sugars
- Cholesterol: 79mg cholesterol
- Protein: 32g protein. Diabetic Exchanges: 3 lean meat

Chapter 5: Mushroom Side Dish Recipes

***

215. Artichoke Spinach Casserole

Serving: 14 servings. | Prep: 25mins | Cook: 25mins | Ready in:

Ingredients

- 1 pound fresh mushrooms, sliced
- 1/3 cup chicken broth
- 1 tablespoon all-purpose flour
- 1/2 cup evaporated milk
- 4 packages (10 ounces each) frozen chopped spinach, thawed and squeezed dry
- 2 cans (14-1/2 ounces each) diced tomatoes, drained
- 2 cans (14 ounces each) water-packed artichoke hearts, rinsed, drained and thinly sliced
- 1 cup sour cream
- 1/2 cup mayonnaise

- 3 tablespoons lemon juice
- 1/2 teaspoon garlic powder
- 1/4 teaspoon salt
- 1/4 teaspoon pepper
- Paprika, optional

Direction

- Cook broth and mushrooms over medium heat in a large skillet until softened, 3 minutes. Use a slotted spoon to take mushrooms out and put aside.
- Beat milk and flour until smooth; pour into skillet. Heat to a boil; cook and stir in 2 minutes. Take away from the heat; blend in mushrooms, tomatoes, and spinach.
- Pour 1/2 the artichoke into an ungreased 13x9-inch baking dish. Spread 1/2 the spinach mixture on top. Repeat the layers. Mix pepper, salt, garlic powder, lemon juice, mayonnaise, and sour cream; dollop over casserole. Scatter with paprika if wanted.
- Bake without covering at 350° about 25 to 30 minutes, until bubbling.

Nutrition Information

- Calories: 136 calories
- Sodium: 249mg sodium
- Fiber: 2g fiber)
- Total Carbohydrate: 8g carbohydrate (3g sugars
- Cholesterol: 17mg cholesterol
- Protein: 4g protein.
- Total Fat: 10g fat (3g saturated fat)

216. Asparagus Mushroom Casserole

Serving: 6 servings. | Prep: 10mins | Cook: 35mins | Ready in:

Ingredients

- 4 cups sliced fresh mushrooms
- 1 cup chopped onion
- 4 tablespoons butter, divided
- 2 tablespoons all-purpose flour
- 1 teaspoon chicken bouillon granules
- 1/2 teaspoon salt
- 1/8 teaspoon ground nutmeg
- 1/8 teaspoon pepper
- 1 cup 2% milk
- 1 package (12 ounces) frozen cut asparagus, thawed and drained
- 1/4 cup diced pimientos
- 1-1/2 teaspoons lemon juice
- 3/4 cup soft bread crumbs

Direction

- Cook onion and mushrooms with 3 tablespoons of butter in a nonstick skillet until softened. Using a slotted spoon, take out the vegetables and put aside. Stir the bouillon, flour, pepper, nutmeg and salt into drippings until smooth. Add milk gradually. Boil; cook while stirring for 2 minutes, until thickened. Stir in the mushroom mixture, lemon juice, pimientos and asparagus.
- Pour into a 1-1/2-qt. baking dish greased with cooking spray. Melt the rest of butter and toss with breadcrumbs. Sprinkle over top. Bake without a cover for 35-40 minutes at 350°, until thoroughly heated.

Nutrition Information

- Calories: 162 calories
- Sodium: 532mg sodium
- Fiber: 2g fiber)
- Total Carbohydrate: 16g carbohydrate (0 sugars
- Cholesterol: 24mg cholesterol
- Protein: 6g protein. Diabetic Exchanges: 1 starch
- Total Fat: 9g fat (5g saturated fat)

217. Asparagus Stir Fry

Serving: 8 | Prep: 15mins | Cook: 10mins | Ready in:

Ingredients

- 1/2 cup chicken broth
- 1 tablespoon sherry
- 1 tablespoon soy sauce
- 1 tablespoon cider vinegar
- 1 tablespoon cornstarch
- 1/4 teaspoon sugar
- 1/4 teaspoon dry mustard
- 1/4 teaspoon salt
- 1 tablespoon vegetable oil
- 2 pounds fresh asparagus, trimmed and cut into 1 inch pieces

Direction

- Mix sherry, salt, dry mustard, sugar, cornstarch, cider vinegar, soy sauce, and the broth in a bowl.
- Over medium heat, heat the oil in a skillet. Mix the asparagus into the skillet and coat with the oil. Next, cook and stir until soft but firm, about 5 minutes. Then pour the broth mixture over the asparagus, and keep cooking until heated through and thickened, another 5 minutes.

Nutrition Information

- Calories: 46 calories;
- Protein: 2.7
- Total Fat: 1.9
- Sodium: 199
- Total Carbohydrate: 5.9
- Cholesterol: 0

218. Asparagus And Mushrooms In Lemon Thyme Butter

Serving: 4 servings. | Prep: 10mins | Cook: 10mins | Ready in:

Ingredients

- 1 pound fresh asparagus, trimmed and cut into 1-inch pieces
- 1/2 pound sliced fresh mushrooms
- 1 tablespoon butter
- 1 teaspoon olive oil
- 1-1/2 teaspoons minced fresh thyme or 1/2 teaspoon dried thyme
- 1 teaspoon grated lemon peel
- 1/2 teaspoon salt
- 1/2 teaspoon lemon juice
- 1/4 teaspoon pepper

Direction

- Sauté mushrooms and asparagus in oil and butter in a large skillet until softened. Add the remaining ingredients and stir to combine.

Nutrition Information

- Calories: 64 calories
- Sodium: 324mg sodium
- Fiber: 2g fiber)
- Total Carbohydrate: 5g carbohydrate (2g sugars
- Cholesterol: 8mg cholesterol
- Protein: 3g protein. Diabetic Exchanges: 1 vegetable
- Total Fat: 4g fat (2g saturated fat)

219. Bacon 'n' Veggie Pasta

Serving: 13 servings. | Prep: 10mins | Cook: 35mins | Ready in:

Ingredients

- 2 cans (14-1/2 ounces each) stewed tomatoes
- 2 cups fresh broccoli florets
- 2 medium carrots, thinly sliced
- 1/2 teaspoon salt
- 1/2 teaspoon Italian seasoning
- 1/2 teaspoon dried oregano
- 1/4 teaspoon dried basil
- 4 bacon strips, diced
- 1/2 pound fresh mushrooms, sliced
- 1/3 cup chopped green pepper
- 1/4 cup chopped onion
- 2 garlic cloves, minced
- 16 ounces uncooked medium shell pasta
- 1/4 cup shredded Parmesan cheese

Direction

- Mix the first 7 ingredients together in a big saucepan. Boil it. Lower the heat, put a cover on and simmer until the carrots and broccoli are soft, or for 25-30 minutes.
- Cook bacon in a big skillet over medium heat until crispy. Transfer onto paper towels to strain, saving 1 tablespoon of drippings. Sauté garlic, onion, green pepper, and mushrooms in the drippings until soft; put into the tomato mixture and thoroughly heat.
- In the meantime, cook pasta following the package instructions. Strain and put in a serving bowl, put the vegetable mixture on top. Use Parmesan cheese and bacon to sprinkle.

Nutrition Information

- Calories: 205 calories
- Total Carbohydrate: 36g carbohydrate (0 sugars
- Cholesterol: 4mg cholesterol
- Protein: 8g protein. Diabetic Exchanges: 2 starch
- Total Fat: 3g fat (1g saturated fat)
- Sodium: 289mg sodium
- Fiber: 3g fiber)

220. Broccoli Noodle Side Dish

Serving: 8 servings. | Prep: 10mins | Cook: 10mins | Ready in:

Ingredients

- 6 cups uncooked wide egg noodles
- 3 to 4 garlic cloves, minced
- 1/4 cup olive oil
- 4 cups broccoli florets (about 1 pound)
- 1/2 pound fresh mushrooms, thinly sliced
- 1/2 teaspoon dried thyme
- 1/4 teaspoon pepper
- 1 teaspoon salt, optional

Direction

- Cook noodles following the package directions. In the meantime, sauté the minced garlic in oil until tender in a skillet. Add broccoli; sauté until crisp-tender, for 4 minutes. Add the thyme, mushrooms, pepper and salt if desired; sauté for 2-3 minutes. Strain the noodles and add to the broccoli mixture. Stir gently over low heat until heated through.

Nutrition Information

- Calories: 188 calories
- Total Carbohydrate: 24g carbohydrate (2g sugars
- Cholesterol: 24mg cholesterol
- Protein: 6g protein. Diabetic Exchanges: 1-1/2 starch
- Total Fat: 8g fat (1g saturated fat)
- Sodium: 17mg sodium
- Fiber: 2g fiber)

221. Broccoli Mushroom Medley

Serving: 6 servings. | Prep: 15mins | Cook: 0mins | Ready in:

Ingredients

- 1-1/2 pounds fresh broccoli, cut into florets
- 1 teaspoon lemon juice
- 1 teaspoon salt, optional
- 1 teaspoon sugar
- 1 teaspoon cornstarch
- 1/4 teaspoon ground nutmeg
- 1 cup sliced fresh mushrooms
- 1 medium onion, sliced into rings
- 1 to 2 garlic cloves, minced
- 3 tablespoons canola oil

Direction

- Steam broccoli until tender-crisp, about 1 to 2 minutes. Rinse under cold water and set aside. Mix together nutmeg, cornstarch, sugar, salt if wanted and lemon juice in a bowl, then set aside.
- Stir-fry garlic, onion and mushrooms with oil in a wok or big skillet on high heat for about 3 minutes. Put in lemon juice mixture and broccoli, then stir-fry for about 1 to 2 minutes. Stir promptly.

Nutrition Information

- Calories: 88 calories
- Protein: 4g protein. Diabetic Exchanges: 2 vegetable
- Total Fat: 5g fat (0 saturated fat)
- Sodium: 22mg sodium
- Fiber: 0 fiber)
- Total Carbohydrate: 10g carbohydrate (0 sugars
- Cholesterol: 0 cholesterol

222. Brown Rice Veggie Stir Fry

Serving: 4 servings. | Prep: 10mins | Cook: 10mins | Ready in:

Ingredients

- 2 tablespoons water
- 2 tablespoons reduced-sodium soy sauce
- 1 tablespoon olive oil
- 1 cup sliced zucchini
- 1 cup shredded cabbage
- 1/2 cup sliced fresh mushrooms
- 1/2 cup chopped onion
- 1 cup cooked brown rice
- 1/4 cup diced fresh tomato
- 1/4 cup grated carrot
- 2 tablespoons slivered almonds

Direction

- Mix together oil, soy sauce and water in a wok or big skillet. Put in onion, mushrooms, cabbage and zucchini, then stir-fry the mixture until tender yet still crisp, about 4 to 5 minutes. Put in carrot, tomato and rice, then stir-fry until heated through, about 2 to 3 minutes. Use almonds to sprinkle over top.

Nutrition Information

- Calories: 263 calories
- Total Fat: 11g fat (1g saturated fat)
- Sodium: 627mg sodium
- Fiber: 6g fiber)
- Total Carbohydrate: 35g carbohydrate (7g sugars
- Cholesterol: 0 cholesterol
- Protein: 7g protein.

223. Bundle Of Veggies

Serving: 6 servings. | Prep: 10mins | Cook: 20mins | Ready in:

Ingredients

- 1/2 pound medium fresh mushrooms
- 1/2 pound cherry tomatoes
- 1 cup sliced zucchini
- 1 tablespoon olive oil
- 1 tablespoon butter, melted
- 1/2 teaspoon salt
- 1/2 teaspoon onion powder
- 1/2 teaspoon Italian seasoning
- 1/8 teaspoon garlic powder
- Dash pepper

Direction

- In a double layer of heavy duty foil (about 18-inch square), add the zucchini, tomatoes and mushrooms. Mix the rest of ingredients together and drizzle on top of the vegetables. Fold the foil around the vegetables and seal carefully.
- Cover and grill for 20 to 25 minutes over medium heat until the mixture gets tender. Take out the foil gently so that the steam can escape.

Nutrition Information

- Calories: 52 calories
- Sodium: 27mg sodium
- Fiber: 0 fiber)
- Total Carbohydrate: 5g carbohydrate (0 sugars
- Cholesterol: 0 cholesterol
- Protein: 1g protein. Diabetic Exchanges: 1 vegetable
- Total Fat: 4g fat (0 saturated fat)

224. Cheesy Bacon Ranch Potato Stuffing

Serving: 16 servings. | Prep: 25mins | Cook: 40mins | Ready in:

Ingredients

- 3-1/3 cups cubed potato dinner rolls, divided
- 2/3 envelope ranch salad dressing mix
- 6 cups mashed potatoes (with added milk and butter)
- 2 medium celery ribs, finely chopped
- 1 cup sliced baby portobello mushrooms
- 5 bacon strips, cooked and crumbled
- 1-1/3 cups shredded Monterey Jack cheese
- Chopped green onions, optional

Direction

- Preheat an oven to 350°F. Bake cubed rolls for 7-10 minutes till toasted on a 15x10x1-in. ungreased baking pan. Meanwhile, mix dressing mix into the mashed potatoes.
- Fold in bacon, mushrooms, celery and 2 cups cubed rolls. Put in a 13x9-in. greased baking dish; put leftover cubed rolls on top. Put pan on the baking sheet. Bake for 35 minutes, uncovered. Sprinkle cheese over; bake for 5-10 minutes more till top is golden brown and cheese melts. Top with green onions, if desired.

Nutrition Information

- Calories: 156 calories
- Protein: 5g protein.
- Total Fat: 7g fat (4g saturated fat)
- Sodium: 473mg sodium
- Fiber: 1g fiber)
- Total Carbohydrate: 17g carbohydrate (2g sugars
- Cholesterol: 20mg cholesterol

225. Cheesy Cauliflower With Peas

Serving: 8 servings. | Prep: 20mins | Cook: 15mins | Ready in:

Ingredients

- 1 large head cauliflower (about 2 pounds), broken into florets
- 1/3 cup butter, cubed
- 1/3 cup all-purpose flour
- 3/4 teaspoon salt
- 1/4 teaspoon pepper
- 2-1/2 cups whole milk
- 1 cup frozen peas
- 1/2 cup sliced fresh mushrooms
- 1-1/2 cups shredded cheddar cheese, divided

Direction

- In a covered saucepan, cook the cauliflower in a small amount of water till tender-crisp. At the same time, in a separate saucepan, melt the butter. Whisk in the pepper, salt and flour till becoming smooth. Slowly whisk in the milk. Boil; cook and whisk till becoming thick or for 2 minutes. Take out of heat. Drain the cauliflower. Put the cauliflower, 1 cup of the cheese, mushrooms and peas into milk mixture; whisk gently. Move into a greased 2.5-quart baking dish. Drizzle with the rest of the cheese. Keep covered and bake at 350 degrees for 15 minutes. Remove the cover; bake till thoroughly heated or for 10 more minutes.

Nutrition Information

- Calories: 174 calories
- Protein: 6g protein.
- Total Fat: 10g fat (6g saturated fat)
- Sodium: 388mg sodium
- Fiber: 4g fiber)
- Total Carbohydrate: 16g carbohydrate (7g sugars
- Cholesterol: 31mg cholesterol

226. Cheesy Pasta Pea Bake

Serving: 12 servings. | Prep: 15mins | Cook: 35mins | Ready in:

Ingredients

- 12 ounces uncooked medium shell pasta
- 1/2 pound fresh mushrooms, quartered
- 1/2 cup chopped green onions
- 1 garlic clove, minced
- 2 tablespoons butter
- 2 tablespoons all-purpose flour
- 1 tablespoon cornstarch
- 3 cups whole milk
- 1/2 cup chicken broth
- 1 cup frozen peas
- 1 teaspoon chopped seeded jalapeno pepper
- 1/2 to 1 teaspoon salt
- 1/4 teaspoon pepper
- Dash hot pepper sauce
- 2 cups shredded cheddar cheese, divided
- 1-1/2 cups shredded Monterey Jack cheese
- 1/4 cup dry bread crumbs

Direction

- Cook pasta following the package directions. In the meantime, sauté garlic, onions, and the mushrooms in butter in a large skillet until tender for 5 minutes. Stir in cornstarch and flour until combined. Add the broth and milk gradually. Boil, then cook and stir until thickened for around 2 minutes. Reduce the heat. Add hot pepper sauce, pepper, salt, jalapeno, and peas; simmer for one minute. Put in 1 1/2 cups cheddar cheese and Monterey Jack cheese, stir until melted. Then, remove from the heat.
- Let the pasta drain and move to a greased 13x9-in. baking dish. Stir in the cheese sauce. Dust with the remaining cheddar cheese and breadcrumbs.

- Bake at 375°, uncovered, for 35-40 minutes, or until bubbly and golden brown.

Nutrition Information

- Calories:
- Fiber:
- Total Carbohydrate:
- Cholesterol:
- Protein:
- Total Fat:
- Sodium:

227. Cherry & Fontina Stuffed Portobellos

Serving: 12 servings. | Prep: 30mins | Cook: 15mins | Ready in:

Ingredients

- 6 large portobello mushrooms
- 1/2 cup butter, cubed
- 1 medium onion, chopped
- 1 cup pecan halves, toasted
- 1 package (5 ounces) dried tart cherries, coarsely chopped
- 1/2 teaspoon poultry seasoning
- 1/2 teaspoon dried thyme
- 7 ounces (about 4-1/2 cups) seasoned stuffing cubes
- 1-1/2 to 2 cups chicken broth
- 1-1/2 cups shredded fontina cheese, divided

Direction

- To preheat: set oven to 375°F. Use a damp paper towel to wipe clean the mushroom caps; get rid of stems and gills then throw them away. Use foil to line a 15x10-in. baking pan then arrange caps on the baking pan.
- Put butter in a large skillet then melt butter on medium heat till it begins to brown and you can smell nutty fragrance. Put in onion and sauté while mixing from time until clear. Add seasonings, cherries, pecans; cook and stir for 3 minutes. Take pan off the heat.
- Mix stuffing cubes and onion mixture, toss to coat evenly. Pour 1-1/2 cups broth to onion-stuffing mixture, stir till everything is mixed thoroughly. If needed, add the remaining of broth. Add a cup of cheese then stir.
- Fill mushroom caps with stuffing until mounded, each mushroom cap needs about a cup of stuffing. Use the remaining cheese to sprinkle. Bake for about 15 to 20 minutes till cheese is melted and mushrooms are heated thoroughly.

Nutrition Information

- Calories: 301 calories
- Sodium: 531mg sodium
- Fiber: 6g fiber)
- Total Carbohydrate: 27g carbohydrate (8g sugars
- Cholesterol: 37mg cholesterol
- Protein: 8g protein.
- Total Fat: 19g fat (8g saturated fat)

228. Citrus Veggie Stir Fry

Serving: 4 servings. | Prep: 10mins | Cook: 15mins | Ready in:

Ingredients

- 1 tablespoon cornstarch
- 1 cup orange juice
- 2 tablespoons balsamic vinegar
- 2 garlic cloves, minced
- 1 teaspoon grated orange zest
- 1/2 teaspoon ground ginger
- 1/8 teaspoon hot pepper sauce
- 1 cup sliced carrots
- 1 cup julienned sweet red pepper
- 1 cup julienned green pepper
- 1 tablespoon canola oil

- 1 cup sliced fresh mushrooms
- 2 cups fresh or frozen snow peas
- 1/2 cup sliced green onions
- 1/3 cup salted cashews
- 4 cups hot cooked rice

Direction

- Mix together the initial 7 ingredients in a bowl till blended; reserve. Stir-fry peppers and carrots with oil in a big nonstick skillet or wok for 5 minutes. Put in snow peas and mushrooms; stir-fry for 6 minutes. Put in green onions; stir-fry till vegetables are crisp-tender, about 3 minutes.
- Mix orange juice mixture and put into pan. Boil; cook and mix till thickened, about 2 minutes. Mix in cashews. Serve along with rice.

Nutrition Information

- Calories: 400 calories
- Fiber: 5g fiber)
- Total Carbohydrate: 71g carbohydrate (0 sugars
- Cholesterol: 0 cholesterol
- Protein: 9g protein. Diabetic Exchanges: 4 starch
- Total Fat: 10g fat (1g saturated fat)
- Sodium: 97mg sodium

229. Colorful Grilled Veggies

Serving: 6 servings. | Prep: 20mins | Cook: 10mins | Ready in:

Ingredients

- 10 cherry tomatoes, halved
- 2 celery ribs, thinly sliced
- 1 medium green pepper, sliced
- 1 medium sweet red pepper, sliced
- 1 medium red onion, sliced and separated into rings
- 1 cup sliced fresh mushrooms
- 1 tablespoon red wine vinegar
- 1 tablespoon olive oil
- 1 teaspoon lemon juice
- 1 garlic clove, minced
- 1 teaspoon dried basil
- 1/2 teaspoon salt
- 1/2 teaspoon pepper

Direction

- Split the vegetables among two of 18-inch square heavy-duty foil piece. Mix the remaining ingredients in a small bowl; drizzle on top of the vegetables. Fold and seal the foil around the veggies tightly. On medium heat, grill for 10-15 mins while covering or until the veggies are tender-crisp.

Nutrition Information

- Calories: 51 calories
- Total Fat: 3g fat (1g saturated fat)
- Sodium: 212mg sodium
- Fiber: 2g fiber)
- Total Carbohydrate: 7g carbohydrate (0 sugars)
- Cholesterol: 0 cholesterol
- Protein: 1g protein. Diabetic Exchanges: 2 vegetable.

230. Contest Winning Grilled Mushrooms

Serving: 4 servings. | Prep: 5mins | Cook: 10mins | Ready in:

Ingredients

- 1/2 pound medium fresh mushrooms
- 1/4 cup butter, melted
- 1/2 teaspoon dill weed
- 1/2 teaspoon garlic salt

Direction

- Thread mushrooms on 4 soaked wooden or metal skewers. Stir together garlic salt, dill, and butter, brush the mixture over the mushrooms.
- Grill over medium-high heat until soft, about 10-15 minutes, basting and flipping every 5 minutes.

Nutrition Information

- Calories:
- Protein:
- Total Fat:
- Sodium:
- Fiber:
- Total Carbohydrate:
- Cholesterol:

231. Contest Winning Mushroom Wild Rice

Serving: 12 servings. | Prep: 01hours20mins | Cook: 30mins | Ready in:

Ingredients

- 4 cups water
- 1 cup uncooked wild rice
- 1 teaspoon butter
- 1-1/2 teaspoons salt, divided
- 1/2 cup uncooked brown rice
- 8 bacon strips, diced
- 2 cups sliced fresh mushrooms
- 1 large onion, chopped
- 1 medium green pepper, chopped
- 1 medium sweet red pepper, chopped
- 1 celery rib, thinly sliced
- 1 can (14-1/2 ounces) beef broth
- 2 tablespoons cornstarch
- 1/4 cup cold water
- 1/2 cup slivered almonds

Direction

- Mix together 1/2 tsp. of salt, butter, wild rice and water in a big saucepan, then bring all to a boil. Lower heat and simmer, covered, about 40 minutes. Stir in brown rice, then place a cover and simmer until rice is softened, about 25 to 30 more minutes.
- In the meantime, cook bacon in a big skillet until crispy. Transfer the bacon to paper towels to drain and save 2 tbsp. of drippings. Sauté celery, peppers, onion and mushrooms in the reserved drippings until vegetables are soft. Stir in leftover salt and broth, then bring the mixture to a boil.
- Mix cold water and cornstarch till smooth, then stir into the mushroom mixture. Cook and stir until thickened, about 2 minutes, then stir in bacon and almonds. Drain rice and put in the mushroom mixture.
- Remove the rice mixture to a 13"x9" baking dish coated with grease. Bake, covered, at 350 degrees about 25 minutes. Take off the cover and bake until heated through, about 5 to 10 minutes more.

Nutrition Information

- Calories: 220 calories
- Total Fat: 12g fat (4g saturated fat)
- Sodium: 533mg sodium
- Fiber: 2g fiber)
- Total Carbohydrate: 23g carbohydrate (2g sugars
- Cholesterol: 11mg cholesterol
- Protein: 6g protein.

232. Creamy Mushroom Potato Bake

Serving: 10 servings. | Prep: 30mins | Cook: 20mins | Ready in:

Ingredients

- 2-1/2 to 3 pounds white potatoes, peeled and cubed
- 1 teaspoon salt, divided
- 1 medium onion, finely chopped
- 1/2 pound fresh mushrooms, chopped
- 3 tablespoons butter, divided
- 1/2 cup sour cream
- 1/4 teaspoon pepper
- 1/4 cup grated Parmesan cheese

Direction

- Put potatoes in a large saucepan and pour in water to cover. Put in a half teaspoon salt. Bring to a boil. Lower the heat; cover and cook until tender, about 10-15 minutes. Drain and mash without adding butter or milk.
- Sauté mushrooms and onion in 2 tablespoons butter in a large skillet until just tender, about 3-4 minutes. Mix into potatoes together with the rest of salt, pepper and sour cream.
- Spoon into a 2-qt. baking dish coated with grease. Scatter with cheese; dot with the rest of butter.
- Bake without a cover at 400° for 20-25 minutes or until heated through and golden brown.

Nutrition Information

- Calories: 141 calories
- Total Fat: 6g fat (4g saturated fat)
- Sodium: 317mg sodium
- Fiber: 2g fiber)
- Total Carbohydrate: 18g carbohydrate (3g sugars
- Cholesterol: 19mg cholesterol
- Protein: 4g protein.

233. Far North Wild Rice Casserole

Serving: 10-12 servings. | Prep: 10mins | Cook: 10mins | Ready in:

Ingredients

- 1 medium onion, chopped
- 1 medium green pepper, chopped
- 3/4 cup chopped celery
- 1/2 pound sliced bacon, diced
- 1/2 pound fresh mushrooms, sliced
- 6 cups cooked wild rice
- 1 cup frozen peas, optional
- 1 to 2 teaspoons soy sauce
- 1/4 teaspoon pepper

Direction

- Cook bacon, celery, green pepper and onion together in a big skillet for 3 minutes, until the vegetables are soft. Put in mushrooms and cook about 2 minutes, then drain. Put in pepper, soy sauce, rice and peas, if you want. Cook and stir on moderate heat gently about 5 minutes.

Nutrition Information

- Calories: 133 calories
- Sodium: 135mg sodium
- Fiber: 2g fiber)
- Total Carbohydrate: 20g carbohydrate (2g sugars
- Cholesterol: 5mg cholesterol
- Protein: 6g protein.
- Total Fat: 3g fat (1g saturated fat)

234. Five Veggie Stir Fry

Serving: 4 | Prep: 10mins | Cook: 30mins | Ready in:

Ingredients

- 1 cup uncooked white rice
- 2 cups reduced-sodium beef broth
- 2 tablespoons cornstarch
- 1/2 teaspoon ground ginger
- 1 cup orange juice
- 1/4 cup reduced-sodium soy sauce

- 1 tablespoon beef broth
- 1 teaspoon Worcestershire sauce
- 2 cloves garlic, minced
- 1 tablespoon olive oil
- 1 cup cubed firm tofu
- 2 large carrots, sliced
- 2 cups broccoli florets
- 2 cups cauliflower florets
- 1 teaspoon olive oil
- 1 cup quartered fresh mushrooms
- 1 cup fresh snow peas
- 1 egg, lightly beaten
- 1/4 cup slivered almonds

Direction

- On high heat, boil beef broth and rice in a saucepan. Lower heat to medium-low, put the cover on, and simmer for 20 to 25 minutes until rice is softened and liquid has been absorbed.
- In a small bowl, mix ginger and cornstarch. Mix in garlic, Worcestershire, beef broth, soy sauce and orange juice until blended.
- On medium-high heat, heat 3 tsp. of oil in a big pan; cook and stir cauliflower, broccoli, and carrots for 4 to 5 minutes until just softened. Put in tofu, snow peas, mushrooms and 1 tsp. of oil then keep on cooking till mushrooms are tender, about 3 minutes. Push vegetable mixture to one side of pan and cook and stir egg in remaining space until set; mix veggies with egg. Mix in orange juice mixture and boil for about 2 minutes until thickened.
- Serve on rice and use silvered almonds to top.

Nutrition Information

- Calories: 445 calories;
- Protein: 19
- Total Fat: 13.8
- Sodium: 676
- Total Carbohydrate: 64
- Cholesterol: 46

235. Flavorful Rice Dressing

Serving: 8 servings. | Prep: 20mins | Cook: 30mins | Ready in:

Ingredients

- 7 slices day-old bread, torn
- 1 cup torn corn bread
- 2/3 cup hot water
- 1/2 cup thinly sliced celery
- 1/2 cup chopped onion
- 1/2 cup sliced fresh mushrooms
- 1 tablespoon vegetable oil
- 1 cup firmly packed sliced fresh spinach
- 1 cup cooked long grain rice
- 1/2 cup cooked wild rice
- 1/2 cup orange juice
- 1 egg, beaten
- 2 teaspoons rubbed sage
- 1/2 teaspoon dried thyme
- 1/2 teaspoon salt
- 1/4 teaspoon sugar
- 1/4 teaspoon pepper

Direction

- Toss water and bread lightly in a big bowl. Sauté mushrooms, onion and celery in oil till tender in a skillet, stirring constantly. Mix into bread mixture. Add leftover ingredients; stir well. Put in a 2-qt. greased baking dish and cover; bake for 30 minutes at 350°.

Nutrition Information

- Calories: 162 calories
- Protein: 5g protein.
- Total Fat: 4g fat (1g saturated fat)
- Sodium: 364mg sodium
- Fiber: 2g fiber)
- Total Carbohydrate: 28g carbohydrate (4g sugars
- Cholesterol: 27mg cholesterol

236. French Peas

Serving: 1 serving. | Prep: 5mins | Cook: 10mins | Ready in:

Ingredients

- 1 teaspoon butter
- 2 teaspoons water
- 2 medium fresh mushrooms, thinly sliced
- 1/2 cup frozen peas
- 2 thin onion slices
- Pinch salt, optional

Direction

- In a small saucepan, melt butter, then put in all leftover ingredients. Cover and cook while stirring frequently, until peas are softened.

Nutrition Information

- Calories: 104 calories
- Sodium: 104mg sodium
- Fiber: 0 fiber)
- Total Carbohydrate: 13g carbohydrate (0 sugars
- Cholesterol: 0 cholesterol
- Protein: 4g protein. Diabetic Exchanges: 1 starch
- Total Fat: 1g fat (0 saturated fat)

237. Fresh Green Beans With Mushrooms

Serving: 1 serving. | Prep: 5mins | Cook: 10mins | Ready in:

Ingredients

- 3/4 cup cut fresh green beans (2-inch pieces)
- 2 tablespoons chopped onion
- 2 teaspoons butter
- 1/4 cup sliced fresh mushrooms
- Pepper to taste

Direction

- Cook beans in water in a saucepan until soft, about 6-8 minutes. Sauté onion in butter in a skillet until softened. Put in the mushrooms; cook and stir for a minute. Drain the beans, then add pepper and the mushroom mixture.

Nutrition Information

- Calories: 105 calories
- Protein: 2g protein. Diabetic Exchanges: 1-1/2 vegetable
- Total Fat: 8g fat (0 saturated fat)
- Sodium: 96mg sodium
- Fiber: 0 fiber)
- Total Carbohydrate: 9g carbohydrate (0 sugars
- Cholesterol: 0 cholesterol

238. Garden Saute

Serving: 6 servings. | Prep: 15mins | Cook: 5mins | Ready in:

Ingredients

- 1/4 cup chopped red onion
- 1 garlic clove, minced
- 2 teaspoons olive oil
- 1 medium yellow summer squash, sliced
- 1 medium zucchini, sliced
- 1/2 cup sliced fresh mushrooms
- 1 medium tomato, cut into wedges
- 1/4 cup chopped celery
- 1/2 teaspoon lemon juice
- 1/4 teaspoon dried rosemary, crushed
- 1/4 teaspoon dill weed
- 1/4 teaspoon Italian seasoning
- 1/8 teaspoon fennel seed
- 1/8 teaspoon pepper

Direction

- Sauté garlic and onion in oil in a large skillet coated with cooking spray until tender. Stir in the remaining ingredients gently. Cook, covered, for 5 to 7 minutes over medium heat until vegetables are softened.

Nutrition Information

- Calories: 36 calories
- Protein: 1g protein. Diabetic Exchanges: 1 vegetable.
- Total Fat: 2g fat (0 saturated fat)
- Sodium: 9mg sodium
- Fiber: 2g fiber)
- Total Carbohydrate: 5g carbohydrate (2g sugars
- Cholesterol: 0 cholesterol

239. Garlic Buttered Green Beans

Serving: 6 servings. | Prep: 5mins | Cook: 10mins | Ready in:

Ingredients

- 1 pound fresh or frozen green beans
- 1/2 cup sliced fresh mushrooms
- 6 tablespoons butter, cubed
- 2 to 3 teaspoons onion powder
- 1 to 1-1/2 teaspoons garlic powder
- Salt and pepper to taste

Direction

- Put green beans with enough water to cover in a big saucepan. Boil, cook while covered until they are crisp-tender, about 8 to 10 minutes.
- In the meantime, sauté mushrooms in butter in a big frying pan until tender. Add garlic powder and onion powder. Drain the beans, mix them into the frying pan. Add pepper and salt for seasoning.

Nutrition Information

- Calories:
- Total Carbohydrate:
- Cholesterol:
- Protein:
- Total Fat:
- Sodium:
- Fiber:

240. Green Beans With Mushrooms

Serving: 6 servings. | Prep: 10mins | Cook: 10mins | Ready in:

Ingredients

- 2 cloves garlic, minced
- 1/4 pound small, fresh mushrooms, trimmed and sliced
- 1 tablespoon butter
- 1 medium red onion, cut in thin strips
- 1 pound fresh green beans, trimmed
- Fresh ground pepper
- 1 teaspoon dill weed
- 2 tablespoons toasted almonds or pine nuts

Direction

- Add mushrooms and garlic to butter, sauté until they get tender. Mix in onions and set aside. Steam or cook beans with a little water until they are crisp-tender then drain. Mix the beans with mushroom mixture, add dill weed and pepper. Use nuts for decoration. Serve right away.

Nutrition Information

- Calories: 75 calories
- Sodium: 35mg sodium
- Fiber: 0 fiber)

- Total Carbohydrate: 10g carbohydrate (0 sugars
- Cholesterol: 6mg cholesterol
- Protein: 3g protein. Diabetic Exchanges: 1 vegetable
- Total Fat: 4g fat (0 saturated fat)

241. Grill Bread

Serving: 4 servings. | Prep: 15mins | Cook: 5mins | Ready in:

Ingredients

- 4 frozen Texas-size white dinner rolls (2 ounces each), thawed
- 2 garlic cloves, minced
- 2 tablespoons olive oil
- 1/2 pound fresh mushrooms, sliced
- 1 small onion, cut into thin wedges
- 1 medium green pepper, sliced
- 1 medium sweet yellow pepper, sliced
- 1 medium sweet red pepper, sliced
- 1/2 cup fresh snow peas
- 3/4 teaspoon salt
- 1/8 teaspoon pepper
- 1/2 teaspoon dried oregano

Direction

- On a surface lightly scattered with flour, roll each roll out into a circle, about 8-10 inches, flipping the dough often; put aside.
- Sauté garlic in oil in a big skillet until soft. Add mushrooms, sauté for 2-3 minutes. Add oregano, pepper, salt, peas, peppers, and onion; cook until crunchy and soft, about 3 minutes.
- In the meantime, grill bread without a cover over medium-high heat until turning light brown, about 30-45 seconds each side. Stuff the vegetable mixture in and enjoy immediately. You can reheat the bread in the microwave.

Nutrition Information

- Calories: 153 calories
- Sodium: 493mg sodium
- Fiber: 3g fiber)
- Total Carbohydrate: 19g carbohydrate (6g sugars
- Cholesterol: 0 cholesterol
- Protein: 4g protein.
- Total Fat: 8g fat (1g saturated fat)

242. Grilled Dijon Summer Squash

Serving: 8 servings. | Prep: 20mins | Cook: 10mins | Ready in:

Ingredients

- 1/4 cup olive oil
- 2 tablespoons red wine vinegar
- 1-1/2 teaspoons minced fresh oregano or 1/2 teaspoon dried oregano
- 1-1/2 teaspoons Dijon mustard
- 1 garlic clove, minced
- 1/4 teaspoon salt
- 1/8 teaspoon pepper
- 2 medium zucchini, cut into 1/2-inch slices
- 2 medium yellow summer squash, cut into 1/2-inch slices
- 1 medium red onions, quartered
- 1 small sweet red pepper, cut into 2-inch pieces
- 1 small sweet yellow pepper, cut into 2-inch pieces
- 6 to 8 whole fresh mushrooms
- 6 cherry tomatoes

Direction

- Blend the pepper, salt, garlic, mustard, oregano, vinegar, and oil in a jar covered by a tight-fitting lid. In a shallow baking dish, arrange the vegetables. Put marinade and coat

by tossing. Allow to stand for 15 minutes. Let the marinade drain and discard.
- On a vegetable grill rack, arrange the vegetables. Put a cover on and grill on medium heat until tender or 10-12 minutes.

Nutrition Information

- Calories:
- Fiber:
- Total Carbohydrate:
- Cholesterol:
- Protein:
- Total Fat:
- Sodium:

243. Grilled Mushroom Kabobs

Serving: 4 servings | Prep: 25mins | Cook: | Ready in:

Ingredients

- 1/2 lb. spaghetti, uncooked
- 1/4 cup BULL'S-EYE Sweet & Tangy Barbecue Sauce
- 2 cloves garlic, minced
- 1 tsp. minced gingerroot
- 1 lb. each cremini and shiitake mushrooms

Direction

- Follow the package directions on how to cook the spaghetti; just omit the salt.
- Combine garlic, ginger, and barbecue sauce until well-blended. Thread the mushrooms alternately on the eight skewers.
- Grill the mushrooms, turning and basting occasionally with the barbecue sauce mixture for 12 minutes.
- Drain the cooked spaghetti and serve it with mushrooms.

Nutrition Information

- Calories: 300
- Total Fat: 2 g
- Saturated Fat: 0 g
- Sugar: 10 g
- Cholesterol: 0 mg
- Protein: 14 g
- Sodium: 180 mg
- Fiber: 6 g
- Total Carbohydrate: 61 g

244. Grilled Vegetable Medley

Serving: 8-10 servings. | Prep: 10mins | Cook: 40mins | Ready in:

Ingredients

- 12 small red potatoes, halved
- 1 medium sweet potato, peeled and cut into chunks
- 4 tablespoons butter, melted, divided
- 4 to 6 garlic cloves, minced, divided
- 2 tablespoons minced fresh parsley, divided
- 1-1/2 teaspoons salt, divided
- 1/2 teaspoon lemon-pepper seasoning, divided
- 3/4 pound whole fresh mushrooms
- 1 large onion, sliced
- 1 medium green pepper, cut into 1/4-inch slices
- 1 small zucchini, cut into chunks
- 1 medium yellow summer squash, cut into chunks
- 1 cup shredded part-skim mozzarella cheese or shredded Swiss cheese
- Sour cream, optional

Direction

- On a 15"x18" heavy-duty foil piece, add potatoes and sweet potato, then drizzle 1/2 of the garlic, lemon-pepper, salt and parsley over top, sealing packet tightly. Grill with a cover

- for 20 minutes per side, on indirect moderately hot heat.
- In the meantime, on a 20"x18" heavy-duty foil piece, place summer squash, zucchini, green pepper, onion and mushrooms. Drizzle leftover butter over top and sprinkle over with leftover seasonings. Seal packet tightly, then grill with a cover on moderately hot heat until vegetables are tender yet still crispy, about 10 minutes per side.
- In a serving bowl, mix the contents of both packets together, then sprinkle cheese over top. Serve together with sour cream, if wanted.

Nutrition Information

- Calories:
- Sodium:
- Fiber:
- Total Carbohydrate:
- Cholesterol:
- Protein:
- Total Fat:

245. Harvest Vegetables

Serving: 6 servings. | Prep: 10mins | Cook: 30mins | Ready in:

Ingredients

- 1 small head cabbage
- 2 tablespoons butter, softened
- 1/2 to 1 teaspoon onion salt, optional
- 1/8 to 1/4 teaspoon pepper
- 4 medium carrots, cut into 1-inch pieces
- 2 celery ribs, cut into 1-inch pieces
- 1 small onion, cut into wedges
- 1/2 pound whole fresh mushrooms
- 1 small green pepper, cut into pieces
- 4 bacon strips, cooked and crumbled, optional

Direction

- Chop the cabbage into six wedges; spread the butter on the cut sides. Arrange the cabbage onto one piece of the heavy-duty foil (roughly 24x18 inch). Drizzle with the onion salt, if you want, and pepper.
- Arrange green pepper, mushrooms, onion, celery and carrots around the cabbage. Drizzle with the bacon if you want. Fold the foil over the mixture and seal it tightly.
- Grill, while covering, on medium hot heat till the veggies soften or for half an hour, flip once in a while. Open the foil carefully to let the steam escape.

Nutrition Information

- Calories: 99 calories
- Total Fat: 4g fat (2g saturated fat)
- Sodium: 89mg sodium
- Fiber: 5g fiber)
- Total Carbohydrate: 14g carbohydrate (7g sugars
- Cholesterol: 10mg cholesterol
- Protein: 3g protein. Diabetic Exchanges: 1 starch

246. Hawaiian Kabobs

Serving: 8 servings. | Prep: 15mins | Cook: 20mins | Ready in:

Ingredients

- 1 can (20 ounces) unsweetened pineapple chunks
- 2 large green peppers, cut into 1-inch pieces
- 1 large onion, quartered, optional
- 12 to 16 fresh mushrooms
- 16 to 18 cherry tomatoes
- 1/2 cup soy sauce
- 1/4 cup olive oil
- 1 tablespoon brown sugar
- 2 teaspoons ground ginger
- 1 teaspoon garlic powder

- 1 teaspoon ground mustard
- 1/4 teaspoon pepper
- Cooked rice, optional

Direction

- Reserve 1/2 cup of the juice from the can of pineapples. Take the pineapple fruit and mix with the vegetables in a large bowl; set aside for later. Stir together the 1/2 cup pineapple juice, olive oil, soy sauce, brown sugar, and seasonings in a small saucepan. Let the mixture boil, then lower the heat to simmer without lid for 5 minutes. Pour this over the fruit and vegetable mix, then cover and refrigerate for 1 hour, minimum. Stir occasionally within the marinating period. Take out the pineapples and vegetables; reserve the marinade. Alternately skewer green peppers, pineapples, mushrooms, tomatoes, and, if desired, the onions. Do this on eight metal or pre-soaked wooden skewers. Grill until soft, about 20 minutes, with frequent turning and brushing with marinade. May serve with warm rice.

Nutrition Information

- Calories: 141 calories
- Protein: 4g protein.
- Total Fat: 7g fat (1g saturated fat)
- Sodium: 932mg sodium
- Fiber: 2g fiber)
- Total Carbohydrate: 16g carbohydrate (12g sugars
- Cholesterol: 0 cholesterol

247. Heavenly Onion Casserole

Serving: 6-8 servings. | Prep: 15mins | Cook: 45mins | Ready in:

Ingredients

- 2 tablespoons butter
- 3 medium sweet Spanish onions, sliced
- 8 ounces fresh mushrooms, sliced
- 1 cup shredded Swiss cheese
- 1 can (10-3/4 ounces) condensed cream of mushroom soup, undiluted
- 1 can (5 ounces) evaporated milk
- 2 teaspoons soy sauce
- 6 to 8 slices French bread (1/2 inch thick)
- 6 to 8 thin slices Swiss cheese (about 4 ounces)

Direction

- In a large skillet, heat butter on medium-high heat until melted. Sauté mushrooms and onions until tender. Transfer into an 11x7-inch baking dish or 2-quart baking dish. Spread top with shredded cheese. Mix soy sauce, milk, and soup; transfer over cheese. Spread top with cheese slices and bread. Cover and put in the refrigerator for 4 hours or overnight.
- Take out from the refrigerator 30 minutes before baking. Use foil to cover loosely and bake at 375° for 30 minutes. Remove the cover and bake for an additional 15 to 20 minutes until heated thoroughly. Allow to stand for 5 minutes before serving.

Nutrition Information

- Calories: 249 calories
- Total Carbohydrate: 16g carbohydrate (6g sugars
- Cholesterol: 46mg cholesterol
- Protein: 12g protein.
- Total Fat: 15g fat (9g saturated fat)
- Sodium: 509mg sodium
- Fiber: 2g fiber)

248. Italian Mushrooms

Serving: 6 servings. | Prep: 10mins | Cook: 04hours00mins | Ready in:

Ingredients

- 1 pound medium fresh mushrooms
- 1 large onion, sliced
- 1/2 cup butter, melted
- 1 envelope Italian salad dressing mix

Direction

- Arrange onion and mushrooms in layer in a 3-quart slow cooker. Stir together salad dressing mix and butter; drizzle over vegetables. Cook, covered, for 4 to 5 hours on low setting until all vegetables are softened. Serve with a slotted spoon.

Nutrition Information

- Calories: 99 calories
- Cholesterol: 20mg cholesterol
- Protein: 3g protein.
- Total Fat: 8g fat (5g saturated fat)
- Sodium: 281mg sodium
- Fiber: 1g fiber)
- Total Carbohydrate: 6g carbohydrate (3g sugars

249. Italian Veggie Skillet

Serving: 2-3 servings. | Prep: 10mins | Cook: 15mins | Ready in:

Ingredients

- 1 medium yellow summer squash, cut into 1/4-inch slices
- 1/2 cup sliced fresh mushrooms
- 1 tablespoon olive oil
- 1 cup cherry tomatoes, halved
- 1/2 teaspoon salt
- 1/2 teaspoon minced garlic
- 2 tablespoons minced fresh parsley
- 1-1/2 teaspoons minced fresh rosemary or 1/2 teaspoon dried rosemary, crushed
- 1-1/2 teaspoons minced fresh thyme or 1/2 teaspoon dried thyme
- 1-1/2 teaspoons plus 2 tablespoons minced fresh basil, divided
- 2 tablespoons sliced green onion
- 2 tablespoons grated Parmesan cheese

Direction

- Sauté mushrooms and squash for 4 to 5 minutes in oil in a large skillet until tender. Add garlic, salt, and tomatoes. Lower heat; simmer without covering for 6 to 8 minutes.
- Mix in 1.5 teaspoons basil, thyme, rosemary, and parsley; cook until thoroughly heated, 1 to 2 minutes more. Ladle into serving bowl to serve. Sprinkle with the remaining basil and onion; toss lightly. Top with Parmesan cheese.

Nutrition Information

- Calories: 86 calories
- Protein: 3g protein.
- Total Fat: 6g fat (1g saturated fat)
- Sodium: 464mg sodium
- Fiber: 2g fiber)
- Total Carbohydrate: 7g carbohydrate (3g sugars
- Cholesterol: 3mg cholesterol

250. Kasha Varnishkes

Serving: Makes 8 servings. | Prep: 5mins | Cook: | Ready in:

Ingredients

- 1/2 lb. (8 oz.) bow tie pasta , uncooked
- 1 cup whole kasha
- 1 egg white
- 2 Tbsp. butter or margarine
- 1 medium onion , chopped
- 1 can (14-1/2 oz.) chicken broth

- 1 env. GOOD SEASONS Garlic & Herb Dressing Mix
- 2 Tbsp. chopped fresh parsley

Direction

- Cook pasta following the package instructions. In a medium-sized bowl, combine egg white and kasha till combined.
- Place a big nonstick skillet on medium-high heat. Add the kasha mixture, cook until the grains have dried out and separated, tossing often, about 3 minutes. Add butter, toss until melted. Add onion; cook until the onion is crunchy and soft, about 3 minutes, mixing often. Pour in dressing mix, 1/2 cup water, and chicken broth; boil it. Put a cover on. Lower the heat to medium-low, simmer until the kasha is tender, about 10-15 minutes. Take away from heat. Let sit with a cover on for 10 minutes.
- Mix in the cooked pasta. Sprinkle parsley over.

Nutrition Information

- Calories: 240
- Total Fat: 4 g
- Sodium: 540 mg
- Cholesterol: 10 mg
- Protein: 8 g
- Saturated Fat: 2 g
- Fiber: 2 g
- Sugar: 3 g
- Total Carbohydrate: 42 g

251. Lentil White Bean Pilaf

Serving: 10 servings. | Prep: 35mins | Cook: 15mins | Ready in:

Ingredients

- 1 cup dried lentils, rinsed
- 1/2 cup quick-cooking barley
- 1/2 cup quinoa, rinsed
- 1/3 cup uncooked long grain rice
- 1/2 pound sliced baby portobello mushrooms
- 3 medium carrots, finely chopped
- 3 celery ribs, finely chopped
- 1 large onion, finely chopped
- 1/4 cup butter, cubed
- 3 garlic cloves, minced
- 2 teaspoons minced fresh rosemary or 1/2 teaspoon dried rosemary, crushed
- 1/2 cup vegetable broth
- 1/2 teaspoon salt
- 1/2 teaspoon pepper
- 2 cups canned white kidney or cannellini beans, rinsed and drained

Direction

- Cook rice, quinoa, barley, and lentils following the package instructions; put aside.
- Sauté onion, celery, carrots, and mushrooms with butter in a Dutch oven until soft. Add rosemary and garlic, cook for another 1 minute. Add pepper, salt, and broth, mixing to loosen up the browned bits from the pan. Mix in the cooked rice, quinoa, barley, lentils, and the beans; cook until heated through.

Nutrition Information

- Calories: 259 calories
- Total Carbohydrate: 41g carbohydrate (3g sugars
- Cholesterol: 12mg cholesterol
- Protein: 11g protein.
- Total Fat: 6g fat (3g saturated fat)
- Sodium: 290mg sodium
- Fiber: 11g fiber)

252. Makeover Sausage Pecan Stuffing

Serving: 12 servings. | Prep: 30mins | Cook: 30mins | Ready in:

Ingredients

- 1 pound lean ground turkey
- 2 cups sliced fresh mushrooms
- 2 celery ribs, chopped
- 1 medium onion, chopped
- 1 teaspoon fennel seed
- 1/4 teaspoon cayenne pepper
- 1/8 teaspoon ground nutmeg
- 3 garlic cloves, minced
- 1 loaf (16 ounces) day-old white bread, cubed
- 1 large tart apple, chopped
- 2 teaspoons rubbed sage
- 1-1/2 teaspoons salt
- 1-1/2 teaspoons poultry seasoning
- 1/2 teaspoon pepper
- 2 eggs
- 1 cup reduced-sodium chicken broth
- 1/2 cup chopped pecans

Direction

- Cook the nutmeg, cayenne, fennel seed, onion, celery, mushrooms and turkey in a Dutch oven on medium heat, until the turkey has no visible pink color. Add garlic and let it cook for an additional 1 minute, then drain.
- Move to a big bowl, then add the pepper, poultry seasoning, salt, sage, apple and bread. Whisk the broth and eggs, then pour it on top of the bread mixture and toss until coated. Move to a cooking spray coated 13x9-inch baking dish and sprinkle pecans on top.
- Let it bake for 30-35 minutes at 350 degrees without cover or until a thermometer registers 160 degrees and the top turns light brown.

Nutrition Information

- Calories: 226 calories
- Fiber: 2g fiber)
- Total Carbohydrate: 25g carbohydrate (5g sugars
- Cholesterol: 65mg cholesterol
- Protein: 12g protein. Diabetic Exchanges: 1-1/2 starch
- Total Fat: 9g fat (2g saturated fat)
- Sodium: 654mg sodium

253. Mixed Veggies

Serving: 8 servings. | Prep: 10mins | Cook: 15mins | Ready in:

Ingredients

- 2 cups sliced fresh mushrooms
- 1/2 cup chopped onion
- 2 tablespoons butter
- 2 packages (16 ounces each) frozen peas, thawed
- 1 can (8 ounces) sliced water chestnuts, drained and halved
- 1/4 cup soy sauce

Direction

- In big saucepan, sauté onion and mushrooms in butter. Put in soy sauce, water chestnuts and peas. Cook for roughly 10 minutes or till thoroughly heated.

Nutrition Information

- Calories: 128 calories
- Cholesterol: 8mg cholesterol
- Protein: 7g protein. Diabetic Exchanges: 1 starch
- Total Fat: 3g fat (2g saturated fat)
- Sodium: 478mg sodium
- Fiber: 8g fiber)
- Total Carbohydrate: 19g carbohydrate (0 sugars

254. Mushroom Barley Bake

Serving: 8-10 servings. | Prep: 15mins | Cook: 01hours30mins | Ready in:

Ingredients

- 3/4 pound sliced fresh mushrooms
- 2 medium onions, chopped
- 1/4 cup butter
- 1-1/2 cups medium pearl barley
- 1 jar (2 ounces) diced pimientos, drained
- 6 teaspoons chicken bouillon, divided
- 4 cups boiling water, divided

Direction

- Sauté onions and mushrooms with butter in a skillet until soft. Mix in pimientos and barley. Remove into a 13x9-in. baking dish coated with oil. Add 3 teaspoons bouillon to 2 cups water to dissolve, then mix into the barley mixture. Put a cover on and bake for 1 hour at 325°.
- Add the leftover bouillon to the leftover water to dissolve; mix into the barley mixture. Bake without a cover until the barley is soft and has absorbed the liquid, about another 30 minutes.

Nutrition Information

- Calories: 171 calories
- Fiber: 6g fiber)
- Total Carbohydrate: 28g carbohydrate (3g sugars
- Cholesterol: 13mg cholesterol
- Protein: 5g protein.
- Total Fat: 5g fat (3g saturated fat)
- Sodium: 556mg sodium

255. Mushroom Cornbread Dressing

Serving: 12 servings. | Prep: 20mins | Cook: 01hours05mins | Ready in:

Ingredients

- 2 cups cornmeal
- 3 teaspoons sugar
- 3 teaspoons baking powder
- 1 teaspoon salt
- 5 large eggs
- 1 can (12 ounces) evaporated milk
- 1/4 cup vegetable oil
- 2 cups chopped fresh mushrooms
- 1 cup chopped celery
- 1/2 cup chopped green onions
- 3 tablespoons butter
- 2 cans (14-1/2 ounces each) chicken broth
- 1 can (10-3/4 ounces) condensed cream of chicken soup, undiluted
- 1/4 cup sliced almonds, toasted
- 1 teaspoon poultry seasoning
- 1/4 teaspoon pepper

Direction

- Mix the first four ingredients in a bowl to make the cornbread. Mix milk, oil, and 2 eggs, and then pour it into the dry mixture. Whisk the mixture until just moistened. Transfer the mixture to the greased 9-inches square baking pan. Bake inside the 400° oven for 18-20 minutes until an inserted toothpick comes out clean. Cool on a wire rack.
- Sauté the onions, mushrooms, and celery in butter in a skillet until tender. Whisk the remaining eggs in a large bowl, and then add the poultry seasoning, vegetables, pepper, broth, almonds, and soup. Crumble the cornbread all over the mixture.
- Transfer the mixture to the greased 13x9-inches baking dish. Let it bake uncovered inside the 350° oven for 45-50 minutes until an inserted knife comes out clean.

Nutrition Information

- Calories: 267 calories
- Fiber: 3g fiber)
- Total Carbohydrate: 26g carbohydrate (5g sugars
- Cholesterol: 108mg cholesterol
- Protein: 8g protein.
- Total Fat: 14g fat (5g saturated fat)

- Sodium: 725mg sodium

256. Mushroom Pea Casserole

Serving: 10 servings. | Prep: 10mins | Cook: 25mins | Ready in:

Ingredients

- 1 tablespoon butter
- 1 pound sliced fresh mushrooms
- 6 cups frozen peas, thawed (about 2 pounds)
- 1 can (10-1/2 ounces) condensed cream of celery soup, undiluted
- 1/2 cup whole milk
- 1 package (2.80 ounces) french-fried onions

Direction

- Turn the oven to 350° to preheat. Heat butter in a big frying pan over medium heat. Put in mushrooms, sauté until soft. Mix in milk, soup, and peas. Transfer into an oil-coated 11x7-inch baking dish. Sprinkle onions over. Bake without a cover for 25-30 minutes until fully heated.

Nutrition Information

- Calories: 163 calories
- Cholesterol: 6mg cholesterol
- Protein: 6g protein.
- Total Fat: 7g fat (2g saturated fat)
- Sodium: 330mg sodium
- Fiber: 5g fiber)
- Total Carbohydrate: 19g carbohydrate (6g sugars

257. Mushroom And Rice Pilaf

Serving: 10 servings. | Prep: 15mins | Cook: 03hours00mins | Ready in:

Ingredients

- 1/2 cup butter, cubed
- 2 cups uncooked long grain rice
- 1/2 pound sliced fresh mushrooms
- 8 green onions, chopped
- 2 teaspoons dried oregano
- 2 cans (10-1/2 ounces each) condensed beef broth, undiluted
- 1-1/2 cups water

Direction

- Heat butter in a big saucepan over medium heat. Put in rice; stir and cook for 5-6 minutes until slightly browned. Remove to a 3-quart slow cooker. Add in oregano, green onions, and mushrooms. Mix in water and broth. Cover and cook on low for 3-4 hours, until liquid is absorbed and rice is tender.

Nutrition Information

- Calories: 246 calories
- Protein: 6g protein.
- Total Fat: 10g fat (6g saturated fat)
- Sodium: 490mg sodium
- Fiber: 1g fiber)
- Total Carbohydrate: 34g carbohydrate (1g sugars
- Cholesterol: 24mg cholesterol

258. Northwoods Wild Rice

Serving: 6-8 servings. | Prep: 25mins | Cook: 50mins | Ready in:

Ingredients

- 1-1/2 cups uncooked wild rice, rinsed
- 4 cups water
- 1 teaspoon salt
- 1/4 cup butter, cubed
- 4 slices bacon, diced
- 1 small onion, chopped

- 1/2 cup celery, sliced
- 1/2 cup sliced fresh mushrooms
- Seasoned salt to taste
- 1/4 teaspoon pepper
- 1/2 cup salted cashews

Direction

- In a heavy saucepan, put salt, water and rice. Boil. Lower heat to simmer; cook till tender, about 45 minutes. Remove cover and fluff using a fork. Let simmer for 5 minutes more. Drain the liquid. Meanwhile, fry bacon till crisp. Drain on paper towels. Melt butter and sauté mushrooms, celery and onion in a skillet till tender. Put in pepper, seasoned salt and rice. Heat through. Put cashews and leftover bacon on top just prior to serving.
- For make-ahead dish, place cooked rice mixture in a 2-qt. casserole; top with cashews and bacon. Chill till ready to reheat. Bake at 350° for 20 minutes to half an hour.

Nutrition Information

- Calories: 306 calories
- Total Fat: 18g fat (7g saturated fat)
- Sodium: 506mg sodium
- Fiber: 2g fiber)
- Total Carbohydrate: 30g carbohydrate (1g sugars
- Cholesterol: 23mg cholesterol
- Protein: 7g protein.

259. Orange Vegetable Kabobs

Serving: 8 kabobs. | Prep: 20mins | Cook: 10mins | Ready in:

Ingredients

- 1 large sweet onion
- 1 large unpeeled navel orange
- 1 medium sweet red pepper, cut into 1-inch pieces
- 1 medium sweet yellow pepper, cut into 1-inch pieces
- 8 medium fresh mushrooms
- 8 cherry tomatoes
- 2 small yellow summer squash, cut into 1-inch slices
- MARINADE:
- 1/2 cup olive oil
- 1/3 cup lemon juice
- 1-1/2 teaspoons sugar
- 1 teaspoon salt, optional
- 1/4 teaspoon garlic powder
- 1/4 teaspoon pepper
- 2 tablespoons orange juice

Direction

- Slice the orange and the onion into eight wedges and proceed to halve the wedges. Skewer the vegetables and the orange wedges alternately, portioned out to eight metal or wooden skewers that have been soaked. Place the skewers in a shallow oval dish. Whisk together lemon juice, oil, sugar, pepper, garlic powder, and some salt, if desired, in a small bowl. Drizzle the mixture over the skewers and let sit for 15 minutes, turning the skewers and basting them frequently. Drain marinade; discard liquid. Grill with cover on medium indirect heat for 10-14 minutes, until vegetables are tender on the inside but still crisp on the outside. Brush the vegetables with orange juice right before serving

Nutrition Information

- Calories: 111 calories
- Fiber: 3g fiber)
- Total Carbohydrate: 12g carbohydrate (0 sugars
- Cholesterol: 0 cholesterol
- Protein: 2g protein. Diabetic Exchanges: 2 vegetable
- Total Fat: 7g fat (0 saturated fat)

- Sodium: 13mg sodium

260. Orange Scented Leeks & Mushrooms

Serving: 7 servings. | Prep: 20mins | Cook: 40mins | Ready in:

Ingredients

- 4 pounds medium leeks (white and light green portions only), thinly sliced (about 8 cups)
- 1 pound sliced fresh mushrooms
- 2 tablespoons olive oil
- 1/4 cup sherry or reduced-sodium chicken broth
- 1/2 cup reduced-sodium chicken broth
- 1 tablespoon balsamic vinegar
- 1 teaspoon orange juice
- 1/2 teaspoon grated orange zest
- 1/4 teaspoon salt
- 1/4 teaspoon minced fresh thyme or dash dried thyme
- 1/8 teaspoon pepper

Direction

- In the Dutch oven, cook the mushrooms and leeks in oil in batches on medium heat till becoming soft or for 15 to 20 minutes, mixing once in a while. Bring all back into the pan. Put in the sherry, whisking to loosen the browned bits from the pan.
- Mix in the rest of the ingredients; cook and stir till the liquid has been nearly evaporated or for 10 to 15 minutes.

Nutrition Information

- Calories: 215 calories
- Protein: 6g protein.
- Total Fat: 5g fat (1g saturated fat)
- Sodium: 180mg sodium
- Fiber: 5g fiber)

- Total Carbohydrate: 40g carbohydrate (12g sugars
- Cholesterol: 0 cholesterol

261. Peas With Mushrooms

Serving: 4 | Prep: 10mins | Cook: 10mins | Ready in:

Ingredients

- 1 small onion, chopped
- 2 cloves garlic, minced
- 2 tablespoons butter
- 1 (10 ounce) package frozen green peas, thawed
- 1 (4.5 ounce) jar sliced mushrooms, drained
- 1 teaspoon white sugar
- 1/2 teaspoon salt
- 1/4 teaspoon dried thyme
- 1 pinch black pepper

Direction

- Cook peas as directed on package. Put to one side.
- In a skillet, melt butter over medium heat. Sauté garlic and onion in butter for about 5 minutes until softened. Mix in mushrooms and peas, then sprinkle with pepper, thyme, salt, and sugar to season. Turn heat down to low and keep cooking until heated through.

Nutrition Information

- Calories: 128 calories;
- Sodium: 546
- Total Carbohydrate: 14.7
- Cholesterol: 15
- Protein: 4.7
- Total Fat: 6.2

262. Roasted Green Vegetable Medley

Serving: 10 servings | Prep: 20mins | Cook: 20mins | Ready in:

Ingredients

- 1 pound fresh green beans, trimmed and cut into 2-inch pieces
- 4 cups fresh broccoli florets
- 10 small fresh mushrooms, halved
- 8 fresh Brussels sprouts, halved
- 2 medium carrots, cut into 1/4-inch slices
- 1 medium onion, halved and sliced
- 3 to 5 garlic cloves, thinly sliced
- 4 tablespoons olive oil, divided
- 1/2 cup grated Parmesan cheese
- 3 tablespoons julienned fresh basil leaves, optional
- 2 tablespoons minced fresh parsley
- 1 tablespoon grated lemon peel
- 2 tablespoons lemon juice
- 1/4 teaspoon salt
- 1/4 teaspoon pepper

Direction

- Preheat the oven to 425 degrees F. In a big bowl, combine the first 7 ingredients and mix with 2tbsp oil. Split among two 15-in x 10-in x 1-in pans coated with cooking spray.
- Roast for 20-25mins until tender, mix from time to time; move to a big bowl. Combine the left ingredients with the leftover oil; mix with the veggies.

Nutrition Information

- Calories: 109 calories
- Sodium: 96mg sodium
- Fiber: 3g fiber)
- Total Carbohydrate: 10g carbohydrate (3g sugars
- Cholesterol: 3mg cholesterol
- Protein: 4g protein. Diabetic Exchanges: 1 vegetable
- Total Fat: 7g fat (1g saturated fat)

263. Roasted Veggie Orzo

Serving: 8 servings. | Prep: 25mins | Cook: 20mins | Ready in:

Ingredients

- 1-1/2 cups fresh mushrooms, halved
- 1 medium zucchini, chopped
- 1 medium sweet yellow pepper, chopped
- 1 medium sweet red pepper, chopped
- 1 small red onion, cut into wedges
- 1 cup cut fresh asparagus (1-inch pieces)
- 1 tablespoon olive oil
- 1 teaspoon each dried oregano, thyme and rosemary, crushed
- 1/2 teaspoon salt
- 1-1/4 cups uncooked orzo pasta
- 1/4 cup crumbled feta cheese

Direction

- In a cooking spray-coated 15x10x1-inch baking pan, put vegetables. Use oil to drizzle and seasonings to sprinkle; stir to coat. Bake at 400° until soft, or for 20-25 minutes, tossing from time to time.
- In the meantime, cook orzo following the package instructions. Strain, remove into a serving bowl. Mix in the roasted vegetables. Use cheese to sprinkle.

Nutrition Information

- Calories: 164 calories
- Total Carbohydrate: 28g carbohydrate (3g sugars
- Cholesterol: 2mg cholesterol
- Protein: 6g protein. Diabetic Exchanges: 1-1/2 starch
- Total Fat: 3g fat (1g saturated fat)
- Sodium: 188mg sodium

- Fiber: 3g fiber)

264. Saucy Mushrooms

Serving: 4 servings. | Prep: 5mins | Cook: 10mins | Ready in:

Ingredients

- 1 pound fresh mushrooms, halved
- 2 tablespoons olive oil
- 1/2 cup water, divided
- 1 tablespoon soy sauce
- 1/4 teaspoon sugar
- 2 teaspoons cornstarch

Direction

- Stir-fry the mushrooms in a nonstick frypan with oil for 2 minutes. Mix together the sugar, soy sauce and a quarter cup of water, then pour on top of the mushrooms and toss until coated. Let it cook and stir for 1 to 2 minutes.
- Mix together the leftover water and cornstarch until it becomes smooth, then slowly mix into the mushrooms and boil. Let it cook and stir until it becomes thick or for 2 minutes.

Nutrition Information

- Calories: 97 calories
- Protein: 4g protein. Diabetic Exchanges: 2 vegetable
- Total Fat: 7g fat (1g saturated fat)
- Sodium: 156mg sodium
- Fiber: 1g fiber)
- Total Carbohydrate: 6g carbohydrate (0 sugars
- Cholesterol: 0 cholesterol

265. Sausage And Mushroom Corn Bread Dressing

Serving: 9 cups. | Prep: 20mins | Cook: 55mins | Ready in:

Ingredients

- 1-1/2 cups yellow cornmeal
- 1/2 cup all-purpose flour
- 1 teaspoon baking powder
- 1/2 teaspoon baking soda
- 1/2 teaspoon salt
- 1-1/2 cups 2% milk
- 2 large eggs
- 1/4 cup plus 1 tablespoon olive oil, divided
- 1 tablespoon honey
- 1 tablespoon cider vinegar
- CORN BREAD DRESSING:
- 1/2 pound Jones No Sugar Pork Sausage Roll sausage
- 8 ounces sliced fresh mushrooms
- 3 celery ribs, chopped
- 1 large onion, chopped
- 1-1/2 cups soft whole wheat bread crumbs (3-4 slices)
- 3 large eggs, beaten
- 1 carton (32 ounces) reduced-sodium chicken broth
- 1 tablespoon minced fresh rosemary
- 1 teaspoon pepper

Direction

- In the oven, put a 10-inch cast-iron skillet; preheat the oven to 425°. Beat together the initial 5 ingredients. Beat vinegar, honey, 1/4 cup olive oil, eggs and milk in a separate bowl; beat into the dry ingredients. Take off skillet from the oven; grease lightly using leftover olive oil. Put in batter. Let bake for about 15 minutes till golden brown. Allow to cool for 10 minutes; take off from the pan to a wire rack to cool fully.
- In the meantime, cook sausage in a big skillet over medium-high heat, crumbling the meat, till not pink anymore. Take off and let drain.

Cook onion, celery and mushrooms using same skillet for about 5 minutes till onion is soft. Into a big bowl, crumble corn bread; mix in mushroom mixture, sausage and the rest of the ingredients. Put to a 13x9-inch greased baking dish. Chill with cover for a minimum of 8 hours.

- Half an hour prior to baking, take off from refrigerator. Preheat the oven to 375°. Let bake without cover for 40 to 45 minutes, till browned and mixture is set.

Nutrition Information

- Calories: 276 calories
- Total Carbohydrate: 29g carbohydrate (5g sugars
- Cholesterol: 90mg cholesterol
- Protein: 11g protein.
- Total Fat: 13g fat (3g saturated fat)
- Sodium: 592mg sodium
- Fiber: 2g fiber)

266. Sausage And Rice Casserole Side Dish

Serving: 6 servings. | Prep: 15mins | Cook: 60mins | Ready in:

Ingredients

- 1 pound Jones No Sugar Pork Sausage Roll
- 1 cup sliced celery
- 1/2 cup chopped onion
- 1/4 cup chopped sweet red pepper
- 1/4 cup chopped green pepper
- 1/2 cup fresh mushrooms, sliced
- 1 can (8 ounces) sliced water chestnuts, drained
- 1 cup converted rice, uncooked
- 2 cups chicken broth
- 1/2 teaspoon salt
- 1/8 teaspoon ground pepper

Direction

- Set a heavy skillet over medium heat; drop the sausage in and fry until it turns brown. Transfer them to a 2-1/2-qt. casserole dish that's greased. Using the sausage drippings in the skillet, sauté the onion, celery, peppers and mushrooms until turns brown lightly; put them on the prepared dish. Pour in the water chestnuts and add the rice, seasonings and broth; blend the mixture well. Tightly cover and let it bake inside the oven for 1 to 1-1/2 hours at 350° or just until the rice looks fluffy and softened.

Nutrition Information

- Calories:
- Sodium:
- Fiber:
- Total Carbohydrate:
- Cholesterol:
- Protein:
- Total Fat:

267. Sauteed Garlic Mushrooms

Serving: 6 servings. | Prep: 5mins | Cook: 10mins | Ready in:

Ingredients

- 3/4 pound sliced fresh mushrooms
- 2 to 3 teaspoons minced garlic
- 1 tablespoon seasoned bread crumbs
- 1/3 cup butter, cubed

Direction

- In a big skillet, sauté bread crumbs, garlic and mushrooms in the butter till the mushrooms soften.

Nutrition Information

- Calories: 109 calories
- Fiber: 1g fiber)
- Total Carbohydrate: 3g carbohydrate (1g sugars
- Cholesterol: 27mg cholesterol
- Protein: 2g protein.
- Total Fat: 10g fat (6g saturated fat)
- Sodium: 123mg sodium

268. Savory Green Bean Casserole

Serving: 12 servings. | Prep: 20mins | Cook: 25mins | Ready in:

Ingredients

- 1 package (16 ounces) frozen cut green beans
- 1 medium onion, chopped
- 1 garlic clove, minced
- 1 teaspoon butter
- 1/2 pound fresh mushrooms, chopped
- 1 can (12 ounces) fat-free evaporated milk
- 1/4 cup all-purpose flour
- 1/2 cup fat-free milk
- 1 teaspoon reduced-sodium soy sauce
- 1/2 teaspoon salt
- 1/4 teaspoon poultry seasoning
- 1/8 to 1/4 teaspoon pepper
- TOPPING:
- 2 cups sliced onions
- 1 teaspoon butter
- 1/2 cup soft bread crumbs

Direction

- In a microwaveable dish, put the beans, then cover and let it cook for 7-9 minutes on high or until it becomes tender, then drain.
- Cook the garlic and onion in a big nonstick fry pan with butter for about 4 minutes on medium heat, until it becomes tender. Put in mushrooms and let it cook until it becomes soft. Lower the heat to medium-low, then slowly mix in the evaporated milk. Mix together the milk and flour until it becomes smooth, then slowly mix into the mushroom mixture. Add the pepper, poultry seasoning, salt and soy sauce, then boil. Let it cook while stirring for 2 minutes until it becomes thick. Mix in beans. Move to a cooking spray coated 2-quart baking dish. Let it bake for 15 minutes at 375 degrees without cover.
- In the meantime, to make the topping, cook the onions in a small nonstick frypan with butter on medium-low heat, until it turns golden brown in color. Put in breadcrumbs and let it cook until it turns golden brown and becomes dry, then sprinkle on top of the casserole. Let it bake for another 7 to 10 minutes or until the topping turns brown and is heated through. Prior to serving, allow to stand for 10 minutes.

Nutrition Information

- Calories: 86 calories
- Total Carbohydrate: 15g carbohydrate (0 sugars
- Cholesterol: 3mg cholesterol
- Protein: 5g protein. Diabetic Exchanges: 2 vegetable
- Total Fat: 1g fat (1g saturated fat)
- Sodium: 200mg sodium
- Fiber: 2g fiber)

269. Scalloped Tomatoes

Serving: 6 | Prep: | Cook: | Ready in:

Ingredients

- 1/4 cup butter
- 1 onion, chopped
- 1 teaspoon salt
- ground black pepper to taste
- 1/2 teaspoon dried basil

- 4 teaspoons brown sugar
- 5 tomatoes, sliced
- 2 cups white bread cubes

Direction

- Set oven to 375°F (190°C) to preheat.
- In a medium saucepan, sauté onion in butter until onion turns translucent. Stir in tomatoes, brown sugar, basil, pepper, and salt. Mix in bread until everything is thoroughly seasoned.
- Transfer the tomato bread mixture to a lightly oiled 9x13-inch casserole. Bake in the preheated oven for 30 to 35 minutes. Serve.

Nutrition Information

- Calories: 140 calories;
- Protein: 2.3
- Total Fat: 8.3
- Sodium: 529
- Total Carbohydrate: 15.6
- Cholesterol: 20

270. Shiitake & Butternut Risotto

Serving: 2 servings. | Prep: 25mins | Cook: 25mins | Ready in:

Ingredients

- 1 cup cubed peeled butternut squash
- 2 teaspoons olive oil, divided
- Dash salt
- 1-1/4 cups reduced-sodium chicken broth
- 2/3 cup sliced fresh shiitake mushrooms
- 2 tablespoons chopped onion
- 1 small garlic clove, minced
- 1/3 cup uncooked arborio rice
- Dash pepper
- 1/4 cup white wine or 1/4 cup additional reduced-sodium chicken broth
- 1/4 cup grated Parmesan cheese
- 1 teaspoon minced fresh sage

Direction

- Arrange squash in an oiled 9-inch square baking dish. Add salt and 1 teaspoon oil; stir until evenly coated.
- Bake, uncovered, for 25 to 30 minutes at 350° until tender, stirring occasionally.
- In the meantime, heat broth in small saucepan and keep warm. Sauté garlic, onion, and mushrooms in the remaining oil in a small skillet until tender for 3 to 4 minutes. Mix in pepper and rice; sauté for 2 to 3 minutes. Lower heat; pour in wine. Cook until all of the liquid is absorbed, stirring well.
- Pour in heated broth, a quarter cup at a time, and stir frequently. Let the liquid absorb after each addition. Cook just until rice is almost tender and risotto is creamy. Cooking time is about 20 minutes. Mix in cheese until melted. Mix in sage and squash. Serve right away.

Nutrition Information

- Calories: 282 calories
- Sodium: 567mg sodium
- Fiber: 3g fiber)
- Total Carbohydrate: 40g carbohydrate (3g sugars
- Cholesterol: 12mg cholesterol
- Protein: 10g protein.
- Total Fat: 9g fat (3g saturated fat)

271. Slow Cooker Mushroom Rice Pilaf

Serving: 6 servings. | Prep: 20mins | Cook: 03hours00mins | Ready in:

Ingredients

- 1 cup medium grain rice
- 1/4 cup butter

- 6 green onions, chopped
- 2 garlic cloves, minced
- 1/2 pound sliced baby portobello mushrooms
- 2 cups warm water
- 4 teaspoons beef base
- Thinly sliced green onions, optional

Direction

- Sauté rice with butter in a big frying pan until turning light brown. Add garlic and green onions, stir and cook until soft. Mix in mushrooms.
- Move into a 1-1/2-quart slow cooker. Stir together beef base and water in a small bowl, add to the rice mixture. Put the lid on and cook on low until the rice is soft and has absorbed the liquid, or about 3 to 3-1/2 hours. Use a fork to fluff. Add sliced green onions if you want.

Nutrition Information

- Calories: 210 calories
- Cholesterol: 20mg cholesterol
- Protein: 4g protein. Diabetic Exchanges: 2 starch
- Total Fat: 8g fat (5g saturated fat)
- Sodium: 512mg sodium
- Fiber: 1g fiber)
- Total Carbohydrate: 30g carbohydrate (2g sugars

272. Spaghetti Squash Casserole Bake

Serving: 6 servings. | Prep: 25mins | Cook: 60mins | Ready in:

Ingredients

- 1 medium spaghetti squash (about 8 inches)
- 1 tablespoon butter
- 1/2 pound sliced fresh mushrooms
- 1 large onion, chopped
- 2 garlic cloves, minced
- 1 teaspoon dried basil
- 1/2 teaspoon dried oregano
- 1/4 teaspoon dried thyme
- 1/2 teaspoon salt
- 1/4 teaspoon pepper
- 2 medium tomatoes, chopped
- 1 cup dry bread crumbs
- 1 cup ricotta cheese
- 1/4 cup minced fresh parsley
- 1/4 cup grated Parmesan cheese

Direction

- Halve squash lengthwise and scrape out seeds. In a baking dish, set the squash cut side facing down. Pour half-inch water and using foil, tightly cover. Allow to bake for 20 minutes to half an hour at 375° or till easily pricked using a fork.
- Meantime, in a big skillet, liquify the butter. Put pepper, salt, thyme, oregano, basil, garlic, onion and mushrooms; sauté till onion is soft. Put tomatoes; let cook till majority of liquid has vaporized. Reserve.
- Scrape out squash, parting strands using fork. Mix parsley, ricotta cheese, bread crumbs, tomato mixture and squash.
- Put to a 2-quart oiled baking dish. Scatter Parmesan cheese on top. Allow to bake without cover at 375° for 40 minutes till top is golden brown and warmed through.

Nutrition Information

- Calories: 263 calories
- Protein: 12g protein.
- Total Fat: 9g fat (5g saturated fat)
- Sodium: 528mg sodium
- Fiber: 5g fiber)
- Total Carbohydrate: 37g carbohydrate (6g sugars
- Cholesterol: 24mg cholesterol

273. Spaghetti Squash With Sweet Peppers

Serving: 4 servings. | Prep: 25mins | Cook: 0mins | Ready in:

Ingredients

- 1 medium spaghetti squash (2 pounds)
- 1/2 medium green pepper, sliced
- 1/2 medium sweet red pepper, sliced
- 4 medium fresh mushrooms, sliced
- 1 small onion, chopped
- 1 tablespoon olive oil
- 2 medium tomatoes, quartered
- 1 garlic clove, minced
- 1/2 cup chicken broth
- 1/4 teaspoon salt
- 3 tablespoons shredded Parmesan cheese

Direction

- Halve squash lengthwise; throw seeds. In a microwave-safe plate or dish, put the squash cut side facing down. Allow to microwave on high without cover for 10 to 12 minutes or till soft. Let cool.
- Sauté onion, mushrooms and peppers with oil in a big nonstick skillet till soft. Put garlic and tomatoes; sauté for 4 to 5 minutes more. Put salt and broth; let simmer for 3 to 4 minutes without cover.
- Once squash is cool enough to the touch, part strands with a fork. On individual plates or a serving platter, put the squash; put pepper mixture over. Scatter Parmesan cheese on top.

Nutrition Information

- Calories: 110 calories
- Protein: 4g protein. Diabetic Exchanges: 3 vegetable
- Total Fat: 5g fat (1g saturated fat)
- Sodium: 372mg sodium
- Fiber: 3g fiber)
- Total Carbohydrate: 13g carbohydrate (0 sugars
- Cholesterol: 4mg cholesterol

274. Special Herb Dressing

Serving: 14-16 servings. | Prep: 30mins | Cook: 35mins | Ready in:

Ingredients

- 1 pound ground beef
- 1 pound Jones No Sugar Pork Sausage Roll sausage
- 1 pound sliced fresh mushrooms
- 1 can (8 ounces) water chestnuts, drained and chopped
- 2 cups diced peeled apples
- 1 cup chopped onion
- 1/4 cup minced fresh parsley
- 1/4 cup chopped fresh celery leaves
- 1 cup chopped fresh or frozen cranberries
- 2 garlic cloves, minced
- 1-1/2 teaspoons salt
- 1 teaspoon dried savory
- 1 teaspoon dried thyme
- 1 teaspoon rubbed sage
- 3/4 teaspoon pepper
- Pinch nutmeg
- 12 cups day-old bread cubes
- 1 cup chicken broth

Direction

- Set an oven to 350 degrees and start preheating. Cook the sausage and beef on medium heat in a large skillet until not pink anymore; drain them. Put in celery leaves, parsley, onion, apples, water chestnuts, and mushrooms; cook until the apples and mushrooms become tender or for 6-8 minutes. Put the seasonings, garlic, and cranberries; cook for 2 more minutes.
- In a large bowl, put the bread cubes. Put in the meat mixture; add in broth and stir. Scoop into

a greased 13x9-inch baking dish. Put a cover on and bake for 35-45 minutes.

Nutrition Information

- Calories: 204 calories
- Sodium: 561mg sodium
- Fiber: 2g fiber)
- Total Carbohydrate: 21g carbohydrate (5g sugars
- Cholesterol: 24mg cholesterol
- Protein: 10g protein.
- Total Fat: 9g fat (3g saturated fat)

275. Spectacular Spaghetti Squash

Serving: 10-12 servings. | Prep: 15mins | Cook: 50mins | Ready in:

Ingredients

- 1 medium spaghetti squash (about 3 pounds)
- 8 ounces fresh mushrooms, sliced
- 1 medium zucchini, sliced
- 1 medium sweet red pepper, julienned
- 3 cups sugar snap peas
- 6 green onions, chopped
- 2 garlic cloves, minced
- 2 tablespoons olive oil
- 1 tablespoon butter
- 2 medium tomatoes, chopped
- 1 tablespoon minced fresh basil or 1 teaspoon dried basil
- 1/2 teaspoon garlic salt
- 1/8 teaspoon pepper
- 3/4 cup shredded Parmesan cheese

Direction

- Halve squash lengthwise; spoon out the seeds. In a baking dish, put the squash cut side facing down. Pour hot water in pan to reach half-inch. Put cover and let bake for 50 minutes to an hour at 375° or till soft.
- Once cool enough to touch, scrape out squash and part strands using a fork. In a big serving bowl, put the squash and retain warmth. Throw shells.
- Meantime, sauté garlic, onions, peas, red pepper, zucchini and mushrooms with butter and oil for 15 minutes in a skillet till soft. Put pepper, garlic salt, basil and tomatoes; warm through. Put on top of squash. Scatter Parmesan cheese on top.

Nutrition Information

- Calories: 117 calories
- Total Carbohydrate: 14g carbohydrate (3g sugars
- Cholesterol: 6mg cholesterol
- Protein: 5g protein.
- Total Fat: 5g fat (2g saturated fat)
- Sodium: 195mg sodium
- Fiber: 4g fiber)

276. Spinach Artichoke Pie

Serving: 6-8 servings. | Prep: 15mins | Cook: 35mins | Ready in:

Ingredients

- 3 tablespoons vegetable oil, divided
- 1/4 cup dry bread crumbs
- 1/2 pound fresh mushrooms, sliced
- 1 pound fresh spinach, chopped and cooked
- 1 jar (6-1/2 ounces) marinated artichoke hearts, drained and quartered
- 1 cup day-old bread cubes
- 1-1/4 cups shredded cheddar cheese, divided
- 1 jar (4 ounces) diced pimientos, drained
- 2 eggs, beaten
- 1/4 to 1/2 teaspoon garlic powder

Direction

- Coat 2 tbsp. oil to the bottom and sides of a 9-inch pie plate and sprinkle with breadcrumbs. Set plate aside.
- Sauté mushrooms with the remaining oil in a skillet, then drain. Take away from the heat. Squeeze spinach dry and put into mushrooms. Stir in garlic powder, eggs, pimientos, 1 cup of cheese, bread cubes and artichokes, then stir well together.
- Scoop into the prepared pie plate. Bake at 350 degrees without a cover for a half hour. Sprinkle with leftover cheese. Bake until cheese has melted, about 5 to 10 more minutes. Allow to stand for about 10 minutes before cutting.

Nutrition Information

- Calories: 210 calories
- Total Carbohydrate: 11g carbohydrate (1g sugars
- Cholesterol: 72mg cholesterol
- Protein: 9g protein.
- Total Fat: 16g fat (6g saturated fat)
- Sodium: 302mg sodium
- Fiber: 2g fiber)

277. Spinach Rice Casserole

Serving: 12 servings. | Prep: 15mins | Cook: 30mins | Ready in:

Ingredients

- 2 cups sliced fresh mushrooms
- 1 cup chopped onion
- 1 garlic clove, minced
- 1 package (10 ounces) frozen chopped spinach, thawed and squeezed dry
- 1 tablespoon all-purpose flour
- 1/4 cup egg substitute
- 2 cups (16 ounces) fat-free cottage cheese
- 2 cups cooked instant brown rice
- 2 tablespoons grated Parmesan cheese, divided
- 1/2 teaspoon dried thyme
- 1/4 teaspoon pepper
- 2 tablespoons sunflower kernels

Direction

- Sauté garlic, onion and mushrooms in a nonstick skillet sprayed with cooking spray until softened. Put in spinach. Mix egg substitute and flour in a big bowl until smooth. Stir in mushroom mixture, pepper, thyme, 1 tbsp. of Parmesan cheese, rice and cottage cheese, then blend well together. Remove to a baking dish with 11x7-inch size that is sprayed with cooking spray, then use leftover Parmesan cheese and sunflower kernels to sprinkle over top. Bake without a cover at 350 degrees until heated through, about a half hour.

Nutrition Information

- Calories: 97 calories
- Sodium: 175mg sodium
- Fiber: 0 fiber)
- Total Carbohydrate: 12g carbohydrate (0 sugars
- Cholesterol: 6mg cholesterol
- Protein: 8g protein. Diabetic Exchanges: 1 starch
- Total Fat: 2g fat (0 saturated fat)

278. Summer Vegetable Medley

Serving: 6-8 servings. | Prep: 5mins | Cook: 10mins | Ready in:

Ingredients

- 1/2 cup butter, melted

- 1-1/4 teaspoons each minced fresh parsley, basil and chives
- 3/4 teaspoon salt
- 1/4 teaspoon pepper
- 3 medium ears sweet corn, husks removed, cut into 2-inch pieces
- 1 medium sweet red pepper, cut into 1-inch pieces
- 1 medium sweet yellow pepper, cut into 1-inch pieces
- 1 medium zucchini, cut into 1/4-inch slices
- 10 large fresh mushrooms

Direction

- Mix together pepper, salt, chives, basil, parsley and butter in a big bowl, then add in vegetables and toss to coat well.
- In a disposable foil pan, place the vegetables, then grill with a cover on medium-high heat for 5 minutes. Stir. Grill until vegetables are soft, about 5 more minutes.

Nutrition Information

- Calories: 148 calories
- Sodium: 345mg sodium
- Fiber: 2g fiber)
- Total Carbohydrate: 10g carbohydrate (4g sugars
- Cholesterol: 31mg cholesterol
- Protein: 3g protein.
- Total Fat: 12g fat (7g saturated fat)

279. Summer's Bounty Soup

Serving: 14 servings (about 3-1/2 quarts). | Prep: 5mins | Cook: 07hours00mins | Ready in:

Ingredients

- 4 medium tomatoes, chopped
- 2 medium potatoes, peeled and cubed
- 2 cups halved fresh green beans
- 2 small zucchini, cubed
- 1 medium yellow summer squash, cubed
- 4 small carrots, thinly sliced
- 2 celery ribs, thinly sliced
- 1 cup cubed peeled eggplant
- 1 cup sliced fresh mushrooms
- 1 small onion, chopped
- 1 tablespoon minced fresh parsley
- 1 tablespoon salt-free garlic and herb seasoning
- 4 cups reduced-sodium V8 juice

Direction

- In a 5-qt. slow cooker, mix all of the ingredients together. Put a cover on and cook on Low until the vegetables are soft, or for about 7-8 hours.

Nutrition Information

- Calories: 67 calories
- Protein: 2g protein. Diabetic Exchanges: 2 vegetable.
- Total Fat: 0 fat (0 saturated fat)
- Sodium: 62mg sodium
- Fiber: 3g fiber)
- Total Carbohydrate: 15g carbohydrate (6g sugars
- Cholesterol: 0 cholesterol

280. Sweet Peas And Mushrooms

Serving: 8 servings. | Prep: 15mins | Cook: 0mins | Ready in:

Ingredients

- 2 packages (10 ounces each) frozen peas
- 2 cups sliced fresh mushrooms
- 1/2 cup chopped onion
- 1/4 cup butter
- 2 teaspoons sugar

- 1 teaspoon salt
- Dash pepper

Direction

- Cook peas following the package directions. In the meantime, sauté onion and mushrooms in butter in a skillet until the onion is crisp-tender.
- Drain the peas and put into the skillet along with the sugar, pepper, and salt. Then cover and cook until heated through.

Nutrition Information

- Calories: 117 calories
- Total Fat: 6g fat (4g saturated fat)
- Sodium: 433mg sodium
- Fiber: 4g fiber)
- Total Carbohydrate: 12g carbohydrate (6g sugars
- Cholesterol: 15mg cholesterol
- Protein: 4g protein.

281. Three Rice Pilaf

Serving: 8-10 servings. | Prep: 25mins | Cook: 60mins | Ready in:

Ingredients

- 1/2 cup uncooked brown rice
- 1/2 cup finely chopped carrots
- 1/2 cup chopped onion
- 1/2 cup sliced fresh mushrooms
- 2 tablespoons canola oil
- 1/2 cup uncooked wild rice
- 3 cups chicken broth
- 1/4 teaspoon dried thyme
- 1/4 teaspoon dried rosemary, crushed
- 1/2 cup uncooked long grain rice
- 1/3 cup chopped dried apricots
- 2 tablespoons minced green onions
- 1/4 teaspoon salt

- 1/8 teaspoon pepper
- 1/2 cup chopped pecans, toasted

Direction

- In a big saucepan, sauté the mushrooms, onion, carrots and brown rice in the oil till the rice turns golden or for 10 minutes.
- Put in the rosemary, thyme, broth and wide rice; boil. Lower the heat; keep covered and let it simmer for 25 minutes.
- Whisk in the long grain rice; keep covered and let it simmer till the wild rice softens and the liquid has been absorbed or for 25 minutes.
- Take off the heat; whisk in the pepper, salt, green onions and apricots. Keep covered and allow it to rest for 5 minutes. Drizzle with the pecans just prior to serving.

Nutrition Information

- Calories: 190 calories
- Sodium: 345mg sodium
- Fiber: 2g fiber)
- Total Carbohydrate: 27g carbohydrate (4g sugars
- Cholesterol: 0 cholesterol
- Protein: 4g protein.
- Total Fat: 8g fat (1g saturated fat)

282. Thyme Roasted Vegetables

Serving: 10 servings (3/4 cup each). | Prep: 25mins | Cook: 45mins | Ready in:

Ingredients

- 2 pounds red potatoes, cubed (about 9 cups)
- 3 cups sliced sweet onions (about 1-1/2 large)
- 3 medium carrots, sliced
- 1/2 pound medium fresh mushrooms, halved
- 1 large sweet red pepper, cut into 1-1/2-inch pieces

- 1 large sweet yellow pepper, cut into 1-1/2-inch pieces
- 2 tablespoons butter, melted
- 2 tablespoons olive oil
- 1 tablespoon minced fresh thyme or 1 teaspoon dried thyme
- 1 teaspoon salt
- 1/4 teaspoon pepper

Direction

- Set oven to 400 degrees and start preheating. Combine vegetables in a big bowl. Add in the rest of ingredients; turn to coat.
- Remove to a 15x10x1-inch baking pan. Roast until tender, mixing from time to time, or about 45-50 minutes.

Nutrition Information

- Calories: 151 calories
- Sodium: 274mg sodium
- Fiber: 4g fiber)
- Total Carbohydrate: 24g carbohydrate (5g sugars
- Cholesterol: 6mg cholesterol
- Protein: 3g protein. Diabetic Exchanges: 1 starch
- Total Fat: 5g fat (2g saturated fat)

283. Tomato Sesame Pasta Toss

Serving: 7 servings. | Prep: 20mins | Cook: 0mins | Ready in:

Ingredients

- 4 quarts water
- 8 ounces uncooked angel hair pasta, broken in half
- 2 cups fresh broccoli florets
- 14 to 16 cherry tomatoes, halved
- 1 cup sliced fresh mushrooms
- 1 cup torn fresh spinach
- 3 green onions, thinly sliced
- 1/4 cup cashews
- 1/4 cup reduced-sodium soy sauce
- 2 tablespoons sesame seeds, toasted
- 2 tablespoons brown sugar
- 2 tablespoons sesame oil
- 2 teaspoons lime juice
- 1 garlic clove, minced
- 1 teaspoon finely chopped jalapeno pepper

Direction

- Boil water in a Dutch oven. Put pasta; allow to boil for 4 minutes. Put broccoli, let boil till pasta is tender for 2 minutes more. Wash with cold water and drain. Put to a big bowl. Put the cashews, onions, spinach, mushrooms and tomatoes; toss.
- Put together the rest of the ingredients in a jar with a tight-fitting lid; shake thoroughly. Put atop pasta mixture; softly toss to coat.

Nutrition Information

- Calories: 260 calories
- Fiber: 4g fiber)
- Total Carbohydrate: 37g carbohydrate (0 sugars
- Cholesterol: 0 cholesterol
- Protein: 8g protein. Diabetic Exchanges: 2 starch
- Total Fat: 10g fat (2g saturated fat)
- Sodium: 399mg sodium

284. Unstuffing Side Dish

Serving: 8 servings. | Prep: 20mins | Cook: 40mins | Ready in:

Ingredients

- 1/2 pound Johnsonville® Ground Mild Italian sausage

- 1/4 cup butter, cubed
- 1/2 pound sliced fresh mushrooms
- 3/4 cup chopped celery
- 1 medium onion, chopped
- 1 teaspoon poultry seasoning
- 1/2 teaspoon salt
- 1/4 teaspoon pepper
- 6 cups unseasoned stuffing cubes or dry cubed bread
- 2-1/2 to 3 cups chicken broth

Direction

- Cook the sausage in a large skillet until it is no longer pink; drain. Add the onion, butter, celery, and mushrooms. Cook the mixture for 3-5 minutes until the onion is tender. Mix in pepper, poultry seasoning, and salt. Pour the mixture into a large bowl. Add the stuffing cubes. Pour in enough broth to moisten.
- Put the mixture into the greased 2-qt baking dish. Cover the dish. Bake it inside the 350° oven for 30 minutes. Remove the cover from the dish. Bake the mixture for 10 more minutes until browned.

Nutrition Information

- Calories: 259 calories
- Sodium: 951mg sodium
- Fiber: 3g fiber)
- Total Carbohydrate: 33g carbohydrate (4g sugars
- Cholesterol: 27mg cholesterol
- Protein: 10g protein.
- Total Fat: 11g fat (5g saturated fat)

285. Vegetable Kabobs

Serving: 4 servings. | Prep: 20mins | Cook: 10mins | Ready in:

Ingredients

- 1 garlic clove, peeled
- 1 teaspoon salt
- 1/3 cup olive oil
- 3 tablespoons lemon juice
- 1 teaspoon Italian seasoning
- 1/4 teaspoon pepper
- 8 medium fresh mushrooms
- 2 small zucchini, cut into 1/2-inch slices
- 2 small onions, cut into six wedges
- 8 cherry tomatoes

Direction

- Mince the garlic with salt in a small bowl to make a paste. Mix in oil, Italian seasoning, lemon juice, and pepper. Alternately skewer the different vegetables onto metal or pre-soaked wooden skewers. Arrange skewers in a shallow dish and pour the garlic mixture over them. Marinate for 15 minutes. Place kabobs in the grill, cover it, and cook over medium heat for 10-15minutes or until vegetables are just about tender. Turn frequently to cook all sides.

Nutrition Information

- Calories: 202 calories
- Fiber: 2g fiber)
- Total Carbohydrate: 9g carbohydrate (5g sugars
- Cholesterol: 0 cholesterol
- Protein: 3g protein.
- Total Fat: 18g fat (2g saturated fat)
- Sodium: 598mg sodium

286. Vegetable Kabobs With Rice

Serving: 4 servings. | Prep: 15mins | Cook: 15mins | Ready in:

Ingredients

- 1/2 cup Italian salad dressing

- 1 tablespoon minced fresh parsley
- 1 teaspoon dried basil
- 2 medium yellow squash, cut into 1-inch pieces
- 8 small boiling onions, peeled
- 8 cherry tomatoes
- 8 medium fresh mushrooms
- 2 cups hot cooked rice

Direction

- Combine dressing, basil, and parsley in a small bowl. Cue the vegetables alternately on eight skewers. Arrange on the grill over medium heat. Turn and baste frequently with dressing for the 15-minute grilling time, or until vegetables are cooked. Plate 2 kabobs over 1/2 cup of rice.

Nutrition Information

- Calories: 171 calories
- Total Fat: 0 fat (0 saturated fat)
- Sodium: 70mg sodium
- Fiber: 0 fiber)
- Total Carbohydrate: 38g carbohydrate (0 sugars
- Cholesterol: 0 cholesterol
- Protein: 5g protein. Diabetic Exchanges: 2 vegetable

287. Vegetable Wild Rice Stuffing

Serving: 7 servings. | Prep: 25mins | Cook: 60mins | Ready in:

Ingredients

- 2 cans (14-1/2 ounces each) chicken broth
- 1-1/2 cups water
- 2/3 cup uncooked wild rice
- 1/2 teaspoon salt
- 1/2 teaspoon dried thyme
- 4 medium carrots, sliced
- 2 celery ribs, chopped
- 1 medium onion, chopped
- 2 tablespoons canola oil
- 1/2 pound fresh mushrooms, sliced
- 1-1/2 cups uncooked long grain rice
- 1/4 cup minced fresh parsley

Direction

- Boil water and broth in a big saucepan. Add thyme, salt and wild rice. Lower heat; cover. Simmer it for 30 minutes.
- Meanwhile, sauté onion, celery and carrots in oil till crisp-tender in another saucepan. Add mushrooms; sauté for 5 more minutes. Stir in long grain rice and veggies to wild rice and cover; cook till rice is tender for 30-35 minutes. Mix in parsley.

Nutrition Information

- Calories: 313 calories
- Sodium: 272mg sodium
- Fiber: 4g fiber)
- Total Carbohydrate: 57g carbohydrate (0 sugars
- Cholesterol: 2mg cholesterol
- Protein: 9g protein. Diabetic Exchanges: 3 starch
- Total Fat: 6g fat (0 saturated fat)

288. Vegetarian Cabbage Rolls

Serving: 8 | Prep: 30mins | Cook: 1hours5mins | Ready in:

Ingredients

- 1/3 cup uncooked brown rice
- 2/3 cup water
- 2 cups textured vegetable protein
- 3/4 cup boiling water
- 2 (10.75 ounce) cans tomato soup

- 10 3/4 fluid ounces water
- 1 large head cabbage, cored
- 1 tablespoon vegetable oil
- 1 large onion, chopped
- 1/2 carrot, finely chopped
- 1/2 red bell pepper, diced
- 3 cloves garlic, minced
- 1 tablespoon white wine
- 1 (14.5 ounce) can whole peeled tomatoes, drained, juice reserved
- 1 egg, lightly beaten
- 1/2 cup frozen peas
- 2 pinches cayenne pepper
- 1/2 teaspoon onion powder
- 1 teaspoon garlic powder
- 1/2 teaspoon dried basil
- 3 drops hot red pepper sauce
- toothpicks
- salt and pepper to taste

Direction

- In a pot, put 2/3 cup of water and the rice then set to a boil. Lower heat to low, simmer while covered for about 40 minutes until tender. In a medium bowl, blend 3/4 cup of boiling water and the textured vegetable protein together. Soak for 15 minutes until rehydrated. Stir in the cooked rice.
- Preheat oven to 350° F (175° C). Stir 10 and 3/4 fluid ounces of (1 soup can) water and tomato soup in a bowl.
- In a pot, put the cabbage and enough water to cover. Boil, then cook for 15 minutes till leaves can be removed with ease. Drain, cool, then separate the leaves.
- In a frying pan, heat the oil over medium heat. Mix in the garlic, red bell pepper, carrot, and onion. Cook until softened. Blend in wine, and keep cooking till most of the liquid has evaporated. Mix in textured vegetable protein and rice, reserved juice from tomatoes, peas, and egg. Flavor with hot pepper sauce, basil, garlic powder, onion powder, and cayenne pepper. Cook and whisk till heated through.
- On a cabbage leaf, position 1 tomato and 2 tablespoons of skillet mixture. Roll firmly, then secure using a toothpick. Do the same with the leftover filling. Line in a casserole dish. Spread water and soup over cabbage rolls. Spice with pepper and salt.
- In the preheated oven, bake, covered, for 35 minutes while basting infrequently with the tomato sauce. Take off the cover, and go on baking for 10 minutes.

Nutrition Information

- Calories: 215 calories;
- Cholesterol: 23
- Protein: 27.3
- Total Fat: 3.8
- Sodium: 435
- Total Carbohydrate: 23.2

289. White Beans With Rigatoni

Serving: 5 servings. | Prep: 10mins | Cook: 25mins | Ready in:

Ingredients

- 8 ounces rigatoni or large tube pasta
- 1/2 cup chopped onion
- 1 garlic clove, minced
- 1 tablespoon olive oil
- 1 package (8 ounces) sliced fresh mushrooms
- 1 can (15 ounces) white kidney or cannellini beans, rinsed and drained
- 1 can (14-1/2 ounces) diced tomatoes, undrained
- 2 tablespoons miced fresh sage
- 1/2 teaspoon salt
- 1/4 teaspoon pepper
- 2 cups chopped fresh kale
- 1/4 cup shredded Parmesan cheese

Direction

- Cook pasta following the package instructions. Sauté garlic and onion in oil in a big saucepan until soft. Mix in mushrooms; cook until the mushrooms are nearly soft, or about another 5 minutes.
- Mix in pepper, salt, sage, tomatoes, and beans. Boil it. Lower the heat; simmer without a cover for 5 minutes. Mix in kale. Boil again. Put a cover on and cook until the kale is soft and wilted, or about 3-4 minutes. Strain the pasta, put on the bean mixture and heat through. Sprinkle Parmesan cheese over.

Nutrition Information

- Calories: 319 calories
- Total Fat: 6g fat (1g saturated fat)
- Sodium: 537mg sodium
- Fiber: 8g fiber)
- Total Carbohydrate: 55g carbohydrate (0 sugars
- Cholesterol: 3mg cholesterol
- Protein: 14g protein.

290. Wild Rice Medley

Serving: 8 servings. | Prep: 01hours15mins | Cook: 30mins | Ready in:

Ingredients

- 1-3/4 cups reduced-sodium chicken broth
- 1 teaspoon dill weed
- 1/2 teaspoon dried basil
- 1/8 teaspoon pepper
- Pinch dried thyme
- 3/4 cup uncooked wild rice
- 1 cup chopped green pepper
- 1 small onion, chopped
- 1 tablespoon olive oil
- 1 garlic clove, minced
- 6 fresh mushrooms, sliced
- 1 large tomato, diced
- 1/4 cup shredded part-skim mozzarella cheese

Direction

- Mix seasonings and broth together in a big saucepan, then bring the mixture to a boil. Put in rice and simmer, covered, until liquid has been absorbed, about 55 to 60 minutes.
- Sauté onion and green pepper in a big skillet with oil, then put in garlic and cook for a minute more. Put in mushrooms and sauté until soft. Stir in tomato and rice.
- Remove to a 1 1/2-quart baking dish coated with grease. Cover and bake at 350 degrees about 25 minutes. Use cheese to sprinkle over, then bake without a cover until cheese has melted, about 5 more minutes.

Nutrition Information

- Calories: 110 calories
- Protein: 5g protein. Diabetic Exchanges: 1 starch
- Total Fat: 3g fat (0 saturated fat)
- Sodium: 48mg sodium
- Fiber: 0 fiber)
- Total Carbohydrate: 17g carbohydrate (0 sugars
- Cholesterol: 3mg cholesterol

291. Wild Rice Mushroom Casserole

Serving: 3 servings. | Prep: 55mins | Cook: 25mins | Ready in:

Ingredients

- 1/2 cup uncooked wild rice
- 1 cup chicken broth
- 1/2 cup water
- 1 celery rib, sliced
- 1 small onion, chopped
- 1/2 cup sliced fresh mushrooms
- 2 teaspoons butter

- 2/3 cup condensed cream of mushroom soup, undiluted
- 1/8 teaspoon salt

Direction

- Boil water, broth, and rice in a small saucepan. Lower the heat, put a cover on and simmer until the rice has absorbed the liquid and soft, 45-50 minutes.
- Start preheating the oven to 450°. Sauté mushrooms, onion, and celery with butter until soft in a big nonstick skillet. Mix in rice, salt, and soup; remove to a cooking spray - coated 3-cup baking dish. Bake with a cover until very heated, 25-30 minutes.

Nutrition Information

- Calories: 188 calories
- Sodium: 708mg sodium
- Fiber: 3g fiber)
- Total Carbohydrate: 31g carbohydrate (2g sugars
- Cholesterol: 6mg cholesterol
- Protein: 6g protein.
- Total Fat: 5g fat (1g saturated fat)

292. Wild Rice Pancakes

Serving: 6 | Prep: 10mins | Cook: 20mins | Ready in:

Ingredients

- 3 eggs
- 3 cups buttermilk
- 1 teaspoon vanilla extract
- 3 cups all-purpose flour
- 1/4 cup white sugar
- 1 tablespoon baking powder
- 1 1/2 teaspoons ground nutmeg
- 3/4 teaspoon salt
- 3 tablespoons butter, melted
- 1 1/4 cups cooked wild rice

Direction

- In a large bowl, whisk the vanilla, buttermilk and eggs. Mix salt, nutmeg, baking powder, sugar and flour in a separate bowl. Combine the dry ingredients with the egg mixture slowly, ensure the mixture appears smooth. Add cooked wild rice and butter.
- Allow a lightly lubricated griddle or skillet to heat over medium-high heat.
- Spoon 1/2 cup of the batter on griddle and cook for 90 seconds until it becomes browned to form each pancake. Brown the other side for about 60 seconds. Repeat with the rest of the batter.

Nutrition Information

- Calories: 437 calories;
- Cholesterol: 113
- Protein: 15.1
- Total Fat: 10.3
- Sodium: 741
- Total Carbohydrate: 70.5

293. Zesty Rice 'N' Bean Casserole

Serving: 8 servings. | Prep: 35mins | Cook: 15mins | Ready in:

Ingredients

- 2 medium green peppers, chopped
- 1-1/2 cups sliced fresh mushrooms
- 1 medium onion, chopped
- 1/2 cup water
- 1 teaspoon canola oil
- 2 garlic cloves, minced
- 1 can (28 ounces) diced tomatoes, undrained
- 1 can (16 ounces) kidney beans, rinsed and drained
- 3/4 cup uncooked long grain rice
- 2 teaspoons ground cumin

- 1 teaspoon chili powder
- 1/4 teaspoon cayenne pepper
- 1 cup shredded part-skim mozzarella cheese, divided

Direction

- Start preheating oven to 350 degrees. Put oil and water in a big nonstick frying pan and sauté onion, green peppers, and mushrooms until the onion is soft. Add the garlic and cook for 1 more minute. Mix in seasonings, beans, tomatoes, and rice. Heat to boiling. Cover, decrease heat, and simmer until the liquid is almost completely absorbed and rice is tender, 25 minutes. Take away from heat and mix in 1/2 cup cheese. Move to a greased 2-1/2-qt. dish. Sprinkle on the rest of cheese. Do not cover; bake until cheese melts, 15-20 minutes.

Nutrition Information

- Calories: 195 calories
- Cholesterol: 8mg cholesterol
- Protein: 10g protein. Diabetic Exchanges: 1-1/2 starch
- Total Fat: 7g fat (2g saturated fat)
- Sodium: 392mg sodium
- Fiber: 7g fiber)
- Total Carbohydrate: 33g carbohydrate (0 sugars

294. Zucchini Mushroom Bake

Serving: 4 servings. | Prep: 10mins | Cook: 30mins | Ready in:

Ingredients

- 3 cups sliced zucchini
- 2 cups sliced fresh mushrooms
- 1/3 cup sliced onion
- 1/2 teaspoon dried basil
- 1/4 teaspoon salt
- 1/2 cup shredded cheddar cheese

Direction

- Turn oven to 350° to preheat. Combine the first 5 ingredients and arrange in a lightly oiled 2-quart shallow baking dish.
- Cover and bake in the preheated oven for half an hour. Scatter over the top with cheese; uncover and bake for approximately 10 minutes longer until vegetables are tender.

Nutrition Information

- Calories: 83 calories
- Protein: 5g protein. Diabetic Exchanges: 1 medium-fat meat
- Total Fat: 5g fat (3g saturated fat)
- Sodium: 249mg sodium
- Fiber: 1g fiber)
- Total Carbohydrate: 5g carbohydrate (3g sugars
- Cholesterol: 14mg cholesterol

Chapter 6: Vegetarian Mushroom Recipes

***

295. All Veggie Lasagna

Serving: 12 servings. | Prep: 20mins | Cook: 60mins | Ready in:

Ingredients

- 2 cups 1% cottage cheese

- 1 carton (15 ounces) reduced-fat ricotta cheese
- 2 tablespoons minced fresh parsley
- 1 jar (26 ounces) meatless spaghetti sauce
- 9 uncooked lasagna noodles
- 2 medium carrots, shredded
- 1-1/2 cups broccoli florets
- 4 ounces fresh mushrooms, sliced
- 1 small zucchini, thinly sliced
- 1 small yellow summer squash, thinly sliced
- 2 cups fresh spinach
- 2 cups shredded part-skim mozzarella cheese

Direction

- Preheat the oven at 350°F. Mix ricotta, parsley and cottage cheese together in a bowl. In a greased 13x9-inch baking dish with cooking spray, put 1/2 cup of spaghetti sauce evenly at the bottom. Put a layer of 3 noodles and 1/3 of the cheese mixture on top. Spread mushrooms, zucchini, 1/2 of the carrots, squash and broccoli on top. Put 1/3 of the remaining spaghetti sauce over the layer of vegetables.
- Put a layer of 1/2 of the spinach and 1/3 of the mozzarella cheese on top of the spaghetti sauce. Make another layer of noodles, cheese mixture, vegetables, spaghetti sauce, spinach and mozzarella cheese. Finish off with a layer of the remaining noodles, cheese mixture, spaghetti sauce and mozzarella cheese.
- Put the tightly covered baking dish in the preheated oven and bake for 45 minutes. Remove the cover and bake for 15 more minutes or until the noodles are soft. Cool down the lasagna for 15 minutes before slicing then serve.

Nutrition Information

- Calories: 234 calories
- Cholesterol: 26mg cholesterol
- Protein: 19g protein. Diabetic Exchanges: 2 lean meat
- Total Fat: 7g fat (4g saturated fat)
- Sodium: 572mg sodium
- Fiber: 4g fiber)

- Total Carbohydrate: 25g carbohydrate (0 sugars

296. Amber's Sourdough Stuffing

Serving: 2 servings. | Prep: 20mins | Cook: 20mins | Ready in:

Ingredients

- 1 tablespoon olive oil
- 1/3 cup sliced fresh mushrooms
- 1/3 cup chopped celery
- 1/3 cup finely chopped carrot
- 1/3 cup finely chopped onion
- 2-1/2 cups cubed sourdough bread
- 1/2 teaspoon poultry seasoning
- 1/4 teaspoon salt
- 1/8 teaspoon pepper
- 2 tablespoons beaten egg
- 1/2 to 3/4 cup chicken broth

Direction

- Start preheating the oven to 350°. Heat oil in a big frying pan over medium-high heat. Add onion, carrot, celery, and mushrooms; stir and cook until soft.
- Remove into a big bowl. Add seasonings and bread cubes; toss to blend. Mix in sufficient broth and egg until reaching the moistness you want.
- Remove into a 1-qt. baking dish or two 10-oz. ramekins coated with oil. Bake until a thermometer displays 160° and the top turns light brown, or about 20-25 minutes.

Nutrition Information

- Calories: 228 calories
- Cholesterol: 58mg cholesterol
- Protein: 7g protein.
- Total Fat: 10g fat (2g saturated fat)

- Sodium: 806mg sodium
- Fiber: 3g fiber)
- Total Carbohydrate: 28g carbohydrate (5g sugars

- Total Carbohydrate: 74g carbohydrate (6g sugars
- Cholesterol: 33mg cholesterol
- Protein: 21g protein.
- Total Fat: 14g fat (9g saturated fat)

297. Artichoke Blue Cheese Fettuccine

Serving: 4 servings. | Prep: 5mins | Cook: 15mins | Ready in:

Ingredients

- 1 package (12 ounces) fettuccine
- 1 cup sliced fresh mushrooms
- 1 can (14 ounces) water-packed artichoke hearts, drained and chopped
- 1-1/2 cups Alfredo sauce
- 1/4 cup crumbled blue cheese

Direction

- Follow the package directions to cook fettuccine.
- At the same time, put a big nonstick skillet coated with cooking spray on moderately high heat. Put in artichoke hearts and mushrooms, then cook and stir until mushrooms are softened. Stir in Alfredo sauce and bring to a boil on moderate heat. Lower heat and simmer without a cover, while stirring sometimes, for 5 minutes.
- Drain fettuccine and put aside 1/3 cup of pasta water. Add into artichoke mixture with fettuccine and toss well to mix while putting in reserved pasta water if wanted. Sprinkle over with blue cheese.

Nutrition Information

- Calories: 499 calories
- Sodium: 770mg sodium
- Fiber: 4g fiber)

298. Asparagus Mushroom Salad

Serving: 8-10 servings. | Prep: 10mins | Cook: 10mins | Ready in:

Ingredients

- 1 pound fresh asparagus
- 1 pound fresh mushrooms, sliced 1/4 inch thick
- 4 tablespoons lemon juice, divided
- 1 cup heavy whipping cream
- 1/2 teaspoon paprika
- 1/2 teaspoon salt
- 1/4 teaspoon pepper
- 1 bunch romaine, torn
- Tomato wedges and additional paprika, optional

Direction

- In boiling salted water, cook asparagus until tender-crisp; drain off and wash under cold water.
- Combine 3 tablespoons of lemon juice and mushrooms in a bowl by tossing. Mix the leftover lemon juice and pepper, salt, paprika, and cream; mix until smooth in consistency. Put on top of the mushrooms; coat by tossing.
- Line romaine on a large serving platter. Spread the asparagus with stems toward middle in spoke fashion. Scoop mushrooms into the middle. If you want, use tomato wedges and paprika to garnish.

Nutrition Information

- Calories: 106 calories
- Total Carbohydrate: 5g carbohydrate (2g sugars
- Cholesterol: 33mg cholesterol
- Protein: 3g protein.
- Total Fat: 9g fat (6g saturated fat)
- Sodium: 135mg sodium
- Fiber: 2g fiber)

299. Asparagus Soup

Serving: 4 | Prep: 20mins | Cook: 15mins | Ready in:

Ingredients

- 1 onion, chopped
- 2 tablespoons butter
- 1 pound fresh asparagus, trimmed and coarsely chopped
- 1 cup vegetable broth
- 1 dash garlic powder
- 1 dash white pepper
- 1 cup 1% milk

Direction

- In a microwave-safe bowl, place butter and onion, and cook in the microwave for 2 minutes on high power. Add vegetable broth, asparagus, white pepper, and garlic powder. Cover the bowl and microwave for 10 to 12 minutes on high power. Pour mixture into the blender to puree.
- Transfer mixture to a microwave-safe dish, add milk, stir, and continue to microwave until heated through.

Nutrition Information

- Calories: 118 calories;
- Cholesterol: 18
- Protein: 5.2
- Total Fat: 6.8
- Sodium: 198

- Total Carbohydrate: 11.2

300. Balsamic Mushroom Bread Pudding

Serving: 12 servings. | Prep: 45mins | Cook: 40mins | Ready in:

Ingredients

- 3 tablespoons butter, divided
- 1-1/2 pounds sliced fresh mushrooms
- 1 large onion, chopped
- 1/2 cup balsamic vinegar
- 1 teaspoon dried marjoram
- 1/2 teaspoon salt
- 1/4 teaspoon pepper
- 1 can (10-1/2 ounces) condensed beef consomme, undiluted
- 1 cup heavy whipping cream
- 2 large eggs
- 2 large egg yolks
- 1 tablespoon minced fresh thyme or 1/4 teaspoon dried thyme
- 6 cups day-old cubed sourdough bread
- 1 package (8 ounces) cream cheese, cut into 1/2-inch cubes

Direction

- Preheat an oven to 350°. Over medium heat, heat 2 tablespoons of butter in a large skillet and then add onion and half of mushrooms. Cook while stirring for 6 to 8 minutes or until the mushrooms become tender. Take out from the pan. Repeat this with the remaining mushrooms and butter.
- Place the onion and mushrooms back into the pan. Add pepper, salt, marjoram and vinegar. Let it cook while stirring often for about 5 minutes until the liquid evaporates. Take out from the heat and cool a bit.
- Whisk thyme, egg yolks, eggs, cream and consommé in a large bowl until blended. Mix in mushroom mixture and bread cubes and

allow to stand for 10 minutes or until the bread is softened.
- Place into a 13x9-inch baking dish that is greased. Add cream cheese on top. Bake without covering for 40 to 45 minutes or until set. You can serve while still warm.

Nutrition Information

- Calories:
- Sodium:
- Fiber:
- Total Carbohydrate:
- Cholesterol:
- Protein:
- Total Fat:

301. Basil Garden Salad

Serving: 6 servings. | Prep: 15mins | Cook: 0mins | Ready in:

Ingredients

- 2 cups torn leaf lettuce
- 1 cup torn Bibb lettuce
- 3 green onions with tops, sliced
- 1 medium tomato, peeled and diced
- 6 fresh mushrooms, sliced
- 9 fresh basil leaves, thinly sliced
- 2 tablespoons red wine vinegar
- 3 tablespoons olive oil
- 1/4 teaspoon pepper
- 1/2 teaspoon salt, optional
- 1/2 teaspoon sugar, optional

Direction

- Mix basil, mushrooms, tomato, onions, and lettuce in a big salad bowl. Blend sugar (optional), salt, pepper, oil, and vinegar in a jar with a tight lid. Cover then shake well. Pour on salad while tossing to coat. Serve quickly.

Nutrition Information

- Calories: 78 calories
- Total Carbohydrate: 3g carbohydrate (0 sugars
- Cholesterol: 0 cholesterol
- Protein: 1g protein. Diabetic Exchanges: 1-1/2 fat
- Total Fat: 7g fat (0 saturated fat)
- Sodium: 6mg sodium
- Fiber: 0 fiber)

302. Black Bean Veggie Enchiladas

Serving: 6 enchiladas. | Prep: 30mins | Cook: 25mins | Ready in:

Ingredients

- 1 small onion, chopped
- 1 small green pepper, chopped
- 1/2 cup sliced fresh mushrooms
- 2 teaspoons olive oil
- 1 garlic clove, minced
- 1 can (15 ounces) black beans, rinsed and drained
- 3/4 cup frozen corn, thawed
- 1 can (4 ounces) chopped green chilies
- 2 tablespoons reduced-sodium taco seasoning
- 1 teaspoon dried cilantro flakes
- 6 whole wheat tortillas (8 inches), warmed
- 1/2 cup enchilada sauce
- 3/4 cup shredded reduced-fat Mexican cheese blend

Direction

- Heat oil in a large pan and sauté onion, green pepper as well as the mushrooms all together until it turns crisp yet tender. Stir in the garlic and let it cook for about a minute, then add the beans and corn, the chilies, cilantro and taco seasonings. Cook them all for roughly 2 to 3 minutes or until completely heated.

- Scoop half a cup of the bean mixture and put down at the middle of every tortilla. Roll up and set them seam side down in a greased baking pan, about 13 x 9-inch size. Top with the enchilada sauce and then the cheese.
- Bake inside the oven for 25 to 30 minutes at 350° without placing any cover or until completely heated.

Nutrition Information

- Calories: 292 calories
- Total Carbohydrate: 43g carbohydrate (4g sugars
- Cholesterol: 10mg cholesterol
- Protein: 13g protein.
- Total Fat: 8g fat (2g saturated fat)
- Sodium: 759mg sodium
- Fiber: 6g fiber)

303. Broccoli Veggie Pasta Primavera

Serving: 4 servings. | Prep: 10mins | Cook: 15mins | Ready in:

Ingredients

- 8 ounces uncooked linguine
- 1 cup thinly sliced fresh broccoli
- 1 medium carrot, thinly sliced
- 1/2 cup sliced green onions
- 1/4 cup butter, cubed
- 1-1/2 cups sliced fresh mushrooms
- 1 garlic clove, minced
- 1 teaspoon dried basil
- 1/2 teaspoon salt
- 1/4 teaspoon pepper
- 6 ounces fresh or frozen snow peas (about 2 cups), thawed
- 1/4 cup dry white wine or chicken broth
- 1/4 cup shredded Parmesan cheese

Direction

- Cook linguine following package instructions.
- In the meantime, cook onions, carrot, and broccoli with butter in a big skillet for 3 minutes. Add pepper, salt, basil, garlic, and mushrooms; cook for another 1 minute. Add wine and snow peas. Put a cover on and cook until the peas are soft and crunchy, about 2 minutes.
- Strain the linguine, add to the skillet and blend by tossing. Use cheese to sprinkle.

Nutrition Information

- Calories: 376 calories
- Total Carbohydrate: 49g carbohydrate (6g sugars
- Cholesterol: 34mg cholesterol
- Protein: 13g protein.
- Total Fat: 14g fat (8g saturated fat)
- Sodium: 514mg sodium
- Fiber: 5g fiber)

304. Cheese Trio Artichoke & Spinach Dip

Serving: 4 cups. | Prep: 20mins | Cook: 02hours00mins | Ready in:

Ingredients

- 1 cup chopped fresh mushrooms
- 1 tablespoon butter
- 2 garlic cloves, minced
- 1-1/2 cups mayonnaise
- 1 package (8 ounces) cream cheese, softened
- 1 cup plus 2 tablespoons grated Parmesan cheese, divided
- 1 cup shredded part-skim mozzarella cheese, divided
- 1 can (14 ounces) water-packed artichoke hearts, rinsed, drained and chopped
- 1 package (10 ounces) frozen chopped spinach, thawed and squeezed dry
- 1/4 cup chopped sweet red pepper

- Toasted French bread baguette slices

Direction

- Sauté mushrooms in a big skillet until tender. Add in garlic and cook for 1 minute more.
- Mix together the cream cheese, mayonnaise, 3/4 cup mozzarella cheese, and 1 cup Parmesan cheese in a big bowl. Add in the artichokes, red pepper, spinach, and mushroom mixture.
- Pour the mixture into a 3-quart slow cooker. Sprinkle top with remaining cheeses. Cook on low heat for 2 to 3 hours covered or until heated through. Best served with slices of baguette.

Nutrition Information

- Calories: 264 calories
- Sodium: 354mg sodium
- Fiber: 1g fiber)
- Total Carbohydrate: 4g carbohydrate (0 sugars
- Cholesterol: 34mg cholesterol
- Protein: 6g protein.
- Total Fat: 25g fat (8g saturated fat)

305. Cheesy Bread

Serving: 16 servings. | Prep: 25mins | Cook: 20mins | Ready in:

Ingredients

- 6 cups sliced fresh mushrooms
- 1 tablespoon butter
- 4 green onions, chopped
- 1 loaf (1 pound) French bread
- 1 carton (8 ounces) spreadable garlic and herb cream cheese
- 2 cups shredded Italian cheese blend
- 1 cup mayonnaise
- 1 cup grated Parmesan cheese

Direction

- Sauté mushrooms in butter in a large skillet until soft. Add onions; sauté until liquid has vaporized. Put to one side.
- Divide French bread in half vertically and then crosswise; spread cream cheese over the cut sides. Combine Parmesan cheese, mayonnaise, and Italian cheese. Spread cheese mixture over bread. Place mushroom mixture over the top.
- Arrange on a baking sheet. Bake for 20 minutes at 350° until cheese is melted. If desired, broil about 4 to 6 inches away from the heat source until it turns golden brown, for 2 to 4 minutes. Cut bread into slices and serve warm.

Nutrition Information

- Calories: 308 calories
- Cholesterol: 41mg cholesterol
- Protein: 10g protein.
- Total Fat: 21g fat (8g saturated fat)
- Sodium: 534mg sodium
- Fiber: 1g fiber)
- Total Carbohydrate: 19g carbohydrate (2g sugars

306. Chili Lime Mushroom Tacos

Serving: 4 servings. | Prep: 15mins | Cook: 10mins | Ready in:

Ingredients

- 4 large portobello mushrooms (about 3/4 pound)
- 1 tablespoon olive oil
- 1 medium sweet red pepper, cut into strips
- 1 medium onion, halved and thinly sliced
- 2 garlic cloves, minced
- 1-1/2 teaspoons chili powder
- 1/2 teaspoon salt
- 1/2 teaspoon ground cumin
- 1/4 teaspoon crushed red pepper flakes

- 1 teaspoon grated lime zest
- 2 tablespoons lime juice
- 8 corn tortillas (6 inches), warmed
- 1 cup shredded pepper jack cheese

Direction

- Get rid of the mushrooms' stems, and remove gills with a spoon, if wanted. Cut mushrooms into slices with 1/2 inch size.
- Heat oil in a big skillet on moderately high heat, then sauté with onion, red pepper and mushrooms for 5 to 7 minutes, until mushrooms are softened. Stir in lime juice, lime zest, seasonings and garlic, then cook and stir for a minute. Serve together with tortillas and put cheese on top.

Nutrition Information

- Calories: 300 calories
- Sodium: 524mg sodium
- Fiber: 6g fiber)
- Total Carbohydrate: 33g carbohydrate (5g sugars
- Cholesterol: 30mg cholesterol
- Protein: 13g protein. Diabetic Exchanges: 2 vegetable
- Total Fat: 14g fat (6g saturated fat)

307. Contest Winning Garden Harvest Chili

Serving: 6 servings (2-1/2 quarts). | Prep: 20mins | Cook: 10mins | Ready in:

Ingredients

- 2 tablespoons vegetable oil
- 2 garlic cloves, minced
- 1 medium green pepper, chopped
- 1 medium sweet red pepper, chopped
- 1-1/2 cups sliced fresh mushrooms
- 1/2 cup chopped onion
- 1 can (28 ounces) diced tomatoes, undrained
- 1 can (15 ounces) tomato sauce
- 2 tablespoons chili powder
- 2 teaspoons sugar
- 1 teaspoon ground cumin
- 1 can (16 ounces) kidney beans, rinsed and drained
- 2 cups sliced zucchini
- 2 cups frozen sweet corn, thawed
- 1-1/2 cups shredded cheddar cheese, optional

Direction

- Heat oil in a skillet on medium-high heat. Sauté onion, mushrooms, peppers, and garlic until tender. Add cumin, sugar, chili powder, tomato sauce, and tomatoes with liquid; boil. Lower heat to low. Add corn, zucchini, and beans. Simmer for 10 minutes, uncovered, until zucchini becomes tender. Serve in bowls. Top with cheese if you want.

Nutrition Information

- Calories: 252 calories
- Fiber: 0 fiber)
- Total Carbohydrate: 44g carbohydrate (0 sugars
- Cholesterol: 0 cholesterol
- Protein: 10g protein. Diabetic Exchanges: 2 starch
- Total Fat: 7g fat (0 saturated fat)
- Sodium: 675mg sodium

308. Creamy Eggs & Mushrooms Au Gratin

Serving: 8 servings. | Prep: 15mins | Cook: 25mins | Ready in:

Ingredients

- 2 tablespoons butter
- 1 pound sliced fresh mushrooms

- 1 green onion, chopped
- SAUCE:
- 2 tablespoons butter, melted
- 3 tablespoons all-purpose flour
- 1/2 teaspoon salt
- 1/8 teaspoon pepper
- 1 cup 2% milk
- 1/2 cup heavy whipping cream
- 2 tablespoons grated Parmesan cheese
- EGGS:
- 16 large eggs
- 1/4 teaspoon salt
- 1/8 teaspoon pepper
- 1/4 cup butter, cubed
- 1/2 cup grated Parmesan cheese
- 1 green onion, finely chopped

Direction

- Heat the butter in a big broiler-safe skillet on medium-high heat. Add the mushrooms and let it cook and stir for 4-6 minutes or until it turns brown. Add the green onion and let it cook for 1 minute more. Using a slotted spoon, take it out of the pan. Wipe the skillet clean.
- To make the sauce, melt the butter in a small saucepan on medium heat. Mix in the pepper, salt and flour until it becomes smooth, then slowly whisk in the cream and milk. Let it boil, mixing continuously, then cook and stir for 2 to 4 minutes or until it becomes thick. Take it out of the heat, then mix in cheese.
- Set the broiler to preheat. To make the eggs, whisk the pepper, salt and eggs in a big bowl until combined. Heat the butter in the same skillet on medium heat. Pour in the egg mixture and let it cook and stir until no liquid egg remains and the eggs become thick. Take it out of the heat.
- Scoop 1/2 of the sauce on top of the eggs, then put mushrooms on top. Add the leftover sauce, then sprinkle cheese on top. Let it broil for 4-6 minutes, placed 4-5 inches from the heat source, or until the top turns light brown. Sprinkle green onion on top.

Nutrition Information

- Calories: 363 calories
- Sodium: 591mg sodium
- Fiber: 1g fiber)
- Total Carbohydrate: 8g carbohydrate (3g sugars
- Cholesterol: 431mg cholesterol
- Protein: 18g protein.
- Total Fat: 29g fat (15g saturated fat)

309. Creamy Pasta With Florets

Serving: 8 servings. | Prep: 20mins | Cook: 10mins | Ready in:

Ingredients

- 1 cup (8 ounces) 1% cottage cheese
- 1/2 cup 1% milk
- 1/4 cup reduced-fat sour cream
- 1/4 cup grated Parmesan cheese
- 1/2 teaspoon salt
- 1/8 teaspoon cayenne pepper
- 5 cups broccoli florets
- 4 cups cauliflowerets
- 4 ounces uncooked angel hair pasta
- 3 garlic cloves, minced
- 2 teaspoons olive oil
- 2-1/2 cups sliced fresh mushrooms

Direction

- Mix together cayenne, salt, Parmesan cheese, sour cream, milk and cottage cheese in a food processor or blender, then cover and blend until smooth. Put the mixture aside.
- Bring 1 inch of water in a saucepan to a boil, then put into a steamer basket set over boiling water with cauliflower and broccoli. Cover and steam vegetables until tender yet still crispy, about 3 to 4 minutes. In the meantime, following package directions to cook pasta, then drain.

- Saute garlic in a big nonstick skillet with oil about 2 minutes. Put in mushrooms and saute for 5 more minutes. Stir in cottage cheese mixture, pasta, cauliflower and broccoli, then heat through.

Nutrition Information

- Calories: 151 calories
- Sodium: 357mg sodium
- Fiber: 2g fiber)
- Total Carbohydrate: 20g carbohydrate (0 sugars
- Cholesterol: 7mg cholesterol
- Protein: 11g protein. Diabetic Exchanges: 1 starch
- Total Fat: 4g fat (2g saturated fat)

310. Diploma Appetizers

Serving: 32 servings. | Prep: 20mins | Cook: 15mins | Ready in:

Ingredients

- 16 to 20 green onions
- 2-1/2 cups chopped fresh mushrooms
- 1/4 cup butter, cubed
- 1 package (8 ounces) cream cheese, cubed
- 1/2 teaspoon Worcestershire sauce
- 1/4 teaspoon salt
- 1/4 teaspoon pepper
- 1/8 teaspoon garlic salt
- 32 slices white or wheat bread, crusts removed
- Melted butter
- 1 cup boiling water

Direction

- Slice off onions' green tops; put aside. Chop enough from the rest of the onions until it reaches half a cup.
- Sauté mushrooms and onions in butter in a large skillet until onions are softened. Put in seasonings and cream cheese; whisk on low heat for about 2 minutes until cheese melts. Take off the heat; let it cool slightly.
- Use a rolling pin to flatten out the bread. Spread on each slice with 1 tablespoon of mushroom mixture; roll up. Arrange in one layer on baking sheets coated with cooking spray. Leave in the freezer for half an hour. You can store frozen unbaked roll-ups in airtight containers in the freezer for a maximum period of 1 month.
- Brush over with melted butter. Bake at 375 degrees until light brown, or for 15 to 20 minutes. Halve onions tops reserved earlier lengthwise. Arrange into boiling water for 60 seconds; drain and allow to cool. Tie a strip around each roll-up.

Nutrition Information

- Calories:
- Fiber:
- Total Carbohydrate:
- Cholesterol:
- Protein:
- Total Fat:
- Sodium:

311. Easy Marinated Mushrooms

Serving: 16 | Prep: 15mins | Cook: 8hours | Ready in:

Ingredients

- 2 cups soy sauce
- 2 cups water
- 1 cup butter
- 2 cups white sugar
- 4 (8 ounce) packages fresh mushrooms, stems removed

Direction

- On low heat, mix butter, water and soy sauce in a medium saucepan. Mix till melted butter, then slowly stir in the sugar till sugar totally dissolved.
- In a slow cooker on Low setting, put mushrooms and coat mushrooms with the soy sauce mixture. Cook 8 to 10 hours while mixing roughly every hour. Keep chilled in the fridge till serving.

Nutrition Information

- Calories: 228 calories;
- Sodium: 1889
- Total Carbohydrate: 29.3
- Cholesterol: 31
- Protein: 3.9
- Total Fat: 11.7

312. Favorite Marvelous Mushroom Soup

Serving: 6 servings. | Prep: 30mins | Cook: 0mins | Ready in:

Ingredients

- 1/2 pound fresh mushrooms, sliced
- 1 large onion, finely chopped
- 1 garlic clove, minced
- 1/2 teaspoon dried tarragon
- 1/4 teaspoon ground nutmeg
- 3 tablespoons butter
- 1/4 cup all-purpose flour
- 2 cans (14-1/2 ounces each) beef or vegetable broth
- 1 cup sour cream
- 1/2 cup half-and-half cream
- 1/2 cup evaporated milk
- 1 teaspoon lemon juice
- Dash hot pepper sauce
- Salt and pepper to taste

Direction

- Sauté nutmeg, tarragon, garlic, onion, and mushrooms in butter in a soup kettle or Dutch oven until vegetables are softened. Add flour and stir until smooth. Slowly pour in broth; bring to a boil, stirring continuously. Turn heat to low; gradually add sour cream. Cook, stirring until no lumps remain. Mix in milk and cream. Add pepper, salt, hot pepper sauce, and lemon juice. Heat through without boiling.

Nutrition Information

- Calories: 229 calories
- Cholesterol: 59mg cholesterol
- Protein: 6g protein.
- Total Fat: 16g fat (11g saturated fat)
- Sodium: 358mg sodium
- Fiber: 1g fiber)
- Total Carbohydrate: 12g carbohydrate (7g sugars

313. Foolproof Mushrooms

Serving: 2-1/2 dozen. | Prep: 15mins | Cook: 10mins | Ready in:

Ingredients

- 1 package (6-1/2 ounces) garlic-herb spreadable cheese
- 3 tablespoons grated Parmesan cheese, divided
- 30 small fresh mushrooms, stems removed
- Thinly sliced fresh basil, optional

Direction

- Turn oven to 400° to preheat. Combine 2 tablespoon Parmesan cheese and spreadable cheese in a small mixing bowl; fill into mushroom caps.
- Remove stuffed mushrooms to a baking sheet lined with aluminum foil; scatter the rest of Parmesan on top. Bake in the preheated oven

until lightly browned for 10 to 12 minutes. If desired, sprinkle top with basil.

Nutrition Information

- Calories: 29 calories
- Sodium: 45mg sodium
- Fiber: 0 fiber)
- Total Carbohydrate: 1g carbohydrate (0 sugars
- Cholesterol: 8mg cholesterol
- Protein: 1g protein.
- Total Fat: 3g fat (2g saturated fat)

314. Fresh Broccoli Salad

Serving: 9 | Prep: 15mins | Cook: 15mins | Ready in:

Ingredients

- 2 heads fresh broccoli
- 1 red onion
- 1/2 pound bacon
- 3/4 cup raisins
- 3/4 cup sliced almonds
- 1 cup mayonnaise
- 1/2 cup white sugar
- 2 tablespoons white wine vinegar

Direction

- On medium high heat, cook bacon in a deep pan till browned evenly. Let it cool off and crumble.
- Chop the broccoli into bite-size pieces and chop the onion into thin bite-size slices. Mix them well with your preferred nuts, raisins and bacon.
- For the dressing, whisk the vinegar, sugar and mayonnaise till smooth in consistency. Mix into the salad, keep it chilled and serve.

Nutrition Information

- Calories: 374 calories;
- Protein: 7.3
- Total Fat: 27.2
- Sodium: 353
- Total Carbohydrate: 28.5
- Cholesterol: 18

315. Fresh Veggie Pizza

Serving: 8 servings. | Prep: 25mins | Cook: 0mins | Ready in:

Ingredients

- 1 tube (8 ounces) reduced-fat crescent rolls
- 1 package (8 ounces) reduced-fat cream cheese
- 1 envelope ranch salad dressing mix
- 2 tablespoons fat-free milk
- 1/2 cup each chopped fresh broccoli, cauliflower, carrots, green pepper, sweet red pepper and mushrooms

Direction

- Unroll crescent dough roll to one long rectangle. Press at the bottom of a 13x9-in. baking pan that's coated with cooking spray. Seal perforations and seams.
- Bake for 11-13 minutes or until golden brown at 375 degrees. Completely cool.
- Beat milk, salad dressing mix and cream cheese until smooth in a big bowl. Spread onto crust. Sprinkle with veggies. Refrigerate, covered, for at least an hour prior to serving. Cut to 16 pieces.

Nutrition Information

- Calories: 164 calories
- Total Fat: 7g fat (3g saturated fat)
- Sodium: 623mg sodium
- Fiber: 1g fiber)
- Total Carbohydrate: 18g carbohydrate (0 sugars
- Cholesterol: 10mg cholesterol

- Protein: 6g protein.

316. Garden Focaccia

Serving: 20 slices. | Prep: 15mins | Cook: 30mins | Ready in:

Ingredients

- 1 loaf (1 pound) frozen bread dough, thawed
- 1 tablespoon olive oil
- 1 tablespoon minced fresh rosemary or 1 teaspoon dried rosemary, crushed
- 1 tablespoon minced fresh thyme or 1 teaspoon dried thyme
- 1 package (8 ounces) cream cheese, softened
- 1/4 cup finely chopped onion
- 1 garlic clove, minced
- 4 large fresh mushrooms, sliced
- 3 medium tomatoes, sliced
- 1 small zucchini, thinly sliced
- 1/4 cup grated Parmesan cheese

Direction

- Roll the dough on a lightly floured surface into a 15x10-inch rectangle. Then arrange in a 15x10x1-inch greased baking pan. Put a cover and allow to rise for half an hour.
- Make indentations in the dough with fingertips. Brush oil over; dust with thyme and rosemary. Bake at 400 degrees until golden brown, for 12-15 minutes. Let slightly cool.
- Mix garlic, onion, and cream cheese in a large bowl. Spread on the crust. Place zucchini, tomatoes, and mushrooms on top; dust with Parmesan cheese.
- Bake until brown lightly, for 12-15 minutes. Before slicing, let cool for 5 minutes.

Nutrition Information

- Calories: 109 calories
- Total Fat: 4g fat (2g saturated fat)
- Sodium: 185mg sodium
- Fiber: 1g fiber)
- Total Carbohydrate: 14g carbohydrate (0 sugars
- Cholesterol: 7mg cholesterol
- Protein: 5g protein. Diabetic Exchanges: 1 vegetable

317. Garlic Mushroom Appetizer

Serving: 12-16 servings. | Prep: 15mins | Cook: 30mins | Ready in:

Ingredients

- 1 cup chopped onion
- 1/2 cup canola oil
- 3 tablespoons butter
- 2 pounds fresh mushrooms, sliced
- 1 can (28 ounces) crushed tomatoes in puree, undrained
- 1 teaspoon salt
- 1/4 teaspoon pepper
- 1/2 cup red wine vinegar
- 1 bunch fresh parsley, finely chopped (about 1-1/2 cups)
- 3 garlic cloves, minced
- Sliced French bread

Direction

- Sauté onion in butter and oil in a large saucepan until crisp-tender. Put in mushrooms; cook for 2 minutes or until vegetables become tender. Put in pepper, salt, and tomatoes; simmer, covered for 20 to 30 minutes.
- Mix in the garlic, parsley, and vinegar. Simmer for 10 minutes, covered. Keep in the refrigerator for several hours or overnight, covered. Scoop onto French bread slices to serve.

Nutrition Information

- Calories: 118 calories
- Total Fat: 9g fat (2g saturated fat)
- Sodium: 240mg sodium
- Fiber: 2g fiber)
- Total Carbohydrate: 8g carbohydrate (1g sugars
- Cholesterol: 6mg cholesterol
- Protein: 3g protein.

318. Gnocchi Alfredo

Serving: 5 servings. | Prep: 10mins | Cook: 15mins | Ready in:

Ingredients

- 2 pounds potato gnocchi
- 3 tablespoons butter, divided
- 1 tablespoon plus 1-1/2 teaspoons all-purpose flour
- 1-1/2 cups whole milk
- 1/2 cup grated Parmesan cheese
- Dash ground nutmeg
- 1/2 pound sliced baby portobello mushrooms
- Minced fresh parsley, optional

Direction

- Cook the gnocchi following the package instructions; drain. In the meantime, melt 1 tbsp. of butter in a small saucepan. Mix in flour until smooth then add milk while stirring gradually; boil while constantly mixing. Cook and stir for 1-2 mins or until thick. Take off the heat; mix in nutmeg and cheese until combined. Keep warm.
- On medium heat, melt the remaining butter in a big heavy skillet. Heat for 5-7 mins while constantly mixing or until golden brown. Add gnocchi and mushrooms immediately; cook and stir for 4-5 mins or until the gnocchi are slightly brown and the mushrooms are tender.

Serve with sauce. Top with sprinkled parsley if desired.

Nutrition Information

- Calories: 529 calories
- Protein: 19g protein.
- Total Fat: 14g fat (8g saturated fat)
- Sodium: 996mg sodium
- Fiber: 5g fiber)
- Total Carbohydrate: 81g carbohydrate (15g sugars
- Cholesterol: 46mg cholesterol

319. Goat Cheese Mushrooms

Serving: 2 dozen. | Prep: 15mins | Cook: 15mins | Ready in:

Ingredients

- 24 baby portobello mushrooms (about 1 pound), stems removed
- 1/2 cup crumbled goat cheese
- 1/2 cup chopped drained roasted sweet red peppers
- Pepper to taste
- 4 teaspoons olive oil
- Chopped fresh parsley

Direction

- Heat the oven to 375°. Put caps of mushroom in an oiled baking pan, 15x10x1-inch in size. Stuff a teaspoon of cheese into each; put in a teaspoon red pepper on top of each. Scatter pepper over; sprinkle with oil.
- Bake to soften mushrooms, about 15 to 18 minutes. Scatter parsley on top.

Nutrition Information

- Calories: 19 calories
- Fiber: 0 fiber)

- Total Carbohydrate: 1g carbohydrate (1g sugars
- Cholesterol: 3mg cholesterol
- Protein: 1g protein.
- Total Fat: 1g fat (0 saturated fat)
- Sodium: 31mg sodium

320. Green Bean Quiche

Serving: 6 servings. | Prep: 30mins | Cook: 25mins | Ready in:

Ingredients

- 1 package (9 ounces) frozen cut green beans
- 1/2 cup water
- 1/2 cup chopped onion
- 2 tablespoons butter
- 1/2 cup sliced fresh mushrooms
- 1/4 cup diced green pepper
- 1/2 cup mayonnaise
- 1/4 cup sour cream
- 1/4 teaspoon salt
- 1/4 cup crushed saltines (about 8 crackers)
- 6 eggs, lightly beaten
- 1 medium tomato, seeded and chopped
- 3/4 cup shredded sharp cheddar cheese

Direction

- Arrange beans in a saucepan; cover with water; allow to boil. Turn the heat down. Simmer with a cover till crisp-tender, or for 6-8 minutes; strain; set aside.
- Sauté onion in butter till tender in a small skillet. Include in green pepper and mushrooms; sauté till tender.
- In a large bowl, mix salt, sour cream and mayonnaise; mix in the cracker crumbs, mushroom mixture and beans. Gradually mix in eggs. Place into a greased deep-dish 9-inch pie plate. Top with cheese and tomato.
- Bake at 350° till a knife come out clean after being inserted in the center, or for 25-30 minutes. Allow to stand, 5-10 minutes before cutting.

Nutrition Information

- Calories: 349 calories
- Cholesterol: 251mg cholesterol
- Protein: 11g protein.
- Total Fat: 30g fat (10g saturated fat)
- Sodium: 479mg sodium
- Fiber: 2g fiber)
- Total Carbohydrate: 9g carbohydrate (4g sugars

321. Grilled Mediterranean Eggplant & Tomato Salad

Serving: 6 servings. | Prep: 15mins | Cook: 15mins | Ready in:

Ingredients

- 1 medium eggplant, cut into 1/2-inch slices
- 1/4 cup olive oil, divided
- 1-1/2 teaspoons minced fresh thyme or 1/2 teaspoon dried thyme
- 1-1/2 teaspoons minced fresh oregano or 1/2 teaspoon dried oregano
- 1/2 pound sliced fresh mushrooms
- 1 large onion, coarsely chopped
- 1 garlic clove, minced
- 1/4 teaspoon salt
- 1/4 teaspoon coarsely ground pepper
- 1/3 cup dry red wine
- 1-1/2 cups cherry tomatoes, halved
- 1/4 cup minced fresh parsley
- 2 tablespoons balsamic vinegar
- 1/2 cup crumbled feta cheese

Direction

- Use a brush to coat the eggplant with 2 tablespoons of oil then season it with oregano and thyme. Put the seasoned eggplant on a grill over medium heat then cover and let it grill for 3-4 minutes on every side until softened. Slice the grilled eggplant into bite-size pieces once it is cool to the touch.

- While the eggplant is grilling, put the remaining oil in a big skillet and heat it up on medium-high heat. Put in the onion and mushrooms and sauté for 5-7 minutes until soft. Mix in the pepper, garlic and salt and let it cook for 1 more minute. Pour in the wine and let the mixture cook while stirring the browned bits off the skillet. Let it boil and continue cooking for 2-3 minutes until the liquid has reduced.
- Mix the tomatoes, eggplant, vinegar, mushroom mixture and parsley together in a big bowl. Put in the cheese and mix until well-blended.

Nutrition Information

- Calories:
- Protein:
- Total Fat:
- Sodium:
- Fiber:
- Total Carbohydrate:
- Cholesterol:

322. Grilled Vegetable Orzo Salad

Serving: 8 servings. | Prep: 35mins | Cook: 10mins | Ready in:

Ingredients

- 1-1/4 cups uncooked orzo pasta
- 1/2 pound fresh asparagus, trimmed
- 1 medium zucchini, cut lengthwise into 1/2-inch slices
- 1 medium sweet yellow or red pepper, halved
- 1 large portobello mushroom, stem removed
- 1/2 medium red onion, halved
- DRESSING:
- 1/3 cup olive oil
- 1/4 cup balsamic vinegar
- 3 tablespoons lemon juice
- 4 garlic cloves, minced
- 1 teaspoon lemon-pepper seasoning
- SALAD:
- 1 cup grape tomatoes, halved
- 1 tablespoon minced fresh parsley
- 1 tablespoon minced fresh basil
- 1/2 teaspoon salt
- 1/4 teaspoon pepper
- 1 cup (4 ounces) crumbled feta cheese

Direction

- Follow packaging instructions to cook the orzo. In a big bowl, add vegetables. Beat the dressing ingredients in a small-sized bowl; toss with the vegetables until coated.
- Take out the vegetables and reserve dressing. On medium heat, grill with cover the pepper, mushroom, and onion for 5 to 10 minutes until tender, flipping occasionally. For 3 to 4 minutes, grill with cover the zucchini and asparagus until cooked to the desired doneness, flipping occasionally.
- Let vegetables cool enough to handle; slice into bite-size pieces. Mix together tomatoes, pepper, basil, reserved dressing, parsley, cooked orzo, salt, and grilled vegetables in a big bowl; tossing until blended. Keep in refrigerator until cold or eat at room temperature. Add in cheese just before serving.

Nutrition Information

- Calories: 260 calories
- Protein: 8g protein. Diabetic Exchanges: 2 fat
- Total Fat: 12g fat (3g saturated fat)
- Sodium: 352mg sodium
- Fiber: 2g fiber)
- Total Carbohydrate: 30g carbohydrate (4g sugars
- Cholesterol: 8mg cholesterol

323. Grilled Veggies With Caper Butter

Serving: 8 servings. | Prep: 25mins | Cook: 10mins | Ready in:

Ingredients

- 1/4 cup butter, cubed
- 2 garlic cloves, minced
- 1 tablespoon lemon juice
- 2 teaspoons capers, drained and chopped
- 1 tablespoon minced fresh parsley
- 2 medium zucchini, cut in half lengthwise
- 2 medium crookneck or yellow summer squash, cut in half lengthwise
- 1 medium sweet yellow or orange pepper, quartered
- 1 medium sweet red pepper, quartered
- 2 large portobello mushrooms, stems removed
- 3 green onions, trimmed
- 2 tablespoons olive oil
- 1/2 teaspoon salt
- 1/4 teaspoon pepper

Direction

- Over medium-low heat, melt butter in a small saucepan. Add garlic and cook for 2 minutes. Add capers and lemon juice; continue to cook for another 2 minutes. Stir in parsley.
- Sweep the vegetables with oil; then dust with pepper and salt.
- Cover and grill peppers, squash, and zucchini over medium heat until crisp-tender, around 4-5 minutes on each side; occasionally basting with the butter mixture. Grill onions and mushrooms, covered, until tender, 1-2 minutes on each side; basting infrequently with the butter mixture.
- Cut the vegetables as desired; then transfer to a serving dish. Spray with the remaining butter mixture.

Nutrition Information

- Calories: 117 calories
- Cholesterol: 15mg cholesterol
- Protein: 2g protein.
- Total Fat: 10g fat (4g saturated fat)
- Sodium: 219mg sodium
- Fiber: 2g fiber)
- Total Carbohydrate: 7g carbohydrate (3g sugars

324. Hearty Portobello Linguine

Serving: 4 servings. | Prep: 15mins | Cook: 10mins | Ready in:

Ingredients

- 1 package (9 ounces) refrigerated linguine
- 1/4 cup olive oil
- 4 large portobello mushroom caps (about 3/4 pound), halved and thinly sliced
- 3 garlic cloves, minced
- 3 plum tomatoes, chopped
- 1/3 cup pitted Greek olives, halved
- 1 teaspoon Greek seasoning
- 3/4 cup crumbled tomato and basil feta cheese

Direction

- Following the package directions to cook linguine. At the same time, heat oil in a big skillet on moderately high heat. Put in mushrooms then cook and stir until softened. Put in garlic then cook for one more minute. Stir in Greek seasoning, olives and tomatoes, then cook and stir for 2 minutes.
- Drain linguine and put into pan, then toss to coat well. Serve together with cheese.

Nutrition Information

- Calories: 422 calories

- Total Carbohydrate: 43g carbohydrate (4g sugars
- Cholesterol: 11mg cholesterol
- Protein: 14g protein.
- Total Fat: 21g fat (4g saturated fat)
- Sodium: 763mg sodium
- Fiber: 5g fiber)

325. Herbed Portobello Pasta

Serving: 4 servings. | Prep: 20mins | Cook: 15mins | Ready in:

Ingredients

- 1/2 pound uncooked multigrain angel hair pasta
- 4 large portobello mushrooms (3/4 pound), stems removed
- 1 tablespoon olive oil
- 2 garlic cloves, minced
- 4 plum tomatoes, chopped
- 1/4 cup pitted Greek olives
- 1/4 cup minced fresh basil
- 1 teaspoon minced fresh rosemary or 1/4 teaspoon dried rosemary, crushed
- 1 teaspoon minced fresh thyme or 1/4 teaspoon dried thyme
- 1/4 teaspoon salt
- 1/8 teaspoon pepper
- 2/3 cup crumbled feta cheese
- 1/4 cup shredded Parmesan cheese

Direction

- Follow al dente directions on package to cook pasta. In the meantime, cut mushrooms first in half, then thinly slice. Heat oil in a big frying pan on medium heat. Add the mushrooms and sauté 8-10 minutes or until tender. Mix in garlic and cook for 1 more minute. Mix in olives and tomatoes. Put heat on low. Do not cover; cook until thick, 5 minutes. Mix in pepper, herbs, and salt. Drain water from pasta, keep 1/4 cup of cooking water. Mix the pasta into the mushroom mixture, use the cooking water to adjust consistency. Sprinkle on cheeses.

Nutrition Information

- Calories: 375 calories
- Total Carbohydrate: 48g carbohydrate (5g sugars
- Cholesterol: 14mg cholesterol
- Protein: 18g protein. Diabetic Exchanges: 3 starch
- Total Fat: 12g fat (4g saturated fat)
- Sodium: 585mg sodium
- Fiber: 7g fiber)

326. Homemade Marinated Vegetables

Serving: 6 servings. | Prep: 10mins | Cook: 0mins | Ready in:

Ingredients

- 1 head fresh broccoli, separated into florets
- 4 ounces fresh mushrooms, sliced
- 1 can (5 ounces) sliced water chestnuts, rinsed and drained
- 1 red onion, sliced, separated into rings
- 1 bottle (8 ounces) Italian dressing
- 1 to 2 cups cherry tomatoes, halved

Direction

- In a big bowl, mix together the dressing, onion, water chestnuts, mushrooms and broccoli florets. Cover the mixture; let it marinate for a few hours, stirring once in a while. Just prior to serve, put in cherry tomatoes, stirring lightly to combine.

Nutrition Information

- Calories: 190 calories

- Sodium: 649mg sodium
- Fiber: 5g fiber)
- Total Carbohydrate: 14g carbohydrate (6g sugars
- Cholesterol: 0 cholesterol
- Protein: 4g protein.
- Total Fat: 14g fat (2g saturated fat)

327. Italian Salad Bowl

Serving: 4 servings. | Prep: 15mins | Cook: 0mins | Ready in:

Ingredients

- 1 bunch leaf lettuce, torn into bite-size pieces
- 8 cherry tomatoes, halved
- 8 fresh mushrooms, sliced
- 4 radishes, sliced
- 1 small zucchini, thinly sliced
- 1/2 yellow, red or green pepper, thinly sliced
- 1/4 cup shredded mozzarella cheese
- Italian salad dressing to taste

Direction

- Mix all ingredients together in a big salad bowl. Serve right away.

Nutrition Information

- Calories: 57 calories
- Protein: 4g protein.
- Total Fat: 2g fat (1g saturated fat)
- Sodium: 52mg sodium
- Fiber: 2g fiber)
- Total Carbohydrate: 7g carbohydrate (3g sugars
- Cholesterol: 5mg cholesterol

328. Italian Spaghetti Squash

Serving: 4 | Prep: 15mins | Cook: 1hours25mins | Ready in:

Ingredients

- 1/2 cup water
- 1 spaghetti squash, halved and seeded
- 2 tablespoons butter
- 1 tablespoon olive oil
- 1 onion, diced
- 1 clove garlic, minced
- 1 (14.5 ounce) can diced tomatoes with onion, celery, and green pepper
- 2 teaspoons dried basil
- 1 teaspoon salt
- 1 teaspoon ground black pepper
- 1/4 cup shredded Parmesan cheese, plus more for topping

Direction

- Preheat an oven to 175°C/350°F.
- Put water in baking dish; put halved squash in dish, cut side down.
- In preheated oven, bake squash for 45 minutes till fork easily pierces skin. Cook squash while prepping the rest of the recipe.
- Melt olive oil and butter in big skillet on medium high heat. In hot butter, sauté onion for 5 minutes till soft. Add garlic; sauté for 1 more minute till fragrant. Put diced tomatoes on onion mixture; use basil to season. Cover skillet; lower heat to medium low. At a simmer, cook for 30 minutes till tomatoes are soft. Use pepper and salt to season.
- Strip flesh from skin to strands with a fork when squash is cool to handle. Mix parmesan cheese and squash into tomato mixture; cover skillet again. Cook for 5-10 more minutes till squash heats through. Sprinkle extra parmesan cheese on dish; serve.

Nutrition Information

- Calories: 204 calories;

- Total Fat: 12.5
- Sodium: 1230
- Total Carbohydrate: 22.4
- Cholesterol: 20
- Protein: 5.2

329. Italian Style Pizzas

Serving: 2 pizzas. | Prep: 15mins | Cook: 10mins | Ready in:

Ingredients

- 2 prebaked mini pizza crusts
- 1/2 cup prepared pesto
- 2/3 cup shredded part-skim mozzarella cheese
- 1/2 cup sliced sweet onion
- 1/2 cup thinly sliced fresh mushrooms
- 1/4 cup roasted sweet red peppers, drained
- 2 tablespoons grated Parmesan cheese

Direction

- On a cookie sheet without grease, place the crusts. Spread on the pesto. Layer mozzarella, onion, mushrooms, and the peppers. Sprinkle Parmesan on top. Bake in a 400-degree oven until cheese melts, 10-12 minutes.

Nutrition Information

- Calories: 429 calories
- Fiber: 2g fiber)
- Total Carbohydrate: 37g carbohydrate (3g sugars
- Cholesterol: 23mg cholesterol
- Protein: 19g protein.
- Total Fat: 23g fat (7g saturated fat)
- Sodium: 820mg sodium

330. Makeover Meatless Lasagna

Serving: 12 servings. | Prep: 30mins | Cook: 45mins | Ready in:

Ingredients

- 10 uncooked whole wheat lasagna noodles
- 1-1/2 cups sliced fresh mushrooms
- 1/4 cup chopped onion
- 2 garlic cloves, minced
- 1 can (14-1/2 ounces) Italian diced tomatoes, undrained
- 1 can (12 ounces) tomato paste
- 1 package (14 ounces) firm tofu, drained and cubed
- 2 eggs, lightly beaten
- 3 cups (24 ounces) 2% cottage cheese
- 1/2 cup grated Parmesan cheese
- 1/2 cup packed fresh parsley leaves
- 1/2 teaspoon pepper
- 2 cups shredded part-skim mozzarella cheese, divided

Direction

- Set oven temperature to 375 degrees and leave aside for preheating. Follow package instructions to cook noodles al dente. Using a large saucepan, cook onion and mushrooms at medium heat setting until tenderized. Mix garlic into pan and continue cooking for another minute. Introduce tomato paste and tomatoes while stirring until heated thoroughly. Blend tofu in a food processor until it has a smooth consistency. Then mix in the following five ingredients and continue blending until evenly blended. Strain water from noodles. Coat a baking tray measuring 13x9-in with cooking spray, and place five noodles at the bottom of the tray, overlapping if necessary. Layer as follows; half of tofu blend, half of sauce mix, and half of the mozzarella. Add the remaining noodles, tofu blend and sauce on top. Cover the tray and bake for 35 minutes. Remove cover to scatter remaining mozzarella. Continue baking while uncovered for another 10-15 minutes until the cheese has melted. Allow to sit for 10 minutes before serving.

Nutrition Information

- Calories: 258 calories
- Total Fat: 9g fat (4g saturated fat)
- Sodium: 498mg sodium
- Fiber: 3g fiber)
- Total Carbohydrate: 26g carbohydrate (9g sugars
- Cholesterol: 48mg cholesterol
- Protein: 19g protein. Diabetic Exchanges: 2 medium-fat meat

331. Manchester Stew

Serving: 6 servings. | Prep: 25mins | Cook: 08hours00mins | Ready in:

Ingredients

- 2 tablespoons olive oil
- 2 medium onions, chopped
- 2 garlic cloves, minced
- 1 teaspoon dried oregano
- 1 cup dry red wine
- 1 pound small red potatoes, quartered
- 1 can (16 ounces) kidney beans, rinsed and drained
- 1/2 pound sliced fresh mushrooms
- 2 medium leeks (white portion only), sliced
- 1 cup fresh baby carrots
- 2-1/2 cups water
- 1 can (14-1/2 ounces) no-salt-added diced tomatoes
- 1 teaspoon dried thyme
- 1/2 teaspoon salt
- 1/4 teaspoon pepper
- Fresh basil leaves

Direction

- Heat oil in a big frying pan over medium-high heat. Add onions, stir and cook for 2-3 minutes until the onions are soft. Add oregano and garlic, stir and cook for another 1 minute. Mix in wine. Boil it; cook for 3-4 minutes until the liquid decreases by half.
- Move to a 5- or 6-qt. slow cooker. Add carrots, leeks, mushrooms, beans, and potatoes. Mix in pepper, salt, thyme, tomatoes, and water. Put a cover on and cook for 8-10 hours on low until the potatoes are soft. Put the basil on top.

Nutrition Information

- Calories: 221 calories
- Protein: 8g protein. Diabetic Exchanges: 2 starch
- Total Fat: 5g fat (1g saturated fat)
- Sodium: 354mg sodium
- Fiber: 8g fiber)
- Total Carbohydrate: 38g carbohydrate (8g sugars
- Cholesterol: 0 cholesterol

332. Marinated Garden Platter

Serving: 8-10 servings. | Prep: 15mins | Cook: 0mins | Ready in:

Ingredients

- 1-1/2 pounds fresh green beans
- 3/4 cup canola oil
- 1/3 cup cider vinegar
- 1 tablespoon sugar
- 2 teaspoons Dijon mustard
- 1/2 teaspoon salt
- 1/2 teaspoon pepper
- 1 pint cherry tomatoes, halved
- 2 tablespoons finely chopped red onion
- 1/2 cup sliced fresh mushrooms

Direction

- Cover beans with water in a saucepan, cooking until crisp yet tender. As it cooks, mix the next 6 ingredients in a small jar with a tight lid, shaking well. Mix 1/4 cup of dressing, onion, and tomatoes in a bowl. Blend 2 tablespoons dressing and mushrooms in a separate bowl. Drain beans and put in a bowl. Add the rest of the dressing. Chill vegetables in their separate bowls for a minimum of an hour. Assemble vegetables on a platter to serve.

Nutrition Information

- Calories: 178 calories
- Protein: 2g protein.
- Total Fat: 17g fat (2g saturated fat)
- Sodium: 150mg sodium
- Fiber: 2g fiber)
- Total Carbohydrate: 8g carbohydrate (4g sugars
- Cholesterol: 0 cholesterol

333. Marinated Mushrooms & Artichokes

Serving: 16 servings (1/2 cup each). | Prep: 15mins | Cook: 0mins | Ready in:

Ingredients

- 2 pounds medium fresh mushrooms, halved
- 2 cans (14 ounces each) water-packed quartered artichoke hearts, drained
- 1-1/2 cups water
- 1 cup cider vinegar
- 1/2 cup olive oil
- 1 bay leaf
- 1-1/2 teaspoons salt
- 1-1/2 teaspoons minced fresh tarragon or 1/2 teaspoon dried tarragon
- 1-1/2 teaspoons minced fresh thyme or 1/2 teaspoon dried thyme
- 1 garlic clove, minced
- 1/2 teaspoon pepper
- 1 tablespoon minced fresh parsley
- Additional parsley

Direction

- Combine the initial 12 ingredients in a nonreactive bowl. Cover and keep in the refrigerator for 3-4 hours to let flavors combine. Put in more parsley to serve.

Nutrition Information

- Calories: 43 calories
- Total Fat: 1g fat (0 saturated fat)
- Sodium: 162mg sodium
- Fiber: 0 fiber)
- Total Carbohydrate: 5g carbohydrate (0 sugars
- Cholesterol: 0 cholesterol
- Protein: 3g protein. Diabetic Exchanges: 1 vegetable.

334. Marinated Vegetables

Serving: Serves 6 as a first course | Prep: | Cook: | Ready in:

Ingredients

- 1/3 cup fresh lemon juice
- 1/2 cup olive oil
- 2 cups chicken broth
- 3 garlic cloves, crushed lightly with the flat side of a knife
- a pinch of dried hot red pepper flakes, or to taste
- 3/4 teaspoon salt, or to taste
- 2 teaspoons coriander seeds
- 2 fresh thyme sprigs or 1/4 teaspoon dried thyme, crumbled
- 2 fresh oregano sprigs or 1/4 teaspoon dried oregano, crumbled
- 1 teaspoon sugar

- 2 leeks (about 1/2 pound), trimmed, washed well, and cut crosswise into 1-inch pieces
- 1 yellow squash, trimmed, halved lengthwise, and cut crosswise into 1-inch pieces
- 4 ribs of celery, trimmed and cut into 1-inch pieces
- 2 red bell peppers, cut into 1-inch pieces
- 1/4 pound green beans, trimmed and cut into 1-inch pieces
- 1/2 pound mushrooms, halved if large and the stems reserved for another use

Direction

- Preparation: Combine pepper, sugar, oregano, thyme, coriander seeds, salt, red pepper flakes, garlic, broth, oil and lemon juice to taste in a kettle. Boil the mixture, let it simmer, stirring once in a while, for 5 minutes. Boil the mixture, put in the leeks, and let simmer for 2 minutes. Put in the celery and the squash, and simmer the vegetables while stirring lightly for 2 minutes. Put in the green beans and bell peppers, and simmer the vegetables while stirring lightly for 2 minutes. Put in the mushrooms and simmer the vegetables while stirring lightly for 1/2 minute.
- Use a slotted spoon to transfer veggies to a bowl or shallow baking dish, boil the cooking liquid until it is decreased to half a cup, about 2 minutes, and through a fine sieve, strain it onto the vegetables. Let the vegetables marinate, with cover, keep chilled for a minimum of 3 hours or overnight. Use salt and pepper to season, then let cool to room temperature prior to serve.

Nutrition Information

- Calories: 270
- Cholesterol: 2 mg(1%)
- Protein: 5 g(11%)
- Total Fat: 20 g(30%)
- Saturated Fat: 3 g(14%)
- Sodium: 438 mg(18%)
- Fiber: 4 g(17%)
- Total Carbohydrate: 22 g(7%)

335. Mixed Mushroom Tartlets

Serving: 8 servings. | Prep: 40mins | Cook: 15mins | Ready in:

Ingredients

- 1-1/2 pounds sliced fresh assorted mushrooms
- 1 medium onion, chopped
- 1/2 cup butter
- 3 tablespoons olive oil
- 1/2 cup white wine or dry vermouth
- 1 teaspoon minced fresh thyme or 1/2 teaspoon dried thyme
- 1 teaspoon salt
- 1 cup heavy whipping cream
- 1 package (17.3 ounces) frozen puff pastry, thawed
- 1 egg yolk
- 1 teaspoon water

Direction

- Stir-fry the onion and mushroom in oil and butter by batches on a large pan until tender. Lower heat to medium and add the salt, wine, and thyme. Cook until wine is reduced to half then add the cream; stir. Continue to cook until mixture is thick, about 10 minutes. Take out from heat and put on one side.
- Roll out one puff pastry sheet; form into a 12x8-inch rectangle. Slice into 8 rectangle pieces. Mark 1/2 inch from the corner of each pastry with a sharp knife (don't slice through the pastry).
- Place into the baking sheets. Repeat procedure with the rest of the puff pastry. Scoop the mushroom mixture and spread at the middle. Beat water and egg yolk; brush onto the edges of the pastry.
- Bake for 13 to 16 minutes at 400 degrees F, until golden brown.

Nutrition Information

- Calories: 610 calories
- Protein: 8g protein.
- Total Fat: 44g fat (19g saturated fat)
- Sodium: 593mg sodium
- Fiber: 6g fiber)
- Total Carbohydrate: 42g carbohydrate (2g sugars
- Cholesterol: 96mg cholesterol

336. Mushroom & Leek Strudel

Serving: 2 strudels (12 slices each). | Prep: 50mins | Cook: 20mins | Ready in:

Ingredients

- 2 tablespoons butter, divided
- 2 pounds fresh mushrooms, finely chopped, divided
- 1 medium leek (white portion only), chopped, divided
- 2 garlic cloves, minced
- 1/4 cup white wine
- 1/4 cup heavy whipping cream
- 2 tablespoons minced fresh parsley
- 1 tablespoon minced fresh thyme or 1 teaspoon dried thyme
- 1/2 teaspoon salt
- 1/4 teaspoon pepper
- ASSEMBLY:
- 12 sheets phyllo dough (14x9 inches)
- 3/4 cup butter, melted
- 4 tablespoons grated Parmesan cheese, divided

Direction

- Heat a tablespoon of butter in big skillet on moderately-high heat. Put in leek and 1/2 of mushrooms. Cook and mix to slightly brown the mushrooms and soften the leek; take out of pan. Redo with leftover mushrooms, leek and butter, putting in garlic on the final minute of cooking time. Put in everything back to pan.
- Mix in cream and wine; cook till liquid is nearly vaporized, for 1 to 2 minutes. Mix in salt, pepper and herbs. Take out of pan; cool fully.
- Heat the oven to 375°. Put a phyllo dough sheet on work counter; brush using butter. Pile with 5 more sheets of phyllo, brushing every pile. Use plastic wrap and moist towel to cover the rest of the phyllo to avoid drying out. Scoop 1/2 of mushroom mixture on the middle third of phyllo dough, leaving an-inch of border from ends. Scatter 2 tablespoons of cheese on filling. Fold short sides up to seal the filling. Roll up like jelly-roll, beginning with the long side.
- Turn, seam side facing down, onto a baking pan, 15x10x1-inch in size, lined with parchment paper. Brush using more butter. Redo with the rest of the ingredients. Bake till golden brown, for 18 to 22 minutes.
- Let stand 10 minutes before slicing. Serve warm.

Nutrition Information

- Calories: 100 calories
- Protein: 2g protein.
- Total Fat: 8g fat (5g saturated fat)
- Sodium: 135mg sodium
- Fiber: 1g fiber)
- Total Carbohydrate: 6g carbohydrate (1g sugars
- Cholesterol: 22mg cholesterol

337. Mushroom & Peas Rice Pilaf

Serving: 6 servings. | Prep: 5mins | Cook: 20mins | Ready in:

Ingredients

- 1 package (6.6 ounces) rice pilaf mix with toasted almonds
- 1 tablespoon butter
- 1-1/2 cups fresh or frozen peas
- 1 cup sliced baby portobello mushrooms

Direction

- Follow the package directions to prepare pilaf.
- Heat butter in a big skillet on moderate heat. Put in mushrooms and peas, then cook and stir for 6 to 8 minutes, until softened. Whisk in rice.

Nutrition Information

- Calories: 177 calories
- Sodium: 352mg sodium
- Fiber: 3g fiber)
- Total Carbohydrate: 28g carbohydrate (3g sugars
- Cholesterol: 10mg cholesterol
- Protein: 5g protein. Diabetic Exchanges: 2 starch
- Total Fat: 6g fat (2g saturated fat)

338. Mushroom Bisque

Serving: 4 servings. | Prep: 25mins | Cook: 0mins | Ready in:

Ingredients

- 1/2 pound fresh mushrooms, sliced
- 1 medium onion, sliced
- 1 cup minced fresh parsley
- 1/4 cup butter, cubed
- 1 tablespoon all-purpose flour
- 1 can (14-1/2 ounces) beef broth
- 1 cup (8 ounces) sour cream

Direction

- Sauté parsley, onion and mushrooms in butter in a big saucepan till tender. Mix flour in till blended. Add broth slowly; boil. Mix and cook till thick for 2 minutes. Slightly cool.
- Put into a blender; process till pureed, covered. Put into pan. Mix sour cream in; heat through, occasionally mixing, without boiling.

Nutrition Information

- Calories: 271 calories
- Protein: 6g protein.
- Total Fat: 22g fat (14g saturated fat)
- Sodium: 529mg sodium
- Fiber: 2g fiber)
- Total Carbohydrate: 11g carbohydrate (6g sugars
- Cholesterol: 71mg cholesterol

339. Mushroom Brunch Toast

Serving: 4 servings. | Prep: 10mins | Cook: 15mins | Ready in:

Ingredients

- 1/4 cup butter
- 8 ounces fresh mushrooms, sliced
- 2 garlic cloves, minced
- 1/4 cup heavy whipping cream
- 1 teaspoon lemon juice
- 1/2 teaspoon salt
- Dash pepper
- Dash nutmeg
- 4 slices white bread, toasted
- 2 tablespoons chopped fresh parsley

Direction

- Melt butter in a skillet and sauté mushrooms until browned a bit. Put in nutmeg, pepper, salt, lemon juice, cream and garlic. Cook until cream has thickened and the volume is decreased by half, while stirring continuously.
- Split the mushroom mixture and scoop over the toast. Sprinkle 1/2 tbsp. of parsley to each

serving. Bake for 5 to 8 minutes at 450° until sauce bubbles. Serve promptly.

Nutrition Information

- Calories:
- Total Fat:
- Sodium:
- Fiber:
- Total Carbohydrate:
- Cholesterol:
- Protein:

340. Mushroom Cheesecake Appetizers

Serving: 1 dozen. | Prep: 25mins | Cook: 15mins | Ready in:

Ingredients

- 2 teaspoons butter
- 1/2 cup soft bread crumbs
- 1 carton (8 ounces) whipped cream cheese
- 2 eggs
- 1/4 cup sour cream
- 2 tablespoons minced fresh thyme or 2 teaspoons dried thyme, divided
- 1/2 teaspoon salt
- 1/2 teaspoon pepper
- 1/2 cup shredded fontina cheese
- TOPPING:
- 1/2 pound sliced baby portobello mushrooms
- 3 tablespoons butter
- 1 garlic clove, minced
- Toasted French bread baguette slices

Direction

- Use butter to grease halfway up the sides and the bottoms of muffin cups. Press bread crumbs onto the bottoms and halfway up the sides of the prepared cups.
- Beat cream cheese in a small bowl until smooth. Beat in pepper, salt, 1 tablespoon thyme, sour cream, and eggs. Distribute among the prepared muffin cups; dust with the remaining thyme and fontina cheese. Bake for 12-15 minutes at 350°, or until set.
- In the meantime, sauté mushrooms in butter in a large skillet until soft. Put in garlic and continue to sauté for 1 minute more. Put the mushroom mixture on top of the cheesecakes. Serve with baguette slices.

Nutrition Information

- Calories:
- Fiber:
- Total Carbohydrate:
- Cholesterol:
- Protein:
- Total Fat:
- Sodium:

341. Mushroom Marsala With Barley

Serving: 6 servings. | Prep: 20mins | Cook: 04hours15mins | Ready in:

Ingredients

- 1-1/2 pounds baby portobello mushrooms, cut into 3/4-in. chunks
- 1 cup thinly sliced shallots
- 3 tablespoons olive oil
- 1/2 teaspoon minced fresh thyme
- 3/4 cup Marsala wine, divided
- 3 tablespoons reduced-fat sour cream
- 2 tablespoons all-purpose flour
- 1-1/2 teaspoons grated lemon zest
- 1/4 teaspoon salt
- 1/4 cup crumbled goat cheese
- 1/4 cup minced fresh parsley
- 2-1/2 cups cooked barley

Direction

- Mix together thyme, olive oil, shallots and mushrooms in a 4- or 5-qurater slow cooker. Put in 1/4 cup Marsala wine then cook on low with a cover for 4 hours, until vegetables are softened.
- Stir in leftover Marsala, salt, lemon zest, flour and sour cream then cook on low with a cover for 15 more minutes. Sprinkle over with parsley and goat cheese. Serve along with hot cooked barley.

Nutrition Information

- Calories: 235 calories
- Sodium: 139mg sodium
- Fiber: 5g fiber)
- Total Carbohydrate: 31g carbohydrate (6g sugars
- Cholesterol: 7mg cholesterol
- Protein: 7g protein. Diabetic Exchanges: 2 starch
- Total Fat: 9g fat (2g saturated fat)

342. Mushroom Spinach Dip

Serving: 3 cups. | Prep: 15mins | Cook: 0mins |Ready in:

Ingredients

- 1 package (10 ounces) frozen chopped spinach, thawed and squeezed dry
- 1-1/2 cups (12 ounces) sour cream
- 1 cup mayonnaise
- 1 package vegetable soup mix
- 1 cup chopped fresh mushrooms
- 3 green onions, finely chopped
- Raw vegetables or crackers

Direction

- Mix the onions, soup mix, mayonnaise, spinach, mushrooms, and sour cream in a bowl. Cover the bowl and place it inside the fridge for 2 hours. Serve this together with crackers or vegetables.

Nutrition Information

- Calories:
- Protein:
- Total Fat:
- Sodium:
- Fiber:
- Total Carbohydrate:
- Cholesterol:

343. Mushroom Spinach Omelet

Serving: 2 | Prep: 15mins | Cook: 15mins |Ready in:

Ingredients

- 1 (8 ounce) carton liquid egg substitute
- 1 tablespoon shredded Cheddar cheese
- 1 tablespoon shredded Parmesan cheese
- 1/4 teaspoon salt
- 1/8 teaspoon ground black pepper
- 1/8 teaspoon garlic powder
- 1/8 teaspoon red pepper flakes
- 1 teaspoon olive oil
- 1/2 cup chopped fresh mushrooms
- 1 tablespoon chopped onion
- 1/2 cup chopped fresh spinach, or more to taste

Direction

- In a bowl, whisk together red pepper flakes, garlic powder, black pepper, salt, Parmesan cheese, cheddar cheese and egg substitute.
- In a nonstick skillet, heat olive oil over medium heat; cook onion and mushroom for 4 to 5 minutes until softened, remember to stir while cooking. Add spinach and cook for another 3-4 minutes until wilted. Pour in egg mixture; swirl skillet around in order that egg

mixture is distributed evenly. Cook for 5 to 10 minutes until egg is completely cooked and set in the center. Cut into wedges.

Nutrition Information

- Calories: 164 calories;
- Sodium: 584
- Total Carbohydrate: 2.8
- Cholesterol: 8
- Protein: 18.1
- Total Fat: 8.8

344. Mushroom Turnovers

Serving: 10 | Prep: 25mins | Cook: 15mins | Ready in:

Ingredients

- 1 (8 ounce) package cream cheese
- 1 cup butter
- 1 1/2 cups all-purpose flour
- 2 tablespoons butter
- 3/4 pound fresh mushrooms, finely chopped
- 1/2 medium onion, chopped
- 1/8 teaspoon dried thyme
- 1/4 teaspoon salt
- 1/2 teaspoon ground black pepper
- 1 1/2 teaspoons all-purpose flour
- 1/2 cup sour cream

Direction

- Combine together the 1 cup of butter and cream cheese in a medium bowl till well mixed. Add in flour till completely blended. Form into a ball, and chill while making the filling.
- In a big skillet, melt 2 tablespoons butter. Put onion and mushrooms. Add pepper, salt and thyme to season. Cook and mix for 5 minutes till soft. To prevent from getting lumpy, scatter flour all over, then turn heat to low, and mix in sour cream. Heat just till thickened, then take off from heat.
- Preheat an oven to 175 °C or 350 °F. Unroll dough to approximately quarter-inch thickness, on a slightly floured surface. Cut into 3-inch circles. On 1 side of every round, put a little amount of mushroom mixture, then fold dough on top and seal by pressing. Puncture tops using fork to release steam, and put pastries on baking sheet. They be frozen at this time till using.
- In the prepped oven, bake till golden brown for 15 minutes. It may take 5 minutes longer incase baking frozen turnovers.

Nutrition Information

- Calories: 366 calories;
- Sodium: 280
- Total Carbohydrate: 17.4
- Cholesterol: 85
- Protein: 5.4
- Total Fat: 31.3

345. Mushroom And Spinach Saute

Serving: 2 servings. | Prep: 5mins | Cook: 5mins | Ready in:

Ingredients

- 2 teaspoons olive oil
- 2 cups sliced fresh mushrooms
- 2 garlic cloves, minced
- 1 package (5 to 6 ounces) fresh baby spinach
- 1/8 teaspoon salt
- 1/8 teaspoon pepper

Direction

- Heat oil in a big skillet on moderately high heat. Put in mushrooms and sauté for 2 minutes, until soft. Put in garlic and cook for another minute. Working in batches, put in spinach, then cook and stir for a minute until wilted. Use pepper and salt to season, then serve instantly.

Nutrition Information

- Calories: 76 calories
- Total Carbohydrate: 6g carbohydrate (2g sugars
- Cholesterol: 0mg cholesterol
- Protein: 4g protein. Diabetic Exchanges: 1 vegetable
- Total Fat: 5g fat (1g saturated fat)
- Sodium: 208mg sodium
- Fiber: 2g fiber)

346. Mushroom, Walnut & Thyme Cheesecake

Serving: 24 servings. | Prep: 35mins | Cook: 25mins | Ready in:

Ingredients

- 1 cup dry bread crumbs
- 1/4 cup butter, melted
- FILLING:
- 1 tablespoon butter
- 1/2 pound baby portobello mushrooms, chopped
- 1 garlic clove, minced
- 1/3 cup chopped walnuts
- 1 tablespoon minced fresh thyme or 1 teaspoon dried thyme
- 1 teaspoon reduced-sodium soy sauce
- 1/4 teaspoon white pepper
- 2 packages (8 ounces each) cream cheese, softened
- 1/2 cup plain Greek yogurt
- 2 large eggs, lightly beaten
- Assorted crackers, baguette slices or sliced apples

Direction

- Prepare the oven by preheating to 325 degrees. Combine butter and bread crumbs in a small bowl. Press onto bottom of a 9-inch springform pan that is greased. Transfer pan to a baking sheet. Bake for 15 to 17 minutes or until golden brown. Transfer to a wire rack to cool.
- Put butter in a large skillet and heat over medium-high heat. Put in mushrooms; stir and cook until softened. Put in garlic; cook for 1 more minute. Mix in walnuts; cook until toasted. Mix in pepper, soy sauce, and thyme. Take away from the heat; let fully cool.
- Whip cream cheese in a large bowl until smooth. Whisk in yogurt. Put in eggs; whisk on low speed just until combined. Add mushroom mixture and fold. Put the mixture over crust. Put the pan back to the baking sheet.
- Bake for 25 to 30 minutes or until the center of cheesecake is just set and top looks dull. Transfer to a wire rack and cool for 10 minutes. Use a knife to loosen sides from pan. Allow to cool for 1 more hour. Keep in the fridge overnight.
- Take off the rim from pan. Serve with crackers.

Nutrition Information

- Calories: 130 calories
- Fiber: 0 fiber)
- Total Carbohydrate: 5g carbohydrate (1g sugars
- Cholesterol: 46mg cholesterol
- Protein: 3g protein.
- Total Fat: 11g fat (6g saturated fat)
- Sodium: 123mg sodium

347. Nutty Stuffed Mushrooms

Serving: 20 servings. | Prep: 15mins | Cook: 15mins | Ready in:

Ingredients

- 20 large fresh mushrooms
- 3 tablespoons butter
- 1 small onion, chopped
- 1/4 cup dry bread crumbs
- 1/4 cup finely chopped pecans
- 3 tablespoons grated Parmesan cheese
- 1/4 teaspoon salt
- 1/4 teaspoon dried basil
- Dash cayenne pepper

Direction

- Prepare the oven by preheating to 400 degrees. Take off the stems from mushrooms; reserve caps. Finely chop stems. Put butter in a large skillet and heat over medium heat. Add onion and chopped mushrooms; stir-fry for about 5 minutes, until liquid has evaporated. Take away from the heat; reserve.
- In the meantime, mix the rest of the ingredients; mix in mushroom mixture. Fill firmly into the mushroom caps. Place in a greased 15x10x1-inch baking pan and bake for 15 to 18 minutes, without cover, until tender. Serve warm.

Nutrition Information

- Calories: 44 calories
- Sodium: 67mg sodium
- Fiber: 0 fiber)
- Total Carbohydrate: 3g carbohydrate (0 sugars
- Cholesterol: 5mg cholesterol
- Protein: 2g protein.
- Total Fat: 3g fat (1g saturated fat)

348. Onion Stuffed Portobellos

Serving: 4 servings. | Prep: 25mins | Cook: 15mins | Ready in:

Ingredients

- 1 large onion, sliced
- 3 garlic cloves, minced
- 1 tablespoon minced fresh thyme or 1 teaspoon dried thyme
- 1/4 teaspoon salt, divided
- 1/4 teaspoon pepper, divided
- 1/4 cup olive oil, divided
- 1 cup port wine
- 2-1/2 cups coarsely chopped fresh spinach
- 4 medium portobello mushrooms
- 1/2 cup crumbled blue cheese

Direction

- Cook 1/8 teaspoon salt and pepper, thyme, garlic and the onion in two tablespoons oil on medium heat for 15 to 20 minutes or till onion turns golden brown, remember to stir once in a while. Pour in wine and stir. Bring to a boil; cook till the liquid is reduced by 2/3, about 8 to 10 minutes. Put in spinach; cook until wilted.
- Get rid of the stems and gills from mushrooms then throw them away. Put mushrooms in a large skillet and cook in the remaining oil on medium heat for 2 minutes per side. Use the remaining salt and pepper to sprinkle.
- Use onion mixture to fill mushroom; cover and cook for 5 to 7 minutes or just till mushrooms are soft. Use cheese to sprinkle; cover and cook for 2 minutes more or till cheese melts.

Nutrition Information

- Calories: 267 calories
- Fiber: 2g fiber)
- Total Carbohydrate: 13g carbohydrate (5g sugars
- Cholesterol: 13mg cholesterol
- Protein: 7g protein.
- Total Fat: 19g fat (5g saturated fat)
- Sodium: 408mg sodium

349. Overnight Baked Eggs Bruschetta

Serving: 9 servings. | Prep: 45mins | Cook: 10mins | Ready in:

Ingredients

- 1 tube (13.8 ounces) refrigerated pizza crust
- 1 tablespoon cornmeal
- 3 tablespoons olive oil, divided
- 1-1/2 cups shredded part-skim mozzarella cheese, divided
- 3/4 pound sliced baby portobello mushrooms
- 3/4 teaspoon garlic powder
- 3/4 teaspoon dried rosemary, crushed
- 1/2 teaspoon pepper
- 1/4 teaspoon salt
- 2 cups pizza sauce
- 1 tablespoon white vinegar
- 9 large eggs
- 2 ounces fresh goat cheese, crumbled
- 1/2 cup French-fried onions
- Fresh basil leaves

Direction

- Set an oven to 400 degrees and start preheating. Roll out the pizza dough and press onto the bottom of a 15x10x1-inch baking pan coated with cooking spray and sprinkled with cornmeal. Brush 1 tbsp. of oil over the dough and sprinkle 3/4 cup of mozzarella cheese on top. Bake for 8 minutes.
- In the meantime, heat the leftover oil in a big skillet on medium-high heat. Add the mushrooms, then cook and stir until it becomes tender. Mix in the seasonings, rosemary and garlic powder. Mix pizza sauce into the mushrooms and spread the mushroom mixture on top of the crust.
- Boil 2-3 inch of water and vinegar in a big skillet with high sides. Lower the heat to keep a gentle simmer. Crack cold eggs, one by one, into a small bowl; hold the bowl near the surface of water and slip eggs into the water.
- Cook for 3 to 5 minutes without a cover or until the yolks start to thicken, but not yet hard, and the whites are fully set. Take out the eggs using a slotted spoon, then put it on top of the mushrooms in the baking pan. Sprinkle the leftover mozzarella and goat cheese on top of the mushrooms and eggs. Let chill in the fridge overnight with a cover.
- Take the pan out of the fridge 30 minutes prior to baking. Start preheating oven to 400 degrees. Sprinkle onions on top. Bake for 10 to 15 minutes without a cover until heated through and turns golden brown. Put basil on top just prior to serving.

Nutrition Information

- Calories: 345 calories
- Protein: 17g protein.
- Total Fat: 17g fat (5g saturated fat)
- Sodium: 798mg sodium
- Fiber: 2g fiber)
- Total Carbohydrate: 29g carbohydrate (6g sugars
- Cholesterol: 227mg cholesterol

350. Pepper Salad

Serving: 8 | Prep: 15mins | Cook: 20mins | Ready in:

Ingredients

- 14 green bell peppers
- 6 cloves garlic, minced
- 1 cup fresh lemon juice
- salt and pepper to taste

Direction

- Take seeds out of the peppers and slice into strips. Put peppers in a big baking pan. Put in garlic cloves. Drizzle with half of the lemon juice, pepper and salt. Toss them gently to spread the seasonings.

- Broil on the top rack that is closest to the heat source while stirring once in a while till all peppers are tender and some are a bit charred, about 20 minutes. In a bowl or container, put any accumulated liquid and peppers. Put in leftover lemon juice and mix well.
- Serve warm or after it has been chilled in the fridge for a minimum of several hours. Toss prior to serve.

Nutrition Information

- Calories: 53 calories;
- Protein: 2
- Total Fat: 0.4
- Sodium: 7
- Total Carbohydrate: 13
- Cholesterol: 0

351. Peppered Portobello Penne

Serving: 4 servings. | Prep: 15mins | Cook: 15mins | Ready in:

Ingredients

- 2 cups uncooked penne pasta
- 4 large portobello mushrooms, stems removed, halved and thinly sliced
- 2 tablespoons olive oil
- 1/2 cup heavy whipping cream
- 3/4 teaspoon salt
- 1/4 teaspoon pepper
- 1 cup shredded pepper jack cheese

Direction

- Following package directions to cook pasta.
- In the meantime, saute mushrooms in a big skillet with oil until softened. Stir in pepper, salt and cream, then heat through. Stir in cheese until melted. Drain pasta and put into the skillet, tossing to coat well.

Nutrition Information

- Calories: 503 calories
- Protein: 17g protein.
- Total Fat: 28g fat (13g saturated fat)
- Sodium: 632mg sodium
- Fiber: 3g fiber)
- Total Carbohydrate: 48g carbohydrate (3g sugars
- Cholesterol: 71mg cholesterol

352. Pickled Mushrooms

Serving: Makes about 3 cups | Prep: 15mins | Cook: 9hours | Ready in:

Ingredients

- 2 cups dry white wine
- 1 teaspoon whole coriander seeds
- 1/2 teaspoon whole black peppercorns
- 3/4 teaspoon salt
- 1 Turkish or 1/2 California bay leaf
- 3 garlic cloves, peeled and smashed
- 1 lb small (1-inch) white or cremini mushrooms, trimmed
- 1/4 cup extra-virgin olive oil

Direction

- In one 10-inch heavy deep skillet, boil garlic, bay leaf, salt, spices and wine for 5 minutes. Put in oil and mushrooms, then lower the heat and simmer gently with no cover for 15 minutes, till mushrooms are just soft. Turn onto bowl and let mushrooms cool in liquid with no cover. Refrigerate with cover, for a minimum of 8 hours to blend the flavors. Throw whole spices and bay leaf. Serve at room temperature.
- Note: Pickled mushrooms may be refrigerated up to a week.

Nutrition Information

- Calories: 211
- Fiber: 1 g(4%)
- Total Carbohydrate: 8 g(3%)
- Protein: 3 g(6%)
- Total Fat: 14 g(21%)
- Saturated Fat: 2 g(9%)
- Sodium: 447 mg(19%)

353. Portobello Bruschetta With Rosemary Aioli

Serving: 2 dozen. | Prep: 01hours20mins | Cook: 15mins | Ready in:

Ingredients

- AIOLI:
- 1/3 cup mayonnaise
- 1 garlic clove, minced
- 1-1/2 teaspoons lemon juice
- 1-1/2 teaspoons balsamic vinegar
- 1 teaspoon minced fresh rosemary
- 1 teaspoon Dijon mustard
- MARINADE:
- 1/4 cup packed brown sugar
- 1/4 cup balsamic vinegar
- 1/4 cup honey
- 4 teaspoons minced fresh thyme or 1 teaspoon dried thyme
- BRUSCHETTA:
- 6 large portobello mushrooms, stems and gills removed
- 1/2 cup olive oil, divided
- 3 medium red onions, halved and thinly sliced
- 2 large sweet red peppers
- 3 tablespoons thinly sliced green onions
- 3 tablespoons minced fresh basil
- 1 garlic clove, minced
- 1/4 teaspoon salt
- 1/8 teaspoon pepper
- 24 slices French bread baguette (1/4-inch thick)
- 1 cup fresh arugula

Direction

- Combine aioli ingredients in a small bowl. Put cover and chill till serving time.
- Preheat the oven to 375°. Mix marinade ingredients till incorporated in a small bowl. Put the mushrooms in a baking dish 13x9-inch in size; sprinkle with quarter cup marinade. Bake with cover for 35 to 40 minutes till soft. Take off from baking dish; slightly cool down. Slice into half-inch strips.
- Heat 2 tablespoons oil in a big skillet over medium heat. Put red onions; cook and mix for 8 to 10 minutes till softened. Turn heat to medium-low; allow to cook for 30 to 40 minutes till deep golden brown, mixing from time to time. Put the leftover marinade; let cook for 4 to 6 minutes till onions are glazed, mixing from time to time.
- On a baking sheet lined with foil, put the red peppers. Let broil 4 inches from heat till skins blister for 5 minutes. Rotate peppers a quarter turn using tongs. Broil and rotate till every side are blackened and blistered. Quickly put peppers in a bowl; with cover, allow to sit for 20 minutes.
- Remove and throw charred skin of peppers. Take off seeds and stems. Slice peppers; bring back to bowl. Put 1 tablespoon oil, pepper, salt, garlic, basil and green onions. Combine by tossing.
- On not greased baking sheets, put the baguette slices; brush with leftover oil. Bake at 375° for 4 to 6 minutes on per side till golden brown.
- To serve, atop toasts with pepper mixture, onions, arugula and mushrooms. Allow to bake for 5 to 8 minutes more till heated through. Sprinkle with aioli.

Nutrition Information

- Calories: 109 calories
- Protein: 1g protein.
- Total Fat: 7g fat (1g saturated fat)
- Sodium: 75mg sodium

- Fiber: 1g fiber)
- Total Carbohydrate: 11g carbohydrate (7g sugars
- Cholesterol: 1mg cholesterol

354. Portobello Gouda Grilled Sandwiches

Serving: 2 servings. | Prep: 10mins | Cook: 10mins | Ready in:

Ingredients

- 1 cup sliced baby portobello mushrooms
- 1 tablespoon plus 4 teaspoons butter, divided
- 4 ounces smoked Gouda cheese, sliced
- 4 slices rye bread
- 1 plum tomato, sliced

Direction

- Sauté the mushrooms in 1 tbsp. of butter in a big frying pan until it becomes soft. Put the cheese on 2 slices of bread. Put tomato, mushrooms and leftover bread on top. Spread the leftover butter on the exteriors of the sandwiches.
- Toast the sandwiches in a small frying pan for 2 to 3 minutes per side on medium heat or until the cheese melts.

Nutrition Information

- Calories: 498 calories
- Protein: 21g protein.
- Total Fat: 31g fat (19g saturated fat)
- Sodium: 984mg sodium
- Fiber: 5g fiber)
- Total Carbohydrate: 35g carbohydrate (5g sugars
- Cholesterol: 100mg cholesterol

355. Quick Italian Salad

Serving: 1-1/2 cups dressing. | Prep: 20mins | Cook: 0mins | Ready in:

Ingredients

- Salad greens
- Sliced tomatoes, zucchini, mushrooms and green pepper or vegetables of your choice
- 1 cup canola oil
- 1/2 cup white wine vinegar
- 1 garlic clove, minced
- 2 tablespoons minced fresh parsley
- 1 tablespoon grated Parmesan cheese
- 1-1/2 teaspoons dried basil
- 1 teaspoon dried oregano
- 1/2 teaspoon pepper

Direction

- On separate salad dishes or in a salad bowl, arrange vegetables and greens. Mix all leftover ingredients in a tight-fitting lidded jar; shake the mixture well. Serve on top of salad.

Nutrition Information

- Calories: 167 calories
- Total Carbohydrate: 1g carbohydrate (0 sugars
- Cholesterol: 0 cholesterol
- Protein: 0 protein.
- Total Fat: 18g fat (2g saturated fat)
- Sodium: 8mg sodium
- Fiber: 0 fiber)

356. Rainbow Quiche

Serving: 8 servings. | Prep: 30mins | Cook: 40mins | Ready in:

Ingredients

- Pastry for single-crust pie (9 inches)
- 2 tablespoons butter

- 1 small onion, finely chopped
- 1 cup sliced fresh mushrooms
- 1 cup small fresh broccoli florets
- 1/2 cup finely chopped sweet orange pepper
- 1/2 cup finely chopped sweet red pepper
- 3 large eggs, lightly beaten
- 1-1/3 cups half-and-half cream
- 3/4 teaspoon salt
- 1/2 teaspoon pepper
- 1 cup shredded Mexican cheese blend, divided
- 1 cup fresh baby spinach

Direction

- Turn the oven to 425° and start preheating. Unroll and place pastry sheet onto a lightly floured surface, roll to a 12-in. circle. Place in a 9-in. deep-dish pie plate; trim and flute the edge. Keep in the fridge while you prepare the filling.
- Heat butter over medium-high heat in a large skillet; sauté peppers, broccoli, mushrooms and onion for 6-8 minutes until mushrooms become lightly browned. Allow to slightly cool.
- Beat pepper, salt, cream and eggs together. Place 1/2 cup of cheese over crust; top with vegetable and spinach mixture. Dust with remaining cheese. Pour in egg mixture.
- Bake for 15 minutes on the lower oven rack. Lower the heat to 350°; bake for 25-30 minutes until the inserted knife in the center comes out clean (Use foil to cover the edge loosely if needed to not be over browned.) Allow to rest 10 minutes before cutting.

Nutrition Information

- Calories: 347 calories
- Cholesterol: 140mg cholesterol
- Protein: 10g protein.
- Total Fat: 25g fat (15g saturated fat)
- Sodium: 537mg sodium
- Fiber: 1g fiber)
- Total Carbohydrate: 20g carbohydrate (3g sugars

357. Refried Bean Tostadas

Serving: 6 servings. | Prep: 15mins | Cook: 15mins | Ready in:

Ingredients

- 6 flour tortillas (8 inches)
- 1/2 pound sliced fresh mushrooms
- 1 cup diced zucchini
- 2 tablespoons canola oil
- 1 jar (16 ounces) chunky salsa
- 1 can (7 ounces) white or shoepeg corn, drained
- 1 can (16 ounces) vegetarian refried beans, warmed
- 1-1/2 cups shredded lettuce
- 1-1/2 cups shredded cheddar cheese
- 2 medium ripe avocados, peeled and sliced
- 1-1/2 cups chopped tomatoes
- 6 tablespoons sour cream

Direction

- Cook tortillas in an ungreased big frying pan until light brown, 1-2 minutes. Remove tortillas and set aside. Put oil in the same pan and sauté zucchini and mushrooms until tender and crispy. Mix in the corn and salsa and cook until heated, 2-3 minutes. Spread each tortilla with refried beans. Put lettuce, cheese, avocados, salsa mixture, sour cream, and tomatoes on top.

Nutrition Information

- Calories: 588 calories
- Fiber: 12g fiber)
- Total Carbohydrate: 60g carbohydrate (9g sugars
- Cholesterol: 40mg cholesterol
- Protein: 19g protein.
- Total Fat: 31g fat (10g saturated fat)

- Sodium: 1250mg sodium

358. Salad With Vinaigrette Dressing

Serving: 1 cup dressing. | Prep: 10mins | Cook: 0mins | Ready in:

Ingredients

- 3/4 cup canola oil
- 1/4 cup white wine vinegar
- 1 teaspoon salt
- 1 teaspoon ground mustard
- 1/2 teaspoon sugar
- 1/2 teaspoon garlic powder
- 3 to 4 drops hot pepper sauce
- Salad greens
- Bell peppers, mushrooms, tomatoes and/or other vegetables of your choice

Direction

- Mix the initial 7 ingredients in a tight-fitting lidded jar and shake the mixture well. Spread salad greens and vegetables on separate salad dishes or mix them in a big bowl. Serve alongside dressing.

Nutrition Information

- Calories: 186 calories
- Protein: 0 protein.
- Total Fat: 21g fat (3g saturated fat)
- Sodium: 295mg sodium
- Fiber: 0 fiber)
- Total Carbohydrate: 1g carbohydrate (0 sugars
- Cholesterol: 0 cholesterol

359. Satisfying Cremini Barley

Serving: 5 servings. | Prep: 20mins | Cook: 15mins | Ready in:

Ingredients

- 2 cups vegetable broth
- 1 cup quick-cooking barley
- 1 medium red onion, finely chopped
- 1 celery rib, finely chopped
- 1 medium carrot, finely chopped
- 2 teaspoons olive oil
- 1/2 pound sliced baby portobello (cremini) mushrooms
- 2 garlic cloves, minced
- 1 package (6 ounces) fresh baby spinach
- 1 can (15 ounces) white kidney or cannellini beans, rinsed and drained
- 1/4 teaspoon pepper
- 3 tablespoons minced fresh parsley

Direction

- Heat broth to boiling in a big pot. Mix in barley. Cover, decrease heat, and simmer until barley is tender, 10-12 minutes. Take away from heat; let it sit for 5 minutes. In the meantime, put oil in a big frying pan and sauté carrot, onion, and celery, 3 minutes. Mix in mushrooms; sauté until veggies are tender, 3-4 minutes. Add the garlic and cook for 1 more minute. Stir in barley, spinach, pepper, and beans. Stirring constantly, cook until spinach wilts. Mix in parsley.

Nutrition Information

- Calories: 255 calories
- Sodium: 532mg sodium
- Fiber: 12g fiber)
- Total Carbohydrate: 47g carbohydrate (4g sugars
- Cholesterol: 0 cholesterol
- Protein: 11g protein.
- Total Fat: 3g fat (0 saturated fat)

360. Savory Marinated Mushroom Salad

Serving: 6-8 servings. | Prep: 25mins | Cook: 0mins | Ready in:

Ingredients

- 2-1/2 quarts water
- 3 tablespoons lemon juice
- 3 pounds small fresh mushrooms
- 2 medium carrots, sliced
- 2 celery ribs, sliced
- 1/2 medium green pepper, chopped
- 1 small onion, chopped
- 1 tablespoon minced fresh parsley
- 1/2 cup sliced pimiento-stuffed olives
- 1 can (2-1/4 ounces) sliced ripe olives, drained
- DRESSING:
- 1/2 cup prepared Italian salad dressing
- 1/2 cup red or white wine vinegar
- 1 garlic clove, minced
- 1/2 teaspoon salt
- 1/2 teaspoon dried oregano

Direction

- Boil lemon juice and water in a big saucepan. Add and cook mushrooms for 3 minutes, stirring once in a while. Drain it off; let it cool down.
- In a big bowl, add mushrooms with olives, parsley, onion, green pepper, celery and carrots. Combine the dressing ingredients in a small bowl. Put on top of the salad. Keep it covered and chilled in the fridge overnight.

Nutrition Information

- Calories: 142 calories
- Total Fat: 9g fat (1g saturated fat)
- Sodium: 671mg sodium
- Fiber: 3g fiber)
- Total Carbohydrate: 14g carbohydrate (5g sugars
- Cholesterol: 0 cholesterol
- Protein: 6g protein.

361. Spinach Dip Stuffed Mushrooms

Serving: 16 appetizers. | Prep: 25mins | Cook: 15mins | Ready in:

Ingredients

- 16 large fresh mushrooms (about 1-1/2 pounds)
- 1 tablespoon olive oil
- 2 cups fresh baby spinach, coarsely chopped
- 2 garlic cloves, minced
- 1/2 cup reduced-fat sour cream
- 3 ounces reduced-fat cream cheese
- 1/3 cup shredded part-skim mozzarella cheese
- 3 tablespoons grated Parmesan cheese
- 1/4 teaspoon salt
- 1/4 teaspoon cayenne pepper
- 1/4 teaspoon pepper

Direction

- Set an oven to preheat to 400 degrees. Take off stems from the mushrooms and put the caps aside; get rid of the stems or reserve for later use. Heat the olive oil in a small frying pan on medium heat. Add the spinach and sauté until it wilts, then add the garlic and cook for 1 minute more.
- Mix together the leftover ingredients with the spinach mixture, then stuff it into the mushroom caps. Put it on a cooking spray coated 15x10-inch baking pan. Let it bake for 12 to 15 minutes without cover, or until the mushrooms become tender. Serve it warm.

Nutrition Information

- Calories: 44 calories
- Cholesterol: 9mg cholesterol

- Protein: 2g protein.
- Total Fat: 3g fat (2g saturated fat)
- Sodium: 100mg sodium
- Fiber: 0 fiber)
- Total Carbohydrate: 1g carbohydrate (1g sugars

362. Stuffed Asiago Basil Mushrooms

Serving: 2 dozen. | Prep: 25mins | Cook: 10mins | Ready in:

Ingredients

- 24 baby portobello mushrooms (about 1 pound), stems removed
- 1/2 cup reduced-fat mayonnaise
- 3/4 cup shredded Asiago cheese
- 1/2 cup loosely packed basil leaves, stems removed
- 1/4 teaspoon white pepper
- 12 cherry tomatoes, halved
- Sliced Parmesan cheese, optional

Direction

- Set oven to 375° to preheat. Arrange mushroom caps in an oiled 15x10x1-inch baking pan. Bake in the preheated oven for 10 minutes. In the meantime, bring pepper, basil, Asiago cheese, and mayonnaise in a food processor, then process until blended.
- Drain mushroom caps. Put 1 rounded teaspoon mayonnaise mixture into each cap; place a tomato half on top of each.
- Bake until lightly browned, 8 to 10 minutes. Top with Parmesan cheese, if desired.

Nutrition Information

- Calories: 35 calories
- Total Fat: 3g fat (1g saturated fat)
- Sodium: 50mg sodium

- Fiber: 0 fiber)
- Total Carbohydrate: 2g carbohydrate (1g sugars
- Cholesterol: 5mg cholesterol
- Protein: 2g protein.

363. Summer Salad With Lemon Vinaigrette

Serving: 16 servings (1 cup each). | Prep: 15mins | Cook: 0mins | Ready in:

Ingredients

- 1/4 cup lemon juice
- 1/4 cup olive oil
- 2 tablespoons balsamic vinegar
- 2 garlic cloves, minced
- 1 teaspoon salt
- 1 teaspoon grated lemon peel
- 1 teaspoon Dijon mustard
- 1/2 teaspoon pepper
- 2 packages (5-1/2 ounces each) torn mixed salad greens
- 1 medium red onion, sliced
- 2 cups sliced fresh mushrooms
- 2 cups fresh raspberries
- 1 cup chopped walnuts

Direction

- Combine the initial 8 ingredients in a small bowl. Keep chilled in the fridge till serving.
- Mix walnuts, raspberries, mushrooms, onion and salad greens in a salad bowl. Sprinkle with dressing; coat by tossing. Serve right away.

Nutrition Information

- Calories: 96 calories
- Fiber: 2g fiber)
- Total Carbohydrate: 5g carbohydrate (2g sugars

- Cholesterol: 0 cholesterol
- Protein: 3g protein. Diabetic Exchanges: 1-1/2 fat
- Total Fat: 8g fat (1g saturated fat)
- Sodium: 161mg sodium

364. Swiss Mushroom Loaf

Serving: 12 servings. | Prep: 15mins | Cook: 40mins | Ready in:

Ingredients

- 1 loaf (1 pound) Italian bread, unsliced
- 1 block (8 ounces) Swiss cheese, cut into cubes
- 1 cup sliced fresh mushrooms
- 1/4 cup softened butter, cubed
- 1 small onion, finely chopped
- 1-1/2 teaspoons poppy seeds
- 2 garlic cloves, minced
- 1/2 teaspoon seasoned salt
- 1/2 teaspoon ground mustard
- 1/2 teaspoon lemon juice

Direction

- Set oven to 350 degrees and start preheating. Slice bread diagonally into 1-inch slices to within 1-inch of bottom of loaf. Repeat cutting in opposite direction. Arrange mushrooms and cheese cubes in cuts.
- Mix the rest ingredients in a microwave-safe bowl. Cover and microwave on high for 30-60 seconds or until butter melts. Stir until combined, then spoon over the bread.
- Use a foil to wrap the loaf and put on a baking tray. Bake in 40 minutes until the cheese melts.

Nutrition Information

- Calories: 214 calories
- Total Fat: 11g fat (6g saturated fat)
- Sodium: 372mg sodium
- Fiber: 1g fiber)

- Total Carbohydrate: 21g carbohydrate (2g sugars
- Cholesterol: 28mg cholesterol
- Protein: 9g protein.

365. Tuscan Portobello Stew

Serving: 4 servings. | Prep: 20mins | Cook: 20mins | Ready in:

Ingredients

- 2 large portobello mushrooms, coarsely chopped
- 1 medium onion, chopped
- 3 garlic cloves, minced
- 2 tablespoons olive oil
- 1/2 cup white wine or vegetable broth
- 1 can (28 ounces) diced tomatoes, undrained
- 2 cups chopped fresh kale
- 1 bay leaf
- 1 teaspoon dried thyme
- 1/2 teaspoon dried basil
- 1/2 teaspoon dried rosemary, crushed
- 1/4 teaspoon salt
- 1/4 teaspoon pepper
- 2 cans (15 ounces each) white kidney or cannellini beans, rinsed and drained

Direction

- Sauté garlic, onion, and mushrooms in oil in a large skillet until softened. Pour in wine. Bring to a boil; cook until liquid mixture is reduced by half. Mix in seasonings, kale, and tomatoes. Bring to a boil. Lower heat; simmer, covered for 8 to 10 minutes.
- Add beans, cook through. Remove bay leaf.

Nutrition Information

- Calories: 309 calories
- Sodium: 672mg sodium
- Fiber: 13g fiber)

- Total Carbohydrate: 46g carbohydrate (9g sugars
- Cholesterol: 0 cholesterol
- Protein: 12g protein. Diabetic Exchanges: 2 starch
- Total Fat: 8g fat (1g saturated fat)

366. Ultimate Breakfast Burritos

Serving: 2 servings. | Prep: 10mins | Cook: 10mins | Ready in:

Ingredients

- 1 teaspoon olive oil
- 1/2 cup chopped fresh mushrooms
- 1/4 cup chopped green pepper
- 1/4 cup chopped sweet red pepper
- 1 cup egg substitute
- 1/4 teaspoon pepper
- 2 whole wheat tortillas (8 inches), warmed
- 1/4 cup shredded reduced-fat cheddar cheese
- 2 tablespoons salsa
- 2 tablespoons fat-free sour cream

Direction

- Heat the oil in a cooking spray coated small nonstick frypan on medium-high heat. Put vegetables and let it cook while stirring until it becomes tender. Take it out of the pan and keep it warm.
- Add the pepper and egg substitute into the same frypan and let it cook and stir on medium heat until no liquid egg was retained, and the eggs become thick. Take it out of the heat.
- Scoop the scrambled eggs and vegetable mixture across the middle of every tortilla, then put sour cream, salsa and cheese on top. Fold the sides and bottom of the tortilla atop the filling, then roll it up.

Nutrition Information

- Calories: 294 calories
- Sodium: 585mg sodium
- Fiber: 3g fiber)
- Total Carbohydrate: 31g carbohydrate (6g sugars
- Cholesterol: 13mg cholesterol
- Protein: 21g protein. Diabetic Exchanges: 2 starch
- Total Fat: 8g fat (2g saturated fat)

367. Vegetable Quiche

Serving: 8 | Prep: 35mins | Cook: 40mins | Ready in:

Ingredients

- 1 teaspoon vegetable oil
- 1 onion, chopped
- 1/2 large green bell pepper, chopped
- 2 teaspoons minced garlic
- 3 eggs, beaten
- 1 zucchini, peeled and grated
- 1 yellow squash, peeled and grated
- 1 carrot, grated
- 1 green onion, sliced
- 1 cup buttermilk baking mix
- 1/2 cup shredded sharp Cheddar cheese
- 1/4 cup vegetable oil
- 1 teaspoon salt
- 3/4 teaspoon Italian seasoning
- 1/2 teaspoon paprika
- 1/2 teaspoon red pepper flakes
- ground black pepper to taste
- 1/2 cup shredded Cheddar cheese

Direction

- Set oven at 350° F (175°C) to preheat. Spray oil over an 8-inch square baking dish.
- Heat 1 teaspoon of vegetable oil over medium heat in a skillet; keep cooking and stirring garlic, bell pepper, and onion in skillet until

tender, in 5 minutes. Pour the mixture in a large bowl.
- Blend black pepper, red pepper flakes, paprika, Italian seasoning, salt, 1/4 cup of vegetable oil, 1/2 cup of Cheddar cheese, baking mix, green onion, carrot, yellow squash, zucchini, and eggs in onion mixture. Pour the vegetable mixture in the prepared baking dish, and add the 1/2 cup of Cheddar cheese on top.
- Bake in the prepared oven for 35 minutes, until the top is brown.

Nutrition Information

- Calories: 228 calories;
- Cholesterol: 86
- Protein: 8.5
- Total Fat: 14.9
- Sodium: 713
- Total Carbohydrate: 16.2

368. Vegetable Salad

Serving: 8 | Prep: 10mins | Cook: 5mins | Ready in:

Ingredients

- 1 (15 ounce) can peas, drained
- 1 (15 ounce) can green beans, drained
- 1 (14 ounce) can shoepeg corn, drained
- 1 onion, chopped
- 2 stalks celery, chopped, or more to taste
- 1/2 teaspoon salt
- 1/4 teaspoon ground black pepper
- 3/4 cup white sugar
- 1/2 cup cooking oil
- 1/2 cup red wine vinegar

Direction

- In a bowl, combine pepper, salt, celery, onion, corn, green beans and peas.

- On medium heat, mix vinegar, oil and sugar in a saucepan; cook and stir till sugar dissolves for about 5 minutes. Put mixture on top of vegetable mixture and coat by mixing; keep in the refrigerator till flavors blend, for 8 hours to overnight.

Nutrition Information

- Calories: 297 calories;
- Total Fat: 14.2
- Sodium: 481
- Total Carbohydrate: 39.5
- Cholesterol: 0
- Protein: 3.8

369. Vegetable Stuffed Portobellos

Serving: 4 servings. | Prep: 20mins | Cook: 15mins | Ready in:

Ingredients

- 1 can (15 ounces) white kidney or cannellini beans, rinsed and drained
- 2 tablespoons olive oil, divided
- 1 tablespoon water
- 1 teaspoon dried rosemary, crushed
- 1 garlic clove, peeled and halved
- 1/4 teaspoon salt
- 1/4 teaspoon pepper
- 4 large portobello mushrooms (4 to 4-1/2 inches), stems removed
- 1 medium sweet red pepper, finely chopped
- 1 medium red onion, finely chopped
- 1 medium zucchini, finely chopped
- 1/2 cup shredded pepper Jack cheese

Direction

- Combine pepper, salt, garlic, rosemary, water, a tablespoon of oil and beans in a food

processor. Process, covered, until pureed. Put aside.
- Put the mushrooms on the broiler pan coated with cooking spray. Broil 4 in. from the heat until mushrooms are tender, or about 6 to 8 minutes on each side.
- In the meantime, in a small nonstick frying pan coated with cooking spray, cook zucchini, red onion and red pepper in the remaining oil until tender.
- Put 1/3 cup of the reserved bean mixture over each mushroom. Add half cup of the vegetable mixture on top. Top with cheese. Broil until the cheese is melted, or about 2 to 3 minutes more.

Nutrition Information

- Calories: 252 calories
- Total Fat: 12g fat (4g saturated fat)
- Sodium: 378mg sodium
- Fiber: 7g fiber)
- Total Carbohydrate: 26g carbohydrate (5g sugars
- Cholesterol: 15mg cholesterol
- Protein: 11g protein. Diabetic Exchanges: 2 lean meat

370. Vegetarian Black Bean Pasta

Serving: 6 servings. | Prep: 15mins | Cook: 10mins | Ready in:

Ingredients

- 9 ounces uncooked whole wheat fettuccine
- 1 tablespoon olive oil
- 1-3/4 cups sliced baby portobello mushrooms
- 1 garlic clove, minced
- 1 can (15 ounces) black beans, rinsed and drained
- 1 can (14-1/2 ounces) diced tomatoes, undrained
- 1 teaspoon dried rosemary, crushed
- 1/2 teaspoon dried oregano
- 2 cups fresh baby spinach

Direction

- Following the package directions to cook fettuccine. At the same time, heat oil in a big skillet on moderately high heat. Put in mushrooms, then cook and stir until softened, about 4 to 6 minutes. Put in garlic and cook for 1 minute more.
- Stir in oregano, rosemary, tomatoes and black beans, then heat through. Stir in spinach until wilted. Drain fettuccine and put into the bean mixture, then toss to mix.

Nutrition Information

- Calories: 255 calories
- Total Carbohydrate: 45g carbohydrate (4g sugars
- Cholesterol: 0 cholesterol
- Protein: 12g protein. Diabetic Exchanges: 3 starch
- Total Fat: 3g fat (0 saturated fat)
- Sodium: 230mg sodium
- Fiber: 9g fiber)

371. Vegetarian Egg Strata

Serving: 12 servings. | Prep: 25mins | Cook: 45mins | Ready in:

Ingredients

- 1 medium zucchini, finely chopped
- 1 medium sweet red pepper, finely chopped
- 1 cup sliced baby portobello mushrooms
- 1 medium red onion, finely chopped
- 2 teaspoons olive oil
- 3 garlic cloves, minced
- 2 teaspoons minced fresh thyme or 1/2 teaspoon dried thyme

- 1/2 teaspoon salt
- 1/4 teaspoon pepper
- 1 loaf (1 pound) day-old French bread, cubed
- 2 packages (5.3 ounces each) fresh goat cheese, crumbled
- 1-3/4 cups grated Parmesan cheese
- 6 eggs, lightly beaten
- 2 cups fat-free milk
- 1/4 teaspoon ground nutmeg

Direction

- Sauté onion, mushrooms, red pepper and zucchini in oil in a large skillet until they become tender. Put in pepper, salt, thyme, and garlic; sauté for 1 more minute.
- In a greased 13x9-inch baking dish, arrange Parmesan cheese, goat cheese, zucchini mixture, and 1/2 bread cubes in a layer in reverse order. Repeat the process.
- Beat together nutmeg, milk, and eggs in a small bowl. Place the blend over the top. Put in the fridge, covered, overnight.
- Before baking, take out from the fridge for half an hour. Set an oven to 350 degrees and start preheating. Uncover and bake until a knife comes out clean after inserted in the center, or for 45-50 minutes. Before cutting, allow to stand for 10 minutes.

Nutrition Information

- Calories: 281 calories
- Total Carbohydrate: 27g carbohydrate (4g sugars
- Cholesterol: 140mg cholesterol
- Protein: 17g protein.
- Total Fat: 12g fat (6g saturated fat)
- Sodium: 667mg sodium
- Fiber: 2g fiber)

372. Very Veggie Frittata

Serving: 4 servings. | Prep: 20mins | Cook: 5mins | Ready in:

Ingredients

- 5 large eggs
- 1/4 cup sour cream
- 1/4 teaspoon salt
- 1/8 teaspoon pepper
- 1 cup shredded cheddar cheese, divided
- 2 green onions, chopped
- 1 cup chopped fresh mushrooms
- 1/2 cup each chopped sweet red, yellow and green pepper
- 1/4 cup chopped onion
- 1 tablespoon butter
- Hot pepper sauce, optional

Direction

- Whisk sour cream and eggs together in a large bowl with pepper and salt. Mix in green onions and 3/4 cup cheese; put to one side. Sauté onion, sweet peppers, and mushrooms in butter in a 9-inch oven-safe skillet until tender. Lower the heat; pour egg mixture on top. Cook, covered, until almost firm, about 4 to 6 minutes.
- Remove the cover and sprinkle with remaining cheese. Broil 3 to 4 inches away from the heat source until eggs are completely firm, 2 to 3 minutes. Let stand for 5 minutes. Divide into wedges. Enjoy with pepper sauce, if desired.

Nutrition Information

- Calories: 269 calories
- Protein: 16g protein.
- Total Fat: 20g fat (12g saturated fat)
- Sodium: 434mg sodium
- Fiber: 1g fiber)
- Total Carbohydrate: 7g carbohydrate (3g sugars
- Cholesterol: 312mg cholesterol

373. Whole Wheat Veggie Pizza

Serving: 2 pizzas (6 slices each). | Prep: 40mins | Cook: 20mins | Ready in:

Ingredients

- 1/2 cup whole wheat flour
- 2 packages (1/4 ounce each) quick-rise yeast
- 1 teaspoon garlic powder
- 1/2 teaspoon salt
- 2-1/2 cups all-purpose flour
- 1 cup water
- 2 tablespoons olive oil
- SAUCE:
- 1 can (14-1/2 ounces) diced tomatoes, undrained
- 1 tablespoon minced fresh parsley
- 1-1/2 teaspoons sugar
- 1-1/2 teaspoons Italian seasoning
- 1-1/2 teaspoons dried basil
- 1/2 teaspoon garlic powder
- 1/4 teaspoon pepper
- TOPPINGS:
- 1 teaspoon olive oil
- 1 cup chopped zucchini
- 1 cup sliced fresh mushrooms
- 1/2 cup chopped green or red pepper
- 1/4 cup chopped onion
- 1-1/4 cups shredded part-skim mozzarella cheese

Direction

- Combine 1 cup of all-purpose flour with the first four ingredients in a large bowl. Heat oil and water in a small saucepan to 120-130°. Include into the dry ingredients; beat for 3 minutes on medium speed. To make a soft dough, mix in enough of the remaining flour.
- Place onto a floured surface; knead for around 5 minutes, or till elastic and smooth. Arrange on a greased bowl, flipping once to grease the top. Use plastic wrap to cover; allow to rise for around 30 minutes in a warm place, or till doubled.
- Allow sauce ingredients to boil in a small saucepan. Lower the heat; simmer without a cover, stirring occasionally, for 15-18 minutes, or till slightly thickened. Take away from the heat.
- Set the oven at 400° and start preheating. Punch the dough down. On a lightly floured surface, separate the dough in half; roll each into a 12-in. circle. Arrange on two 12-in. pizza pans coated with a grease; use a fork to prick. Bake for around 8-10 minutes, or till lightly browned.
- Meanwhile, place a skillet on medium-high heat; heat oil; sauté in vegetables till the zucchini becomes crisp-tender. Spread the crusts with the sauce; place cheese and vegetables on top. Bake for 12-15 minutes, or till the cheese is melted.

Nutrition Information

- Calories: 190 calories
- Fiber: 3g fiber)
- Total Carbohydrate: 28g carbohydrate (3g sugars
- Cholesterol: 8mg cholesterol
- Protein: 7g protein. Diabetic Exchanges: 1-1/2 starch
- Total Fat: 6g fat (2g saturated fat)
- Sodium: 234mg sodium

374. Wild Rice And Squash Pilaf

Serving: 10 servings. | Prep: 15mins | Cook: 20mins | Ready in:

Ingredients

- 1-1/2 cups sliced fresh mushrooms

- 1-1/2 cups finely chopped peeled winter squash
- 2 medium onions, finely chopped
- 1 small green pepper, chopped
- 2 tablespoons olive oil
- 2 to 3 garlic cloves, minced
- 3 cups cooked wild rice
- 1/2 cup chicken broth or vegetable broth
- 1 tablespoon reduced-sodium soy sauce
- 1/2 teaspoon dried savory
- 1/4 cup sliced almonds, toasted

Direction

- Sauté green pepper, onions, squash and mushrooms in a big saucepan with oil until tender-crisp. Put in garlic and sauté for 1 more minute.
- Stir in savory, soy sauce, broth and rice, then cover and cook on moderately low heat until squash is softened, about 13 to 15 minutes. Whisk in almonds.

Nutrition Information

- Calories: 118 calories
- Fiber: 3g fiber)
- Total Carbohydrate: 18g carbohydrate (3g sugars
- Cholesterol: 0 cholesterol
- Protein: 4g protein. Diabetic Exchanges: 1 starch
- Total Fat: 4g fat (1g saturated fat)
- Sodium: 114mg sodium

375. Zucchini Harvest Salad

Serving: 8 servings. | Prep: 15mins | Cook: 0mins | Ready in:

Ingredients

- 4 cups thinly sliced zucchini
- 1 cup sliced celery
- 1/2 cup sliced fresh mushrooms
- 1/2 cup sliced ripe olives
- 1/4 cup chopped green pepper
- 1/4 cup chopped sweet red pepper
- 1 cup mild or medium picante sauce or salsa
- 1/2 cup vinegar
- 3 tablespoons olive oil
- 3 tablespoon sugar
- 1/2 teaspoon oregano
- 1 garlic clove, minced
- Lettuce leaves

Direction

- Mix the initial 6 ingredients together in a big bowl, toss to mix. Mix together all the leftover ingredients excluding lettuce in a jar or small bowl and shake/mix well. Put on top of the veggies. Keep it covered and chilled for a few hours or overnight. Serve in large lettuce-lined salad bowl or in individual "cups".

Nutrition Information

- Calories: 113 calories
- Sodium: 37mg sodium
- Fiber: 0 fiber)
- Total Carbohydrate: 13g carbohydrate (0 sugars
- Cholesterol: 0 cholesterol
- Protein: 2g protein. Diabetic Exchanges: 1-1/2 vegetable
- Total Fat: 7g fat (0 saturated fat)

Chapter 7: Awesome Mushroom Recipes

***

376. 10 Minute Mushroom Carbonara

Serving: 6 | Prep: 5mins | Cook: 12mins | Ready in:

Ingredients

- 1 (16 ounce) package spaghetti
- 1/2 pound sliced fresh mushrooms
- 1 tablespoon olive oil
- 2 cloves garlic
- 3 eggs
- 1/2 cup freshly grated Parmesan cheese divided

Direction

- Boil a big pot with slightly salted water. In boiling water, let spaghetti cook for 12 minutes, mixing from time to time, till tender but firm to bite. Strain.
- Meantime, in dry skillet, put mushrooms on moderate heat. Cook for 3 to 5 minutes, till they render moisture and start to brown. Put in garlic and oil. Fry for an additional of 3 minutes, till softened.
- In a bowl, whip the eggs. Put in half of Parmesan cheese. Combine thoroughly and mix into the cooked mixture of mushroom.
- Put mushroom sauce and the rest of Parmesan cheese over pasta and serve.

Nutrition Information

- Calories: 371 calories;
- Total Carbohydrate: 57.8
- Cholesterol: 99
- Total Fat: 7.9
- Protein: 16.7
- Sodium: 144

377. A Simple Seafood Bisque

Serving: 4 | Prep: 20mins | Cook: 8mins | Ready in:

Ingredients

- 1 (12 ounce) can evaporated milk
- 1/2 cup half-and-half
- 1/2 cup dry white wine
- 1 roasted red pepper, chopped
- 2 teaspoons butter
- 1 bay leaf
- 1 pinch salt
- 1 dash hot pepper sauce (such as Tabasco®)
- 2 (8 ounce) cans oysters, drained and rinsed
- 2 (6.5 ounce) cans chopped clams with juice
- 1 cup chopped portobello mushrooms
- 2 green onions, minced

Direction

- In saucepan, heat hot pepper sauce, salt, bay leaf, butter, roasted red pepper, white wine, half and half and evaporated milk on medium low heat, mixing often, for about 5 minutes till very hot yet not simmering. Mix mushrooms, clams with juice and oysters in; cook for about 3 minutes till canned oyster just heat through, covered. Don't boil. Discard bay leaf; sprinkle green onions. Serve.

Nutrition Information

- Calories: 427 calories;
- Protein: 39.3
- Total Fat: 16.7
- Sodium: 433
- Total Carbohydrate: 22.8
- Cholesterol: 165

378. Absolutely Fabulous Portobello Mushroom Tortellini

Serving: 4 | Prep: 10mins | Cook: 15mins | Ready in:

Ingredients

- 1 pound cheese tortellini

- 2 large portobello mushrooms
- 1/4 cup white wine
- 1 tablespoon chopped fresh parsley
- 2 cloves garlic, minced
- 8 ounces Alfredo-style pasta sauce
- salt and pepper to taste
- 1/3 cup grated Parmesan cheese

Direction

- Boil lightly salted water in a large pot. Add pasta and cook until al dente, about 8 to 10 minutes then drain.
- In the meantime, prepare mushrooms by washing and slicing the mushroom caps thinly; discard the stems.
- Combine mushrooms, garlic, parsley, and wine in a medium skillet over low heat. Stir it frequently and sauté until mushrooms are cooked thoroughly, approximately 5 minutes.
- Remove the skillet from heat and slowly add the Alfredo sauce. Stir it to blend and season with desired amount of pepper and salt.
- Separate the hot pasta into four equal portions and pour spoonful of sauce over the pasta. Garnish pasta with cheese. Serve immediately.

Nutrition Information

- Calories: 470 calories;
- Protein: 18.3
- Total Fat: 25.4
- Sodium: 933
- Total Carbohydrate: 42.2
- Cholesterol: 55

379. Alice Chicken

Serving: 4 | Prep: 5mins | Cook: 15mins | Ready in:

Ingredients

- 4 skinless, boneless chicken breast halves
- 5 fluid ounces Worcestershire sauce
- 8 slices bacon
- 2 tablespoons butter
- 8 ounces fresh mushrooms, sliced
- 1 (8 ounce) package Monterey Jack cheese, shredded
- 1 (16 ounce) container honey mustard salad dressing

Direction

- In a glass bowl or dish, put chicken; use a fork to poke a few times, and then add Worcestershire sauce and flip to coat. Put a cover on the bowl or dish and chill for approximately 60 minutes.
- In a big, deep skillet, put bacon. Cook until turning brown evenly over medium-high heat. Strain and put aside.
- In a small skillet, heat butter over medium heat. Add, then sauté mushrooms until tender, about 10 minutes. Put aside.
- Turn on the oven's broil setting to preheat.
- Take the chicken out of the marinade (dispose any leftover liquid), and broil for approximately 5 minutes per side. Once the chicken has nearly done, put 2 slices bacon and then cheese on top of each breast. Keep broiling until the cheese melts, and then take out of the oven. Enjoy with salad dressing and mushrooms for topping.

Nutrition Information

- Calories: 930 calories;
- Protein: 46.8
- Total Fat: 69.5
- Sodium: 1975
- Total Carbohydrate: 31.9
- Cholesterol: 152

380. Allison's Trout

Serving: 6 | Prep: 15mins | Cook: 35mins | Ready in:

Ingredients

- 1/2 cup butter
- 3 lemons, juiced
- 14 fresh mushrooms, sliced
- 1/4 cup sherry wine
- 3 pounds trout fillets
- salt to taste
- cracked black pepper to taste

Direction

- Preheat the oven to 175 degrees C/350 degrees F. Line foil on a shallow baking dish.
- In a skillet, heat butter on medium heat. Pour lemon juice in. Stir and cook mushrooms for 5 minutes until tender. Stir sherry in. Put trout fillets on prepped baking dish, skin sides down. Sprinkle with cracked pepper and salt. Pour mushroom mixture on fish.
- Bake in preheated oven for 30 minutes until fish easily flakes with a fork and sauce reduces.

Nutrition Information

- Calories: 390 calories;
- Total Carbohydrate: 3
- Cholesterol: 228
- Protein: 39.5
- Total Fat: 23.7
- Sodium: 302

381. Angela's Alfredo Ham

Serving: 4 | Prep: | Cook: |Ready in:

Ingredients

- 8 ounces fresh tortellini pasta
- 1 slice ham
- 16 ounces frozen green peas
- 8 ounces fresh mushrooms, sliced
- 1 1/2 (16 ounce) jars Alfredo-style pasta sauce

Direction

- To Cook the Tortellini: Put pasta in a big pot of boiling salted water. Allow to cook until tortellini is al dente, about 8 to 10 minutes. Thoroughly drain then reserve.
- Heat your skillet to medium heat setting. Add mushrooms, peas and ham, and toss them together until heated thoroughly. Add reserved tortellini and sauce, and stir together. Let it simmer for about 3 to 5 minutes then serve.

Nutrition Information

- Calories: 716 calories;
- Total Carbohydrate: 42.9
- Cholesterol: 82
- Protein: 21.5
- Total Fat: 53.6
- Sodium: 1917

382. Antipasto Skewers

Serving: 12 | Prep: 15mins | Cook: |Ready in:

Ingredients

- 10 ounces Havarti cheese, cubed
- 2 cloves garlic, minced
- 3 tablespoons olive oil
- 1 tablespoon fresh parsley, chopped
- salt and pepper to taste
- 1 (6 ounce) jar mushroom caps, drained
- 6 slices cocktail rye bread, quartered

Direction

- In an average-sized bowl, combine olive oil, garlic, salt, pepper and parsley. Mix well then toss in mushrooms. Leave for 20 minutes to marinate.
- On small skewers or cocktail toothpicks, stick one piece each, mushroom, Havarti and bread.

Assemble skewers on a serving plate and pour remaining marinade over them. Serve.

Nutrition Information

- Calories: 169 calories;
- Protein: 6.6
- Total Fat: 13
- Sodium: 449
- Total Carbohydrate: 7.5
- Cholesterol: 29

383. Asian Noodle Bowl With Sausage And Kale

Serving: 6 | Prep: | Cook: | Ready in:

Ingredients

- 1 tablespoon vegetable oil
- 1 (13 ounce) package Farmland® Hickory Smoked Sausage, bias-sliced
- 3 cups sliced fresh mushrooms
- 1 red sweet pepper, chopped
- 1 tablespoon grated fresh ginger
- 4 cloves garlic, minced
- 3 cups reduced-sodium chicken broth
- 1/4 cup reduced-sodium soy sauce
- 3 cups chopped fresh kale
- 1 cup fresh bean sprouts
- 12 ounces dried rice noodles, cooked according to package and drained
- Toasted sesame seeds
- Crushed red pepper flakes

Direction

- Heat oil on medium-high heat in a 4-5 quart pot. Add the smoked sausage. Sauté until browned for 2-3 minutes. Take out and put aside.
- Add garlic, ginger, sweet pepper, and mushrooms in the pot. Sauté for 6-8 minutes until liquid evaporates and mushrooms are brown. Add soy sauce and broth to the pot. Boil. Add kale then reduce the heat. Cook for 3 minutes, uncovered, until wilted. Mix in smoked sausage and sprouts then heat through.
- Serve on top of rice noodles then top with crushed red pepper and sesame seeds.

384. Asian Veggie Packets

Serving: 4 | Prep: | Cook: | Ready in:

Ingredients

- 2 sheets (18x15 inches each) Reynolds Wrap® Heavy Duty Aluminum Foil
- 2 tablespoons butter, melted
- 2 tablespoons soy sauce
- 2 tablespoons rice vinegar
- 2 tablespoons packed brown sugar
- 4 medium carrots, peeled and sliced thin
- 6 ounces snow peas
- 8 ounces white button mushrooms, sliced
- 4 scallions (green onions), sliced thin
- 1 (1 inch) piece fresh ginger, peeled and minced
- 2 cloves garlic, minced
- 4 teaspoons sesame seeds

Direction

- Turn oven to 450°F to preheat. In a small mixing bowl, combine brown sugar, rice vinegar, soy sauce, and melted butter; put aside.
- In a large mixing bowl, combine the remaining ingredients. Arrange 1/2 veggie mix in the center of a sheet of foil. Ladle 1/2 butter mixture over the vegetables.
- Fold the upsides of the Reynolds Wrap(R) Heavy Duty Aluminum Foil over the veggie mix, then fold down 2 times. Double fold 2 ends of the foil to seal packet, leaving space for heat circulation. Do the same with the second

- packet. Transfer packets to a baking sheet with 1-inch sides.
- Bake in the preheated oven until veggies reach desired crispness, about 15 to 20 minutes. Cut along top folds using a sharp knife to carefully open the packets; let steam release gradually. Stir until evenly coated.

Nutrition Information

- Calories: 161 calories;
- Total Fat: 7.7
- Sodium: 543
- Total Carbohydrate: 20.7
- Cholesterol: 15
- Protein: 5

385. Asian Style Watercress Soup

Serving: 6 | Prep: 10mins | Cook: 15mins | Ready in:

Ingredients

- 6 cups water
- 1 small onion, diced
- 1/4 cup soy sauce
- 1 1/2 tablespoons soy-based liquid seasoning (such as Maggi®)
- 2 tablespoons chopped garlic
- 1 tablespoon chopped fresh ginger root
- 2 tablespoons cornstarch
- 2 tablespoons boiling water
- 1 1/2 pounds sliced fresh mushrooms
- 1 1/2 tablespoons vegetarian chicken-flavored bouillon
- 1/4 pound tofu, diced
- 1 bunch watercress, coarsely chopped
- 2 eggs, beaten

Direction

- In a saucepan, place in the ginger root, garlic, soy-based liquid seasoning, soy sauce, onion, and water, then set to boil.
- Mix the cornstarch with 2 tablespoons of boiling water. Add to the saucepan. Add in bouillon and mushrooms. Decrease the heat to medium-high and simmer for 7 minutes until the flavors blend. Add in the watercress and tofu. Simmer the soup for another 2 minutes.
- Slowly pour in the eggs, constantly whisking, for 1-2 minutes until cooked.

Nutrition Information

- Calories: 95 calories;
- Protein: 9.6
- Total Fat: 3
- Sodium: 715
- Total Carbohydrate: 10.2
- Cholesterol: 62

386. Asparagus Portobello Pasta

Serving: 4 | Prep: 10mins | Cook: 20mins | Ready in:

Ingredients

- 2 (15 ounce) cans asparagus
- 1 (2.25 ounce) can sliced black olives
- 1/2 pound fettuccini pasta
- 1 tablespoon olive oil
- 3 large portobello mushrooms, sliced
- 1 (8 ounce) can peas, drained
- 2 teaspoons Italian seasoning
- 1 (6 ounce) can tomato paste
- 1/2 cup grated Parmesan cheese

Direction

- Boil drained liquids of olives and asparagus and water in big pot. Cook pasta till al dente for 8-10 minutes. Drain.

- Meanwhile, heat oil in big skillet on medium heat; sauté Italian seasoning, peas and mushrooms till mushrooms are tender.
- Puree Parmesan, tomato paste, black olives and asparagus in blender/food processor. Put in small saucepan, then heat through on medium-low heat. Put asparagus sauce on fettuccine using spoon; top with peas and mushrooms.

Nutrition Information

- Calories: 390 calories;
- Total Carbohydrate: 61.5
- Cholesterol: 9
- Protein: 19.6
- Total Fat: 10.1
- Sodium: 1248

387. Asparagus And Morel Risotto

Serving: 4 | Prep: 20mins | Cook: 21mins | Ready in:

Ingredients

- 3 1/2 cups chicken stock
- 1/4 cup olive oil, or more to taste, divided
- 1/4 cup unsalted butter, divided
- 1/2 pound asparagus, cut into 1-inch pieces on the bias
- 1/3 pound fresh morel mushrooms, halved
- 1 shallot, minced
- 1 cup Arborio rice
- 1/4 cup dry white wine
- 1 teaspoon fresh thyme leaves
- 1/3 cup freshly grated Parmigiano-Reggiano cheese, or to taste
- 1 tablespoon finely chopped fresh parsley
- salt and ground black pepper to taste
- 1 1/2 tablespoons high-quality balsamic vinegar (optional)

Direction

- In a small saucepan, put the chicken stock on medium heat; simmer.
- In a big saucepan on medium-high heat, heat a tablespoon of the butter and 2 tablespoons of the olive oil till butter begins to bubble. Put in the morel mushrooms and asparagus; sauté for around 4 minutes till soft. Turn out onto a plate including any accumulated juices.
- In the same saucepan, heat a tablespoon of butter and the leftover 2 tablespoons of the olive oil. Put in the shallot; cook and mix for around a minute till softens. Mix in the arborio rice and cook for approximately a minute till it begins to toast. Add wine and cook till it evaporates. Mix in the thyme.
- Add a quarter cup of simmering stock on top of the rice. Cook till stock is absorbed, mixing continuously. Repeat with the rest of the stock for around 12 minutes till rice is soft but firm to the bite. Mix in mushrooms including their juices and asparagus and continue for approximately 3 minutes longer till flavors incorporate.
- Take rice off the heat. Mix in parsley, Parmigiano-Reggiano cheese and the leftover 2 tablespoons of the butter. Add black pepper and salt to season. Jazz up with more olive oil and balsamic vinegar prior to serving.

Nutrition Information

- Calories: 508 calories;
- Sodium: 748
- Total Carbohydrate: 54.3
- Cholesterol: 37
- Protein: 9.5
- Total Fat: 27.6

388. Asparagus And Mushroom Casserole

Serving: 6 | Prep: 20mins | Cook: 40mins | Ready in:

Ingredients

- 1 pound fresh asparagus, trimmed and cut into 1 1/2-inch pieces
- 1 tablespoon olive oil
- 1 (8 ounce) package sliced fresh mushrooms
- 1/4 onion, thinly sliced
- 1 (4 ounce) packet saltine crackers, crushed
- 1 cup shredded sharp Cheddar cheese
- 1/4 teaspoon ground black pepper
- 1 (10.75 ounce) can condensed cream of mushroom soup
- 1/2 cup milk
- 1/2 cup coarsely chopped pecans

Direction

- Preheat oven to 175 degrees C/350 degrees C.
- Grease a 1 1/2-qt. baking dish.
- In a saucepan, put a steamer insert. Fill water to reach below the steamer's bottom. Cover pan. Boil. Add asparagus. Steam for 5-8 minutes, covered, until tender.
- In a big skillet, heat olive oil. Sauté onions and mushrooms for 5-8 minutes until mushrooms release liquid. Mix in asparagus. Toss veggies until hot. Take off heat.
- In a bowl, mix black pepper, sharp cheddar cheese and saltine cracker crumbs. Spread half of mixture on the bottom of a prepped baking dish.
- Spoon asparagus mixture on crumb mixture.
- Mix milk and cream of mushroom soup until smooth in a bowl. Pour soup mixture on asparagus mixture.
- Spread remaining crumb-cheese mixture on casserole. Sprinkle pecans on top.
- Bake for about 30 minutes in the preheated oven until casserole bubbles.

Nutrition Information

- Calories: 336 calories;
- Total Fat: 21.2
- Sodium: 700
- Total Carbohydrate: 27
- Cholesterol: 21
- Protein: 12

389. Asparagus Spinach Artichoke Casserole

Serving: 10 | Prep: 10mins | Cook: 33mins | Ready in:

Ingredients

- 2 (15 ounce) cans asparagus, drained
- 1 (6.5 ounce) jar marinated artichoke hearts, drained
- 1 (13.5 ounce) can spinach, drained
- 1 (4 ounce) can sliced mushrooms, drained
- 1 cup heavy whipping cream
- 1 (8 ounce) package cream cheese
- 1/2 cup vegetable broth, or to taste
- 1/2 teaspoon dried Italian seasoning, or to taste
- 1/2 teaspoon garlic powder, or to taste
- 1 (8 ounce) package cream cheese
- 1/2 (8 ounce) package sharp Cheddar cheese (such as Kerrygold™ Dubliner), sliced

Direction

- Across the bottom of a 9x13-inch casserole dish, spread the asparagus. On top, scatter artichoke hearts. Put the casserole dish inside the oven; as the oven heats, some of the remaining moisture from the vegetables will be removed.
- Set an oven to preheat to 175°C (350°F).
- In a microwave-safe bowl, put the mushrooms and spinach and heat it in the microwave for about 5 minutes, until the moisture evaporates.
- Into a pot on medium heat, transfer the mushrooms and spinach. Add the broth, cream cheese and heavy cream. Let it cook and stir constantly for about 5 minutes until the sauce becomes thick and the cheese has melted. Lower the heat to low. Stir in garlic powder and Italian seasoning and cook for about 3 minutes until the flavors combine.

- Take the casserole out of the oven. Over the vegetables, pour the sauce and top it with slices of Cheddar cheese.
- Let it bake in the preheated oven for about 20 minutes until the top becomes light brown and the edges turned crumbly. Allow it to cool for about 10 minutes prior to serving.

Nutrition Information

- Calories: 326 calories;
- Total Fat: 29.5
- Sodium: 600
- Total Carbohydrate: 8.3
- Cholesterol: 94
- Protein: 10.2

390. Aunty Pasto's Seafood Lasagna

Serving: 8 | Prep: 5mins | Cook: 1hours15mins | Ready in:

Ingredients

- 8 lasagna noodles
- 2 tablespoons butter
- 1 cup chopped onion
- 1 (8 ounce) package cream cheese, softened
- 1 1/2 cups cottage cheese, creamed
- 1 egg, beaten
- 2 teaspoons dried basil
- 1/2 teaspoon salt
- 1/8 teaspoon ground black pepper
- 2 (10.75 ounce) cans condensed cream of mushroom soup
- 1/3 cup milk
- 1/3 cup dry white wine
- 1 (6 ounce) can crabmeat
- 1 pound cooked salad shrimp
- 1/4 cup grated Parmesan cheese
- 1/2 cup shredded sharp Cheddar cheese
- 2 cups fresh sliced mushrooms

Direction

- In a large pot of boiling salted water, cook noodles until done. Rinse; drain noodles. Put aside.
- Over medium heat, in a small saucepan, melt margarine or butter. Add onion; cook while stirring until tender. Add pepper, salt, basil, egg, cottage cheese and cream cheese.
- Mix wine, milk and soup in a medium bowl. Stir in mushrooms, shrimp and crab.
- In the bottom of a well-oiled 9x13 inch pan, place 4 noodles. Top with half cheese mixture and spread; scoop half soup mixture over cheese. Do the same layers again.
- Bake without a cover for 45 minutes at 350°F (175°C). Top with Parmesan cheese and sharp cheese. Brown lasagna under broiler. Take out of the heat; rest 15 minutes; serve.

Nutrition Information

- Calories: 475 calories;
- Total Fat: 25
- Sodium: 1217
- Total Carbohydrate: 28.2
- Cholesterol: 209
- Protein: 33.1

391. BBQ Teriyaki Pork Kabobs

Serving: 6 | Prep: 30mins | Cook: 20mins | Ready in:

Ingredients

- 3 tablespoons soy sauce
- 3 tablespoons olive oil
- 1 clove garlic, minced
- 1/2 teaspoon crushed red pepper flakes
- salt and pepper to taste
- 1 pound boneless pork loin, cut into 1 inch cubes
- 1 (14.5 ounce) can low-sodium beef broth

- 2 tablespoons cornstarch
- 2 tablespoons soy sauce
- 1 tablespoon brown sugar
- 2 cloves garlic, minced
- 1/4 teaspoon ground ginger
- 3 portobello mushrooms, cut into quarters
- 1 large red onion, cut into 12 wedges
- 12 cherry tomatoes
- 12 bite-size chunks fresh pineapple

Direction

- Mix 3 tbsp. of soy sauce, red pepper flakes, pepper, salt, a clove of minced garlic, and olive oil in a shallow dish. Add the pork cubes, flipping them until coated evenly with the marinade. Cover the dish and chill inside the fridge for 3 hours.
- Mix beef broth, brown sugar, ginger, 2 cloves of minced garlic, 2 tbsp. of soy sauce, and cornstarch in a saucepan. Bring the mixture to a boil while constantly stirring it. Lower the heat and simmer for 5 minutes.
- Set the outdoor grill over high heat for preheating. Oil the grate lightly. Use skewers to thread the pork cubes, making sure you arrange them alternately with mushrooms, onion, tomatoes, and chunks of pineapple.
- Cook the pork on the grill for 15 minutes until cooked through. Flip the skewers over and baste them with the sauce while cooking.

Nutrition Information

- Calories: 297 calories;
- Protein: 19.4
- Total Fat: 17
- Sodium: 867
- Total Carbohydrate: 17.6
- Cholesterol: 48

392. Babushka's Slow Cooker Root Vegetable And Chicken Stew

Serving: 10 | Prep: 40mins | Cook: 7hours10mins | Ready in:

Ingredients

- 2 ½ pounds skin-on, bone-in chicken thighs
- 1 yellow onion, coarsely chopped
- 1 red onion, coarsely chopped
- 4 stalks celery with some leaves, coarsely chopped
- 4 mediums red potatoes - peeled, halved, and cubed
- 1 rutabaga - peeled, halved, and cubed
- 2 mediums turnips - peeled, halved, and cubed
- 2 mediums carrots, peeled and sliced
- 1 ½ cups cremini mushrooms, coarsely chopped
- 4 cloves garlic, peeled and crushed
- 2 teaspoons salt
- 1 teaspoon herbes de Provence
- 1 teaspoon onion powder
- 1 teaspoon garlic powder
- freshly ground black pepper
- 1 (32 fluid ounce) container vegetable broth

Direction

- On medium low heat, heat a sauté pan. In batches, cook chicken thighs, 2-3 minutes per side, until skin begins to brown. Do not overcook. Meat should be raw and pink inside. Put chicken in a bowl, keeping juices in the pan.
- In the pan, sauté celery and onion for 5 minutes until edges brown and is translucent. Put in a big bowl.
- Add in garlic, mushrooms, carrots, turnips, rutabaga and potatoes to celery-onion mixture. Sprinkle on pepper, garlic powder, onion powder, herbes de Provence and salt. Mix and stir veggies until coated.

- In a slow cooker, put 1/2 of veggie mixture. Add 1/2 of chicken. Layer leftover chicken and veggies on top. Put vegetable broth on mixture in the slow cooker.
- Cook for 7 hours on low, stirring gently every several hours if you want.
- Take chicken from stew with tongs. Cool. Separate bones and skin from meat. Shred meat. Put meat back in slow cooker.

Nutrition Information

- Calories: 296 calories;
- Protein: 21.4
- Sodium: 756
- Total Carbohydrate: 26.2
- Cholesterol: 64
- Total Fat: 11.8

393. Baby Bok Choy And Shiitake Stir Fry

Serving: 4 | Prep: 20mins | Cook: 10mins | Ready in:

Ingredients

- 1/2 cup low-sodium chicken or mushroom broth
- 2 tablespoons oyster sauce
- 2 tablespoons rice wine or dry sherry
- 2 teaspoons cornstarch
- 1 1/2 tablespoons peanut or vegetable oil
- 2 medium garlic cloves, minced
- 1 (1 1/2 inch) piece ginger root, peeled and minced
- 1/2 teaspoon kosher salt
- 3 1/2 ounces shiitake mushrooms, stems discarded and caps sliced
- 1 1/4 pounds baby bok choy, chopped

Direction

- In a small bowl, mix in oyster sauce, rice wine, broth, and cornstarch together.
- Using a large skillet or wok over medium-high heat, heat the oil until it starts to shimmer. Cook garlic and ginger and stir-fry with salt for 30 seconds or until fragrant. Stir-fry the shiitake for 1 to 2 minutes or until it softens. Stir-fry the bok choy in for 2 to 3 minutes or until it is crisp and tender.
- Stir the cornstarch mixture again. Create a hole in the vegetables then add in the cornstarch mixture. Once it boils, toss the vegetables to coat. Serve warm.

Nutrition Information

- Calories: 95 calories;
- Total Fat: 5.4
- Sodium: 407
- Total Carbohydrate: 7.2
- Cholesterol: < 1
- Protein: 3.3

394. Bacon Wrapped Delights

Serving: 6 | Prep: 25mins | Cook: 15mins | Ready in:

Ingredients

- 12 spears white asparagus
- 4 ounces enoki mushrooms
- 4 ounces shiitake mushrooms, stemmed and sliced 1/4-inch thick
- 24 slices bacon

Direction

- Turn oven to 425°F (220°C) to preheat.
- Bring water in a large pot to a boil. Blanch asparagus for 2 to 4 minutes, until still crisp and barely cooked. Once done, plunge asparagus into ice water to stop cooking. Once asparagus is cool, trim into 8-inch lengths. Wrap 6 bacon strips around a bundle of 6 spears of asparagus, arranging side by side, secure each slice using a toothpick. Bacon

should be wrapped around 2 times so that there will be 2 layers.
- Trim enoki mushrooms, and divide into 12 pieces. Stuff 4 pieces of shiitake into each enoki piece. Wrap a bacon slice around each bundle, wrapping around 2 times; secure with a toothpick. Arrange bundles on a wire rack set over a baking sheet.
- Roast for 6 minutes in the preheated oven; turn over the bundles; keep cooking until bacon is crispy and brown, for 4 to 6 minutes longer.
- Pick out 24 toothpicks, and cut asparagus bundles between the bacon to serve. Allow bundles to drain on paper towels for a while until ready to serve.

Nutrition Information

- Calories: 225 calories;
- Sodium: 859
- Total Carbohydrate: 4.9
- Cholesterol: 41
- Protein: 15.6
- Total Fat: 15.6

395. Bacon Wrapped Stuffed Mushrooms

Serving: 20 | Prep: 10mins | Cook: 20mins | Ready in:

Ingredients

- 1/2 cup chopped green onions
- 2 (8 ounce) packages cream cheese, softened
- 20 fresh mushrooms, stems removed
- 1 pound sliced bacon, cut in half

Direction

- Preheat oven to 175°C or 350°F.
- Combine cream cheese and green onions in a medium bowl. Scoop the mixture in mushroom caps and wrap with half a slice of bacon. Secure the mushrooms using toothpicks and place on a baking dish.
- Bake in the preheated oven for 20 minutes until the bacon is cooked through.

Nutrition Information

- Calories: 123 calories;
- Total Fat: 11
- Sodium: 241
- Total Carbohydrate: 1.5
- Cholesterol: 33
- Protein: 5.1

396. Bacon And Cheddar Stuffed Mushrooms

Serving: 8 | Prep: 15mins | Cook: 15mins | Ready in:

Ingredients

- 3 slices bacon
- 8 crimini mushrooms
- 1 tablespoon butter
- 1 tablespoon chopped onion
- 3/4 cup shredded Cheddar cheese

Direction

- In a large and deep skillet, cook the bacon over medium-high heat until evenly browned all over. Let it drain and dice; put aside.
- Set the oven to 400°F (200°C) for preheating.
- Remove the mushroom stems and chop them; set the caps aside.
- Melt butter in a large saucepan over medium heat. Stir in chopped stems and onion and cook them slowly, stirring until the onion is tender. Remove from the heat.
- Mix the mushroom stem mixture, a 1/2 cup of Cheddar, and bacon in a medium bowl. Once the mixture is well-combined, scoop it into the mushroom caps.

- Place it inside the preheated oven and bake for 15 minutes or until the cheese has melted completely.
- Remove them from the oven and sprinkle them with the remaining cheese.

Nutrition Information

- Calories: 110 calories;
- Total Carbohydrate: 0.9
- Cholesterol: 22
- Protein: 4.7
- Total Fat: 9.7
- Sodium: 170

397. Bacon, Brussels Sprouts, And Mushroom Linguine

Serving: 6 | Prep: 15mins | Cook: 25mins | Ready in:

Ingredients

- 1 (16 ounce) package linguine
- 2 tablespoons olive oil, or as needed
- 1 pound bacon, cut into bite-size pieces
- 1/2 teaspoon dried rosemary
- 1 1/2 pounds crimini mushrooms, sliced
- salt and ground black pepper to taste
- 1 1/2 pounds Brussels sprouts, trimmed and chopped
- 1/2 cup grated Parmesan cheese

Direction

- Boil a large pot of lightly salted water. Cook linguine for 11 mins at a boil until tender but firm to bite; drain the paste, keeping half cup of pasta water for later use. Take pasta back to the pot and drizzle with olive oil, toss to coat.
- In a large skillet, put bacon; cook while stirring for 10 mins, until bacon starts to crisp. Drain and discard half of bacon fat, leave bacon in skillet and mix in rosemary.
- Mix black pepper, salt, and mushrooms into bacon mixture. Put in Brussels sprouts; cook while stirring for 1-2 mins, until heated through. Pour the reserved pasta water in the bacon mixture, put Parmesan cheese and linguine, mix vegetable with pasta until heated through, about 2 mins. Flavor with pepper and salt.

Nutrition Information

- Calories: 557 calories;
- Sodium: 778
- Total Carbohydrate: 69
- Cholesterol: 33
- Protein: 30.5
- Total Fat: 18.9

398. Bacon Wrapped Venison Tenderloin With Garlic Cream Sauce

Serving: 6 | Prep: 15mins | Cook: 1hours10mins | Ready in:

Ingredients

- 6 thick slices bacon
- 2 (3/4 pound) venison tenderloin roasts
- 2 teaspoons olive oil, divided
- 1/4 teaspoon onion powder, divided
- kosher salt and ground black pepper to taste
- 2 tablespoons butter
- 1 (8 ounce) package sliced cremini mushrooms
- 2 cloves garlic, chopped
- 1 tablespoon chopped green onion, or more to taste
- 1/2 cup heavy whipping cream, or more to taste

Direction

- Set oven to 375°F (190°C) for preheating.
- Put the bacon on slotted pan.

- Let bacon bake in oven for 6-8 minutes, until partly cooked, but still flexible.
- Take olive oil and brush tenderloins; use black pepper, salt and onion powder to season. Arrange tenderloin roasts beside each other and use strips of the partly cooked bacon to wrap them. Put on roasting pan.
- Roast for an hour until the bacon appears brown and an instant-read thermometer measures at least 65°C (145°F) when poked into the thickest part of the tenderloin, about 60 minutes.
- In a pot placed on medium heat, heat butter; cook mushrooms and garlic while stirring for 8-10 minutes, until mushrooms are tender. Stir in green onion and add cream. Cook while stirring frequently until the sauce is well heated. Serve sauce with tenderloins.

Nutrition Information

- Calories: 310 calories;
- Total Fat: 20.3
- Sodium: 443
- Total Carbohydrate: 2.4
- Cholesterol: 130
- Protein: 28.2

399. Baked Asparagus With Portobello Mushrooms And Thyme

Serving: 4 | Prep: 10mins | Cook: 15mins | Ready in:

Ingredients

- 2 pounds fresh asparagus, trimmed
- 2 portobello mushroom caps, cut into strips
- 2 tablespoons olive oil
- 3 sprigs fresh thyme, leaves removed
- salt and freshly ground black pepper

Direction

- Set the oven to 230°C or 450°F to preheat and grease a baking sheet slightly.
- In a bowl, mix together portobello mushrooms and asparagus then drizzle olive oil over. Season with pepper, salt and thyme. Mix well to blend, then spread onto the prepared baking sheet in a single layer.
- In the preheated oven, bake for 8 minutes until asparagus is softened. Turn and bake for 8 to 12 minutes more, depending on the asparagus spears' thickness, then season with pepper and salt.

Nutrition Information

- Calories: 109 calories;
- Cholesterol: 0
- Protein: 5.4
- Total Fat: 7.1
- Sodium: 44
- Total Carbohydrate: 9.6

400. Baked Brie And Mushroom Sourdough Appetizer

Serving: 8 | Prep: 15mins | Cook: 25mins | Ready in:

Ingredients

- 2 tablespoons butter
- 1 teaspoon minced garlic
- 12 ounces sliced fresh mushrooms
- 1 (8 ounce) wedge Brie cheese, rind removed, cubed
- 1 (1 pound) loaf round sourdough bread
- 2 1/2 tablespoons grated Parmesan cheese

Direction

- Heat the broiler beforehand.
- Melt the butter over low heat in a saucepan. Sauté mushrooms and garlic till soft. Add in

the Brie. Cook while stirring until blended well and melted.
- Remove the sourdough bread's top and empty the center. Fill the bread with the brie mixture. Use Parmesan cheese to dredge on top.
- On a baking sheet, place the filled bread; allow to broil in the preheated oven till the top gets browned lightly for 10 minutes. Let cool down slightly; cut into wedges to serve.

Nutrition Information

- Calories: 299 calories;
- Total Fat: 12.3
- Sodium: 589
- Total Carbohydrate: 33.3
- Cholesterol: 37
- Protein: 14.4

401. Baked Chicken On Rice

Serving: 8 | Prep: | Cook: | Ready in:

Ingredients

- 4 skinless, boneless chicken breast halves
- 2 (10.75 ounce) cans condensed cream of mushroom soup
- 2 1/2 cups milk
- 1 1/2 cups uncooked white rice
- 2 (4.5 ounce) cans sliced mushrooms
- 2 (1 ounce) packages dry onion soup mix

Direction

- Turn the oven to 350°F (175°C) to preheat. Halve each chicken breast to have 8 pieces in total, put aside.
- Stir together milk and cream of mushroom soup. Save 1 cup of the mixture. Mix together the leftover mixture with 1 envelope of dry onion soup mix, undrained mushrooms, and rice.
- Add the rice mixture to a 9x13-in. baking dish. Top with the chicken pieces. Pour over the chicken with the saved soup mixture and sprinkle the remaining envelope of onion soup mix over. Put on aluminum foil to securely cover and bake for 60 minutes in the preheated oven. Uncover and bake for another 15 minutes. Let cool for 10 minutes and enjoy.

Nutrition Information

- Calories: 326 calories;
- Protein: 20.8
- Total Fat: 7.2
- Sodium: 1314
- Total Carbohydrate: 43.7
- Cholesterol: 40

402. Baked Eggs, Grandma Style

Serving: 12 | Prep: 10mins | Cook: 45mins | Ready in:

Ingredients

- cooking spray (such as Pam®)
- 1 cup shredded Cheddar-Monterey Jack cheese blend
- 1 cup shredded mozzarella cheese
- 1/4 cup butter, divided
- 1/2 pound fresh mushrooms, sliced
- 6 green onions, sliced
- 2 cups fresh spinach
- 1/2 cup chopped tomatoes
- 12 eggs
- 1 cup half-and-half
- 1 teaspoon prepared yellow mustard
- 1 teaspoon dried marjoram
- 1 teaspoon dried tarragon
- ground black pepper to taste

Direction

- Start preheating the oven to 350°F (175°C). Spray cooking spray over a 9x13-in. baking dish.
- In the prepared baking dish, place Cheddar-Monterey Jack cheese blend then the mozzarella cheese in layer.
- In a big frying pan, heat 2 tablespoons butter over medium-high heat. Sauté green onions and mushrooms for 5-10 minutes until the mushrooms turn golden brown. Add tomatoes and spinach, sauté for 3-5 minutes until the spinach barely wilts. Add the vegetable mixture to the cheese mixture.
- In a bowl, combine black pepper, tarragon, marjoram, mustard, half-and-half, and eggs; add to the vegetable mixture. Dot on the egg mixture with the leftover butter.
- Put in the preheated oven and bake for 35-45 minutes until a knife will come out clean when you insert it near the middle. Allow to sit before eating, about 5 minutes.

Nutrition Information

- Calories: 199 calories;
- Total Fat: 15.5
- Sodium: 232
- Total Carbohydrate: 3.7
- Cholesterol: 218
- Protein: 12.2

403. Baked Mushrooms With Thyme And White Wine

Serving: 2 | Prep: 10mins | Cook: 35mins | Ready in:

Ingredients

- 1 1/2 tablespoons minced onion
- 1/2 teaspoon minced garlic
- 1/4 teaspoon dried thyme
- 1 1/2 tablespoons white wine
- 1 tablespoon olive oil
- 8 ounces fresh mushrooms, quartered
- salt and pepper to taste

Direction

- Set the oven to 190°C or 375°F.
- In a big bowl, whisk together olive oil, white wine, thyme, garlic and onion, then put in mushrooms and toss to coat well. Season with pepper and salt to taste.
- Turn out the mushroom mixture to a small baking dish, then cover and bake for 35 minutes while stirring from time to time.

Nutrition Information

- Calories: 98 calories;
- Total Fat: 7.2
- Sodium: 7
- Total Carbohydrate: 5
- Cholesterol: 0
- Protein: 3.6

404. Baked Potato With Mushrooms

Serving: 1 | Prep: 10mins | Cook: 30mins | Ready in:

Ingredients

- 1 large baking potato
- 1 tablespoon unsalted butter
- 1/4 cup chopped onions
- 1/2 cup chopped mushrooms
- salt to taste
- 2 tablespoons nonfat plain yogurt

Direction

- Preheat the oven to 230 degrees C (450 degrees F).
- Pierce the potato several times using a fork. Add onto the microwave-safe dish, and cook for 10 minutes in the microwave over high heat, till becoming soft yet not mushy. Move

the potato into the baking dish, and bake in the preheated oven for 15 minutes.
- Melt the butter on medium heat in the saucepan. Stir in the onion. Cook and stir till becoming soft. Stir in the mushrooms. Use the salt to season. Lower the heat to low, keep covered, and allow it to rest till the mushrooms soften or for 5 minutes. Add the yogurt and mushrooms on top of the potato to serve.

Nutrition Information

- Calories: 427 calories;
- Cholesterol: 31
- Protein: 10.9
- Total Fat: 12.1
- Sodium: 51
- Total Carbohydrate: 71.7

405. Baked Rice And Vegetables In Broth

Serving: 4 | Prep: 15mins | Cook: 30mins | Ready in:

Ingredients

- 3/4 cup uncooked long-grain rice
- 1 tablespoon uncooked wild rice
- 1/4 cup uncooked brown rice
- 1/4 cup sliced fresh mushrooms
- 1/4 chopped fresh broccoli
- 1/4 cup chopped carrots
- 1/4 cup chopped red bell pepper
- 1/4 cup finely chopped onion
- 1 teaspoon salt
- 1 teaspoon dried onion flakes
- 1 teaspoon paprika
- 1/4 teaspoon black pepper
- 2 1/2 cups vegetable broth

Direction

- Set the oven to 425°F (220°C) and start preheating.
- Combine broth, black pepper, paprika, onion flakes, salt, onion, bell pepper, carrots, broccoli, mushrooms, brown rice, wild rice and white rice in a 9 x 13-inch baking dish. Combine well; cover.
- Bake in the prepared oven until cooked through or for half an hour; stir once during baking.

Nutrition Information

- Calories: 210 calories;
- Protein: 5.1
- Total Fat: 1
- Sodium: 877
- Total Carbohydrate: 44.3
- Cholesterol: 0

406. Baked Spaghetti From Borden® Cheese

Serving: 4 | Prep: 15mins | Cook: 30mins | Ready in:

Ingredients

- 1 (16 ounce) package spaghetti, cooked and drained
- 1 cup chopped onion
- 1 cup chopped green bell pepper
- 1 tablespoon butter
- 1 pound ground beef
- 1 (28 ounce) can tomatoes with liquid, chopped
- 1 (4 ounce) can mushrooms, drained
- 1 (2.25 ounce) can sliced ripe olives, drained
- 2 cups Borden® Shredded Mild Cheddar Cheese
- 1 (10.75 ounce) can condensed cream of mushroom soup, undiluted
- Grated Parmesan cheese
- 2 teaspoons dried oregano

Direction

- Preheat the oven to 350°F. Use the nonstick cooking spray to spray the 9x13-in. baking plate. Cook the spaghetti based on the instruction on the packages.
- Heat the butter on medium-high heat in the big nonstick skillet till hot. Sauté the pepper and onion till softened. Put in the ground beef and cook till the beef is browned, drain off.
- Whisk in the oregano, olives, mushrooms and tomatoes. Boil and lower the heat to medium. Let simmer for 10 minutes.
- Add 1/2 spaghetti into prepped baking plate. Add 1/2 of the meat-veggie mixture on top. Drizzle with 1/2 Cheddar cheese. Repeat the layers. Mix the soup along with half cup of the water; add on top of the casserole. Drizzle with the Parmesan cheese. Bake, uncovered, till heated through or for 30 - 35 minutes.

Nutrition Information

- Calories: 990 calories;
- Protein: 55.6
- Total Fat: 38.7
- Sodium: 1642
- Total Carbohydrate: 102.9
- Cholesterol: 131

407. Balsamic Chicken Salad

Serving: 4 | Prep: 20mins | Cook: 10mins | Ready in:

Ingredients

- 1 (16 ounce) bottle light balsamic vinaigrette salad dressing (such as Newman's Own® Lighten Up® Balsamic Vinaigrette Dressing), divided
- 8 chicken tenders
- 1 (6 ounce) package sliced portobello mushroom caps
- 2 hearts of romaine lettuce, chopped
- 2 green onions, sliced diagonally
- 1 pint cherry tomatoes, cut into quarters
- 1 cup shredded mozzarella cheese
- 1/4 cup sliced fresh basil leaves

Direction

- In a bowl, mix 1/3 bottle of balsamic vinaigrette dressing with the chicken tenders. Toss mushroom slices with 1/3 bottle of dressing in another bowl. Set the remaining 1/3 bottle aside. Let mushrooms and chicken tenders to marinate for at least half an hour.
- Preheat the oven's broiler; place the oven rack about 6 inches from the heat source.
- Take the mushrooms and chicken tenders out of the marinade; drain off excess. Broil mushroom and chicken for 5-8 minutes until cooked through and chicken turns brown. Take the mushrooms and chicken out of the heat; slice chicken tenders into bite-sized pieces.
- When serving, distribute chopped romaine lettuce between four plates; place mushrooms and broiled chicken on top of each. Place basil leave slices, mozzarella cheese and cherry tomatoes on top of each plate; serve with the rest of the vinaigrette dressing.

Nutrition Information

- Calories: 240 calories;
- Cholesterol: 81
- Protein: 32.8
- Total Fat: 7.8
- Sodium: 248
- Total Carbohydrate: 10.3

408. Balsamic Mushrooms

Serving: 8 | Prep: | Cook: | Ready in:

Ingredients

- 1/3 cup olive oil

- 3 cloves garlic, minced
- 1 pound fresh mushrooms, sliced
- 3 tablespoons balsamic vinegar
- 3 tablespoons white wine
- salt and pepper to taste

Direction

- Sauté garlic in olive oil for around 1 - 2 minutes. Avoid browning the garlic. Put in mushrooms and cook for 2 minutes more while sometimes stirring. Mix in wine and balsamic vinegar, cook for another 2 minutes. Spice with pepper and salt.

Nutrition Information

- Calories: 94 calories;
- Protein: 1.9
- Total Fat: 8.3
- Sodium: 5
- Total Carbohydrate: 3.3
- Cholesterol: 0

409. Banh Mi Style Vietnamese Baguette

Serving: 2 | Prep: 20mins | Cook: 25mins | Ready in:

Ingredients

- 2 portobello mushroom caps, sliced
- 2 teaspoons olive oil
- salt and pepper to taste
- 1 carrot, sliced into sticks
- 1 daikon (white) radish, sliced into sticks
- 1 cup rice vinegar
- 1/2 cup fresh lime juice
- 1/2 cup cold water
- 1/2 cup chilled lime juice
- 2 teaspoons soy sauce
- 1 teaspoon nuoc mam (Vietnamese fish sauce)
- 1/2 teaspoon toasted sesame oil
- 2 tablespoons canola oil
- 2 teaspoons minced garlic
- 1/3 cup white sugar
- 1/3 cup cold water
- 1 jalapeno pepper, thinly sliced
- 8 sprigs fresh cilantro with stems
- 1 medium cucumber, sliced into thin strips
- 2 sprigs fresh Thai basil
- 2 (7 inch) French bread baguettes, split lengthwise

Direction

- Set the oven to 450°F (230°C) for preheating. Arrange the mushrooms on a baking sheet. Drizzle with a bit of olive oil and spice up with pepper and salt. Roast the mushroom for about 25 minutes inside the prepped oven. Let it cool slightly, and cut into strips.
- Meanwhile, put a water in a saucepan and let it boil. Drop the radish sticks and carrot into the boiling water and remove after a few seconds, and submerge them in an ice water placed in a bowl to prevent the vegetables from cooking. In another bowl, stir a half cup of lime juice, rice vinegar and half cup cold water together. Place the radish and carrot to the vinegar and lime marinade and allow soaking for 15 minutes, much longer if it's convenient.
- Make the sandwich sauce: Combine together 1/3 cup water, the remaining lime juice, fish sauce, 1/3 cup sugar, sesame oil, soy sauce and canola oil, mix in a small bowl,.
- To arrange the sandwiches, drizzle a bit of a sandwich sauce on each half of the French loaves. Put the roasted mushrooms on the bottom half of each roll and drizzle with a little more sauce. Top it off with a couple sticks of carrot and radish (without the marinade), a few slices of jalapeno, basil, cilantro and cucumber. Place the other half of the bread on top to close. Serve.

Nutrition Information

- Calories: 760 calories;
- Total Fat: 22.8

- Sodium: 1282
- Total Carbohydrate: 128.4
- Cholesterol: 0
- Protein: 19.5

410. Barilla® Spicy Sriracha Pasta Bowl

Serving: 8 | Prep: 25mins | Cook: 7mins | Ready in:

Ingredients

- 1 (16 ounce) box Barilla® Spaghetti
- 1/4 cup Sriracha chile sauce
- 1/4 cup honey
- 1 lime, juiced
- 2 tablespoons neutral oil (such as coconut or canola)
- 2 cups thinly sliced mushrooms
- 2 medium carrots, cut into matchstick-size pieces
- 1 cup thinly sliced yellow or green bell pepper
- 1 cup sugar snap peas, halved lengthwise
- 1 (26 ounce) jar Barilla® Spicy Marinara Sauce
- Sesame seeds (optional)
- 3 green onions, thinly sliced

Direction

- In the small-sized bowl, mix lime juice, honey, and Sriracha; put them aside.
- In the big pot, boil to rolling 4-6 qt. of water; put in the salt to taste and the Spaghetti; mix lightly.
- Based on the instruction on package, cook pasta; take out of the heat and drain it well.
- At the same time, in the big skillet, heat oil on medium heat; put in the sugar snap peas, bell pepper, carrots, and mushrooms.
- Cook, mixing often, till becoming soft or for 5 - 7 minutes; put in Spicy Marinara and mix; put in pasta and combine by tossing.
- Serve in bowls and as you want, add a drizzle of the sesame seeds, green onions and a sprinkle of Sriracha-honey mixture on top.

Nutrition Information

- Calories: 345 calories;
- Total Fat: 6
- Sodium: 692
- Total Carbohydrate: 66
- Cholesterol: 0
- Protein: 10.4

411. Barley Bake

Serving: 6 | Prep: 25mins | Cook: 1hours25mins | Ready in:

Ingredients

- 1/4 cup butter
- 1 medium onion, diced
- 1 cup uncooked pearl barley
- 1/2 cup pine nuts
- 2 green onions, thinly sliced
- 1/2 cup sliced fresh mushrooms
- 1/2 cup chopped fresh parsley
- 1/4 teaspoon salt
- 1/8 teaspoon pepper
- 2 (14.5 ounce) cans vegetable broth

Direction

- Pre heat the oven to 175 degrees C (350 degrees F).
- Melt the butter on medium high heat in the skillet. Whisk in the pine nuts, barley and onion. Cook and stir till the barley turns brown a bit. Stir in the parsley, mushrooms and green onions. Use the pepper and salt to season. Move mixture into the 2 qt. casserole dish, and whisk in vegetable broth.
- Bake in preheated oven for 75 minutes till the barley softens and the liquid is absorbed.

Nutrition Information

- Calories: 280 calories;
- Total Fat: 14.2
- Sodium: 437
- Total Carbohydrate: 33.2
- Cholesterol: 20
- Protein: 7.4

412. Barley Chicken Casserole

Serving: 4 | Prep: | Cook: |Ready in:

Ingredients

- 4 slices bacon, fat removed and meat finely chopped
- 1 onion, thinly sliced
- 2 carrots, diced
- 12 button mushrooms, quartered
- 2 1/2 cups chicken stock
- 1 cup barley
- 1 teaspoon dried thyme
- 1 teaspoon dried marjoram
- 1 teaspoon dried parsley
- 1 bay leaf, crushed
- ground black pepper to taste
- 1 green bell pepper, chopped
- 4 dark meat chicken pieces

Direction

- Set an oven to preheat to 190°C (375°F).
- Fry the bacon in a big fry pan until it turns brown. Set aside the bacon fat for sautéing the chicken later. Add carrots and onions into the fry pan and sauté for 2 minutes. Add pepper to taste, bay leaf, parsley, marjoram, thyme, barley, stock and mushrooms. Stir it all together. In a 9x13-inch baking dish, spread the mixture, then top it with green bell pepper and mix to settle.
- In a fry pan, heat the reserved bacon fat, then cook the chicken until brown. Put the browned chicken over the barley mixture. Put the lid on the baking dish and let it bake for an hour and 10 minutes in the preheated oven.

Nutrition Information

- Calories: 381 calories;
- Sodium: 292
- Total Carbohydrate: 43.5
- Cholesterol: 67
- Protein: 28.5
- Total Fat: 11

413. Barley, Lentil And Mushroom Soup

Serving: 8 | Prep: 20mins | Cook: 1hours10mins |Ready in:

Ingredients

- 1/4 cup olive oil
- 1 medium onion, chopped
- 1 stalk celery, chopped
- 2 carrots, chopped
- 3/4 cup pearl barley
- 3/4 cup dry brown lentils
- 1/3 cup dried porcini mushrooms, rinsed
- 2 quarts low-sodium beef broth
- 1/4 teaspoon dried thyme
- 1 teaspoon dried parsley
- 1/4 teaspoon freshly ground black pepper
- 1 bay leaf
- 4 cups sliced button mushrooms
- 1 tablespoon dry sherry (optional)

Direction

- Add the olive oil to a big pot and heat over medium heat. Add the onion, stir and cook for about 5 minutes until it gets soft but not brown. Mix in the carrot and celery, cook for 5 more minutes. Mix in the lentils and barley until oil forms a coat outside, keep cooking and stir until they are lightly toasted.
- Add in the beef broth, the bay leaf, pepper, parsley and thyme for seasoning. Boil them

up. Add the porcini mushrooms, let simmer while covered over low heat for 25 minutes. Add the button mushroom, cover and keep cooking for half an hour more, stir sporadically. Mix in sherry at the last 5 minutes. Add more seasoning if necessary then serve.

Nutrition Information

- Calories: 265 calories;
- Total Fat: 8.9
- Sodium: 107
- Total Carbohydrate: 33
- Cholesterol: 0
- Protein: 14

414. Basil Mushrooms In Cream Sauce

Serving: 4 | Prep: 15mins | Cook: 15mins | Ready in:

Ingredients

- 2 tablespoons butter
- 1 tablespoon olive oil
- 6 cups sliced fresh mushrooms
- 1 tablespoon chopped fresh basil
- 3 tablespoons rum
- 2 tablespoons cooking sherry
- 1 tablespoon lemon juice
- 1 1/4 cups sour cream
- 1/2 cup grated Parmesan cheese
- 1/4 teaspoon sea salt

Direction

- In a skillet, melt butter with olive oil over medium heat. Cook basil and mushrooms in the mixture until the mushrooms are warm. Add sherry and rum to the mushrooms and keep cooking until the mushrooms are tender. Mix in Parmesan cheese, sour cream, and lemon juice; simmer until fully heated. Use salt to season and enjoy.

Nutrition Information

- Calories: 344 calories;
- Sodium: 430
- Total Carbohydrate: 8.5
- Cholesterol: 58
- Protein: 10.4
- Total Fat: 28.1

415. Bavarian Chanterelle Mushrooms With Bacon

Serving: 4 | Prep: 10mins | Cook: 15mins | Ready in:

Ingredients

- 1 tablespoon butter
- 2 slices lean bacon, chopped
- 1 small onion, finely chopped
- 1 pound chanterelle mushrooms, cut lengthwise
- salt and freshly ground black pepper to taste
- 2 tablespoons chopped fresh parsley, or to taste

Direction

- Melt the butter on medium heat in a skillet. Cook the onion and bacon for roughly 5 minutes till the bacon turns crispy and the onion softens and translucent.
- Put in the chanterelle mushrooms and let it simmer in skillet for roughly 10 minutes till the liquid is totally boiled off. Drizzle with the parsley and serve right away.

Nutrition Information

- Calories: 101 calories;
- Total Carbohydrate: 8.1
- Cholesterol: 13

- Total Fat: 4.8
- Protein: 4.4
- Sodium: 190

416. Beef Stroganoff For Instant Pot®

Serving: 8 | Prep: 20mins | Cook: 37mins |Ready in:

Ingredients

- 2 tablespoons canola oil
- 1/2 onion, diced
- 2 teaspoons salt, divided
- 2 pounds beef stew meat, cut into 1-inch cubes
- 1 teaspoon freshly ground black pepper
- 3 cloves garlic, minced
- 1/2 teaspoon dried thyme
- 2 tablespoons soy sauce
- 3 cups chopped mushrooms
- 2 tablespoons all-purpose flour
- 3 cups chicken broth
- 1 (16 ounce) package wide egg noodles
- 3/4 cup sour cream, or to taste

Direction

- Set the multi-cooker, an Instant Pot® for example, into Sauté function. Heat oil for 60 seconds and then cook the onion and half tsp. of salt. Allow it to cook for 3-4 minutes until the onion is tender.
- Spice the beef with pepper and a tsp. of salt. Stir it in to the pot and allow it to cook for 2 minutes until browned equally on all sides. Mix in thyme and garlic and let it cook for another 30 seconds until fragrant. Stir in soy sauce.
- Add mushrooms and mix the flour until well-combined. Pour the remaining half tsp. of salt together with the chicken broth. Close and secure the lid tightly and set the timer for 10 minutes. Follow the manufacturer's guide to set the cooker to high pressure for 10-15 minutes.
- Use the quick-release method to carefully release its pressure. Slowly unlock the lid and stir in egg noodles. Lock it again and set it to high pressure for 5 minutes. Allow it to cook for 5 minutes more.
- Use the natural release method to release the pressure for 5 minutes. Once done, use quick-release method to remove all the remaining pressure inside. Unlock the pressure cooker and mix in sour cream.

Nutrition Information

- Calories: 536 calories;
- Total Fat: 26.2
- Sodium: 1312
- Total Carbohydrate: 45.2
- Cholesterol: 121
- Protein: 29

417. Beef Sukiyaki

Serving: 4 | Prep: 30mins | Cook: 15mins |Ready in:

Ingredients

- 1 1/2 cups prepared dashi stock
- 3/4 cup soy sauce
- 3/4 cup mirin
- 1/4 cup white sugar
- 8 ounces shirataki noodles
- 2 tablespoons canola oil
- 1 pound beef top sirloin, thinly sliced
- 1 onion, thinly sliced
- 1 tablespoon canola oil
- 2 stalks celery, thinly sliced
- 2 carrots, thinly sliced
- 5 green onions, cut into 2 inch pieces
- 4 ounces sliced fresh mushrooms (button, shiitake, or enoki)
- 1 (14 ounce) package firm tofu, cut into cubes

Direction

- In a bowl, mix sugar, dashi, mirin, and soy sauce; set aside.
- In boiling water, soak noodles for a minute then drain; rinse under cold water.
- Heat 2 tbsp. canola oil; cook and stir beef for 2-3 mins in hot oil, or until the meat is not pink anymore. Drain the beef then set aside.
- Heat a tablespoon of canola oil in the pan; cook and stir mushrooms, onion, carrot, and celery for 4 mins, or until soft. Mix in tofu, green onions, beef, noodles, and the dashi mixture; simmer. Split the hot sukiyaki between 4 bowls. Serve.

Nutrition Information

- Calories: 576 calories;
- Protein: 34.4
- Total Fat: 25.6
- Sodium: 2941
- Total Carbohydrate: 44.9
- Cholesterol: 61

418. Beefy Mushroom Barley Soup

Serving: 8 | Prep: 20mins | Cook: 1hours10mins | Ready in:

Ingredients

- 1 pound cubed beef stew meat
- 1 tablespoon vegetable oil
- 2 cups water
- 2 tablespoons margarine
- 2 large carrots, diced
- 3 cloves garlic, minced
- 1 onion, chopped
- 2 stalks celery, chopped
- 1 pound fresh mushrooms, sliced
- 6 cups water
- 3 cubes beef bouillon cube
- 1/4 cup pearl barley
- 1/4 cup sour cream

Direction

- Over medium heat, brown tiny cubes of stew meat in vegetable oil, until the juices have a rich brown color. Add 2 cups water, and simmer meat while preparing the vegetables.
- In a big soup pot, melt margarine or butter over medium heat. Sauté onion, carrots, celery, mushrooms, and garlic.
- Add 6 cups water, meat, barley, and bouillon cubes to vegetable mixture. Cook for about 1 hour until barley is soft. Adjust liquid and seasoning if wished. Take away from heat, then mix in sour cream. Serve instantly.

Nutrition Information

- Calories: 249 calories;
- Total Fat: 17.2
- Sodium: 422
- Total Carbohydrate: 11
- Cholesterol: 41
- Protein: 13.7

419. Belle And Chron's Spinach And Mushroom Quiche

Serving: 8 | Prep: 15mins | Cook: 35mins | Ready in:

Ingredients

- 6 slices bacon
- 4 eggs, beaten
- 1 1/2 cups light cream
- 1/4 teaspoon ground nutmeg
- 1/2 teaspoon salt
- 1/2 teaspoon pepper
- 2 cups chopped fresh spinach
- 2 cups chopped fresh mushrooms
- 1/2 cup chopped onions
- 1 cup shredded Swiss cheese
- 1 cup shredded Cheddar cheese
- 1 (9 inch) deep dish pie crust

Direction

- Set the oven to 400°F or 200°C for preheating.
- In a large and deep skillet, cook the bacon over medium-high heat until browned all over. Drain the bacon, and then crumple; put aside.
- Mix the pepper, eggs, nutmeg, salt, and cream together in a large bowl. Mix in spinach, 3/4 cup of Cheddar cheese, mushrooms, bacon, onions, and 3/4 cup of Swiss cheese. Spread the mixture over the pie crust and sprinkle the remaining cheese on top.
- Let it bake uncovered inside the preheated oven for 35 minutes, or until lightly browned and bubbly.

Nutrition Information

- Calories: 534 calories;
- Total Fat: 42.4
- Sodium: 694
- Total Carbohydrate: 17.3
- Cholesterol: 183
- Protein: 21.4

420. Beth's Portobello Mushroom Burgers

Serving: 2 | Prep: 5mins | Cook: 15mins | Ready in:

Ingredients

- 2 portobello mushroom caps
- 4 slices turkey bacon
- 3 teaspoons horseradish sauce
- 2 leaves romaine lettuce
- 2 slices tomato
- 2 hamburger buns

Direction

- Preheat the oven to 230°C or 450°Fahrenheit. Place a sheet of foil in a cookie sheet then coat with a cooking spray. Clean the mushrooms using a damp cloth to remove the dirt. Cut the stem off the mushroom to let it sit evenly.
- Envelop each mushroom with two turkey bacon pieces and slip the ends beneath the stem; arrange on the prepared cookie sheet. Bake mushrooms for 10-15 mins; drain on paper towels.
- Slather 1 1/2 tsp. horseradish sauce on top of each buns, tweak depending on your preference. Add a piece of lettuce, a slice of tomato, and 1 mushroom burger on every bun.

Nutrition Information

- Calories: 313 calories;
- Sodium: 934
- Total Carbohydrate: 29.9
- Cholesterol: 53
- Protein: 15.5
- Total Fat: 15.3

421. Better Slow Cooker Robust Chicken

Serving: 6 | Prep: 5mins | Cook: 8hours | Ready in:

Ingredients

- 1 1/2 pounds skinless, boneless chicken breast halves - cut into 1 inch strips
- 2 tablespoons bacon bits
- 1/4 cup chopped green olives
- 1 (14.5 ounce) can diced tomatoes, drained
- 1 (4.5 ounce) can sliced mushrooms, drained
- 1 (1.25 ounce) envelope dry chicken gravy mix
- 1/2 cup red wine
- 3 tablespoons Dijon mustard
- 1/4 cup balsamic vinegar

Direction

- Mix vinegar, mustard, wine, gravy mix, mushrooms, tomatoes, olives, bacon bits, and chicken in a slow cooker. Combine together.

- Put the lid on the slow cooker and cook for 6-8 hours on Low.

Nutrition Information

- Calories: 198 calories;
- Cholesterol: 62
- Protein: 24.5
- Total Fat: 4.7
- Sodium: 946
- Total Carbohydrate: 10.1

422. Black Olive, Mushroom, And Sausage Stuffing

Serving: 8 | Prep: 25mins | Cook: 50mins | Ready in:

Ingredients

- 20 slices bread
- 1 pound breakfast sausage
- 3/4 cup butter
- 1 cup chopped onion
- 2 cups chopped celery
- 2 cups sliced fresh mushrooms
- 1 (15 ounce) can black olives, drained and chopped
- 2 teaspoons garlic, minced
- 1 tablespoon poultry seasoning
- 1/4 teaspoon salt (optional)
- 1/4 teaspoon ground black pepper
- 1 egg, beaten

Direction

- Set the oven to 350°F (175°C) for preheating. Grease the 9x13-inches baking dish.
- On the baking sheets, arrange the slices of bread in a single layer. Let them bake inside the preheated oven until the bread slices turn golden brown, and then flip the bread over and bake the other side until they turn golden brown, for about 15 minutes. Remove it from the oven and let them cool. Cut the bread into 1/2-inch cubes once they are cool.
- In the meantime, place the large skillet over medium-high heat. Mix in sausage and cook it until it is no longer pink and the sausage is crumbly. Mix in celery, butter, and onion. Cook for 5 minutes until the onion is translucent and softened. Scrape the mixture into the large mixing bowl. Mix in garlic, pepper, salt, mushrooms, poultry seasoning, and olives. Mix in half of the bread cubes. Stir the mixture until evenly-blended. Whisk in beaten eggs together with the remaining bread cubes. Pack the mixture into the prepared baking dish.
- Bake inside the preheated oven for 30 minutes until the top is golden brown and crispy.

Nutrition Information

- Calories: 641 calories;
- Total Fat: 48
- Sodium: 1428
- Total Carbohydrate: 38.9
- Cholesterol: 110
- Protein: 14.3

423. Blue Cheese Stuffed Mushrooms With Grilled Onions

Serving: 8 | Prep: 30mins | Cook: 5mins | Ready in:

Ingredients

- 1 pound fresh mushrooms, stems removed
- 8 ounces blue cheese
- 3 medium onions, sliced into rings
- 1/4 cup olive oil

Direction

- Preheat an outdoor grill for high heat, then slightly oil grate. Spoon crumbled blue cheese into the mushroom caps.
- On the prepared grill, position mushrooms (cheese side up) and onion slices. Flip onions often until tender. Don't flip mushrooms. Grill till mushrooms become softened and blue cheese has melted. Transfer mushrooms to a serving plate, cover with grilled onions.

Nutrition Information

- Calories: 189 calories;
- Sodium: 400
- Total Carbohydrate: 6.4
- Cholesterol: 21
- Protein: 8.3
- Total Fat: 15.1

424. Bow Tie Tuna Florentine

Serving: 4 | Prep: 15mins | Cook: 30mins | Ready in:

Ingredients

- 1 (8 ounce) package farfalle (bow tie) pasta
- 1 tablespoon margarine
- 1 1/4 cups milk
- 1 (1.2 ounce) package creamy pesto sauce mix
- 2 cups fresh spinach, rinsed and thinly sliced
- 1/2 cup sliced fresh mushrooms
- 3 (5 ounce) cans tuna, drained
- 3 roma (plum) tomatoes, chopped

Direction

- Boil a big pot of lightly salted water. Put pasta and cook till al dente or for 8 to 10 minutes; let drain.
- Liquefy the margarine in a big saucepan, over medium-high heat. Put in pesto sauce mix and milk; boil, mixing continuously with a wire whisk till well incorporated and boiling. Lower heat, and put mushrooms and spinach. Allow to simmer for 3 to 4 minutes, mixing from time to time.
- Put tomatoes, tuna and cooked pasta, mixing softly to coat. Cook 3 to 5 minutes till heated well.

Nutrition Information

- Calories: 437 calories;
- Total Fat: 7.6
- Sodium: 664
- Total Carbohydrate: 53.4
- Cholesterol: 34
- Protein: 37

425. Bow Tie Pasta With Sausage, Peas, And Mushrooms

Serving: 4 | Prep: 10mins | Cook: 35mins | Ready in:

Ingredients

- 1/2 cup olive oil, divided
- 1 pound Italian sausage, casings removed
- 1 (10 ounce) package portobello mushrooms, sliced
- 3/4 teaspoon sea salt, or more to taste, divided
- 3/4 teaspoon freshly ground black pepper, divided
- 1 (10 ounce) package frozen peas, partially thawed
- 1 (16 ounce) package farfalle (bow-tie) pasta
- 1/2 cup Parmesan cheese

Direction

- In a big skillet over high heat, heat 2 tablespoons olive oil; in the hot oil, cook and mix sausage for 5 minutes till crumbly and browned, cutting up any big chunks. Move cooked sausage to a plate.
- Using the same big skillet, heat 2 additional tablespoons olive oil over medium heat; in the hot oil, cook and mix 1/2 teaspoon pepper,

1/2 teaspoon salt and mushrooms till mushrooms are soft and all the liquid has evaporated for 8 minutes.
- Mix peas into mushroom mixture and cook for 2 minutes till peas are warmed. Put sausage back to mushroom mixture; cook and mix for 3 minutes till flavors have incorporated and sausage is heated through.
- Boil a big pot of lightly salted water. Let bowtie pasta cook at a boil for 12 minutes, mixing from time to time till cooked through yet firm to the bite; drain pasta, set aside half cup pasta water. Put pasta back to pot and mix in sausage-mushroom mixture; cook and mix for 5 minutes till mixture is equally mixed, putting in reserved pasta water as necessary.
- Sprinkle leftover quarter cup olive oil atop pasta mixture and season with leftover quarter teaspoon salt and quarter teaspoon pepper; coat by tossing. Put in Parmesan cheese; toss to incorporate.

Nutrition Information

- Calories: 1026 calories;
- Sodium: 1518
- Total Carbohydrate: 98.9
- Cholesterol: 53
- Protein: 39.2
- Total Fat: 54.2

426. Braised Tofu

Serving: 4 | Prep: 10mins | Cook: 20mins | Ready in:

Ingredients

- 1 (14 ounce) package firm tofu
- cooking spray
- 3 teaspoons sesame oil, divided
- 1 (8 ounce) can water chestnuts, drained
- 3 ounces fresh shiitake mushrooms, stems removed
- 1 1/2 cups snow peas, trimmed
- 1/2 teaspoon oyster flavored sauce
- 1 cup water

Direction

- Cut tofu block lengthwise into 3 long slabs. Use paper towels to wrap each slab, and press to remove any excess water.
- In a skillet coated with cooking spray, heat 2 teaspoons sesame oil; add tofu slabs to the skillet when oil is hot. Fry each side for about 5 minutes until nicely browned.
- Take browned tofu out of the skillet, and slice into smaller cubes. Add the rest teaspoon of sesame oil to the skillet and sauté snow peas, mushrooms, and water chestnuts. Combine oyster sauce and water, then pour into the skillet along with the tofu. Cook, covered, for about 10 minutes over low heat.

Nutrition Information

- Calories: 153 calories;
- Sodium: 62
- Total Carbohydrate: 12.7
- Cholesterol: 0
- Protein: 10
- Total Fat: 7.8

427. Bratwurst Pot Pie

Serving: 4 | Prep: 20mins | Cook: 25mins | Ready in:

Ingredients

- 2 tablespoons vegetable oil
- 3 links Farmland® Beer Bratwurst
- 1 pound mushrooms, sliced
- 1 1/2 cups diced yellow onion
- 3/4 cup diced carrots
- 3/4 cup diced celery
- 4 garlic cloves, sliced
- 1/2 teaspoon red pepper flakes
- 1 teaspoon fresh thyme leaves

- 3 tablespoons all-purpose flour
- 2 cups chicken stock
- 1 cup heavy cream
- 1 tablespoon whole-grain mustard
- 2 cups Cheddar cheese, grated
- Salt and pepper, to taste
- 3 soft pretzels
- 3 tablespoons melted butter

Direction

- Set the oven to 350°F to preheat.
- Heat vegetable oil in a heavy-based sauté pan over medium-high heat. Add sausages and cook until barely cooked through and all sides are brown. Take out, and when cool, cut into rounds.
- Add mushrooms to the same pan and cook until turning very brown. Add celery, carrots, and onions. Cook until tender, add garlic and cook for another 2 minutes.
- Add fresh thyme and red pepper flakes, and then flour. Lower the heat and cook for another 2 minutes to cook raw taste from the flour.
- Add heavy cream and chicken stock, and simmer while stirring often.
- Add cheddar cheese and mustard, and mix to blend. Add the saved sausage and use pepper and salt to season. Remove to individual oven-safe serving plates.
- Roughly chop pretzels by hands or in a food processor to create crumbs. Mix with melted butter and put the crumb mixture on top of each serving plate.
- Bake for about 12-15 minutes until fully warm and golden brown.

Nutrition Information

- Calories: 1012 calories;
- Total Carbohydrate: 51.7
- Cholesterol: 167
- Protein: 35.1
- Total Fat: 74.9
- Sodium: 2145

428. Brazilian Chicken Stroganoff

Serving: 4 | Prep: 20mins | Cook: 32mins | Ready in:

Ingredients

- 3 tablespoons olive oil, divided
- 1 onion, thinly sliced
- 3 cups mushrooms, sliced
- 2 cloves garlic cloves, crushed
- 2 skinless, boneless chicken breasts, thinly sliced
- salt and ground black pepper to taste
- 1 (14.5 ounce) can stewed tomatoes, blended
- 1 (7.6 ounce) can table cream

Direction

- In a skillet, heat 2 tablespoons olive oil over medium-low heat. Add in onions; cook and stir for 5 to 7 minutes, until onions are soft, Add garlic and mushroom; cook and stir for 7 to 10 minutes longer until mushrooms becomes soft,. In a bowl, transfer the mushroom mixture.
- In the skillet heat 1 tablespoon olive oil over medium-high heat. Add chicken; cook for 7 to 10 minutes per side until the chicken is no longer pink in the center and becomes golden brown. Transfer the mushroom mixture into the chicken and stir well; add salt and pepper to taste. Pour in tomatoes; cook and stir in 5 to 7 minutes, until tomato juice start to simmer. Add table cream, stir and let it simmer in 1 to 3 minutes, until flavors are combined.

Nutrition Information

- Calories: 440 calories;
- Cholesterol: 73
- Protein: 28.4
- Total Fat: 28.7

- Sodium: 366
- Total Carbohydrate: 14.4

429. Brazilian Stroganoff

Serving: 10 | Prep: 15mins | Cook: 21mins | Ready in:

Ingredients

- 1 pound stew beef, tenderized and diced
- 1/2 teaspoon vinegar
- salt to taste
- 1 teaspoon oil, or as needed
- 1 onion, diced
- 1 (15 ounce) can corn, drained
- 1 (15 ounce) can sweet peas, drained
- 1 (4.5 ounce) can mushrooms, drained and diced
- 1 (6 ounce) can tomato sauce
- 1/2 quart heavy whipping cream

Direction

- In a bowl, place in beef and cover with salt and vinegar.
- On medium-high heat, heat oil in a big skillet and stir the onion in. Cook until it is soft, about 3-5 minutes. Mix the meat in with the onions, cooking and stirring for 5 minutes until the meat starts to brown and the onions become soft. Add mushrooms, peas and corn in the skillet and stir for 10 minutes until the flavors merge. Stir the cream and tomato sauce in then cook for another 3 minutes. It is ready when the meat is salmon pink. Sprinkle with salt to taste.

Nutrition Information

- Calories: 327 calories;
- Sodium: 387
- Total Carbohydrate: 16.7
- Cholesterol: 90
- Protein: 11.6

- Total Fat: 24.7

430. Brie And Mushroom Phyllo Puffs

Serving: 25 | Prep: 2hours | Cook: 30mins | Ready in:

Ingredients

- 1 cup butter, divided
- 8 crimini mushrooms, sliced
- 6 shiitake mushrooms, sliced
- 3 cloves garlic, chopped
- 1 (8 ounce) wedge Brie cheese
- 1 (16 ounce) package frozen phyllo pastry, thawed

Direction

- Place a skillet over medium heat and melt 2 1/2 tablespoons of butter. Sauté garlic, shiitake mushrooms, and crimini until tender. Remove from the heat, set aside. Microwave the leftover butter in a dish until melted.
- Preheat oven to 190°C/375°F.
- Roll out phyllo dough and cut equally into three 3 x 12-inch strips using kitchen shears. Place two phyllo sheets on either a cutting board or another work surface. Use a damp paper towel to cover the pile of remaining sheets to prevent them from drying.
- Brush melted butter on the top sheet. Put a dab of brie (around the size of a raspberry) on one end of the sheet. Then add a small amount of mushroom mixture on top of brie. Make a triangle by folding the dough over the filling. Continue to fold back and forth in a triangle shape and brush the exposed side with melted butter as you go. Seal the last fold with a little butter or water. Place the phyllo triangle on an ungreased baking sheet. Repeat process with the rest of the dough and filling.
- Bake in preheated oven for 20 to 25 minutes, or until triangles are golden brown. Turnover once while baking to brown the other side.

Nutrition Information

- Calories: 153 calories;
- Protein: 3.6
- Total Fat: 11
- Sodium: 199
- Total Carbohydrate: 10
- Cholesterol: 29

431. Broccoli And Carrot Lasagna

Serving: 12 | Prep: | Cook: | Ready in:

Ingredients

- 4 cups chopped broccoli
- 2 cups chopped carrots
- 9 lasagna noodles
- 2 (10.75 ounce) cans condensed cream of mushroom soup
- 3/4 cup grated Parmesan cheese
- 3/4 cup cottage cheese
- 3 cups mozzarella cheese, shredded
- 1 teaspoon garlic powder
- 1 teaspoon dried rosemary, crushed
- 2 teaspoons paprika

Direction

- Put carrots and broccoli in a steamer, and let it steam until soft. Boil lasagna pasta.
- Mix well 1/2 cup parmesan, cream of mushroom soup, cottage cheese and 2 cups mozzarella in a bowl. Set aside 1 1/4 cup mixture.
- Add the cooked vegetables, garlic powder and rosemary to the remaining sauce. Set aside.
- To create lasagna: using a 9x13 in. pan, place 3 noodles and pour 1/2 of vegetable mixture, 3 noodles, spread rest of veggie mixture, 3 noodles, the reserved 1 1/4 cup of cheese mixture. Pour the 1 cup mozzarella on top. Combine, paprika and 1/4 cup parmesan. Drizzle on top of mozzarella.
- Cover and bake at 375 degrees F (190 degrees C) for 1/2 hour, then remove cover and bake 10 more minutes! Enjoy, it's really wonderful!

Nutrition Information

- Calories: 249 calories;
- Total Fat: 12
- Sodium: 662
- Total Carbohydrate: 22.1
- Cholesterol: 29
- Protein: 14.2

432. Broken Pasta With Mushroom, Onion, And Crispy SPAM®

Serving: 4 | Prep: 15mins | Cook: 30mins | Ready in:

Ingredients

- 1/3 (8 ounce) package bucatini (dry)
- 1/3 (12 ounce) can fully cooked luncheon meat (such as SPAM®), cut into small cubes
- 2 tablespoons olive oil, divided
- 1/4 teaspoon crushed black peppercorns
- 1 onion, sliced
- 1 tablespoon white sugar
- 6 mushrooms, sliced
- 1/2 teaspoon Italian seasoning
- 1/2 teaspoon garlic powder
- 1/4 teaspoon red pepper flakes
- salt and ground black pepper to taste
- 1 tablespoon unsalted butter
- 2 tablespoons grated Parmesan cheese
- 1 (1 ounce) slice mozzarella cheese, cut into small cubes

Direction

- Break each bucatini piece into 4 pieces.

- In a pan, on medium heat, toast luncheon meat with 1 tablespoon of olive oil. Put in crushed peppercorns and cook for about 5 minutes until meat seems crispy. Put aside.
- In a different pan, heat over medium-low heat the remaining oil. Cover and cook the onion for 5 to 7 minutes until softened. Put in sugar; cook, stirring every 2 to 3 minutes, for 10 to 15 minutes until browned and very tender.
- In the meantime, pour in a large pot with lightly salted water and heat to a rolling boil. Cook bucatini at a boil for about 5 minutes until softened yet set to the bite. Drain.
- Put black pepper, salt, red pepper flakes, garlic powder, Italian seasoning, Parmesan cheese, and mushrooms in the pan with the onions. Combine then cover. Cook for 5 minutes until mushrooms release some moisture and shrink. Add butter; cook for an extra 3 minutes until flavors are well-combined. Put in Parmesan cheese and crispy meat. Stir.
- Drain pasta; stir in the mushroom mixture. Put in mozzarella cheese. Turn up the heat to high and close the pan. Cook, stirring several times, for an extra 3 to 5 minutes until pasta has a light crust.

Nutrition Information

- Calories: 303 calories;
- Total Fat: 19.7
- Sodium: 513
- Total Carbohydrate: 22.2
- Cholesterol: 34
- Protein: 10.1

433. Buffalo Cheesy Chicken Lasagna

Serving: 10 | Prep: 15mins | Cook: 1hours15mins | Ready in:

Ingredients

- 1 pound skinless, boneless chicken breast - cooked and diced
- 4 cups spaghetti sauce
- 2 tablespoons hot sauce
- 2 tablespoons apple cider vinegar
- 1 1/2 cups water
- 1 teaspoon garlic powder
- 1 small onion, chopped
- 1 small green bell pepper, chopped
- 1 (6 ounce) can mushrooms, drained
- 1 egg, beaten
- 1 (15 ounce) container ricotta cheese
- 12 uncooked lasagna noodles
- 2 cups shredded mozzarella cheese
- 3/4 cup crumbled blue cheese

Direction

- Start preheating the oven to 350°F (175°C). Grease a lasagna pan lightly.
- Combine mushrooms, bell pepper, onion, garlic powder, water, vinegar, hot sauce, spaghetti sauce and chicken in a large bowl. Mix well, then put aside. Mix ricotta cheese and egg beat together in a medium bowl.
- Spread into bottom of the prepared pan with one cup of the spaghetti/chicken mixture. Layer with the lasagna noodles, then another 1 1/2 cups chicken mixture. Spread half of the egg/ ricotta mixture over all. Sprinkle with half of mozzarella cheese. Place on another layer of the noodles, one and a half cups of chicken mixture, the remaining ricotta mixture and the remaining mozzarella. Add 1 last layer of the noodles and the remaining chicken mixture on top.
- Bake, covered, for 70 mins at 350°F (175°C). Put away the cover, top with a sprinkle of the crumbled blue cheese. Bake without covering for 5 mins longer.
- Discard from the oven, allow to stand with a cover for about 15-20 mins before enjoying.

Nutrition Information

- Calories: 435 calories;

- Total Carbohydrate: 40
- Cholesterol: 94
- Protein: 33.3
- Total Fat: 15.4
- Sodium: 932

434. Busted Up Veggie Omelet

Serving: 2 | Prep: 10mins | Cook: 5mins | Ready in:

Ingredients

- 2 tablespoons extra-virgin olive oil
- 2 egg whites
- 1 egg
- 2 tablespoons milk
- 1/2 tomato, coarsely chopped
- 1/3 cup coarsely chopped red onion
- 1/3 cup sliced mushrooms
- 1/3 cup coarsely chopped spinach
- 1/4 cup shredded mozzarella cheese
- 2 tablespoons grated Parmesan cheese
- salt and ground black pepper to taste

Direction

- In a medium-sized skillet, heat oil over medium heat.
- In a small bowl, whisk together milk, egg and egg whites. In another bowl, toss together spinach, mushrooms, onion and tomato.
- In the hot skillet, pour and cook the egg mixture about 1 minute, until firm on the bottom. Use a spatula to flip the omelette; don't worry as it would be busted up. Add the tomato mixture immediately and top with Parmesan and mozzarella cheeses. Wait about 2 minutes for cheeses to melt slightly.
- Use the spatula to push omelette onto a plate. Add salt and pepper to season.

Nutrition Information

- Calories: 260 calories;
- Total Fat: 20.1
- Sodium: 348
- Total Carbohydrate: 6.4
- Cholesterol: 108
- Protein: 13.9

435. Busy Day Chicken Rice Casserole

Serving: 8 | Prep: 10mins | Cook: 2hours | Ready in:

Ingredients

- 1 (10.75 ounce) can condensed cream of mushroom soup
- 1 (10.75 ounce) can condensed cream of celery soup
- 1 cup water
- 1 cup uncooked white rice
- 1 (4.5 ounce) can mushrooms, drained
- 1 pinch garlic powder
- ground black pepper to taste
- 1 (1 ounce) package dry onion soup mix
- 8 skinless, boneless chicken breast halves

Direction

- Preheat an oven to 165°C/325°F.
- Mix black pepper, garlic powder, mushrooms, rice, water, celery soup and mushroom soup in a big bowl together. Put mixture into 9x13-in. baking dish; spread onto the bottom.
- Over soup mixture, lay chicken pieces. Sprinkle over all with dry onion soup mix. Use aluminum foil to tightly cover. In preheated oven, bake for 1-1 1/2 hours or till chicken isn't pink inside and is cooked through.

Nutrition Information

- Calories: 291 calories;
- Total Fat: 5.7
- Sodium: 988

- Total Carbohydrate: 27.7
- Cholesterol: 73
- Protein: 30.5

436. Cajun Crab Stuffed Mushrooms

Serving: 4 | Prep: 20mins | Cook: 10mins | Ready in:

Ingredients

- 1 (8 ounce) package cream cheese, softened
- 1/2 cup shredded Colby-Monterey Jack cheese
- 1 teaspoon seafood seasoning (such as Old Bay®)
- 1/2 teaspoon Cajun seasoning
- 1/4 teaspoon cayenne hot pepper sauce, or to taste (optional)
- 1/4 teaspoon garlic powder
- 1 (8 ounce) package imitation crabmeat, flaked
- 1/4 cup Italian seasoned bread crumbs
- 1 (8 ounce) package crimini mushrooms, stems removed

Direction

- Preheat an oven to 175°C (350°F). Oil a 9x5-inch baking dish.
- In a mixing bowl, mix garlic powder with hot pepper sauce, Cajun seasoning, seafood seasoning, Colby-Monterey Jack cheese and cream cheese until smooth. Toss in the bread crumbs and crabmeat until uniformly mixed. Pour the cheese blend into the mushroom caps; put them in the prepared baking dish, filling-side up.
- Bake for 7 minutes in the preheated oven; set the oven to broil then broil for about 3 minutes until the tops are crisp and brown.

Nutrition Information

- Calories: 364 calories;
- Total Carbohydrate: 17.9

- Cholesterol: 89
- Protein: 15.9
- Total Fat: 25.7
- Sodium: 1124

437. California Grilled Pizza

Serving: 6 | Prep: 15mins | Cook: 5mins | Ready in:

Ingredients

- 2 sheets (12x12 inches each) Reynolds Wrap® Aluminum Foil
- 2 (8 inch) pre-baked pizza crusts
- 2 tablespoons olive oil
- 1 teaspoon chopped garlic
- 1/2 medium red onion, sliced thin
- 1 sliced vine ripe tomato
- 1/4 cup marinated artichoke hearts, sliced thin
- 4 baby portabella mushrooms, sliced thin
- 2 tablespoons chopped fresh basil
- 1/2 cup shredded mozzarella cheese

Direction

- Start preheating the grill to medium-high. Put each pizza crust on a sheet of Reynolds Wrap(R) Aluminum Foil; put aside.
- In a small skillet, heat olive oil over medium heat. Put in onion and garlic. Cook until the onion is softened, stirring frequently.
- Brush olive oil mixture over the pizza crust. Place basil, mushrooms, artichoke hearts, tomatoes and onion on the crust. Top with cheese.
- Grill the pizza for 5-7 minutes on the foil sheets in the covered grill, until the cheese is melted.

Nutrition Information

- Calories: 224 calories;
- Total Carbohydrate: 27
- Cholesterol: 11

- Protein: 10
- Total Fat: 9.2
- Sodium: 361

438. California Melt

Serving: 4 | Prep: 15mins | Cook: 2mins | Ready in:

Ingredients

- 4 slices whole-grain bread, lightly toasted
- 1 avocado, sliced
- 1 cup sliced mushrooms
- 1/3 cup sliced toasted almonds
- 1 tomato, sliced
- 4 slices Swiss cheese

Direction

- Set the oven broiler to preheat.
- On a baking sheet, lay out the toasted bread, then put slices of tomato, almonds, mushrooms and 1/4 cup of avocado on top of each bread slice, then top each with Swiss cheese slice.
- Broil the open-face sandwiches for about 2 minutes, until starts to bubble and the cheese has melted. Serve the sandwiches while it's still warm.

Nutrition Information

- Calories: 335 calories;
- Total Carbohydrate: 21.1
- Cholesterol: 26
- Protein: 15.6
- Total Fat: 22.5
- Sodium: 170

439. Cally's Omelet

Serving: 2 | Prep: 10mins | Cook: 25mins | Ready in:

Ingredients

- 2 tablespoons butter
- 1/2 green bell pepper, chopped
- 1/2 red bell pepper, chopped
- 1/2 Bermuda onion, sliced
- 7 baby portobello mushrooms, sliced
- 1/2 pound beef tip
- 1/2 cup egg substitute

Direction

- Melt butter in a medium saucepan placed over medium heat. Stir in Portobello mushrooms, onion, red bell pepper and green bell pepper. Cook for about 5 minutes until softened.
- Stir beef into vegetable mixture and cook for 5 to 10 minutes until evenly brown.
- Stir egg beaters into the mixture and cook for 10 minutes or until solidified.

Nutrition Information

- Calories: 511 calories;
- Sodium: 284
- Total Carbohydrate: 26
- Cholesterol: 105
- Protein: 40.2
- Total Fat: 29.5

440. Cauliflower "Risotto" With Porcini Mushrooms And Peas

Serving: 4 | Prep: 20mins | Cook: 27mins | Ready in:

Ingredients

- 1 1/4 cups dried porcini mushrooms
- 3 cups low-sodium chicken broth, or more if needed
- 1 large head cauliflower, chopped
- 3 tablespoons unsalted butter
- 1 shallot, minced

- 2 teaspoons sea salt
- 1 teaspoon freshly ground black pepper
- 1 1/2 cups frozen petite peas, thawed
- 1 tablespoon balsamic vinegar
- 1 teaspoon chopped fresh thyme

Direction

- Add 2 cups of the boiling water to a large bowl. Put in the dried mushrooms; allow to stand for 20 minutes until rehydrated. Use a slotted spoon to take the mushrooms out, then pat them dry; chop the mushrooms into smaller pieces. Save the soaking liquid.
- Add the chicken broth to a saucepan over medium-low heat. Put on a cover and keep it warm.
- Put cauliflower into a food processor with a shredding disc and process into rice-sized grains.
- In a large pot, melt the butter over medium heat. Put in shallot; then cook for 2 minutes until soft. Put pepper, salt, and cauliflower rice. Cook and stir from time to time for 5 minutes until the flavors are blended.
- Mix a cup of the warm chicken broth into the pot; simmer for 5 minutes until absorbed. Pour in the remaining broth, 1 cup at a time, simmering for 10 minutes until the cauliflower rice becomes tender and the broth is absorbed.
- Stir thyme, balsamic vinegar, peas and the chopped mushrooms into the pot. Stir and cook for 5 minutes until peas and mushrooms are heated through.

Nutrition Information

- Calories: 263 calories;
- Total Fat: 10.3
- Sodium: 1043
- Total Carbohydrate: 29.5
- Cholesterol: 26
- Protein: 16.3

441. Champinones A La Sevillana (Seville Style Mushrooms)

Serving: 4 | Prep: 15mins | Cook: 3mins | Ready in:

Ingredients

- 2/3 cup olive oil
- 1 tablespoon crushed fresh garlic
- 1 pinch dried parsley
- 8 mushrooms, stemmed and sliced
- 2 slices Parma ham
- 1 loaf crusty bread, cut into chunks

Direction

- In a bowl, combine the garlic, parsley and olive oil together.
- Distribute the mushrooms evenly among 2 4-inch stovetop-safe round clay dishes. Pour the olive oil mixture on top of the mushrooms.
- Let the mushrooms cook for 3-5 minutes on medium-high heat while stirring the mixture from time to time using a small spoon until the oil is bubbling. Carefully remove the clay dishes from heat.
- Crumble the parma ham and spread it evenly on top of the mushrooms.
- Serve together with bread.

Nutrition Information

- Calories: 662 calories;
- Total Fat: 41.6
- Sodium: 1050
- Total Carbohydrate: 59.4
- Cholesterol: 13
- Protein: 13.8

442. Chanterelle Mushroom And Bacon Tartlets

Serving: 12 | Prep: 15mins | Cook: 25mins | Ready in:

Ingredients

- 2 teaspoons olive oil
- 2 tablespoons minced shallots
- 1 clove garlic, minced
- 1 1/2 cups chanterelle mushrooms, finely chopped
- 1 tablespoon brandy
- 1/2 teaspoon minced fresh thyme
- 1 tablespoon minced fresh parsley
- 1/4 teaspoon salt and pepper to taste
- 1 egg
- 1/4 cup milk
- 1/4 cup shredded Swiss cheese
- 2 tablespoons cream cheese, softened
- 2 slices bacon, cooked and crumbled
- 24 mini phyllo tart shells

Direction

- Preheat the oven to 325°F or 165°C.
- Place the large skillet over medium heat and heat the olive oil. Stir in shallots and cook until they start to brown. Mix in mushrooms and garlic and cook until tender. Use brandy to deglaze the pan. Season the mixture with parsley, salt, pepper, and thyme. Remove the mixture from the heat and set aside to cool.
- Mix cream cheese, bacon, egg, Swiss cheese, and milk in a large bowl. Fold in the mushroom mixture. Fill the phyllo cups with the mixture and arrange them on a baking sheet.
- Let it bake inside the preheated oven for 15-20 minutes until the filling is completely set.

Nutrition Information

- Calories: 109 calories;
- Sodium: 132
- Total Carbohydrate: 7
- Cholesterol: 25
- Protein: 4.3
- Total Fat: 6.2

443. Chanterelle Shazam

Serving: 4 | Prep: 15mins | Cook: 13mins | Ready in:

Ingredients

- 3 tablespoons olive oil
- 2 cloves crushed garlic
- 1 pound fresh wild chanterelle mushrooms, cleaned and quartered
- 1 teaspoon butter
- 1 pinch kosher salt and freshly ground black pepper to taste
- 1/2 cup port

Direction

- In a cast iron skillet, heat olive oil over medium heat till sizzling yet not smoking. Mix in the garlic. Put in butter and chanterelles. Turn heat down to medium-low and cook for 10 minutes, mixing often, till most of the excess liquid has vaporized. Put in pepper and salt to season.
- Raise heat to high and cautiously put port into the skillet, mix for 2 minutes till reduced. Serve steaming hot.

Nutrition Information

- Calories: 169 calories;
- Sodium: 134
- Total Carbohydrate: 7.5
- Cholesterol: 3
- Protein: 2.6
- Total Fat: 11.1

444. Chanterelle And Caramelized Onion Bruschetta

Serving: 8 | Prep: 10mins | Cook: 40mins | Ready in:

Ingredients

- 2 pounds onion, chopped

- 1 pound chanterelle mushrooms, halved and very thinly sliced
- 4 tablespoons olive oil, divided
- 1 teaspoon white sugar
- salt to taste
- 1 French baguette, sliced into 1/2-inch rounds
-

Direction

- Prepare the oven by preheating to 350°F (175°C).
- Place a skillet on the stove and turn on medium heat then put in 2 tablespoons of olive oil. Stir and cook onions for 25 minutes until they start to turn golden in color and soft. Sprinkle on sugar and keep on cooking for 10 to 15 minutes, whisking as needed, until dark brown in color and soft, but not at all crispy. Lower heat if onions are crisping.
- Place another skillet on the stove and turn on medium heat then put in the 2 tablespoons left olive oil. Cook the chanterelle mushrooms for 15 to 20 minutes until golden in color and soft.
- Put baguette rounds in one layer on a baking sheet.
- Place inside the preheated oven and bake for 3 to 5 minutes until toasted.
- On top of each piece of toast, pile a small amount of onions. Place a few mushrooms slices on top and serve hot.

Nutrition Information

- Calories: 293 calories;
- Total Fat: 7.9
- Protein: 9.2
- Sodium: 405
- Total Carbohydrate: 46.3
- Cholesterol: 0

445. Cheese Stuffed Mushroom Appetizer

Serving: 6 | Prep: 30mins | Cook: 15mins | Ready in:

Ingredients

- 6 tablespoons butter
- 2 pounds medium fresh mushrooms, stems removed
- 1 (8 ounce) package Neufchatel cheese
- 1 (4 ounce) package goat cheese crumbles
- 2 tablespoons finely chopped onion
- 1/2 cup mushroom stems, chopped
- 1/4 cup butter
- 1 tablespoon finely chopped garlic

Direction

- Start heating two large skillets on medium-high heat; in each skillet, let 3 tablespoons of butter melt and evenly fill each with the mushroom caps. Stir and cook the mushroom caps for around 5 minutes until the edges slightly become soft. To drain and cool the mushrooms, arrange them in a colander.
- Combine goat cheese and cream cheese together until mixed thoroughly. Stir in mushroom stems and the onions. Fill each mushroom cap generously with all the fillings and arrange in a baking pan with filling side up.
- Set the oven broiler and start preheating on high heat.
- In a small saucepan, let the remaining 1/4 cup of butter melt with the garlic on medium heat; when the butter has melted properly, cook the garlic for a minute. Use the garlic butter to lightly sprinkle on the filled mushroom caps.
- Put the pan of mushrooms in the prepared oven to broil for around 5 minutes until they turn golden brown.

Nutrition Information

- Calories: 373 calories;
- Total Fat: 34.1

- Sodium: 391
- Total Carbohydrate: 7.5
- Cholesterol: 94
- Protein: 13

446. Cheesy Chicken Bundles

Serving: 4 | Prep: 30mins | Cook: 40mins | Ready in:

Ingredients

- 4 skinless, boneless chicken breast halves
- 1 teaspoon butter
- 1 (4.5 ounce) can sliced mushrooms, drained
- 1 egg
- 1/2 cup cheese-flavored crackers (such as Cheez-It Duoz Sharp Cheddar and Parmesan®), crushed
- 1 (8 ounce) package cream cheese
- 1 1/4 cups shredded Cheddar cheese, divided
- 6 tablespoons grated Parmesan cheese

Direction

- Set an oven to 190°C (375°F) and start preheating. Coat a 9x12-inch baking dish with cooking spray.
- Arrange between 2 sheets of heavy plastic (or resealable freezer bags) with a chicken breast on a solid and level surface. Use the smooth side of a meat mallet to pound the chicken breast firmly to 1/4-inch thick. Repeat using the other chicken breasts.
- In a small skillet, melt butter and cook the mushrooms for 8 minutes until they start browning. Put aside. In a shallow bowl, whisk the egg. In a different bowl, arrange cracker crumbs.
- Combine parmesan cheese, a cup of Cheddar cheese, cream cheese, and mushrooms in a bowl; spread on the chicken generously with the mixture. Roll up the chicken breasts and dip each in the whisked egg, then roll the bundles into cracker crumbs. Arrange in the greased baking dish. Scatter the rest of 1/4 cup of Cheddar cheese over the bundles.
- In the prepared oven, bake for half an hour, until the crumbs turn golden brown, the filling melts, and the chicken is cooked thoroughly. An instant-read thermometer needs to register a minimum of 74°C (165°F) when inserted in the center of a roll.

Nutrition Information

- Calories: 680 calories;
- Protein: 44.3
- Total Fat: 46.4
- Sodium: 973
- Total Carbohydrate: 20.5
- Cholesterol: 222

447. Cheesy Chicken Tetrazzini

Serving: 6 | Prep: 30mins | Cook: 55mins | Ready in:

Ingredients

- 2 tablespoons butter
- 1 1/2 pounds boneless, skinless chicken breasts, cut in 1-inch strips
- 1 1/2 cups sliced fresh mushrooms
- 1 small red bell pepper, cut into strips
- 1/2 cup sliced green onions
- 1/4 cup all-purpose flour
- 1 3/4 cups chicken broth
- 1 cup light cream
- 2 tablespoons dry sherry
- 1/2 teaspoon salt
- 1/4 teaspoon pepper
- 1/4 teaspoon dried thyme, crushed
- 1 (8 ounce) package rotelle pasta
- 1/4 cup grated Parmesan cheese
- 2 tablespoons chopped fresh parsley
- 1 cup shredded Jarlsberg cheese

Direction

- Set oven to 165°C (325°F) and begin preheating.
- In a big skillet, bring butter to medium heat. Stir in chicken pieces and brown them. Mix in mushrooms until browned. Put in green onion and red pepper; cook, stirring often, for a few minutes. Blend in flour; cook and stir for a few minutes until incorporated. Slowly mix in sherry, cream and chicken broth, then cook and stir until mixture is thick and smoothened. Add thyme, pepper and salt into the mixture to season.
- In the meantime, boil lightly salted water in a large pot. Put in pasta and cook for about 8 minutes until just softened; let drain.
- Combine parsley, Parmesan cheese and pasta with chicken mixture. Transfer to a 1 1/2-qt. baking dish.
- Bake for 35 minutes in prepared oven. Remove from the heat, set atop Jarlsberg cheese, and put back into the oven; bake until cheese melts.

Nutrition Information

- Calories: 490 calories;
- Cholesterol: 122
- Protein: 40.1
- Total Fat: 20
- Sodium: 432
- Total Carbohydrate: 36.8

448. Cheesy Grits Mexicano

Serving: 3 | Prep: 15mins | Cook: 30mins | Ready in:

Ingredients

- Sauce:
- 1 tablespoon olive oil
- 1 onion, chopped
- 1 large portobello mushroom cap, cut into bite-size pieces
- 1 (7.75 ounce) can enchilada sauce (such as El Pato Salsa de Chile Fresco ®)
- 1 cup water
- Grits:
- 3 cups water
- 1 cup coarse yellow cornmeal
- 1/4 cup milk
- 1/2 cup shredded sharp Cheddar cheese
- 1 teaspoon bacon salt
- 1 dash black pepper

Direction

- In a saucepan, heat olive oil on medium heat and stir in onions, then cook for 5 minutes until translucent and tender. Decrease heat to medium-low and cover, then continue to cook, occasionally stirring, for 15-20 minutes until the onions turn to dark brown. Once the onions have caramelized, stir in 1 cup water, enchilada sauce, and Portobello mushroom. Simmer and cook for 5 minutes, then keep warm on low heat.
- At the same time, boil 3 cups water in a big saucepan on high heat, and whisk in cornmeal, then bring down the heat to low. Simmer, whisking frequently, until the grits thicken for 10 minutes. Once thick, whisk in the milk and continue to cook until the grits become soft. Take off the heat once cooked, then whisk in bacon salt and Cheddar cheese. Season with salt and black pepper along with more bacon salt to taste. To serve, top the grits with the prepared sauce.

Nutrition Information

- Calories: 363 calories;
- Total Fat: 13.5
- Sodium: 510
- Total Carbohydrate: 49.8
- Cholesterol: 21
- Protein: 10.6

449. Cheesy Hash Brown Cups

Serving: 12 | Prep: 25mins | Cook: 15mins | Ready in:

Ingredients

- 3 cups Simply Potatoes® Shredded Hash Browns
- 1/4 cup butter or margarine
- 1/4 teaspoon salt
- 1/2 pound ground Italian sausage
- 1/2 cup finely chopped mushrooms
- 1/2 cup finely chopped red bell pepper
- 2 cups AllWhites® egg whites
- 1/2 teaspoon dried Italian seasoning
- 1/2 cup Crystal Farms® Finely Shredded Cheddar Cheese

Direction

- Heat an oven to 400°F then grease a 12-cup regular muffin cup pan; put aside. Mix salt, melted butter and hash browns well in a medium bowl. Press 1/4 cup of hash brown mixture in each muffin cup, lining sides and bottom. Bake till edges are golden brown for 12-15 minutes.
- Meanwhile in a 10-inch skillet, brown Italian sausage; drain fat. Add red bell pepper and mushrooms; cook, occasionally mixing, till vegetables are tender. Use sausage mixture to equally fill every baked hash brown cup.
- Mix Italian seasoning and AllWhites well in small bowl. Put AllWhites on sausage mixture filling in every muffin cup evenly. Sprinkle cheese; bake till a toothpick inserted in the middle of cup exits cleanly for 12-14 minutes.

Nutrition Information

- Calories: 155 calories;
- Total Fat: 8.9
- Sodium: 357
- Total Carbohydrate: 9.9
- Cholesterol: 23
- Protein: 8.2

450. Cheesy Mashed Potato Stuffed Mushrooms

Serving: 12 | Prep: | Cook: | Ready in:

Ingredients

- 1 (14.1 ounce) package Idahoan® Buttery Golden Selects Mashed Potatoes
- 1 1/2 cups shredded white Cheddar cheese
- 1/2 cup chives, chopped
- 1 cup chopped, cooked bacon or prepared bacon bits
- 6 tablespoons olive oil
- 4 tablespoons minced garlic
- 24 large mushrooms, or more depending on size

Direction

- Preheat oven to 350 °F.
- Prepare mashed potatoes following the instruction of the package.
- Add bacon, chives, and shredded cheese (reserve enough to top mushrooms).
- Eliminate stems from clean mushrooms and stuff potato mixture into caps.
- On the bottom of baking dish or walled cookie sheet, spread minced garlic and olive oil. Place mushrooms on top.
- Sprinkle top of mushrooms with shredded cheddar.
- Bake for around 20-25 minutes.

451. Cheesy Spinach Chicken Rolls

Serving: 6 | Prep: 30mins | Cook: 25mins | Ready in:

Ingredients

- 3 skinless, boneless chicken breasts, halved lengthwise
- salt and ground black pepper to taste
- 1/4 cup olive oil, divided
- 6 mushrooms, chopped
- 2 cloves garlic, minced
- 1 (8 ounce) package cream cheese
- 1/2 (10 ounce) package frozen chopped spinach, thawed
- 2 tablespoons chopped green onions
- 1/2 teaspoon red pepper flakes
- 12 toothpicks

Direction

- On a hard, smooth surface, put chicken breasts between 2 heavy plastic sheets; using the smooth side of a meat mallet, firmly pound on the chicken breasts until the thickness is 1/4-inch. Use pepper and salt to season.
- In a frying pan, heat 1 tablespoon olive oil over medium heat. Add garlic and mushrooms; stir and cook for 5 minutes, or until tender.
- Turn the oven to 400°F (200°C) to preheat.
- In a bowl, mix together red pepper flakes, green onions, spinach, cream cheese, and the garlic-mushroom mixture.
- In the center of each chicken breast, scoop 1 tablespoon of the cream cheese mixture. Roll up the chicken breasts around the filling mixture and hold with toothpicks.
- In an ovenproof frying pan, heat the leftover 3 tablespoons over medium heat. In the frying pan, arrange one layer of the chicken rolls; cook for 5 minutes per side until turning golden.
- Remove the frying pan to the preheated oven; bake for 10-15 minutes longer until the middle of the chicken is not pink anymore.

Nutrition Information

- Calories: 289 calories;
- Sodium: 185
- Total Carbohydrate: 3.2
- Cholesterol: 75
- Protein: 16.6
- Total Fat: 23.7

452. Chef John's Bigos (Polish Hunter's Stew)

Serving: 6 | Prep: 30mins | Cook: 2hours30mins | Ready in:

Ingredients

- 1/4 cup dried porcini mushrooms
- 1/2 cup warm water
- 2 tablespoons unsalted butter
- 2 cups packed, drained sauerkraut (not rinsed)
- 1 small head green cabbage, quartered and sliced
- 4 strips bacon, cut into 1-inch pieces
- 1 pound pork shoulder, cut into 1 1/2-inch pieces
- 1 pound boneless beef chuck, cut into 1-inch pieces
- 1 pound Polish sausage links, sliced (or any other sausage)
- 1 large onion, peeled and chopped
- 3 pitted prunes, diced
- 1 cup dry red wine
- 1 teaspoon paprika
- 1/2 teaspoon caraway seeds
- 1 teaspoon dried thyme leaves
- 1/4 teaspoon allspice
- 1 large bay leaf
- freshly ground black pepper
- salt to taste

Direction

- In warm water, put the mushrooms and let it soak for 10-15 minutes to soften. Drain it then chop.
- In a Dutch oven or a heavy pot, heat the butter. Add in the chopped cabbage and sauerkraut, then cook on medium low while stirring often. Cook the meat until brown, then

- stir it into the pot while sauerkraut is cooking per directions below.
- On medium-high heat, heat the pan. Put the bacon and cook until it turns brown but not crisp. Move the bacon into the pot with the cabbage; reserve the bacon grease in the pan.
- In bacon grease, cook the pork shoulders pieces until brown on medium-high heat. Sprinkle salt on top, then cook and stir for 4-5 minutes until all sides turn brown. Move the pork into the pot. Put the beef chunks in the pan and sprinkle it with salt. Let it cook and stir for about 4-5 minutes until it turns brown. Put sausage slices into the pan and cook and stir until it turns brown. Move the slices into the pot.
- Under the pan, minimize the heat to medium. Put chopped onion then a sprinkle salt on top. Let it cook and stir until the onion begins to take on some color and turns translucent. Mix in diced prunes and chopped mushrooms. Let it cook and stir for about 2 minutes. Put dry red wine then increase the heat to medium-high. Simmer until the wine is reduced and a very small amount of liquid remains. Move the onion mixture into the pot with the meat and cabbage. Add salt, pepper, bay leaf, allspice, thyme, caraway seeds and paprika. Mix until all ingredients are distributed evenly.
- Tightly cover. Simmer for 1-1 1/2 hours on medium-low heat, stirring once in a while, until the meat becomes tender. Separate from heat, then let the stew cool a bit. Let it chill in the fridge overnight to allow the flavors to combine.
- On low to medium-low heat, place the pot then pour a splash of water. Let the stew cook on low simmer for 10-15 minutes, stirring often, until hot.

Nutrition Information

- Calories: 640 calories;
- Total Fat: 44.9
- Sodium: 1174
- Total Carbohydrate: 19
- Cholesterol: 135
- Protein: 32.2

454. Chef John's Chicken Cacciatore

Serving: 6 | Prep: 20mins | Cook: 1hours30mins | Ready in:

Ingredients

- 2 tablespoons olive oil
- 1 whole roasting chicken, cut in quarters
- 1 large onion, sliced
- 8 ounces fresh mushrooms, quartered
- 1 pinch salt
- 1 pinch ground black pepper
- 4 cloves garlic, sliced
- 3 sprigs rosemary
- 1 teaspoon dried oregano
- 1/2 teaspoon red pepper flakes, or to taste
- 1 cup tomato sauce
- 1/2 cup water
- salt and ground black pepper to taste
- 2 red bell peppers, sliced
- 2 green bell peppers, sliced

Direction

- Preheat an oven to 175 °C or 350 °F.
- In a big Dutch oven over medium-high heat, heat the olive oil; put chicken and allow to cook till outside are browned. Take off to a bowl to get the juices.
- Mix in mushrooms and onions; let cook till soft for 5 to 6 minutes. Put a huge pinch of pepper and salt. Mix in water, tomato sauce, oregano, red pepper flakes, rosemary and garlic.
- In the bowl, put any accumulated juices and chicken portions over cooked vegetables. Put additional pepper and salt. Set slices of pepper over the chicken.

- Put cover and in the prepped oven, allow to cook for 1 hour and 15 minutes.

Nutrition Information

- Calories: 513 calories;
- Sodium: 401
- Total Carbohydrate: 11.1
- Cholesterol: 149
- Protein: 50.2
- Total Fat: 29.1

454. Chef John's Chicken Marsala

Serving: 2 | Prep: 20mins | Cook: 40mins | Ready in:

Ingredients

- 2 skin-on, boneless chicken breast halves
- 1 teaspoon salt and ground black pepper to taste
- 3 tablespoons butter, divided
- 2 tablespoons olive oil
- 5 white mushrooms, sliced
- 1 shallot, minced
- 1 tablespoon all-purpose flour
- 1 cup Marsala wine
- 2 cups chicken stock
- 2 tablespoons chopped fresh parsley
- 1 teaspoon cold butter

Direction

- Sprinkle pepper and salt all over the chicken breast to season.
- On medium heat, pour olive oil and melt 1/12 tbsp. of butter in a pan. Place the chicken breasts with the skin-side down in the pan and cook for 5 minutes in the hot butter until brown. Turn and cook for another 5 minutes until the chicken breasts are nearly cooked through. Move the chicken to a plate.
- On medium-high heat, melt 1 1/2 tbsp. butter in the same pan. Add mushrooms, season with a pinch each of pepper and salt and sear for 5-7 minutes in the hot butter until golden brown. Put in minced shallot and cook while stirring for 2-3 minutes until soft. Dust flour on top, cook and stir for another 3-4 minutes until the flour's bitter taste cooks off.
- Pour wine into the pan and boil. Cook and stir for 3-4 minutes until the wine reduces and the mixture thickens. Pour in the chicken stock and let it simmer. Cook for another 3-5 minutes until it reduces a bit.
- Place the chicken back in the pan. Turn heat to low and cook for 10 minutes until the chicken is not pink in the center and the juice is clear, flip once. An inserted instant-read thermometer in the center of the chicken should register at least 74°C or 165°F. Take off heat.
- Place chicken in one corner of the pan. Turn the pan to the side until the sauce gathers at the bottom. Add 1 teaspoon of cold butter and parsley, keep stirring until the butter melts completely and the mixture is glossy. Move chicken to plates and serve with sauce and mushrooms on top.

Nutrition Information

- Calories: 799 calories;
- Total Fat: 39
- Sodium: 2391
- Total Carbohydrate: 26.8
- Cholesterol: 185
- Protein: 51.1

455. Chef John's Chicken Riggies

Serving: 4 | Prep: 20mins | Cook: 1hours15mins | Ready in:

Ingredients

- 1 tablespoon olive oil
- 4 ounces hot Italian ground sausage meat
- 1 cup sliced mushrooms
- 1 onion, sliced
- salt and ground black pepper to taste
- 1 1/2 pounds skinless, boneless chicken thighs, roughly chopped
- 1/2 cup Marsala wine
- 1 (28 ounce) can whole Italian plum tomatoes (such as San Marzano), crushed
- 1 cup chicken broth
- 1/2 cup heavy whipping cream
- 1/2 cup water, or as needed
- 1 1/2 cups chopped hot and sweet peppers
- 1/2 cup pitted and chopped kalamata olives
- 3 cloves garlic, minced
- 1/4 cup chopped Italian flat leaf parsley
- 1 pound rigatoni
- 1/2 cup grated Parmigiano-Reggiano or Romano cheese

Direction

- In a big saucepan, heat olive oil on medium heat. Let mushrooms, salt, onions, black pepper and sausage cook in the oil for 6-7 minutes until vegetables are soft and sausage becomes brown.
- Mix in and cook sliced chicken with the sausage mixture on medium-high heat for five minutes until it becomes brown. Place in wine and let it cook for 2-3 minutes while stirring so that the bottom of the pan does not have brown bits and until majority of the wine vaporized. Simmer chicken broth, cream and tomatoes for half an hour. Create a thick sauce by adding water if necessary.
- Mix in olives, garlics and peppers. Allow to simmer for 15-20 minutes until it becomes thick. Spice with pepper and salt and the mix in parsley.
- Boil a big pot of lightly salted water. In the boiling water, cook rigatoni for around 11 minutes with constant stirring until it is al dente. Drain.
- Mix in cooked pasta and sauce then mix in cheese. Place a cover on then put aside. Wait for 1-2 minutes until pasta absorbs the sauce.

Nutrition Information

- Calories: 1051 calories;
- Sodium: 1002
- Total Carbohydrate: 110.2
- Cholesterol: 167
- Protein: 56.4
- Total Fat: 41

456. Chef John's Chicken A La King

Serving: 4 | Prep: 15mins | Cook: 30mins | Ready in:

Ingredients

- 6 tablespoons unsalted butter
- 1/2 pound sliced mushrooms
- 2 large shallots, minced
- 1 cup diced sweet bell peppers
- Salt and freshly ground black pepper to taste
- 1/3 cup all-purpose flour
- 1/4 cup dry sherry
- 3 1/2 cups chicken stock or broth
- 1 pinch freshly grated nutmeg
- 1 pinch cayenne pepper
- 2 teaspoons fresh thyme
- 1 tablespoon chopped fresh Italian parsley
- 1/3 cup creme fraiche or heavy cream
- 4 cups cubed roasted chicken
- Chopped fresh chives for garnish

Direction

- Melt butter in big skillet on medium high heat. Add salt and mushrooms; sauté till mushrooms release moisture. Cook for 8-10 minutes till mushrooms start to brown and moisture evaporates. Add shallots; mix and cook for 3-4 minutes till shallots just soften.

- Lower heat to medium. Mix flour in to coat mushrooms; cook for 5 minutes to make roux till flour starts to be golden. Add peppers; mix and cook for 1 minute. Add sherry wine; sizzle for 30 seconds. Mix stock in; put heat on medium high. Simmer; lower heat to medium low when it begins to bubble. Cook for 10-15 minutes till slightly thicken, occasionally mixing. Add cayenne pepper and nutmeg.
- Mix chicken, cream, parsley and thyme in; lower heat to low. Cook for 5 minutes till chicken heats through. Check seasonings, as needed, adjust. Put some chopped fresh chives on top of each serving.

Nutrition Information

- Calories: 583 calories;
- Cholesterol: 179
- Protein: 43.7
- Total Fat: 36.2
- Sodium: 833
- Total Carbohydrate: 20.8

457. Chef John's Classic Beef Stroganoff

Serving: 8 | Prep: 15mins | Cook: 1hours30mins | Ready in:

Ingredients

- 1 tablespoon vegetable oil
- 2 pounds beef chuck roast, cut into 1/2-inch thick strips
- salt and pepper to taste
- 1 tablespoon butter
- 1/2 medium onion, sliced or diced
- 8 ounces sliced mushrooms
- 2 cloves garlic, minced
- 1 1/2 tablespoons all-purpose flour
- 1/2 cup white wine
- 2 cups beef broth, divided
- 3/4 cup creme fraiche
- 1 tablespoon fresh chopped chives
- salt and pepper to taste

Direction

- Season beef with salt and pepper generously.
- In a large frying pan, heat oil on high heat until almost smoking. Add in beef, then cook and stir once in a while for 6-7 minutes, until the meat browns and the liquid evaporates. Remove from pan and set aside.
- In the pan, stir in butter, onions and mushrooms. Cook and stir on medium heat until the vegetables turn light brown. Add garlic and stir for half a minute. Mix in flour and cook for 1-2 minutes until combined.
- Pour 1 cup of stock and wine, scraping the pan's bottom to release any browned bits. Simmer and cook for 3-4 minutes until the sauce becomes thick.
- Put the beef back into the pan. Mix in leftover cup of stock and make it simmer. Cook on low heat for about 1 hour, covered, until the sauce is thick, and the beef is tender. Mix every 20 minutes.
- Add in chives and crème fraiche; stir. Season with salt and pepper to taste.

Nutrition Information

- Calories: 307 calories;
- Sodium: 288
- Total Carbohydrate: 4.1
- Cholesterol: 86
- Protein: 15.8
- Total Fat: 24.5

458. Chef John's Mushroom Gravy

Serving: 6 | Prep: 10mins | Cook: 50mins | Ready in:

Ingredients

- 1/4 cup butter
- 1 (16 ounce) package sliced mushrooms
- salt to taste
- 1/4 cup all-purpose flour, or as needed
- 1 quart beef stock
- 1 pinch ground black pepper to taste
- fresh thyme leaves, to taste (optional)

Direction

- In a saucepan, heat butter over medium heat till it foams. Mix in mushrooms. Add salt to taste. Allow to simmer for 20 minutes till liquid evaporates.
- Mix in the flour, cooking and mixing for approximately 5 minutes. Put in approximately 1 cup of beef stock, mixing briskly till blended, then add in the leftover stock and mix well. Spice with thyme and black pepper. Lower heat to medium-low, and allow to simmer for half an hour till thickened, mixing frequently.

Nutrition Information

- Calories: 133 calories;
- Sodium: 63
- Total Carbohydrate: 8.9
- Cholesterol: 20
- Protein: 5.7
- Total Fat: 8.7

459. Chef John's Truffled Potato Gratin

Serving: 6 | Prep: 15mins | Cook: 1hours | Ready in:

Ingredients

- 1 1/3 tablespoons butter
- 1 tablespoon olive oil
- 5 cups sliced mushrooms
- 2 teaspoons butter, softened
- 1 clove garlic, minced (optional)
- 5 russet potatoes, peeled and very thinly sliced
- salt and freshly ground black pepper to taste
- 1 teaspoon minced fresh thyme, divided
- 6 ounces sottocenere (Italian semi-soft truffle cheese), shredded
- 1 cup chicken stock
- 2 cups heavy whipping cream

Direction

- In a big saucepan over medium-high heat, melt 1 1/3 tablespoons butter together with olive oil; cook mushrooms in hot butter-oil mixture for 15 to 20 minutes, mixing frequently, till edges are browned.
- Preheat the oven to 175 °C or 350 °F. In a small bowl, mix together garlic and 2 teaspoons softened butter; grease a baking dish of 9x13-inches square with garlic butter.
- In the bottom of the prepped baking dish, scatter 1/3 of potatoes in 1 layer; put in black pepper and salt to season, half of thyme leaves and half of cooked mushrooms. Scatter nearly 1/2 of sottocenere cheese on top of potatoes, setting aside approximately 3 tablespoons for top. Layer the following 1/3 of potatoes on top of cheese, put in salt and black pepper to season, leftover half of thyme leaves, half of the leftover cheese, leftover mushrooms, and final layer of potatoes. Put in additional black pepper and salt on potatoes to season. Spread chicken stock and cream over the top. Scatter additional black pepper and salt and reserved 3 tablespoons sottocenere cheese. Loosely cover the dish using aluminum foil; tent foil a bit to keep it from touching the potatoes.
- In the prepped oven, bake for 45 minutes till potatoes are bubbly. Take off foil and cook for 15 minutes longer till top turns brown. Allow to cool slightly prior to serving.

Nutrition Information

- Calories: 641 calories;
- Total Carbohydrate: 47.6
- Cholesterol: 152
- Protein: 15.9

- Total Fat: 44.8
- Sodium: 414

460. Chicago Style Pan Pizza

Serving: 6 | Prep: 30mins | Cook: 35mins | Ready in:

Ingredients

- 1 (1 pound) loaf frozen bread dough, thawed
- 1 pound bulk Italian sausage
- 2 cups shredded mozzarella cheese
- 8 ounces sliced fresh mushrooms
- 1 small onion, chopped
- 2 teaspoons olive oil
- 1 (28 ounce) can diced tomatoes, drained
- 3/4 teaspoon dried oregano
- 1/2 teaspoon salt
- 1/4 teaspoon fennel seed
- 1/4 teaspoon garlic powder
- 1/2 cup freshly grated Parmesan cheese

Direction

- Heat the oven to 350°F (175°C). Press the dough into up the sides and bottom of a 9x13-inch greased baking dish. Place sausage in a large skillet over medium-high heat and crumble. Stir and cook until brown evenly. Use a slotted spoon to take the sausage, and scatter over the dough crust. Scatter mozzarella cheese evenly over the sausage.
- Add onion and mushrooms to the skillet; stir and cook until the onion soften. Mix in the garlic powder, fennel seeds, salt, oregano, and tomatoes. Scoop over the mozzarella cheese. Scatter Parmesan cheese on top.
- Place in the preheated oven and bake for 25-35 minutes or until the crust turn golden brown.

Nutrition Information

- Calories: 578 calories;
- Total Fat: 27.4

- Sodium: 1816
- Total Carbohydrate: 46.8
- Cholesterol: 61
- Protein: 32.3

461. Chicken And Artichoke Penne With A White Sauce

Serving: 4 | Prep: | Cook: | Ready in:

Ingredients

- 2 skinless, boneless chicken breast halves - cut into 1 inch cubes
- 1 (8 ounce) can artichoke hearts in water, drained
- 8 fresh mushrooms, sliced
- 3/4 (6 ounce) can black olives, drained and chopped
- 1 pinch paprika
- 1 tablespoon olive oil
- 10 ounces penne pasta
- 2 cups homemade bechamel sauce

Direction

- In a large pot, cook pasta with boiling water. Drain.
- In a pan, heat olive oil over medium heat. Sauté chicken pieces till light-to-golden brown.
- In a pan, put in mushrooms, olives and artichoke hearts; heat in about 1-1/2 seconds. Reduce the heat to low, put in cooked pasta, then heat until warm.
- Pour in the pan with warm bechamel sauce, then toss the ingredients 3 - 4 times. Use fresh Parmesan cheese and freshly grated black pepper to taste, serve. If desired, sprinkle a dash of paprika on top for color.

Nutrition Information

- Calories: 598 calories;
- Total Fat: 22.7

- Sodium: 847
- Total Carbohydrate: 70.5
- Cholesterol: 49
- Protein: 30.6

462. Chicken Breasts Stuffed With Perfection

Serving: 6 | Prep: 1hours | Cook: 45mins | Ready in:

Ingredients

- 6 skinless, boneless chicken breast halves - pounded thin
- 1 (8 ounce) bottle Italian-style salad dressing
- 8 slices of stale wheat bread, torn
- 3/4 cup grated Parmesan cheese
- 1 teaspoon chopped fresh thyme
- 1/8 teaspoon pepper
- 1 1/2 cups feta cheese, crumbled
- 1/2 cup sour cream
- 1 tablespoon vegetable oil
- 3 cloves garlic, minced
- 4 cups chopped fresh spinach
- 1 bunch green onions, chopped
- 1 cup mushrooms, sliced
- 1 (8 ounce) jar oil-packed sun-dried tomatoes, chopped

Direction

- Position chicken breasts into a big resealable plastic bag. Pour in Italian dressing, tightly seal, and let refrigerate for at least 1 hour.
- In a food processor, place the pepper, thyme, Parmesan, and stale bread. Pulse till the bread is processed into crumbs. Leave aside.
- In a big bowl, stir the sour cream and feta together. Leave aside.
- In a large skillet, heat the oil over medium heat. Whisk in the garlic. Then add in the spinach, and cook till it wilts. Mix in green onions, cook for 2 minutes. Transfer spinach into a plate, and reserve leftover liquid in the pan. Mix in mushrooms, then sauté until soft. Transfer mushrooms into a plate along with spinach. Let it cool briefly, then blend mushrooms and spinach with sour cream mixture and feta.
- Whisk into the mixture the sun-dried tomatoes, then pour onto a big cookie sheet. Set in the freezer for around 30 minutes.
- Preheat the oven to 400 °F (200 °C).
- On a cookie sheet, position the chicken breasts then set the middle of each breast with about 3 tablespoons of the filling mixture. Roll the breasts, and use a toothpick to secure. Transfer chicken breasts into a baking dish, then sprinkle the chicken breasts with breadcrumb mixture.
- In a preheated oven, bake while uncovered for 25 minutes.

Nutrition Information

- Calories: 622 calories;
- Total Carbohydrate: 34.7
- Cholesterol: 119
- Protein: 43.4
- Total Fat: 35.2
- Sodium: 1517

463. Chicken Breasts Supreme

Serving: 6 | Prep: 25mins | Cook: 1hours35mins | Ready in:

Ingredients

- 6 skinless, boneless chicken breast halves
- salt and pepper to taste
- 1 pinch paprika, or to taste
- 3 tablespoons butter
- 1 (10.75 ounce) can condensed cream of mushroom soup
- 1/3 cup milk
- 2 tablespoons minced onion
- 1/2 cup processed cheese (such as Velveeta®), diced

- 2 tablespoons Worcestershire sauce
- 1 (4.5 ounce) can sliced mushrooms, drained and chopped
- 2/3 cup sour cream

Direction

- Start preheating the oven to 350°F (175°C). Oil a 2-qt. casserole dish.
- Sprinkle paprika, pepper, and salt over chicken breasts. In a big frying pan, heat butter and brown the chicken breasts for 5 minutes each side until both sides have thoroughly browned. In the bottom of the prepared casserole dish, put the chicken breasts.
- In a saucepan, combine mushrooms, Worcestershire sauce, processed cheese, onion, milk, and mushroom soup over medium-low heat. Let the mixture heat to melt the cheese without boiling. Whisk to blend well, stir in sour cream until smooth. Add the sauce to the dish of the chicken breasts and put on foil to cover.
- Bake for 45 minutes in the preheated oven until the juices run clear and the chicken is soft. Remove the cover, use the sauce to baste, and bake for another 30 minutes, basting sometimes.

Nutrition Information

- Calories: 335 calories;
- Total Fat: 20.6
- Sodium: 769
- Total Carbohydrate: 8.9
- Cholesterol: 100
- Protein: 28.2

464. Chicken Casserole Del Sol

Serving: 6 | Prep: 30mins | Cook: 30mins | Ready in:

Ingredients

- 1 (16 ounce) package uncooked rigatoni pasta
- 2 skinless, boneless chicken breast halves
- 2 (10.75 ounce) cans condensed cream of chicken soup
- 1 cup mayonnaise
- 2 teaspoons lemon juice
- 1/2 teaspoon curry powder
- 1 (14.5 ounce) can French-style green beans, drained
- 1 (4 ounce) can sliced mushrooms, drained
- 1 cup shredded Cheddar cheese
- 1/4 cup melted butter
- 1 cup crushed cornflakes cereal
- 2 teaspoons chopped fresh parsley

Direction

- Set oven to 375°F (190°C) to preheat.
- Cook rigatoni until al dente as directed on the package. In the meantime, boil chicken breasts in another saucepan until cooked through.
- Combine mushrooms, green beans, curry powder, lemon juice, mayonnaise, and soup in a large mixing bowl. Drain rigatoni; mix into soup mixture in the bowl. Cut cooked chicken breasts into cubes; mix into pasta mixture. Pour mixture into a large casserole dish.
- Scatter cheese over top of the casserole. Combine corn flakes and butter in a medium mixing bowl; distribute all over the cheese layer. Sprinkle parsley over top.
- Bake for 20 to 30 minutes in the preheated oven until cheese is bubbly.

Nutrition Information

- Calories: 840 calories;
- Total Carbohydrate: 70.3
- Cholesterol: 82
- Protein: 26.5
- Total Fat: 51.5
- Sodium: 1392

465. Chicken Diane Style

Serving: 6 | Prep: | Cook: |Ready in:

Ingredients

- 2 small onions, chopped
- 1 pound fresh mushrooms
- 8 skinless, boneless chicken breast halves
- 1/2 teaspoon salt
- 1/2 teaspoon ground black pepper
- 1/2 teaspoon paprika
- 2 teaspoons chopped fresh chives
- 2 teaspoons dried parsley
- 1/2 cup chicken broth
- 1/4 cup brandy
- 2 tablespoons prepared Dijon-style mustard

Direction

- In a big frying pan, sauté mushrooms and onions over medium heat. Take the mushroom/onions mixture out of the frying pan and put aside. In the frying pan, put chicken breasts. Sauté for 4 minutes, and then flip and top with the mushroom mixture.
- Combine parsley, chives, paprika, pepper, and salt in a small bowl, and then sprinkle over the chicken with this mixture. Mix mustard, brandy, and broth together in a medium-sized bowl and combine. Add to the chicken, lower the heat low and simmer until the chicken has fully cooked (the inside is not pink anymore), about 20-25 minutes.

Nutrition Information

- Calories: 235 calories;
- Sodium: 425
- Total Carbohydrate: 6.5
- Cholesterol: 91
- Protein: 38.1
- Total Fat: 2.3

466. Chicken Divan

Serving: 6 | Prep: 25mins | Cook: 30mins |Ready in:

Ingredients

- 2 1/2 cups cooked chopped broccoli
- 2 cups shredded, cooked chicken meat
- 2 (4.5 ounce) cans mushrooms, drained
- 1 (8 ounce) can water chestnuts, drained (optional)
- 2 (10.75 ounce) cans condensed cream of chicken soup
- 1 cup mayonnaise
- 1 teaspoon lemon juice
- 1/4 teaspoon curry powder
- 1 tablespoon melted butter
- 1/2 cup shredded Cheddar cheese

Direction

- Set the oven to 350°F (175°C) for preheating. Grease the 3-qt casserole dish.
- Place the cooked broccoli into the prepared baking dish. Arrange the chicken over the broccoli. Add the water chestnuts and mushrooms.
- Mix the lemon juice, melted butter, curry powder, soup, and mayonnaise in a medium-sized bowl. Drizzle sauce mixture over the vegetables and chicken. Sprinkle the top with cheese. Bake it inside the preheated oven for 30-45 minutes until the cheese is golden brown and the casserole is bubbling.

Nutrition Information

- Calories: 524 calories;
- Total Fat: 42.2
- Sodium: 1164
- Total Carbohydrate: 18
- Cholesterol: 72
- Protein: 20

467. Chicken Hekka

Serving: 8 | Prep: 30mins | Cook: 15mins | Ready in:

Ingredients

- 1 1/2 pounds skinless, boneless chicken breast meat
- 3/4 cup white sugar
- 3/4 cup soy sauce
- 3/4 cup mirin (Japanese sweet wine)
- 2 tablespoons vegetable oil
- 1 tablespoon grated fresh ginger
- 3 carrots, julienned
- 2 onions, thinly sliced
- 1 (14 ounce) can shredded bamboo, drained
- 1/2 pound fresh mushrooms, sliced
- 1 cup trimmed and coarsely chopped watercress
- 1 (8 ounce) package rice noodles, soaked and cut into 2 inch pieces

Direction

- Cut the chicken meat to bite-sized pieces. Mix mirin wine, soy sauce, and sugar in a medium-sized bowl. Combine well then put aside.
- In a wok or skillet, heat oil on medium-high heat. Squeeze grated ginger juice in the wok then add grated ginger, stir fry it until brown. Get rid of ginger fibers. Bring heat up to high then mix in chicken. Season with the soy sauce mixture then cook for another 2 minutes.
- Add watercress, mushrooms, bamboo shoots, onions, and carrots one at a time. Mix after every addition. Put in rice noodles and cook for another 3 minutes while stirring, or until done.

Nutrition Information

- Calories: 399 calories;
- Total Fat: 5
- Sodium: 1483
- Total Carbohydrate: 58.4
- Cholesterol: 49
- Protein: 24.6

468. Chicken Livers With Gorgonzola Polenta

Serving: 4 | Prep: 15mins | Cook: 45mins | Ready in:

Ingredients

- 2 tablespoons olive oil
- 1 pound chicken livers, trimmed and chopped
- 1 medium onion, sliced
- 1 green bell pepper, chopped
- 4 cloves garlic, minced
- 7 mushrooms, sliced
- 1 (14.5 ounce) can peeled and diced tomatoes, drained
- 1 cup white wine
- salt and pepper to taste
- 2 cups chicken stock
- 3/4 cup milk
- 1 cup dry polenta
- 4 ounces Gorgonzola cheese, crumbled

Direction

- In a big skillet, heat olive oil over medium heat. Add bell pepper and onion, and use a small amount of pepper and salt to season. Cook until soft, tossing often. Add garlic and mushrooms to the skillet; cook until aromatic, about several minutes. Transfer the vegetables to the sides of the skillet, and add chicken livers. Cook the livers, flipping often, about 5 minutes.
- Mix wine and tomatoes into the skillet, and adjust the heat to medium-high. Simmer until the liquid has mostly gone, about 20 minutes. Taste and use pepper and salt to season.
- In the meantime, add chicken stock to a saucepan, and boil it. Gradually add polenta while whisking thoroughly. Cook for several minutes, then mix in milk. Lower the heat to low; put a cover on and simmer until thick, about 5 minutes. Mix into the polenta with gorgonzola until melted.

- Ladle polenta onto plates, and put in the chicken liver sauce to cover.

Nutrition Information

- Calories: 648 calories;
- Sodium: 918
- Total Carbohydrate: 45.4
- Cholesterol: 676
- Protein: 43.2
- Total Fat: 26.6

in spinach; cook for about 2 minutes. Serve over the chicken.

Nutrition Information

- Calories: 671 calories;
- Sodium: 693
- Total Carbohydrate: 24.6
- Cholesterol: 160
- Protein: 32
- Total Fat: 43.4

469. Chicken Marsala Florentine

Serving: 4 | Prep: 10mins | Cook: 25mins | Ready in:

Ingredients

- 4 boneless, skinless chicken breast halves
- 1/4 cup all-purpose flour
- salt and pepper to taste
- 1 tablespoon dried oregano
- 2 tablespoons olive oil
- 3/4 cup butter
- 3 cups sliced portobello mushrooms
- 3/4 cup sun-dried tomatoes
- 1/2 cup packed fresh spinach
- 1 cup Marsala wine

Direction

- Put chicken breasts between 2 pieces of wax paper, with a meat mallet, pound to 1/4 inch thick. Sprinkle with oregano, pepper, salt and flour.
- Fry chicken in olive oil over medium heat in a skillet. Cook until done, turn to cook evenly. Put aside; keep warm.
- Melt the butter over medium heat in the same pan; add Marsala wine, sun-dried tomatoes and mushrooms. Cook while stirring occasionally for approximately 10 minutes. Stir

470. Chicken Marsala Meatballs

Serving: 4 | Prep: 15mins | Cook: 19mins | Ready in:

Ingredients

- 3 tablespoons olive oil
- 4 leaves fresh sage
- 1 pound ground chicken
- 1 egg
- 1/4 cup almond flour
- 2 tablespoons grated Parmesan cheese
- 1 teaspoon dried sage
- 1 teaspoon dried parsley
- 1 teaspoon sea salt
- 1/2 teaspoon freshly ground black pepper
- 1 (8 ounce) package sliced fresh mushrooms
- 1 large shallot, minced
- 1 cup low-sodium chicken broth
- 1/3 cup Marsala wine
- 1 tablespoon unsalted butter
- 2 teaspoons arrowroot flour

Direction

- Over moderately-high heat, heat a big skillet. Swirl in the olive oil and heat till extremely hot. Put sage leaves; fry for a minute each side till crisp. With tongs, put sage leaves onto paper towels-lined plate. Take skillet off heat, setting oil aside.

- In a big bowl, combine pepper, salt, parsley, sage, Parmesan cheese, almond flour, egg and ground chicken together. With ice cream scoop, a tablespoon or using hands, shape into balls.
- In a skillet, reheat the oil over moderate heat. Let meatballs cook for 7 minutes till browned on every side. Put the shallot and mushrooms; cook for 5 minutes till soft.
- Into skillet, mix arrowroot flour, butter, Marsala wine and chicken broth. Place a cover and let cook for 5 to 7 minutes, mixing one time, till sauce partially thickens.

Nutrition Information

- Calories: 382 calories;
- Total Fat: 20.6
- Sodium: 605
- Total Carbohydrate: 10.8
- Cholesterol: 123
- Protein: 33.5

471. Chicken Marsala With Portobello Mushrooms

Serving: 6 | Prep: 20mins | Cook: 40mins | Ready in:

Ingredients

- 8 tablespoons butter, divided
- 2 tablespoons olive oil, divided
- 4 portobello mushroom caps, sliced
- 1 clove garlic, chopped
- 1 tablespoon all-purpose flour
- 1 (14.5 ounce) can beef broth
- 1/2 cup dry Marsala wine
- 1 tablespoon browning sauce
- kosher salt, or to taste
- 1/4 teaspoon ground black pepper, or to taste
- 6 skinless, boneless chicken breast halves - pounded to 1/2 inch thickness
- 1 pinch kosher salt and pepper to taste
- 3/4 cup all-purpose flour, or as needed

Direction

- Set an oven to 175°C (350°F) and start preheating.
- In a skillet, heat a tablespoon of olive oil and melt 4 tablespoons of butter on medium heat. In the skillet, stir and cook the mushroom slices until they become tender. Take the pan out of the heat and put aside.
- In a saucepan, heat a tablespoon olive oil and melt a tablespoon of butter on medium-high heat. Add the garlic and stir, cook until it is tender, then beat in a tablespoon of flour gradually. Cook and stir continuously for a minute.
- Turn up the heat to high, then beat in the browning sauce, Marsala, and beef broth. Flavor the sauce with 1/4 teaspoon pepper and 1/2 teaspoon of salt. Boil the sauce and turn down the heat to low. Combine in the cooked mushrooms; you will need a skillet to cook the chicken. Put a cover on the saucepan and take away from the heat.
- Flavor the chicken with pepper and salt, then dredge the chicken breasts into flour. In the skillet used to cook the mushrooms, melt the remaining 3 tablespoons butter on medium heat. Cook the chicken until it is browned, for 2 minutes on each side. In the bottom of a 9x13-inch baking dish, place the chicken, cover it with the mushroom mixture and sauce.
- Put a cover on the baking dish and bake in the prepared oven for 25 minutes or until juices from the chicken run clear.

Nutrition Information

- Calories: 426 calories;
- Total Fat: 23.1
- Sodium: 622
- Total Carbohydrate: 19.9
- Cholesterol: 108
- Protein: 29.1

472. Chicken Pasta Shannon Style

Serving: 8 | Prep: 15mins | Cook: 20mins | Ready in:

Ingredients

- 1 pound farfalle (bow tie) pasta
- 4 tablespoons olive oil, divided
- 1 egg
- 2 tablespoons water
- 1 cup Italian seasoned bread crumbs
- 1 pound skinless, boneless chicken breast halves - cut into bite-size pieces
- 1 clove garlic, minced
- 1 onion, chopped
- 1/2 green bell pepper, chopped
- 1/2 red bell pepper, chopped
- 1/2 yellow bell pepper, chopped
- 1/2 cup chopped fresh mushrooms
- 1 cup Greek salad dressing
- 1/2 pint grape tomatoes
- 1/2 cup grated Parmesan cheese

Direction

- Boil a big pot of lightly salted water, and mix in the pasta. Allow to cook for 8 to 10 minutes till al dente, and drain.
- In a skillet, heat 3 tablespoons olive oil over medium heat. In a bowl, beat together the water and egg. In another bowl, put bread crumbs. Into the egg mixture, dunk first the chicken pieces, then dip into bread crumbs to coat. In the skillet, put coated chicken pieces, and cook for 5 minutes on every side or till juices run clear and coating is golden brown. Allow to drain on paper towels.
- In another skillet, heat leftover 1 tablespoon olive oil over medium heat. Add in mushrooms, yellow bell pepper, red bell pepper, green bell pepper, onion and garlic. Cook and mix till vegetables are soft.
- Toss the vegetables, chicken and pasta with the Greek dressing in a big bowl. Serve atop with Parmesan cheese and tomatoes.

Nutrition Information

- Calories: 552 calories;
- Total Carbohydrate: 57.8
- Cholesterol: 62
- Protein: 26.2
- Total Fat: 23.8
- Sodium: 565

473. Chicken Riggies I

Serving: 4 | Prep: 30mins | Cook: 1hours | Ready in:

Ingredients

- 1 (8 ounce) package uncooked rigatoni pasta
- 4 skinless, boneless chicken breast halves, cubed
- 2 cups red spaghetti sauce
- 1 green bell pepper, chopped
- 1 red bell pepper, chopped
- 1 onion, chopped
- 1 (8 ounce) package sliced fresh mushrooms
- 1 (15 ounce) can sliced black olives, drained
- 1 (8 ounce) jar hot cherry peppers, drained
- 2 cups Alfredo sauce

Direction

- Boil a large pot filled with lightly salted water. Add pasta and cook until firm to the bite for 8-10 minutes, then drain the pasta.
- Sauté the chicken in a large skillet on medium-high heat until browned thoroughly, 5-7 minutes. Add spaghetti sauce, turn down the heat to low, then let simmer for 20 minutes.
- Add hot peppers, olives, mushrooms, onion, red bell pepper, and green bell pepper. Stir them together and bring to a simmer for 40 minutes.
- Add Alfredo sauce and stir until combined, then bring to a simmer for 10 more minutes. Spread on the hot, cooked pasta to serve.

Nutrition Information

- Calories: 978 calories;
- Total Fat: 54.2
- Sodium: 3048
- Total Carbohydrate: 79.6
- Cholesterol: 122
- Protein: 46

474. Chicken Supreme II

Serving: 6 | Prep: | Cook: |Ready in:

Ingredients

- 2 tablespoons butter
- 2 tablespoons vegetable oil
- 6 skinless, boneless chicken breasts
- 1 (10.75 ounce) can condensed cream of chicken soup
- 1/2 cup light whipping cream
- 1/2 cup dry sherry
- 1 teaspoon dried tarragon
- 1 teaspoon Worcestershire sauce
- 1 teaspoon chopped fresh cilantro
- 1/4 teaspoon garlic powder
- 1 (6 ounce) can sliced mushrooms

Direction

- Preheat an oven to 175°C/350°F.
- Pound the chicken breasts to an even thickness. Heat oil and margarine/butter in a 9x13-in. baking dish. Add chicken; coat the chicken with margarine/butter mixture. In the preheated oven, bake till breast is just cooked for 10-15 minutes; the middle should be slightly pink.
- Warm mushrooms, garlic powder, cilantro, Worcestershire sauce, tarragon, sherry, cream and soup in a medium saucepan on medium heat. Put sherry cream mixture on baked chicken. Put back in the oven, uncovered; bake for 15-20 minutes more. Slightly cool; serve.

Nutrition Information

- Calories: 317 calories;
- Total Fat: 16.8
- Sodium: 693
- Total Carbohydrate: 9.3
- Cholesterol: 96
- Protein: 29.6

475. Chicken Supreme IV

Serving: 4 | Prep: 15mins | Cook: 40mins |Ready in:

Ingredients

- 1 1/2 cups grated Parmesan cheese
- 3 eggs, beaten
- 1 1/2 cups Italian-style seasoned bread crumbs
- 3 tablespoons vegetable oil
- 4 skinless, boneless chicken breast halves
- 2 cups white Zinfandel wine
- 2 cups sliced fresh mushrooms
- 3 cups shredded Monterey Jack cheese

Direction

- Preheat oven to 375°F (190°C). Grease a medium baking dish lightly.
- In three separate small bowls, place breadcrumbs, eggs, and Parmesan cheese. In a large skillet, heat oil over medium-high heat. Dip each piece of chicken in order: first into the Parmesan cheese, second into the egg, and lastly into the breadcrumbs. In the hot skillet, brown the chicken on both sides; place them on the prepared baking dish.
- Pour wine into skillet and scrape up to loosen the browned bits. Add mushrooms and cook for around 5 minutes until softened. Use even amounts of Monterey Jack cheese to top each chicken breast, then spoon mushrooms over the cheese. Pour the remaining wine from the skillet over all. Use aluminum foil to cover dish.

- In the preheated oven, bake for 30 to 35 minutes until juices run clear and chicken is no longer pink.

Nutrition Information

- Calories: 977 calories;
- Total Fat: 52
- Sodium: 1695
- Total Carbohydrate: 34.6
- Cholesterol: 310
- Protein: 71

- Total Carbohydrate: 34.1
- Cholesterol: 167
- Protein: 52
- Total Fat: 26.5
- Sodium: 558

476. Chicken Susan

Serving: 4 | Prep: 30mins | Cook: 30mins | Ready in:

Ingredients

- 2 (8 ounce) packages egg noodles, cooked
- 1/2 pound Swiss cheese, cubed
- 2 cups sliced fresh mushrooms
- 4 stalks celery, chopped
- 2 cups chicken stock
- 4 chicken breast halves with skin and bone, steamed

Direction

- Preheat an oven to 200°C/400°F>
- In a 9x13-in. lightly greased baking dish, put cooked egg noodles. Add celery, mushrooms and cheese; stir well. Add chicken stock; add more stock if chicken stock level can't be seen through the noodles, keep adding till it is visible. Put chicken breasts, bone side down, over noodle mixture.
- Bake for 30 minutes at 200°C/400°F or till chicken juices are clear and skin is crisp and brown.

Nutrition Information

- Calories: 589 calories;

477. Chicken Tetrazzini

Serving: 8 | Prep: | Cook: | Ready in:

Ingredients

- 8 chicken tenderloins
- salt and pepper to taste
- 3/4 cup fresh sliced mushrooms
- 1 red bell pepper, chopped
- 1/2 yellow bell pepper, chopped
- 1 (8 ounce) package uncooked spaghetti
- 1/4 cup butter
- 1/4 cup all-purpose flour
- 1 cup chicken broth
- 1 cup half-and-half
- 1 teaspoon garlic salt
- ground black pepper to taste
- 1/2 cup shredded Swiss cheese
- 1/3 cup grated Parmesan cheese
- 1/4 cup grated Parmesan cheese for topping (optional)

Direction

- Sauté the tenderloins in a large non-skillet. Season to taste with pepper and salt. Add yellow bell peppers, red bell peppers, and mushrooms; cook until the greens are tender.
- Cook the spaghetti following the package directions. Let drain and put aside.
- Melt margarine or butter in a large saucepan, then blend in flour. Stir in half-and-half and the chicken broth gradually. Over medium-low heat, cook until the sauce starts to thicken, stirring constantly. Add ground black pepper and garlic salt to taste. Blend in the Parmesan and Swiss cheeses, then continue to heat until the cheeses melt, stirring constantly.

- Stir in the vegetable/chicken mixture and heat thoroughly. Then toss with the cooked pasta; if desired, put grated Parmesan cheese on top.

Nutrition Information

- Calories: 329 calories;
- Sodium: 421
- Total Carbohydrate: 27.7
- Cholesterol: 70
- Protein: 22.3
- Total Fat: 14

478. Chicken Tetrazzini For A Crowd

Serving: 20 | Prep: | Cook: | Ready in:

Ingredients

- 1 pound spaghetti, broken into pieces
- 3 (10.75 ounce) cans condensed cream of mushroom soup
- 12 ounces shredded Cheddar cheese
- 6 cups shredded boiled chicken breast meat
- 1 pound sauteed mushrooms
- 1 (4 ounce) jar sliced pimento peppers, drained
- 2 cups reserved chicken broth

Direction

- Preheat the oven to 175 ° C or 350 ° F. Boil a big pot of salted water. Break uncooked spaghetti into thirds and put to pot, let cook till al dente, for 8 to 10 minutes. Allow to drain and reserve.
- Heat soup in a big saucepan on low heat. Put in shredded cheese, set some aside for the topping, and mix together. Then put in cooked spaghetti, pimento peppers, mushrooms and cooked shredded chicken, and mix everything. Put in sufficient of reserved broth to turn it 'sloppy' and stir all together.
- Put the mixture into one baking dish, 9x13 inch in size. Scatter the reserved shredded cheese over and in prepped oven, bake till bubbly, for 25 to 35 minutes.

Nutrition Information

- Calories: 279 calories;
- Total Fat: 12
- Sodium: 506
- Total Carbohydrate: 21.4
- Cholesterol: 49
- Protein: 20.7

479. Chicken Thigh Fricassee With Mushrooms And Rosemary

Serving: 4 | Prep: 15mins | Cook: 1hours15mins | Ready in:

Ingredients

- 4 tablespoons olive oil, divided
- 5 ounces fresh mushrooms, sliced
- 4 cloves garlic, peeled and halved
- 2 tablespoons fresh rosemary, chopped
- 1 pound chicken thighs
- salt and freshly ground black pepper to taste
- 1/4 teaspoon crushed red pepper flakes
- 3/4 cup dry white wine
- 12 cherry tomatoes
- 12 Nicoise olives

Direction

- In a large skillet, heat 2 tablespoons of the olive oil over medium heat. Mix in the mushrooms. Cook until soft. Transfer to a plate.
- Clean the skillet, then heat 2 tablespoons of the olive oil over medium-high heat. Put chicken thighs, rosemary, and garlic into the hot oil. Add pepper and salt for seasonings. Cook,

turning the chicken, until the garlic and chicken are well browned.
- Put the mushrooms back into the pan. Add red pepper flakes over the chicken. Add white wine, using a wooden spoon to scrape the bottom of the pan. Cook for 3 minutes.
- Lower the heat to low; gently simmer, covered, for 60 minutes.
- Uncover and add olives and tomatoes over top of the chicken. Cover and cook for 5 minutes longer.

Nutrition Information

- Calories: 402 calories;
- Total Fat: 28.6
- Sodium: 257
- Total Carbohydrate: 7.1
- Cholesterol: 71
- Protein: 21

480. Chicken Thighs With Mushroom Leek Sauce

Serving: 8 | Prep: 10mins | Cook: 30mins | Ready in:

Ingredients

- 1 tablespoon extra-virgin olive oil
- 8 boneless, skinless chicken thighs
- 4 cups baby bella mushrooms, thinly sliced
- 2 leeks, thinly sliced
- 2/3 cup dry white wine
- 1 1/2 cups reduced-sodium chicken broth
- 2 teaspoons cornstarch
- 2/3 cup low-fat sour cream
- 1 1/2 teaspoons Dijon mustard
- salt to taste
- ground black pepper to taste

Direction

- Put oil in a large skillet and heat it over medium-high. Add the chicken and cook each side for 4-5 minutes until evenly browned and the center of the chicken is no longer pink. Place the chicken onto a plate. Cover the chicken and keep it warm.
- Add leeks and mushrooms to the skillet. Cook and stir the mixture frequently over medium heat for 4-6 minutes until the mushrooms start to brown and the moisture has been evaporated. Pour in the wine. Cook for 1 minute. In a small bowl, mix the cornstarch and broth, and then pour the mixture into the skillet. Cook for 2-3 more minutes until thickened. Mix in the mustard and sour cream. Cook and stir for 1 minute until combined. Season the sauce with salt and pepper.
- Lay the chicken thighs into the sauce and cook for 8-10 more minutes until the inserted instant-read thermometer into the thickest portion of the thigh registers 165°F or 74°C.

Nutrition Information

- Calories: 198 calories;
- Protein: 13.8
- Total Fat: 11.2
- Sodium: 113
- Total Carbohydrate: 7.2
- Cholesterol: 47

481. Chicken Valdostano

Serving: 6 | Prep: 15mins | Cook: 25mins | Ready in:

Ingredients

- 2 tablespoons all-purpose flour
- 6 skinless, boneless chicken breast halves - pounded thin
- 1/4 cup unsalted butter
- 10 fresh mushrooms, sliced
- 3/4 cup dry white wine
- 3/4 cup chicken stock
- 3 tablespoons chopped fresh parsley
- 1 teaspoon freshly ground white pepper

- 6 slices thinly sliced prosciutto
- 6 slices fontina cheese

Direction

- Flour chicken breasts lightly; shake off excess flour. Melt margarine/butter over low heat in a large skillet. Add chicken; sauté for about 2 minutes per side until lightly browned. Take it out with a slotted spatula; put aside.
- Increase the heat to medium-low. Add mushrooms; sauté for about 4 minutes until juices are rendered. Add wine; simmer for about 3-4 minutes until it reduces by 1/4. Increase the heat to medium-high. Add pepper, parsley and stock; simmer for about 10 minutes until sauce reduces to 1 cup.
- Lower the heat to low. Place a slice of fontina cheese and a slice of prosciutto on top of each chicken breast. Transfer the chicken back to the skillet; cook just until cheese is melted. Place chicken on individual plates and pour some of the mushroom sauce over each plate before serving.

Nutrition Information

- Calories: 396 calories;
- Total Fat: 23.7
- Sodium: 706
- Total Carbohydrate: 4.8
- Cholesterol: 127
- Protein: 34.5

482. Chicken Wild Rice Soup I

Serving: 8 | Prep: 15mins | Cook: 2hours10mins | Ready in:

Ingredients

- 1/2 cup butter
- 1 finely chopped onion
- 1/2 cup chopped celery
- 1/2 cup sliced carrots
- 1/2 pound fresh sliced mushrooms
- 3/4 cup all-purpose flour
- 6 cups chicken broth
- 2 cups cooked wild rice
- 1 pound boneless skinless chicken breasts, cooked and cubed
- 1/2 teaspoon salt
- 1/2 teaspoon curry powder
- 1/2 teaspoon mustard powder
- 1/2 teaspoon dried parsley
- 1/2 teaspoon ground black pepper
- 1 cup slivered almonds
- 3 tablespoons dry sherry
- 2 cups half-and-half

Direction

- Over medium heat, melt butter in a large saucepan. Mix in carrots, onion, and celery and then sauté for five minutes. Place in mushrooms and then sauté for two minutes. Pour in flour and mix thoroughly. Slowly add in chicken broth while stirring continuously until all is added. Heat to boil, decrease the heat to low and simmer.
- Add the rice, ground black pepper, chicken, sherry, salt, parsley, mustard powder, almonds and curry powder and heat through. Add in half-and-half and allow to simmer for about 1 to 2 hours. (Note: Avoid boiling because the roux will break.)

Nutrition Information

- Calories: 529 calories;
- Total Carbohydrate: 28.7
- Cholesterol: 97
- Protein: 32.7
- Total Fat: 32
- Sodium: 1514

483. Chicken With Mushrooms

Serving: 4 | Prep: 15mins | Cook: 30mins | Ready in:

Ingredients

- 3 cups sliced mushrooms
- 4 skinless, boneless chicken breast halves
- 2 eggs, beaten
- 1 cup seasoned bread crumbs
- 2 tablespoons butter
- 6 ounces mozzarella cheese, sliced
- 3/4 cup chicken broth

Direction

- Turn the oven to 350°F (175°C) to preheat.
- In a 9x13-in. pan, put 1/2 of the mushrooms. Dip the chicken in beaten eggs, and then roll in bread crumbs.
- Melt butter in a frying pan over medium heat. In the frying pan, brown the chicken on both sides. Top the mushrooms with the chicken. On the chicken, put the leftover mushrooms, and put mozzarella cheese on top. Pour chicken broth into the pan.
- Bake for 30-35 minutes in the preheated oven until the juices run clear and the chicken is not pink anymore.

Nutrition Information

- Calories: 454 calories;
- Total Carbohydrate: 23.8
- Cholesterol: 204
- Protein: 44.1
- Total Fat: 19.8
- Sodium: 1108

484. Chicken With Portobello Mushrooms And Artichokes

Serving: 4 | Prep: 5mins | Cook: 30mins | Ready in:

Ingredients

- 4 skinless, boneless chicken breast halves
- 2 tablespoons olive oil
- 1/4 cup all-purpose flour
- salt and pepper to taste
- 1 small onion, thinly sliced
- 2 portobello mushrooms
- 1/2 cup beef broth
- 2 teaspoons dried tarragon
- 5 canned quartered artichoke hearts
- 1/2 cup brandy
- 1/4 cup lemon juice

Direction

- Pound the chicken breasts lightly to even thickness. Dust flour over the chicken, season with pepper and salt to taste.
- Heat one tablespoon of olive oil in a heavy skillet over medium heat. Put the chicken in skillet, brown both sides, and cook through, about 8-10 minutes. Take out of skillet; put aside.
- Put in the remaining one tablespoon of olive oil; sauté mushrooms and onions for 3-5 minutes over medium heat.
- Put artichoke hearts, tarragon, lemon juice and beef broth into the pan; heat about 2-3 minutes, stirring gently. Mix in brandy then simmer for 2-3 more minutes. Put the chicken back to the skillet and heat through.

Nutrition Information

- Calories: 344 calories;
- Total Fat: 8.6
- Sodium: 290
- Total Carbohydrate: 13.7
- Cholesterol: 68
- Protein: 30.9

485. Chicken A La Can Can

Serving: 5 | Prep: | Cook: |Ready in:

Ingredients

- 2 cups diced, cooked chicken meat
- 1 (10.75 ounce) can condensed cream of celery soup
- 2 cups cooked white rice
- 1 (4.5 ounce) can sliced mushrooms
- 1 onion, diced and cooked until soft
- ground black pepper to taste
- 2 stalks celery, chopped
- 1 (8 ounce) can water chestnuts
- 1/2 cup peanuts
- 1 (6 ounce) can French fried onions

Direction

- Preheat the oven to 175 degrees F (350 degrees F).
- Mix peanuts, water chestnuts, celery, ground pepper, diced onion, mushrooms, rice, soup and chicken. Add the mixture into the 9x13-in. casserole dish. Drizzle half can of French fried onions over the top and bake in preheated oven till becoming bubbling and the onions turn crisp. Drizzle the rest half of the fried onions over the top and serve.

Nutrition Information

- Calories: 553 calories;
- Protein: 22.4
- Total Fat: 29.4
- Sodium: 905
- Total Carbohydrate: 49
- Cholesterol: 49

486. Chicken A La King III

Serving: 4 | Prep: 10mins | Cook: 20mins |Ready in:

Ingredients

- 2 tablespoons butter
- 1 green bell pepper, chopped
- 1 cup sliced fresh mushrooms
- 1 cup chicken broth
- 2 tablespoons all-purpose flour
- 2 1/4 cups cooked, cubed chicken breast meat
- 1 cup sour cream
- 2 egg yolks
- 1 pimento, chopped
- 4 teaspoons cooking sherry
- salt and pepper to taste

Direction

- In a large skillet, melt butter over medium high heat. Sauté mushrooms and bell pepper until softened, then mix in flour and broth and cook, stirring, until thickened. Add chicken, heat through and take away from heat.
- Combine egg yolks, sour cream, sherry, pimento, pepper and salt in a small bowl and mix together. Add into chicken mixture in skillet and thoroughly heat, stirring. Serve while it is still hot.

Nutrition Information

- Calories: 365 calories;
- Sodium: 167
- Total Carbohydrate: 10
- Cholesterol: 210
- Protein: 28.8
- Total Fat: 23

487. Chicken A La Queen

Serving: 6 | Prep: 45mins | Cook: 25mins |Ready in:

Ingredients

- 1 (10 ounce) can large refrigerated flaky biscuits
- 1 (3 pound) rotisserie-roasted chicken

- 2 tablespoons olive oil
- 1 large onion, chopped
- 1 cup shredded carrots
- 1 cup fresh mushrooms
- salt and ground black pepper to taste
- 1/2 red bell pepper, sliced into thin strips
- 3 tablespoons butter
- 3 tablespoons all-purpose flour
- 1/2 cup white wine
- 4 cups chicken broth
- 1 cup heavy whipping cream
- 1/2 pound fresh asparagus, trimmed and cut into 1 inch pieces
- 1 cup frozen petite peas, thawed
- 1 tablespoon chopped fresh tarragon

Direction

- Set the oven to 175 ° C or 350 ° F to preheat. Arrange the biscuits on an unoiled baking sheet, spacing 1 - 2 inch apart.
- Bake for 13 - 17 minutes in prepped oven till biscuits turn golden brown in color. Take out the biscuits and let them cool, then put aside. Slice meat from rotisserie chicken into bite-size portions; put aside.
- In a skillet, heat olive oil on medium heat. Mix in black pepper, salt, mushrooms, carrots and onion. Cook while mixing for 7 minutes till carrots turn tender, mushrooms releases their liquid and onion is soft. Mix in red bell pepper; then cook about 2 minutes longer. Take off from the heat; put aside.
- In a saucepan, melt butter on medium heat. Mix in flour for making a paste with thick consistency. Carry on cooking, mixing continuously for 5 minutes, till the raw smell of flour is gone. Mix in white wine, raise the heat to medium-high; let it simmer about a minute. Mix in whipping cream and chicken broth and boil the sauce. Lower the heat, mix in shredded chicken; let it simmer about 7 minutes.
- Transfer the mixture of chicken into skillet with vegetables and turn to medium heat. Pour in asparagus; then cook for 4 minutes, till asparagus pieces are softened. Mix in tarragon and peas, stir thoroughly.
- Arrange a split biscuit on each plate and top the biscuits with chicken mixture.

Nutrition Information

- Calories: 766 calories;
- Total Fat: 49
- Sodium: 672
- Total Carbohydrate: 35
- Cholesterol: 182
- Protein: 42.5

488. Chicken And Bacon Fajitas

Serving: 4 | Prep: 30mins | Cook: 30mins | Ready in:

Ingredients

- 3 boneless, skinless chicken breast halves
- salt to taste
- 3 slices peppered bacon, diced
- 1/2 cup chopped onion
- 1 chopped green bell pepper
- 1 chopped red bell pepper
- 1 1/2 cups chopped mushrooms
- 1 cup cherry tomatoes, cut in half
- 3/4 cup chopped cilantro
- 8 large flour tortillas (burrito size), warmed to soften

Direction

- Heat a large skillet over medium-high heat. Cook chicken breasts until juices run clear and outside of chicken turns golden brown. Season the breasts to taste with salt. Put aside.
- In the hot skillet, cook bacon until it starts to release some oil. Mix in bell peppers and onion. Cook until onions become translucent and bacon become crispy. Mix in mushrooms

and tomatoes. Keep cooking until mushrooms soften.
- Cut cooked chicken breasts into the bite-sized pieces. Put into skillet along with cilantro. Combine by stirring. Cook to reheat for one minute. Put into the warmed tortillas to enjoy.

Nutrition Information

- Calories: 682 calories;
- Protein: 36.9
- Total Fat: 22.1
- Sodium: 1305
- Total Carbohydrate: 82.1
- Cholesterol: 66

489. Chicken And Bowtie Pasta With Asiago Cream Sauce

Serving: 6 | Prep: 20mins | Cook: 40mins | Ready in:

Ingredients

- 1 (16 ounce) package farfalle (bow tie) pasta
- 2 tablespoons vegetable oil
- 1 pound skinless, boneless chicken breast halves - cubed
- 2 1/4 cups heavy cream, divided
- 1/4 cube chicken bouillon, crumbled
- 3/4 cup grated Asiago cheese
- 1/2 tablespoon cornstarch
- 2 tablespoons butter
- 1/4 cup chopped prosciutto
- 1 tablespoon chopped fresh garlic
- 1/4 cup sliced mushrooms
- 1/2 tablespoon parsley flakes

Direction

- Boil a big pot of lightly salted water. Allow pasta to cook till al dente for 8 to 10 minutes. Let drain, and reserve.
- In a skillet over medium-high heat, heat 2 tablespoons vegetable oil. Cook and mix chicken cubes, lower heat if needed, till juices run clear and not pink anymore in middle. Reserve.
- Simmer 2 cups cream in a medium saucepan, mixing frequently. Mix in cheese and bouillon till well incorporated and bouillon has fully dissolved. In 2 tablespoons water, melt cornstarch, and stir into mixture. Cook and mix for 2 minutes longer, then take off heat and reserve.
- In a medium skillet, liquefy butter over medium high heat. Mix in mushrooms, garlic and prosciutto and cook for 3 minutes till mushrooms are soft. Put in chicken, lower heat, and keep cooking till chicken is heated through. Put sauce back to the stove and put the leftover quarter cup cream and parsley flakes. Heat mixture through.
- In a serving or big mixing bowl, put the pasta to serve. Put mushroom and chicken mixture and add in cream sauce. Toss thoroughly, then serve.

Nutrition Information

- Calories: 837 calories;
- Cholesterol: 193
- Protein: 33.2
- Total Fat: 50.7
- Sodium: 425
- Total Carbohydrate: 61.5

490. Chicken And Herbs In White Wine

Serving: 6 | Prep: 20mins | Cook: 1hours45mins | Ready in:

Ingredients

- 2 tablespoons olive oil
- 1 (4 pound) chicken, cut into pieces
- garlic powder to taste
- 1/2 pound fresh mushrooms, sliced

- 1 large onion, diced
- 1/2 teaspoon dried basil
- 1/2 teaspoon dried oregano
- 1/2 teaspoon dried rosemary
- 1/2 teaspoon dried thyme
- 1 teaspoon garlic salt
- 1/4 teaspoon black pepper
- 1 teaspoon poultry seasoning
- 1 cup dry white wine
- 1 (10.5 ounce) can chicken broth

Direction

- In a large Dutch oven, heat olive oil over medium heat. Drizzle garlic powder over chicken, then brown on both sides. Transfer the chicken to paper towels.
- Spoon off chicken fat, then move the pan back to stove. Mix in onions and mushrooms; cook while sometimes stirring until onions become softened. Transfer to a medium bowl.
- In a different bowl, blend thyme, rosemary, oregano, and basil. Flavor with poultry seasoning, pepper, and garlic salt together. Mix in wine, then add to mushrooms and onion.
- Transfer chicken back to the Dutch oven. Spread broth and mushroom mixture over chicken; cook, covered, over low heat for around 1 and a half hours till meat starts to fall off the bone.

Nutrition Information

- Calories: 750 calories;
- Sodium: 760
- Total Carbohydrate: 5.6
- Cholesterol: 228
- Protein: 58.1
- Total Fat: 50.4

491. Chicken And Mushroom Chowder

Serving: 4 | Prep: 15mins | Cook: 45mins | Ready in:

Ingredients

- 3 cups chicken broth
- 1/2 cup water
- 1 pound cubed cooked chicken breast meat
- 1 1/2 teaspoons dried oregano
- 1/4 teaspoon pepper
- 1/2 cup uncooked long grain rice
- 1 tablespoon olive oil
- 3 cloves garlic, minced
- 1 onion, finely chopped
- 1 carrot, finely chopped
- 3/4 pound mushrooms, sliced
- 3 tablespoons all-purpose flour
- 1 cup milk

Direction

- Bring water and chicken broth to a boil in a large saucepan. Stir in chicken, season with oregano and pepper. Put in rice; reduce the heat.
- In a medium saucepan, heat olive oil over medium heat; sauté mushrooms, carrot, onion, and garlic until softened. Mix in thoroughly the flour. Add to the broth mixture.
- Stir in milk; continue to cook, stirring irregularly, about 30 minutes or until thickened.

Nutrition Information

- Calories: 416 calories;
- Total Fat: 13.6
- Sodium: 113
- Total Carbohydrate: 33.8
- Cholesterol: 90
- Protein: 38.6

492. Chicken And Mushroom Crepes

Serving: 5 | Prep: 25mins | Cook: 32mins | Ready in:

Ingredients

- Filling:
- 5 tablespoons butter, divided
- 2 tablespoons canola oil
- 3 boneless, skinless chicken breasts, cut into chunks
- 1 (8 ounce) package sliced fresh mushrooms
- 1/3 cup finely chopped onion
- 1/4 cup all-purpose flour
- 2 cups milk
- 2 cubes chicken bouillon
- 1/4 teaspoon salt
- 1/8 teaspoon ground black pepper
- 1/2 cup sour cream
- 3 tablespoons dry sherry
- 2 teaspoons dried parsley, divided
- Crepes:
- 1 cup milk
- 3/4 cup all-purpose flour
- 1 egg
- 1 tablespoon butter, melted
- 1 1/2 teaspoons white sugar
- 1/4 teaspoon vanilla extract
- 1/4 teaspoon baking powder

Direction

- In a large skillet over medium heat, put 1 tablespoons butter and oil to heat. Add chicken then stir and cook for about 5 minutes until not pink in the middle. Place to a plate.
- In the same skillet over medium heat, put remaining 1/4 cup butter to dissolve. Place in onion and mushrooms; stir and cook for about 5 minutes until tender. Mix in 1/4 cup flour and cook for 2 minutes. Lower heat. Stir in pepper, salt, chicken bouillon cubes and 2 cups milk; whisk and cook for about 5 minutes until thickened into a sauce. Mix in sherry and sour cream.
- In a bowl, place 1 cup sauce; remain warm. In the skillet with remaining sauce, add 1 teaspoon parsley and chicken. Boil for about 5 minutes until chicken is heated well.
- In a bowl, whisk baking powder, vanilla extract, sugar, 1 tablespoon dissolved butter, egg, 3/4 cup flour and 1 cup milk to create a crepe batter.
- Lightly grease a 7-inch skillet; then heat over medium. Put 2 tablespoons batter into the skillet, whirling to scatter equally. Then cook crepe for about 30 seconds each side, until golden brown. Place crepe to plate. Continue with remaining batter, using waxed paper to separate crepes and covering to remain warm.
- Onto each crepe, place 1/4 cup chicken mixture and turn up. On filled crepes, put reserved 1 cup sauce. Decorate with remaining 1 teaspoon parsley.

Nutrition Information

- Calories: 501 calories;
- Sodium: 872
- Total Carbohydrate: 32.8
- Cholesterol: 131
- Protein: 24.6
- Total Fat: 30

493. Chicken And Portobello Rollups

Serving: 4 | Prep: 30mins | Cook: 40mins | Ready in:

Ingredients

- 1 tablespoon olive oil
- 1 teaspoon minced garlic
- 1 portobello mushroom cap, cut into 1/2-inch slices
- 1 large red bell pepper, cut into strips
- 8 asparagus spears, trimmed
- 1/2 teaspoon seasoned salt
- 1/2 teaspoon dried oregano

- 4 (6 ounce) skinless, boneless chicken breast halves
- 1 (10.5 ounce) can cream of mushroom soup
- 1 cup milk

Direction

- Place a skillet on the stove and turn on to medium heat then put olive oil. Put in the garlic, and cook for about 1 minute until it starts to turn golden brown in color. Stir in the asparagus, red pepper and mushroom; put seasoned salt and oregano to season, then slowly cook until tender. Put the mixture onto a plate, and let it cool.
- Prepare the oven by preheating to 375 degrees F (190 degrees C). Get a small glass baking dish and use cooking spray to coat then reserve.
- Between two sheets of plastic wrap, put each chicken breast, and smash to 1/4-inch thick. Equally split among the flattened chicken breasts the asparagus, red pepper and portobello. Reel up and use toothpicks to secure. Then put into prepared baking dish.
- Place inside the preheated oven and bake for about 30 minutes until pink color fades. In the meantime, in a saucepan over medium-high heat, stir together the milk and cream of mushroom soup. Simmer then lower the heat, and let it stay warm while cooking chicken.
- To present, get toothpicks out the chicken, cut each in half at an angle, and put onto individual plates or serving platter. Scoop cream of mushroom soup all over the top.

Nutrition Information

- Calories: 342 calories;
- Total Fat: 13.3
- Sodium: 709
- Total Carbohydrate: 13.8
- Cholesterol: 102
- Protein: 40.7

494. Chicken And Spinach Alfredo Lasagna

Serving: 12 | Prep: 30mins | Cook: 1hours30mins | Ready in:

Ingredients

- 1 (8 ounce) package lasagna noodles
- 3 cups heavy cream
- 2 (10.75 ounce) cans condensed cream of mushroom soup
- 1 cup grated Parmesan cheese
- 1/4 cup butter
- 1 tablespoon olive oil
- 1/2 large onion, diced
- 4 cloves garlic, sliced
- 5 mushrooms, diced
- 1 roasted chicken, shredded
- salt and ground black pepper to taste
- 1 cup ricotta cheese
- 1 bunch fresh spinach, rinsed
- 3 cups shredded mozzarella cheese

Direction

- Let oven warm up to 350°F or to 175°C. Let boil lightly salted water in a big pot. Once boiling, allow lasagna noodles to cook until it becomes al dente for 8-10 minutes. Discard excess water and wash noodles with cold water.
- In a saucepan, mix cream of mushroom soup, heavy cream, butter and parmesan cheese over low fire. Allow to simmer until well blended with constant stirring.
- In a skillet, warm olive oil over medium fire. Let onion cook in olive oil with stirring until softened then mix in mushrooms and garlic. Add chicken and allow to cook through. Spice with pepper and salt to taste.
- In 9x13-inch baking dish lightly coated with oil, even out ample cream mixture. On top of it, arrange 1/3 of the lasagna noodles, half ricotta cheese, half spinach, half of the chicken mixture, and one cup mozzarella. Even out 1/3 of the cream sauce mixture then make

another layer. Finish it off with remaining noodles and sauce.
- Let it bake for 60 minutes in a warmed up oven until it becomes brown and forms bubbles. Embellish with leftover mozzarella and let it bake until cheese is lightly browned and melted.

Nutrition Information

- Calories: 591 calories;
- Total Fat: 43.7
- Sodium: 847
- Total Carbohydrate: 22
- Cholesterol: 159
- Protein: 28.7

495. Chicken And Wild Rice Casserole

Serving: 10 | Prep: 30mins | Cook: 2hours | Ready in:

Ingredients

- 3 pounds bone-in chicken breast halves, with skin
- 1 cup water
- 1 cup dry white wine
- 1 1/2 teaspoons salt
- 1 teaspoon curry powder
- 1 onion, sliced
- 1 cup chopped celery
- 2 (6 ounce) packages long grain and wild rice mix
- 1 (16 ounce) can sliced mushrooms, drained
- 1 cup sour cream
- 1 (10.75 ounce) can condensed cream of mushroom soup

Direction

- In a big pot, put celery, onion, curry powder, salt, wine, water and chicken breasts. Cover; boil. Lower heat to low. Simmer for an hour.
- Take off heat; strain (keep broth). Refrigerate to cool. Take chicken meat from bone. Cut to bite-sized pieces.
- Following package directions, prep rice mix. Substitute the specified liquid amount with same amount of leftover broth.
- Preheat an oven to 175°C/350°F. Grease a 9x13-in. baking dish lightly.
- Mix mushrooms, rice and chicken in a big bowl. Blend soup and sour cream in. put into prepped baking dish.
- Bake for 1 hour at 175°C/350°F.

Nutrition Information

- Calories: 385 calories;
- Total Fat: 10.3
- Sodium: 1326
- Total Carbohydrate: 33.7
- Cholesterol: 88
- Protein: 33.8

496. Chicken With Mushrooms, Prosciutto, And Cream Sauce

Serving: 6 | Prep: 10mins | Cook: 1hours | Ready in:

Ingredients

- 2 tablespoons butter or margarine, melted
- 6 chicken thighs
- salt and pepper to taste
- 6 slices prosciutto (thin sliced)
- 2 tablespoons minced garlic, divided
- 1 cup sliced fresh mushrooms
- 1/4 cup dry white wine (optional)
- 1 cup sour cream

Direction

- Preheat an oven to 175 degrees C (350 degrees F).

- Drizzle butter into a casserole dish. Season the chicken with 1 tablespoon of garlic, pepper and salt. Encase the chicken thighs in prosciutto and transfer into casserole dish. Sprinkle remaining garlic and mushrooms over chicken.
- Bake in the preheated oven for about 1 hour until the juices run clear. Transfer the chicken onto a platter and then keep warm by covering with aluminum foil.
- Transfer the drippings from the casserole to a skillet that is placed on top of medium-low heat. Whisk in sour cream and wine and then cook for about 5 to 7 minutes until warmed through. Pour atop chicken and then serve.

Nutrition Information

- Calories: 383 calories;
- Total Fat: 30.8
- Sodium: 425
- Total Carbohydrate: 3.3
- Cholesterol: 119
- Protein: 20.7

497. Chicken With Red Grapes And Mushrooms

Serving: 5 | Prep: 5mins | Cook: 25mins | Ready in:

Ingredients

- 2 tablespoons butter
- 1 tablespoon olive oil
- 4 skinless, boneless chicken breast halves
- 1 cup sliced fresh mushrooms
- 1 cup red wine
- 1 cup heavy cream
- 1 tablespoon dried thyme
- 1 teaspoon salt
- 1 teaspoon ground black pepper
- 1 cup seedless red grapes, rinsed and dried

Direction

- In a large skillet over medium high heat, melt butter with oil. When hot, place chicken breast and brown for 3 to 5 minutes each side until golden in color.
- Add mushroom and sauté for 2 to 3 minutes or until mushrooms are softened. Pour wine in the pan and deglaze, remember to loosen any brown parts from the bottom of pan. Simmer for 5 minutes.
- Stir in cream, add thyme, pepper and salt. Lower the heat to low and simmer, covered, for 5 to 7 minutes, stir occasionally while simmering.
- Remove cover and reduce cream until thickened, 3 minutes. Add red grapes and heat through.

Nutrition Information

- Calories: 402 calories;
- Protein: 23.5
- Total Fat: 26.4
- Sodium: 581
- Total Carbohydrate: 9.6
- Cholesterol: 132

498. Chicken, Cheese, And Biscuits

Serving: 4 | Prep: | Cook: | Ready in:

Ingredients

- 1 tablespoon margarine
- 3 tablespoons all-purpose flour, divided
- 1/2 teaspoon ground mustard
- 1/4 teaspoon rubbed sage
- 1 1/2 cups milk
- 2 cubes chicken bouillon
- 1 pinch ground white pepper
- 2 ounces shredded Cheddar cheese
- 1 cup cooked, diced chicken breast
- 1 cup fresh mushrooms, sliced
- 1 cup chopped fresh green beans

- 1 (10 ounce) can refrigerated biscuit dough

Direction

- In a sauce pan, heat the margarine till becoming hot and bubbling. Put in the sage, mustard and flour; whisk quickly to mix. Whisk continuously, pour in the milk. Cook and whisk till becoming smooth.
- Put in the pepper and bouillon, and combine them well. Lower the heat to low. Cook, whisk once in a while, for 5-10 minutes till the mixture thickens.
- Whisk in cheese, and cook till melted. Put in green beans, mushrooms and chicken. Cook for 3-5 minutes till thoroughly heated.
- Add the chicken mixture into the slightly greased 9x13-in. baking dish. Divide the biscuits into 2 layers, creating 10 circles. Arrange the biscuits on top of the chicken mixture.
- Bake, while uncovering, at 205 degrees C (400 degrees F) for roughly 10-12 minutes till the biscuits turn golden.

Nutrition Information

- Calories: 448 calories;
- Sodium: 1457
- Total Carbohydrate: 42.8
- Cholesterol: 50
- Protein: 23.7
- Total Fat: 20.2

499. Chicken, Fennel And Mushroom Soup

Serving: 4 | Prep: 10mins | Cook: 25mins | Ready in:

Ingredients

- 2 skinless, boneless chicken breast halves
- 1 tablespoon olive oil
- 1 teaspoon butter
- 1 teaspoon lemon pepper
- 1 bulb fennel, trimmed and thinly sliced
- 1/4 cup cream sherry
- 1 1/2 cups sliced crimini mushrooms
- 1/4 cup diced red bell pepper
- 3 tablespoons finely minced fresh parsley
- 1 cup buttermilk
- 1/2 cup half-and-half cream
- 1 1/2 cups water
- 2 teaspoons chicken soup base

Direction

- Put butter and oil in a saucepan and heat it over medium-high heat. Brown both sides of the chicken. Adjust the heat to medium. Add the cream sherry, lemon pepper, and fennel. Simmer the mixture until the chicken is cooked through but not dry. Once the chicken is cooked, take it out of the pan and put it aside to cool.
- While waiting for the chicken to cool, add the parsley, red pepper, water, half-and-half, mushrooms, chicken soup base, and buttermilk; stir. Tear the chicken into bite-sized pieces. Bring the chicken pieces back into the soup. Heat the soup until warmed through but not boiling. Take note that the peppers and mushrooms must still be firm.

Nutrition Information

- Calories: 221 calories;
- Cholesterol: 51
- Protein: 19.5
- Total Fat: 9.5
- Sodium: 763
- Total Carbohydrate: 13.4

500. Chicken, Sweet Potato, And Mushroom Stew

Serving: 4 | Prep: 20mins | Cook: 45mins | Ready in:

Ingredients

- 3 tablespoons olive oil
- 1 large onion, chopped
- 2 carrots, shredded
- 1 (8 ounce) package baby bella mushrooms, halved
- 1 chicken breast, cut into small pieces, or more to taste
- 5 sweet potatoes, quartered, or more to taste
- 4 cloves garlic, minced
- 3 cups chicken broth
- salt and ground black pepper to taste
- 1 (15 ounce) can kidney beans, drained and rinsed

Direction

- Over medium heat, heat olive oil in a 5-quart saucepan. Put in onion; cook and stir about 5 minutes until onion turns translucent. Add carrots; cook and stir for 3 to 4 minutes until softened. Stir in mushrooms; cook 4-5 minutes until browned.
- In the saucepan, add chicken breast; cook and stir 5-7 minutes until juices run clear. Mix in garlic and sweet potatoes. Pour in broth. Add salt and pepper to season. Cook for 25 minutes approximately until sweet potatoes are soft. Add kidney beans and stir; cook about 3 minutes until heated through.

Nutrition Information

- Calories: 559 calories;
- Sodium: 502
- Total Carbohydrate: 97.4
- Cholesterol: 15
- Protein: 19.4
- Total Fat: 11.6

501. Chicken Stuffed Mushrooms

Serving: 6 | Prep: | Cook: | Ready in:

Ingredients

- 1 pound medium button or mini-bella mushrooms
- 2 tablespoons unsalted butter
- 1 large onion, finely chopped
- 1 large clove garlic, minced
- 1 cooked boneless chicken breast half, finely diced*
- 1 1/2 tablespoons Diamond Crystal® Kosher Salt
- 3/4 teaspoon coarsely ground pepper
- 1 tablespoon all-purpose flour
- 1 cup whipping cream
- 5 tablespoons chopped fresh parsley, divided
- finely shredded mozzarella or Parmesan cheese (optional)

Direction

- Heat oven to 350 °F.
- Eliminate stems from mushrooms, but do not discard. Scoop out insides of mushrooms with a small melon baller, leaving at least half shell to make more room for filling. Chop mushroom stems and centers finely.
- In a large skillet, melt butter over medium heat. Add garlic and onion; cook for about 1 minute. Mix in chopped mushrooms, chicken, pepper, and Diamond Crystal(R) Kosher Salt. Cook and stir for an addition of 3 minutes. Blend in 3 tablespoons parsley, cream and flour. Cook and stir until bubbly and thickened. Take away from heat.
- Spoon mushroom caps evenly with the mixture. Place in lightly oiled, shallow baking dish. Bake for approximately 10 minutes. Put leftover 2 tablespoons parsley on top and jazz up with mozzarella or Parmesan cheese for garnish, if wished. Bake for about 5 to 10 minutes or until hot and cheese melts. If you want, garnish with additional parsley.

Nutrition Information

- Calories: 228 calories;
- Total Fat: 19.8
- Sodium: 1476
- Total Carbohydrate: 7.6
- Cholesterol: 73
- Protein: 7

502. Chicken Stuffed Shells With Sherry Sauce

Serving: 4 | Prep: 30mins | Cook: 30mins | Ready in:

Ingredients

- 1 tablespoon olive oil
- 4 ounces button mushrooms, sliced
- 2 ounces shiitake mushrooms, thinly sliced
- 1/4 cup dry sherry
- 1 tablespoon olive oil
- 2 skinless, boneless chicken breast halves
- 1 teaspoon minced garlic
- 1/2 teaspoon dried thyme
- 1/2 cup chicken broth
- 1 cup ricotta cheese
- 1/4 cup shredded Gruyere cheese
- 1 (8 ounce) package jumbo pasta shells
- 2 tablespoons butter
- 2 tablespoons all-purpose flour
- 1/4 cup dry sherry
- 1/2 teaspoon salt
- 1/2 teaspoon white pepper
- 3/4 cup milk
- 1/4 cup shredded Gruyere cheese
- 3 tablespoons grated Parmesan cheese

Direction

- Heat a tablespoon of olive oil in a nonstick skillet over moderately-high heat. Add shiitake and button mushrooms and cook for 2 minutes, mixing continuously. Mix in a quarter cup of sherry and keep cooking till liquid has cooked down by half and mushrooms are tender. Using a slotted spoon, take mushrooms out; reserve. Set mushroom sherry liquid aside; reserve.
- Over moderately-high heat, heat a tablespoon of olive oil in same skillet. In pan, put the garlic and chicken breasts and brown chicken on each side. Scatter thyme over, add chicken broth, reduce the heat and place a cover on skillet. Allow to simmer for 10 minutes till chicken is not pink anymore and cooked through. Take chicken out of broth and allow to cool. Set broth aside; reserve.
- Pulse in food processor or use 2 forks to shred the cooled chicken. In big bowl, mix together mushroom mixture, 1/4 cup Gruyere, ricotta and shredded chicken till well incorporated.
- Mix reserved sherry-mushroom liquid and reserved chicken broth to equal a half cup. Remove any oil that floats on the surface.
- Boil a big pot of slightly salted water. Put the pasta and cook till al dente, about 8 to 10 minutes; drain.
- Preheat the oven to 175 °C or 350 °F. Oil a 9x13 in. baking dish. Liquify butter over moderate heat in a small saucepan. Add the flour all at once, and using whisk, mix briskly to create a roux. Put in a quarter cup of sherry and reserved mushroom liquid or broth, a small amount at a time, mixing continuously till smooth. Scatter with pepper and salt, turn the heat down to low, and mix continuously till thickened. Gradually mix in a quarter cup Gruyere and milk till smooth and fully blended.
- Fill approximately 2 tablespoons of chicken mixture into each pasta shell; and in prepped baking dish, set the shells tightly packed in 1 layer. Scoop sauce on top of shells and scatter Parmesan over top. Bake for 30 minutes, or till bubbly and heated through. Serve right away.

Nutrition Information

- Calories: 545 calories;

- Total Fat: 22.8
- Sodium: 662
- Total Carbohydrate: 55.5
- Cholesterol: 67
- Protein: 26.4

503. Chinese Chicken Rice Salad

Serving: 6 | Prep: 15mins | Cook: 45mins | Ready in:

Ingredients

- 1 cup brown rice
- 2 1/2 cups water
- 2 tablespoons olive oil
- 3 tablespoons lemon juice
- 3 tablespoons soy sauce
- 1 teaspoon minced fresh ginger root
- 1 teaspoon teriyaki sauce
- salt and black pepper to taste
- 2 cups chopped, cooked chicken breast meat
- 1 cup sliced celery
- 1 cup sliced water chestnuts
- 1 cup sliced fresh mushrooms
- 1/2 cup diced green onion
- 1/2 cup diced red bell pepper

Direction

- Boil water and rice together in a pot. Turn to low heat, let it simmer, covered, for 45mins until the rice absorbs the water. Set the rice aside to cool.
- Prepare the dressing. In a bowl, mix teriyaki sauce, oil, ginger, lemon juice, soy sauce, and together; sprinkle pepper and salt to season.
- Stir chicken and cooked rice together in a big bowl. Toss in red pepper, celery, green onion, water chestnuts, mushrooms, and the dressing to coat evenly. Place in the refrigerator, covered, for 8hrs or overnight. Gently toss then serve.

Nutrition Information

- Calories: 231 calories;
- Protein: 17.1
- Total Fat: 6.7
- Sodium: 606
- Total Carbohydrate: 25.5
- Cholesterol: 36

504. Chinese Clay Pot Chicken Rice

Serving: 4 | Prep: 15mins | Cook: 45mins | Ready in:

Ingredients

- 1 whole chicken breast, cut into big chunks
- 6 chicken wings, cut into thirds, tips discarded
- 1 cup dark soy sauce
- 1 tablespoon sesame oil
- 8 cloves garlic, smashed
- ground white pepper to taste
- 2 links lop chong (Chinese-style sausage)
- 6 dried shiitake mushrooms
- 2 tablespoons vegetable oil
- 1/2 cup dark soy sauce
- 1 2/3 cups jasmine rice
- 5 tablespoons chile paste
- 2 tablespoons grated fresh ginger root
- 2 tablespoons fresh lime juice
- 1 cup shredded iceberg lettuce

Direction

- In a mixing bowl, combine garlic, a cup of dark soy sauce, chicken wings, chicken breast, and sesame oil. Add white pepper for seasoning. Prepare the Chinese sausages (sliced on an angle) and mix in the chicken mixture. Cover the container and leave to chill for at least 10 minutes. Pour hot water over well-rinsed shiitake mushrooms. Let the mushrooms be submerged for about 15 minutes or until they are bloated and well-soaked. Drain off the mushrooms and reserve

the liquid. Discard the mushroom stalks and slice the tops in half and set aside.
- In a large and deep pan set over medium heat, heat oil and cook the chicken in the hot oil for 7 to 10 minutes or until the chicken juices run clear and they are no longer pink in the center. Top the chicken with a drizzle of half a cup of dark soy sauce.
- Rinse the rice in water until the water runs almost clear and completely drain. In a non-stick skillet, combine 1 and a half of the reserved mushroom liquid and rice. Let the mixture come to a boil. Adjust the heat to low. Cover the pan and allow the mixture to simmer for 10 minutes while keeping the heat on. Mix in the mushrooms and chicken mixture and take off the heat. Let the pot stand while covered for 15 to 20 minutes or until the rice is completely cooked and tender.
- In a small bowl, combine ginger, chili paste, and lime juice. Top chicken rice with a drizzle of the sauce and shredded lettuce before serving.

Nutrition Information

- Calories: 725 calories;
- Total Fat: 29.2
- Sodium: 5990
- Total Carbohydrate: 87.7
- Cholesterol: 46
- Protein: 34.2

505. Chinese Ham Stew

Serving: 8 | Prep: | Cook: |Ready in:

Ingredients

- 1 (5 pound) pork leg, cut into bite size pieces
- 4 ounces dried wood ear mushrooms
- 5 tablespoons soy sauce
- 10 cloves minced garlic
- 4 cups water

Direction

- Wash garlic, leaving skin intact; wash the mushrooms and allow to sit in water until tender.
- In a large pot, place garlic, soy sauce, mushrooms and pork. Add water, set the heat to low and allow to simmer for 60 to 90 minutes or until a thermometer inserted in the center of pork shows 160°F (70°C)

Nutrition Information

- Calories: 437 calories;
- Protein: 55.9
- Total Fat: 17.4
- Sodium: 686
- Total Carbohydrate: 12.4
- Cholesterol: 172

506. Chipotle Burgers With Avocado Salsa

Serving: 4 | Prep: 30mins | Cook: 10mins |Ready in:

Ingredients

- 1 bunch fresh cilantro, chopped
- 1 pound ground beef
- 1 (7 ounce) can chipotle peppers in adobo sauce
- 1 cup chopped fresh mushrooms
- 1 tablespoon Worcestershire sauce
- 1 avocado - peeled, pitted, and diced
- 1 onion, diced
- 1 tomato, diced
- 2 jalapeno peppers, seeded and chopped
- 1 lime, juiced
- salt and ground black pepper to taste
- 4 onion rolls, split

Direction

- Preheat the outdoor grill for medium-high heat and grease grate lightly.
- Into a big bowl, put half of the chopped cilantro and combine with Worcestershire sauce, mushrooms, chipotle peppers in adobo sauce and ground beef. Reserve the rest of cilantro. Shape beef mixture into 4 patties.
- In a bowl with black pepper, salt, lime juice, jalapeno peppers, tomato, onion and avocado, gently toss the rest of cilantro.
- On the prepped grill, let the burgers grill for 5 minutes each side till browned and not pink anymore on the inside. Serve burgers on onion rolls with avocado salsa on top.

Nutrition Information

- Calories: 503 calories;
- Total Fat: 24.6
- Sodium: 593
- Total Carbohydrate: 42.3
- Cholesterol: 71
- Protein: 28

507. Chunky Broccoli Cheese Soup

Serving: 10 | Prep: 5mins | Cook: 20mins | Ready in:

Ingredients

- 1 large onion, diced
- 1/2 cup butter
- 1 (10.75 ounce) can condensed cream of chicken soup
- 1 (10.75 ounce) can condensed cream of mushroom soup
- 1 (10.75 ounce) can condensed cream of celery soup
- 2 (10 ounce) packages chopped frozen broccoli, thawed
- 2 (10 ounce) cans chunk chicken, drained
- 1 (2 pound) loaf processed cheese, cubed
- 1 (16 ounce) can sliced mushrooms, drained
- 4 cups milk

Direction

- Cook onion in butter over medium heat in a large soup pot until onion is translucent. Mix in milk, mushrooms, processed cheese, chicken, broccoli, cream of celery, cream of mushroom, and cream of chicken. Cook for 10 to 20 minutes until broccoli is tender and cheese is melted, stirring frequently when cooking. Serve right away.

Nutrition Information

- Calories: 630 calories;
- Total Fat: 43.7
- Sodium: 2368
- Total Carbohydrate: 24.6
- Cholesterol: 145
- Protein: 36.5

508. Cindy's Beef Tips

Serving: 6 | Prep: 15mins | Cook: 3hours15mins | Ready in:

Ingredients

- 1 cup all-purpose flour
- 1 teaspoon seasoned salt
- 1 teaspoon ground black pepper
- 1/2 teaspoon garlic powder
- 1/2 teaspoon onion powder
- 1 pound cubed beef stew meat
- 1/4 cup canola oil, divided
- 1 large onion, coarsely chopped
- 3 cups beef broth
- 1 (10.75 ounce) can fat free condensed cream of mushroom soup
- 1 (10.75 ounce) can skim milk
- 1 (8 ounce) can sliced mushrooms, drained
- 2 tablespoons cornstarch (optional)
- 1 tablespoon water (optional)

Direction

- Put onion powder, garlic powder, black pepper, seasoned salt and flour into a large resealable plastic zipper bag. Mix the seasonings and flour together; include in beef stew meat. Seal the bag; shake for several times so that the seasoned flour coat the beef cubes properly. Brush off any excess flour.
- Place a large skillet on medium-high heat; heat half of the canola oil. Fry in half of the beef cubes for 5-10 minutes, turning over till nicely browned on all sides. Take the browned beef away and place on a plate; repeat with the remaining beef cubes and canola oil. Transfer onto a plate; cook while stirring onion in the hot skillet for around 5 minutes, or till translucent.
- Whisk skim milk, mushroom soup and beef broth together till smooth. Transfer the beef cubes back to the skillet along with any juices on the plate; include in mushrooms; transfer the broth mixture over the mushrooms and beef. Lower the heat; simmer for around 3 hours, or till the meat is very tender. To make a thicker gravy, combine water and cornstarch into a smooth paste; mix into the gravy. Simmer for around 2 minutes to thicken.

Nutrition Information

- Calories: 343 calories;
- Total Fat: 15.5
- Sodium: 1130
- Total Carbohydrate: 29.5
- Cholesterol: 43
- Protein: 20.6

509.   Classic Meatloaf

Serving: 10 | Prep: 30mins | Cook: 45mins | Ready in:

Ingredients

- Meatloaf Ingredients:
- 1 carrot, coarsely chopped
- 1 rib celery, coarsely chopped
- 1/2 onion, coarsely chopped
- 1/2 red bell pepper, coarsely chopped
- 4 white mushrooms, coarsely chopped
- 3 cloves garlic, coarsely chopped
- 2 1/2 pounds ground chuck
- 1 tablespoon Worcestershire sauce
- 1 egg, beaten
- 1 teaspoon dried Italian herbs
- 2 teaspoons salt
- 1 teaspoon ground black pepper
- 1/2 teaspoon cayenne pepper
- 1 cup plain bread crumbs
- 1 teaspoon olive oil
- Glaze Ingredients:
- 2 tablespoons brown sugar
- 2 tablespoons ketchup
- 2 tablespoons Dijon mustard
- hot pepper sauce to taste

Direction

- Set the oven to 325°F and start preheating.
- In a food processor, place garlic, mushrooms, red bell pepper, onion, celery and carrot; pulse until very finely chopped, almost to a puree. In a large mixing bowl, place minced vegetables; combine in egg, Worcestershire sauce and ground chuck. Add cayenne pepper, black pepper, salt and Italian herb. Using a wooden spoon, combine gently to incorporate egg and vegetables into the meat. Add bread crumbs. Mix in the crumbs gently with your fingertips for about a minute just until combined.
- Shape the meatloaf into a ball. In a baking dish, place olive oil and arrange meat balls into the dish. Form the ball into a loaf, about 4 inches in height and 6 inches across.
- Bake in the prepared oven for about 15 minutes until the meatloaf turns hot.
- At the meantime, combine hot sauce, Dijon mustard, ketchup and brown sugar in a small bowl. Stir until brown sugar dissolves.

- Take the meatloaf out of the oven. Smooth this glaze on top its top, using the back of the spoon; pull a small amount of glaze down the sides of meatloaf, using the back to the spoon.
- Transfer the meatloaf back to the oven; bake for 30-40 minutes more until the inside is no longer pink and glaze has baked onto the meatloaf. The inserted instant-read thermometer into the thickest part of the loaf should register at least 160°F (70°C). Depending on the thickness and shape of the meatloaf, cooking time will be different.

Nutrition Information

- Calories: 284 calories;
- Sodium: 755
- Total Carbohydrate: 14.8
- Cholesterol: 85
- Protein: 21.6
- Total Fat: 14.9

510. Company Liver With Onions

Serving: 6 | Prep: 15mins | Cook: 33mins | Ready in:

Ingredients

- 1/2 cup butter
- 2 onions, sliced
- 1 1/2 pounds calf's liver
- 1/2 teaspoon salt
- 1/8 teaspoon freshly ground black pepper
- 1 (8 ounce) can mushrooms, with liquid
- 2 cups sour cream
- 1 teaspoon Worcestershire sauce

Direction

- Melt the butter in a big skillet on medium-high heat. Cook and stir the onions for about 7 minutes until it becomes tender. Sprinkle pepper and salt to season the slices of liver, then add it to the skillet. Cook the slices of liver until brown, flipping once, for about 5 minutes. Pour in the mushrooms with their liquid. Lower the heat, put on the cover and let it simmer for 8-10 minutes. Mix in Worcestershire sauce and sour cream and keep on simmering for an additional of 8-10 minutes. Serve right away.

Nutrition Information

- Calories: 449 calories;
- Sodium: 567
- Total Carbohydrate: 12.5
- Cholesterol: 344
- Protein: 22.5
- Total Fat: 34.9

511. Coq Au Vin Alla Italiana

Serving: 8 | Prep: 10mins | Cook: 50mins | Ready in:

Ingredients

- 4 pounds dark meat chicken pieces
- 1 tablespoon vegetable oil
- 5 cloves crushed garlic
- 1/2 cup all-purpose flour
- 1 teaspoon poultry seasoning
- 3 (4 ounce) links sweet Italian sausage, sliced
- 1 cup chopped onion
- 3 carrots, sliced
- 1/2 pound fresh mushrooms, sliced
- 1/2 teaspoon dried rosemary
- 1 cup red wine
- 1 (14.5 ounce) can whole peeled tomatoes
- salt and pepper to taste

Direction

- Heat oil in a big skillet. Add 1/2 garlic. Use poultry seasoning to season flour. In flour, dredge chicken parts. Brown for 4-5 minutes in skillet. Add sausage. Sauté for several

minutes. Add leftover garlic, rosemary, mushrooms, carrots and onion; mix all together.
- Add tomatoes and wine; mix. Cover. Simmer for 25 minutes on low heat. Season with pepper and salt to taste; simmer for 10 minutes more. Cool for 10 minutes, covered. Serve.

Nutrition Information

- Calories: 616 calories;
- Sodium: 519
- Total Carbohydrate: 20.4
- Cholesterol: 150
- Protein: 43.5
- Total Fat: 36.9

512. Corey's Steak, Cheese, And Mushroom Subs

Serving: 4 | Prep: 10mins | Cook: 11mins | Ready in:

Ingredients

- 1 tablespoon olive oil
- 1 pound fresh mushrooms, sliced
- 1 1/2 pounds shaved steak
- 1 teaspoon soy sauce, or to taste
- 1 pinch garlic powder, or to taste
- 1 pinch onion powder, or to taste
- salt and ground black pepper to taste
- 4 (6 inch) hoagie rolls, split lengthwise
- 8 slices sharp American cheese

Direction

- In a skillet, heat olive oil on medium heat. Put in mushrooms and cook for 5 minutes until it gets tender. Set the heat to high, put in the steak and taste with pepper, salt, onion powder, garlic powder and soy sauce. Cook for 5 minutes while stirring until it gets hot and starts sizzling. Remove it from heat and cover.
- Put the rack into with about 6 inches apart from the heat source, preheat the broiler in the oven.
- Toast the rolls for 1 or 2 minutes with the broiler. On each roll, put 2 slices of American cheese and pour steak-mushroom mixture over the roll.

Nutrition Information

- Calories: 732 calories;
- Cholesterol: 131
- Protein: 42.8
- Total Fat: 43.2
- Sodium: 1432
- Total Carbohydrate: 42.8

513. Corn And Porcini Mushroom Cornbread Dressing

Serving: 12 | Prep: 20mins | Cook: 33mins | Ready in:

Ingredients

- cooking spray
- 1/2 cup dried porcini mushrooms
- 1 cup hot tap water
- 3/4 cup all-purpose flour
- 3/4 cup yellow cornmeal
- 1/4 cup white sugar
- 1 teaspoon fine salt
- 1/2 teaspoon baking soda
- 1/4 teaspoon freshly ground black pepper
- 1 pinch cayenne pepper, or to taste
- 1/2 cup unsalted butter
- 2 large eggs
- 1 cup buttermilk
- 1/4 cup milk
- 1 (16 ounce) package frozen corn, thawed and drained
- 1/4 cup chopped green onions

Direction

- In a small bowl, put mushrooms, soak in hot water, allow to submerge for half an hour till mushrooms have softened. Take off mushrooms from bowl, drain by squeezing, and finely chop.
- Preheat the oven to 175 °C or 350 °F. With cooking spray, oil a baking dish, 9x13-inch in size.
- In a big bowl beat cayenne pepper, black pepper, baking soda, salt, sugar, cornmeal and flour.
- In a big skillet, liquefy butter over medium heat. Put chopped mushrooms and mix for 3 to 4 minutes till cooked slightly and softened. Take off from heat and let it cool for 10 minutes.
- Mix milk, buttermilk and eggs into the flour mixture. Put corn and mushroom mixture; mix till well combined. Fold in the green onions. To the prepared baking dish, put batter and pat on a flat work surface for 2 to 3 times to get rid of any air bubbles.
- In the prepared oven, bake for 30 to 35 minutes till golden on top. An inserted paring knife into the middle should come out clean.

Nutrition Information

- Calories: 215 calories;
- Total Fat: 9.5
- Sodium: 287
- Total Carbohydrate: 28.2
- Cholesterol: 53
- Protein: 5.8

514. Crab Stuffed Mushrooms II

Serving: 20 | Prep: 20mins | Cook: 15mins | Ready in:

Ingredients

- 1 pound large mushrooms
- 3 tablespoons butter
- 2 tablespoons finely chopped onion
- 1 (3 ounce) package cream cheese, softened
- 2 tablespoons prepared Dijon-style mustard
- 6 1/2 ounces crabmeat
- 1/4 cup chopped water chestnuts
- 2 tablespoons chopped pimento peppers
- 4 tablespoons grated Parmesan cheese

Direction

- Prepare the oven by preheating to 400°F (200°C).
- Take the stems off from the mushrooms, keeping the caps. Then chop the stems. Place butter in a medium saucepan and dissolve. Brush with melted butter the mushroom caps.
- Using the rest of the butter, stir and cook the onions and chopped mushrooms until soft. Slowly stir the mustard and cream cheese into the saucepan. Keep on stirring until smooth. Mix in the pimentos, water chestnuts, and crab meat. Heat until warm.
- Fill the mushroom caps with the crab meat mixture. Dust the filled caps with Parmesan cheese. Place the caps in a shallow pan, then bake for 10 to 15 minutes at 400° or until hot.

Nutrition Information

- Calories: 52 calories;
- Sodium: 110
- Total Carbohydrate: 1.6
- Cholesterol: 18
- Protein: 3.4
- Total Fat: 3.7

515. Crab And Lobster Stuffed Mushrooms

Serving: 8 | Prep: 10mins | Cook: 10mins | Ready in:

Ingredients

- 3/4 cup melted butter, divided

- 1 pound fresh mushrooms, stems removed
- 1 cup crushed seasoned croutons
- 1 cup shredded mozzarella cheese
- 1 (6 ounce) can crabmeat, drained
- 1 pound lobster tail, cleaned and chopped
- 3 tablespoons minced garlic
- 1/4 cup shredded mozzarella cheese (optional)

Direction

- Preheat an oven to 190 degrees C (375 degrees F). Use about 1/4 cup of melted butter to rub a large baking sheet. Spread a single layer of mushroom caps on the baking sheet.
- Combine crushed croutons, garlic, remaining 1/2 cup of butter, lobster, crabmeat, and shredded cheese in a medium bowl. Place a spoonful of mixture into mushroom caps where stems were in place.
- Bake in the preheated oven for about 10 to 12 minutes or until browned lightly on top. If desired, drizzle with more cheese and then serve while still hot!

Nutrition Information

- Calories: 310 calories;
- Sodium: 535
- Total Carbohydrate: 6.9
- Cholesterol: 130
- Protein: 21.9
- Total Fat: 22

516. Crab And Mushroom Enchiladas

Serving: 8 | Prep: 15mins | Cook: 20mins | Ready in:

Ingredients

- 1 pound imitation crabmeat, chopped
- 1 (10 ounce) can red enchilada sauce
- 1 (10.75 ounce) can condensed cream of mushroom soup
- 1/2 pound fresh mushrooms, sliced
- 1 (8 ounce) package shredded Mexican-style cheese blend
- 8 (10 inch) flour tortillas

Direction

- Preheat an oven to 190°C/375°F. Grease medium baking dish lightly.
- Mix 1/2 of the cheese, mushrooms, cream of mushroom soup, red enchilada sauce and imitation crabmeat in big bowl. Roll even amount of mixture in every tortilla. Put filled tortillas in the prepared baking dish; cover using enchilada sauce. Put leftover cheese on top.
- In preheated oven, bake till cheese is bubbly for 20 minutes. Before serving, let sit for 5 minutes.

Nutrition Information

- Calories: 465 calories;
- Total Fat: 21.1
- Sodium: 1361
- Total Carbohydrate: 50.4
- Cholesterol: 51
- Protein: 18.5

517. Crab Stuffed Filet Mignon With Whiskey Peppercorn Sauce

Serving: 4 | Prep: 1hours | Cook: 30mins | Ready in:

Ingredients

- CRAB STUFFING:
- 2 tablespoons olive oil
- 1 teaspoon minced onion
- 1 teaspoon minced green onion
- 1 teaspoon minced garlic

- 1 teaspoon minced celery
- 1 teaspoon minced green bell pepper
- 2 tablespoons shrimp stock or water
- 1 (6 ounce) can crab meat, drained
- 2 tablespoons bread crumbs
- 1 teaspoon Cajun seasoning
- PEPPERCORN SAUCE
- 1 1/4 cups beef broth
- 1 teaspoon cracked black pepper
- 1 fluid ounce whiskey
- 1 cup heavy cream
- STEAKS:
- 4 (6 ounce) filet mignon steaks
- 4 slices bacon, cooked lightly
- salt and cracked black pepper to taste
- 1 tablespoon olive oil
- 1 clove garlic, minced
- 1 teaspoon minced shallot
- 1 cup crimini mushrooms, sliced
- 1 fluid ounce whiskey
- 1 teaspoon Dijon mustard

Direction

- Making crab stuffing: In a big skillet, heat 2 tablespoons of olive oil. Sauté green pepper, celery, garlic, green onion and onion until tender. Stir Cajun seasoning, bread crumbs, crab meat and shrimp stock in. Move it away from heat. Set it aside.
- Preparing peppercorn sauce: Over medium heat, combine cracked black pepper, and beef broth in a small saucepan. Let it simmer, frequently stirring, until reduced to 1 cup. Put 1 cup of cream and 1 ounce whiskey. Continue simmering until reduced to 1 cup, then, move it away from heat, setting it aside.
- Preparing the steaks: In the side of each steak, slice a pocket and stuff it with crab stuffing generously. Wrap bacon around side and use toothpicks to secure it. Use pepper and salt to season and set it aside. In a big cast iron skillet, heat olive oil over medium heat. For a minute, sauté shallot and garlic, then, stir mushrooms in. Sauté until tender. Remove mushroom mixture. Set it aside.
- In a skillet, cook steaks into desired doneness. Take out from the skillet, keep it warm. Use 1 ounce whiskey to deglaze the skillet. Reduce heat, then, stir in Dijon mustard and peppercorn sauce. Mix in mushroom mixture then, reduce sauce until it thickens. Take the toothpicks out and bacon from steaks. Arrange steaks into a plate. Put sauce on top.

Nutrition Information

- Calories: 748 calories;
- Total Fat: 57.3
- Sodium: 1175
- Total Carbohydrate: 6.7
- Cholesterol: 215
- Protein: 41.4

518. Crab Stuffed Mushrooms

Serving: 10 | Prep: | Cook: | Ready in:

Ingredients

- 1 pound large fresh mushrooms
- 4 tablespoons butter, divided
- 1/4 cup Kikkoman Panko Bread Crumbs
- 1/2 cup imitation crabmeat, flaked
- 1/4 teaspoon onion powder
- 1/8 teaspoon salt
- 2 tablespoons Kikkoman Panko Bread Crumbs
- 1/8 teaspoon black pepper

Direction

- Heat oven to 375 °F. Use a damp paper towel to wipe mushrooms gently. Take and finely chop stems. In a large skillet, melt 3 tablespoons of the butter over medium heat. Add mushroom stems and cook for 5 minutes or until tender. Take away from heat and stir in the shredded crab, 1/4 cup of the panko, onion powder, pepper and salt.

- Fill crab mixture into mushrooms caps and arrange them on unoiled baking sheet with rim, stuffing side facing up. Mix panko and remaining butter in a small bowl. Sprinkle the mixture evenly over the mushroom tops and bake for approximately 15 minutes.

Nutrition Information

- Calories: 770 calories;
- Total Carbohydrate: 158.3
- Cholesterol: 14
- Protein: 20.9
- Total Fat: 8.1
- Sodium: 392

519. Crabby Cliff's Mushroom Puffs

Serving: 18 | Prep: 20mins | Cook: 20mins | Ready in:

Ingredients

- 2 tablespoons olive oil
- 3 cups fresh chopped mushrooms
- 2 green onions, chopped
- 1 clove garlic, crushed
- 1/2 teaspoon ground cayenne pepper
- 4 ounces cream cheese, softened
- 1 (6 ounce) can crabmeat, drained and flaked
- 1 (17.5 ounce) package frozen puff pastry sheets, thawed

Direction

- Prepare the oven by preheating to 400°F (200°C).
- Heat olive oil in a medium saucepan set over medium heat. Place in the cayenne pepper, garlic, green onions, and mushrooms then stir. Cook for 10 minutes, or until softened. Place the mushroom mixture into a medium bowl. Mix in the crabmeat and cream cheese.
- Roll each pastry sheet into a 12x12-inch square on a lightly floured flat surface. Slice each sheet into nine 4x4-inch squares. Put 1 tablespoon of the mushroom mixture onto each pastry square. Then fold the squares by bringing the corners to the middle, making an X. Transfer the squares to a medium baking sheet.
- Bake in the preheated oven for 20 minutes, or until golden brown.

Nutrition Information

- Calories: 199 calories;
- Cholesterol: 15
- Protein: 4.9
- Total Fat: 14.3
- Sodium: 119
- Total Carbohydrate: 13.2

520. Crazy Good Stuffing And Baked Chops

Serving: 6 | Prep: 20mins | Cook: 55mins | Ready in:

Ingredients

- 1/2 pound sliced fresh mushrooms, or more to taste
- 1 onion, chopped
- 1/4 cup dry sherry, or to taste
- 2 tablespoons all-purpose flour, or as needed
- 2/3 cup milk, or as needed
- 1 (10.75 ounce) can condensed cream of mushroom soup
- 1 (14 ounce) package dry bread stuffing mix
- 1/4 cup butter
- 6 boneless pork chops
- 1/2 cup water
- 1 (10.75 ounce) can condensed cream of mushroom soup
- 1/2 (10.75 ounce) can milk

Direction

- Start preheating the oven to 375°F (190°C). Spray cooking spray over a 9x13 inches baking dish.
- In a large saucepan, cook while stirring onion and mushrooms over medium-low heat for 5 mins or until mushrooms have given up the liquid and turn soft. Mix in sherry, boil and simmer for 2-3 more mins until onions become tender. Sprinkle the mixture with flour. Cook until thick while stirring constantly. Mix in 2/3 cup of milk gradually to create the creamy gravy, stirring constantly to prevent it from burning. Mix in dry stuffing and one can of cream of mushroom soup. Simmer, then cook for 5 mins until stuffing mix becomes moist.
- Melt butter in a large pan over medium heat until no longer foamy. Pan-fry chops for 5 mins on each side until browned but not cooked through. In the prepared baking dish, place chops. Stir the water into skillet, boil, then scrape and dissolve all the remaining flavor bits in skillet. Allow mixture to boil for 10 mins until reduced by half. Put skillet drippings into stuffing mix. Then mix thoroughly.
- Scoop up the generous amounts of the stuffing then mound on each chop. Whisk one can of the cream of the mushroom soup with half of soup can of the milk together. Cover each chop with soup mixture.
- Bake in prepared oven for 20 mins until the chops are cooked through and tender. An instant-read thermometer should register at least 165°F (74°C) when inserted into middle of chop.

Nutrition Information

- Calories: 633 calories;
- Sodium: 1878
- Total Carbohydrate: 66.1
- Cholesterol: 84
- Protein: 35.9
- Total Fat: 24.1

521. Cream Cheese Chicken

Serving: 6 | Prep: 15mins | Cook: 15mins | Ready in:

Ingredients

- 1 teaspoon butter
- 8 ounces fresh mushrooms, sliced
- 6 ounces cream cheese, softened
- 6 skinless, boneless chicken breast halves
- 1 cup brown sugar
- 1/2 cup Dijon mustard
- 1/2 cup chopped walnuts

Direction

- Preheat the oven to 230 degrees C (450 degrees F).
- Melt the butter on medium heat in the skillet. Sauté the mushrooms till soft. Lower the heat, and whisk in the cream cheese till melted. Take out of the heat.
- Pound the chicken breasts thin using the meat mallet. Spread with the mushroom mixture, and roll them up. In the small-sized bowl, combine the Dijon mustard and brown sugar together. Press the mustard mixture onto the chicken. Roll the chicken into the chopped nuts. Add into the baking plate.
- Bake in the preheated oven till the juices come out clear and the chicken is not pink anymore or for 15-20 minutes.

Nutrition Information

- Calories: 468 calories;
- Total Carbohydrate: 43.5
- Cholesterol: 101
- Protein: 32.1
- Total Fat: 18.7
- Sodium: 678

522. Cream Of Mushroom Chicken

Serving: 7 | Prep: | Cook: | Ready in:

Ingredients

- 2 tablespoons butter
- 1 (10.75 ounce) can condensed cream of mushroom soup
- 1 1/4 cups water, or as needed
- 1 (12 fluid ounce) can evaporated milk
- 1 onion, chopped
- salt and pepper to taste
- 2 pounds skinless, boneless chicken breast halves - cubed
- 1 (6 ounce) can sliced mushrooms, drained

Direction

- Melt butter or margarine in a large saucepan. Add milk, water, and soup. Mix together over medium heat. Add pepper, salt, and onion; bring to a boil.
- When mixture begins to boil, put in chicken meat; let simmer altogether until chicken is thoroughly cooked. Add sliced mushrooms; boil over medium heat, stirring constantly, for about 5 minutes. Serve.

Nutrition Information

- Calories: 294 calories;
- Total Fat: 11.6
- Sodium: 549
- Total Carbohydrate: 11
- Cholesterol: 100
- Protein: 35

523. Creamy Chicken Marsala Fettuccine

Serving: 4 | Prep: 30mins | Cook: 40mins | Ready in:

Ingredients

- 4 skinless, boneless chicken breast halves
- 1/2 cup all-purpose flour
- 1/4 teaspoon paprika
- 1/4 teaspoon cayenne pepper
- salt and freshly ground black pepper (optional)
- 2 tablespoons olive oil
- 2 tablespoons butter, divided
- 1 sweet onion, chopped
- 1 cup shiitake mushrooms, cut in half
- 1 cup fresh oyster mushrooms, cut in half
- 1 cup cremini mushrooms, cut in half
- 1 (12 ounce) package dry fettuccine pasta
- 2 tablespoons butter
- 2 tablespoons minced garlic
- 3/4 cup Marsala wine
- 1 (8 ounce) container mascarpone cheese
- 2 tablespoons Dijon mustard
- 1 cup chicken broth
- 2 tablespoons chopped fresh flat-leaf parsley

Direction

- Arrange chicken breasts between two sheets of the heavy plastic (resealable freezer bags could also do the trick well) onto a solid and flat surface. Use smooth side of the meat mallet to pound the chicken firmly to a thickness that is roughly a quarter in. In a shallow bowl, stir black pepper, salt, cayenne pepper, paprika and flour. Press each of the chicken breasts to flour mixture on both of the sides. Tap off the excess flour.
- Heat the olive oil and 1 tbsp. of butter on medium heat in a skillet till butter gives off a lightly toasted fragrance, and pan-fry chicken for roughly 3 minutes on each side till turning brown on both of the sides. Put them aside. Melt 1 additional tbsp. of butter in the skillet, and cook and whisk onion for roughly 5 minutes till becoming translucent; whisk in garlic, cremini mushrooms, oyster mushrooms and shiitake mushrooms, and cook for 10-12 minutes till mushrooms give off the juice and start to become browned.

- Fill a big pot with lightly-salted water and heat to a rolling boil on high heat. When water is boiling, whisk in fettuccini, and bring back to a boil. Cook pasta, without covering, whisk once in a while, for roughly 8 minutes till pasta becomes thoroughly cooked but still firm to bite. Drain them well in a colander that is placed in the sink. Arrange pasta to a serving dish, and toss along with 2 tbsp. of butter; use black pepper and salt to season to taste, and keep them warm.
- After mushroom juices have evaporated, add the Marsala wine to the sauce, and scrape up and dissolve any browned flavor bits in skillet's bottom. Switch the heat to high, and whisk for roughly 3 minutes till 1/2 of the wine is evaporated; whisk in the chicken broth, Dijon mustard and mascarpone; cook, whisk continuously, for 3 more minutes till sauce becomes thick slightly. Lower the heat to medium low; bring back cooked chicken breasts to the sauce. Cook for roughly 5 minutes till sauce becomes thick and chicken juices run clear. Whisk in the parsley. Serve along with the buttered fettuccine.

Nutrition Information

- Calories: 1028 calories;
- Total Fat: 49.4
- Sodium: 391
- Total Carbohydrate: 90.8
- Cholesterol: 168
- Protein: 44.9

524. Creamy Chicken And Mushroom Tart With Nabisco® Chicken In A Biscuit Cracker Crust

Serving: 8 | Prep: 30mins | Cook: 58mins | Ready in:

Ingredients

- Crust:
- 1 3/4 cups crushed chicken-flavored crackers (such as Nabisco® Chicken in a Biscuit)
- 6 tablespoons melted butter
- 1 egg white, beaten
- Filling:
- 3/4 pound boneless chicken breast, cut into small pieces
- salt and ground black pepper to taste
- 1 tablespoon olive oil
- 2 tablespoons butter
- 1/2 cup chopped shallot
- 6 ounces cremini mushrooms, thinly sliced
- 1 tablespoon minced garlic
- 2 teaspoons finely chopped fresh rosemary
- 1 cup heavy whipping cream
- 2 eggs
- 6 tablespoons grated Parmesan cheese, divided
- 1/4 cup finely chopped Italian parsley, divided
- 1/2 teaspoon salt
- 1/2 teaspoon ground black pepper

Direction

- Set the oven at 1750C (3500F) and preheat.
- In a bowl, combine melted butter and cruched cracker together. Press down the mixture and up the sides of a 9 inch springform pan.
- Bake in the prepared oven for 10 minutes. Move out the crust, brush in egg white to seal. Bake for 4 additional minutes. Move out and let it cool at room temperature.
- Flavor chicken with pepper and salt.
- In a large skillet, heat the olive oil over medium heat, cook while stirring chicken for 2 minutes per sides or just until it looks brown. Put it into a plate.
- Decrease the heat to medium low, put in 2 tablespoons butter. In hot butter, cook while stirring shallot for 2 minutes, until it start to soften. Add 1 pinch salt, rosemary, garlic and mushroom, cook and stir for 8 minutes or until mushrooms look tender and juices evaporate.
- In a bowl, whisk together 1/2 teaspoon pepper, 1/2 teaspoon salt, 2 tablespoons

parsley, 1/4 cup grated Parmesan cheese, eggs and cream.
- Put the baked crust on a baking tray, place chicken and mushrooms on the top. Top with the egg mixture then the remaining 2 tablespoons Parmesan cheese.
- Bake in the prepared oven for 30 to 35 minutes until it is set in the center and lightly golden on the top. Allow to rest for 10 minutes. Take away the outer ring. Sprinkle 2 tablespoons remaining parsley on the top.

Nutrition Information

- Calories: 454 calories;
- Total Fat: 35.1
- Sodium: 598
- Total Carbohydrate: 18.3
- Cholesterol: 145
- Protein: 16

525. Creamy Drunken Mushroom Pork Chops

Serving: 4 | Prep: 10mins | Cook: 6hours | Ready in:

Ingredients

- 4 thick cut bone-in pork chops
- 1 (10.75 ounce) can reduced-fat, reduced-sodium cream of mushroom soup
- 1 (3 ounce) can chopped mushrooms, drained
- 1/3 cup red wine
- 2 cloves garlic, minced
- ground black pepper to taste

Direction

- In bottom of the slow cooker, put pork chops. In a bowl, stir together pepper, garlic, red wine, mushrooms and mushroom soup. Add over pork chops. Cook, covered, for 6-8 hours on Low.

Nutrition Information

- Calories: 276 calories;
- Sodium: 421
- Total Carbohydrate: 8.4
- Cholesterol: 73
- Protein: 29.4
- Total Fat: 11.3

526. Creamy Morel Mushroom Grits

Serving: 4 | Prep: 10mins | Cook: 45mins | Ready in:

Ingredients

- 1 cup stone-ground white corn grits
- 3 cups vegetarian chicken-flavored broth
- 4 dried morel mushrooms, or more to taste
- 3 cups whole milk
- 1/2 cup shredded Parmesan cheese

Direction

- In a bowl add grits and water to cover. Put aside to soak for 8 hours or overnight. Skim any debris floating on the top, then rinse well and drain.
- In a saucepan, bring broth to a boil, then take away from the heat. Put in mushrooms and soak for a half hour, until tender. Strain mushrooms and save the broth. Chop mushrooms.
- In a saucepan, bring milk and reserved broth to a boil on high heat. Mix grits in slowly, then put in mushrooms and lower heat to low. Cook for 40-50 minutes, covered, while stirring sometimes, until grits are creamy and softened. Add in Parmesan cheese and stir until melted.

Nutrition Information

- Calories: 310 calories;
- Total Fat: 9.3

- Sodium: 564
- Total Carbohydrate: 41.9
- Cholesterol: 27
- Protein: 14.3

- Total Carbohydrate: 45.5
- Cholesterol: 17
- Protein: 10.1

527. Creamy Mushroom Pasta

Serving: 6 | Prep: 5mins | Cook: 20mins | Ready in:

Ingredients

- 1 (12 ounce) package dry fettuccine noodles
- 1 tablespoon olive oil
- 1 tablespoon butter
- 4 fresh mushrooms, sliced
- 1 tablespoon minced garlic
- 1 tablespoon Italian seasoning
- 1 teaspoon salt
- 1/2 cup white wine
- 1 cup chicken stock
- 1/2 cup sour cream
- 1 tablespoon cornstarch
- 1/4 cup grated Parmesan cheese for topping

Direction

- Boil big pot of lightly salted water. Add olive oil and pasta; cook till tender for 7 minutes. Drain.
- Meanwhile, melt butter in skillet on low heat. Add mushrooms; cook till dark and soft. Mix chicken broth, white wine, salt, Italian seasoning and garlic; put heat on medium. Cook for 5 minutes, constantly mixing.
- Lower heat to low; mix sour cream in till smooth. Mix cornstarch in; simmer to thicken for 1 minute. Mix pasta in; put sauce on pasta. Serve with grated parmesan cheese on top.

Nutrition Information

- Calories: 326 calories;
- Total Fat: 10.7
- Sodium: 582

528. Creamy Mushroom Risotto

Serving: 6 | Prep: 15mins | Cook: 40mins | Ready in:

Ingredients

- 1/2 cup dried porcini mushrooms
- 1/2 (10 ounce) can cream of mushroom soup
- 1/4 cup boiling water
- 4 cups chicken stock
- 1 tablespoon butter
- 1 tablespoon olive oil
- 1 onion, finely chopped
- 1 clove garlic, crushed
- 1 3/4 cups Arborio rice
- salt and pepper to taste
- fresh thyme, chopped
- chopped fresh basil

Direction

- Into the small bowl, put the dried mushrooms and cover with hot water to soak for 10 minutes. Remove using a slotted spoon; using paper towels, softly squeeze dry. Slice the mushrooms and reserve.
- Into a bowl, ladle cream of mushroom soup and slowly mix in the boiling water till mixture is smooth yet not runny.
- Let the stock come to a gentle simmer in the saucepan over moderate heat.
- In a big pot, heat olive oil and butter over moderate heat. Mix in chopped mushrooms, garlic and onion; let cook for 3 minutes. Slowly mix in rice; let cook for 2 minutes, mixing continuously to cover rice with oil. Add pepper and salt to season. Mix in basil and thyme to taste.
- Add mushroom soup mixture, mixing till absorbed. Slowly put in 1/3 of stock, mixing

till liquid is soaked in. Keep mixing in stock slowly, a cup at a time, letting the liquid to be soaked in prior to putting another cup. It will take approximately 20 minutes to soak in total the stock and the rice turns al dente (soft yet firm to the bite).

Nutrition Information

- Calories: 337 calories;
- Protein: 8
- Total Fat: 6.3
- Sodium: 627
- Total Carbohydrate: 61.3
- Cholesterol: 6

529. Creamy Mushroom Soup

Serving: 4 | Prep: 10mins | Cook: 15mins | Ready in:

Ingredients

- 1/4 cup butter
- 1 cup chopped shiitake mushrooms
- 1 cup chopped portobello mushrooms
- 2 shallots, chopped
- 2 tablespoons all-purpose flour
- 1 (14.5 ounce) can chicken broth
- 1 cup half-and-half
- salt and pepper to taste
- 1 pinch ground cinnamon (optional)

Direction

- In a large saucepan, melt butter over medium high heat. Sauté for about 5 minutes or until tender the Portobello mushrooms, shallots and shiitake mushrooms. Add the flour until smooth. Stir in chicken broth little by little. Stir while cooking for 5 minutes, until soup is thick and bubbly.
- Mix in the half-and-half; add salt, pepper and cinnamon to taste. Simmer the soup but do not bring to a boil.

Nutrition Information

- Calories: 234 calories;
- Total Carbohydrate: 13.3
- Cholesterol: 53
- Protein: 4.4
- Total Fat: 18.6
- Sodium: 119

530. Creamy Shrimp Pasta With Mushrooms

Serving: 4 | Prep: 10mins | Cook: 35mins | Ready in:

Ingredients

- 2 tablespoons olive oil
- 1 pound uncooked medium shrimp, peeled and deveined
- 3 cloves garlic, finely chopped
- 1 pinch salt to taste
- 1 pinch dried basil, or to taste
- 1 pinch paprika, or to taste
- 1 (8 ounce) package sliced fresh mushrooms
- 1 cup half-and-half
- 3/4 cup shredded mozzarella cheese
- 1/2 cup grated Parmesan cheese
- 1/2 (16 ounce) package dry fettuccine pasta
- 1 pinch red pepper flakes, or to taste

Direction

- Heat olive oil in big skillet on medium heat then add garlic and shrimp immediately; cook for 3-4 minutes till shrimp is pink. Sprinkle paprika, basil and salt on shrimp; mix and cook, leaving shrimp slightly undercooked to complete cooking in sauce for 1 minute.
- Take shrimp mixture from skillet. Put mushrooms in same skillet; mix and cook for 5 minutes till juicy, seasoning with salt. Add shrimp; add parmesan cheese, mozzarella cheese and half and half immediately then

boil. Lower heat; simmer for 5-8 minutes till cheese melts, constantly mixing. Cover; take off heat.
- Put big pot of lightly salted water on rolling boil; cook fettuccine at boil for 8 minutes till tender yet firm to chew; in small amounts, add some pasta water if cream sauce is thick. Drain pasta and rinse; use cold water to rinse. Add to cream sauce.

Nutrition Information

- Calories: 544 calories;
- Total Carbohydrate: 47.9
- Cholesterol: 217
- Protein: 38.8
- Total Fat: 22.5
- Sodium: 552

531. Creamy Slow Cooker Beef Stroganoff

Serving: 16 | Prep: 25mins | Cook: 5hours10mins | Ready in:

Ingredients

- 1 cup Shamrock Farms® Premium Sour Cream
- 3 tablespoons vegetable oil, divided
- 1 pound white mushrooms, trimmed and cut into thick slices
- 1 pinch salt
- 1 large white onion, minced
- 1/4 cup tomato paste
- 6 cloves garlic, minced
- 2 teaspoons dried thyme
- 1/3 cup all-purpose flour
- 1 1/2 cups low-sodium beef broth
- 1/2 cup dry white wine
- 1/3 cup soy sauce
- 2 bay leaves
- 4 pounds boneless beef chuck roast, trimmed of excess fat and cut into 1 1/2-inch chunks
- salt and ground black pepper to taste
- 1 tablespoon Dijon mustard
- 1/2 teaspoon dried dill

Direction

- Put a 12-inch skillet on medium heat. Pour in 1 tablespoon oil. Then add mushrooms and sprinkle a pinch of salt on top. Cook mushrooms for 5 – 10 minutes or until mushrooms soften. Transfer mushrooms into a 5-quart slow cooker.
- Heat 2 tablespoon oil in the empty 12-inch skillet. Then put thyme, garlic, tomato paste, onion into the skillet. Cook everything until onion have softened, keep stirring while cooking, about 5 – 10 minutes. Fold in flour and cook for 1 more minute.
- Add in broth, wine and whisk, remove any browned pieces. Make sure to keep whisking until there are no flour lumps left. Transfer the mixture into the slow cooker. Add soy sauce, bay leaves and stir.
- Use salt and pepper to season beef chunks. Put the seasoned beef chunks into the slow cooker, cover the whole chunk in the sauce.
- Put the lid on and cook till the beef is tender, 5 – 7 hours on High or 9 – 11 hours on Low. Skim from the top any formed fat. Remove bay leaves.
- Transfer 1 cup of cooking liquid from slow cooker to a bowl. Whisk in mustard and Shamrock Farms Premium Sour Cream. Put the mixture back to the slow cooker and stir well to mix. Season with dill, pepper and more salt to taste.

Nutrition Information

- Calories: 246 calories;
- Protein: 15.8
- Total Fat: 16.8
- Sodium: 426
- Total Carbohydrate: 6.5
- Cholesterol: 57

532. Creamy Spinach & Mushroom Risotto

Serving: 4 | Prep: 10mins | Cook: 30mins | Ready in:

Ingredients

- 2 tablespoons butter
- 1/2 cup sliced mushrooms
- 1/2 cup chopped onion
- 2 1/2 cups water
- 1 (8 ounce) package ZATARAIN'S® Yellow Rice
- 1/2 cup heavy cream
- 1/2 cup shredded Monterey Jack cheese
- 1 cup baby spinach leaves

Direction

- In medium saucepan, melt butter on medium high heat. Add onion and mushrooms; mix and cook till onion starts to soften for 2 minutes.
- Mix in Rice Mix and water. Boil, occasionally mixing. Lower heat to low; cover and simmer for 20 minutes. Mix in cheese and cream; cover and cook till rice is tender for 5 minutes more. Mix in spinach. Take it off the heat. Let stand for 5 minutes. Before serving, fluff using a fork.

Nutrition Information

- Calories: 420 calories;
- Sodium: 1101
- Total Carbohydrate: 46.9
- Cholesterol: 69
- Protein: 4.8
- Total Fat: 21.6

533. Creamy Spinach Tortellini

Serving: 4 | Prep: 15mins | Cook: 20mins | Ready in:

Ingredients

- 1 (9 ounce) package refrigerated cheese tortellini
- 2 tablespoons Butter
- 1 small onion, chopped
- 1 (8 ounce) package cream cheese
- 1/2 cup grated Parmesan cheese
- 1/2 cup milk
- fresh mushrooms, sliced
- 1 (10 ounce) package frozen chopped spinach, thawed and drained
- cherry tomatoes, halved

Direction

- Cook the tortellini following the package instructions.
- Grab a large skillet and heat butter on medium heat. Stir in the onion; cook until translucent and soft. Mix in spinach, mushrooms, milk, parmesan and cream cheese.
- Slowly mix in cherry tomatoes and tortellini with the skillet contents. Warm thoroughly and serve.

Nutrition Information

- Calories: 546 calories;
- Total Fat: 35
- Sodium: 671
- Total Carbohydrate: 40.2
- Cholesterol: 116
- Protein: 21.8

534. Creamy Spinach And Zucchini Soup

Serving: 4 | Prep: 20mins | Cook: 45mins | Ready in:

Ingredients

- 1 large onion, chopped
- 6 cups water, divided

- 3 potatoes, chopped
- 3 zucchini, sliced
- 1 tablespoon low-sodium soy sauce
- 2 cups tightly packed spinach leaves
- ground black pepper to taste
- 1/3 cup sliced fresh enoki mushrooms

Direction

- In a big saucepan, mix together 1/2 cup of water and onion over medium-high heat, stir and cook for 3 minutes until the onion is tender.
- Add the leftover water to the saucepan; add soy sauce, zucchini, and potatoes. Boil the water, lower the heat to low, put a cover on the saucepan, and cook for 35 minutes.
- Mix spinach into the soup, use black pepper to season. Keep cooking for another 2 minutes; take the saucepan away from heat.
- Put the soup in a blender to blend in batches until totally pureed. Put the pureed soup back to the saucepan and put on medium-low heat.
- Mix mushrooms into the pureed soup, cook for 5 minutes until the mushrooms are thoroughly warmed.

Nutrition Information

- Calories: 162 calories;
- Sodium: 176
- Total Carbohydrate: 36
- Cholesterol: 0
- Protein: 5.6
- Total Fat: 0.4

535. Creme Fraiche Chicken

Serving: 5 | Prep: | Cook: | Ready in:

Ingredients

- 6 skinless, boneless chicken breast halves
- 1/4 cup white wine
- salt and pepper to taste
- 1 (8 ounce) package pasta, your choice of shape
- 1 large white onion, chopped
- 1 tablespoon chopped garlic
- 2 (8 ounce) packages sliced fresh mushrooms
- 2 cups creme fraiche
- 1/2 cup grated Parmesan cheese for topping
- 3 tablespoons sour cream

Direction

- Sauté chicken breasts in oil in a large skillet over medium-high heat. Add pepper and salt to taste, and white wine when breasts are browned. Simmer until juices from the chicken run clear and the chicken is cooked through, 15-20 minutes.
- To cook pasta: At the same time, boil a large pot with salted water. Put pasta into the boiling water and cook until tender but firm to bite, 8-10 minutes. Then drain the pasta.
- Take the chicken out of the skillet once it is cooked, then cube. Put aside. In the remaining juices, sauté garlic and onion. Put in mushrooms and sauté until they become soft when onions turn translucent. Add sour cream, crème Fraiche, and the cubed chicken (to the desired thickness). Stir them together and heat through. Place the hot cooked pasta onto the plate, then put sauce and chicken on top and dust with grated Parmesan cheese.

Nutrition Information

- Calories: 708 calories;
- Sodium: 270
- Total Carbohydrate: 35.1
- Cholesterol: 256
- Protein: 47.6
- Total Fat: 43.1

536. Crispy Tofu And Bacon Wraps

Serving: 10 | Prep: 30mins | Cook: 30mins | Ready in:

Ingredients

- 1 (16 ounce) package tofu, drained and cubed
- 1 yellow onion, roughly chopped
- 6 large green onions, chopped
- 1 medium red bell pepper, coarsely chopped
- 8 cloves garlic
- 20 mushrooms
- 1 tomato, coarsely chopped
- 3/4 cup crumbled cooked bacon
- 1 tablespoon fish sauce
- 2 tablespoons red wine
- 1/4 cup chopped fresh Italian parsley
- 1/4 teaspoon salt
- 1/2 teaspoon black pepper
- 1/4 teaspoon curry powder
- 1/4 teaspoon mustard powder
- 1/4 teaspoon dill weed
- 1/2 teaspoon ground ginger
- 1 (12 ounce) package egg roll wrappers
- canola oil for frying

Direction

- In the bowl of a processor, combine bacon, tomato, mushrooms, garlic, red pepper, green onion, yellow onion, and tofu. Season with ginger, dill, mustard powder, curry powder, pepper, salt, parsley, red wine, and fish sauce; process the mixture until smooth.
- In a work surface, place an egg roll wrapper with a corner pointing towards you. Ladle 1-2 tablespoons of tofu puree between the center and bottom corner of the wrapper. Fold the closest corner over the filling, then fold the two sides. Moisten the furthest corner with some water and roll up carefully.
- In a large pot, heat a few inches of canola oil to 350°F (175°C). Fry a few tofu wraps at a time until center is cooked and outside turns golden brown. Transfer to paper towels to drain and serve hot.

Nutrition Information

- Calories: 296 calories;
- Sodium: 634
- Total Carbohydrate: 26.7
- Cholesterol: 9
- Protein: 12.7
- Total Fat: 16

537. Crock Pot® Mushrooms

Serving: 4 | Prep: 5mins | Cook: 3hours | Ready in:

Ingredients

- 1 pound mushrooms
- 1/2 cup butter
- 1 (1 ounce) envelope ranch salad dressing mix

Direction

- In a slow cooker, add ranch salad dressing mix, butter and mushrooms.
- Cook on low heat about 3 to 4 hours.

Nutrition Information

- Calories: 246 calories;
- Sodium: 659
- Total Carbohydrate: 7.2
- Cholesterol: 61
- Protein: 3.7
- Total Fat: 23.4

538. Crustless Spinach, Mushroom, And Tomato Quiche (Keto)

Serving: 8 | Prep: 15mins | Cook: 40mins | Ready in:

Ingredients

- cooking spray
- 1 tablespoon butter
- 1 onion, sliced
- 1/2 cup halved cherry tomatoes
- 1 cup sliced mushrooms
- 2 cups fresh spinach
- 1 cup heavy cream
- 3 eggs
- 1/2 teaspoon salt
- 1/4 teaspoon ground black pepper
- 1/4 teaspoon ground nutmeg
- 1 cup shredded Gouda cheese

Direction

- Set an oven to preheat to 190°C (375°F). Use cooking spray to grease a 9-inch pie plate.
- In a medium cast-iron frying pan, melt the butter on medium heat. Add onion, then cook and stir for about 5 minutes, until it becomes translucent and tender. Stir in cherry tomatoes for about 3 minutes, until it becomes a bit tender. Add mushrooms and let it cook for about 3 minutes, until soft. Stir in spinach, then cook for a minute more.
- In a bowl, whisk together the nutmeg, pepper, salt, eggs and cream.
- In the prepped pie plate, spread 1/2 of the Gouda cheese, then put spinach mixture on top. Cover it with egg mixture then sprinkle the remaining Gouda cheese on top.
- Let it bake in the preheated oven for about 25 minutes, until the top turns golden and the eggs are set.

Nutrition Information

- Calories: 208 calories;
- Total Fat: 18.6
- Sodium: 324
- Total Carbohydrate: 3.7
- Cholesterol: 131
- Protein: 7.5

539.   Cubed Steak And Wild Rice

Serving: 4 | Prep: 10mins | Cook: 25mins | Ready in:

Ingredients

- 2 tablespoons butter
- 1 pound cube steak, cut into bite size pieces
- 1 (4.5 ounce) package long grain and wild rice mix
- 2 cups water
- 5 fresh mushrooms, sliced
- 2 tablespoons Worcestershire sauce
- 2 tablespoons garlic powder
- 1 tablespoon onion powder

Direction

- Melt butter in skillet on medium heat; sauté cube steak till browned evenly.
- Mix onion powder, garlic powder, Worcestershire sauce, mushrooms, water, rice and cooked steak and juices in medium pot; boil. Lower heat to low; simmer till all liquid is absorbed for 25 minutes.

Nutrition Information

- Calories: 272 calories;
- Protein: 18.4
- Total Fat: 12
- Sodium: 160
- Total Carbohydrate: 23.5
- Cholesterol: 43

540.   Curried Celery Apple Soup With Shiitake

Serving: 10 | Prep: 20mins | Cook: 30mins | Ready in:

Ingredients

- 1 head garlic, peeled
- 1/4 teaspoon sea salt
- 2 tablespoons butter
- 1/4 cup white miso paste
- 2 tablespoons ground cumin
- 2 tablespoons yellow curry powder
- 1 teaspoon celery seed
- 1 tablespoon ground black pepper
- 1 tablespoon sea salt
- 1 bunch celery, chopped
- 1 small apple - peeled, cored, and chopped
- 1 cup chicken broth
- 2 large skinless, boneless chicken breasts, cut into bite-size pieces
- 1/4 cup water
- 1 cup dried sliced shiitake mushrooms
- 2 tablespoons balsamic vinegar
- 1 teaspoon black truffle oil

Direction

- Grind the garlic with 1/4 teaspoon sea salt into a paste using a mortar and pestle.
- In a large skillet placed over medium heat, melt the butter. Stir in the miso paste, curry powder, black pepper, celery, apple, celery seed, 1 tablespoon sea salt, cumin and garlic paste to the skillet and cook for 5 to 7 minutes, until the celery is slightly tender.
- Transfer about half of the mixture to a blender along with the chicken broth. Pulse the blender a few times then leave it to blend, while holding the lid in place with a folded kitchen towel. In a stockpot placed over medium heat, pour the mixture with the half remaining in the skillet. Keep some drippings in the skillet.
- Cook the chicken with the drippings in the skillet over medium heat, for 5 minutes, until it becomes browned completely. Add water and boil in the skillet while scraping the brown particles of food off the base of the pan with a wooden spoon. Empty the whole contents of skillet in the stockpot along with shiitake mushrooms. Let simmer for about 20 minutes, until the mushrooms become tender.

Stir in the truffle oil and balsamic vinegar to the soup and serve.

Nutrition Information

- Calories: 163 calories;
- Sodium: 915
- Total Carbohydrate: 19.9
- Cholesterol: 30
- Protein: 12.3
- Total Fat: 4.9

541. Deer Soup With Cream Of Mushroom And Celery

Serving: 7 | Prep: 15mins | Cook: |Ready in:

Ingredients

- 1 onion, chopped
- 4 carrots, chopped
- 1 pound venison (deer meat)
- 1 pound boneless pork loin, cubed
- 1/2 teaspoon salt
- 1 teaspoon white sugar
- 1 pint water
- 1 (10.75 ounce) can condensed cream of mushroom soup
- 1 (10.75 ounce) can condensed cream of celery soup

Direction

- In a crockpot, put water, sugar, salt, pork, deer meat, carrots, and onion. Cook for 30 minutes.
- Add cream of celery soup and cream of mushroom soup. Cook for 3 1/2 to 4 hours.

Nutrition Information

- Calories: 308 calories;
- Protein: 29.6
- Total Fat: 15.3
- Sodium: 869

- Total Carbohydrate: 12
- Cholesterol: 99

542. Delicious Potato Salad Bake

Serving: 6 | Prep: 20mins | Cook: 1hours5mins | Ready in:

Ingredients

- 8 potatoes
- 12 slices bacon
- 2 onions, finely chopped
- 1 cup sliced mushrooms
- 1 cup heavy cream
- 1/2 cup milk
- 1 1/2 cups shredded mozzarella cheese
- salt and pepper to taste

Direction

- Set the oven to 325°F (165°C) and start preheating. Grease or butter an 8x16-inch baking plate.
- Boil a big pot of salted water. Put potatoes and cook for 15 minutes until softened but still firm. Strain and let cool.
- In a big, deep frying pan, put bacon. Cook on medium-high heat until evenly brown. Add pepper, salt, mushrooms, and onions. Cook until mushrooms and onions are tender.
- Cut the potatoes and put a thin layer on the baking plate. Then add a layer of bacon mixture and redo the layers until there are no ingredients left. Put milk and cream on the layers, use grated cheese to drizzle.
- Bake until milk and cream almost reduced entirely, about 35 minutes.

Nutrition Information

- Calories: 553 calories;
- Total Carbohydrate: 56.3

- Cholesterol: 94
- Protein: 21.7
- Total Fat: 27.6
- Sodium: 641

543. Deviled Chicken Breasts

Serving: 4 | Prep: | Cook: | Ready in:

Ingredients

- 1/8 cup Italian-style dried bread crumbs
- 4 skinless, boneless chicken breasts
- 1 tablespoon olive oil
- 1/2 cup dry white wine
- 1/2 teaspoon ground savory
- 1/4 teaspoon salt
- 1 (4.5 ounce) can sliced mushrooms
- 1 tablespoon lemon juice
- 1 tablespoon honey mustard

Direction

- Put breadcrumbs in a large, resealable plastic bag. Add chicken; seal the bag and shake to coat the chicken with breadcrumbs.
- In a large nonstick skillet over medium heat, heat oil. Add chicken. Cook each side until browned or for 3 minutes. Add mushrooms, salt, savory and wine to the chicken. Cover and lower the heat. Simmer until chicken is done or for 15 minutes. Take the mushrooms and chicken out with a slotted spoon; transfer to a serving plate.
- Add mustard and lemon juice to the skillet; stir well. Heat through. Serve the sauce with chicken.

Nutrition Information

- Calories: 217 calories;
- Protein: 28.6
- Total Fat: 5.4
- Sodium: 454

- Total Carbohydrate: 7.2
- Cholesterol: 69

544. Diane's Chicken Dish

Serving: 6 | Prep: 20mins | Cook: 35mins | Ready in:

Ingredients

- 1/4 cup vinegar
- 1/4 cup olive oil
- 1/4 cup water
- 1 (.7 ounce) package dry Italian salad dressing mix (such as Good Seasons®)
- 1 pound boneless chicken pieces, cut into bite-size chunks
- 1 tablespoon butter
- 1 large onion, chopped
- 1 large green bell pepper, chopped
- 1 (10 ounce) package sliced crimini mushrooms
- 1 large tomato, chopped
- 2 cups shredded sharp Cheddar cheese

Direction

- In a bowl, stir Italian dressing mix, water, olive oil and vinegar together. Whisk in chicken; let the chicken marinate when preparing the rest of ingredients.
- Heat butter on medium high heat in a skillet. Whisk in bell pepper and onion; cook and whisk for roughly 5 minutes till onion softens and becomes translucent. Take chicken out of marinade with a slotted spoon, and move into the skillet; save rest of the marinade. Cook and whisk chicken for 3-5 minutes till not pink in middle anymore
- Whisk in mushrooms; cook and whisk for roughly 2 minutes till they start to become tender. Put in the reserved marinade and tomato, and then drizzle the cheese over the top. Don't whisk. Keep covered and let it simmer over low heat for roughly 20 minutes till the chicken softens and the cheese melts.

Let the dish stand for several minutes prior to serving.

Nutrition Information

- Calories: 370 calories;
- Protein: 26.9
- Total Fat: 25.1
- Sodium: 832
- Total Carbohydrate: 8.5
- Cholesterol: 84

545. Earth, Sea And Fire Salmon

Serving: 8 | Prep: 15mins | Cook: 45mins | Ready in:

Ingredients

- 2 tablespoons olive oil
- 4 (8 ounce) salmon fillets
- 4 medium potatoes, peeled and sliced
- 2 large red onions, sliced into rings
- 1 jarred roasted red pepper, drained and cut into strips
- 8 ounces portobello mushrooms
- 1 tablespoon fresh lemon juice
- salt and pepper to taste
- 1 teaspoon sesame oil

Direction

- Heat the oven to 350 degrees beforehand. Prepare a 9x13-inch baking dish and use olive oil to generously cover its bottom.
- On the bottom of the baking dish, place slices of potatoes in a layer. Use a little pepper and salt for seasoning. Lay a layer of onions over the potatoes, then a layer of roasted peppers. Use pepper and salt to season every layer according to your taste. In the dish, lay salmon fillets over the vegetables, then use pepper, salt and lemon juice to season. Lay whole

mushrooms over the fillets and use sesame oil to drizzle.
- In the preheated oven, bake for 45 minutes till potatoes get tender and fish flakes easily with a fork.

Nutrition Information

- Calories: 325 calories;
- Total Fat: 15.1
- Sodium: 134
- Total Carbohydrate: 24.4
- Cholesterol: 55
- Protein: 22.9

546. Easier Chicken Marsala

Serving: 4 | Prep: 10mins | Cook: 20mins | Ready in:

Ingredients

- 1/4 cup all-purpose flour
- 1/2 teaspoon garlic salt
- 1/4 teaspoon ground black pepper
- 1/2 teaspoon dried oregano
- 4 boneless, skinless chicken breast halves
- 1 tablespoon olive oil
- 1 tablespoon butter
- 1 cup sliced fresh mushrooms
- 1/2 cup Marsala wine

Direction

- Stir oregano, pepper, garlic salt and flour together in a medium bowl. Coat the chicken lightly with the mixture.
- In a large skillet over medium heat, heat butter and olive oil. In the skillet, fry the chicken until it turns light brown on one side or for 2 minutes. Turn the chicken over; add mushrooms. Cook until the second side of chicken turns light brown, about 2 minutes. Stir mushrooms to cook them evenly.
- Pour Marsala wine over the chicken. Cover the skillet, lower the heat to low; simmer until chicken is no longer pink and juices run clear or for 10 minutes.

Nutrition Information

- Calories: 286 calories;
- Total Fat: 10.1
- Sodium: 313
- Total Carbohydrate: 11.4
- Cholesterol: 80
- Protein: 27.9

547. Easy Baked Cheese And Vegetable Twist

Serving: 16 | Prep: 20mins | Cook: | Ready in:

Ingredients

- 2 eggs
- 4 ounces PHILADELPHIA Cream Cheese, softened
- 1/2 cup KRAFT 2% Milk Shredded Italian* Three Cheese Blend
- 3 cups frozen broccoli cuts, thawed, drained
- 1/2 cup fresh mushrooms, cut into quarters
- 1/2 cup cherry tomatoes, cut in half
- 4 green onions, sliced
- 2 (8 ounce) cans refrigerated crescent dinner rolls

Direction

- Heat oven to 375°F.
- In large bowl, mix the first three ingredients until blended well. Mix in next four ingredients.
- Unroll the dough; then divide into 16 triangles. Place on foil-covered baking sheet in 11-in. circle, the short sides of triangles overlapping in the middle and the triangles points toward outside. (In middle of circle

should have a 5-in. diameter opening). Put the cheese mixture onto the dough near middle of the circle. Bring the outside points of triangles up over the filling and cover the filling by tucking under the dough in middle of the ring.
- Bake until filling is heated through and crust turns golden brown, about 35-40 mins.

548. Easy Barbeque Chicken And Red Potatoes

Serving: 4 | Prep: 15mins | Cook: 1hours |Ready in:

Ingredients

- 4 skinless, boneless chicken breast halves
- 1 Vidalia onion, sliced
- 1 pound sliced fresh mushrooms
- 8 red potatoes, sliced 1/2 inch thick
- 1 (18 ounce) bottle barbeque sauce

Direction

- Preheat oven to 350 °F (175 °C).
- In a lightly greased baking dish (9x13 inches), place onion, chicken breasts, potatoes and mushrooms and pour the sauce to cover all.
- Cover dish and bake for approximately 1 hour.

Nutrition Information

- Calories: 676 calories;
- Total Fat: 4.2
- Sodium: 1502
- Total Carbohydrate: 123.5
- Cholesterol: 67
- Protein: 35.3

549. Easy Beef Stroganoff In The Slow Cooker

Serving: 5 | Prep: 10mins | Cook: 4hours17mins |Ready in:

Ingredients

- 1 1/3 pounds cubed beef stew meat
- 2 cups fresh mushrooms, thickly sliced
- 1 (10.75 ounce) can condensed cream of mushroom soup
- 1 cup milk
- 2 onions, chopped
- 2 tablespoons Worcestershire sauce
- 6 ounces herb and garlic-flavored cream cheese
- 1 cup fusilli pasta
- 1/4 cup sour cream (optional)

Direction

- In a slow cooker, mix Worcestershire sauce, onions, milk, mushrooms, beef and cream of mushroom soup together.
- Cook for 3 to 4 hours on a high setting and for 5 to 7 hours on low. Whisk in the cream cheese until it is thoroughly dissolved then cook for another hour.
- Boil a big pot filled with lightly salted water and put the fusilli. Cook for about 12 minutes until it's firm to the bite yet tender, stirring every now and then. Drain the noodles and Place the stroganoff over fusilli and garnish with sour cream. Serve.

Nutrition Information

- Calories: 450 calories;
- Sodium: 738
- Total Carbohydrate: 23.9
- Cholesterol: 106
- Protein: 29.4
- Total Fat: 25.3

550. Easy Chanterelle Mushrooms In Cream Sauce

Serving: 4 | Prep: 20mins | Cook: 15mins | Ready in:

Ingredients

- 2 tablespoons butter
- 3 shallots, minced
- 3 cups chanterelle mushrooms, finely chopped
- 1/2 cup heavy whipping cream
- 1 1/2 teaspoons all-purpose flour
- 1/2 teaspoon cold water, or as needed
- 1/2 teaspoon salt
- 1/2 teaspoon herbes de Provence, or to taste
- fresh ground black pepper, to taste

Direction

- Melt the butter on medium heat in a pan and cook the shallots for roughly 5 minutes till becoming tender and translucent. Put in the chanterelle mushrooms and cook for 2 more minutes. Put in the cream and cook for 5-10 minutes till the mushrooms soften.
- Whisk together the water and flour and put to the mushrooms. Boil. Use the pepper, herbes de Provence and salt to season.

Nutrition Information

- Calories: 227 calories;
- Total Fat: 16.8
- Sodium: 372
- Total Carbohydrate: 14
- Cholesterol: 56
- Protein: 4.2

551. Easy Chicken Casserole

Serving: 4 | Prep: | Cook: | Ready in:

Ingredients

- 4 skinless, boneless chicken breast halves
- 1 (10.75 ounce) can condensed cream of chicken soup
- 1 cup sour cream
- 32 buttery round crackers
- 1/4 cup chopped onion (optional)
- 1/4 cup chopped mushrooms (optional)

Direction

- Set oven to 175° C (350° F) and start preheating.
- Boil chicken for 20-30 minutes until cooked through (the meat is not pink inside anymore). Cut into bite-size chunks and put in a 9x13-inch baking dish.
- Combine sour cream, soup, and if wished, mushrooms and onions. Spread the mixture over chicken, place crumbled crackers over top. Put on cover and bake at 350 degrees F (175 degrees C) for 30 minutes (or keep in the fridge and bake at another time).

Nutrition Information

- Calories: 466 calories;
- Cholesterol: 120
- Protein: 33.1
- Total Fat: 23.9
- Sodium: 797
- Total Carbohydrate: 29

552. Easy Chicken With Mushrooms And Zucchini In Cream Sauce

Serving: 2 | Prep: 10mins | Cook: 15mins | Ready in:

Ingredients

- 1 tablespoon butter
- 2 (5 ounce) boneless, skinless chicken breasts, cubed
- salt and freshly ground pepper to taste
- 1 tablespoon olive oil

- 4 green onions, chopped
- 2 green zucchini, cut in half lengthwise and into 1/4-inch slices
- 8 large fresh mushrooms, sliced
- 1 tablespoon all-purpose flour
- 3/4 cup heavy whipping cream
- 1 tablespoon chopped fresh parsley

Direction

- Take a skillet and melt butter on medium heat then cook chicken for 5-7 minutes until it becomes brown while frequently stirring. Use salt and pepper to season; then transfer chicken onto a plate. Keep it warm by covering it with foil or a bowl.
- Use the same skillet to heat olive oil on medium heat; then cook green onions for 2 minutes until they become soft. Add in the zucchini slices and cook for 5 minutes until they softened. Mix in mushrooms. Put chicken back in skillet and drizzle on flour. Mix in cream and cook for 3-5 minutes until the sauce starts to thicken. Top with chopped parsley.

Nutrition Information

- Calories: 671 calories;
- Total Carbohydrate: 17.9
- Cholesterol: 224
- Protein: 39.7
- Total Fat: 50.8
- Sodium: 257

553. Easy Lentil Feta Wraps

Serving: 6 | Prep: 15mins | Cook: 20mins | Ready in:

Ingredients

- 6 (8 inch) whole wheat tortillas
- 3 tablespoons olive oil
- 2 cloves garlic, minced
- 2 shallots, finely chopped
- 1/2 pound fresh mushrooms, sliced
- 1/4 cup dry white wine
- 1 (15 ounce) can brown lentils
- 1 (4 ounce) package feta cheese, crumbled
- 1/4 cup chopped kalamata olives
- 1/2 cup chopped tomatoes

Direction

- Set an oven to 120°C (250°F) and start preheating. Use aluminum foil to wrap the tortillas, then put in the oven to warm until they become soft, for 10 minutes.
- In a saucepan, heat olive oil over medium heat, then sauté mushrooms, shallots, and garlic until they are browned slightly, for 5 minutes. Add the wine and loosen all browned bits from the bottom of the saucepan. Stir in lentils and cook until they are just heated through, 2 minutes.
- Spoon a portion of the lentil mixture into each tortilla, then roll or fold them. Put tomatoes, olives, and feta cheese on top.

Nutrition Information

- Calories: 309 calories;
- Total Fat: 13
- Sodium: 614
- Total Carbohydrate: 42.1
- Cholesterol: 17
- Protein: 12.8

554. Easy Mushroom Rice

Serving: 4 | Prep: 5mins | Cook: 1hours | Ready in:

Ingredients

- 1 cup uncooked long-grain rice
- 1 (10.5 ounce) can condensed French onion soup
- 1 (10.5 ounce) can beef broth
- 1 (4 ounce) can sliced mushrooms, drained

- 1/4 cup butter

Direction

- Set the oven to 175°C or 350°F to preheat.
- Mix in an 8"x8" casserole dish with butter, mushrooms, beef broth, onion soup and rice.
- In the preheated oven, bake, covered, about one hour.

Nutrition Information

- Calories: 336 calories;
- Protein: 9.1
- Total Fat: 13
- Sodium: 1216
- Total Carbohydrate: 45.4
- Cholesterol: 33

555. Easy Salmon

Serving: 6 | Prep: 15mins | Cook: 30mins | Ready in:

Ingredients

- 6 (4 ounce) fillets salmon
- 1 (.7 ounce) package dry Italian-style salad dressing mix
- 1/2 cup water
- 2 tablespoons lemon juice
- 1 cup fresh sliced mushrooms

Direction

- Turn oven to 350°F (175°C) to preheat. Lightly grease a 9x13-inch baking dish with butter.
- Mix lemon juice, water, and salad dressing mix together in a cup.
- Place salmon fillets in 1 layer in the baking dish. Stream the water mixture over the fish and top with sliced mushrooms.
- Cover and bake fish for 15 minutes in the preheated oven. Uncover; keep baking, basting with cooking juices, for 15 more minutes.

Nutrition Information

- Calories: 217 calories;
- Total Fat: 12.2
- Sodium: 597
- Total Carbohydrate: 2.5
- Cholesterol: 66
- Protein: 22.7

556. Easy Slow Cooker Stroganoff

Serving: 6 | Prep: 15mins | Cook: 8hours | Ready in:

Ingredients

- 2 (10.75 ounce) cans cream of mushroom soup
- 1 (8 ounce) package sliced fresh mushrooms (optional)
- 1/2 cup butter
- 1 small onion, chopped
- 3 pounds beef tips, cut into bite-size pieces
- 1 (8 ounce) package wide egg noodles

Direction

- Mix mushrooms, onion, butter, and mushroom soup in a slow cooker. Place in beef tips. Cook on low for 8 hours.
- Boil a big pot of lightly salted water. Cook the egg noodles in boiling water with occasional stirring for about 5 minutes until cooked through yet has a firm bite. Drain it.
- Serve the cooked egg noodles with sauce and beef tips on top.

Nutrition Information

- Calories: 663 calories;
- Sodium: 857
- Total Carbohydrate: 35.8
- Cholesterol: 170
- Protein: 47.8
- Total Fat: 36.1

557. Easy Spaghetti With Tomato Sauce

Serving: 5 | Prep: | Cook: | Ready in:

Ingredients

- 12 ounces spaghetti
- 1 pound lean ground beef
- 1 teaspoon salt
- 3/4 teaspoon white sugar
- 1 teaspoon dried oregano
- 1/4 teaspoon ground black pepper
- 1/8 teaspoon garlic powder
- 2 tablespoons dried minced onion
- 2 1/2 cups chopped tomatoes
- 1 1/3 (6 ounce) cans tomato paste
- 1 (4.5 ounce) can sliced mushrooms

Direction

- Brown beef on moderate heat and get rid of the fat.
- Mix together mushrooms, tomato paste, diced tomatoes, onion flakes, garlic powder, pepper, oregano, sugar, salt and beef in a big pot. Simmer about 2 hours at low heat while stirring sometimes.
- Following package directions, cook pasta, then drain well. Serve sauce on top of the spaghetti.

Nutrition Information

- Calories: 557 calories;
- Total Fat: 20.3
- Sodium: 1002
- Total Carbohydrate: 65.7
- Cholesterol: 68
- Protein: 28.2

558. Easy Turkey Tetrazzini

Serving: 6 | Prep: 20mins | Cook: 25mins | Ready in:

Ingredients

- 1 (8 ounce) package cooked egg noodles
- 2 tablespoons butter
- 1 (6 ounce) can sliced mushrooms
- 1 teaspoon salt
- 1/8 teaspoon pepper
- 2 cups chopped cooked turkey
- 1 (10.75 ounce) can condensed cream of celery soup
- 1 cup sour cream
- 1/2 cup grated Parmesan cheese

Direction

- Fill a big pot up with lightly salted water and bring it to a boil. Insert the pasta and cook until al dente, about 8-10 minutes. Drain. Preheat the oven to 375°F (190°C).
- In a big heavy skillet, melt butter and sauté the mushrooms in it for 1 minute. Sprinkle salt and pepper to season then stir in the turkey, sour cream and condensed soup. Transfer the cooked noodles into a 9x13-inch baking dish then pour the sauce mixture atop evenly. Scatter some Parmesan cheese over it. Put the dish into the preheated oven. Bake until the sauce is bubbling, about 20-25 minutes.

Nutrition Information

- Calories: 411 calories;
- Sodium: 1082
- Total Carbohydrate: 33.5
- Cholesterol: 105
- Protein: 24
- Total Fat: 20.1

559. Easy Vegetarian Pasta

Serving: 8 | Prep: 10mins | Cook: 25mins | Ready in:

Ingredients

- 1 (16 ounce) package uncooked whole wheat spaghetti
- 3 tablespoons olive oil
- 2 tablespoons garlic, minced
- 3 large tomatoes, diced
- 1 red onion, chopped
- 1 yellow bell pepper, chopped
- 1 red bell pepper, chopped
- 1 cup chopped zucchini
- 1/2 cup sliced fresh mushrooms
- 2 tablespoons balsamic vinegar
- 2 tablespoons crumbled feta cheese

Direction

- Boil a big pot of lightly salted water. Put in pasta and cook for 8 - 10 minutes or until al dente; let drain.
- Heat the oil in a frying pan over medium heat, then sauté the garlic until lightly browned. Stir in the mushrooms, zucchini, red bell pepper, yellow bell pepper, onion, and tomatoes. Cook and mix until tender.
- Stir the balsamic vinegar into the pan. Mix with the cooked spaghetti, then top with feta cheese and serve.

Nutrition Information

- Calories: 263 calories;
- Total Fat: 6.6
- Sodium: 39
- Total Carbohydrate: 45.6
- Cholesterol: 2
- Protein: 9.5

560. Easy Vegetarian Stroganoff

Serving: 7 | Prep: 5mins | Cook: 10mins | Ready in:

Ingredients

- 1 (12 ounce) package textured vegetable protein
- 2 (10.75 ounce) cans condensed cream of mushroom soup
- 1 (6 ounce) can sliced mushrooms, drained
- 2 tablespoons minced onion
- 1 tablespoon garlic powder
- 1 tablespoon seasoning salt
- 2 1/2 cups water
- 1 cup rolled oats
- 1 tablespoon olive oil

Direction

- Mix olive oil, oats, water, seasoning salt, garlic powder, onion, mushrooms, mushroom soup, and textured vegetable protein in a big and heavy skillet on medium heat. Mix till the ingredients become well mixed, oats become moist and soup has been dissolved. Lower the heat to low and simmer for roughly 10 minutes till thick.

Nutrition Information

- Calories: 310 calories;
- Total Carbohydrate: 20
- Cholesterol: 0
- Protein: 42.4
- Total Fat: 9.6
- Sodium: 1541

561. Egg Foo Yung II

Serving: 5 | Prep: 5mins | Cook: 25mins | Ready in:

Ingredients

- 8 eggs, beaten
- 1 cup thinly sliced celery
- 1 cup finely chopped onion
- 1 cup bean sprouts
- 1/2 cup diced fresh mushrooms
- 1/3 cup chopped cooked chicken breast
- 1/3 cup cooked and crumbled ground beef
- 1/3 cup chopped cooked pork
- 1 teaspoon salt
- 1/4 teaspoon ground black pepper
- FOO YUNG SAUCE
- 2 cubes chicken bouillon
- 1 1/2 cups hot water
- 1 1/2 teaspoons white sugar
- 2 tablespoons soy sauce
- 6 tablespoons cold water
- 1 1/2 tablespoons cornstarch

Direction

- In a big bowl, beat the eggs. Put in pepper, salt, pork, beef, chicken, mushrooms, bean sprouts, onion and celery. Blend together.
- In a medium work or skillet, heat the oil and brown 1/2 cup of egg mixture at a time until done. When the entire of the mixture turns brown, put aside.
- For the sauce, in a small saucepan with hot water, dissolve the bouillon; put in soy sauce and sugar and mix well over medium heat. Put in cornstarch and cold water and blend until the mixture is smooth and thickened. Serve the sauce with Egg Foo Yung.

Nutrition Information

- Calories: 240 calories;
- Protein: 22
- Total Fat: 12.6
- Sodium: 1443
- Total Carbohydrate: 9.6
- Cholesterol: 330

562. Egg Foo Yung For Two

Serving: 2 | Prep: 20mins | Cook: 10mins | Ready in:

Ingredients

- 3 extra large eggs
- 2 teaspoons soy sauce
- 1 teaspoon oyster sauce
- 1/2 teaspoon sesame oil
- 3 tablespoons vegetable oil
- 6 slices fresh ginger
- 1 large clove garlic, smashed
- 1 cup fresh bean sprouts
- 1/2 cup chopped roast pork loin
- 1/2 cup chopped cooked chicken breast
- 1/4 cup chopped mushrooms
- 1/4 cup chopped green onions

Direction

- In a glass measuring cup, stir together the sesame oil, oyster sauce, soy sauce, and eggs. Pour in enough water to make one cup and stir until blended.
- In an 11-inch nonstick omelet pan, heat the vegetable oil on medium-high heat. Cook garlic and ginger while stirring for 1-2 minutes until browned. Remove the garlic and ginger.
- In the same skillet, cook while stirring the green onions, mushrooms, chicken breast, pork loin, and bean sprouts for about 2 minutes until heated through. Move to a bowl.
- Heat the skillet on medium-high heat again. Put in half of the egg mixture, tilting the skillet to coat the bottom. Cook for half a minute. Add half of the bean sprout mixture and spread over one side of the egg layer. Lower the heat to low, cook until the eggs are set for 3-5 minutes. Fold over omelet and slide onto a plate.
- Repeat the process with the remaining half cup egg mixture and bean sprout mixture for the second omelet.

Nutrition Information

- Calories: 474 calories;
- Cholesterol: 378
- Protein: 31.5
- Total Fat: 36.2
- Sodium: 489
- Total Carbohydrate: 6.2

563. Eggplant Mixed Grill

Serving: 6 | Prep: 15mins | Cook: 12mins | Ready in:

Ingredients

- 2 tablespoons olive oil
- 2 tablespoons chopped fresh parsley
- 2 tablespoons chopped fresh oregano
- 2 tablespoons chopped fresh basil
- 1 tablespoon balsamic vinegar
- 1 teaspoon kosher salt
- 1/2 teaspoon black pepper
- 6 cloves garlic, minced
- 1 red onion, cut into wedges
- 18 spears fresh asparagus, trimmed
- 12 crimini mushrooms, stems removed
- 1 (1 pound) eggplant, sliced into 1/4 inch rounds
- 1 red bell pepper, cut into wedges
- 1 yellow bell pepper, cut into wedges

Direction

- Mix the garlic, pepper, kosher salt, vinegar, basil, oregano, parsley and olive oil in a big resealable plastic bag. Put yellow and red bell peppers, together with the eggplant, mushrooms, asparagus and onion into the bag; seal. Marinate it in the fridge, occasionally turning, for 2 hours.
- Preheat a grill to high heat.
- Oil the grill grate lightly. Grill vegetables till tender, 6 minutes per side.

Nutrition Information

- Calories: 107 calories;
- Total Carbohydrate: 13.3
- Cholesterol: 0
- Protein: 4.3
- Total Fat: 4.9
- Sodium: 340

564. Eggplant Zucchini Pasta Bake With Mushrooms

Serving: 6 | Prep: 30mins | Cook: 1hours15mins | Ready in:

Ingredients

- 1 eggplant, diced into 1/2-inch squares
- 2 tablespoons extra-virgin olive oil, divided
- 1 tablespoon butter
- 1 zucchini, diced
- 2 cloves garlic, chopped
- 4 mushrooms, chopped
- 1 onion, chopped
- 1 (26 ounce) jar plain tomato sauce
- 1 large tomato, diced
- 1/4 teaspoon dried basil, or to taste
- 1/4 teaspoon dried marjoram, or to taste
- salt and ground black pepper to taste
- 1/2 cup dry white wine
- 1 1/4 cups farfalle (bow tie) pasta
- 1 3/4 cups grated Parmesan cheese
- 2 tablespoons grated Parmesan cheese
- 1 (7 ounce) package mozzarella cheese, cut into strips

Direction

- Boil a saucepan of water and place in the eggplant to cook for 8 minutes until mostly soft, then drain.
- In a skillet, heat butter with 1 tablespoon olive oil over a medium-high heat, then sauté garlic and zucchini for 5 minutes until zucchini becomes tender. Add in the mushrooms and cook for 3 minutes until they begin to brown,

then add eggplant, sauté for 2 minutes until brown.
- In another saucepan, heat the leftover oil over medium-high heat, then sauté onions for 4 minutes until golden. Add pepper, salt, majoram, basil, diced tomato, and tomato sauce, decrease the heat to a medium-low, then allow the sauce to just boil.
- Pour the wine into the zucchini mixture, lower the heat and simmer for 6 minutes until liquid is almost gone, then add the tomato sauce, blend thoroughly.
- Set the oven to 350 degrees F or 175 degrees C.
- Allow a large pot of moderately salted water to boil, then cook the farfalle pasta in the boiling water, stirring periodically, for 12 minutes until al dente, then drain.
- In the bottom of a lasagna dish, pour a fine layer of the sauce, then add a helping of a 1 3/4 cups and 2 tablespoons of Parmesan cheese and Mozzarella strips. Add a layer of pasta on top. Repeat the layering process and end with the cheese mixture.
- Place in the preheated oven to bake for 20 minutes until the cheese melts completely.

Nutrition Information

- Calories: 376 calories;
- Sodium: 1282
- Total Carbohydrate: 26.5
- Cholesterol: 48
- Protein: 22.8
- Total Fat: 19.7

565. Eggs Over Toast

Serving: 8 | Prep: 15mins | Cook: 15mins | Ready in:

Ingredients

- 2 (10.75 ounce) cans condensed cream of mushroom soup, undiluted
- 6 hard-cooked eggs, sliced
- 1 (16 ounce) package frozen mixed vegetables, thawed
- 2 cups milk
- salt and pepper to taste
- 8 slices white bread, toasted

Direction

- Mix together the pepper, salt, milk, mixed vegetables, sliced eggs and cream of mushroom soup in a big saucepan. Let the mixture simmer over medium heat and continue to cook until vegetables are heated completely. To serve, arrange the toast on the plates, and scoop the sauce on top.

Nutrition Information

- Calories: 256 calories;
- Total Fat: 10.8
- Sodium: 760
- Total Carbohydrate: 28.7
- Cholesterol: 164
- Protein: 11.8

566. Enoki Protein Egg Bakes

Serving: 12 | Prep: 25mins | Cook: 28mins | Ready in:

Ingredients

- 1 bunch enoki mushrooms, cut from stalk and separated
- 2 tablespoons garlic salt
- 2 tablespoons safflower oil
- 1/2 large shallot, chopped
- 2 cloves garlic, minced
- 1 pound extra-lean ground turkey breast
- 2 yellow bell peppers, finely chopped
- 12 eggs
- 2 tablespoons Italian seasoning
- salt and ground black pepper to taste

Direction

- Preheat the oven to 150 degrees C (300 degrees F).
- Toss the enoki mushrooms along with the garlic salt on a big plate.
- Heat the oil in a big wok or skillet. Put in the enoki mushrooms; cook and whisk for 2-3 minutes till firm and lightly browned on bottom. Bring back to the plate. Put the garlic and shallot into the skillet; cook and whisk for 1-2 minutes till becoming fragrant. Put to the mushrooms.
- Whisk the turkey into the skillet. Cook, whisk to crumble the clumps, for roughly 5 minutes till brown.
- Mix the turkey along with the mushroom mixture; cut finely. Whisk in the yellow bell peppers.
- Whip together the pepper, salt, Italian seasoning and eggs in a big bowl. Whisk in the turkey mixture and add into two a-third-cup muffin tins.
- Bake in preheated oven for roughly 20 minutes till the edges turn brown and a toothpick inserted in middle comes out clean.

Nutrition Information

- Calories: 140 calories;
- Sodium: 1008
- Total Carbohydrate: 1.8
- Cholesterol: 209
- Protein: 15.8
- Total Fat: 7.6

567. Essanaye's Sesame Beef Stir Fry

Serving: 6 | Prep: 25mins | Cook: 15mins | Ready in:

Ingredients

- 1/2 cup soy sauce
- 1/2 cup white sugar
- 1/3 cup rice wine vinegar
- 1/3 cup minced garlic
- 1 tablespoon sesame seeds
- 1 pound round steak, thinly sliced
- 1/4 cup peanut oil
- 2 cups 1-inch sliced asparagus
- 1 cup sliced fresh mushrooms, or more to taste
- 1 sweet onion, chopped
- 1 red bell pepper, sliced
- 1 bunch green onions, chopped into 1-inch pieces
- 1 cup whole cashews
- 1 tablespoon sesame seeds
- 1 tablespoon cornstarch (optional)
- 1 tablespoon water (optional)
- 1 tablespoon sesame seeds

Direction

- Mix rice wine vinegar, soy sauce, 1 tablespoon of sesame seeds, garlic and sugar together in a bowl then put the mixture in a ziplock plastic bag. Put in the beef and seal the ziplock bag pushing as much air out then gently massage the beef to evenly coat with the marinade. Keep the marinated beef in the fridge overnight.
- Heat a big skillet or wok with peanut oil on medium-high heat then cook and stir the marinated beef along with the marinade for 5 minutes or until the beef is browned well. Add in the mushrooms, bell pepper, asparagus, green onions and onion then cook and stir for 3-4 minutes or until the vegetables are starting to soften. Put in 1 tablespoon of sesame seeds and cashews and continue to cook the mixture for 2-3 more minutes until the vegetables are soft.
- In a small bowl, mix water and cornstarch together until the cornstarch has fully dissolved then pour it into the beef stir-fry and cook for 3 minutes or until the sauce is thick in consistency. Top off with the leftover 1 tablespoon of sesame seeds.

Nutrition Information

- Calories: 476 calories;

- Total Fat: 27.2
- Sodium: 1380
- Total Carbohydrate: 38.3
- Cholesterol: 40
- Protein: 23.7

568. Farro With Wild Mushrooms

Serving: 6 | Prep: 15mins | Cook: 55mins | Ready in:

Ingredients

- 1/2 ounce dried porcini mushrooms
- 2 tablespoons olive oil
- 10 brown mushroom caps, diced
- salt to taste
- 1/2 onion, diced small
- 2 cloves garlic, minced
- 1 cup pearled farro, rinsed, or more to taste
- 3 cups chicken stock, divided
- 2 tablespoons creme fraiche
- 2 tablespoons chopped fresh flat-leaf parsley
- freshly ground black pepper to taste
- 2 tablespoons freshly grated Parmigiano-Reggiano cheese, or to taste

Direction

- Arrange porcini mushrooms in a bowl and pour in warm water to cover; submerge for 20 to 30 minutes until mushrooms are reconstituted. Drain and chop mushrooms.
- Heat olive oil over medium-high heat in a pot. Sauté brown mushrooms with a dash of salt in hot oil, for 5 to 10 minutes until moisture evaporates and mushrooms turn golden slightly for 2-4 minutes.
- Stir onion into mushrooms. Sauté for 5 to 7 minutes until golden and transparent. Add garlic; sauté for another minute until aromatic.
- Pour in farro into the mushroom mixture; mix until coated with olive oil. Raise heat to high; pour in 1 cup chicken broth and sprinkle with a pinch of salt to mushroom mixture; bring to a boil. Turn the heat to medium low; simmer, covered for about 10 minutes, stirring once, until liquid is absorbed.
- Raise the heat to high and mix the remaining chicken broth into farro mixture; bring to a boil; turn the heat to medium low; simmer, covered for about 15 minutes, stir sometimes, until farro is just softened. Uncover the pan; keep simmering for about 15 minutes more until a desired doneness of farro is reached.
- Turn the heat to low; mix in parsley and creme fraiche into the farro mixture. Sprinkle with black pepper and salt to season. Mix in Parmigiano-Reggiano cheese into farro and pour into bowls.

Nutrition Information

- Calories: 193 calories;
- Total Fat: 8.2
- Sodium: 401
- Total Carbohydrate: 27.8
- Cholesterol: 9
- Protein: 6.5

569. Fast And Easy Ricotta Cheese Pizza With Mushrooms, Broccoli, And Chicken

Serving: 8 | Prep: 15mins | Cook: 25mins | Ready in:

Ingredients

- 1 tablespoon butter
- 1 skinless, boneless chicken breast, cut into bite-sized chunks
- 1 (8 ounce) container ricotta cheese
- 1 tablespoon butter
- 1 teaspoon garlic powder
- 1 teaspoon dried oregano
- salt and ground black pepper to taste
- 1 (12 inch) pre-baked pizza crust
- 2 cups shredded mozzarella cheese

- 1/2 cup chopped fresh broccoli
- 1 (3 ounce) can sliced mushrooms, drained

Direction

- Preheat the oven to 165°C/325°F.
- Melt 1 tbsp. butter on medium heat in a skillet; cook chicken in butter for 7-10 minutes till juices are clear and not pink. Take off heat; put aside.
- Heat pepper, salt, oregano, garlic powder, 1 tbsp. butter and ricotta cheese in microwave-safe bowl for 1 minute in microwave; stir to mix. Spread mixture on pizza crust; evenly scatter mozzarella cheese on pizza. Evenly put mushrooms, broccoli and cooked chicken over pizza.
- In the preheated oven, bake for 20 minutes till cheese melts.

Nutrition Information

- Calories: 310 calories;
- Total Carbohydrate: 28.6
- Cholesterol: 48
- Protein: 20.7
- Total Fat: 13.1
- Sodium: 575

570. Fettuccine And Zoodles Topped With Chicken Sausage, Asparagus, And Mushrooms

Serving: 4 | Prep: 20mins | Cook: 30mins | Ready in:

Ingredients

- 3 tablespoons olive oil, divided
- 1 (16 ounce) package chicken Italian sausage, casings removed
- 1 (8 ounce) package sliced fresh mushrooms
- 1/2 cup diced onion
- 1 cup chicken broth
- 1/2 pound fresh asparagus, cut into 1-inch pieces
- salt and ground black pepper to taste
- 1/2 cup half-and-half
- 2 tablespoons all-purpose flour
- 1 tablespoon butter
- 1 (9 ounce) package fresh fettuccine (such as Buitoni®)
- 3 cloves garlic, thinly sliced
- 2 zucchini, cut into spirals using a spiral slicer
- 1/4 teaspoon red pepper flakes
- 2 tablespoons shaved Parmesan cheese, or to taste

Direction

- In a skillet, heat a tablespoon of olive oil on medium heat; stir and cook the sausage for 5-7 minutes until it becomes crumbly and browned. Place the sausage into a bowl.
- In the same skillet, heat a tablespoon of olive oil; stir and cook the onion and mushrooms for 5 minutes until the mushrooms soften yet still firm and the onions soften. Add asparagus and chicken broth; stir and cook for 3 minutes. Flavor the mixture with pepper and salt.
- Transfer the vegetables to the edge of the skillet, then add butter, flour, and half-and-half; stir and cook for 5-7 minutes until a smooth and thick sauce is formed. Put the sausage into the skillet, add the vegetables into the sauce and stir.
- Boil a large pot with lightly salted water. In the boiling water, cook the fettuccine for 1-3 minutes until al dente but tender, then drain the fettuccine.
- In another skillet, heat the remaining tablespoon of olive oil on medium heat; stir and cook the garlic for half a minute until it becomes fragrant. Add red pepper flakes and zoodles (zucchini noodles); stir and cook for 5-7 minutes until al dente but tender. Combine the fettuccine into the zoodle mixture.
- Fill the serving plates with the fettuccine-zoodle mixture and place the sausage mixture on top. Dust each with the Parmesan cheese.

Nutrition Information

- Calories: 599 calories;
- Total Fat: 29.3
- Sodium: 1382
- Total Carbohydrate: 53.7
- Cholesterol: 139
- Protein: 30.3

571. Fettuccine In Creamy Mushroom And Sage Sauce

Serving: 2 | Prep: 10mins | Cook: 20mins | Ready in:

Ingredients

- 8 ounces spinach fettuccine pasta
- 1 tablespoon extra virgin olive oil
- 1 shallot, chopped
- 1 clove garlic, chopped
- 4 ounces chopped fresh oyster mushrooms
- 1/2 cup heavy cream
- 1 tablespoon chopped fresh sage
- salt and pepper to taste

Direction

- Boil a big pot of slightly salted water. Put in the pasta and cook till al dente or for 8 to 10 minutes; drain.
- In a medium saucepan, heat the olive oil over medium heat, and cook garlic and shallots till clear. Mix in the mushrooms, and cook till soft. Stir in sage and heavy cream. Cook and mix till thickened.
- Toss cooked fettucine and sauce together, and add pepper and salt to season and serve.

Nutrition Information

- Calories: 612 calories;
- Cholesterol: 82
- Protein: 16.5
- Total Fat: 31.4
- Sodium: 289
- Total Carbohydrate: 70.2

572. Fireball Mushrooms

Serving: 8 | Prep: 20mins | Cook: 25mins | Ready in:

Ingredients

- 1/4 cup margarine
- 1/2 bunch celery, diced
- 3 large onions, diced
- 1 1/2 tablespoons minced garlic
- 2 (6.5 ounce) cans chopped clams, drained
- 1/2 pound salad shrimp, chopped
- 2 teaspoons chicken bouillon granules
- 1/4 teaspoon cayenne pepper
- 1/4 teaspoon white pepper
- 2 cups croutons
- 1/4 cup seasoned bread crumbs
- 1/2 pound cooked lump crabmeat
- 1/4 cup margarine
- 1/4 cup dry white wine
- 16 large fresh white mushrooms, cleaned and stems removed
- 1 cup shredded Italian blend cheese

Direction

- In a big frying pan, heat a quarter cup of margarine then cook and mix the garlic, onion, and celery over medium heat for approximately 5 minutes, till onion becomes translucent. Blend in the salad shrimp and chopped clams, then cook and mix for about 3 minutes more, till the mixture becomes hot. Drain almost all the liquid from the pan, keeping about 1 tablespoon.
- Dust in the white pepper, cayenne pepper, and chicken bouillon granules, then mix. Gently mix in the crab meat, bread crumbs, and croutons.
- Preheat an oven to 400° F (200° C).
- In the bottom of a 9x13-inch baking dish, melt a quarter cup of margarine, then add the white

wine. Mound approximately 1/3 cup of filling into each mushroom cap, then transfer them to the baking dish. Dust the mushroom caps with the Italian blend cheese.
- In the preheated oven, bake for about 20 minutes till the cheese becomes bubbling and starts to brown.

Nutrition Information

- Calories: 341 calories;
- Total Carbohydrate: 19.7
- Cholesterol: 91
- Protein: 25.3
- Total Fat: 17.4
- Sodium: 584

573. Flaky Crescent Mushroom Turnovers

Serving: 8 | Prep: 20mins | Cook: 15mins | Ready in:

Ingredients

- 1/4 pound fresh mushrooms, coarsely chopped
- 2 tablespoons minced fresh parsley
- 2 tablespoons minced onion
- 3 tablespoons butter, divided
- 1 (8 ounce) can refrigerated crescent roll dough
- 2 1/2 tablespoons grated Parmesan cheese
- 2 tablespoons sesame seeds

Direction

- Preheat an oven to 190 °C or 375 °F.
- In a medium saucepan, gently cook and mix onion, parsley and mushrooms in 2 tablespoons of butter over medium heat till soft. Let drain and reserve.
- Split dough into 4 rectangles. Halve each rectangle, creating 8 squares, and set on a big baking sheet. On every square, put 1 tablespoon mushroom mixture. Put 1 teaspoon Parmesan cheese on top of every square. Fold squares forming triangles.
- Melt the rest of butter in a small saucepan. With butter, glaze triangles and scatter sesame seeds on top.
- In the prepped oven, bake till golden brown for 10 to 15 minutes. Serve while warm.

Nutrition Information

- Calories: 172 calories;
- Total Carbohydrate: 12.5
- Cholesterol: 13
- Protein: 3.4
- Total Fat: 11.9
- Sodium: 276

574. Flank Steak With Mushroom Sauce

Serving: 4 | Prep: 20mins | Cook: 20mins | Ready in:

Ingredients

- 2 tablespoons olive oil
- 1 beef flank steak
- 2 tablespoons butter
- 8 ounces mushrooms, sliced
- 1 shallot, diced
- 1 clove garlic, minced
- 1 tablespoon chopped fresh rosemary leaves
- 2 packets Swanson® Flavor Boost™ Concentrated Beef Broth
- 1/4 cup water

Direction

- In a 10-inch pan, heat 1 tablespoon of oil on medium heat. Insert the beef into the skillet. Cook until both sides are browned well or until desired doneness is achieved, 10 minutes for medium-rare. Move the beef out of the skillet.

- In the skillet, heat the remaining oil with 1 tablespoon of butter. Mix the mushrooms in and cook 5 minutes until tender, stirring every now and then. Stir constantly the rosemary, garlic and shallot in and cook for 30 seconds. Pour in the combination of water, concentrated broth and left butter. Cook until the butter melts entirely.
- Diagonally slice the beef against the grain into thin pieces. Place the mushroom mixture in with the beef. Serve.

Nutrition Information

- Calories: 260 calories;
- Protein: 18.7
- Total Fat: 18.3
- Sodium: 493
- Total Carbohydrate: 5.3
- Cholesterol: 46

575. Flat Iron Steak And Spinach Salad

Serving: 6 | Prep: 25mins | Cook: 25mins | Ready in:

Ingredients

- 1 (2 pound) flat iron steak
- salt and ground black pepper to taste
- 2 tablespoons olive oil
- 1 large red onion, thinly sliced
- 1/2 cup Italian salad dressing
- 3 large red bell peppers, cut into 1/2 inch strips
- 2 portobello mushrooms, sliced
- 1/2 cup red wine
- 4 cups baby spinach leaves
- 1/2 cup crumbled blue cheese

Direction

- Set an outdoor grill to preheat to medium-high heat; lightly glaze the grate with oil.
- Season both sides of the flat iron steak with salt and pepper. Cook on preheated grill grate for about 5 minutes each side for medium-rare or until meat reaches desired doneness. Allow to rest in a warm area while proceed the remaining ingredients.
- In a large skillet, heat olive oil over medium-high heat. Stir in onion and cook for about 4 minutes or until onion starts to turn soft. Pour the Italian salad dressing over onion, and bring to a boil, then stir in mushrooms and red peppers. Lower the heat to medium, cook for about 5 minutes or until peppers become soft.
- Use a slotted spoon to remove vegetables from skillet; set aside. Increase the heat to medium-high; add red wine and simmer for about 5 minutes or until the mixture of salad dressing and wine becomes a syrupy sauce.
- In the meantime, distribute spinach leaves onto serving plates. Slice the flat iron steak thinly across the grain. Place the warm, cooked vegetable mixture over spinach leaves, then place steak slices on top. Drizzle with reduced red wine sauce, add blue cheese on top and serve.

Nutrition Information

- Calories: 486 calories;
- Sodium: 601
- Total Carbohydrate: 12.7
- Cholesterol: 112
- Protein: 36.2
- Total Fat: 31.1

576. Foil Pack Mushrooms

Serving: 4 | Prep: 15mins | Cook: 20mins | Ready in:

Ingredients

- 24 fresh crimini mushrooms, stems removed
- 4 green onions, chopped
- 2 tablespoons pine nuts

- 1/4 cup olive oil
- salt and freshly ground black pepper to taste

Direction

- Preheat a grill to high heat. Grease 4 big heavy-duty aluminum foil sheets lightly.
- Stuff even amounts of pine nuts and green onions in every mushroom. On each aluminum foil piece, put 6 mushrooms. Drizzle olive oil on. Season with pepper and salt. Seal foil around mushrooms, making 4 packets.
- On preheated grill, put foil packets. Cook till mushrooms are tender for about 20 minutes.

Nutrition Information

- Calories: 184 calories;
- Total Fat: 15.7
- Sodium: 45
- Total Carbohydrate: 5.3
- Cholesterol: 0
- Protein: 6.1

577. Frank's Famous Spaghetti Sauce

Serving: 8 | Prep: 15mins | Cook: 30mins | Ready in:

Ingredients

- 1 tablespoon olive oil
- 1 onion, chopped
- 1 green bell pepper, chopped
- 3 cloves garlic, minced
- 4 fresh mushrooms, sliced
- 1 pound ground turkey
- 1 pinch dried basil
- 1 pinch dried oregano
- ground black pepper to taste
- 1 (14.5 ounce) can stewed tomatoes
- 2 (15 ounce) cans tomato sauce
- 1 (6 ounce) can tomato paste

Direction

- The first part of this dish is simply sautéing garlic, green bell pepper, and onions together in olive oil in a big skillet over medium heat until the bell pepper is tender and onions are translucent. Put in the ground black pepper, oregano, basil, ground turkey, and mushrooms; fry while stirring frequently until the turkey is cooked.
- To the same pan you used for the first part, add the can of stewed tomatoes with the liquid. Lower the heat once you've added this and allow it to simmer until the tomatoes turn soft and start to fall apart. Put in tomato sauce and stir; thicken it by adding tomato paste. Turn the heat down to very low and allow the sauce to simmer for 15 minutes. Serve this with your preferred pasta.

Nutrition Information

- Calories: 168 calories;
- Total Fat: 6.8
- Sodium: 885
- Total Carbohydrate: 15.6
- Cholesterol: 45
- Protein: 13.3

578. French Onion Casserole

Serving: 6 | Prep: 10mins | Cook: 1hours | Ready in:

Ingredients

- 1 pound lean ground beef
- 1 cup uncooked white rice
- 1 (10.5 ounce) can condensed French onion soup
- 1 (10.75 ounce) can condensed cream of mushroom soup
- 1/2 cup chopped celery
- 1/2 cup chopped green onions
- 1/2 cup chopped green bell pepper

Direction

- Preheat an oven to 175°C/350°F.
- Mix green bell pepper, green onions, celery, cream of mushroom soup, French onion soup, rice and ground beef in a 2-qt. casserole dish. Mix everything well.
- Bake, covered, for 1 hour at 175°C/350°F.

Nutrition Information

- Calories: 342 calories;
- Protein: 20
- Total Fat: 13.6
- Sodium: 804
- Total Carbohydrate: 33.8
- Cholesterol: 54

579. French Onion Chicken

Serving: 8 | Prep: 10mins | Cook: 1hours | Ready in:

Ingredients

- cooking spray (optional)
- 4 frozen whole chicken breasts
- 1 (8 ounce) package sliced fresh mushrooms
- 1 (10.75 ounce) can condensed cream of mushroom soup
- 8 ounces sour cream
- 1 (1 ounce) package dry onion soup mix

Direction

- Set the oven to 190°C or 375°F to preheat. Coat the bottom of a 3-qt casserole dish with cooking spray.
- In the prepped baking dish, arrange the chicken breasts and put mushrooms on top. In a bowl, combine together onion soup mix, sour cream and cream of mushroom soup, then drizzle this mixture over mushrooms as well as chicken. Use aluminum foil to cover the dish.
- In the preheated oven, bake for an hour, until juices run clear and is not pink in the middle anymore. An instant-read thermometer should reach at least 74°C or 165°F after being inserted in the center.

Nutrition Information

- Calories: 239 calories;
- Total Fat: 11.2
- Sodium: 630
- Total Carbohydrate: 6.9
- Cholesterol: 80
- Protein: 27.1

580. Fried Tilapia With Oyster Mushrooms

Serving: 4 | Prep: 10mins | Cook: 15mins | Ready in:

Ingredients

- 2 tablespoons butter
- 3 cups fresh oyster mushrooms, stemmed and sliced
- 1 cup heavy whipping cream
- salt and freshly ground black pepper to taste
- 4 (8 ounce) fillets tilapia
- 2 tablespoons all-purpose flour
- 2 tablespoons vegetable oil

Direction

- In a frying pan, melt butter over medium heat and cook mushroom for 5 minutes until browned. Add in pepper, salt and cream and let them simmer for about 5 minutes to get desired thickness.
- Divide tilapia into large chunks and use pepper and salt for seasoning. Sprinkle flour over the top.
- In a frying pan over medium heat, heat oil and cook tilapia for 3 minutes each side until

heated through and browned. Set on a plate and pour mushroom-cream sauce on top.

Nutrition Information

- Calories: 580 calories;
- Sodium: 213
- Total Carbohydrate: 8
- Cholesterol: 180
- Protein: 50
- Total Fat: 37.9

581. Garbanzo Stir Fry

Serving: 4 | Prep: 15mins | Cook: 30mins | Ready in:

Ingredients

- 2 tablespoons olive oil
- 1 tablespoon chopped fresh oregano
- 1 tablespoon chopped fresh basil
- 1 clove garlic, crushed
- ground black pepper to taste
- 1 (15 ounce) can garbanzo beans, drained and rinsed
- 1 large zucchini, halved and sliced
- 1/2 cup sliced mushrooms
- 1 tablespoon chopped fresh cilantro
- 1 tomato, chopped

Direction

- In a big frying pan, heat the oil on medium heat. Stir in pepper, garlic, basil and oregano, then add the zucchini and garbanzo beans and stir well to coat it with herbs and oil. Let it cook for 10 minutes with cover, stirring from time to time.
- Stir in cilantro and mushrooms and let it cook until it becomes tender, stirring from time to time. Put the chopped tomato over the mixture. Put cover and allow the tomatoes to steam for several minutes but avoid it from getting mushy. Serve right away.

Nutrition Information

- Calories: 167 calories;
- Total Fat: 7.7
- Sodium: 216
- Total Carbohydrate: 21.2
- Cholesterol: 0
- Protein: 4.6

582. Garden Tomato Soup

Serving: 10 | Prep: 15mins | Cook: 30mins | Ready in:

Ingredients

- 3 (16 ounce) cans whole peeled tomatoes
- 2 tablespoons vegetable oil
- 2 zucchini, cubed
- 2 large onions, chopped
- 2 cups sliced fresh mushrooms
- 2 teaspoons salt, or to taste
- 3 bay leaves
- 1/2 teaspoon dried thyme
- 2 teaspoons dried basil
- 1/2 teaspoon ground white pepper

Direction

- Puree whole tomatoes using a food processor or blender, until smooth.
- Over medium heat, cook in oil the zucchini, mushrooms and onions, until tender in a big pot. Add pureed tomatoes. Sprinkle salt, thyme, bay leaves, basil and white pepper to season. Boil mixture and lower heat; for 15 minutes, simmer mixture. Before serving, take out bay leaves.

Nutrition Information

- Calories: 71 calories;
- Total Fat: 3.1
- Sodium: 752

- Total Carbohydrate: 10.9
- Cholesterol: 0
- Protein: 2

583. Garlic Chicken Marinara

Serving: 8 | Prep: | Cook: |Ready in:

Ingredients

- 2 (8 ounce) packages angel hair pasta
- 6 skinless, boneless chicken breast halves, cut into bite size pieces
- 2 tablespoons olive oil
- 1 medium head garlic, minced
- 4 cups stewed tomatoes
- 1 large onion, chopped
- 2 cups fresh sliced mushrooms
- 4 large tomatoes, diced
- 1/2 red bell pepper, diced
- 1/2 green bell pepper, diced
- 1 1/2 cups corn
- 1/2 cup light beer

Direction

- With olive oil, pan fry half of the head of minced garlic and the boneless skinless chicken breasts in a big skillet. Cook till chicken's juices run clear.
- Boil beer, corn, red and green bell pepper, fresh tomatoes, mushrooms, onion, the other half of the garlic and stewed tomatoes in a big saucepan. Once sauce boils, put the cooked chicken, let simmer for an hour.
- Cook angel hair pasta with boiling salted water till al dente in a large pot. Drain pasta.
- Mix garlic chicken sauce and pasta. Serve while warm.

Nutrition Information

- Calories: 398 calories;
- Total Carbohydrate: 55.4

- Cholesterol: 51
- Protein: 30.7
- Total Fat: 6.9
- Sodium: 468

584. Garlic Herb Cheese Stuffed Mushrooms

Serving: 10 | Prep: 25mins | Cook: 25mins |Ready in:

Ingredients

- 1 (5.2 ounce) package garlic and herb cheese spread (such as Boursin®)
- 1 (8 ounce) package cream cheese, softened
- 1 (8 ounce) package grated Parmesan cheese, divided
- 1 cup olive oil
- 20 mushrooms, stems removed

Direction

- Set oven to 325°F (165°C) to preheat. In a mixing bowl, combine 1/2 package of Parmesan cheese, cream cheese, and cheese spread until well combined; chill in the fridge with cover.
- Pour olive oil into a bowl. Immerse each mushroom in oil to coat completely. Position the mushroom face down on a parchment paper-lined-baking sheet. Place another sheet of parchment paper over the mushrooms.
- Bake mushrooms for about 12 minutes in the preheated oven until soft. Take out of the oven and let mushrooms cool slightly. Place a clean sheet of parchment paper over the baking sheet.
- Over-fill each mushroom cap with the prepped cheese mixture; place stuffed mushroom caps on the baking sheet.
- Put the baking sheet back into the oven, and keep baking for about 12 minutes longer until cheese melts. Sprinkle top with the remainder 1/2 package of Parmesan cheese before serving.

Nutrition Information

- Calories: 435 calories;
- Total Carbohydrate: 3.2
- Cholesterol: 62
- Protein: 12.5
- Total Fat: 42.5
- Sodium: 505

585. Garlic Mushroom Burgers

Serving: 3 | Prep: 5mins | Cook: 10mins | Ready in:

Ingredients

- 1 egg, beaten
- 1 tablespoon minced garlic
- 1/4 teaspoon salt
- 1 (4.5 ounce) can sliced mushrooms, drained
- 1 pound ground beef

Direction

- Preheat the outdoor grill on medium-high heat; grease the grate lightly.
- In a bowl, combine mushrooms, egg, salt, and garlic; mix in ground beef thoroughly. Split the mixture into 3 patties.
- Grill patties for 5-7mins on each side for well done in the preheated grill or until cooked to your preferred doneness. An inserted instant-read thermometer in the middle should register 70°C or 160°Fahrenheit.

Nutrition Information

- Calories: 306 calories;
- Sodium: 483
- Total Carbohydrate: 3.2
- Cholesterol: 154
- Protein: 28.3
- Total Fat: 19.5

586. Garlic Mushroom Pasta

Serving: 4 | Prep: 10mins | Cook: 20mins | Ready in:

Ingredients

- 2 tablespoons olive oil
- 1/2 large onion, diced
- 5 large mushrooms, sliced
- 8 cloves garlic, crushed
- 1 teaspoon olive oil, or as needed
- 1 (12 ounce) package spaghetti
- 2 eggs, beaten
- 1/4 cup grated Parmesan cheese, plus more for garnish

Direction

- In a frying pan, heat 2 tablespoons olive oil over medium heat. In the hot oil, stir and cook garlic, mushrooms, and onion for 5-7 minutes until the onion turns translucent.
- Boil lightly salted water in a big pot; add approximately 1 teaspoon olive oil to prevent the spaghetti from sticking. In the boiling water, cook spaghetti for 12 minutes until fully cooked but remain firm to bite, tossing from time to time. Strain and return the hot spaghetti to the pot.
- Mix the spaghetti with eggs, cooking the eggs with the heat from the spaghetti. Mix 1/4 cup Parmesan cheese and mushroom and onion mixture into the spaghetti over low heat until the cheese melts and the eggs have fully cooked. Use more Parmesan cheese to garnish.

Nutrition Information

- Calories: 467 calories;
- Protein: 17.7
- Total Fat: 13.3
- Sodium: 120
- Total Carbohydrate: 68.8
- Cholesterol: 97

587. Garlic Pork Tenderloin With Mushroom Gravy

Serving: 6 | Prep: 15mins | Cook: 55mins | Ready in:

Ingredients

- kosher salt to taste
- ground black pepper to taste
- 2 (1 pound) pork tenderloins
- 3/4 cup butter
- 6 cloves garlic, minced
- 1 (16 ounce) can sliced mushrooms, drained
- 1 tablespoon balsamic vinegar
- 1 (14 ounce) can chicken broth, or as needed
- 1/4 cup all-purpose flour

Direction

- Start preheating the oven at 350°F (175°C).
- Rub pepper and salt over all sides of pork tenderloins; in a 9x13-inch baking dish, nestle tenderloins next to each other.
- Heat butter over medium heat in a saucepan until melted; put in mushrooms and garlic. Heat to a boil, lower the heat to medium-low, and simmer, stirring often, for about 5 minutes until sauce is aromatic. Whisk vinegar into the mushroom sauce. Spread the mushroom sauce over tenderloins, allowing the sauce to seep between the two tenderloins.
- Bake in the prepared oven for about 45 minutes until tenderloins turn light pink in the center. An instant-read thermometer should show at least 145°F (63°C) when inserted into the center. Place tenderloins onto a serving dish.
- Drain the drippings from the baking dish, including mushrooms, into a measuring cup, scraping the bottom to dislodge all the brown bits. Transfer 1/4 cup of the grease from the mixture and add to a saucepan. Pour enough chicken broth to the drippings to get 2 cups; blend flour into drippings until well-combined. Stir the broth-drippings mixture into the saucepan with grease over medium heat for about 5 minutes until thick; flavor with pepper and salt.
- Cut tenderloins into medallions and spread 1/2 of the gravy on top. Pour the leftover gravy in a gravy boat for serving.

Nutrition Information

- Calories: 384 calories;
- Total Fat: 27
- Sodium: 913
- Total Carbohydrate: 9.6
- Cholesterol: 128
- Protein: 26.1

588. Garlic Wine Chicken

Serving: 1 | Prep: 15mins | Cook: 10mins | Ready in:

Ingredients

- 1 skinless, boneless chicken breast half - pounded thin
- 1 tablespoon vegetable oil
- 1/4 cup all-purpose flour
- ground black pepper to taste
- 1/2 tablespoon chopped garlic
- 4 mushrooms, chopped
- 1/2 lemon
- 1 1/2 cups Chablis or other dry white wine
- 2 tablespoons butter, room temperature
- 2 ounces cooked angel hair pasta

Direction

- Heat the oil for frying in a medium skillet. Use flour to dredge the chicken breast in then put it in the hot skillet. To taste, put pepper. Cook for 3 to 4 minutes until golden brown on one side.
- Flip the chicken (presentation side up) and put wine, juice from 1/2 lemon, mushrooms and garlic. Mix them all together. Increase heat as high as possible letting liquid evaporate until

what's left in the skillet is about 1/4 cup of liquid.
- Take chicken out from the skillet and put the butter at room temperature. In the skillet sauce, swirl it around until the sauce is slightly thickened and it is incorporated. Put sauce over chicken. Serve together with the pasta.

Nutrition Information

- Calories: 1015 calories;
- Cholesterol: 130
- Protein: 40.2
- Total Fat: 40.5
- Sodium: 379
- Total Carbohydrate: 67

589. Garlicky Ham, Mushroom, And Spinach Frittata

Serving: 6 | Prep: 20mins | Cook: 50mins | Ready in:

Ingredients

- 2 tablespoons butter
- 8 cloves garlic, smashed
- 1 shallot, sliced
- 1 (8 ounce) package sliced fresh mushrooms
- 4 cups bagged fresh spinach
- 3/4 cup diced cooked ham
- 9 eggs, beaten
- 1 cup shredded Cheddar cheese (optional)
- salt and ground black pepper to taste (optional)

Direction

- Preheat an oven to 175°C/350°F.
- In a big ovenproof skillet, heat butter on medium heat; mix and cook shallot and garlic in hot butter for 5 minutes till shallot is soft. Mix mushrooms into garlic and shallot; stir and cook for 8-10 minutes till mushrooms start to brown. Mix spinach into mushroom mixture and cover; cook for 5 more minutes, occasionally mixing, till spinach wilts.
- Mix ham in; cook for 5 minutes till ham starts to brown. Evenly put eggs in skillet; cover.
- In the preheated oven, bake for 25 minutes till frittata is lightly puffed and set in the middle. A knife inserted in middle of frittata should exit cleanly. Sprinkle Cheddar cheese. Let stand for 5 minutes till cheese melts; season with black pepper and salt.

Nutrition Information

- Calories: 283 calories;
- Protein: 19.5
- Total Fat: 20.9
- Sodium: 485
- Total Carbohydrate: 5.5
- Cholesterol: 318

590. Glenda's Mandarin Orange Salad

Serving: 6 | Prep: 15mins | Cook: | Ready in:

Ingredients

- Dressing
- 1 onion, minced
- 2/3 cup white sugar
- 1 tablespoon dry mustard
- 1 teaspoon celery seed
- 1 teaspoon black pepper
- 1/2 cup distilled white vinegar
- 1/2 cup olive oil
- Salad
- 1 head romaine lettuce, chopped
- 1 (10 ounce) can mandarin oranges, drained
- 5 ounces fresh mushrooms, sliced
- 3 tablespoons slivered almonds
- 3 tablespoons crumbled cooked bacon

Direction

- In a small bowl, place black pepper, celery seed, mustard, sugar and onion. Stir in vinegar to dissolve the sugar. Add olive oil and whisk till the dressing is thickened. Cover and store for at least 3 hours in the fridge.
- For the salad, in a large bowl, toss bacon, almonds, mushrooms, oranges and lettuce together. Drizzle dressing over and toss again till coated.

Nutrition Information

- Calories: 332 calories;
- Sodium: 120
- Total Carbohydrate: 34.1
- Cholesterol: 2
- Protein: 4.6
- Total Fat: 21.2

591. Gluten Free Elbows With Mixed Mushrooms And Italian Sausage Soup

Serving: 6 | Prep: 15mins | Cook: 30mins | Ready in:

Ingredients

- 1 (12 ounce) box Barilla® Gluten Free Elbows
- 3 quarts chicken stock
- 3 cloves garlic, minced
- 4 tablespoons extra-virgin olive oil
- 1 sprig rosemary
- 4 (6 ounce) packages mixed mushrooms
- 1 pound Italian sausage, boiled for 10 minutes and cut into 1/3 inch slices
- 1 (15 ounce) can cannellini beans, drained
- 1 pint cherry tomatoes, halved
- Salt and black pepper to taste
- 1 tablespoon parsley, chopped

Direction

- Bring chicken stock to a simmer in a big soup pot.
- In the meantime, sauté garlic with rosemary and olive oil in a saucepan until turning light yellow, about 1 minute. Add mushrooms and sauté until turning light brown. Add sausage and sauté for 2 minutes.
- Add sausage and mushrooms to the broth, mix in Barilla® Gluten Free Elbows, tomatoes, and beans. Cook for 1/2 of the time the box recommends.
- Allow the soup to sit for 10 minutes before eating. Use pepper and salt to season. Use parsley to garnish and use olive oil to drizzle on top.

Nutrition Information

- Calories: 818 calories;
- Sodium: 2094
- Total Carbohydrate: 99.2
- Cholesterol: 59
- Protein: 24
- Total Fat: 36.6

592. Gluten Free Penne With Cajun Chicken

Serving: 6 | Prep: | Cook: | Ready in:

Ingredients

- 1 (12 ounce) box Barilla Gluten Free Penne
- 4 tablespoons extra-virgin olive oil
- 4 boneless, skinless chicken thighs
- 1 Vidalia onion, cut julienne style
- 1 red bell pepper, cut julienne style
- 6 domestic mushrooms, quartered
- 3 cloves garlic, chopped
- 1 tablespoon Cajun seasoning
- 1/2 cup dry white wine
- 1/2 cup heavy cream
- 1/2 cup Parmesan cheese, grated
- Salt and black pepper to taste

Direction

- Bring a big pot of water to a boil.
- At the meantime, brown chicken in a hot skillet in olive oil for about 5 minutes over high heat. Add Cajun seasoning, garlic, mushrooms, bell pepper and onion; sauté for 3 more minutes. Stir in wine; sprinkle with pepper and salt; reduce liquid by 1/2.
- Add cream; heat up to a simmer.
- At the meantime, cook pasta as directed on the package.
- Drain; toss with sauce; stir in cheese, then serve.

Nutrition Information

- Calories: 527 calories;
- Total Fat: 24.5
- Sodium: 415
- Total Carbohydrate: 52.3
- Cholesterol: 79
- Protein: 21.1

593. Gnocchi And Peppers In Balsamic Sauce

Serving: 4 | Prep: 30mins | Cook: 30mins | Ready in:

Ingredients

- 2 tablespoons olive oil
- 3 cloves garlic, chopped
- 1/2 cup diced red onion
- salt to taste
- 6 crimini mushrooms, chopped
- 4 small mixed sweet peppers, julienned
- 1/2 cup cherry tomatoes, halved
- 4 leaves fresh basil, chopped
- 1/2 cup balsamic vinegar
- 1 (16 ounce) package potato gnocchi
- 1 cup Additional butter or margarine

Direction

- Following the package instructions, cook the gnocchi; then drain the gnocchi.
- In a skillet, heat olive oil over medium heat. Put the garlic into the skillet, cook for 2 minutes. Stir in the chopped onions, then flavor with salt; cook for 5 minutes until the onions start to soften. Stir in basil, tomatoes, peppers, and mushrooms; cook for 5 more minutes. Add the butter, stirring to melt. Pour the balsamic vinegar into the skillet, stir it, then turn down the heat and simmer the sauce for 15-20 minutes. Toss the sauce and the cooked gnocchi together.

Nutrition Information

- Calories: 693 calories;
- Sodium: 435
- Total Carbohydrate: 33.8
- Cholesterol: 143
- Protein: 5.9
- Total Fat: 61

594. Golden Lasagna

Serving: 5 | Prep: 15mins | Cook: 50mins | Ready in:

Ingredients

- 6 lasagna noodles
- 1/4 cup chopped onion
- 1 (4.5 ounce) can sliced mushrooms, drained
- 3 tablespoons chicken broth
- 1 (10.75 ounce) can condensed cream of chicken soup
- 1/3 cup milk
- 1/2 teaspoon dried basil
- 2 cups diced chicken breast meat
- 1 pound ricotta cheese
- 1 1/2 cups shredded Cheddar cheese
- 1/8 cup grated Parmesan cheese

Direction

- Turn the oven to 350°F (175°) to preheat. Boil lightly salted water in a big pot. Put in noodles and cook until al dente, about 8-10 minutes; strain.
- Sauté mushrooms and onion in chicken broth in a small saucepan. Take away from heat. Mix in basil, milk, and soup. Stir thoroughly. Put aside.
- Arrange 3 cooked lasagna noodles in a lightly oiled 9x13-in. baking dish. Make the layers as follows: half of the chicken, half of the ricotta cheese, half of the Cheddar cheese, half of the Parmesan cheese, and half of the soup/mushroom mixture. Put on 3 more lasagna noodles and duplicate layers. Bake without a cover for about 50 minutes in the preheated oven.

Nutrition Information

- Calories: 545 calories;
- Total Carbohydrate: 33.4
- Cholesterol: 124
- Protein: 46.6
- Total Fat: 24.7
- Sodium: 928

595. Goldy's Special Salad

Serving: 4 | Prep: 20mins | Cook: | Ready in:

Ingredients

- 10 ounces fresh spinach - trimmed, washed and dried
- 1 mango - peeled, seeded, and cubed
- 1 avocado - peeled, pitted and diced
- 1 tomato, cut into wedges
- 1/2 red onion, julienned
- 1/2 pound fresh mushrooms, sliced
- 2 tablespoons extra virgin olive oil
- 1/2 cup white wine vinegar
- 1/2 teaspoon ground black pepper
- 1 pinch white sugar

Direction

- Mix together mushrooms, onion, tomato, avocado, mango and spinach in a big salad bowl.
- Mix sugar, pepper, vinegar and oil in a jar to prepare for the dressing. Seal the jar and shake well, then drizzle over salad and toss to coat well.

Nutrition Information

- Calories: 216 calories;
- Sodium: 68
- Total Carbohydrate: 20.4
- Cholesterol: 0
- Protein: 5.5
- Total Fat: 14.8

596. Gourmet Cream Of Wild Mushroom Soup

Serving: 4 | Prep: 25mins | Cook: 28mins | Ready in:

Ingredients

- 3 tablespoons extra-virgin olive oil
- 1 pound assorted wild mushrooms, thinly sliced
- 1 large yellow onion, finely chopped
- 2 portobello mushrooms, thinly sliced
- 1 tablespoon chopped fresh thyme
- 1 teaspoon chopped fresh rosemary
- 1/2 teaspoon sea salt
- 1/4 cup dry white wine
- 3 cups gluten-free chicken broth
- 1 cup heavy whipping cream
- 1/2 cup chopped fresh parsley, divided
- 1 tablespoon gluten-free all-purpose flour
- sea salt and ground white pepper to taste

Direction

- In a large saucepan over low heat, put olive oil. Add sea salt, rosemary, thyme, Portobello mushrooms, yellow onion, and wild mushrooms; cook for about 3 minutes, covered, until mushrooms soften.
- Remove the cover of the saucepan and add white wine; stir and cook for about 5 minutes until most of the wine vaporizes. Add chicken broth; simmer the soup for about 15 minutes until flavors blend.
- In a small bowl, mix flour, 1/4 cup parsley, and heavy cream. Add into the soup; cook for about 5 minutes, whisking occasionally, until heated through. Add pepper and salt to the soup to taste; put the rest 1/4 cup parsley on top.

Nutrition Information

- Calories: 375 calories;
- Sodium: 1056
- Total Carbohydrate: 13
- Cholesterol: 85
- Protein: 6.7
- Total Fat: 33.1

597. Grandma Sylvia's Brisket

Serving: 6 | Prep: 30mins | Cook: 2hours30mins | Ready in:

Ingredients

- 2 1/2 pounds beef brisket
- 2 (6 ounce) cans tomato paste
- 2 (6 ounce) cans water
- 2 onions, cut into 1-inch wedges
- 3 carrots, sliced
- 1/4 pound fresh mushrooms, sliced
- 1 tablespoon garlic powder
- 1 tablespoon white sugar
- salt and ground black pepper to taste

Direction

- Set a big skillet over medium-high heat. Place the brisket on pan and brown on both sides; transfer to a deep pot.
- Pour in the water and stir in tomato paste, carrots, onions, mushrooms, sugar, pepper, garlic powder and salt. Allow the mixture to boil.
- Lessen the heat to low and make it to a simmer while covered for roughly 2 1/2 hours, until the meat is softened. Place the brisket on a baking dish, allow to cool, and keep on the fridge overnight.
- Roughly 1 1/2 hours before serving, set the oven for preheating to 300°F (150°C). Scoop out the fat residue from sauce and cut the meat across the grain. Layer the beef, followed by the vegetables, and sauce in a baking dish.
- Cover the pan using a foil and let it bake inside the oven for roughly an hour until warm.

Nutrition Information

- Calories: 349 calories;
- Cholesterol: 77
- Protein: 26.6
- Total Fat: 16.6
- Sodium: 532
- Total Carbohydrate: 24.9

598. Grandma's Pork Chops In Mushroom Gravy

Serving: 6 | Prep: 15mins | Cook: 1hours | Ready in:

Ingredients

- 1 tablespoon butter
- 1 clove garlic, pressed
- 6 pork chops
- salt and pepper to taste
- 1 (8 ounce) can mushrooms, drained
- 1 cup dry sherry
- 1 (10.5 ounce) can beef broth

- 2 tablespoons cornstarch
- 2 tablespoons water

Direction

- Start preheating oven to 350°F (175°C).
- In a large skillet, melt butter over medium heat. Put in garlic, sauté until fragrant. Add pepper and salt to the pork chops to taste. In the skillet, fry for 3 mins each side just until browned on both sides. Transfer pork chops to a Dutch oven or baking pan.
- Place mushrooms into skillet with garlic and pork drippings. Stir in beef broth and sherry, scrape all the bits of pork that are stuck to pan. Boil, transfer over pork chops in baking pan. Close the lid or cover with aluminum foil.
- Bake in prepared oven for 45 mins. Discard the foil or lid, keep baking for 15 mins. more. Transfer the chops from pan to a serving platter. Put dish onto stove over medium heat. Stir water and cornstarch together. Stir in the cornstarch mixture slowly when juices in pan come to a boil. Cook for 2 mins until thickened. Spoon the sauce over chops. Enjoy!

Nutrition Information

- Calories: 209 calories;
- Sodium: 609
- Total Carbohydrate: 10.7
- Cholesterol: 59
- Protein: 19.2
- Total Fat: 8.1

599. Grandpa's Beef, Mushroom, And Barley Soup

Serving: 8 | Prep: 15mins | Cook: 6hours | Ready in:

Ingredients

- 1 cup pearl barley
- 2 1/2 cups water
- 8 ounces broken dried mushrooms
- 1/2 cup water
- 1 (3 pound) boneless chuck roast
- 5 quarts water
- 1/2 cup chopped fresh parsley
- 1/2 cup chopped fresh dill
- 1 (14 ounce) can beef broth
- 1 tablespoon kosher salt
- 1 teaspoon pepper

Direction

- In a bowl, mix 2 and 1/2 cups of water and barley, cover and allow to soak overnight. Add dried mushrooms in a bowl with 1/2 cup of water, cover and allow to soak them overnight.
- In a large stockpot, put the chuck roast over medium heat, cover it with 5 quarts of water. Start boiling the water, remove any foam on the surface. Keep boiling for about 15 minutes until there is no foam forming on the water. Add in the mushrooms, barley and water from 2 bowls into stockpot, mix in with pepper, salt, broth, dill and parsley. Boil the mixture again, lower the heat to low, let it simmer for 4 to 6 hours, stir every hour until the soup gets the wanted thickness.
- Remove large chunks of beef from the soup, trim and drain fat. Cut the rest of the meat into bite-sized pieces and take back to the soup

Nutrition Information

- Calories: 416 calories;
- Cholesterol: 74
- Protein: 29
- Total Fat: 19.1
- Sodium: 993
- Total Carbohydrate: 34.1

600. Great Grilled Smoky Vegetables With Avocado And Goat Cheese Crumbles

Serving: 6 | Prep: 25mins | Cook: 5mins | Ready in:

Ingredients

- 6 portobello mushroom caps
- 4 red bell peppers, cored and quartered
- 1 red onion, thickly sliced
- 1/2 cup olive oil
- 2 limes, juiced
- 2 tablespoons grill seasoning
- 2 cloves garlic, minced
- 1 pinch cayenne pepper, or to taste
- 2 tablespoons balsamic vinegar
- 1 avocado - peeled, pitted, and cubed
- 1/2 cup crumbled goat cheese
- salt to taste
- freshly ground black pepper to taste
- 2 tablespoons finely chopped fresh basil

Direction

- In a 9x13-inches baking dish, put the red onion, red bell peppers and mushrooms. In a small bowl, whisk the cayenne pepper, garlic, grill seasoning, lime juice and olive oil; toss to coat. Let vegetables marinate for at least 30 minutes.
- Preheat the grill to medium heat; oil the grate lightly.
- Take vegetables out from the marinade; shake the excess off. Reserve the leftover marinade.
- On preheated grill, grill vegetables for 5 minutes till tender. Put grilled vegetables on a big platter. Whisk leftover marinade with balsamic vinegar and pour it on the vegetables. Put goat cheese and avocado on top. Season it with pepper and salt. Sprinkle basil on and serve.

Nutrition Information

- Calories: 331 calories;
- Total Fat: 27
- Sodium: 563
- Total Carbohydrate: 18.7
- Cholesterol: 9
- Protein: 7.4

601. Greek Pasta

Serving: 4 | Prep: 15mins | Cook: 15mins | Ready in:

Ingredients

- 1 pound linguine pasta
- 3 tomatoes
- 1/3 cup olive oil
- 3 cloves garlic, minced
- 1 pound mushrooms, sliced
- 1 teaspoon dried oregano
- 3/4 cup crumbled feta cheese
- 1 (2 ounce) can sliced black olives, drained

Direction

- Boil a big pot of lightly salted water; briefly plunge whole tomatoes in water till skin begins to peel. Use a slotted spoon to remove; put in cold water. Put pasta in boiling water; cook till al dente or for 8-10 minutes. Drain.
- Peel then chop blanched tomatoes as pasta cooks.
- Heat olive oil in a big skillet on medium heat. Mix in mushrooms and garlic; sauté till mushrooms start to give up their juices. Mix in oregano and tomatoes; cook till tomatoes are tender.
- Serving: Plate pasta then put hot tomato sauce on top; sprinkle olives and feta.

Nutrition Information

- Calories: 759 calories;
- Protein: 23.3
- Total Fat: 31
- Sodium: 866

- Total Carbohydrate: 102.4
- Cholesterol: 25

602. Greek Pita Pockets

Serving: 4 | Prep: 15mins | Cook: 10mins | Ready in:

Ingredients

- 1/2 cup Greek-style (thick) unflavored yogurt
- 1 lemon, juiced
- 4 ounces bulk pork sausage
- 1 small onion, diced
- 1/3 cup Greek olives, diced
- 3/4 cup wild mushrooms, chopped
- 1 cup fresh baby spinach leaves, packed
- 6 eggs, beaten
- 2/3 cup Nikos® feta cheese crumbles
- 2 pitas, halved crosswise

Direction

- Combine lemon juice and yogurt in a small bowl; put aside.
- Cook sausage, stirring often and crumbling, on medium-high heat for 2 minutes in a non-stick skillet. Put in mushrooms, olives and onion, then cook for another 4 minutes.
- Put in spinach leaves and cook for about 1-3 minutes until vegetables give up all liquid and the sausage is cooked through. Crack in eggs and cook while stirring constantly until almost dry. Take off the heat and whisk in feta.
- Pack feta-egg mixture into each pita half. Serve at once with lemon yogurt.

Nutrition Information

- Calories: 382 calories;
- Cholesterol: 317
- Protein: 21
- Total Fat: 23.4
- Sodium: 896
- Total Carbohydrate: 23.4

603. Green Bean Casserole My Way

Serving: 6 | Prep: 15mins | Cook: 1hours6mins | Ready in:

Ingredients

- 2 tablespoons vegetable oil
- 1 small onion, chopped
- 2 cups chopped mushrooms
- 1/2 cup whiskey
- 2/3 cup sour cream
- 1/2 cup vegetable broth
- 2 tablespoons all-purpose flour
- 1 whole roasted chicken, dark meat removed from bones and shredded
- 4 cups frozen cut green beans
- salt and ground black pepper to taste
- 1 1/2 cups French-fried onion rings
- 1/2 (12 ounce) jar pork gravy (optional)

Direction

- Pre heat the oven to 200 degrees C (400 degrees F).
- Heat the oil on medium high heat in the big ovenproof skillet. Put in the onion; cook and whisk for roughly 5 minutes till becoming tender and translucent. Put in the mushrooms and cook for 1-2 minutes. Add whiskey carefully to the hot skillet. Lower the heat to medium and allow the whiskey to cook down, roughly 5 minutes.
- Stir together flour, vegetable broth and sour cream in a bowl. Whisk into skillet. Boil; lower the heat and let it simmer for roughly 5 minutes till the sauce becomes thickened.
- Mix the green beans and chicken in a big bowl; add the sauce and toss till well-coated. Use pepper and salt to season. Add the mixture back to skillet and cover using the tight-fitting lid or aluminum foil.

- Bake in preheated oven for roughly half an hour till thoroughly heated. Remove the cover and scatter the onion rings over the top. Keep baking for roughly 15 minutes longer till the rings become crispy and golden brown. Whisk the gravy into hot casserole.

Nutrition Information

- Calories: 715 calories;
- Total Fat: 45.2
- Sodium: 772
- Total Carbohydrate: 36.2
- Cholesterol: 78
- Protein: 24.9

604. Green Bean And Portobello Mushroom Casserole

Serving: 10 | Prep: 15mins | Cook: 35mins | Ready in:

Ingredients

- 4 slices bacon
- 1/4 cup olive oil
- 1 pound baby portobello mushrooms, sliced
- 1/2 medium onion, chopped
- 3 cloves garlic, finely chopped
- 1/2 cup slivered almonds
- 1 (10.75 ounce) can condensed cream of mushroom soup with roasted garlic
- 3/4 teaspoon seasoned salt with no MSG
- 1/3 teaspoon white pepper
- 2 (15.5 ounce) cans French cut green beans, drained
- 1 cup shredded Cheddar cheese

Direction

- Set oven to 375°F (190°C) to preheat.
- Cook bacon over medium-high heat in a large skillet until crisp. Transfer cooked bacon to paper towels to drain. Add olive oil to the skillet, and lower heat to medium. Once oil is hot, add onion and mushrooms; cook vegetables, mixing often, until onions begin to turn transparent. Add garlic, sauté for a few minutes barely until aromatic. Mix in almonds and mushroom soup, and bring to a boil. Sprinkle mixture with white pepper and seasoned salt to taste, and crush bacon in. Gradually mix in green beans, then pour the mixture into a casserole dish.
- Bake without covering for half an hour in the preheated oven. Take the dish out of the oven, and scatter Cheddar cheese on top. Put back into the oven and bake until cheese is melted, for 5 minutes. Allow to stand for 5 minutes, and serve.

Nutrition Information

- Calories: 244 calories;
- Sodium: 656
- Total Carbohydrate: 10.3
- Cholesterol: 23
- Protein: 8.5
- Total Fat: 19.3

605. Green Olive Chicken II

Serving: 6 | Prep: 10mins | Cook: 1hours | Ready in:

Ingredients

- 3 tablespoons butter
- 1/2 cup chopped onion
- 1 (16 ounce) can whole peeled tomatoes, drained and chopped
- 1 cup water
- 1/2 cup chopped green bell pepper
- 1 (4 ounce) can sliced mushrooms
- 1 tablespoon chopped fresh parsley
- 1 teaspoon paprika
- 1 tablespoon salt
- 1/4 teaspoon ground black pepper
- 1 cup uncooked long-grain white rice
- 1/2 cup sliced green olives

- 4 skinless, boneless chicken breast halves

Direction

- Melt butter on medium heat in a big skillet. Add onion; sauté till browned lightly. Mix in olives, rice, salt, pepper, paprika, parsley, mushrooms, bell pepper, water and tomatoes. Put chicken in skillet; cover. Boil.
- Lower heat to medium low; simmer for 1 hour. Remove chicken then let rice complete cooking if rice is unfinished yet chicken is cooked through. Serve: Slice chicken; put over cooked rice.

Nutrition Information

- Calories: 295 calories;
- Total Fat: 9.7
- Sodium: 1766
- Total Carbohydrate: 32.5
- Cholesterol: 56
- Protein: 19.3

606. Grilled Beef Sirloin & Farmer's Market Skewers

Serving: 4 | Prep: | Cook: | Ready in:

Ingredients

- 1 (1 1/4 pound) beef top sirloin steak boneless, cut 1 inch thick
- 1 medium yellow squash, sliced (1/2-inch)
- 1 medium zucchini, sliced (1/2-inch)
- 1 small red onion, cut into 1/2-inch thick wedges
- 8 medium mushrooms
- 1 tablespoon Dijon-style mustard
- 1 tablespoon olive oil
- Mustard-Thyme Glaze:
- 2 tablespoons Dijon-style mustard
- 2 tablespoons apricot preserves
- 1 teaspoon lemon juice
- 1/2 teaspoon dried thyme leaves
- 1/4 teaspoon black pepper

Direction

- In 1-cup glass measure, mix all the glaze ingredients together. Put in the microwave set on high for 45 seconds, stir the mixture 1 time. Use a brush to coat the beef steak with the prepared glaze mixture.
- Insert the vegetables in an alternating pattern on four 12-inch metal skewers. Mix the oil and mustard together and use a brush to coat the vegetables with the mustard mixture.
- Put the vegetable skewers and the steak on a grill grid placed on top of medium, ash-covered coals. Let the steak cook in a covered grill for 11-15 minutes (13-16 minutes if cooked on a preheated gas grill over medium heat) if you want the meat doneness to be medium rare (145°F) to medium (160°F), flip the steak from time to time. Let the vegetable skewers grill for 6-10 minutes until soft, flip the skewers from time to time.
- Slice the grilled steak and sprinkle with salt to taste. Serve it alongside the grilled vegetables.

Nutrition Information

- Calories: 277 calories;
- Total Carbohydrate: 15.5
- Cholesterol: 61
- Protein: 27.1
- Total Fat: 11.9
- Sodium: 345

607. Grilled Chicken And Portobello Lasagna Rollups

Serving: 9 | Prep: 30mins | Cook: 1hours | Ready in:

Ingredients

- 18 lasagna noodles, cooked and drained

- 2 cups marinara sauce
- 1 teaspoon vegetable oil
- 2 portobello mushrooms, diced
- 1 cup frozen chopped spinach
- 2 cups diced cooked chicken
- 1 (15 ounce) container ricotta cheese
- 1/2 cup grated Parmesan cheese
- 1 teaspoon dried oregano
- salt and ground black pepper to taste
- 2 cups Alfredo sauce
- 1 cup shredded mozzarella cheese
- 1/4 cup pine nuts

Direction

- Use the slightly-salted water to fill the big pot and boil to the rolling boil on high heat. Whisk in lasagna noodles, and bring back to the boil. Cook pasta, uncovered, whisk once in a while, for roughly 8 minutes or till noodles become cooked yet still firm to bite; drain off and wash.
- Preheat the oven to 190 degrees C (375 degrees F). Spread marinara sauce in the bottom of the 9x13 glass baking plate; put aside.
- Heat the oil on medium heat in the skillet; cook and whisk the mushrooms for roughly 5 minutes or till tender. Whisk in the spinach, and cook till hot; take out of the heat.
- Whisk cooked spinach mixture, oregano, Parmesan cheese, ricotta cheese and chicken together in the big bowl. Use the black pepper and salt to season. Spread roughly a quarter cup mixture onto each lasagna noodle. Roll noodle up, and position with the seam side down to prepped baking plate. Repeat the process for each noodle. Scoop the Alfredo sauce on rollups.
- Bake, covered, in preheated oven for 40 minutes. Remove the cover; drizzle with the pine nuts and mozzarella cheese. Bring back to oven and bake for roughly 10 minutes or till pine nuts toast and cheese melts and bubbly. Serve while hot.

Nutrition Information

- Calories: 603 calories;
- Sodium: 1004
- Total Carbohydrate: 50.8
- Cholesterol: 74
- Protein: 30
- Total Fat: 32.1

608. Grilled Kansas City Smothered BBQ Chicken

Serving: 4 | Prep: 15mins | Cook: 25mins | Ready in:

Ingredients

- 4 skinless, boneless chicken breasts, pounded to 1/2-inch thickness
- 2 cups Kansas City BBQ Sauce, divided (see below for recipe)
- 1/3 cup sliced white mushrooms
- 1/2 medium onion, thinly sliced
- 8 slices provolone cheese
- Fresh cilantro or parsley (optional)
- Reynolds Wrap® Non-Stick Foil
- Kansas City BBQ Sauce:
- 1 cup ketchup
- 1/2 cup brown sugar
- 1/4 cup yellow mustard
- 1/4 cup apple cider vinegar
- 1/4 cup Worcestershire sauce
- 2 tablespoons honey
- 2 tablespoons dark molasses
- 2 teaspoons chili powder
- 2 teaspoons garlic powder
- 1 teaspoon liquid smoke
- 1 teaspoon onion powder
- 1 teaspoon crushed red pepper flakes
- 1/2 teaspoon salt
- 1/2 teaspoon black pepper

Direction

- Whisk all sauce ingredients in a medium saucepan; boil. Lower to simmer; cook for 10-

- 15 minutes. Take off heat; cool for 15 minutes to room temperature.
- Measure 1/2 cup of sauce; put aside. Put leftover sauce in a big sealable bag; put chicken breasts in bag. Seal; refrigerate for half an hour.
- Preheat a grill on medium heat; put 4 12x12-inch Reynold Wrap Nonstick Foil pieces on grill. Transfer a chicken breast with tongs on each foil square; throw marinade away.
- Brush some leftover 1/2 cup of BBQ sauce on each chicken breast; top with onions and mushrooms. Fold the foil around every chicken breast to enclose veggies and chicken. Cook for 10-12 minutes on medium heat till a meat thermometer inserted in middle reads 170°C, juices are clear and chicken is tender.
- Unwrap the foil packets; put 2 provolone cheese slices on each chicken breast so cheese lies over onions and mushrooms; cook for 2-3 more minutes, uncovered, till cheese melts. Use fresh parsley/cilantro to garnish; serve.

Nutrition Information

- Calories: 605 calories;
- Sodium: 1884
- Total Carbohydrate: 67.9
- Cholesterol: 104
- Protein: 40.8
- Total Fat: 20.2

609. Grilled Mushroom Sandwich With Citrus Mayo

Serving: 4 | Prep: 10mins | Cook: 15mins | Ready in:

Ingredients

- 2 tablespoons olive oil
- 1/4 cup balsamic vinegar
- 1 clove garlic, minced
- 4 portobello mushroom caps
- 1/3 cup mayonnaise
- 2 tablespoons orange juice
- 1 (12 ounce) jar roasted red bell peppers
- 4 rolls sourdough bread
- 4 slices smoked Gouda cheese
- 1 (10 ounce) bag mixed salad greens

Direction

- Beat garlic, balsamic vinegar and olive oil until combined thoroughly. In a resealable bag, transfer on top of the mushroom caps to coat, then seal the bag and let it marinate for half an hour. Stir orange juice and mayonnaise together, then put aside.
- Set an outdoor grill on medium heat and start preheating.
- Take the mushroom caps out of the marinade, then shake off to remove the excess. On a square piece of foil, arrange each mushroom cap upside down. Top with the roasted peppers, then seal. Cook on the prepared grill, turning from time to time, for 15 minutes until tender. Slice open the sourdough rolls once the mushrooms are almost finished, then grill on the sliced sides until golden brown.
- Spread orange mayonnaise over the sliced sides of the rolls and place the mixed greens, Gouda cheese, roasted pepper, and mushrooms into layers to assemble the sandwiches.

Nutrition Information

- Calories: 519 calories;
- Protein: 17
- Total Fat: 30.3
- Sodium: 848
- Total Carbohydrate: 49.2
- Cholesterol: 39

610. Grilled Mushroom Swiss Burgers

Serving: 6 | Prep: 15mins | Cook: 15mins | Ready in:

Ingredients

- 1 1/2 pounds lean ground beef
- 1/2 teaspoon seasoned meat tenderizer
- salt and pepper to taste
- 2 teaspoons butter
- 2 (4 ounce) cans sliced mushrooms, drained
- 2 tablespoons soy sauce
- 4 slices Swiss cheese
- 6 hamburger buns

Direction

- Prepare the grill for medium heat. Grease grate lightly with oil.
- Split the ground beef into 6 patties. Put meat tenderizer, pepper and salt to taste. Reserve.
- In a skillet, liquefy butter over medium heat. Put in the soy sauce and mushrooms; cook and mix till browned. Reserve and retain warmth.
- Grill patties till cooked through, about 6 minutes each side. Distribute the mushroom mixture equally between the burgers and put atop each one with 1 slice of Swiss cheese. To let the cheese melt, cover the grill for a minute. Take away from the grill and put on hamburger buns, serve.

Nutrition Information

- Calories: 520 calories;
- Total Fat: 32.4
- Sodium: 868
- Total Carbohydrate: 25
- Cholesterol: 106
- Protein: 30

611. Grilled Steak And Vegetable Salad From Publix®

Serving: 4 | Prep: 30mins | Cook: |Ready in:

Ingredients

- 1 1/2 pounds grilling steaks (strip, rib eye, tenderloin)
- 1 teaspoon kosher salt, divided
- 1/2 teaspoon ground black pepper
- 1 medium zucchini, halved lengthwise
- 3 plum (Roma) tomatoes, halved
- 1 (6 ounce) package fresh sliced portobello mushrooms, stems and gills removed
- 2 tablespoons olive oil
- 8 tablespoons balsamic glaze (reduced balsamic vinegar), divided
- 1 (5 ounce) bag mixed salad greens with arugula
- 4 tablespoons Caesar salad dressing, divided

Direction

- Preheat grill pan (or grill).
- Use pepper and a half teaspoon of salt to season steaks. Put steaks on grill pan (or grill). Grill each side for 3-4 minutes or till the internal temperature of the steak reaches 145°F. Take the steaks out of the grill and allow them to sit about 5 minutes then slice.
- Put portobellos, tomatoes, zucchini, oil and the remaining a half teaspoon of salt together. Transfer the vegetables to the grill, grill each side of the vegetables for 2-3 minutes or until they becomes tender and you can see grill marks on the vegetables.
- Take vegetables out of the grill; chop them into bite-size pieces. Cut steaks into slices.
- Distribute salad greens among four serving plates. Put vegetables and steak on top of the salad. Pour drizzles of balsamic glaze, salad dressing on each salad. The dish is ready to serve.

Nutrition Information

- Calories: 385 calories;
- Total Fat: 25.1
- Sodium: 683
- Total Carbohydrate: 15.3
- Cholesterol: 99
- Protein: 22.9

612. Grilled Stuffed Duckling

Serving: 4 | Prep: 25mins | Cook: 1hours5mins | Ready in:

Ingredients

- 1 cup couscous
- 3 1/2 tablespoons butter, or as needed, divided
- 1 cup finely chopped white onion
- 1/2 cup diced mushrooms
- 4 serrano peppers, diced, or more to taste
- cayenne pepper
- 1 whole duckling - thawed, neck and giblets removed, rinsed
- 1 1/2 teaspoons dried basil, or to taste
- sea salt and ground black pepper to taste

Direction

- Pour water in a saucepan and bring to boil, and then remove from heat and add couscous in water. Then cover saucepan with lid and let stand for 10 minutes, or until the water has been completely absorbed. Use a fork to ensure the couscous stays fluffy.
- In a skillet, heat butter (1 1/2 tablespoons) over medium heat, and then add Serrano peppers, mushrooms, and onions. Cook until onions, mushrooms, and peppers are lightly brown, stirring; should take about 5 minutes. Add cayenne pepper and the cooked couscous.
- Take the couscous mixture and use it to fill the duckling's cavity, and then spread a thin layer of butter over the entire duckling's skin; about 1 tablespoon. Season by rubbing salt, pepper, and basil into the skin. Use aluminum foil to wrap.
- Lightly oil your grill's grate, and then preheat grill to about 300 F°/150 C° on medium heat.
- Cook the duckling on the grill for 30 minutes, turning once. You can remove the aluminum foil. Keep grilling. Turning occasionally and basting with butter each time. Cook for about 25 – 30 minutes, or until you can see the juices are clear and the meat is no longer pink at the bone. Use an instant-read thermometer to get the temperature. It should be at 180 F° or 82 C°. Insert the thermometer into the thickest part of the thigh, near the bone.
- Take the duckling off of the grill and prepare a double sheet of aluminum foil for cover. Let it rest for 10 minutes at warm temperature before slicing. Spoon out couscous and serve alongside the duckling.

Nutrition Information

- Calories: 321 calories;
- Total Fat: 13.1
- Sodium: 182
- Total Carbohydrate: 38.4
- Cholesterol: 51
- Protein: 12.3

613. Ground Beef Stroganoff Casserole

Serving: 8 | Prep: 15mins | Cook: 50mins | Ready in:

Ingredients

- cooking spray
- 1 pound extra-lean (94%) ground beef
- 1 teaspoon salt
- 1/2 teaspoon ground black pepper
- 1 (8 ounce) package sliced fresh mushrooms
- 1 large onion, chopped
- 3 cloves garlic, minced
- 1/2 cup dry white wine
- 1 (10.75 ounce) can fat-free condensed cream of mushroom soup (such as Campbell's®)
- 1/2 cup fat-free sour cream
- 1 tablespoon Dijon mustard
- 4 cups cooked egg noodles

Direction

- Preheat an oven to 175 degrees C (350 degrees F). Use cooking spray to coat a 9x13-inch baking dish.
- Use cooking spray to spritz a large nonstick skillet; set on medium-high heat. Place in ground beef and cook for 10 minutes while breaking up until browned. Add pepper and salt to taste.
- Mix garlic, onion and mushrooms into the skillet. Cook while stirring for about 2 minutes until the onion becomes tender. Pour in wine, then decrease the heat to low and let to simmer for three minutes. Add mustard, sour cream, and cream of mushroom soup.
- Place cooked noodles in a large bowl and add the beef mixture on top. Coat by tossing. Transfer to the greased baking dish; cover with aluminum foil.
- In the preheated oven, bake for about 25 minutes until bubbling.

Nutrition Information

- Calories: 298 calories;
- Total Carbohydrate: 28.8
- Cholesterol: 66
- Protein: 18.1
- Total Fat: 10.6
- Sodium: 681

---

614. Grown Up Macaroni And Cheese

Serving: 4 | Prep: 25mins | Cook: 40mins | Ready in:

Ingredients

- 1 ounce dried porcini mushrooms
- 1 (8 ounce) package small shell pasta
- 1/4 cup unsalted butter
- 1 leek, finely chopped
- 1 small shallot, finely chopped
- 1/4 cup all-purpose flour
- 1 teaspoon Worcestershire sauce
- 1/8 teaspoon ground black pepper
- 1 cup milk, warmed
- 1 tomato, chopped
- 2 tofu hot dogs, sliced 1/8-inch thick
- 6 ounces grated Cheddar cheese
- 3 ounces Brie cheese, rind removed and cut into cubes
- 2 ounces grated Asiago cheese
- 1/4 cup milk (optional)
- 1/3 cup bread crumbs
- 1 teaspoon ground paprika

Direction

- In a small bowl, put the porcini mushrooms. Cover with warm water. Allow to immerse for 20 minutes to half an hour till rehydrated. Drain and chop roughly.
- Preheat an oven to 220 °C or 425 °F.
- Boil a big pot of slightly salted water. Cook the shell pasta in boiling water for 8 minutes, mixing from time to time, till soft but firm to the bite. Drain.
- In a big pot, liquify butter over moderate heat. Put in the shallot and leek; cook and mix for 2 minutes till softened. Lower the heat to low; mix in the pepper, Worcestershire sauce and flour. Add a cup of warmed milk gradually, mixing continuously, till blended. Simmer the sauce for 5 minutes till thickened.
- Mix tofu hot dogs, tomato and chopped mushrooms into the sauce; fold in the pasta. Mix in Asiago cheese, Brie cheese and Cheddar cheese till melted.
- In a 9-inch square casserole dish, add cheese mixture and pasta. Sprinkle with a quarter cup of milk in case mixture looks very thick. Put paprika and bread crumbs on top. Cover the dish using aluminum foil.
- In the prepped oven, bake for 20 minutes till bubbling in the middle.

Nutrition Information

- Calories: 771 calories;

- Total Carbohydrate: 67.7
- Cholesterol: 115
- Protein: 38.2
- Total Fat: 39.6
- Sodium: 815

615. Grzybki Marynowane (Pickled Wild Mushrooms)

Serving: 16 | Prep: 30mins | Cook: 17mins | Ready in:

Ingredients

- 4 pounds fresh porcini mushrooms
- 5 1-pint canning jars with lids and rings
- 3 1/2 cups water
- 1 cup white vinegar
- 1 onion, roughly chopped
- 1 tablespoon superfine sugar
- 1 teaspoon salt
- 6 whole black peppercorns, or to taste
- 2 whole allspice berries
- 1 bay leaf

Direction

- Trim the mushrooms and rinse. Put in a big saucepan, cover in water, and boil. Take saucepan off the heat and drain. Put mushrooms back to saucepan, put in fresh water to cover, and boil once more. Take off the heat and drain. Slice bigger mushrooms into bite-sized portions.
- In boiling water, sterilize lids and jars for a minimum of 5 minutes. Into sterilized, hot jars, pack the mushrooms.
- In a big pot, boil bay leaf, allspice, peppercorns, salt, sugar, onion, vinegar and water for 5 minutes. Take off the heat and put aside for approximately 20 minutes to cool. On top of mushrooms, evenly transfer the liquid, filling to within a quarter-inch of surface.
- Around the insides of jars, trace a thin spatula or clean knife after having filled to get rid of any air bubbles. Using a damp paper towel, wipe jar rims to get rid of any food residue. Put on lids and screw on the rings.
- In the big stockpot bottom, put a rack and fill with water midway. Boil and into the boiling water, lower jars with a holder. Retain a 2-inch gap among the jars. Put in additional boiling water if needed to let water level come to at least an-inch over the jar tops. Let water come to a rolling boil, place cover on the pot, and process for 7 minutes.
- Take jars out of stockpot and put onto a wood or cloth-covered surface, a few-inch apart, till cool. Press the surface of every lid using a finger, making sure that seal is tight, lid must not move down or up at all. Keep in a dark, cool place.

Nutrition Information

- Calories: 38 calories;
- Total Fat: 0.1
- Sodium: 154
- Total Carbohydrate: 6.4
- Cholesterol: 0
- Protein: 3

616. Guay Diaw Lawd (Pork Belly, Chicken Wing, And Noodle Stew)

Serving: 5 | Prep: 40mins | Cook: 1hours | Ready in:

Ingredients

- 10 dried shiitake mushrooms
- 1/2 cup peeled and chopped cilantro root
- 1/4 cup coarsely chopped garlic
- 2 tablespoons black peppercorns
- 2 (32 ounce) cartons beef stock
- 9 ounces pork belly, cut into 3/4-inch pieces
- 1 pound chicken wings
- 9 ounces firm tofu, cut into 1/3-inch chunks
- 9 ounces pickled radish (jap chai), diced

- 2 tablespoons oyster sauce, or more to taste
- 2 tablespoons dark sweet soy sauce (pad se ew), or more to taste
- 1 dash fish sauce, or more to taste
- sea salt to taste
- 1 (16 ounce) package wide rice noodles
- 2 cups bean sprouts
- 1 cup green onions, sliced
- 1 cup chopped cilantro leaves

Direction

- In a small bowl, put shiitake mushrooms. Use hot water to cover and soak for about 20 minutes until tender. Drain and squeeze out extra water then slice.
- Pound black peppercorns, garlic, and cilantro root in a mortar and pestle to make a coarse paste. Place paste in a big pot.
- Place beef stock in the pot. Add chicken wings and pork belly. Simmer and cook for 10 minutes. Add pickled radish, tofu, and sliced shiitake mushrooms. Simmer the soup for about 45 minutes until chicken wings are cooked thoroughly. Mix in soy sauce and oyster sauce. Season with sea salt and fish sauce.
- Put a steamer basket in a big pot then pour in water to reach the bottom of the steamer. Boil water. Add noodles, then steam for about 5 minutes, covered, until tender.
- Put noodles in every serving bowl then place soup over it. Top with cilantro, green onions, and bean sprouts.

Nutrition Information

- Calories: 647 calories;
- Total Fat: 15.7
- Sodium: 1612
- Total Carbohydrate: 96.6
- Cholesterol: 34
- Protein: 28.7

617. Gumbo Style Chicken Creole

Serving: 5 | Prep: 15mins | Cook: 45mins | Ready in:

Ingredients

- 1/4 cup oil for frying
- 1/4 cup all-purpose flour
- 1 green bell pepper, chopped
- 1 onion, chopped
- 2 cups cooked, chopped chicken breast meat
- 1 (14.5 ounce) can diced tomatoes with green chile peppers, with liquid
- 1 (4.5 ounce) can sliced mushrooms, drained
- 2 tablespoons chopped fresh parsley
- 2 teaspoons Worcestershire sauce
- 3 cloves garlic, minced
- 1 teaspoon soy sauce
- 1 teaspoon white sugar
- 1/2 teaspoon salt
- 1/2 teaspoon ground black pepper
- 3 dashes hot sauce

Direction

- In a large skillet over high heat, heat oil. Stir in flour and cook for 5 minutes or until mixture has the same color as a cooper penny, remember to stir constantly while cooking. Lower the heat to low and stir in onion and bell pepper. Cook, stirring sometimes, for 10 to 15 minutes until softened.
- Add hot sauce, pepper, salt, sugar, soy sauce, garlic, Worcestershire sauce, parsley, mushrooms, green chile peppers, tomatoes and chicken. Stir together until well combined and simmer, covered, for 20 minutes.

Nutrition Information

- Calories: 167 calories;
- Total Fat: 3.3
- Sodium: 807
- Total Carbohydrate: 14.7
- Cholesterol: 48
- Protein: 19.8

618. Ham Mushroom Barley Soup

Serving: 4 | Prep: 10mins | Cook: 50mins | Ready in:

Ingredients

- 2 tablespoons butter
- 1 cup chopped onion
- 1 (8 ounce) pre-cooked ham steak, diced
- 2 tablespoons curry powder, or to taste
- 3 1/2 cups chicken broth
- 1 (14.5 ounce) can stewed tomatoes
- 1/2 cup pearl barley
- 1 pound quartered mushrooms
- 1 cup thickly sliced carrots

Direction

- In a big saucepan, melt butter over medium heat. Add onions; cook for 5 minutes until clear. Mix in curry and ham for 30-60 seconds until the curry is aromatic. Add barley, tomatoes, and chicken broth. Boil it, lower the heat and bring to a simmer with a cover for 30-35 minutes until the barley is soft. Add carrots and mushrooms and cook for 10-15 minutes until soft.

Nutrition Information

- Calories: 361 calories;
- Cholesterol: 51
- Protein: 20.6
- Total Fat: 15
- Sodium: 2103
- Total Carbohydrate: 39.3

619. Ham, Garden Vegetable And Spring Mix Salad With Swiss Cheese

Serving: 3 | Prep: 15mins | Cook: | Ready in:

Ingredients

- 1 (8 ounce) package DOLE® Extra Veggie™ with Garden Vegetables
- 4 ounces roasted ham or turkey slices, cut into thin strips
- 2 slices Swiss cheese, cut into thin strips
- 1 pound DOLE® Asparagus, cooked, cut into 2-inch pieces
- 4 medium DOLE White or Brown Mushrooms, sliced
- 1/3 cup thinly sliced DOLE Red Onion
- salt and ground black pepper to taste
- Creamy Dijon Dressing*:
- 3 tablespoons Sherry wine vinegar
- 2 teaspoons Dijon-style mustard
- 1 clove garlic, minced
- 1 teaspoon dried oregano, crushed
- 1/2 teaspoon salt
- 1/4 teaspoon black pepper
- 1/4 cup canola oil
- 1 tablespoon mayonnaise

Direction

- In a large bowl, combine onion, mushrooms, asparagus, cheese, ham, vegetables from pouch and salad blend. Season to taste with Cream Dijon Dressing and toss. Add pepper and salt to taste.
- To make Creamy Dijon Dressing: In a small bowl, whisk 1/4 tsp of black pepper, 1/2 tsp of salt, 1 tsp of dried oregano crushed, 1 minced clove garlic, 2 tsp of Dijon-style mustard and 3 tbsp. of Sherry wine vinegar. Gradually whisk in 1 tbsp. of mayonnaise and 1/4 cup of canola oil to blend. Yields 1/2 cup.

Nutrition Information

- Calories: 423 calories;
- Cholesterol: 40
- Protein: 16.3
- Total Fat: 34.6
- Sodium: 1016
- Total Carbohydrate: 11.5

620. Hawaiian Shrimp

Serving: 6 | Prep: 30mins | Cook: 8mins | Ready in:

Ingredients

- 2 pounds medium shrimp, peeled and deveined
- 2 (20 ounce) cans pineapple chunks, juice reserved
- 1/2 pound bacon slices, cut into 2 inch pieces
- 2 large red bell peppers, chopped
- 1/2 pound fresh mushrooms, stems removed
- 2 cups cherry tomatoes
- 1 cup sweet and sour sauce
- skewers

Direction

- Preheat grill on high.
- Alternately thread shrimp, red bell peppers, pineapple, bacon, cherry tomatoes, and mushroom caps on skewers. Arrange them in a shallow baking dish. In a small bowl, combine sweet and sour sauce with reserved pineapple juice and save a small amount for basting. Sauce over the skewers with this mixture.
- Grease the grill grates lightly. Grill for 6 to 8 minutes, or until shrimps are opaque, basting regularly with reserved sauce.

Nutrition Information

- Calories: 385 calories;
- Sodium: 714
- Total Carbohydrate: 47.1
- Cholesterol: 244
- Protein: 32.4
- Total Fat: 8.1

621. Hazelnut Mushroom Pilaf

Serving: 6 | Prep: 10mins | Cook: 30mins | Ready in:

Ingredients

- 1/4 cup butter
- 1/2 cup uncooked long-grain rice
- 1/4 cup uncooked orzo pasta
- 1/2 cup sliced fresh mushrooms
- 1/2 cup chopped onion
- 1/4 cup minced celery
- 2 cups chicken broth
- 2 tablespoons chopped fresh parsley
- 1/4 teaspoon dried marjoram
- 1/4 teaspoon ground black pepper
- 1/2 cup chopped toasted hazelnuts

Direction

- Put a big pan on medium-low heat. Melt the butter and sauté the celery, onion, mushrooms, orzo and rice. Stir continuously until the rice is light brown.
- Stir in hazelnuts, pepper, marjoram, parsley and chicken broth; boil. Lower the heat to low; cover the pan and let it simmer for 15 minutes. Take off from heat and allow to stand for 10 minutes prior to serving.

Nutrition Information

- Calories: 256 calories;
- Total Carbohydrate: 23.9
- Cholesterol: 21
- Protein: 8.1
- Total Fat: 14.7
- Sodium: 584

622. Healthy Mince Pies

Serving: 4 | Prep: 25mins | Cook: 25mins | Ready in:

Ingredients

- 1 tablespoon vegetable oil
- 8 ounces lean ground beef
- 1/2 onion, finely chopped
- 1/2 cup spaghetti sauce
- 1 small zucchini, peeled and grated
- 4 button mushrooms, finely chopped
- 1 small carrot, peeled and grated
- salt and ground black pepper to taste
- olive oil cooking spray
- 4 sheets phyllo pastry
- 4 teaspoons grated Parmesan cheese

Direction

- Preheat the oven to 400°F (200°C).
- In a large skillet, heat oil over medium heat. Cook and stir onion and beef in the hot oil for about 5 minutes, until browned. Mix in carrot, mushrooms, zucchini and spaghetti sauce; season with pepper and salt. Allow to simmer for about 5 minutes, until flavors combine.
- Spray cooking spray on half of each phyllo dough sheet and fold lengthwise in half. On one edge of each phyllo sheet, add a half cup of the beef mixture; add 1 teaspoon of Parmesan cheese on top. Fold up into rectangular parcels.
- Place parcels on a baking sheet. Coat the parcels with cooking spray.
- Bake in the prepped oven in about 15 minutes, until golden brown.

Nutrition Information

- Calories: 299 calories;
- Protein: 14.1
- Total Fat: 17.9
- Sodium: 344
- Total Carbohydrate: 19.8
- Cholesterol: 45

623. Hearty Meat Sauce

Serving: 4 | Prep: 15mins | Cook: 30mins | Ready in:

Ingredients

- 1/2 pound ground beef
- 2 (16 ounce) jars spaghetti sauce
- 1 diced yellow pepper
- 1 diced red bell pepper
- 1 (14.5 ounce) can peeled and diced tomatoes, drained
- 6 fresh mushrooms, coarsely chopped

Direction

- Place a skillet over medium heat and brown the ground beef till no pink shows; drain.
- In a large pot over medium heat, mix spaghetti sauce and browned beef together, about 5-10 minutes. Put in mushrooms, canned tomatoes, red peppers and yellow peppers. Turn the heat down; simmer with a cover while stirring every once in a while, about 30 minutes.

Nutrition Information

- Calories: 351 calories;
- Total Fat: 14
- Sodium: 1111
- Total Carbohydrate: 39.3
- Cholesterol: 39
- Protein: 15.8

624. Hearty Vegetable Lasagna

Serving: 12 | Prep: 25mins | Cook: 1hours | Ready in:

Ingredients

- 1 (16 ounce) package lasagna noodles
- 1 pound fresh mushrooms, sliced
- 3/4 cup chopped green bell pepper
- 3/4 cup chopped onion
- 3 cloves garlic, minced
- 2 tablespoons vegetable oil
- 2 (26 ounce) jars pasta sauce
- 1 teaspoon dried basil
- 1 (15 ounce) container part-skim ricotta cheese
- 4 cups shredded mozzarella cheese
- 2 eggs
- 1/2 cup grated Parmesan cheese

Direction

- Cook lasagna noodles for about 10 minutes in a large pot containing boiling water or until al dente. Then rinse under cold water and drain them.
- Cook while stirring garlic, onion, green peppers and mushrooms in oil in a large saucepan. Mix in basil and pasta sauce. Heat to boil. Decrease the heat and let to simmer for 15 minutes.
- Combine eggs, 2 cups mozzarella cheese, and ricotta.
- Preheat an oven to 175 degrees C (350 degrees F). Scatter one cup of tomato sauce on the bottom of a 9x13 inch baking dish that is greased. Then layer 1/2 each, Parmesan cheese, sauce, ricotta mix and lasagna noodles. Repeat layering and add the remaining two cups of mozzarella cheese on top.
- Bake without covering for 40 minutes. Leave to sit for 15 minutes prior to serving.

Nutrition Information

- Calories: 462 calories;
- Total Fat: 19.5
- Sodium: 843
- Total Carbohydrate: 49.6
- Cholesterol: 77
- Protein: 23.2

625. Hemp Seed Soup

Serving: 4 | Prep: 20mins | Cook: 30mins | Ready in:

Ingredients

- 4 cups water
- 1 cube vegetable bouillon, or more to taste
- 3/4 cup red lentils
- 2 bay leaves
- 1/2 pound carrots, chopped
- 1/4 pound fresh mushrooms, finely chopped
- salt and ground black pepper to taste
- 1 tablespoon olive oil
- 1 onion, chopped
- 2 cloves garlic, minced, or more to taste
- 1/4 pound hemp seeds
- 1 bunch cilantro, chopped

Direction

- Boil the water in a big pot and add vegetable bouillon to taste. Add the bay leaves and lentils and let it simmer for 15 minutes. Add pepper, salt, mushrooms and carrots, then keep on simmering.
- In a frying pan, heat the olive oil on medium-high heat, then sauté the onion for around 5 minutes, until it becomes tender. Add the garlic and sauté for 1-2 minutes until it becomes aromatic. Mix the onion mixture into the soup.
- In another frying pan, cook and stir the hemp seeds on medium-high heat for 2-3 minutes, until it becomes aromatic and toasted. Mix the toasted hemp seeds into the soup, then add the cilantro and let it cook for an additional 5 minutes.

Nutrition Information

- Calories: 372 calories;
- Sodium: 100
- Total Carbohydrate: 37.7
- Cholesterol: 0

- Protein: 21
- Total Fat: 16.5

626. Homemade Chicken A La King

Serving: 8 | Prep: 10mins | Cook: 20mins | Ready in:

Ingredients

- 3 tablespoons butter
- 1 green bell pepper, finely chopped
- 1/2 cup chopped celery
- 1 (4.5 ounce) can mushrooms, drained
- 1 small onion, chopped
- 3 tablespoons all-purpose flour
- 2 cups milk, divided
- 2 egg yolks, beaten
- 2 cups diced, cooked chicken breast meat
- 1 tablespoon lemon juice
- 1 tablespoon sherry
- 1 teaspoon paprika
- salt and pepper to taste
- 1 (8 ounce) can peas, drained
- 1 (4 ounce) jar diced pimento peppers, drained

Direction

- In a large skillet, melt butter over medium heat. Sauté mushrooms, celery and bell pepper for about 5 minutes, until soft. Mix in onion. In a small bowl, stir together 1/2 cup milk and flour; then stir mixture into skillet. Beat egg yolks into the remaining 1 1/2 cups milk and add in the skillet. Cook and stir, until thicken.
- Put in chicken and cook, stirring constantly, about 3 - 5 minutes. Mix in pepper, salt, paprika, sherry and lemon juice. Finally, mix in pimento peppers and peas. Heat through then serve.

Nutrition Information

- Calories: 178 calories;

- Protein: 13.5
- Total Fat: 9.4
- Sodium: 174
- Total Carbohydrate: 9.8
- Cholesterol: 94

627. Honey Curried Chicken

Serving: 18 | Prep: | Cook: | Ready in:

Ingredients

- 18 cut up chicken pieces
- 1/4 cup prepared mustard
- 1 cup honey
- 3 tablespoons curry powder
- 2 (4.5 ounce) cans mushrooms, drained
- 1 (4.5 ounce) can mushrooms, drained, liquid reserved

Direction

- Pre heat the oven to 150 degrees C (300 degrees F).
- Lay the chicken pieces into the 9x13-in. baking dish. In the small-sized microwave-safe bowl, whisk the curry powder, honey and mustard together. Microwave on HIGH (with full power) for 60 seconds. Put in all mushrooms, stir them together, and add the mixture on top of the chicken. Bake in preheated oven till the juices come out clear and the chicken is thoroughly cooked or for 45 - 50 minutes. Flip the chicken pieces over after half an hour of baking. Once done, the chicken should have the beautiful golden brown.

Nutrition Information

- Calories: 315 calories;
- Total Fat: 17.7
- Sodium: 210
- Total Carbohydrate: 17.4
- Cholesterol: 86

- Protein: 22.1

628. Honey Roasted Potatoes And Mushrooms

Serving: 6 | Prep: 20mins | Cook: 25mins | Ready in:

Ingredients

- 1 pound potatoes, cut into bite-sized chunks
- 2 tablespoons olive oil
- 1 pound cremini mushrooms, trimmed and halved
- 1/2 white onion, chopped
- 1 tablespoon honey
- 1 teaspoon dried rosemary
- 1/2 teaspoon dried thyme
- 1/8 teaspoon dried sage
- 1 pinch dry mustard powder
- 1 pinch garlic powder
- salt and ground black pepper to taste

Direction

- Set oven to 450°F (230°C) to preheat.
- In a 9x13-inch baking dish, arrange potato chunks, drizzle olive oil over potatoes, and toss until evenly coated.
- Bake for 10 minutes in the preheated oven.
- Take out of the oven, and mix black pepper, salt, garlic powder, mustard powder, sage, thyme, rosemary, honey, onion, and cremini mushrooms into the potatoes.
- Put the baking dish back into the oven; bake for about 15 minutes longer until potatoes and mushrooms are tender.

Nutrition Information

- Calories: 131 calories;
- Total Carbohydrate: 19.8
- Cholesterol: 0
- Protein: 4.1
- Total Fat: 4.9

- Sodium: 9

629. Hunter Style Chicken

Serving: 4 | Prep: | Cook: | Ready in:

Ingredients

- 4 tablespoons olive oil
- 1 (3 pound) whole chicken, cut into pieces
- 6 slices bacon, diced
- 2 onions, chopped
- 1 cup fresh sliced mushrooms
- 1 tablespoon chopped fresh parsley
- 1 tablespoon chopped fresh basil
- 1 teaspoon salt
- freshly ground black pepper
- 1 cup white wine
- 1 pound tomatoes, diced

Direction

- In a large skillet, heat oil; brown the chicken; remove. Add bacon; sauté for about 2 minutes over medium heat.
- Add onions and mushrooms and keep sautéing until onions become translucent. Transfer chicken back to the skillet; scatter with pepper, salt, basil and parsley. Add tomatoes and wine. Simmer, covered, for 25-30 minutes; during cooking, turning the chicken once. Take the chicken out of the skillet; pour the sauce over the chicken.

Nutrition Information

- Calories: 1142 calories;
- Sodium: 1182
- Total Carbohydrate: 12.1
- Cholesterol: 284
- Protein: 70.4
- Total Fat: 84

630. Imitation Hamburger Gravy

Serving: 4 | Prep: 5mins | Cook: 15mins | Ready in:

Ingredients

- 1 (12 ounce) package textured vegetable protein
- 1 (10.75 ounce) can condensed cream of mushroom soup
- 1 (4 ounce) jar sliced mushrooms
- 1 onion, chopped
- 1 tablespoon soy sauce
- 1 teaspoon seasoning salt
- 1/2 teaspoon dried savory
- 1 cup water

Direction

- Combine sliced mushrooms (including liquid), textured vegetable protein, soup, water, onion, seasoning salt, soy sauce and savory in a 3 qt. saucepan on a stove set on medium heat. Simmer until the gravy has reached the desired consistency and the onions have become tender.

Nutrition Information

- Calories: 371 calories;
- Protein: 70.2
- Total Fat: 7.5
- Sodium: 1977
- Total Carbohydrate: 16.1
- Cholesterol: 0

631. Individual Grilled Veggie Pizzas

Serving: 2 | Prep: 25mins | Cook: 14mins | Ready in:

Ingredients

- 1 large portobello mushroom, sliced
- 1 small zucchini, sliced
- 1/4 pound butternut squash - peeled, seeded, and thinly sliced
- 1 cup bite-size broccoli florets
- 1/4 cup chopped red onion
- 1 tablespoon olive oil
- 2 ounces refrigerated pizza crust
- 1/4 cup pesto
- 1/4 cup crumbled Gorgonzola or blue cheese
- 1/4 cup fontina cheese, cubed

Direction

- Prepare outdoor grill and set to high heat.
- In a grill pan, put in onion, broccoli, squash, zucchini and mushrooms. Brush them with 2 tablespoons of olive oil. Cook the vegetables on the preheated grill, covered, for about 5 minutes until they are tender when pierced with fork. Take out vegetables from grill and set aside.
- On a floured surface, roll out the pizza dough and create two 8-in. circles, 1/4 –in. thick. Apply with a leftover tablespoon of olive oil on top of the pizza dough with a brush then put them on pizza pans.
- Bake pizza dough on the preheated grill, covered, for 3 about minutes per side. Take away pizza dough from the grill then spread with pesto. Take the cooked vegetables and place on top. Sprinkle with fontina and blue cheeses. Put pizza back on the grill, cover, then grill for about 3 minutes until the cheese has melted.

Nutrition Information

- Calories: 486 calories;
- Total Carbohydrate: 29
- Cholesterol: 52
- Protein: 19.5
- Total Fat: 33.4
- Sodium: 790

632. Individual Mushroom Tortilla Pizza

Serving: 1 | Prep: 15mins | Cook: 13mins | Ready in:

Ingredients

- 2 teaspoons garlic oil
- 1 teaspoon butter
- 3 white mushrooms, sliced
- 1 (9 inch) flour tortilla
- 1/4 cup shredded mozzarella cheese
- 6 cherry tomatoes, sliced
- 1 teaspoon dried oregano, or to taste
- 1/2 teaspoon garlic powder, or to taste
- 1 teaspoon olive oil, or more to taste

Direction

- Set oven to 400°F (200°C) to preheat.
- Heat butter and garlic oil over medium heat in a skillet. Cook, stirring, mushrooms in heated oil and butter for about 5 minutes or until dark and soft.
- Arrange tortilla on a baking stone or pizza pan. Top with mushrooms and accumulated juices. Sprinkle cherry tomatoes and mozzarella cheese over mushrooms. Scatter with garlic and oregano. Drizzle with olive oil.
- Bake for 8 to 10 minutes in the preheated oven until edges begin to brown.

Nutrition Information

- Calories: 453 calories;
- Total Carbohydrate: 39
- Cholesterol: 29
- Protein: 14.6
- Total Fat: 27.5
- Sodium: 585

633. Instant Pot® Easy Chicken Marsala

Serving: 4 | Prep: 15mins | Cook: 35mins | Ready in:

Ingredients

- 3 boneless chicken breasts, cut into strips
- 1 1/2 teaspoons salt, divided
- 1/2 teaspoon ground black pepper, divided
- 3 tablespoons butter, divided
- 2 tablespoons olive oil, divided
- 2 cloves garlic, chopped
- 2 tablespoons minced shallots
- 1 cup button mushrooms, sliced
- 1 cup chicken broth
- 2/3 cup Marsala wine
- 1/4 cup water
- 1 tablespoon cornstarch
- 1/2 cup heavy whipping cream
- 1 tablespoon chopped fresh parsley

Direction

- Use half teaspoon salt and quarter teaspoon pepper to season the chicken breasts. Set the multi-function cooker like the Instant Pot® to Sauté mode. Put a tablespoon each of olive oil and butter in; heat. Cook the chicken breasts on both sides for 5 minutes until all sides are golden; take it out of the pot. Melt the leftover tablespoon of olive oil and 2 tbsp. butter. Cook shallots and garlic for 2 minutes until soft. Add the mushrooms and cook for 3 minutes until tender. Add the chicken broth; boil. Stir using a wooden spoon to deglaze and scrape the browned bits at the base of the pan for 3 minutes. Place the chicken back in the pot. Pour Marsala wine until the chicken is covered. Close then lock lid and set the cooker to Poultry mode and set the timer for 10 minutes. Let the pressure build for 10-15 minutes.
- Relieve pressure with the natural-release method following the cooker's manual for 10 minutes. Use the quick release method to let out the leftover pressure for 5 minutes.

Uncover and set to Sauté mode. Melt cornstarch in water then mix in the pot. Stir heavy whipping cream in the pot. Add the leftover teaspoon salt and a quarter teaspoon of pepper. Cook and stir for 5 minutes until slightly thick. Garnish with fresh parsley, serve.

Nutrition Information

- Calories: 415 calories;
- Cholesterol: 109
- Protein: 18.6
- Total Fat: 28.4
- Sodium: 1279
- Total Carbohydrate: 10.9

634. Instant Pot® Goulash

Serving: 6 | Prep: 15mins | Cook: 20mins | Ready in:

Ingredients

- 1 pound ground beef
- 1 pint sliced mushrooms
- 1/2 onion, chopped
- 3 cloves garlic
- salt and ground black pepper to taste
- 2 (15 ounce) cans tomato sauce
- 2 (15 ounce) cans diced tomatoes
- 2 1/2 cups water
- 2 cups noodles
- 3 tablespoons soy sauce
- 2 tablespoons Italian seasoning
- 3 bay leaves

Direction

- Turn on and select the "Sauté" menu of the multi-functional pressure cooker such as Instant Pot ®. Stir in pepper, onion, beef, salt, mushrooms, and garlic, and let it cook for 5-7 minutes until crumbly and browned. Slowly drain and remove fats.
- Stir in bay leaves, dry noodles, diced tomatoes, tomato sauce, Italian seasoning, water, and soy sauce. Close and secure the lid. Follow the manufacturer's directions in setting the cooker to high pressure and set the timer for 4 minutes. Let the pressure to build for 10-15 minutes.
- Use the quick-release method and release its pressure carefully for about 5 minutes. Slowly unlock and remove the lid. Discard bay leaves before serving.

Nutrition Information

- Calories: 278 calories;
- Total Carbohydrate: 26.8
- Cholesterol: 58
- Protein: 20.1
- Total Fat: 10.3
- Sodium: 1486

635. Instant Pot® Shredded Flank Steak

Serving: 4 | Prep: 10mins | Cook: 50mins | Ready in:

Ingredients

- 1 (1 1/4 pound) flank steak, cut into 8 pieces
- 2 tablespoons avocado oil
- 1 (8 ounce) package cremini mushrooms, roughly chopped
- 1 onion, finely chopped
- 2 large cloves garlic, grated
- 1 teaspoon dried thyme
- 1/4 cup dry red wine
- 1 1/2 cups beef broth
- 1 tablespoon Worcestershire sauce
- 3/4 teaspoon salt, or to taste
- freshly ground black pepper to taste
- 1/4 cup water
- 3 tablespoons all-purpose flour

Direction

- Set a multi-functional cooker like Instant Pot® on and select sauté mode. Cook the steak, working in batches for 3-5 minutes on each side until brown. Transfer in a plate and set aside.
- In a pot, heat avocado oil; sauté onion and mushrooms for 5 minutes until the onion is translucent. Cook in thyme and garlic for a minute until aromatic. Add wine and cook for about 2 minutes until almost evaporated; stir. Put pepper, salt, Worcestershire sauce, and broth; simmer.
- Place the beef with broth mixture; flip to coat. Secure lid; set the cooker on Meat mode following the cooker's manual. Secure lid and set the timer on 20 minutes. Let the pressure build up for 10-15 minutes.
- Relieve pressure for at least 20 minutes in accordance with the cooker's manual using the natural release method. Take the beef out of the pot and let it rest. Make a slurry by combining flour and water. Set the cooker on Sauté mode then gradually pour in the slurry. Cook and stir for 3-5 minutes until thick. Use two forks to shred the beef. Put the beef back in the liquid.
- Release pressure using the natural-release method according to manufacturer's instructions, at least 20 minutes. Remove the beef and set aside. Stir water and flour together to make a slurry. Select the Sauté option and add the slurry slowly. Cook until liquid thickens, 3 to 5 minutes. Pull the beef apart using 2 forks. Stir beef back into the liquid.

Nutrition Information

- Calories: 264 calories;
- Sodium: 831
- Total Carbohydrate: 11.3
- Cholesterol: 31
- Protein: 21.5
- Total Fat: 13

636. Italian Meat And Spinach Pie

Serving: 8 | Prep: 45mins | Cook: 1hours20mins | Ready in:

Ingredients

- 1 recipe pastry for a 9-inch pie crust
- 1/2 pound ground beef
- 1/2 pound mild or hot turkey Italian sausage, casings removed
- 1 clove garlic, minced
- 1 onion, chopped
- 3/4 cup chopped red bell pepper
- 10 ounces sliced fresh mushrooms
- 1 clove garlic, minced
- 1 (6 ounce) can tomato paste
- 1 1/4 cups water
- 1/2 teaspoon salt
- 1 teaspoon dried basil
- 1/2 teaspoon dried oregano
- 1 (10 ounce) package frozen chopped spinach, thawed and well drained
- 1 cup part-skim ricotta cheese
- 1 1/2 cups shredded mozzarella cheese, divided
- 1 cup chopped, seeded plum tomatoes
- 1 (6 ounce) can sliced black olives, drained

Direction

- Use the pastry to line a 9-inch pie pan; use a fork to press the edges of the crust so that it will be sealed to the pie dish. Loosely cover with plastic wrap and let chill while making the sauce.
- Over medium-high heat, heat a large skillet and stir in 1 clove of minced garlic, turkey sausage, and ground beef. Cook and stir until the meat is crumbly, no more pink and evenly browned. Let drain and remove any excess oil. Add the mushrooms, red bell pepper, and onion; cook, stirring often for about 5 minutes, or until the mushrooms have given off their

liquid and the onion is transparent and soft. Put in the leftover garlic and continue to cook for 30 seconds.
- Next, stir in oregano, basil, salt, water, and tomato paste; boil the sauce. Lower the heat to low, simmer, covered, for 10 minutes. Then remove from the heat and put aside.
- Set an oven at 230°C (450°F) to preheat.
- Use a double thickness of aluminum foil to line the chilled pie crust. Bake for about 9 minutes. Next, discard the foil and keep baking for about 7 minutes more, or until the crust's bottom is set (see Editor's Note for tips). Then transfer from the oven and put aside. Lower the oven temperature to 175°C (350°F).
- Combine 1/2 cup mozzarella cheese, ricotta, and spinach. Scoop the filling into the baked crust. Put the meat mixture on top. Prevent over-browning by using foil to cover the edges of the pie crust, put the pie on a baking sheet, then bake for around 45 minutes.
- Next, remove the pie from the oven. Use sliced olives, chopped tomatoes, and 1 cup of mozzarella cheese to top the meat mixture. Bring it back to the oven and continue to bake for another 10 minutes, or until the cheese is melted. Prior to serving, allow to sit for 10 minutes.

Nutrition Information

- Calories: 398 calories;
- Total Fat: 22.9
- Sodium: 1098
- Total Carbohydrate: 25.4
- Cholesterol: 60
- Protein: 24.7

637. Italian Sausage Delight!

Serving: 6 | Prep: 30mins | Cook: 30mins | Ready in:

Ingredients

- 6 (3.5 ounce) links hot Italian sausage
- 1 large onion, chopped
- 1 red bell peppers, seeded and diced
- 1 green bell pepper, seeded and diced
- 1 (4 ounce) can mushrooms, drained
- 1 (16 ounce) package penne pasta
- 1/2 cup Italian salad dressing
- 1/4 cup grated Parmesan cheese for topping

Direction

- Bring water in a large pot to a boil. Cook penne pasta for about 10 minutes until tender. Drain.
- In a small skillet over medium heat, arrange Italian sausage links. Cook until firm and thoroughly cooked, turning sometimes.
- Sauté Italian dressing, mushrooms, green and red bell peppers in a separate large skillet for about 5 minutes until vegetables are tender. Cut Italian sausages into round slices, and mix into the vegetables. Continue to cook and stir for 5 more minutes.
- Arrange servings of pasta on plates to serve. Spoon sausage and vegetable mixture over the top. Scatter generously with Parmesan cheese.

Nutrition Information

- Calories: 680 calories;
- Total Fat: 36.9
- Sodium: 1126
- Total Carbohydrate: 62.8
- Cholesterol: 72
- Protein: 25.3

638. Jagerschnitzel

Serving: 4 | Prep: 15mins | Cook: 25mins | Ready in:

Ingredients

- 1 cup bread crumbs
- 1 tablespoon all-purpose flour

- salt and pepper to taste
- 2 tablespoons vegetable oil
- 4 pork steaks or cutlets, pounded thin
- 1 egg, beaten
- 1 medium onion, diced
- 1 (8 ounce) can sliced mushrooms
- 1 1/2 cups water
- 1 cube beef bouillon
- 1 tablespoon cornstarch
- 1/2 cup sour cream

Direction

- Combine the flour and bread crumbs together in a shallow dish. Add in pepper and salt to taste. In another dish, put in the egg. In a big skillet, let the oil heat up over medium-high heat setting. Coat the pork steaks with egg then dredge it in the bread crumb-flour mixture. Put it into the skillet and let it cook in the hot oil for about 5 minutes on every side until the breaded pork steaks are completely cooked and have turned brown on every side.
- Place the cooked breaded pork steaks onto a platter and let it stay warm. Put the mushrooms and onion into the skillet and sauté the mixture until it turns light brown in color. Add in the water and bouillon cube and dissolved the bouillon cube. Let the mixture simmer for about 20 minutes. Combine the sour cream and cornstarch together and mix it into the mushroom mixture. Allow the mixture to cook over low heat setting, without boiling, until it is thick in consistency. Drizzle the cooked mushroom mixture on top of the cooked breaded pork steaks and serve it right away.

Nutrition Information

- Calories: 556 calories;
- Total Fat: 33.5
- Sodium: 683
- Total Carbohydrate: 29.9
- Cholesterol: 157
- Protein: 32.9

639. Jan's Peppered Pork Chops With Mushrooms And Herb Sherry Sauce

Serving: 6 | Prep: 10mins | Cook: 12mins | Ready in:

Ingredients

- 6 thick-cut boneless pork chops
- 1 tablespoon crushed black peppercorns
- 1 (9.74 ounce) package Idahoan Signature™ Russets Mashed Potatoes
- 1/4 cup butter
- 2 tablespoons olive oil
- 4 cloves garlic, chopped
- 1/2 teaspoon salt, or to taste
- 2 tablespoons chopped fresh parsley
- 1 teaspoon chopped fresh rosemary
- 1 teaspoon chopped fresh sage
- 1 teaspoon chopped fresh thyme
- 1 (8 ounce) package sliced fresh mushrooms
- 1/4 cup dry sherry
- 2 teaspoons cornstarch (optional)
- 1 teaspoon water (optional)

Direction

- Onto every side of pork chops, press crushed peppercorns.
- Ready Idahoan Signature Russets Mashed Potatoes based on the package directions. Keep it warm.
- In a big skillet set on medium heat, heat olive oil, and butter. Put the garlic and cook for 1-2 minutes until the garlic starts to become golden yet not brown.
- Add thyme, sage, rosemary, and parsley; then cook for 2 minutes.
- Add pork chops into the skillet then cook for 5 minutes; flip. Put in the mushrooms; add salt to season. Gradually add in dry sherry. Cook for 5 more minutes, covered. An instant-read thermometer poked in the middle should register 145°F (63°C).

- Place pork chops on a warm dish. Cook mushrooms until they are tender, if necessary. Combine water and cornstarch; mix in the skillet. Keep on stirring for approximately 1 minute until the sauce slightly thickens.
- Place mushroom sauce on chops and serve right away with of prepared Idahoan Signature Russets Mashed Potatoes.

Nutrition Information

- Calories: 380 calories;
- Sodium: 363
- Total Carbohydrate: 5.1
- Cholesterol: 109
- Protein: 36.8
- Total Fat: 22.8

640. Japanese Beef Rolls

Serving: 8 | Prep: 30mins | Cook: 10mins | Ready in:

Ingredients

- 1 tablespoon vegetable oil
- 12 shiitake mushrooms, sliced
- 24 spears fresh asparagus, trimmed
- 8 thin-cut top round steaks
- 1/4 cup soy sauce
- 1 bunch green onions, green parts only

Direction

- On medium heat, heat oil in a pan; put in mushrooms then cover. On low heat, let the mushrooms sweat until soft but avoid browning. In the meantime, boil water in a big pot or pan. Put the asparagus in a strainer then blanch in boiling water for half a minute, or until bright green; place in ice water to stop cooking. Set it aside.
- Place an oven rack approximately six inches from heat; preheat the broiler. Oil a broiling pan.
- To make the rolls, lay out the steaks flat. Pound the thick steaks until a quarter-inch thick. Slather soy sauce over the steak; add a couple of green onions and some mushrooms then three spears of asparagus at one end of every steak. Roll up to enclose towards the opposite end then secure with a toothpick. Arrange rolls on the broiling pan with the seam-side down.
- Roast for 3 mins in the preheated oven, or until the tops are brown. Turn then roast for 2-3 mins longer, or until the other side is brown. Do not overcook since it can burn or toughen the steak.

Nutrition Information

- Calories: 689 calories;
- Sodium: 583
- Total Carbohydrate: 5.9
- Cholesterol: 242
- Protein: 95.1
- Total Fat: 29.1

641. Japanese Onion Soup

Serving: 6 | Prep: 15mins | Cook: 45mins | Ready in:

Ingredients

- 1/2 stalk celery, chopped
- 1 small onion, chopped
- 1/2 carrot, chopped
- 1 teaspoon grated fresh ginger root
- 1/4 teaspoon minced fresh garlic
- 2 tablespoons chicken stock
- 3 teaspoons beef bouillon granules
- 1 cup chopped fresh shiitake mushrooms
- 2 quarts water
- 1 cup baby portobello mushrooms, sliced
- 1 tablespoon minced fresh chives

Direction

- Mix a few of the mushrooms, celery, garlic, onion, ginger, and carrot in a big stockpot or saucepan. Add water, beef bouillon, and chicken stock; let it come to a rolling boil on high heat. Cover once boiling then turn to medium heat; cook for 45 mins.
- Put all the rest of the mushrooms into another pot. Put a strainer on top of the mushroom pot once the boiling mixture is done. Strain the cooked soup into the mushroom pot; get rid of the strained materials.
- In small porcelain bowls, serve the broth along with mushrooms and sprinkle on top with fresh chives. To make it more elegant, Asian soup spoons.

Nutrition Information

- Calories: 25 calories;
- Sodium: 257
- Total Carbohydrate: 4.4
- Cholesterol: < 1
- Protein: 1.4
- Total Fat: 0.2

642. Japanese Style Grilled Mushrooms

Serving: 2 | Prep: 5mins | Cook: 10mins |Ready in:

Ingredients

- 4 portobello mushroom caps
- 3 tablespoons soy sauce
- 2 tablespoons sesame oil
- 1 tablespoon minced fresh ginger root
- 1 small clove garlic, minced

Direction

- Preheat the broiler in your oven and place the oven rack about 6 inches away from the source of heat.
- Rinse the mushrooms and place it onto a baking sheet, top-side down. In a small bowl, combine the ginger, soy sauce, garlic and sesame oil and use a brush to coat on top of the mushrooms evenly with the prepared soy sauce mixture.
- Put the prepared mushrooms in the preheated broiler and let it roast for about 10 minutes until it becomes soft.

Nutrition Information

- Calories: 196 calories;
- Protein: 7.3
- Total Fat: 14.1
- Sodium: 1367
- Total Carbohydrate: 14.2
- Cholesterol: 0

643. Jeff's Bordelaise Sauce

Serving: 4 | Prep: 15mins | Cook: 20mins |Ready in:

Ingredients

- 1/2 cup butter
- 1 small onion, sliced
- 1/4 cup sliced carrots
- 1/4 cup sliced celery
- 25 peppercorns
- 16 whole cloves
- 3 tablespoons flour
- 1 cup beef broth
- water, as needed (optional)
- 2 tablespoons chopped fresh parsley, divided
- salt and ground black pepper to taste
- 1/3 cup red wine
- 1 tablespoon olive oil, or to taste
- 3/4 cup sliced mushrooms

Direction

- In big skillet, liquefy butter over moderately-high heat. In liquefied butter, sauté cloves,

peppercorns, celery, carrots and onion for 7 to 10 minutes till onions turn brown.
- Into onion mixture, mix the flour; cook and mix for 1 to 2 minutes till flour is fully moistened. Into the skillet, let beef broth stream while mixing onion mixture; cook for 5 to 10 minutes, mixing continuously, till broth turn thick into gravy. Into thin gravy, put water as necessary to prevent it from turning into paste.
- Into the gravy, mix a tablespoon of parsley; keep cooking for 5 to 10 minutes, mixing often, till parsley imparts its flavor to gravy; through a strainer with fine mesh, filter into clean saucepan. Throw away the vegetables.
- Set saucepan on low heat. Add pepper, salt and majority of leftover parsley to taste the sauce. Into the sauce, mix red wine.
- In skillet, heat olive oil over moderately-high heat; in hot oil, sauté the mushrooms for about 5 minutes till fully softened. Into the sauce, mix the mushrooms; scoop on top of steaks and jazz up with the rest of parsley.

Nutrition Information

- Calories: 320 calories;
- Total Fat: 27.1
- Sodium: 389
- Total Carbohydrate: 14.6
- Cholesterol: 61
- Protein: 3.4

644. Jen's One Pan Penne With Mushrooms And Arugula

Serving: 6 | Prep: 5mins | Cook: 10mins | Ready in:

Ingredients

- 1 box Barilla® Pronto™ Penne
- 1 (4 ounce) can mushrooms, quartered
- 1 cup arugula, packed
- 1/2 cup Parmigiano-Reggiano cheese, grated
- Salt and black pepper to taste

Direction

- In a 12-inches diameter large skillet, pour the whole box of pasta.
- Pour in 3-cups of cold water into the pan. Make sure that the pasta is well-covered with water.
- Add the mushrooms. Set the burner to High and your timer for 10 minutes. (You can add a bit of salt to taste.)
- Let it cook on High, stirring occasionally until the liquid is completely evaporated.
- Remove the pasta from the heat when the desired texture is reached. Mix in cheese and arugula. Serve it immediately.

Nutrition Information

- Calories: 237 calories;
- Cholesterol: 6
- Protein: 10.1
- Total Fat: 3
- Sodium: 209
- Total Carbohydrate: 43.9

645. Jerk Chicken Pizza

Serving: 6 | Prep: 20mins | Cook: 40mins | Ready in:

Ingredients

- 1 green bell pepper
- 4 teaspoons olive oil, divided
- 1 skinless, boneless chicken breast half - finely chopped
- 1 tablespoon jerk sauce, or to taste
- 3 cloves garlic, diced
- 1 portobello mushroom, finely chopped
- 1 (10 ounce) package pre-baked thin pizza crust
- 1/2 cup pizza sauce
- 1 (4 ounce) package thinly sliced salami

- 1 1/2 cups shredded mozzarella cheese

Direction

- Let your oven broiler heat. Put on a baking sheet the green pepper that has been brushed with a teaspoon olive oil. Let it broil for 5 minutes per side until the skin starts to blister. Remove from the heat and, for about 15 minutes, seal in a plastic container. Cut into strips. Then remove the skin, pulp, and seeds; dice.
- Let the oven heat to 175°C (350°F).
- Over medium heat, warm the extra olive oil in a pan. Heat through the chicken for up to 10 minutes or once its juice is clear. Stir in the garlic, roasted green pepper, portobello mushroom, and jerk sauce. Cook through and stir for 5 minutes.
- Put pizza crust on a pan then add on the sauce. Then arrange evenly the salami and chicken mixture over the sauce. Add mozzarella cheese as toppings.
- Bake pizza in the preheated oven for up to 10 minutes or once the cheese is bubbly and melted.

Nutrition Information

- Calories: 358 calories;
- Sodium: 1012
- Total Carbohydrate: 29.6
- Cholesterol: 53
- Protein: 23
- Total Fat: 16.7

646. Jet Tila's Tom Yum Goong Soup

Serving: 6 | Prep: 10mins | Cook: 15mins | Ready in:

Ingredients

- 6 whole Thai chiles
- 2 quarts Thai chicken broth
- 1 cup peeled and deveined medium shrimp
- 1 (15 ounce) can whole straw mushrooms, drained
- 6 tablespoons fish sauce
- 6 tablespoons lime juice
- 3 tablespoons Thai garlic chile paste
- 6 kaffir lime leaves
- 6 sprigs fresh cilantro

Direction

- Set the oven's broiler ready and start preheating; place the oven rack at around 6-in. from the heat source. Cover inside the baking sheet with aluminum foil. Put the peppers on the prepared baking sheet.
- Cook under the prepared broiler, turning around occasionally till the skin of peppers has become blackened and blistered, around 5 minutes. In a bowl, add the blackened peppers; firmly cover with plastic wrap. Keep the peppers steaming as they cool, approximately 20 minutes. Once cool, remove the stem, seeds and skin and throw them away. Cut the roasted chiles.
- Place a large saucepan on medium-high heat; pour in the chicken broth; simmer it. Mix in chopped roasted chiles, mushrooms and shrimp. Take back to the simmer; cook till the shrimps are not translucent in the middle anymore, about 1 minute. Mix in the chile paste, lime juice and fish sauce till the chile paste has melted. Ladle into bowls; dress with a sprig of cilantro and a lime leaf for each bowl.

Nutrition Information

- Calories: 66 calories;
- Cholesterol: 32
- Protein: 7
- Total Fat: 0.7
- Sodium: 1470
- Total Carbohydrate: 9.6

647. Jim's Beer Battered Portobello Mushrooms

Serving: 4 | Prep: 15mins | Cook: 15mins | Ready in:

Ingredients

- oil for frying
- 2 cups bitter ale (such as Goose Island Honkers Ale®)
- 1 3/4 cups all-purpose flour
- 1/2 cup sesame seeds
- 2 tablespoons cornstarch
- 1 tablespoon baking powder
- 3 large portobello mushroom caps, cut into 1/2-inch slices

Direction

- In a large saucepan or a deep-fryer, heat oil to 375°F (190°C).
- In a large bowl, whisk baking powder, cornstarch, sesame seeds flour and ale until the batter is thick and slightly lumpy.
- Dip 7 - 8 strips of mushroom at once into the batter, shake off to get rid of the excess.
- Fry mushrooms in the hot oil in batches for 5-6 minutes until they turn golden brown.

Nutrition Information

- Calories: 574 calories;
- Total Carbohydrate: 54.6
- Cholesterol: 0
- Protein: 9.7
- Total Fat: 31.5
- Sodium: 257

648. Joe's Homemade Mushroom Soup

Serving: 20 | Prep: 10mins | Cook: 10mins | Ready in:

Ingredients

- 1 1/4 cups butter
- 1 large onion, chopped
- 5 pounds sliced fresh mushrooms
- 1 1/4 cups all-purpose flour
- 2 1/2 teaspoons ground black pepper
- 1 1/2 teaspoons salt
- 10 cups milk
- 10 cups chicken broth
- 1/2 cup minced fresh parsley
- 1 pinch ground nutmeg, or to taste
- 1/4 cup sour cream, or as needed

Direction

- In a large saucepan, melt butter over medium heat. Sauté mushrooms and onion in melted butter for about 3 minutes until tender. Mix salt, pepper, and flour into the onion mixture. Slowly stream in chicken broth and milk and stir until incorporated.
- Bring the mixture to a boil; cook at a boil for about 2 minutes until thickened. Turn off the heat. Add nutmeg and parsley into the soup. Spoon soup into serving bowls and top each portion with a dollop of sour cream.

Nutrition Information

- Calories: 227 calories;
- Sodium: 315
- Total Carbohydrate: 16.5
- Cholesterol: 42
- Protein: 8.7
- Total Fat: 15

649. Kale And Mushroom Vegan "Quiche"

Serving: 8 | Prep: 25mins | Cook: 40mins | Ready in:

Ingredients

- 1 (9 inch) vegan pie crust
- 2 tablespoons olive oil
- 2 cloves garlic, diced
- 1 (8 ounce) package button mushrooms, diced
- 4 cups chopped kale
- 1 medium red onion, diced
- 1 (12 ounce) package extra-firm tofu, diced
- 3 tablespoons dry vegan egg replacer
- 1 tablespoon Dijon mustard
- 1 tablespoon nutritional yeast
- 1 tablespoon lemon juice
- 1 teaspoon onion powder
- 1 teaspoon garlic powder
- 1/2 teaspoon ground turmeric
- 1/2 teaspoon salt, or more to taste

Direction

- Set the oven at 350°F (175°C) and start preheating. Put the pie crust in a 9-inch pie plate.
- In a large saucepan, heat olive oil over medium heat. Sauté the garlic about 2 minutes until slightly toasted. Put in onion, kale, and mushrooms; sauté them for about 5 minutes until the onion is translucent and leaves are wilted.
- In a food processor, mix salt, turmeric, garlic powder, onion powder, lemon juice, nutritional yeast, Dijon mustard, egg replacer and tofu. Blend it smoothly. Transfer the mixture in a bowl then fold in the kale mixture.
- Transfer the mixture onto the pie crust and spread it evenly with a spatula.
- Bake for about 30-40 minutes in the preheated oven until the center is firm and have a golden color on the top. Let it cool for 10 minutes before enjoying the dish.

Nutrition Information

- Calories: 221 calories;
- Total Carbohydrate: 19.4
- Cholesterol: 0
- Protein: 7.7

- Total Fat: 13.6
- Sodium: 325

650. Kansas Quail

Serving: 4 | Prep: 10mins | Cook: 10mins | Ready in:

Ingredients

- wooden skewers
- 12 slices bacon
- 12 mushrooms

Direction

- In a bowl of water, soak wooden skewers for 10 minutes.
- Preheat the grill to medium heat. Oil the grate lightly.
- Around each mushroom, wrap 1 bacon slice. Thread onto skewers. Leave 1/2-inch space between every wrapped mushrooms.
- Cook on preheated grill, frequently rotating skewers, for 10-15 minutes until bacon is crispy.

Nutrition Information

- Calories: 161 calories;
- Total Carbohydrate: 2.2
- Cholesterol: 30
- Protein: 11.9
- Total Fat: 11.7
- Sodium: 638

651. Kelly's Slow Cooker Beef, Mushroom, And Barley Soup

Serving: 6 | Prep: 20mins | Cook: 6hours | Ready in:

Ingredients

- 1 (32 ounce) carton beef stock
- 1 (8 ounce) can tomato sauce
- 1 cup water
- 1/2 onion, diced
- 3/4 cup diced carrots
- 1 cup barley
- 1 (6 ounce) package sliced fresh mushrooms
- 4 cloves garlic, minced
- 2 pounds beef sirloin, cut into chunks
- 1 pinch garlic salt, or to taste
- salt and ground black pepper to taste
- 2 bay leaves

Direction

- In a slow cooker, stir the beef stock, garlic, mushrooms, barley, carrot, onion, tomato sauce, and water together.
- Dust black pepper, salt, and garlic salt to season the beef chunks; add to the beef stock mixture. Put bay leaves into the slow cooker.
- Cook on Low heat for about 6 hours, until the soup is thickened and the beef is tender.
- Take out and omit the bay leaves to serve.

Nutrition Information

- Calories: 359 calories;
- Total Fat: 10.3
- Sodium: 381
- Total Carbohydrate: 31.7
- Cholesterol: 65
- Protein: 34.6

652. Keto Buffalo Cauliflower Chorizo "Mac" N Cheese

Serving: 6 | Prep: 20mins | Cook: 30mins | Ready in:

Ingredients

- 1 head cauliflower, cut into florets
- 2 tablespoons coconut oil
- 1/2 pound chorizo, cut into small pieces
- 1 cup chopped mushrooms
- 1/2 onion, chopped
- 2 tablespoons butter
- 1/4 cup heavy cream
- 1 cup shredded Cheddar cheese
- 1/4 cup grated Parmesan cheese
- 1/2 cup hot pepper sauce (such as Frank's RedHot®)

Direction

- Set an oven to preheat to 165°C (325°F).
- In a microwave-safe bowl, put the cauliflower florets. Let it cook for 10 minutes in the microwave oven.
- While the cauliflower is cooking, in a pan, heat coconut oil on medium heat; then add onion, mushrooms and chorizo. Let it cook for 5-7 minutes until it becomes soft, then move to a baking dish.
- Into the cauliflower, stir the butter, cream, Cheddar cheese, and Parmesan cheese, respectively. Stir in the hot sauce and move the mixture to the baking dish with the chorizo mixture.
- Let it bake in the preheated oven for 15-20 minutes, until it becomes bubbly.

Nutrition Information

- Calories: 403 calories;
- Total Fat: 33.9
- Sodium: 1189
- Total Carbohydrate: 8.1
- Cholesterol: 80
- Protein: 17.9

653. Keto Omelet With Zucchini And Chanterelle Mushrooms

Serving: 1 | Prep: 10mins | Cook: 10mins | Ready in:

Ingredients

- 1 tablespoon salted butter
- 1 clove garlic, finely chopped
- 1/3 medium zucchini, thinly sliced
- 4 chanterelle mushrooms, thinly sliced
- 2 eggs, beaten
- 1/4 cup shredded mozzarella cheese
- salt and pepper to taste

Direction

- In a nonstick skillet over high heat, melt butter. Cook garlic for 2 to 3 minutes until garlic turns golden brown and quite crispy, remember to stir while cooking. Lower the heat to medium. Add chanterelle mushrooms and zucchini, cook while stirring for about 5 minutes until golden brown.
- Increase the heat to medium-high and evenly spread mushrooms and zucchini over the bottom of skillet. Add eggs to the skillet. Pick up and tilt the skillet in order to evenly distribute the egg. Working quickly, drizzle cheese on top and add salt and pepper to season, lower the heat to medium. Keeping an eye on the skillet, when the top of omelet starts to bubble, wiggle the pan to loosen the base. When egg reaches desired consistency and cheese is fully melted on top, fold omelet in half. Serve.

Nutrition Information

- Calories: 264 calories;
- Protein: 13.3
- Total Fat: 20.4
- Sodium: 379
- Total Carbohydrate: 6.7
- Cholesterol: 358

654. Killer Chicken With Mushroom, Asparagus, And Red Bell Pepper

Serving: 4 | Prep: 20mins | Cook: 50mins | Ready in:

Ingredients

- 2 cups basmati rice
- 4 cups water
- 1 tablespoon vegetable oil
- 1 red onion, cut into 1/2-inch slices
- 3 1/2 pounds skinless, boneless chicken thighs, cut into 2-inch strips
- 1 tablespoon minced fresh ginger root
- 6 cloves garlic, minced
- 3 cups cremini mushrooms, cut in half
- 12 fresh asparagus, trimmed and cut into 2-inch pieces
- 2 small red bell peppers, cut into 1/2-inch strips
- 1 tablespoon fish sauce
- 1 egg
- 2 cups fresh basil leaves
- 1 cup fresh cilantro leaves, chopped
- 2 tablespoons sesame seeds, for garnish
- tamari soy sauce to taste

Direction

- In a saucepan, boil water and rice together. Lower the heat to medium-low, put a cover on and simmer for 35-40 minutes until the rice is soft and liquid is absorbed.
- Once the rice has almost done, in a big skillet, heat oil over high heat. In the hot oil, cook the onion for 2-3 minutes until tender. Add ginger, garlic and chicken to the skillet and keep stirring and cooking for 7-10 minutes until the chicken is entirely browned. Fold fish sauce, bell peppers, asparagus and mushrooms into the chicken mixture, keep cooking for 5 minutes until just hot. Crack the egg and scramble it into the mixture. Add basil leaves to the mixture, cook for 30 seconds until the leaves have slightly wilted. Take the pan away from heat immediately. Enjoy on

top of the basmati rice, drizzle tamari soy sauce over and use sesame seeds and cilantro to garnish.

Nutrition Information

- Calories: 1095 calories;
- Sodium: 610
- Total Carbohydrate: 86.7
- Cholesterol: 270
- Protein: 77.8
- Total Fat: 47.7

655. Kobe Beef And Oyster Mushroom Meatballs

Serving: 15 | Prep: 30mins | Cook: 20mins | Ready in:

Ingredients

- 14 cups minced oyster mushrooms
- 9 cups panko bread crumbs
- 1/4 cup minced garlic
- 3 tablespoons ground black pepper
- 3 tablespoons kosher salt
- 5 pounds ground Kobe beef, at room temperature
- 3 tablespoons dried parsley

Direction

- Set oven to 350° F (175 degrees C) and preheat. Take 3 baking sheets and line them with parchment paper.
- Mix together oyster mushrooms, garlic, panko, salt and black pepper in a large bowl. Mix well using your hands. Stir in ground beef until the mixture is combined well and sticky.
- Scoop the beef mixture using an ice scream scooper and lightly roll to form into balls. Place each piece on the prepared baking sheet.
- Bake in the preheated oven for about 20 minutes until brown. An instant-read thermometer inserted in the middle should read 165° F (74 degrees C). Take out of the oven and allow the meatballs to rest for 10 minutes prior to serving.
- Using a coffee or spice grinder, grind the dried parsley into a fine dust. Sprinkle parsley dust over meatballs and serve.

Nutrition Information

- Calories: 500 calories;
- Cholesterol: 91
- Protein: 33.3
- Total Fat: 24.3
- Sodium: 1545
- Total Carbohydrate: 50.9

656. Korean Beef Short Rib Stew (Galbi Jjim)

Serving: 4 | Prep: 15mins | Cook: 2hours50mins | Ready in:

Ingredients

- 2 pounds Korean-style short ribs (beef chuck flanken), cut into 3-inch segments
- 4 cups water
- 6 tablespoons soy sauce
- 8 cloves garlic, minced
- 1 small onion, sliced
- 1 tablespoon rice wine
- 1 tablespoon brown sugar
- 2 carrots, cut into chunks
- 2 small potatoes, cut into chunks
- 1/2 cup fresh shiitake mushrooms, sliced
- 2 tablespoons light corn syrup
- 1 tablespoon Asian (toasted) sesame oil
- 6 chestnuts, peeled (optional)
- 6 dates, pitted (optional)
- sliced green onion

Direction

- Add cold water to cover the ribs, chill and let to soak for one hour. Drain ribs, transfer to a saucepan containing four cups of water. Heat to boil. Let the ribs cook for ten minutes. Drain and save two cups of liquid. Transfer ribs and reserved liquid into a large pot.
- In a bowl, combine together the brown sugar, rice wine, onion, garlic, and soy sauce until sugar is dissolved. Add mixture atop the broth and ribs. Mix to combine, heat to boil, decrease heat, and let to simmer for 1 1/2 hours.
- Stir in the dates, chestnuts, sesame oil, corn syrup, shiitake mushrooms, potatoes and carrots and let to simmer for about 1 hour until the veggies and meat are very tender.
- Transfer the veggies and beef into a serving dish. Decrease liquid in pot to form a thickened gravy. Add the sauce atop the veggies and ribs. Drizzle with chopped green onion and then serve.

Nutrition Information

- Calories: 749 calories;
- Total Carbohydrate: 57.5
- Cholesterol: 93
- Protein: 26.7
- Total Fat: 45.6
- Sodium: 1454

657. Korean Kalbi Jjim (Braised Beef Short Ribs)

Serving: 6 | Prep: 30mins | Cook: 1hours25mins | Ready in:

Ingredients

- 2 pounds beef short ribs, or more to taste
- 1 onion, quartered
- 1 (1 inch) piece fresh ginger, sliced
- 2 cloves garlic
- 5 tablespoons soy sauce
- 1/4 cup brown sugar
- 2 tablespoons Korean red pepper flakes (gochugaru)
- 4 cloves garlic, minced
- 1 tablespoon rice vinegar
- 1 tablespoon sesame oil
- 2 potatoes, peeled and cut into 2-inch pieces
- 2 carrots, peeled and cut into 2-inch pieces
- 1/2 cup Japanese beech mushrooms
- 7 chestnuts (bam), or more to taste
- 7 dried Korean dates (daechu)
- 1 tablespoon corn syrup (mulyeot)
- 2 green onions, sliced

Direction

- Soak the beef short ribs for about 30 minutes in a large bowl containing cold water to get rid of residual blood.
- Transfer 2 cloves garlic, ginger, onion and short ribs into a large pot and then add water to cover. Heat to boil for 20 to 30 minutes while skimming the foam that rises to the top. Then measure out two cups of broth and set aside. Drain the short ribs and then rinse with cold water. Get rid of garlic, ginger, and onion. Let to cool until easy to handle.
- Form slits in each short rib to get rid or chop away the excess fat.
- Place the short ribs back into the pot. Add sesame oil, rice vinegar, 4 minced garlic cloves, red pepper flakes, brown sugar, soy sauce and reserved broth. Let to simmer for about 45 minutes on low heat until the flavors have combined. Add dates, chestnuts, mushrooms, carrots and potatoes. Continue to simmer for about 10 minutes until the sauce thickens and the potatoes are tender.
- Mix the corn syrup into sauce. Then simmer for about 5 minutes until the sauce has a slightly syrupy consistency. Garnish with slices of green onion before serving.

Nutrition Information

- Calories: 547 calories;
- Protein: 18.7
- Total Fat: 31

- Sodium: 841
- Total Carbohydrate: 50.2
- Cholesterol: 62

658. Korean Short Ribs (Kalbi Jjim)

Serving: 4 | Prep: 35mins | Cook: 2hours | Ready in:

Ingredients

- 6 dried shiitake mushrooms
- 2 pounds beef short ribs
- 2 cups water
- 1 onion, sliced
- 2 tablespoons soy sauce
- 7 cloves garlic, minced
- 1 1/2 tablespoons brown sugar
- 1 tablespoon rice wine
- 1 Korean radish, peeled and cut into chunks
- 2 carrots, cut into chunks
- 6 roasted and peeled chestnuts (optional)
- 6 hard-boiled eggs, peeled (optional)
- 2 tablespoons corn syrup (mulyeot)
- 1 tablespoon sesame oil
- 1 teaspoon ground black pepper
- 1 green onion, chopped

Direction

- Soak the shiitake mushrooms for about 3 hours in bowl containing very warm water until softened. Drain off water and chop into strips.
- Soak the short ribs for 20 minutes in a bowl containing cold water and change water several times. Drain off the water and bring the ribs to room temperature for about half an hour.
- Heat water to boil in a large pot and then add short ribs. Cook for about 10 minutes until no pink color remains. Drain the ribs and then rinse under cold water. Take out any loose particles and the excess fat. Place in a large pot.
- In a bowl, combine rice wine, brown sugar, garlic, soy sauce, sliced onion and 2 cups of water. Spread on top of ribs in pot. Heat to boil. Cook for about 20 to 25 minutes. Mix in carrot, radish, and shiitake mushrooms. Decrease the heat to low and let to simmer while stirring often for about 1 hour until the short ribs become tender.
- Mix black pepper, sesame oil, corn syrup and eggs into the pot. Raise the heat to medium-high and cook while stirring often for about 15 minutes until most of the cooking liquid is evaporated. Place the short ribs onto a serving platter and then add chopped green onion on top.

Nutrition Information

- Calories: 782 calories;
- Sodium: 652
- Total Carbohydrate: 40.3
- Cholesterol: 411
- Protein: 34.2
- Total Fat: 53.5

659. Kung Pao Tofu Stir Fry

Serving: 4 | Prep: 35mins | Cook: 46mins | Ready in:

Ingredients

- 1 (16 ounce) package firm tofu, cut into 3 slices
- 1 cup low-sodium soy sauce, divided
- 1 (1 inch) piece ginger, finely grated
- 1 tablespoon canola oil
- 1 yellow onion, sliced
- 1 large green bell pepper, cut into chunks
- 2 small zucchini, chopped
- 6 small mushrooms, chopped
- 3 tablespoons rice wine vinegar
- 1 tablespoon Asian hot-chile sauce
- 2 tablespoons crushed roasted peanuts

Direction

- Lay out the slices of tofu on a plate lined with paper towel and use more paper towels to cover. Place a heavy object on top to press out the extra water for around 15 minutes, then drain and get rid of the accumulated liquid.
- In a big dish, combine the ginger and 1/2 cup soy sauce. Add the slices of tofu and allow to marinate for around 15 minutes.
- Set an oven to 175°C (350°F) to preheat. Use parchment paper to line a baking tray.
- Turn the slices of tofu and allow to marinate for about 15 more minutes on the other side. Take the tofu away from the marinade and put onto a prepped baking tray.
- Let bake for about 40 minutes in the preheated oven, until they become dry, turning once halfway through. Slice into smaller pieces.
- In a big frying pan or wok, heat the oil on medium-high heat. Add the green bell pepper and onion and cook for 3-5 minutes, until the onion becomes a bit translucent. Add the mushrooms and zucchini then cook and stir for 2-3 minutes, until light brown. Mix in the baked tofu.
- In a small bowl, stir the chile sauce, rice wine vinegar and the leftover 1/2 cup soy sauce. Pour into the wok and mix for around 1 minute, until the tofu and onion mixture is thoroughly coated. Put roasted peanuts on top to garnish.

Nutrition Information

- Calories: 213 calories;
- Total Fat: 10.6
- Sodium: 2184
- Total Carbohydrate: 18.3
- Cholesterol: 0
- Protein: 15.7

660. LaDonna's Spaghetti With Sauce

Serving: 11 | Prep: | Cook: | Ready in:

Ingredients

- 2 pounds lean ground beef
- 1 onion, chopped
- 1 (46 fluid ounce) can tomato juice
- 1 (29 ounce) can tomato sauce
- 2 (6 ounce) cans tomato paste
- 1 cup finely grated carrots
- 4 tablespoons Italian seasoning
- 1 pound fresh mushrooms, quartered
- 5 cloves garlic, minced
- salt to taste
- ground black pepper to taste
- 2 pounds spaghetti

Direction

- Cook onion and ground beef over medium heat until done. Drain off the grease.
- In a large pot, combine pepper and salt, garlic, mushrooms, seasoning, grated carrots, tomato sauce, tomato paste, tomato juice and onion and beef. Simmer on very low heat for 2-3 hours.
- Cook pasta following the package instructions. Drain. Add sauce over the pasta. Serve.

Nutrition Information

- Calories: 611 calories;
- Total Fat: 19
- Sodium: 1018
- Total Carbohydrate: 81.2
- Cholesterol: 62
- Protein: 30.3

661. Leftover Ham And Bacon Hash

Serving: 4 | Prep: 10mins | Cook: 50mins | Ready in:

Ingredients

- 1 tablespoon Dijon mustard
- 2 tablespoons olive oil
- 3/4 teaspoon kosher salt
- 1 teaspoon freshly ground black pepper
- 2 pounds yellow potatoes, diced
- 8 ounces button mushrooms, quartered
- 1 1/2 cups cubed ham (Smithfield® Anytime Favorites Cubed Ham or Smithfield® Hickory Smoked Spiral Sliced Ham, cubed)
- 4 slices Smithfield® Hometown Original Bacon
- 2/3 cup jarred roasted red peppers, drained and roughly chopped
- 3/4 cup fresh mozzarella cheese, cubed
- 4 eggs, fried, poached, or to preference (optional)
- 1/3 cup thinly sliced fresh basil leaves

Direction

- Preheat an oven to 425°F. Whisk pepper, salt, oil and mustard till combined in a big bowl; add mushrooms and potatoes. Toss till coated.
- Evenly spread potato mixture on 2 nonstick/lightly oiled rimmed baking pans. Roast for 35-40 minutes in oven till mushrooms and potatoes start to brown, mixing halfway through cooking. Add any leftover ham/bacon into mixture; mix.
- Add roasted peppers into oven-safe serving casserole (optional). Put cheese on top. Bake till cheese starts to melt and is soft for 10-15 more minutes. Top hash using sliced basil and eggs cooked to your preference.

Nutrition Information

- Calories: 555 calories;
- Total Fat: 24.4
- Sodium: 2023
- Total Carbohydrate: 49.7
- Cholesterol: 237
- Protein: 35.2

662. Leftover Roast Beef Hash

Serving: 6 | Prep: 20mins | Cook: 17mins | Ready in:

Ingredients

- 3 russet potatoes
- 2 cups 1/2-inch cubes roast beef
- 1 onion, finely chopped
- 1 green bell pepper, thinly sliced
- 1/2 cup sliced fresh mushrooms
- 1 tablespoon vegetable oil

Direction

- In a microwaveable plate, put the potatoes and pierce the skins using a fork. Microwave for 7-8 minutes until a bit tender; slice the potatoes into 1-inch cubes.
- In a bowl, mix mushrooms, potatoes, green bell pepper, onion, and roast beef together.
- Preheat the electric skillet to 175°C or 350°F; grease with oil.
- Evenly spread the potato mixture in the pan. Cook without stirring for 5 minutes until brown. Flip then cook the other side for another 5 minutes until crisp.

Nutrition Information

- Calories: 165 calories;
- Total Fat: 3.6
- Sodium: 390
- Total Carbohydrate: 23.8
- Cholesterol: 18
- Protein: 10.5

663. Lemony Grilled Vegetable Kabobs

Serving: 12 | Prep: 15mins | Cook: 15mins | Ready in:

Ingredients

- 4 pounds assorted vegetables such as:
- zucchini
- summer squash
- cherry tomatoes
- mushrooms
- bell peppers
- onion
- 12 (12-inch) skewers*
- 1/4 cup olive oil
- lemon, juiced
- 1 clove garlic, minced, or more to taste
- 1/2 teaspoon salt
- ground black pepper

Direction

- Cut any big vegetables to 1-in. pieces. Thread the vegetables on the skewers. In a small bowl, whisk leftover ingredients.
- Heat the grill. Brush the kabobs with the lemon mixture. Grill till vegetables are at desired tenderness or for 10-15 minutes, turning it in between as needed to cook it evenly. Drizzle it with the leftover lemon mixture and serve while it's warm.

Nutrition Information

- Calories: 56 calories;
- Cholesterol: 0
- Protein: 0.9
- Total Fat: 4.7
- Sodium: 101
- Total Carbohydrate: 4.2

664. Leslie's Broccoli, Wild Rice, And Mushroom Stuffing

Serving: 12 | Prep: 15mins | Cook: 1hours15mins | Ready in:

Ingredients

- 1/2 cup uncooked wild rice
- 1 1/2 cups water
- 2 cups chopped fresh broccoli
- 1/2 cup butter
- 1 1/2 cups sliced mushrooms
- 1 cup chopped onion
- 1 (16 ounce) package herb seasoned stuffing mix
- 1 (14 ounce) can chicken broth
- 1/2 cup sliced almonds (optional)

Direction

- In a pot, bring 1 1/2 cups of water and rice to a boil. Cover and set heat to low. Let it simmer for 45 minutes.
- In a pot with enough water to cover broccoli, boil broccoli until slightly tender or for 5 minutes. Remove from heat and drain water.
- Preheat oven to 175 degrees C (350 degrees F). Mildly grease baking dish.
- In a skillet over medium heat, melt butter and sauté the onion and mushrooms until soft. Mix in almonds, broth, stuffing mix, cooked broccoli and cooked rice. Move to a prepared baking dish or you can use it as turkey stuffing just before roasting.
- In a preheated oven, bake it until golden brown in color or for 30 minutes.

Nutrition Information

- Calories: 271 calories;
- Total Fat: 11.2
- Sodium: 739
- Total Carbohydrate: 35.9
- Cholesterol: 21
- Protein: 7

665. Less Butter Steak Diane

Serving: 4 | Prep: 20mins | Cook: 30mins | Ready in:

Ingredients

- 1/2 cup beef broth
- 1/2 cup dry red wine
- 1 1/2 cups sliced mushrooms
- 1/4 cup finely chopped shallot
- 3 cloves garlic, crushed
- 3 teaspoons fresh lemon juice
- 3 teaspoons Worcestershire sauce
- 1/4 teaspoon salt, or to taste
- 1 pinch ground black pepper, or to taste
- 2 teaspoons chopped fresh parsley
- 2 teaspoons all-purpose flour
- 1 tablespoon butter
- 1 pound trimmed beef tenderloin, slightly pounded

Direction

- In a large saucepan, stir beef broth and wine, then add shallot, mushrooms, lemon juice, garlic, and Worcestershire sauce. Over medium heat, simmer with frequent stirring for about 20 minutes, until mushrooms shrink. Sprinkle with pepper and salt to taste.
- Remove 2 tablespoons of liquid from the surface of the mushroom mixture and put it in a small dish. Add flour and whisk to blend until it turns into a smooth paste. Sift the flour mixture into the mushroom mixture. Cook sauce while stirring until thickened. If you prefer much thicker sauce, add small amounts of more flour. Add parsley; stir. Keep the sauce warm in the pan until needed.
- Melt butter over medium heat using the same saucepan. Arrange tenderloin in the pan and fry over medium-high heat until desired doneness is achieved; flip over once. Serve coked tenderloin with mushroom sauce.

Nutrition Information

- Calories: 228 calories;
- Sodium: 352
- Total Carbohydrate: 6.4
- Cholesterol: 63
- Protein: 20.4
- Total Fat: 10.8

666. Linguine With Clam Sauce And Baby Portobello Mushrooms

Serving: 4 | Prep: 15mins | Cook: 45mins | Ready in:

Ingredients

- 1 tablespoon olive oil
- 3 cloves garlic, chopped
- 1 (8 ounce) package baby portobello mushrooms, sliced and chopped
- 4 (6.5 ounce) cans chopped clams with juice
- 4 cubes chicken bouillon
- 1 tablespoon chopped fresh parsley
- 1 teaspoon dried basil
- 1 teaspoon dried oregano
- 1 tablespoon Worcestershire sauce
- 1 (16 ounce) package uncooked linguini pasta
- 1/2 cup butter

Direction

- Warm olive oil in a saucepan on medium heat. Mix in mushrooms and garlic; cook till mushrooms are tender. Mix in Worcestershire sauce, oregano, basil, parsley, chicken bouillon and clam juice. Put heat on high; put on a quick boil. Lower heat to medium then simmer for 30 minutes.
- Meanwhile, boil a big pot of lightly salted water. Add pasta; cook for 8-10 minutes till al dente. Drain; put aside.
- Mix butter and chopped clams into sauce; simmer for 15 more minutes. Put on cooked pasta; serve.

Nutrition Information

- Calories: 941 calories;
- Total Carbohydrate: 97
- Cholesterol: 185
- Protein: 64.7
- Total Fat: 33
- Sodium: 1574

667. Linguine With Clams

Serving: 12 | Prep: 15mins | Cook: 43mins | Ready in:

Ingredients

- 1 (16 ounce) package linguine pasta
- 8 tablespoons unsalted butter
- 1 medium white onion, chopped
- 8 ounces fresh mushrooms, sliced
- 4 cloves garlic, pressed
- 1 cup dry white wine
- 4 (6.5 ounce) cans chopped clams, drained and rinsed with juices reserved
- 2 tablespoons sour cream
- freshly ground black pepper
- 1/4 cup chopped flat leaf parsley

Direction

- Boil a big pot of lightly salted water. Add pasta and cook until al dente, about 8-10 minutes. Strain and put aside.
- In a big frying pan, melt butter over medium-high heat. Add garlic, mushrooms, and onions, and sauté until softened. Add wine and simmer for 10 minutes. Lower the heat if needed.
- Mix in parsley, pepper, sour cream, the saved clam juice, and clams, and simmer for an addition of 20 minutes. Mix with linguine and serve. Enjoy!

Nutrition Information

- Calories: 323 calories;
- Sodium: 75
- Total Carbohydrate: 32.2
- Cholesterol: 63
- Protein: 21.1
- Total Fat: 10.1

668. Linguine With Clams And Porcini Mushrooms

Serving: 8 | Prep: 20mins | Cook: 30mins | Ready in:

Ingredients

- 1 ounce dried porcini mushrooms
- 1/4 cup olive oil
- 10 cloves garlic, minced
- 1 teaspoon dried red pepper flakes
- 36 fresh clams, cleaned
- 2 cups dry white wine
- 4 tomatoes, cubed
- 3 (8 ounce) jars clam juice
- 1 1/2 cups chopped fresh parsley
- 1 (16 ounce) package linguine pasta

Direction

- In cold water, add mushrooms and soak for 20-30 minutes to rehydrate. Dry the mushroom; chop coarsely.
- Over medium heat, put a medium saucepan and heat oil. Add red pepper, garlic and mushrooms; cook and stir until they turn browned. Mix in white wine and clams. When the clams open, transfer them to a medium bowl, remove those that don't open.
- Stir parsley, clam juice and tomatoes into the mushroom mixture. Let the mixture simmer in 15 minutes to lightly thicken.
- Boil lightly salted water in a large pot. Cook linguine until al dente, about 8-10 minutes. Drain the pasta.
- Add the clams back to the broth mixture; cook until heated through. Combine the mixture with cooked linguine thoroughly when ready to serve.

Nutrition Information

- Calories: 359 calories;
- Total Fat: 8.6
- Sodium: 209
- Total Carbohydrate: 49.2
- Cholesterol: 8
- Protein: 12

669. Linguine With Portobello Mushrooms

Serving: 8 | Prep: 15mins | Cook: 30mins | Ready in:

Ingredients

- 4 portobello mushroom caps
- 2 tablespoons extra virgin olive oil
- 1 pound linguine pasta
- 1 teaspoon red wine vinegar
- 1 teaspoon chopped fresh oregano
- 1 teaspoon chopped fresh basil
- 1/2 teaspoon chopped fresh rosemary
- 2 cloves garlic, peeled and crushed
- 2 teaspoons lemon juice
- salt and pepper to taste

Direction

- Preheat oven broiler.
- Boil big pot of lightly salted water. Add linguine; cook till al dente or for 9-13 minutes. Drain.
- Brush 1/2 of the olive oil on mushrooms; put on a medium baking sheet. In the prepped oven, broil for 6-8 minutes till tender and browned, frequently turning.
- Slice the mushrooms into 1/4-in. slices; put in a medium bowl. Mix with lemon juice, garlic, rosemary, basil, oregano, red wine vinegar and leftover olive oil; season with pepper and salt.
- Toss mushroom mixture and cooked linguine together in a big bowl.

Nutrition Information

- Calories: 250 calories;
- Cholesterol: 0
- Protein: 9
- Total Fat: 4.8
- Sodium: 152
- Total Carbohydrate: 44.6

670. Loaded Sweet Potato Lasagna

Serving: 10 | Prep: 30mins | Cook: 1hours21mins | Ready in:

Ingredients

- 1/4 cup olive oil, or as needed, divided
- 1 pound ground beef
- 2 cloves garlic, minced
- 2 teaspoons Italian seasoning, divided, or to taste
- 1/2 teaspoon kosher salt, or to taste
- 1/2 teaspoon ground black pepper, or to taste
- 2 cups marinara sauce, divided
- 1 eggplant, sliced
- 2 small zucchini, sliced
- 2 Cubanelle peppers, chopped
- 2 cups sliced fresh mushrooms
- 2 small sweet potatoes, thinly sliced, or more to taste

Direction

- Put oven to 190°C (375°F). Coat a 13 in. x 9 in. pan with a tbsp. of olive oil.
- Put 1 tbsp. of oil in a big skillet on medium heat. Cook the beef; break in smaller pieces with a wooden spoon until it browns, 5 minutes. Transfer to a bowl with slotted spoon.

- Wipe the skillet with paper towel. Put in remaining 1 tbsp. of oil. Cook garlic until aromatic, 30 seconds. Put with beef. Season with salt, pepper and 1 tsp. Italian seasoning. Add 1 1/2 cups of marinara sauce. Blend well.
- Stir and cook eggplant in skillet until tender, 2 minutes a side. Sprinkle with salt. Put on a plate. Do the same with zucchini. Stir and cook mushrooms on medium heat until tender, 5 minutes. Place in a bowl. Stir and cook cubanelle peppers until soft, 3 minutes.
- Place sweet potatoes in bottom of pan. Reserve a few pieces. On top layer the eggplant, beef, zucchini, cubanelle peppers, and mushrooms. Pour the left 1/2 cup marinara sauce over. Place the reserved sweet potato slices on top. Spritz with oil, season with the remaining 1 tsp. Italian seasoning, pepper, and salt. Cover with foil.
- Bake in the oven until potatoes are soft, 45 minutes. Discard the aluminum foil; bake until golden brown, 15 minutes longer. Let it rest 5 minutes then serve.

Nutrition Information

- Calories: 223 calories;
- Total Carbohydrate: 16.3
- Cholesterol: 28
- Protein: 9.8
- Total Fat: 13.5
- Sodium: 339

671. Loaded Vegetarian Quiche

Serving: 8 | Prep: 20mins | Cook: 55mins | Ready in:

Ingredients

- 1 (9 inch) unbaked deep dish pie crust
- 1 tablespoon olive oil
- 1/2 cup sliced onion
- 1/2 cup chopped green bell pepper
- 1/2 cup mushrooms, sliced
- 1/2 cup chopped zucchini
- 1 large tomato, sliced
- 2 tablespoons all-purpose flour
- 2 teaspoons dried basil
- 3 eggs, beaten
- 1/2 cup milk
- 1/2 teaspoon salt
- 1/4 teaspoon ground black pepper
- 1 1/2 cups shredded Colby-Monterey Jack cheese, divided

Direction

- Set the oven at 400°F (200°C) and start preheating.
- Bake the pie crust at about 8 minutes in the preheated oven until firm. Take out the crust from the oven then put aside. Lower the oven heat to 350°F (175°C).
- In a large frying pan, heat olive oil over medium heat. Mix zucchini, mushrooms, green bell pepper and onion in the hot oil at 5-7 minutes until softened. Take out the vegetables from the pan and put aside.
- Put basil and flour over the tomato slices; cook them for about 1 minute each side in the pan.
- In a small bowl, combine pepper, salt, milk, and eggs.
- At the bottom of the pie crust, spread 1 cup of Colby-Monterey Jack cheese. Then place the vegetable mixture over the cheese and top it off with tomatoes. Add the egg mixture in the pie shell. Put the remaining 1/2 cup of cheese onto the quiche.
- Bake for 40-45 minutes in the preheated oven until the knife comes out clean when inserting near the center of the pie. Cool it down about 5 minutes before enjoying the meal.

Nutrition Information

- Calories: 284 calories;
- Cholesterol: 95
- Protein: 10.5
- Total Fat: 19.6

- Sodium: 524
- Total Carbohydrate: 17.2

672. Lobster Salad With Red Devil Dressing

Serving: 4 | Prep: 30mins | Cook: 15mins | Ready in:

Ingredients

- 1 1/2 pounds cooked lobster tails - peeled, shredded and chilled
- 1 medium head garlic
- 1/2 large onion
- salt to taste
- 1/3 cup extra virgin olive oil
- 2 large red bell peppers
- 1 large portobello mushroom, chopped
- 1/2 lemon, juiced
- 1 tablespoon fennel seed
- 1 tablespoon ketchup
- 1 tablespoon cider vinegar
- ground black pepper to taste
- 4 cups mixed salad greens

Direction

- Preheat the oven to broil. Set the rack in the middle of oven. Coat a baking sheet lightly with oil.
- Chop off garlic top and transfer to a square of aluminum foil. Sprinkle with one teaspoon of olive oil and then drizzle with a dash of salt on top. Wrap with foil and transfer to baking sheet. Prepare the onion using the same way.
- Put the baking sheet in the middle of oven and then bake the onion and garlic for 15 minutes. Put the red bell peppers on the sheet and then broil for 15 minutes while flipping to blacken all the sides. Take out the peppers only and transfer to a brown paper bag. Put the mushroom in the baking sheet and then broil for about 15 minutes. Take garlic, onion and mushroom out of the oven. Let the veggies stand until they are cool to handle.
- Peel the peppers and then take out the seeds. Transfer to a blender and get rid of seeds and the peel. Press onion and garlic from the skins and place them into the blender and get rid of the skins. Cut the mushroom coarsely and transfer to the blender along with vinegar, ketchup, fennel, lemon juice and the remaining olive oil. Blend until the resulting mixture is smooth. Add ground black pepper and salt to taste.
- Put the shredded lobster meat in the middle of a large layer of salad greens. Spread the dressing all over the lobster meat.

Nutrition Information

- Calories: 449 calories;
- Protein: 37.8
- Total Fat: 24.6
- Sodium: 736
- Total Carbohydrate: 19.7
- Cholesterol: 130

673. Low 'N Slow Mushroom Barley Soup

Serving: 6 | Prep: 15mins | Cook: 1hours20mins | Ready in:

Ingredients

- 1/4 cup pearl barley
- 1 cup boiling water
- 2 tablespoons canola oil
- 1 onion, finely chopped
- 1 stalk celery, finely chopped
- 1 carrot, finely chopped
- 6 cups white mushrooms, halved if large
- 3 cloves garlic, minced
- 1 tablespoon tomato paste
- 6 cups beef stock
- 1 teaspoon dried oregano
- 1/2 teaspoon salt
- 1/2 teaspoon freshly ground black pepper

- 1 tablespoon Worcestershire sauce

Direction

- In a bowl, mix boiling water and pearl barley; put aside for 10 minutes to soak.
- Heat canola oil on medium heat in a big saucepan; mix and cook carrot, celery and onion in hot oil for 5-7 minutes till soft.
- Mix mushrooms into onion mixture; mix and cook for 5 minutes till brown and soft.
- Drain barley; discard leftover soaking water. Mix barley into mushroom mixture.
- Mix tomato paste and garlic into mixture till combined. Put beef stock into saucepan. Season with Worcestershire sauce, black pepper, salt and oregano.
- Boil soup. Lower heat to low; cook for 1 hour at a simmer.

Nutrition Information

- Calories: 163 calories;
- Total Carbohydrate: 19.8
- Cholesterol: 0
- Protein: 8.7
- Total Fat: 6.2
- Sodium: 353

674. Low Calorie Vegan Chili

Serving: 6 | Prep: 20mins | Cook: 35mins | Ready in:

Ingredients

- 1 (28 ounce) can diced tomatoes
- 3 cups water
- 1 (15.5 ounce) can kidney beans, drained
- 1 (15.5 ounce) can red beans, drained
- 1 yellow onion, diced
- 1 (6 ounce) can tomato paste
- 1 (6 ounce) can mushroom stems and pieces, drained
- 1/2 yellow bell pepper, diced
- 1/2 orange bell pepper, diced
- 3 tablespoons chili powder
- 2 tablespoons garlic powder
- 2 pinches salt

Direction

- In a big saucepan, mix and boil salt, garlic powder, chili powder, orange and yellow bell pepper, mushrooms, tomato paste, onion, red beans, kidney beans, water, and diced tomatoes on high heat; stir occasionally. Lower heat to medium-low. Simmer, occasionally mixing, for 30 minutes until all veggies are tender.

Nutrition Information

- Calories: 220 calories;
- Total Fat: 1.6
- Sodium: 1009
- Total Carbohydrate: 42.5
- Cholesterol: 0
- Protein: 11.9

675. Low Carb, Gluten Free Black Bean And Lentil Burgers

Serving: 8 | Prep: 30mins | Cook: 25mins | Ready in:

Ingredients

- 1 (14 ounce) can black beans, rinsed and drained
- 1 medium onion, finely chopped
- 1 bell pepper, finely chopped
- 1/2 cup finely chopped mushrooms
- 1 jalapeno pepper, finely chopped (optional)
- 2 cloves garlic, minced
- salt and ground black pepper to taste
- 1 tablespoon olive oil
- 3/4 cup ground lentils, or as needed
- 1 egg
- 2 tablespoons ground cumin

- 1 tablespoon chili powder
- 1/2 teaspoon smoked paprika

Direction

- Use a fork to mash black beans until chunky but not totally smooth.
- In a mixing bowl, combine garlic, jalapeno pepper, mushrooms, bell pepper, and onion. Sprinkle with pepper and salt to season.
- Heat olive oil over medium heat in a large skillet. Sauté vegetable mixture in heated oil for 5 to 8 minutes until tender. Sprinkle with pepper and salt to taste.
- Pour vegetable mixture into a food processor; process for 1 to 2 minutes. Stir blended vegetables into black beans. Stir in egg and ground lentils. Add paprika, chili powder, and cumin. Chill mixture for half an hour in the fridge.
- Turn oven to 375°F (190°C) to preheat. Line parchment paper over a baking sheet.
- Form cooled mixture into patties. Place on the prepared baking sheet.
- Bake in the preheated oven until browned for 10 to 15 minutes on each side.

Nutrition Information

- Calories: 154 calories;
- Total Fat: 3.2
- Sodium: 233
- Total Carbohydrate: 23.3
- Cholesterol: 20
- Protein: 9.4

676. Lyn's Chicken

Serving: 4 | Prep: 10mins | Cook: 40mins | Ready in:

Ingredients

- 4 skinless, boneless chicken breast halves
- 2 cups sliced fresh mushrooms
- 1 teaspoon coarse ground black pepper
- 1 1/2 cups shredded Cheddar cheese

Direction

- Set an oven broiler to 190°C (375°F) and start preheating. Use aluminum foil to line a broiler pan. On the broiling pan, arrange the chicken.
- In the prepared oven, broil the chicken breasts until they are cooked thoroughly and juices from the chicken run clear, or for 25-35 minutes.
- In the meantime, in a medium skillet, arrange the mushrooms and flavor to taste with pepper and salt, put a cover on the skillet and cook on high heat until juices run. When that happens, turn down the heat and uncover, keep cooking until the liquid evaporates. Add the mushrooms into the chicken and scatter over the top with the shredded cheese.
- Broil until the cheese is bubbling and golden, 8-10 minutes.

Nutrition Information

- Calories: 350 calories;
- Protein: 41.7
- Total Fat: 18.8
- Sodium: 401
- Total Carbohydrate: 2.6
- Cholesterol: 123

677. Magic Chicken

Serving: 2 | Prep: 5mins | Cook: 35mins | Ready in:

Ingredients

- 2 skinless, boneless chicken breast halves
- 1 cup red cooking wine
- 1 (4 ounce) can sliced mushrooms, drained
- 1 (6.5 ounce) jar marinated artichoke hearts, undrained

Direction

- Set an oven to 175°C (350°F) and start preheating.
- In both sides of the chicken breasts, use a fork to poke holes, then arrange into a baking dish. Pour the cooking wine on top. Cover with the artichoke marinade and artichokes. Scatter over with mushrooms.
- In the prepared oven, bake until the chicken is not pink anymore and juices from the chicken run clear, or for 35 minutes.

Nutrition Information

- Calories: 339 calories;
- Total Fat: 6.5
- Sodium: 1377
- Total Carbohydrate: 31.2
- Cholesterol: 68
- Protein: 31.6

678. Mahi Mahi With Onions And Mushrooms

Serving: 4 | Prep: 10mins | Cook: 20mins | Ready in:

Ingredients

- 2 tablespoons olive oil
- 3 small onions, chopped
- 4 cloves garlic, minced
- 5 button mushrooms, sliced
- 1 1/2 pounds mahi mahi
- salt and pepper to taste
- 1/4 cup white cooking wine
- 1 tablespoon fresh lemon juice
- 1 teaspoon cornstarch
- 2 tablespoons water

Direction

- Pour olive oil into a big skillet. At medium heat, heat the oil. Insert the garlic, mushrooms and onions, cooking until the onions become translucent. Slice the fillets up fish up into fillets, about 3 inches long. On top of the garlic, mushrooms and onions, set the mahi-mahi fillets down. Add pepper and salt to the fillet's first side to your liking. Pour in lemon juice and white cooking wine. Leave it cooking with the cover on for 4-5 minutes. After turning the fillets over, add pepper and salt onto the second side to your liking. Leave it cooking until the flesh starts flaking with ease, about another 4-5 minutes. Transfer the fish along onto a heated plate. Maintain the warmth until the sauce is done. Inside of the skillet with cooking wine, garlic, mushrooms and onion, turn the heat up to medium-high. Boil. Mix 2 tablespoons of water with cornstarch until dissolved, stirring this into the skillet. Keep stirring the sauce consistently until the sauce is at personal preference of consistency. Before serving at once, empty the sauce out atop the mahi-mahi fillets.

Nutrition Information

- Calories: 251 calories;
- Total Fat: 8.1
- Sodium: 155
- Total Carbohydrate: 8
- Cholesterol: 124
- Protein: 33

679. Mahi And Mushrooms

Serving: 2 | Prep: 15mins | Cook: 15mins | Ready in:

Ingredients

- 1 clove garlic, minced, or more to taste
- 1 tablespoon minced shallot, or more to taste
- 1 pinch red pepper flakes, or to taste
- 2 tablespoons olive oil
- 2 (4 ounce) mahi mahi fillets
- salt and ground black pepper to taste
- 2 teaspoons olive oil

- 1 cup fresh oyster mushrooms, stemmed and sliced
- 1/2 cup halved yellow and red grape tomatoes, or more to taste
- 1/4 cup white wine (optional)
- 1 tablespoon butter (optional)

Direction

- In a low dish, combine 2 tablespoons of olive oil, red pepper flakes, shallot and garlic. In the olive oil mixture, set the mahi-mahi down and turn until coated. Put black pepper and salt on the fillets to season. Move the dish into the fridge. Leave the fish marinating for 1/2 hour or through the night. Pour 2 teaspoons of olive oil into a skillet then heat it at medium high heat. Insert the oyster mushrooms, cooking and stirring for around 5 minutes until they tenderize. Add black pepper and salt to season. Add white wine atop mushrooms. Simmer. Leave it cooking as you prep the fish fillets. Extract the mahi-mahi fillets out of the marinade, shaking to get rid of any extra marinade. At medium heat, put the skillet atop until heated. Insert the fillets gently, cooking for around 5 minutes. Empty the marinade out into the skillets on top of the fillets. Proceed to cook until the fillet's center starts flaking. Move it away from the heat and move it onto a serving dish. Maintain the warmth. Insert the butter and tomatoes to wine and mushroom mixture, cooking and stirring until the butter just about melts. Before serving, spoon the mixture atop mahi-mahi fillets. If desired, serve with some bread and a salad for a complete meal.

Nutrition Information

- Calories: 363 calories;
- Total Fat: 25.2
- Sodium: 152
- Total Carbohydrate: 6.4
- Cholesterol: 97
- Protein: 22.6

680. Make Ahead Marsala Turkey Gravy

Serving: 12 | Prep: 15mins | Cook: 5hours | Ready in:

Ingredients

- 2 teaspoons vegetable oil
- 3 turkey necks
- 1 onion, chopped
- 1 stalk celery, chopped
- 1 carrot, chopped
- 1/3 cup Marsala wine
- 2 quarts cold water
- 1/4 ounce dried porcini mushrooms
- 2 cloves garlic, peeled
- 1 bay leaf
- 1/4 cup butter
- 1/4 ounce dried porcini mushrooms
- 3 tablespoons flour
- 2 tablespoons heavy cream
- salt and freshly ground black pepper to taste

Direction

- Over medium-high heat, heat oil in Dutch oven. Put the turkey necks in Dutch oven and then cook for around 5-7 minutes, or until the turkey necks are golden brown. Stir in the carrot, celery, and onion; and continue to cook and mix for around five minutes, until the onion is slightly brown and soft.
- Pour in the Marsala wine over turkey necks, then turn up stove to high heat; boil mixture and scrape off brown-colored bits from the bottom of the pan. Let the turkey necks and Marsala mixture simmer for around 3-4 minutes, until wine has been reduced by half.
- Mix in 1/4 oz. dried porcini mushrooms, bay leaf, garlic, and water. Allow mixture to boil, then reduce heat to low; simmer, skimming any foam or fat that rises to the top. Cover the Dutch oven almost completely; let the turkey necks mixture simmer for about 4-5 hours, until the meat separates from the bones.

Carefully strain the resulting turkey stock into a clean container, and let the mixture cool completely, which should take about 2 hours.
- In a bowl, put 1/4 oz. of dried porcini mushrooms and pour warm water over; keep porcini mushrooms soaked for around 15 minutes, until they're soft enough to be diced. Squeeze out any excess water from the porcini mushrooms, and then drain. Set the mushrooms aside.
- Over medium heat, melt butter in a saucepan. Mix in the diced porcini mushrooms; continue to cook and stir for around five minutes, until porcini mushrooms have turned brown.
- Mix in flour into the butter and mushrooms mixture; cook and mix for around three minutes, until flour no longer appears gritty.
- Mix in turkey stock into the mixture, turning up heat to medium high, and bringing it to a simmer. Let the resulting mixture simmer for around 15-20 minutes, until sauce has thickened and has been reduced by 1/3. Mix in the cream, and season with pepper and salt, to taste.

Nutrition Information

- Calories: 163 calories;
- Total Fat: 8.9
- Sodium: 79
- Total Carbohydrate: 5.6
- Cholesterol: 68
- Protein: 13.1

681. Make Ahead Turkey Gravy With Porcini Mushrooms And Marsala Wine

Serving: 16 | Prep: 5hours | Cook: 45mins | Ready in:

Ingredients

- For the turkey neck stock:
- 2 teaspoons vegetable oil
- 4 turkey necks
- 1 onion, chopped
- 1 stalk celery, chopped
- 1 carrot, chopped
- 1/3 cup Marsala wine
- 2 quarts cold water
- 1 bay leaf
- 2 garlic cloves
- 1/4 ounce dried porcini mushrooms
- For the sauce:
- 1/4 ounce dried porcini mushrooms
- 1 cup hot water
- 1/4 cup butter
- 3 tablespoons all-purpose flour
- 2 tablespoons heavy cream
- salt and ground black pepper to taste

Direction

- Over medium-high heat, heat vegetable oil in a big stockpot. In hot oil, brown turkey necks for about 6 minutes on each side. Put carrots, celery, and onion. Cook for 5 to 10 minutes until the vegetables begin to soften and brown. Put into Marsala wine. At the bottom of the pan, scrape and dissolve any vegetable bits and browned meat off. Turn heat to high and cook until liquid is reduced by half.
- Stir 1/4 ounce dried porcini mushrooms, garlic cloves, bay leaves and 2 quarts of cold water in. Bring to a simmer. Reduce heat to low. Skim and dispose any foam that comes to the top as stock simmers. Partially cover, and simmer for 4 to 5 hours on very low heat. Strain solids out and to cool, set broth aside.
- In a bowl, cover 1 cup hot water to cover 1/4 ounce dried porcini. For 10 minutes, allow to rehydrate. Take mushrooms out from water and chop it finely. Over medium heat, heat 1/4 cup of butter in a big saucepan and brown mushrooms for about 10 minutes. Stir in flour into butter and mushrooms and over medium heat, cook for 3 minutes, constantly stirring. Whisk in about 1/2 cup of broth at a time. Turn heat to medium high and bring gravy to boil.

- Allow to simmer by reducing heat, and cook gravy for about 30 minutes until thickened and reduced. Stir often and stir cream in before serving. Use black pepper and salt to season.

Nutrition Information

- Calories: 140 calories;
- Sodium: 56
- Total Carbohydrate: 3.5
- Cholesterol: 65
- Protein: 12.7
- Total Fat: 7.5

682. Mandarin Chicken Skillet

Serving: 4 | Prep: 10mins | Cook: 25mins | Ready in:

Ingredients

- 1 cup fresh broccoli florets
- 1 tablespoon butter
- 2 pounds skinless, boneless chicken breast meat - cubed
- 1 1/2 cups sliced fresh mushrooms
- 3 teaspoons all-purpose flour
- 2/3 cup water
- 1/3 cup undiluted, thawed orange juice concentrate
- 2 cubes chicken bouillon
- 1 (11 ounce) can mandarin orange segments, drained
- 1/4 cup sliced green onion

Direction

- In a steamer above a 1-in. of boiling water, put broccoli and put a cover on. Cook for 2-6 minutes until soft but not mushy. Strain, let cool and put aside.
- In a big frying pan, melt butter over medium-high heat. In the butter, sauté chicken until turning brown. Take out of the frying pan and put aside.
- In the frying pan, sauté mushrooms for 1 minute, take out of the frying pan and put aside. Stir in seasoning, orange juice concentrate, water, and flour.
- Boil it, whisking. Simmer for 4 minutes, whisking. Put the mushrooms and chicken back into the frying pan, stir in broccoli, green onion, and orange segments. Thoroughly heat and enjoy.

Nutrition Information

- Calories: 369 calories;
- Sodium: 759
- Total Carbohydrate: 21.6
- Cholesterol: 140
- Protein: 55.3
- Total Fat: 6.1

683. Manicotti Italian Casserole

Serving: 8 | Prep: 10mins | Cook: 30mins | Ready in:

Ingredients

- 1 pound rigatoni pasta
- 1 pound ground beef
- 1 pound Italian sausage
- 1 (8 ounce) can mushrooms, drained
- 2 (32 ounce) jars spaghetti sauce
- 1 1/2 pounds shredded mozzarella cheese
- thinly sliced pepperoni

Direction

- Preheat the oven to 175 °C or 350 °F.
- Boil a big pot of slightly salted water. Add the rigatoni, and cook for 8 to 10 minutes till al dente. Drain, and reserve pasta.
- In the meantime, in a big skillet over moderate heat, brown Italian sausage and ground beef.

Transfer sausage and beef to a baking dish using a slotted spoon. Mix cooked pasta, spaghetti sauce and mushrooms into baking dish. Over the top, scatter the pepperoni and cheese.
- In prepped oven, bake for 20 minutes till cheese is bubbly and brown.

Nutrition Information

- Calories: 909 calories;
- Sodium: 2248
- Total Carbohydrate: 77.6
- Cholesterol: 127
- Protein: 52.1
- Total Fat: 43

684. Marcel's Spicy Slow Cooker Chicken Thighs

Serving: 4 | Prep: 20mins | Cook: 6hours6mins | Ready in:

Ingredients

- 4 large tomatoes, chopped
- 2 large onions, chopped
- 1 green bell pepper, chopped
- 1 red bell pepper, chopped
- 1 yellow bell pepper, chopped
- 8 mushrooms, chopped
- 6 skinless chicken thighs
- 4 teaspoons hot pepper sauce, divided, or to taste
- 1 tablespoon vegetable oil
- 10 ounces salsa
- 1 3/4 cups chicken broth

Direction

- In the slow cooker, combine mushrooms, yellow bell pepper, red bell pepper, green bell pepper, onions, and tomatoes.
- Brush chicken thighs with 2 teaspoons of hot pepper sauce. In a frying pan over medium-high heat, heat the oil. Cook each side of chicken thighs for 3 – 5 minutes until lightly browned.
- Move chicken thighs to the slow cooker. Pour in salsa and 2 teaspoons of hot pepper sauce. Add chicken broth, then stir to incorporate.
- Cook on Low for around 6 hours until chicken thighs become soft.

Nutrition Information

- Calories: 251 calories;
- Protein: 23
- Total Fat: 8.1
- Sodium: 1126
- Total Carbohydrate: 23.6
- Cholesterol: 65

685. Marinated Chanterelle Mushroom Canapes

Serving: 12 | Prep: 45mins | Cook: 30mins | Ready in:

Ingredients

- 1 teaspoon olive oil, or as needed
- 2 pounds chanterelle mushrooms, cleaned and chopped
- 1 teaspoon salt
- 1 leek, thinly sliced
- 1/2 yellow onion, thinly sliced
- 1 small carrot, thinly sliced
- 1/2 stalk celery, thinly sliced
- 1 clove garlic, minced
- 1 bay leaf
- 1 sprig thyme
- 1 teaspoon ground coriander
- 3 tablespoons sherry vinegar
- 1/3 cup chicken stock
- 3 tablespoons chopped fresh parsley

- 2 French baguettes, sliced into 1/2-inch rounds
- 1/3 cup extra-virgin olive oil
- 1 teaspoon lemon juice, or to taste
- salt and pepper to taste
- 2 tablespoons olive oil

Direction

- In a large pan, heat 1 teaspoon of olive oil over medium-high heat. Add salt and mushrooms. Sauté for about 10 minutes till almost all water from the mushrooms has evaporated. Shift mushrooms to a bowl while keeping oil in the pan.
- Add celery, carrot, onion, and leek then lower heat to medium. Cook and mix for 5 -7 minutes till vegetables turn golden brown. Put in coriander, thyme, bay leaf, and garlic. Transfer mushrooms back to the pan; cook and whisk for around 3 minutes. Put in vinegar and cook for 1 minute. Add stock then bring to a simmer for 1 minute more. Move the contents of pan to a heat-resistant bowl then pour in 1/3 cup of olive oil. Allow to sit for 2 hours. Flavor with pepper, salt, and lemon juice.
- Preheat the oven to 350° F (175° C).
- On a baking sheet, position baguette slices. Lightly brush with olive oil then spice with salt.
- In the preheated oven, bake while turning once, around 8 minutes on each side until golden.
- On a plate, arrange toasted bread. Spoon marinated mushrooms atop bread.

Nutrition Information

- Calories: 288 calories;
- Protein: 8.8
- Sodium: 618
- Total Carbohydrate: 39.4
- Cholesterol: < 1
- Total Fat: 10

686. Marinated Mushrooms

Serving: 8 | Prep: 15mins | Cook: 10mins | Ready in:

Ingredients

- 1 cup red wine
- 1/2 cup red wine vinegar
- 1/3 cup olive oil
- 2 tablespoons brown sugar
- 2 cloves garlic, minced
- 1 teaspoon crushed red pepper flakes
- 1/4 cup red bell pepper, diced
- 1 pound small fresh mushrooms, washed and trimmed
- 1/4 cup chopped green onions
- 1/4 teaspoon dried oregano
- 1/2 teaspoon salt
- 1/4 teaspoon ground black pepper

Direction

- Mix together the mushrooms, red pepper flakes, bell pepper, garlic, sugar, oil, vinegar and wine in a saucepan on medium heat, then boil. Put cover and put aside to let it cool.
- Mix in pepper, salt, oregano and green onions once cooled. Serve it at room temperature or chilled.

Nutrition Information

- Calories: 139 calories;
- Sodium: 151
- Total Carbohydrate: 8.1
- Cholesterol: 0
- Protein: 2
- Total Fat: 9.3

687. Marinated Mushrooms II

Serving: 16 | Prep: 15mins | Cook: 12mins | Ready in:

Ingredients

- 1/3 cup red wine vinegar
- 1/3 cup olive oil
- 1 small onion, thinly sliced
- 1 teaspoon salt
- 2 tablespoons dried parsley
- 1 teaspoon ground dry mustard
- 1 tablespoon brown sugar
- 2 cloves garlic, peeled and crushed
- 1 pound small fresh button mushrooms

Direction

- Combine the garlic, brown sugar, dry mustard, parsley, salt, onion, olive oil and red wine vinegar in a medium saucepan, then boil. Lower the heat. Mix in mushrooms. Let it simmer for 10-12 minutes, stirring from time to time. Move to sterile containers and chill in the fridge until ready to serve.

Nutrition Information

- Calories: 54 calories;
- Total Fat: 4.6
- Sodium: 148
- Total Carbohydrate: 2.8
- Cholesterol: 0
- Protein: 1

688. Marinated Mushrooms For Antipasto

Serving: 8 | Prep: 15mins | Cook: 10mins |Ready in:

Ingredients

- 1 pound small mushrooms, stemmed
- 4 tablespoons extra-virgin olive oil
- 3 tablespoons white wine vinegar
- 1/2 red onion, finely chopped
- 2 tablespoons finely chopped fresh oregano
- 2 tablespoons finely chopped fresh thyme
- 2 cloves garlic cloves, pressed
- 1/2 teaspoon salt
- 1/2 teaspoon freshly ground black pepper

Direction

- Place lightly salted water in a large pot and make it boil. Put in mushrooms and cook for 10 minutes until softened. Strain and reserve to cool.
- In a large jar with a lid, mix together the pepper, salt, garlic, thyme, oregano, red onion, white wine vinegar and olive oil. Cover jar and shake well. Put in the cooked mushrooms and place inside the refrigerator for at minimum 5 hours. Before serving, get from refrigerator for 10 minutes.

Nutrition Information

- Calories: 79 calories;
- Total Fat: 7
- Sodium: 149
- Total Carbohydrate: 3.1
- Cholesterol: 0
- Protein: 2

689. Marinated Mushrooms With Blue Cheese

Serving: 12 | Prep: 20mins | Cook: |Ready in:

Ingredients

- 1/4 cup blue cheese, crumbled
- 1 cup vegetable oil
- 2 tablespoons lemon juice
- 1/4 cup white wine vinegar
- 2 cloves garlic, minced
- 2 teaspoons seasoning salt
- 1 teaspoon white sugar
- 1/2 teaspoon dry mustard
- hot sauce to taste
- 2 cups fresh mushrooms, stems removed

Direction

- In a medium bowl, combine the hot sauce, dry mustard, white sugar, seasoning salt, garlic, white wine vinegar, lemon juice, vegetable oil and blue cheese. Mix in the mushrooms. Refrigerate while covered for 4 - 6 hours before enjoying.

Nutrition Information

- Calories: 178 calories;
- Sodium: 194
- Total Carbohydrate: 1.5
- Cholesterol: 2
- Protein: 1.2
- Total Fat: 19.1

690. Marinated Mushrooms With Red Bell Peppers

Serving: 12 | Prep: 20mins | Cook: 10mins | Ready in:

Ingredients

- 1/2 cup red wine vinegar
- 1/3 cup water
- 2 tablespoons corn oil
- 1 teaspoon white sugar
- 1 tablespoon chopped onion
- 1 tablespoon chopped fresh parsley
- 1/2 teaspoon dried basil
- 2 cloves garlic, minced
- 1/4 teaspoon salt
- 1/4 teaspoon fresh ground black pepper
- 2 (16 ounce) packages fresh mushrooms, stems removed
- 1/2 red bell pepper, diced

Direction

- Mix together pepper, salt, garlic, basil, parsley, onion, sugar, oil, water and vinegar; come to a boil. Stir in red bell pepper and mushrooms; bring the mixture to a boil again; lower the heat and allow it to simmer for 5-10 minutes, until the mushrooms are tender. Take it out of the heat and cool to room temperature. Put in a container, cover up and keep in fridge for at least 4 hours to serve.

Nutrition Information

- Calories: 44 calories;
- Total Carbohydrate: 4.2
- Cholesterol: 0
- Protein: 2.5
- Total Fat: 2.6
- Sodium: 53

691. Mediterranean Vegetable Stew

Serving: 6 | Prep: | Cook: | Ready in:

Ingredients

- 2 tablespoons olive oil, divided
- 1 cup chopped red onion
- 2 cups coarsely chopped green pepper
- 2 large garlic cloves, crushed
- 1 cup sliced mushrooms
- 1 small eggplant, unpeeled, cut in 1- to 2-inch chunks
- 1 (28 ounce) can crushed tomatoes
- 1/2 cup kalamata olives, pitted and sliced
- 1 (15 ounce) can chickpeas, drained and rinsed
- 1 tablespoon chopped fresh rosemary
- 1 cup coarsely chopped parsley

Direction

- Heat 1 tablespoon of oil in a big frying pan. Sauté pepper and onion for 10 minutes until tender. Add eggplant, mushrooms, garlic, and 1 tablespoon of oil. Simmer for 15 minutes until the eggplant is tender but still firm, tossing sometimes. Add rosemary, chickpeas, olives, and tomatoes. Simmer for 10 minutes until fully heated. Mix in parsley. Sprinkle over the stew with feta cheese if wanted.

Nutrition Information

- Calories: 222 calories;
- Cholesterol: 0
- Protein: 6.7
- Total Fat: 8.8
- Sodium: 505
- Total Carbohydrate: 33.4

692. Melt In Your Mouth Meat Loaf

Serving: 6 | Prep: 15mins | Cook: 5hours15mins | Ready in:

Ingredients

- 2 eggs
- 3/4 cup milk
- 2/3 cup seasoned bread crumbs
- 2 teaspoons dried minced onion
- 1 teaspoon salt
- 1/2 teaspoon rubbed sage
- 1/2 cup sliced fresh mushrooms
- 1 1/2 pounds ground beef
- 1/4 cup ketchup
- 2 tablespoons brown sugar
- 1 teaspoon ground mustard
- 1/2 teaspoon Worcestershire sauce

Direction

- In a big bowl, mix mushrooms, sage, salt, onion, breadcrumbs, milk and eggs then crush ground beef on the mixture and stir it well until combined. Use the mixture to form a round loaf and put it on a 5-quart slow cooker. Cover it then adjust the setting to low and cook for 5-6 hours. It is ready when a meat thermometer registers at 71°F or 160°F.
- In a small bowl, whisk Worcestershire sauce, mustard, brown sugar and ketchup together. Ladle this on the meat loaf and place it back in the slow cooker. Adjust the setting to low and cook until thoroughly heated, around 15 minutes. Leave it rest for 10 minutes before slicing.

Nutrition Information

- Calories: 328 calories;
- Sodium: 841
- Total Carbohydrate: 18.4
- Cholesterol: 136
- Protein: 24.7
- Total Fat: 16.9

693. Microwave Steamed Mushroom Rice

Serving: 4 | Prep: 5mins | Cook: 20mins | Ready in:

Ingredients

- 1 cup white rice
- 1 dried shiitake mushroom
- 3/4 cup very hot water
- 1 ounce enoki mushrooms
- 1/2 ounce shimeji mushrooms
- 2 teaspoons sake
- 1 pinch salt
- 1 (1 inch) piece kombu (dried kelp)

Direction

- Rinse the rice and steep into water about half an hour.
- Soak in the hot water with shiitake mushroom for 5-10 minutes, until softened.
- Meanwhile, cut off the root of enoki mushrooms. Cut off the root of shimeji mushrooms and split individual mushrooms. Cut off the stem of shiitake mushroom and slice the clap thinly. Save the soaking water.

- Drain rice and mix into a microwavable bowl together with mushrooms.
- Combine together salt, sake and saved soaking water, then add over mushrooms as well as rice. Put in kombu and place a microwavable lid to cover the bowl.
- Cook in the microwave for 5 minutes, at 600W, then stir. Microwave for 12 minutes longer at 200W. Keep bowl covered about 5 minutes before serving.

Nutrition Information

- Calories: 201 calories;
- Sodium: 81
- Total Carbohydrate: 43.8
- Cholesterol: 0
- Protein: 4.4
- Total Fat: 0.4

694. Mike's Mushroom Bread

Serving: 12 | Prep: 15mins | Cook: 15mins | Ready in:

Ingredients

- 1 loaf Italian bread
- 1/2 cup softened butter
- 1 pound sliced fresh mushrooms
- 2 cups shredded mozzarella cheese
- 6 green onions, chopped
- 3 cloves garlic, minced

Direction

- Preheat an oven to 400 °F (200 °C).
- Slice bread horizontally in half. To form a hollow shell, pull out most of the soft bread using your fingers. Save pulled-out bread for another use.
- Mix mushrooms, butter, cheese, garlic, and green onions together. Smear both cut sides of bread with mixture. Put the bread on baking sheet, cut sides facing up.
- In preheated oven, bake for approximately 10 to 15 minutes until the cheese has melted. Cut into wedges and serve.

Nutrition Information

- Calories: 279 calories;
- Protein: 10.9
- Total Fat: 12.8
- Sodium: 501
- Total Carbohydrate: 30.6
- Cholesterol: 32

695. Minnesota Pork Chops

Serving: 4 | Prep: 20mins | Cook: 2hours | Ready in:

Ingredients

- 6 pork chops
- salt and pepper to taste
- 1 cup uncooked wild rice
- 1 1/2 cups water
- 1 (8 ounce) can canned mushrooms
- 1 tablespoon chicken bouillon granules
- 1 (10.75 ounce) can condensed cream of mushroom soup

Direction

- Preheat the oven to 175 degrees C (350 degrees F).
- Brown the chops seasoned with pepper and salt in a skillet with a little amount of oil. Use nonstick spray to spritz a large 9x13 inch casserole dish. Evenly drizzle washed rice on bottom of dish.
- Add mushrooms and water. Drizzle with the chicken bouillon. Spread chops at the top and spoon the soup atop rice and chops. Use aluminum foil to cover the casserole and then seal tightly. Bake for about 1 1/2 hours to 2 hours or until the chops and rice become tender.

Nutrition Information

- Calories: 352 calories;
- Total Fat: 14.4
- Sodium: 791
- Total Carbohydrate: 29.3
- Cholesterol: 56
- Protein: 26.9

696. Miso Soup With Shiitake Mushrooms

Serving: 4 | Prep: 10mins | Cook: 10mins | Ready in:

Ingredients

- 4 cups vegetable broth
- 4 shiitake mushrooms, thinly sliced
- 1/4 cup miso paste
- 4 teaspoons soy sauce
- 1/3 cup diced firm tofu
- 2 green onions, trimmed and thinly sliced

Direction

- Boil vegetable broth in a pot; put in mushrooms. Turn to low heat then simmer for 4 mins. In a small bowl, mix soy sauce and miso paste together; pour into the broth then add tofu. Cook continuously for another minute. Ladle soup in bowls then add green onions on top to serve.

Nutrition Information

- Calories: 92 calories;
- Total Fat: 2.5
- Sodium: 1406
- Total Carbohydrate: 11.8
- Cholesterol: 0
- Protein: 5.5

697. Mom's Chicken Cacciatore

Serving: 8 | Prep: | Cook: | Ready in:

Ingredients

- 2 cups all-purpose flour for coating
- 1/2 teaspoon salt
- 1/4 teaspoon ground black pepper
- 1 (4 pound) chicken, cut into pieces
- 2 tablespoons vegetable oil
- 1 onion, chopped
- 2 cloves garlic, minced
- 1 green bell pepper, chopped
- 1 (14.5 ounce) can diced tomatoes
- 1/2 teaspoon dried oregano
- 1/2 cup white wine
- 2 cups fresh mushrooms, quartered
- salt and pepper to taste

Direction

- In a plastic bag, combine pepper, salt and the flour. Shake chicken pieces in flour until covered. Heat oil in a large pan (one that has a lid/cover). Fry chicken pieces until browned on both sides. Take off from the pan.
- Add bell pepper, garlic and onion to the pan and sauté until onion is slightly browned. Transfer the chicken back into the pan and put in wine, oregano and tomatoes. Simmer, covered, over medium low heat for half an hour.
- Add pepper, salt and mushrooms to taste. Simmer for 10 mins longer.

Nutrition Information

- Calories: 670 calories;
- Total Carbohydrate: 28.9
- Cholesterol: 170
- Protein: 46.9
- Total Fat: 38.1
- Sodium: 423

- Total Fat: 28.9

698. Mom's Sweet Spaghetti Sauce

Serving: 7 | Prep: 30mins | Cook: 30mins | Ready in:

Ingredients

- 2 tablespoons vegetable oil
- 1/2 onion, minced
- 1/2 green bell pepper, chopped
- 1 pound ground beef
- 4 slices bacon
- 2 (4 ounce) jars mushrooms, drained
- 1 (29 ounce) can tomato sauce
- 1 (6 ounce) can tomato paste
- 2 tablespoons garlic powder
- 2 tablespoons dried oregano
- 1/2 cup white wine
- 3/4 cup sugar
- salt and pepper to taste

Direction

- Cook bell pepper and onion in a skillet with oil over medium heat until transparent. Put beef into the peppers and onions then cook until brown. Put aside.
- In a big, deep skillet, put the bacon then cook on medium-high heat until evenly browned. Save the crumble bacon and drippings; mix them with the beef mixture.
- Put in oregano, garlic powder, tomato paste, tomato sauce and mushrooms. Put in wine while stirring then mix in sugar, then pepper and salt. Let it cook until hot.

Nutrition Information

- Calories: 480 calories;
- Sodium: 1117
- Total Carbohydrate: 38.4
- Cholesterol: 66
- Protein: 16.6

699. Mozzarella Chicken Marsala

Serving: 6 | Prep: 20mins | Cook: 45mins | Ready in:

Ingredients

- 1 cup all-purpose flour
- 1 tablespoon Creole-style seasoning
- 6 skinless, boneless chicken breast halves
- oil for frying
- 1 cup sliced fresh mushrooms
- 3 large onions, thinly sliced
- 1 (14 ounce) can chicken broth
- 1 cup Marsala wine
- 1 (16 ounce) package shredded mozzarella cheese
- 1/2 cup freshly grated Parmesan cheese

Direction

- In a resealable plastic bag, put flour and dust with seasoning. Put chicken breast into bag, one at a time, seal and shake in order to coat. Take out each breast, allow to rest for about 5 minutes, after that put in bag, seal and shake once again to evenly coat.
- In a large skillet, heat oil over medium high heat. Put in chicken and fry until the juices run clear and the chicken turn golden brown. Move chicken to a 9x13 inch baking dish.
- Heat the oven to 350°F (175°C) beforehand.
- In the same skillet, sauté onions and mushrooms in pan drippings; cook while stirring until lightly tender. Mix in wine and broth, lower heat to medium low and simmer while stirring occasionally for 10 minutes. Pour the mixture over chicken, bake with a cover in prepared oven for half an hour.
- Combine together Parmesan and mozzarella cheese and sprinkle over the chicken. Raise oven temperature to 450°F (230°C) and bake

for 5-7 minutes, or until cheese is golden brown and melted.

Nutrition Information

- Calories: 662 calories;
- Total Carbohydrate: 31.9
- Cholesterol: 124
- Protein: 52
- Total Fat: 30.7
- Sodium: 1204

700. Mozzarella Mushroom Chicken

Serving: 2 | Prep: 15mins | Cook: 30mins |Ready in:

Ingredients

- 3 tablespoons olive oil
- 2 skinless, boneless chicken breast halves
- 1 tablespoon garlic powder
- 1 clove garlic, minced
- 6 fresh mushrooms, sliced
- 2 cups shredded mozzarella cheese

Direction

- Heat olive oil over medium heat in a skillet. Put chicken into the skillet; season with garlic and garlic powder. Cook until chicken juices run clear, or about 12 minutes per side. Put aside the chicken and keep warm.
- Mix mushrooms into the skillet; cook until soft. Put chicken back into the skillet, layer with mushrooms, and sprinkle on top with cheese. Keep cooking, covered until cheese is melted, or about 5 minutes.

Nutrition Information

- Calories: 642 calories;
- Total Fat: 42.2
- Sodium: 766
- Total Carbohydrate: 8.8
- Cholesterol: 144
- Protein: 56.3

701. Muenster Chicken And Mushrooms

Serving: 6 | Prep: 25mins | Cook: 20mins |Ready in:

Ingredients

- 6 skinless, boneless chicken breasts
- 1 1/2 cups milk
- 2 cups dried bread crumbs, seasoned
- 6 slices Muenster cheese
- 1 cup fresh sliced mushrooms
- 1/2 cup chicken broth

Direction

- Start preheating the oven to 350°F (175°C).
- Dip the chicken in milk, then in the breadcrumbs. In a large skillet, brown the coated chicken lightly. Transfer into a 9x13 inch baking dish.
- Add a slice of cheese over top of each chicken. Arrange mushrooms on top, add the broth over and around the chicken. Wrap the dish with the aluminum foil.
- Bake for half an hour at 350°F (175°C). Discard the cover, baste using any remaining broth over the chicken. Bake for 15-20 minutes more.

Nutrition Information

- Calories: 420 calories;
- Total Fat: 13.4
- Sodium: 984
- Total Carbohydrate: 31
- Cholesterol: 101
- Protein: 41.9

702. Mushroom Artichoke Sandwich

Serving: 2 | Prep: 10mins | Cook: 15mins | Ready in:

Ingredients

- 1 (12 inch) French baguette
- 1 tablespoon olive oil
- 12 ounces fresh mushrooms, sliced
- 1 (14 ounce) can quartered artichoke hearts in water, drained
- 2 tablespoons grated Parmesan cheese
- 2 teaspoons garlic and onion seasoning
- salt and pepper to taste

Direction

- Heat the oven to 350°F (175°C).
- Slice lengthwise the baguette in half, split open, and toast in the oven for 7 - 9 minutes, till slightly browned.
- In a skillet, heat the olive oil over medium heat; cook and stir the artichoke hearts and mushrooms for about 10 minutes, until the mushrooms start to brown and their liquid is released. Mix in onion seasoning, garlic and Parmesan cheese, and pepper and salt; cook and stir for about 5 minutes longer, until the mixture thickens.
- Fill the mushroom filling into the toasted bread, close the sandwich, cut in half and serve.

Nutrition Information

- Calories: 466 calories;
- Protein: 22.7
- Total Fat: 10.5
- Sodium: 1893
- Total Carbohydrate: 73.4
- Cholesterol: 4

703. Mushroom Bagna Cauda

Serving: 6 | Prep: 15mins | Cook: 45mins | Ready in:

Ingredients

- 1 tablespoon butter
- 1 (2 ounce) can anchovy fillets, drained
- 8 cloves garlic, minced
- 1 (10 ounce) can condensed cream of mushroom soup
- 1 cup whipping cream
- 2 cups half and half

Direction

- In a sauté pan, melt butter over medium heat. Sauté anchovies and garlic for 2-3 minutes until the garlic has mellowed. Add half and half, cream, and the mushroom soup; lower the heat to low and cook for 45 minutes without boiling the mixture.

Nutrition Information

- Calories: 321 calories;
- Cholesterol: 96
- Protein: 6.4
- Total Fat: 29.4
- Sodium: 643
- Total Carbohydrate: 9.1

704. Mushroom Barley Soup

Serving: 6 | Prep: 25mins | Cook: 40mins | Ready in:

Ingredients

- 1 cup barley
- 3 cups water
- 1 1/2 tablespoons olive oil
- 2 onions, chopped
- 1 carrot, thinly sliced
- 2 stalks celery, thinly sliced
- 2 (10 ounce) packages sliced mushrooms

- 5 cups beef broth
- 1/2 teaspoon salt
- 1/4 teaspoon ground black pepper

Direction

- Boil water and barley in a saucepan. Cover the saucepan. Adjust the heat to low and let it simmer for 30 minutes until tender.
- Put olive oil in a large saucepan and heat it over medium heat. Mix in carrots, celery, and onions. Cook for 10 minutes, stirring until the onion is translucent and soft. Mix in mushrooms. Cook for 5 more minutes.
- Add the beef broth. Simmer the soup over medium-high heat. Adjust the heat to medium-low and continue to simmer for 15 more minutes. Mix in barley. Season the mixture with salt and pepper before serving.

Nutrition Information

- Calories: 194 calories;
- Total Fat: 4.9
- Sodium: 882
- Total Carbohydrate: 30.5
- Cholesterol: 0
- Protein: 9.6

705. Mushroom Bok Choy Soup

Serving: 6 | Prep: 15mins | Cook: 7mins | Ready in:

Ingredients

- 1/4 cup unsalted butter
- 1 head bok choy, chopped
- 1 pound white and crimini mushrooms, cut into quarters
- 4 green onions, sliced
- 2 tablespoons minced garlic, or more to taste
- 8 slices fresh ginger, quartered
- 1/4 cup lime juice
- 7 cups chicken broth
- 1/2 cup chopped fresh cilantro

Direction

- Using a stock pot on medium heat, heat the butter and mix in the mushrooms, green onions, garlic, ginger, and bok choy. Drizzle in lime juice with the mushroom mixture. Stir and cook for 2 to 3 minutes until it turns a light brown color. Adjust the heat to medium-high and pour the chicken broth in. Once it starts boiling, lower the heat and let it simmer for 5 minutes or until the vegetables become soft. Present the dish with cilantro.

Nutrition Information

- Calories: 125 calories;
- Cholesterol: 26
- Protein: 5.3
- Total Fat: 8.7
- Sodium: 1178
- Total Carbohydrate: 8.4

706. Mushroom Bouchees

Serving: 10 | Prep: 20mins | Cook: 15mins | Ready in:

Ingredients

- cooking spray
- 3 green onions
- 1 (10 ounce) can mushroom pieces, drained
- 2 tablespoons butter
- 2 tablespoons cornstarch
- 1/2 cup half-and-half
- salt and ground black pepper to taste
- 1 pinch garlic powder, or to taste
- 10 slices sandwich bread

Direction

- Start preheating the oven to 350°F (175°C). Use cooking spray to grease a cookie sheet.

- Cut mushrooms and green onions very finely to a consistency close to a paste.
- In a small saucepan, heat butter over medium heat, mix in mushrooms and green onions, stir and cook for 2 minutes until aromatic. Mix cornstarch into half-and-half, put onto the mushroom mixture and cook, tossing regularly for 3 minutes until it becomes thick. Use garlic powder, pepper, and salt to season the mushroom mixture.
- Use a rolling pin to roll bread slices until very thin and flat. Spread onto the flattened bread the mushroom mixture then roll up bread slices securely. Cut each bread pipe into 1-inch thick rounds and put them on a cookie sheet.
- Put in the preheated oven and bake for 10 minutes until the bread turns brown.

Nutrition Information

- Calories: 118 calories;
- Total Fat: 4.6
- Sodium: 328
- Total Carbohydrate: 16.5
- Cholesterol: 11
- Protein: 2.9

707. Mushroom Bundles

Serving: 8 | Prep: 20mins | Cook: 20mins | Ready in:

Ingredients

- 1 stick unsalted butter
- 4 cups chopped mushrooms
- 4 cloves garlic, minced
- 1/2 cup dry white wine
- salt to taste
- 1 (17.5 ounce) package frozen puff pastry, thawed
- 1/3 cup grated Parmesan cheese

Direction

- In a skillet, melt butter over medium heat; then cook and mix garlic and mushrooms in the melted butter for about 1 minute. Add white wine; cook and mix the mixture for about 5 minutes until all the liquid has evaporated. Spice with salt. Take away from heat.
- Preheat oven to 375° F (190° C). Use a parchment paper to line a baking sheet.
- Slice each puff pastry sheet into 4 even rectangles, making a total of 8 rectangles. Spoon the mushroom mixture onto the middle of each rectangle; dust with Parmesan cheese. Assemble all 4 corners of the rectangle together around the filling; pinch edges and corners of puff pastry to form a seal. Redo with the rest rectangles. On the prepped baking sheet, line bundles. Gently press the bundles for flat bottoms.
- In the preheated oven, bake for around 15 minutes until bundles turn golden brown,

Nutrition Information

- Calories: 476 calories;
- Total Fat: 35.9
- Sodium: 208
- Total Carbohydrate: 29.8
- Cholesterol: 33
- Protein: 7.1

708. Mushroom Cap Chorizo Burger

Serving: 8 | Prep: 15mins | Cook: 27mins | Ready in:

Ingredients

- 8 large portobello mushrooms, stems removed
- 1 tablespoon vegetable oil, or more as needed
- salt and ground black pepper to taste
- 1 pound ground beef
- 1 pound chorizo sausage
- 1/2 onion, diced

- 4 slices cooked bacon, chopped
- 1 egg
- 2 cloves garlic, minced
- 1/4 cup chopped fresh cilantro
- 1/2 teaspoon salt
- 1/2 teaspoon ground black pepper
- 1/2 teaspoon garlic powder
- 1/2 teaspoon onion powder
- 1/2 teaspoon chili powder

Direction

- Turn oven to 375°F (190°C) to preheat.
- Remove gills from each mushroom. Brush top and bottom of each mushroom with olive oil; season with pepper and salt. Place mushroom on a baking sheet, gill-side up.
- Bake mushrooms for about 7 minutes in the preheated oven until tender.
- In a large mixing bowl, combine chili powder, onion powder, garlic powder, 1/2 teaspoon black pepper, 1/2 teaspoon salt, cilantro, garlic, egg, bacon, onion, chorizo, and ground beef until incorporated; form mixture into 8 patties. Top each mushroom with a patty.
- Bake for about 20 minutes in the preheated oven until burgers are cooked through or when and instant-read thermometer inserted into the center registers at least 160°F (70°C)

Nutrition Information

- Calories: 427 calories;
- Total Fat: 34.2
- Sodium: 980
- Total Carbohydrate: 3.2
- Cholesterol: 111
- Protein: 25.2

709. Mushroom Cheese Puffs

Serving: 8 | Prep: 10mins | Cook: 10mins | Ready in:

Ingredients

- 1 (8 ounce) package refrigerated crescent rolls
- 1 (8 ounce) can mushrooms, drained
- 1 cup shredded Cheddar cheese

Direction

- Preheat an oven to 190 °C or 375 °F. Slightly oil a cookie sheet.
- Roll out a crescent dough package and put on cookie sheet. Pinch seams together till sheet is form to a rectangle. Onto the dough, put the drained mushrooms and place grated cheese on top. Put another roll of crescent dough over, pinching the seams once more. Slightly press to flatten and pinch seams across but retaining a slit for steam to release.
- Let bake till golden brown for 10 minutes. Cut into 8 separate servings and serve right away.

Nutrition Information

- Calories: 167 calories;
- Sodium: 356
- Total Carbohydrate: 13.7
- Cholesterol: 29
- Protein: 6.8
- Total Fat: 9.4

710. Mushroom Chicken Piccata

Serving: 6 | Prep: 20mins | Cook: 30mins | Ready in:

Ingredients

- 1/2 cup all-purpose flour
- 1 teaspoon salt
- 1/2 teaspoon paprika
- 1 egg
- 2 tablespoons milk
- 6 skinless, boneless chicken breast halves
- 4 tablespoons butter
- 1/2 pound fresh mushrooms, sliced
- 1/4 cup chopped onion

- 1 cup chicken broth
- 1/2 cup white wine
- 2 tablespoons lemon juice
- 1 tablespoon cornstarch
- 1 tablespoon chopped fresh parsley, for garnish

Direction

- Combine paprika, salt and flour in a bowl or a shallow dish. Combine milk and egg in a separate bowl or dish. Dredge chicken pieces to the egg mixture then transfer them to the seasoned flour mixture.
- Heat margarine or butter in a large skillet over medium-high heat. Sauté chicken pieces until they are golden brown in color. Stir in onion and mushrooms; sauté for 3-5 minutes.
- Mix together cornstarch, lemon juice, wine and broth in a medium bowl. Stir well and transfer it onto the mushrooms and chicken. Lower the heat to medium-low; simmer the mixture until juices run clear and the chicken is cooked through or for 25 minutes. Use parsley to sprinkle before serving.

Nutrition Information

- Calories: 288 calories;
- Total Fat: 10.4
- Sodium: 697
- Total Carbohydrate: 12.6
- Cholesterol: 121
- Protein: 31.1

711. Mushroom Chicken Tetrazzini

Serving: 4 | Prep: 15mins | Cook: 20mins | Ready in:

Ingredients

- 1/2 (8 ounce) package spaghetti
- 3 skinless, boneless chicken breast halves
- 1 onion, chopped
- 8 ounces fresh mushrooms, quartered
- 1 cube chicken bouillon
- water to cover
- salt and pepper to taste
- 4 cups heavy cream
- 1/4 cup grated Parmesan cheese

Direction

- Boil a big pot with slightly salted water. Put in and cook pasta till al dente, for 8 to 10 minutes; strain. Meantime, let chicken cook in microwave till nearly cooked completely and juices run nearly clear.
- Preheat the oven to 165°C or 325°F.
- In medium size saucepan, sauté mushrooms and onion till soft. Put in bouillon, chicken, and water to submerge. Simmer on moderately low heat, seasoning to taste with pepper and salt. Put in cream and cooked spaghetti and combine everything; lastly, mix cheese in.
- In prepped oven, bake for 20 minutes to half an hour, or till cooked completely. Monitor dish midway through cooking and if wished, put in additional Parmesan cheese to taste.

Nutrition Information

- Calories: 1072 calories;
- Total Carbohydrate: 33.5
- Cholesterol: 382
- Protein: 32.5
- Total Fat: 91.4
- Sodium: 516

712. Mushroom Chile Relleno Casserole

Serving: 4 | Prep: 20mins | Cook: 57mins | Ready in:

Ingredients

- 2 tablespoons butter
- 3 cloves garlic, minced
- 1/2 cup chopped onion
- 1/2 cup seeded and minced sweet peppers
- 1/2 cup minced green bell pepper
- 1/2 cup chopped fresh mushrooms
- 1 (16 ounce) can chopped green chiles, or to taste
- 1/2 cup stewed tomatoes with juice, chopped
- salt and freshly ground black pepper to taste
- 1 1/2 cups soy milk
- 5 eggs
- 1/2 cup all-purpose flour
- 2 tablespoons minced cilantro
- 1/8 teaspoon chili powder
- 1/8 teaspoon dried oregano
- 1/8 teaspoon ground cumin
- 1 cup shredded Cheddar-Monterey Jack cheese blend

Direction

- Start preheating the oven to 350°F (175°C). Lightly coat a 2-qt. casserole dish with oil.
- In a frying pan, heat butter over medium-low heat. Add garlic, mix in green bell pepper, sweet peppers, and onion. Cook for 5 minutes until soft. Add mushrooms and cook for 4-6 minutes until soft. Add stewed tomatoes and green chiles, cook for 3-4 minutes until thoroughly heated. Use pepper and salt to season. On the bottom of the prepared casserole dish, spread the mixture.
- In a big bowl, combine eggs and soy milk until thoroughly mixed. Add cumin, oregano, cilantro, and flour. Use pepper and salt to season. Using a whisk, combine very well until all of the lumps have mostly gone.
- In the casserole, sprinkle over the top of the pepper mixture with 1/2 cup Cheddar-Monterey Jack cheese. Add to the egg mixture and put the leftover cheese on top.
- Put in the preheated oven and bake for 45 minutes until the sides and tops are barely crunchy and a knife will come out clean when you insert it into the middle. Allow to sit before slicing, about 10 minutes.

Nutrition Information

- Calories: 401 calories;
- Total Fat: 22.1
- Sodium: 1772
- Total Carbohydrate: 31.9
- Cholesterol: 273
- Protein: 20.9

713. Mushroom Cream Sauce With Shallots

Serving: 3 | Prep: 10mins | Cook: 15mins | Ready in:

Ingredients

- 2 lobster mushrooms, cut into cubes
- 2 tablespoons water
- 1/3 cup heavy whipping cream
- 2 teaspoons all-purpose flour
- 2 tablespoons grated Asiago cheese
- 1/2 shallot, minced
- 1/2 teaspoon salt
- 1/2 teaspoon ground black pepper

Direction

- Place a nonstick skillet over medium heat; add mushrooms; put in water. Cook while stirring sometimes for around 5 minutes or till water is evaporated.
- Whisk flour and cream into mushrooms till flour is incorporated. Put black pepper, salt, shallot and Asiago cheese into the mushroom mixture, stirring continually. Cook while stirring for around 7 minutes or till sauce thickens.

Nutrition Information

- Calories: 123 calories;
- Total Fat: 11.1
- Sodium: 454

- Total Carbohydrate: 4.1
- Cholesterol: 40
- Protein: 2.5

714. Mushroom Curry With Galangal

Serving: 4 | Prep: 10mins | Cook: 20mins | Ready in:

Ingredients

- 2 cups coconut milk
- 1 (2 inch) piece galangal, peeled and sliced
- 3 kaffir lime leaves, torn
- 2 teaspoons salt
- 1/3 pound sliced fresh mushrooms
- 5 Thai chile peppers, chopped
- 1/4 cup fresh lime juice
- 1 tablespoon fish sauce

Direction

- In a pot, add the galangal and coconut milk and then heat to boil. Add salt and kaffir lime leaves and simmer for ten minutes. Place in mushrooms and cook for 5 to 7 minutes until soft. Take out from the heat. Mix fish sauce and lime juice into the mixture. Transfer to a bowl and add the Thai chilies on top. Serve.

Nutrition Information

- Calories: 261 calories;
- Total Fat: 24.4
- Sodium: 1458
- Total Carbohydrate: 11.8
- Cholesterol: 0
- Protein: 4.9

715. Mushroom Gravy/Sauce

Serving: 8 | Prep: 10mins | Cook: 10mins | Ready in:

Ingredients

- 2 tablespoons butter
- 1 (8 ounce) package button mushrooms, sliced
- 1/4 cup minced shallot
- 2 tablespoons all-purpose flour
- 2 teaspoons all-purpose flour
- 2 cups fat-free reduced-sodium beef broth
- 1/4 cup half-and-half
- 1/2 teaspoon ground black pepper
- 1 dash salt

Direction

- Over medium-high heat, melt butter in a heavy 12 inches skillet. Put shallot and mushrooms. Sauté for about 6 minutes until softened, stirring occasionally. Put 2 tablespoons and 2 teaspoons of flour. For about a minute, cook until incorporated. Put beef broth. Cook for about 2 minutes until thickened slightly, stirring frequently. Stir half-and-half, salt and black pepper in. Cook for 30 more seconds.

Nutrition Information

- Calories: 64 calories;
- Protein: 2.7
- Total Fat: 4.2
- Sodium: 93
- Total Carbohydrate: 4.4
- Cholesterol: 10

716. Mushroom Kabobs

Serving: 4 | Prep: 30mins | Cook: 10mins | Ready in:

Ingredients

- 3/4 cup sliced fresh mushrooms

- 2 red bell peppers, chopped
- 1 green bell pepper, cut into 1 inch pieces
- 1/4 cup olive oil
- 2 tablespoons lemon juice
- 1 clove garlic, minced
- 2 teaspoons chopped fresh thyme
- 1 teaspoon chopped fresh rosemary
- 1/4 teaspoon salt
- 1/4 teaspoon ground black pepper

Direction

- Set grill on medium to pre-heat.
- Alternately thread peppers and mushrooms on skewers.
- Mix salt, pepper, thyme, rosemary, garlic, olive oil, and lemon juice in a small bowl. Brush this oil mixture on the peppers and mushrooms.
- Oil the grate and grill the kabobs, basting frequently with oil mixture. Grill until mushrooms are tender and cooked through, about 4 to 6 minutes.

Nutrition Information

- Calories: 151 calories;
- Sodium: 150
- Total Carbohydrate: 6.5
- Cholesterol: 0
- Protein: 1.4
- Total Fat: 13.8

717. Mushroom Lentil Barley Stew

Serving: 8 | Prep: 15mins | Cook: 12hours | Ready in:

Ingredients

- 2 quarts vegetable broth
- 2 cups sliced fresh button mushrooms
- 1 ounce dried shiitake mushrooms, torn into pieces
- 3/4 cup uncooked pearl barley
- 3/4 cup dry lentils
- 1/4 cup dried onion flakes
- 2 teaspoons minced garlic
- 2 teaspoons dried summer savory
- 3 bay leaves
- 1 teaspoon dried basil
- 2 teaspoons ground black pepper
- salt to taste

Direction

- In a slow cooker, combine together salt, pepper, basil, bay leaves, savory, garlic, onion flakes, lentils, barley, shiitake mushrooms, button mushrooms and the broth.
- Cook with a cover for 10-12 hours on low heat or 4-6 hours on high heat. Discard the bay leaves. Serve.

Nutrition Information

- Calories: 213 calories;
- Total Fat: 1.2
- Sodium: 466
- Total Carbohydrate: 43.9
- Cholesterol: 0
- Protein: 8.4

718. Mushroom Mint Pasta Salad

Serving: 12 | Prep: 15mins | Cook: 20mins | Ready in:

Ingredients

- 1 (16 ounce) package farfalle (bow tie) pasta
- 1/4 cup olive oil, divided
- 2 (8 ounce) packages button mushrooms, sliced
- 4 onions, sliced
- 1 quart heavy cream
- 10 sprigs fresh mint
- 1 1/2 teaspoons white sugar

- 1 pinch salt
- 1 pinch ground black pepper

Direction

- Boil the lightly salted water in a large pot. Put pasta into pot and cook until al dente, about 8-10 mins, then drain. Let cool, then place into a large bowl. Mix with 3 tablespoons of the olive oil.
- In a large skillet, heat the remaining olive oil over medium heat. In the skillet, put onions and mushrooms. Cook while stirring until it is lightly brown. Add heavy cream gradually, stirring continuously. Put mint sprigs into skillet. Cook while stirring for 5 mins.
- Mix the sugar into cream sauce. Add pepper and salt to season. Using slotted spoon, discard the mint sprigs. Stir in cooked pasta until it is well coated.

Nutrition Information

- Calories: 487 calories;
- Sodium: 35
- Total Carbohydrate: 36.4
- Cholesterol: 109
- Protein: 8.7
- Total Fat: 34.9

719. Mushroom Moong Dal Dosas

Serving: 6 | Prep: 45mins | Cook: 22mins | Ready in:

Ingredients

- Dosas:
- 1 cup moong dal (split husked mung beans)
- 1 teaspoon chili powder
- 1 teaspoon minced ginger
- 1/2 cup water, or as needed
- 1/2 teaspoon salt
- 1/2 teaspoon jeera (cumin seeds)
- Filling:
- 3 stalks celery, finely chopped
- 1 onion, chopped
- 2 cups sliced cremini mushrooms
- 1 (10 ounce) package frozen chopped spinach, thawed and drained
- 1 yellow bell pepper, chopped
- 1 cup frozen peas
- 1 cup salsa
- 1/2 cup chopped fresh cilantro
- 2 tablespoons lemon juice
- 2 tablespoons minced garlic
- 2 tablespoons garam masala
- 1 tablespoon ground coriander
- 2 teaspoons chili powder
- 2 teaspoons minced ginger
- 1 teaspoon sea salt
- 1 teaspoon seasoned salt
- 1 teaspoon ground cinnamon
- 1 teaspoon cumin seeds
- 1 teaspoon fennel seeds
- 1 cup cottage cheese

Direction

- In 4 cups water, soak dal for a minimum of 4 hours; drain.
- Blend 1 tsp. ginger, 1 tsp. chili powder and soaked dal, adding 2-3 tbsp. water if needed, till combined well in a blender. Add cumin seeds and salt; keep on blending till dosa batter gets the consistency of pancake batter.
- Sauté 1 tbsp. water, onions and celery in skillet on medium-high heat till soft. Put mushrooms in; cook for 5 minutes till shrunk. Mix frozen peas, yellow bell pepper and spinach in. Add fennel seeds, cumin seeds, cinnamon, seasoning salt, sea salt, 2 tsp. ginger, 2 tsp. chili powder, coriander, garam masala, garlic, lemon juice, cilantro and salsa; add cottage cheese. Lower heat; simmer filling mixture while making dosas.
- Preheat nonstick skillet on medium-high heat till a water drop sizzles when it hits surface. Put 1/2 cup batter on middle of skillet; use back of spoon to evenly spread. Swirl spoon outward till dosa is 7-in. in diameter. Cook for

1 minute till dry on top; flip. Cook for 1 minute longer till golden brown; repeat with leftover batter.
- Put 3/4 cup filling down middle of a dosa then fold 1 side up; turn over so both sides get tucked under. Repeat using leftover dosas.

Nutrition Information

- Calories: 260 calories;
- Total Carbohydrate: 41.3
- Cholesterol: 6
- Protein: 19.6
- Total Fat: 3.7
- Sodium: 1172

720. Mushroom Rice Turnovers

Serving: 16 | Prep: 20mins | Cook: 40mins | Ready in:

Ingredients

- 1 tablespoon butter
- 1 pound sliced fresh mushrooms
- 5 scallions, sliced
- 1 cup cooked brown rice
- 1/2 cup sour cream
- 4 teaspoons dried dill weed
- 1 teaspoon salt
- 1/4 teaspoon ground black pepper
- 1 (17.5 ounce) package frozen puff pastry, thawed

Direction

- Preheat an oven to 200 °C or 400 °F.
- In a big skillet, melt butter over medium heat. Put scallions and mushrooms; allow to cook for 10 minutes, mixing from time to time, till softened. Put to a bowl.
- Into the mushroom mixture, mix pepper, salt, dill, sour cream and brown rice in the bowl.
- Onto a not greased baking sheet, unfold 1 puff pastry sheet. Scatter mushroom mixture equally on top, retaining a 1-inch border on every side. Set another puff pastry sheet on top. Using a fork, press edges together to seal.
- In the prepped oven, bake for half an hour till golden brown on surface and pastry is puffed up. Let cool slightly for 10 minutes prior serving.

Nutrition Information

- Calories: 211 calories;
- Total Fat: 14.1
- Sodium: 233
- Total Carbohydrate: 18.1
- Cholesterol: 5
- Protein: 3.7

721. Mushroom Salad II

Serving: 6 | Prep: 10mins | Cook: | Ready in:

Ingredients

- 1 pound fresh white mushrooms
- 1 cup sliced celery
- 1/4 cup chopped fresh parsley
- 1/4 cup diced Swiss cheese
- 1/2 cup chopped green onions
- 1/2 cup olive oil
- 1/3 cup red wine vinegar
- 1 tablespoon prepared Dijon-style mustard

Direction

- Combine mustard, vinegar and oil in a big bowl. Bring in onions, cheese, parsley, celery and mushrooms and toss until coated thoroughly. Put in the fridge for 2 hours minimum, and then serve.

Nutrition Information

- Calories: 210 calories;
- Total Fat: 19.9
- Sodium: 96
- Total Carbohydrate: 5.6
- Cholesterol: 5
- Protein: 4.2

722. Mushroom Slow Cooker Roast Beef

Serving: 8 | Prep: 5mins | Cook: 9hours | Ready in:

Ingredients

- 1 pound sliced fresh mushrooms
- 1 (4 pound) standing beef rib roast
- 1 (1.25 ounce) envelope onion soup mix
- 1 (12 fluid ounce) bottle beer
- ground black pepper

Direction

- In the bottom of a slow cooker, put the mushrooms, then put the roast on top of the mushrooms. Sprinkle the onion soup mix on top of the beef and pour the beer all over, then sprinkle black pepper to season. Set the slow cooker to Low and let it cook for 9-10 hours, until the meat easily pulls apart using a fork.

Nutrition Information

- Calories: 388 calories;
- Total Carbohydrate: 6.2
- Cholesterol: 82
- Protein: 24.4
- Total Fat: 28.1
- Sodium: 453

723. Mushroom Soup Without Cream

Serving: 8 | Prep: 15mins | Cook: 45mins | Ready in:

Ingredients

- 2 tablespoons butter
- 1 cup peeled and sliced carrots
- 1 cup sliced onions
- 1 cup sliced leeks (optional)
- 1/2 cup sliced celery
- 1 teaspoon fresh thyme leaves
- 2 pounds sliced fresh brown or white mushrooms
- 6 cups chicken stock
- salt and pepper to taste
- 1/2 cup chopped green onion

Direction

- In a stockpot, melt butter on medium heat. Stir and cook celery, leeks, onions and carrots in for about 10 minutes until tender yet not browned. Mix in mushrooms and thyme. Cook for about 5 minutes more until mushrooms are soft.
- Put chicken stock in the pot. Season with pepper and salt. Simmer, covered, for 30 minutes on low heat. Put into bowls. Top with green onions. Serve.

Nutrition Information

- Calories: 81 calories;
- Total Carbohydrate: 9.6
- Cholesterol: 8
- Protein: 4.6
- Total Fat: 3.8
- Sodium: 561

724. Mushroom Spinach Soup

Serving: 10 | Prep: 20mins | Cook: 50mins | Ready in:

Ingredients

- 3 tablespoons butter
- 3 leeks, chopped
- 2 onions, chopped
- 2 cloves garlic, minced
- 2 pounds chopped mushrooms
- 2 teaspoons dried savory
- 1/4 teaspoon dried oregano
- 1/3 cup sherry
- 9 cups chicken stock
- 2 tablespoons tomato paste
- 1 bay leaf
- salt to taste
- ground black pepper to taste
- 10 leaves fresh spinach

Direction

- Sauté garlic, onion, leeks, and butter until clear. Add mushrooms (except the 8 reserved chopped mushrooms), bay leaf, tomato paste, savory, stock, sherry, and oregano. Stew for 30 minutes or more.
- Next, strain out the greens.
- Stir spinach leaves and the reserved mushrooms into the broth; cook until the spinach is wilted. Season with salt and pepper to taste. If desired, garnished with Parmesan cheese. Serve.

Nutrition Information

- Calories: 90 calories;
- Total Carbohydrate: 11.5
- Cholesterol: 9
- Protein: 4
- Total Fat: 3.9
- Sodium: 117

---

725. Mushroom Stuffing

Serving: 14 | Prep: | Cook: |Ready in:

Ingredients

- 1 pound fresh mushrooms, sliced
- 6 tablespoons butter
- 1 cup diced onion
- 1 cup chopped celery
- 1 teaspoon poultry seasoning
- 1 teaspoon salt
- 1/4 teaspoon ground black pepper
- 12 cups dried bread crumbs
- 1 1/2 cups hot chicken broth
- 2 eggs, beaten
- 2 cups diced apple without peel
- 1/4 cup chopped parsley

Direction

- Butter 1 9x13-in. casserole dish; preheat an oven to 190°C/375°F.
- Rinse, pat dry then quarter mushrooms. Heat butter in a big skillet; add celery, onion and mushrooms. Sauté for 5 minutes; discard from heat. Mix in pepper, salt and poultry seasoning.
- Mix breadcrumbs with eggs and broth in a big mixing bowl; put in parsley, mushroom mixture and apples, then mix well. Turn into the casserole dish.
- Cover; bake for 45 minutes at 190°C/375°F. Uncover; bake until brown top, about 15 minutes.

Nutrition Information

- Calories: 443 calories;
- Sodium: 899
- Total Carbohydrate: 71.7
- Cholesterol: 40
- Protein: 14.6
- Total Fat: 10.7

---

726. Mushroom Stuffing Balls

Serving: 24 | Prep: 15mins | Cook: 20mins |Ready in:

Ingredients

- 8 ounces fresh mushrooms, chopped
- 1 medium onion, chopped
- 1/2 cup butter, melted
- 4 eggs, beaten
- 2 teaspoons dried parsley flakes
- 1/8 teaspoon garlic powder
- 1/2 cup grated Parmesan cheese
- 2 1/2 cups seasoned dry bread crumbs

Direction

- Preheat the oven to 350 °F (175 °C).
- Mix the onion, mushrooms, eggs, butter, parsley, Parmesan cheese, and garlic powder together in a large bowl until creamy. Stir in bread crumbs gradually until the mixture is stiff enough to form into balls. Shape into balls of 2-inches, and place on cookie sheets.
- Bake in the prepped oven for 18 minutes, until the undersides are lightly browned. Place on a serving tray and serve while it is still hot or warm.

Nutrition Information

- Calories: 107 calories;
- Total Fat: 6
- Sodium: 291
- Total Carbohydrate: 9.5
- Cholesterol: 43
- Protein: 4

727. Mushroom Toast Cups

Serving: 20 | Prep: 40mins | Cook: 30mins | Ready in:

Ingredients

- 1 1/2 (1 pound) loaves sliced white bread
- 2 tablespoons butter
- 1/2 pound fresh mushrooms, finely diced
- 1/2 cup onion, finely diced
- 1/8 teaspoon ground cayenne pepper
- 1 tablespoon fresh lemon juice
- 1/2 teaspoon salt
- 1/8 teaspoon ground black pepper
- 2 tablespoons chopped fresh parsley
- 1/2 cup half-and-half
- 1 tablespoon all-purpose flour
- 1/2 cup Parmesan cheese, grated

Direction

- Preheat oven to 400° F (200° C).
- Cut rounds out of the bread with a tiny cookie cutter. Push the rounds into ungreased little muffin tins, then bake for around 8 - 9 minutes until golden. Attentively watch them as they bake fast. Take out bread cups and cool.
- In a large frying pan, heat butter over medium heat. Blend in the onions and mushrooms, cook for about 8 minutes until soft. Spice with chopped parsley, pepper, salt, lemon juice, and cayenne pepper. Slowly blend in half-and-half, dust with a little flour until the mixture thickens.
- Fill the mushroom mixture into bread cups, top each with a scatter of Parmesan, and position them on a lightly greased baking sheet. Allow to bake for 10 - 12 minutes.

Nutrition Information

- Calories: 125 calories;
- Sodium: 340
- Total Carbohydrate: 18.8
- Cholesterol: 7
- Protein: 4.2
- Total Fat: 3.7

728. Mushroom And Artichoke Soup

Serving: 50 | Prep: | Cook: | Ready in:

Ingredients

- 4 (14 ounce) cans canned quartered artichoke hearts
- 1 cup olive oil
- 3 pounds thinly sliced shallots
- 3 small red onions, chopped
- 3 cloves garlic, minced
- 3/4 cup all-purpose flour
- 1/2 cup rice vinegar
- 1 gallon water
- 6 tablespoons vegetable base
- 1 1/2 teaspoons salt
- 1/2 teaspoon ground black pepper
- 1/2 teaspoon ground cayenne pepper
- 1/2 teaspoon ground nutmeg
- 2 tablespoons dried thyme
- 6 dried portabella mushrooms, softened in water
- 3 pounds fresh mushrooms, sliced
- 3 pounds carrots, sliced
- 3/4 cup capers
- 3/4 cup chopped fresh parsley

Direction

- In a food processor, add artichokes; slice thinly and put aside. You can use a 3 millimeter slicing disk to do this.
- In an extra-large stock pot, sauté shallots, garlic and onions in olive oil and set on low. Cook for about 15 minutes.
- Sprinkle flour over the onions; cook for 60 seconds. Mix in vinegar and cook for about 3 minutes until vinegar evaporates.
- Mix in sliced artichokes, thyme, nutmeg, cayenne, pepper, salt, vegetable base and water; cook for 25 minutes.
- Put in carrots, fresh mushrooms and the dried mushrooms as well as the water they soaked in. Cook for 15 minutes.
- Mix in parsley and capers, season with salt to taste then serve.

Nutrition Information

- Calories: 102 calories;
- Total Carbohydrate: 13.7
- Cholesterol: 0
- Protein: 3.3
- Total Fat: 4.6
- Sodium: 350

729. Mushroom And Asparagus Casserole

Serving: 4 | Prep: 15mins | Cook: 30mins | Ready in:

Ingredients

- 2 (15 ounce) cans asparagus spears, drained
- 1 (10.75 ounce) can cream of mushroom soup
- 4 hard-cooked eggs, chopped
- 1 (8 ounce) can sliced mushrooms, drained
- 1 (4 ounce) can sliced water chestnuts, drained
- 1 (2 ounce) jar pimentos
- 1 (2.8 ounce) can French-fried onions

Direction

- Set the oven to 175°C or 350°F to preheat and coat an 8-inch square baking dish with grease.
- In the baking dish, place asparagus spears.
- In a bowl, combine together pimientos, water chestnuts, mushrooms, eggs and mushroom soup, then drizzle over asparagus.
- In the preheated oven, bake about 20 minutes. Place French-fried onions on top of the casserole and keep on baking for 10 minutes longer, until onions start to darken.

Nutrition Information

- Calories: 323 calories;
- Total Fat: 20.4
- Sodium: 1562
- Total Carbohydrate: 23.9
- Cholesterol: 212
- Protein: 12.6

730. Mushroom And Bacon Green Beans

Serving: 4 | Prep: 10mins | Cook: 15mins | Ready in:

Ingredients

- 2 tablespoons butter
- 1 (8 ounce) package sliced white mushrooms
- 1 teaspoon minced onion
- 1/2 teaspoon minced garlic
- 2 tablespoons crumbled cooked bacon
- 1 pinch lemon-pepper seasoning
- 1 pinch seasoned salt
- 1 cup frozen green beans

Direction

- Melt the butter on medium heat in a skillet; cook and whisk garlic, onion and mushrooms for roughly 5 minutes or till the mushrooms become softened slightly. Whisk the seasoned salt, lemon pepper and bacon into the onion mixture; cook for 5-10 minutes longer till the mushrooms soften.
- Whisk the green beans into the mushroom mixture; cook, whisk once in a while, for 5-10 minutes till the green beans become tender and thoroughly cooked.

Nutrition Information

- Calories: 105 calories;
- Sodium: 289
- Total Carbohydrate: 4.3
- Cholesterol: 21
- Protein: 4.3
- Total Fat: 8.3

731. Mushroom And Chorizo Stuffed Pork Tenderloin

Serving: 4 | Prep: 15mins | Cook: 25mins | Ready in:

Ingredients

- 1 pork tenderloin
- 2 tablespoons Worcestershire sauce, divided
- 1/2 small onion
- 1/4 cup chopped mushrooms
- 3 cloves garlic, minced
- 1 teaspoon steak seasoning
- 1 small chorizo sausage, thinly sliced, slices cut in half

Direction

- Turn the oven to 375°F (190°C) to preheat.
- Slice pork tenderloin down the middle lengthwise almost all the way through, keeping the two sides attached; sprinkle 1 tablespoon Worcestershire sauce over.
- In a bowl, combine garlic, mushrooms, and onion. Evenly divide the mushroom mixture along the middle of the pork, sprinkle steak seasoning and the leftover Worcestershire sauce over. Evenly lay along the mushroom stuffing with chorizo slices.
- Pierce 4-5 skewers crosswise into the tenderloin through both edges, wrap around the skewers with butcher's twine resembling tying shoelaces and pull the tenderloin tightly around the stuffing. Bind the twine together by the ends; put the tenderloin in a baking dish.
- Bake for 20-30 minutes in the preheated oven until an instant-read thermometer displays a minimum of 145°F (74°C) when you insert it into the middle of the pork and the pork is a little pink in the middle. Discard the skewers and string, slice into medallions with 2-in. thickness and enjoy.

Nutrition Information

- Calories: 179 calories;
- Sodium: 527
- Total Carbohydrate: 3.9
- Cholesterol: 62
- Protein: 21.3
- Total Fat: 8.1

732. Mushroom And Mascarpone Ravioli

Serving: 4 | Prep: 25mins | Cook: 14mins | Ready in:

Ingredients

- 1 tablespoon olive oil
- 2 large shallots, minced
- 8 ounces fresh mushrooms, chopped
- 1 tablespoon chopped fresh thyme
- 2 tablespoons minced garlic
- 1 tablespoon chopped fresh chives
- 1 (8 ounce) container mascarpone cheese
- salt and pepper to taste
- 32 (3.5 inch square) wonton wrappers
- 1 egg, beaten
- 2 tablespoons milk

Direction

- In a big skillet, heat the olive oil over medium-high heat. Put the shallots; cook and mix till beginning to brown. Lower the heat to medium and put the chives, garlic, thyme and mushrooms; keep cooking for 5 to 10 minutes till the liquid from the mushrooms has evaporated. Take off heat and reserve to cool.
- Mix together the mushroom mixture and mascarpone cheese in a medium bowl. Put with salt and pepper to taste; reserve.
- On a clean surface, lay 16 wonton wrappers out. In a small cup, mix together the milk and egg. Onto the wrappers, brush with egg wash. Place a tablespoon of the cheese mixture onto the middle of every square. With a small spoonful of the mushroom mixture, atop the cheese. Put the second wonton wrapper on top of all the filling and pinch edges to seal. Ravioli can be chilled on a baking tray with plastic wrap cover.
- Boil a big pot of lightly salted water. Put the ravioli one at a time and allow to cook till they rises to the top for 3 to 4 minutes.

Nutrition Information

- Calories: 519 calories;
- Total Fat: 32
- Sodium: 424
- Total Carbohydrate: 46
- Cholesterol: 123
- Protein: 14.9

733. Mushroom And Sausage Rice Pilaf

Serving: 6 | Prep: 15mins | Cook: 58mins | Ready in:

Ingredients

- 1/2 cup orzo pasta
- 1/4 cup butter, divided
- 1/2 cup chopped onion
- 3 cloves garlic, minced
- 2 cups sliced mushrooms
- 1 cup long grain white rice
- 1/2 cup chopped smoked sausage, or more to taste
- 3 1/2 cups chicken broth

Direction

- Preheat the oven to 175°C or 350°F.
- Toast the orzo pasta in an ovenproof pan on medium heat for around 5 minutes, until light brown; move to a plate.
- In the same pan, melt 2 tbsp. butter. Cook the garlic and onion for around 5 minutes, until the onion is a bit translucent. Add mushrooms and let it cook for about 5 minutes more until tender. Combine with the orzo pasta.
- Cook the white rice for about 5 minutes in the remaining 2 tbsp. butter, until the rice turns light brown. Mix in sausage, then cook for 3 minutes. Stir in mushroom mixture and cooked orzo pasta; pour in chicken broth, then

boil. Take off from heat. Use an oven-proof lid to cover the pan.
- Bake for half an hour in the preheated oven, until the liquid is absorbed; stir thoroughly.

Nutrition Information

- Calories: 290 calories;
- Total Fat: 10.6
- Sodium: 857
- Total Carbohydrate: 40.7
- Cholesterol: 30
- Protein: 7.5

734. Mushroom And Swiss Burger Meatloaf

Serving: 8 | Prep: 20mins | Cook: 1hours |Ready in:

Ingredients

- 2 slices pumpernickel bread
- 1 pound ground chuck
- 1 pound ground pork
- 1 egg
- 1/2 cup finely chopped sweet onion
- 1/3 cup petite-cut diced tomatoes with sweet onions, drained and juice reserved
- 1/4 cup finely chopped green pepper
- 1 tablespoon onion powder
- 1/2 teaspoon garlic salt
- 1/2 teaspoon ground black pepper
- 2 dashes Worcestershire sauce
- 2 dashes soy sauce
- 6 slices deli-sliced Swiss cheese
- 1 (4.5 ounce) can sliced mushrooms, drained
- 1/2 cup bottled sweet chili sauce

Direction

- Set oven to 175°C (350°F) and begin preheating. Coat a 9x5" loaf pan with cooking spray. Tear the pumpernickel apart into small pieces, then transfer into the work bowl of a food processor. Pulse a few times to create bread crumbs.
- In a bowl, combine soy sauce, Worcestershire sauce, black pepper, garlic salt, onion powder, green pepper, a quarter cup of the reserved tomato juice, diced tomatoes, onion, egg, ground pork, ground chuck, and pumpernickel crumbs and gently, but thoroughly mix until the mixture is well blended. To prevent the loaf from being too tough, try not to over mix the meat mixture.
- In the bottom of the prepared loaf pan, lay 1/2 of the mixture, while lightly pat down to create a smooth surface. Put 3 Swiss cheese slices on the meat mixture, and arrange sliced mushrooms evenly on top of the cheese. Add on another layer of 3 Swiss cheese slices, and cover the top well with the remaining meat mixture. Smoothen the surface by pressing down lightly.
- Bake for 45 minutes in the prepared oven, then take out of the oven and brush the loaf evenly with chili sauce. Put the loaf back into the oven and bake for another 15 minutes until juices run clear and the sauce has achieved the consistency of a glaze. Allow to stand for 10 minutes before cutting.

Nutrition Information

- Calories: 370 calories;
- Total Carbohydrate: 12.8
- Cholesterol: 109
- Protein: 24.7
- Total Fat: 24.3
- Sodium: 617

735. Mushroom And Swiss Chicken

Serving: 4 | Prep: 25mins | Cook: 45mins |Ready in:

Ingredients

- 4 skinless, boneless chicken breasts
- 2 cloves crushed garlic
- 3 tablespoons olive oil
- 3 tablespoons red wine vinegar
- 1 tablespoon Cajun-style seasoning
- 1 cup chopped green onion
- 1 (8 ounce) package sliced fresh mushrooms
- 4 slices Swiss cheese

Direction

- Preheat an oven to 175°F/350°F.
- In a 9x13-in. baking dish, mix garlic and oil. Add chicken breasts; coat with garlic and oil well. Sprinkle Cajun seasoning and vinegar.
- Bake for 30 minutes at 175°C/350°F.
- Take chicken out of the oven; use mushrooms and green onion to cover. Add vinegar and a few extra sprinkles of oil; put dish back into the oven for another 15-20 minutes. Take out of oven; put 1 cheese slice over each chicken breast immediately. Cheese will melt; immediately serve.

Nutrition Information

- Calories: 360 calories;
- Protein: 36.9
- Total Fat: 19.8
- Sodium: 500
- Total Carbohydrate: 7.5
- Cholesterol: 95

---

736. Mushroom And Tomato Bruschetta

Serving: 12 | Prep: 25mins | Cook: 15mins | Ready in:

Ingredients

- 1 loaf Italian bread, cut into 3/4-inch thick slices
- 1/2 cup olive oil
- 1/2 pound diced fresh mushrooms
- 5 green onions, minced
- 4 cloves garlic, minced
- 1 teaspoon salt
- 1 teaspoon ground black pepper
- 1 teaspoon chopped fresh parsley
- 3 large tomatoes, diced
- 1 teaspoon balsamic vinegar
- 2 cups shredded mozzarella cheese

Direction

- Preheat oven's broiler and place oven rack approximately 6 inches from the heat source. On a baking sheet, set slices of bread in 1 layer.
- Broil slices of bread for 1 to 2 minutes till toasted; keep an eye to avoid burning. Take off toasted slices and reserve on baking sheet.
- In a skillet, heat olive oil over medium heat; let cook for 5 minutes and mix parsley, black pepper, salt, garlic, green onions and mushrooms till mushrooms are softened and juicy. Reserve mixture. In a bowl, combine diced tomatoes with balsamic vinegar and reserve.
- Atop each toasted slice of bread with mushroom mixture and scatter tomato mixture over. Scatter mozzarella cheese over every appetizer. Put back to broiler for 5 minutes till cheese has melted and bruschetta are hot.

Nutrition Information

- Calories: 296 calories;
- Total Fat: 14.1
- Sodium: 642
- Total Carbohydrate: 31.9
- Cholesterol: 12
- Protein: 10.7

---

737. Mushroom And Walnut Stuffed Cornish Hens

Serving: 4 | Prep: 20mins | Cook: 1hours | Ready in:

Ingredients

- 1 tablespoon unsalted butter
- 2 tablespoons minced shallot
- 1 teaspoon minced garlic
- 1 (10 ounce) package button mushrooms, finely chopped
- 1 1/2 teaspoons salt, divided
- ground white pepper to taste
- 1/3 cup toasted walnuts
- 3 tablespoons dry white wine
- 4 Cornish game hens
- 1 teaspoon paprika
- 1 teaspoon onion powder
- 1/2 teaspoon garlic powder
- 1/2 teaspoon freshly ground black pepper
- 4 sprigs fresh thyme

Direction

- In a big skillet, melt butter over medium-high heat. Add garlic and shallot, stir and cook for 30 seconds. Add white pepper, 1/2 teaspoon salt and mushrooms. Lower the heat to medium; cook for 12 minutes until the mushrooms begin to turn brown and the moisture is evaporated, tossing frequently.
- Mix white wine and walnuts into the skillet. Cook for 3-5 minutes until the wine is evaporated, scraping to the browned bits off the bottom of the skillet.
- Turn the oven to 400°F (200°C) to preheat.
- Use black pepper, garlic powder, onion powder, paprika and the leftover 1 teaspoon salt to season inside out the Cornish hens. Use your fingers to gently open the cavities; stuff the mushroom mixture into it. Replace the skin to cover the stuffing by pulling back. In a roasting pan, put the hens with the breast-side facing up.
- Roast for 45 minutes in the preheated oven until an instant-read thermometer displays 180°F (82°C) when you insert it into the thickest section of the thigh, basting with the pan juices from the pan for 1-2 times. Use thyme sprigs to decorate.

Nutrition Information

- Calories: 755 calories;
- Sodium: 1028
- Total Carbohydrate: 13.3
- Cholesterol: 310
- Protein: 57.1
- Total Fat: 52.2

738. Mushroom, Cheese, And Haddock Bake

Serving: 4 | Prep: 10mins | Cook: 35mins | Ready in:

Ingredients

- 1 tablespoon olive oil
- 1/2 bunch green onions, chopped
- 1 (6 ounce) package button mushrooms, chopped
- 2 pounds haddock fillets
- salt and pepper to taste
- 1 tablespoon garlic powder
- 1/8 teaspoon dried red chile peppers
- 3 tablespoons butter
- 1/8 teaspoon dried parsley
- 3/4 cup shredded Colby-Monterey Jack cheese
- 1 lemon - cut into wedges, for garnish (optional)

Direction

- Set an oven to 175°C (350°F) and start preheating. Coat a 9x13-inch baking dish with cooking spray.
- In a skillet, heat the olive oil on medium-high heat, add mushrooms and green onions; stir and cook for 5 minutes until tender. Flavor the haddock with dried chile pepper, garlic powder, pepper, and salt, then place in the baking dish. Place the mushroom mixture and green onion on top, use butter to dot. Scatter over the top with parsley.
- Use foil to cover and bake for 15 minutes in the prepared oven. Take off the foil and

arrange cheese atop the haddock, then place the baking dish back into the oven. Carry on baking for 15-20 minutes until the cheese melts and the fish is fork-tender.

Nutrition Information

- Calories: 428 calories;
- Total Fat: 22
- Sodium: 419
- Total Carbohydrate: 5.8
- Cholesterol: 179
- Protein: 51

739. Mushroom, Kale, And Bok Choy Ramen

Serving: 4 | Prep: 25mins | Cook: 10mins | Ready in:

Ingredients

- 3 (3 ounce) packages instant ramen noodles (without flavor packet)
- 2 1/2 cups boiling water
- 3 tablespoons soy sauce
- 3 tablespoons balsamic vinegar
- 2 teaspoons sesame oil
- 1 teaspoon white sugar
- 1 teaspoon minced garlic, or to taste
- 1/4 teaspoon ground ginger
- 2 teaspoons vegetable oil
- 2 cups chopped baby bok choy
- 1/2 medium onion, chopped
- 1/3 cup chopped carrots
- 1/2 cup chopped cremini mushrooms
- 1/2 cup chopped shiitake mushrooms
- 1/2 cup chopped kale

Direction

- Put the bricks of ramen into a heat-safe bowl that is shallow. Pour in some boiling hot water over the ramen and let it sit until the noodles begin to soften and separate.

- Mix the balsamic vinegar, soy sauce, sugar, ginger, garlic, and sesame oil all together in a bowl that's small or a glass jar.
- In a big skillet or a big wok, on medium-high heat add vegetable oil and heat. Sauté the onion, carrots, and bok choy for about 3-5 minutes or until the onion is translucent. Put in the shiitake mushrooms, cremini mushrooms, and kale. Sauté it for 3-5 minutes until the kale starts wilting.
- Separate the noodles using a fork and drain any extra water. Place the drained noodles into skillet and put the heat on high. Pour in the soy and vinegar sauce on top of the noodles and veggies. Mix it up until all the flavors merge together for around 2 minutes.

Nutrition Information

- Calories: 358 calories;
- Sodium: 1010
- Total Carbohydrate: 46.4
- Cholesterol: 0
- Protein: 8.7
- Total Fat: 15.3

740. Mushroom, Leek, Chicken Sausage And Tortellini Soup

Serving: 6 | Prep: 25mins | Cook: 35mins | Ready in:

Ingredients

- 1 tablespoon olive oil
- 5 large mushrooms, chopped
- 2 large leeks, cleaned, and cut into 1/4 inch thick rounds
- 6 cups chicken broth
- 4 chicken sausages, sliced in 1/3-inch rounds
- 1 (9 ounce) package cheese tortellini
- 3 cloves garlic, minced

- 3 tablespoons hot pepper sauce (e.g. Tabasco™), or to taste
- salt and pepper to taste
- 5 sprigs chopped fresh cilantro, for garnish

Direction

- On a skillet pan, heat olive oil on medium-high heat. Stir in the leeks and mushrooms. Cook and stir mixture for about 5 minutes until they soften. Set aside.
- Meanwhile, in a large pan, pour the chicken broth and boil over medium-high heat. Add the hot sauce, garlic, tortellini and sausage. Lower the heat to medium, and stir in the leeks and mushrooms. Cover and for 30 minutes, simmer soup mixture. Sprinkle with cilantro to garnish before serving.

Nutrition Information

- Calories: 313 calories;
- Sodium: 890
- Total Carbohydrate: 30.8
- Cholesterol: 66
- Protein: 18.2
- Total Fat: 13

---

741. Mushroom, Leek, And Sausage Pot Pie

Serving: 6 | Prep: | Cook: 59mins | Ready in:

Ingredients

- 1 (17.5 ounce) package frozen puff pastry, thawed
- 2 links chicken sausage, halved lengthwise and cut into bite-sized pieces
- 3 tablespoons butter
- 4 carrots, cut into bite-sized pieces
- 1 leek, halved lengthwise and cut into bite-sized pieces
- 2 garlic cloves
- 1 (4 ounce) package mushrooms, quartered
- 3 tablespoons all-purpose flour
- 1 1/4 cups vegetable broth
- 1 tablespoon Dijon mustard
- 1 teaspoon ground cayenne pepper
- 1/2 teaspoon ground nutmeg
- salt and ground black pepper to taste
- 1 egg
- 1 tablespoon water

Direction

- Roll each puff pastry sheet out till they have an even thickness. Use a sharp knife to cut two 8-inches rounds from each sheet.
- Use the pastry rounds to line the sides and bottoms of the two 8-inches pie tins, reserving 2 pastry rounds for their tops. Arrange the pie tins and tops onto the baking sheet and place them inside the fridge.
- In a skillet, cook and stir the sausage over medium heat for 5 minutes until browned. Drain all the excess grease. Add the leek, carrots, butter, and garlic. Cook and stir for 5 minutes until the leek has softened.
- Mix mushrooms into the skillet. Cook for 8 minutes until tender. Mix in the flour for 1 minute. Slowly add the vegetable broth, and then followed by the cayenne pepper, pepper, salt, Dijon mustard, and nutmeg. Cook and stir for 5 minutes until the sauce is thick.
- Set the oven to 400°F or 200°C for preheating.
- Distribute the sausage mixture among the pie tins evenly. Use the pastry tops to cover them.
- In a small bowl, prepare the egg wash by mixing water and egg. Coat the pastry tops with the egg wash.
- Let them bake inside the preheated oven for 35 minutes until golden brown. Let them cool briefly for 10 minutes before slicing.

Nutrition Information

- Calories: 623 calories;
- Sodium: 600
- Total Carbohydrate: 49.6

- Cholesterol: 81
- Protein: 13.1
- Total Fat: 41.9

742. Mushroom, Spinach And Cheese Torta

Serving: 6 | Prep: 40mins | Cook: 50mins | Ready in:

Ingredients

- 2 cups chopped onions
- 4 cloves garlic, minced
- 1/4 cup olive oil
- 6 cups fresh mushrooms, sliced
- 10 ounces spinach - rinsed, stemmed, and dried
- 3 eggs
- 1 1/2 cups ricotta cheese
- 1 1/2 cups grated Parmesan cheese
- 1 cup sour cream
- 1/2 cup bread crumbs
- 1/4 cup chopped fresh parsley
- 1/2 cup butter, melted
- 1 (16 ounce) package phyllo dough
- 2 teaspoons sesame seeds

Direction

- Prepare the oven by preheating to 375°F (190°C).
- In a large saucepan, put oil then add garlic and onion and stir-fry until onions turn translucent. Add spinach and mushrooms and keep on cooking until spinach has wilted and mushrooms have released their juices. Keep on cooking until liquid has vaporized. Take away from the heat.
- In a large bowl, whisk eggs slightly. Add parsley, bread crumbs, sour cream, Parmesan and ricotta. Drain excess liquid from the vegetables then put it to the cheese mixture. Whisk until combined well.
- Use some of the melted butter to brush on a large baking sheet. Count out 6 phyllo leaves and gently raise them up and lay flat on a buttered baking sheet.
- Put filling over the center of leaves and spread, keeping a 3-inch border all around. Use butter to brush the edges.
- Lay down 2 leaves of phyllo at a time on top of the filling, using the butter to brush top leaf each time. Fold corners of all phyllo leaves up over the filling after 4 pairs then use the butter to brush on them.
- Put down 2 additional pairs of leaves, applying butter on top of the leaf of every pair. Insert edges under torta, corners first then sides. Dust poppy or sesame seeds on top.
- Bake for 50 minutes at 375°F (190°C) or until phyllo turns golden and crisp and filling is set. Let them rest for 10 minutes before cutting.

Nutrition Information

- Calories: 735 calories;
- Total Fat: 46.5
- Sodium: 1046
- Total Carbohydrate: 58.3
- Cholesterol: 168
- Protein: 23.3

743. Mushroom Walnut Loaf (Garden Loaf)

Serving: 12 | Prep: 15mins | Cook: 45mins | Ready in:

Ingredients

- 3 1/2 cups cooked brown rice
- 6 eggs, beaten
- 4 cups shredded Cheddar cheese
- 2 1/2 cups sliced fresh mushrooms
- 1 1/2 cups chopped raw walnuts
- 3/4 cup finely chopped onion
- 1 1/2 tablespoons tamari
- 1 1/2 teaspoons garlic powder

Direction

- Set the oven to 350°F (175°C) and start preheating.
- In a large bowl, mix garlic powder, tamari, onion, walnuts, mushrooms, Cheddar cheese, beaten eggs and cooked rice; combine well. Transfer to a 9x13-inch baking pan.
- Bake in the prepared oven for about 45 minutes until set.

Nutrition Information

- Calories: 358 calories;
- Total Carbohydrate: 17.6
- Cholesterol: 133
- Protein: 17
- Total Fat: 25.3
- Sodium: 397

744. Mushrooms And Peas Rice

Serving: 5 | Prep: 10mins | Cook: 15mins | Ready in:

Ingredients

- 8 ounces fresh mushrooms, sliced
- 1 tablespoon butter
- 1 (10.75 ounce) can condensed cream of mushroom soup
- 10 3/4 fluid ounces milk
- 1 3/4 cups instant rice
- 1 1/2 cups frozen green peas

Direction

- Sauté mushrooms with butter in a big skillet, then put aside.
- Warm milk and condensed cream of mushroom soup. Once it comes to a slow bubble, put in instant rice and cover. Allow to sit for a minimum of 5 minutes.
- While you are warming the soup mixture, place peas in the microwave to thaw at 30-second intervals. Avoid over-heating the peas.
- Once the rice is softened, stir into rice with peas and mushrooms. Use pepper and salt to season the mixture to taste.

Nutrition Information

- Calories: 269 calories;
- Cholesterol: 11
- Protein: 9.2
- Total Fat: 7.5
- Sodium: 493
- Total Carbohydrate: 41.2

745. Mushrooms And Spinach Italian Style

Serving: 4 | Prep: 20mins | Cook: 10mins | Ready in:

Ingredients

- 4 tablespoons olive oil
- 1 small onion, chopped
- 2 cloves garlic, chopped
- 14 ounces fresh mushrooms, sliced
- 10 ounces clean fresh spinach, roughly chopped
- 2 tablespoons balsamic vinegar
- 1/2 cup white wine
- salt and freshly ground black pepper to taste
- chopped fresh parsley, for garnish

Direction

- In a big skillet, heat olive oil on moderately high heat. Sauté garlic and onion in the oil until they begin to soften. Put in mushrooms and fry for 3-4 minutes, until they start to shrink. Toss in the spinach and fry until wilted, while stirring continuously, or for a several minutes.
- Put in vinegar while stirring continuously until it is absorbed, then stir in white wine. Lower heat to low and simmer until the wine has nearly fully absorbed. Season to taste with

pepper and salt, then sprinkle over with fresh parsley. Serve hot.

Nutrition Information

- Calories: 199 calories;
- Protein: 5.6
- Total Fat: 14.2
- Sodium: 69
- Total Carbohydrate: 10.3
- Cholesterol: 0

746. Mushrooms In White Wine Sauce

Serving: 6 | Prep: 15mins | Cook: 20mins | Ready in:

Ingredients

- 1/4 cup peanut or vegetable oil
- 1/3 cup chopped onion
- 1 clove garlic, minced
- 1 pound mushrooms, sliced
- 3/4 cup water, divided
- 1/4 cup dry white wine
- 1 cube chicken bouillon
- 1/4 teaspoon dried basil
- salt and pepper to taste
- 1 tablespoon cornstarch

Direction

- Over medium heat, heat oil in a large skillet and mix in garlic and onions. Cook for 5 minutes until tender. Mix in wine, mushrooms, chicken bouillon, and 1/2 cup water. Season with pepper, salt, and basil. Heat to boil, decrease the heat and allow to simmer while uncovered for 10 minutes while stirring often. Combine together cornstarch with 1/4 cup of water. Mix into the mushrooms and then cook for about 5 minutes until thickened.

Nutrition Information

- Calories: 115 calories;
- Total Carbohydrate: 4.9
- Cholesterol: < 1
- Protein: 2.6
- Total Fat: 9.3
- Sodium: 198

747. Mushrooms With A Soy Sauce Glaze

Serving: 2 | Prep: 5mins | Cook: 10mins | Ready in:

Ingredients

- 2 tablespoons butter
- 1 (8 ounce) package sliced white mushrooms
- 2 cloves garlic, minced
- 2 teaspoons soy sauce
- ground black pepper to taste

Direction

- In the frying pan, melt the butter on medium heat, then add the mushrooms and let it cook and stir for about 5 minutes, until the mushrooms released its liquid and become soft. Mix in the garlic and keep on cooking and stirring for a minute. Pour in the soy sauce. Cook the mushrooms in the soy sauce for about 4 minutes until the liquid evaporates.

Nutrition Information

- Calories: 135 calories;
- Protein: 4.2
- Total Fat: 11.9
- Sodium: 387
- Total Carbohydrate: 5.4
- Cholesterol: 31

748. Nayza's Mushroom Fiesta Cups

Serving: 3 | Prep: 30mins | Cook: 15mins | Ready in:

Ingredients

- Corn Salsa:
- 1 (15 ounce) can corn, drained
- 3 tablespoons chopped fresh cilantro
- 2 limes, juiced
- 1/2 jalapeno pepper, chopped
- 2 tablespoons ground cumin
- 1 tablespoon onion powder
- 1 tablespoon dried oregano
- 1 1/2 teaspoons chopped garlic
- 1/2 teaspoon Himalayan salt
- 2 teaspoons olive oil
- 2 dashes liquid smoke flavoring
- 3 portobello mushrooms, stems removed
- 2 teaspoons ground cumin
- 2 teaspoons dried oregano
- 2 teaspoons garlic powder
- 2 teaspoons onion powder
- 1 teaspoon ground black pepper
- 1/2 teaspoon sea salt
- 1 (16 ounce) can refried black beans
- 1 tablespoon ground cumin
- 1 tablespoon dried oregano
- 1 tablespoon garlic powder
- 1 tablespoon onion powder
- 1 teaspoon ground black pepper
- 1/2 teaspoon salt
- 1/2 cup shredded Cheddar cheese
- 1 avocado, roughly chopped and slightly mashed
- 1 Roma tomato, diced

Direction

- In a large bowl, combine together 1/2 teaspoon if Himalayan salt, chopped garlic, 1 tablespoon of oregano, 1 tablespoon of onion powder, 2 tablespoons of cumin, jalapeno, lime juice, cilantro and corn until the salsa is well combined.
- In another bowl, combine liquid smoke and olive oil together; rub into mushrooms. Season with 1/2 teaspoon of sea salt, 1 teaspoon of black pepper, 2 teaspoons of onion powder, 2 teaspoons of garlic powder, 2 teaspoons of oregano and 2 teaspoons of cumin. Transfer the mixture onto a grill pan, flat side down. (You can use a countertop induction oven's grill pan instead.)
- Place the pan in the oven; start heating to 445°F (230°C). (If you use a countertop induction oven, turn it on to Combo 1.) Cook for 9-10 minutes until tender.
- Place a pot on medium heat; cook in 1/2 teaspoon of salt, 1 teaspoon of black pepper, 1 tablespoon of onion powder, 1 tablespoon of oregano, 1 tablespoon of cumin and refried beans; stir regularly for about 5 minutes till heated through.
- Take the grill pan away from the oven; using a spoon, move the bean mixture into the prepared mushrooms; put Cheddar cheese on top.
- Turn the pan with mushrooms back to the oven. Set the oven to boil; cook for a half or 1 minute till the cheese is melted.
- Place salsa over the mushrooms; put tomatoes and avocado on top.

Nutrition Information

- Calories: 459 calories;
- Cholesterol: 32
- Protein: 20.9
- Total Fat: 15.6
- Sodium: 2072
- Total Carbohydrate: 68.2

749. Neptune's Favor

Serving: 5 | Prep: 20mins | Cook: 30mins | Ready in:

Ingredients

- 2 (10 ounce) boxes frozen chopped spinach, thawed and squeezed dry
- 1/4 cup mayonnaise
- 1/4 cup all-purpose flour
- 2 cups milk
- 3/4 teaspoon salt
- 1/4 teaspoon paprika
- 1/8 teaspoon crushed rosemary
- 1/8 teaspoon dried thyme leaves
- 2 tablespoons grated onion
- 1/2 (4 ounce) can sliced mushrooms, drained
- 2 hard cooked eggs, chopped
- 1 pound cooked Alaskan snow crab meat
- 1/2 cup shredded Swiss cheese

Direction

- Preheat an oven to 175°C/350°F then butter a square glass 8-in. glass baking dish. Put spinach onto bottom then around sides of the prepped baking dish.
- Mix flour and mayonnaise in a saucepan; mix in milk. Season with thyme, rosemary, paprika and salt. Add mushrooms and onion; simmer on medium high heat and cook till thick, constantly mixing. Mix in eggs; put into a baking dish. Sprinkle cheese and crabmeat.
- In preheated oven, bake for approximately 20 minutes till cheese is melted.

Nutrition Information

- Calories: 435 calories;
- Sodium: 947
- Total Carbohydrate: 17
- Cholesterol: 194
- Protein: 34.8
- Total Fat: 26

750. Night Before Scrambled Eggs

Serving: 8 | Prep: | Cook: |Ready in:

Ingredients

- 3 tablespoons butter or margarine, divided
- 1 1/2 tablespoons all-purpose flour
- 1/2 teaspoon salt
- 1 1/4 cups milk
- 1 3/4 cups shredded cheese (such as Cheddar or Swiss), divided
- 1 cup sliced mushrooms
- 1/3 cup finely chopped onion
- 12 eggs
- 6 slices cooked bacon, chopped*

Direction

- In saucepan, melt 1 tbsp. butter. Whisk salt and flour in. Whisk milk in slowly till smooth. Simmer on medium heat, constantly mixing, till slightly thick. Take off heat. Add 1 1/4 cup cheese, mixing till melted; put aside.
- Melt leftover 2 tbsp. butter in big frying pan. Add onion and mushrooms; sauté till liquid evaporates and tender.
- Whisk eggs; add ham/bacon and eggs into onion/mushroom mixture. Cook till eggs just set yet a bit wet. Mix cheese sauce into the egg mixture.
- Put mixture in greased 23-cm/9-in. square baking pan/2.5L casserole. Sprinkle top with leftover 1/2 cup cheese. Cover; refrigerate overnight.
- Uncover the next morning; bake in preheated 180°C/350°F oven for 20-25 minutes till cheese melts and is heated through.

Nutrition Information

- Calories: 311 calories;
- Sodium: 610
- Total Carbohydrate: 4.9
- Cholesterol: 327
- Protein: 19.8
- Total Fat: 23.6

751. Nikki's Pork Chops With A Mushroom Cream Sauce Over White Jasmine Rice

Serving: 4 | Prep: 20mins | Cook: 58mins | Ready in:

Ingredients

- Rice:
- 2 cups water
- 1 cup white jasmine rice
- 1/2 teaspoon salt
- 1 tablespoon butter
- Pork Chops:
- 4 (1/2-inch thick) pork chops
- 1 tablespoon olive oil, or to taste
- 1/2 teaspoon Creole seasoning, or to taste
- salt and ground black pepper to taste
- 1 green bell pepper, sliced
- 1/2 small onion, sliced
- Cream Sauce:
- 1/4 cup butter
- 1/2 cup sliced fresh mushrooms
- 1/4 cup chopped onion
- 2 cups half-and-half
- 1 tablespoon all-purpose flour
- 1/2 teaspoon ground paprika, or to taste

Direction

- In a saucepan, mix half teaspoon salt, rice and water; bring to a boil. Lower the heat to low; cook with a cover for about 20 minutes until rice becomes tender. Take out of the heat; add a tablespoon of butter; stir until rice becomes fluffy.
- Set the oven to 350°F (175°C) and start preheating. (If you use a countertop induction oven, set the oven to "Combo 1" setting and start preheating.)
- In a 9-inch baking pan, place pork chops (or grill pan if you use countertop induction oven). Drizzle over top with olive oil. Sprinkle pepper, salt and Creole seasoning. Place sliced onions and green bell peppers on and around pork chops.
- Bake in the prepared oven for about 20 minutes with the conventional oven and 10-15 minutes with the countertop induction oven until the inserted instant-read thermometer into the center registers at least 145°F (63°C). Use aluminum foil to cover.
- Over medium heat, in a large skillet, melt 1/4 cup butter. Add chopped onion and mushrooms; cook while stirring for about 5 minutes until onion becomes translucent. Pour in half-and-half. Slowly stir in flour; cook while stirring for about 5 minutes until sauce is thickened.
- Pour sauce on top pork chops; stir to incorporate juices in pan.
- Place pork chops back to the prepared oven; bake for 3-5 minutes until flavors combine. Serve over rice. Top with paprika.

Nutrition Information

- Calories: 673 calories;
- Protein: 31.5
- Total Fat: 38.8
- Sodium: 580
- Total Carbohydrate: 48.9
- Cholesterol: 142

752. No Noodle Zucchini Lasagna

Serving: 8 | Prep: 30mins | Cook: 1hours | Ready in:

Ingredients

- 2 large zucchini
- 1 tablespoon salt
- 1 pound ground beef
- 1 1/2 teaspoons ground black pepper
- 1 small green bell pepper, diced
- 1 onion, diced
- 1 cup tomato paste
- 1 (16 ounce) can tomato sauce
- 1/4 cup red wine

- 2 tablespoons chopped fresh basil
- 1 tablespoon chopped fresh oregano
- hot water as needed
- 1 egg
- 1 (15 ounce) container low-fat ricotta cheese
- 2 tablespoons chopped fresh parsley
- 1 (16 ounce) package frozen chopped spinach, thawed and drained
- 1 pound fresh mushrooms, sliced
- 8 ounces shredded mozzarella cheese
- 8 ounces grated Parmesan cheese

Direction

- Set oven temperature to 325 degrees F (165 degrees C) and leave aside for preheating.
- Cut zucchini into long slices that are as thin as possible. Add a sprinkle of salt on these slices and put aside for draining in a colander.
- Prepare the meat sauce by cooking ground beef and black pepper in a large skillet for 5 minutes on medium-high heat settings. Stir in onions and green pepper and continue cooking until meat no longer appears rare. Mix tomato sauce, tomato paste, basil, wine, and oregano into the pan, consider adding a little hot water if the sauce gets too thick in consistency. Increase the temperature to a boil and then decrease and let simmer for 20 minutes, stirring often.
- In the meantime, combine ricotta, parsley, and egg in a bowl until evenly mixed.
- Assembly the lasagna as follows; 1/2 of the meat sauce is poured into the bottom of prepared pan and spread evenly. Add in the following arrangement, 1/2 zucchini slices, 1/2 ricotta mix, all of the spinach, and all of the mushroom, followed by 1/2 of the mozzarella cheese. Continue the arrangement with the remainder of the meat sauce, zucchini slices, ricotta mixture, and mozzarella cheese. Cover with an even spread of Parmesan cheese and a layer of foil.
- Carefully place in the oven and bake for 45 minutes. Then remove the foil, increase oven temperature to 350 degrees and bake for another 15 minutes. Set aside for 5 minutes before serving.

Nutrition Information

- Calories: 494 calories;
- Total Fat: 27.3
- Sodium: 2200
- Total Carbohydrate: 23.2
- Cholesterol: 118
- Protein: 41.3

753. No Peek Beef Stew

Serving: 6 | Prep: 28mins | Cook: 8hours | Ready in:

Ingredients

- 2 pounds beef stew meat, cut into 1 inch cubes
- 1 (10.5 ounce) can condensed French onion soup
- 1 (10.75 ounce) can condensed cream of mushroom soup
- 1 (4.5 ounce) can mushrooms, drained
- 1/2 cup dry red wine

Direction

- In the slow cooker, mix together dry red wine, mushrooms, condensed cream of mushroom soup, condensed French onion soup and beef stew meat. Cook with a cover for 8 hours on Low.

Nutrition Information

- Calories: 382 calories;
- Total Fat: 24.3
- Sodium: 904
- Total Carbohydrate: 9.3
- Cholesterol: 85
- Protein: 27

754. Noodles Marmaduke

Serving: 4 | Prep: 20mins | Cook: 40mins | Ready in:

Ingredients

- 1/4 cup butter
- 1/2 cup sliced onion
- 1 clove garlic, minced
- 8 ounces fresh mushrooms, sliced
- 1 pound ground beef
- 1/2 cup Burgundy wine
- 3 tablespoons lemon juice
- 1 (10.5 ounce) can condensed beef consomme
- 1/2 teaspoon salt
- 1/4 teaspoon ground black pepper
- 2 cups medium egg noodles
- 1 cup sour cream
- 1 tablespoon chopped fresh parsley for garnish

Direction

- In a large skillet, over medium heat, melt the butter. Add mushrooms, garlic and onions; cook while stirring until lightly browned. Crumble in the ground beef, cook until no longer pink. Drain the excess grease.
- Stir in the Burgundy wine; scrape all the bits of food from the bottom of the pan to flavor the sauce. Stir in pepper, salt, beef consommé and lemon juice. Simmer without a cover for 15 minutes.
- Mix the uncooked noodles into the skillet. Simmer with a cover until noodles become tender or for 10 minutes. Take out of the heat, stir in sour cream. Drizzle over with parsley; serve.

Nutrition Information

- Calories: 555 calories;
- Sodium: 721
- Total Carbohydrate: 22
- Cholesterol: 141
- Protein: 26.6
- Total Fat: 38.1

755. Nutmeg Mushrooms

Serving: 4 | Prep: 5mins | Cook: 10mins | Ready in:

Ingredients

- 1 pound fresh mushrooms
- 3/4 cup white wine
- 1 tablespoon ground nutmeg
- 1 teaspoon salt

Direction

- Wash and cut the mushrooms.
- In skillet, mix every ingredient and cook on moderate heat till wine reaches a boil. Lower heat to low and cook till mushrooms are soft. Take off heat and serve hot.

Nutrition Information

- Calories: 75 calories;
- Sodium: 590
- Total Carbohydrate: 6.1
- Cholesterol: 0
- Protein: 3.7
- Total Fat: 1.2

756. Onion And Mushroom Scrambled Eggs

Serving: 2 | Prep: 15mins | Cook: 20mins | Ready in:

Ingredients

- 1 1/2 tablespoons extra-virgin olive oil
- 1 (8 ounce) package sliced fresh mushrooms
- 1 onion, sliced
- 1 clove garlic, minced
- 1 1/2 tablespoons Italian seasoning

- 5 eggs
- 2 tablespoons garlic and herb cheese spread (such as Boursin®)
- salt and ground black pepper to taste
- 1/3 cup shredded mozzarella cheese

Direction

- In a skillet, warm up the olive oil over medium heat; cook while stirring garlic, onion and mushrooms for about 15 minutes or till the onion is brown. Add Italian seasoning to taste.
- In a bowl, whisk eggs with herb cheese spread and garlic. The mixture will be a bit chunky. Add black pepper and salt to taste.
- Pour the eggs over the mushroom mixture in the skillet; cook while stirring for about 1 minute or until eggs are partially set. Add mozzarella cheese gently into eggs and fold for about 30 seconds or until almost melted.

Nutrition Information

- Calories: 415 calories;
- Total Fat: 31.3
- Sodium: 369
- Total Carbohydrate: 13.3
- Cholesterol: 439
- Protein: 23.9

757. Opa George's Wild Rice

Serving: 6 | Prep: 15mins | Cook: 45mins | Ready in:

Ingredients

- 3 cups water
- 1 cup wild rice
- 1/2 teaspoon salt
- 1/2 cup coarsely chopped fresh morel mushrooms
- 1/2 cup coarsely chopped roasted chestnuts
- 2 green onions, chopped
- 6 ounces sour cream
- 1 green onion, chopped (optional)
- salt and ground black pepper to taste

Direction

- Boil 1/2 tsp. salt, wild rice and water in heavy saucepan. Lower heat to low. Cover; simmer for 30-45 minutes till wild rice is tender.
- Mix 2 chopped green onions, chestnuts and morel mushrooms into rice; simmer for 15 minutes till green onions and mushrooms are tender.
- Drain extra liquid; mix 1 chopped green onion and sour cream into wild rice mixture then season with black pepper and salt. Immediately serve.

Nutrition Information

- Calories: 163 calories;
- Total Fat: 6.5
- Sodium: 216
- Total Carbohydrate: 22.9
- Cholesterol: 12
- Protein: 4.4

758. Orzo Delicioso

Serving: 8 | Prep: 20mins | Cook: 15mins | Ready in:

Ingredients

- 2 tablespoons butter
- 1/4 cup olive oil
- 1 large white onion, chopped
- 2 fresh jalapeno peppers, diced
- 1 red bell pepper, chopped
- 1 green bell pepper, chopped
- 1 yellow bell pepper, chopped
- 1/2 cup white wine
- 1 large tomato, chopped
- 1 (10 ounce) can corn, drained
- 2 tablespoons minced garlic

- 4 fresh mushrooms, sliced
- 1 (16 ounce) package dried orzo pasta

Direction

- Heat the oil and butter in a big pan on medium heat. Mix in yellow, green and red peppers, jalapeno and onion. Pour white wine, then cook for 5 minutes. Mix in mushrooms, garlic, corn and tomato, then cook for 10 minutes.
- In the meantime, cook the orzo following the package instructions; drain. Toss the sautéed veggies with orzo.

Nutrition Information

- Calories: 360 calories;
- Sodium: 132
- Total Carbohydrate: 55.3
- Cholesterol: 8
- Protein: 9.9
- Total Fat: 11

759. Outstanding Chicken Dinner

Serving: 4 | Prep: 20mins | Cook: 30mins | Ready in:

Ingredients

- 2 tablespoons unsalted butter
- 1 (8 ounce) package button mushrooms, chopped
- 2 cups chicken broth
- 4 bone-in chicken breast halves, skinless
- 1 (10 ounce) can artichoke hearts, drained and sliced
- 1/2 cup unsalted butter
- 1/2 cup all-purpose flour
- 1 1/2 cups half-and-half cream
- 1 cup grated Parmesan cheese
- 1 teaspoon dried rosemary
- 1/2 teaspoon salt
- 1/4 teaspoon pepper

Direction

- Heat the oven to 325°F (165°C) for preheating. In a large skillet, melt 2 tablespoons of butter over medium heat. Sauté the mushrooms in butter till tender. Remove it from the skillet; put aside.
- In the skillet, put the chicken, and pour over it with the broth. Cover it, and simmer over medium heat till the chicken is cooked through, about 20 minutes. Save 1/2 cup of broth from the pan for use later; discard or reserve the remaining broth for other uses. Place the chicken in a baking dish of 9x13 inches, and add artichokes on top.
- In a skillet, melt the remaining 1/2 cup of butter over medium heat; whisk in flour till smooth. Slowly stir in the 1/2 cup of saved broth, and half and half cream. Cook and constantly stir for about 5 minutes, until thickened. Shut the heat off, and mix in pepper, salt, rosemary and Parmesan cheese. Pour the sauce over the cooked chicken in a baking dish. Add sautéed mushrooms on top.
- Bake in the prepared oven without a cover for half an hour. Allow to sit for a few minutes to let the sauce thicken before serving.

Nutrition Information

- Calories: 697 calories;
- Total Fat: 48.1
- Sodium: 1130
- Total Carbohydrate: 26.4
- Cholesterol: 195
- Protein: 41.1

760. Owen's Chicken Rice

Serving: 10 | Prep: | Cook: | Ready in:

Ingredients

- 1/2 (3 pound) whole chicken, cut into pieces
- 8 ounces Chinese-style sausages
- 1 teaspoon salt
- 1 tablespoon dark soy sauce
- 2 tablespoons sesame oil
- 1/2 slice fresh ginger root, chopped
- 12 dried shiitake mushrooms, soaked until soft
- 3 cups long-grain white rice
- 2 1/2 cups boiling water
- 3 tablespoons chopped fresh cilantro
- 3 tablespoons thinly sliced green onion

Direction

- Mix soy sauce and 1 teaspoon salt then marinate the sausages and chicken in it and put it aside.
- In a big nonstick wok, heat the sesame oil in it and stir fry the ginger in the oil until it's fragrant. Mix in the chicken and sausages and stir fry them until they are brown. Mix in the mushrooms then fry for 3 more minutes. Add the rice while stirring then add salt and pepper to season.
- Move the mixture to a rice cooker then pour in water. Once the rice has cooked, add spring onions and chopped coriander as toppings then serve.

Nutrition Information

- Calories: 469 calories;
- Sodium: 576
- Total Carbohydrate: 49.4
- Cholesterol: 51
- Protein: 22.1
- Total Fat: 20.1

761. Oxtail Soup I

Serving: 7 | Prep: 20mins | Cook: 3hours10mins | Ready in:

Ingredients

- 3 pounds beef oxtail
- 3 teaspoons salt
- 1/4 teaspoon ground black pepper
- 1 onion, chopped
- 2 carrots, sliced
- 1 parsnip, sliced
- 1 turnip, peeled and diced
- 2 tablespoons brandy (optional)
- 6 cups water
- 1/2 teaspoon dried savory
- 1 bay leaf
- 1/2 cup barley
- 2 ounces dried mushrooms

Direction

- Let the dried mushrooms soak in hot water for 30-45 minutes to let them rehydrate. Drain the soaked mushrooms and cut them.
- Remove all the fat from the oxtails. Distribute the oxtails on a shallow roasting pan. Put it in the preheated 450°F (230°C) oven and let it roast for 45 minutes. Drain the excess fat from the roasting pan, keeping only about 2 tablespoons of the excess fat aside.
- Pour 1 cup of water into the roasting pan where the browned roasted oxtails are. Allow the mixture to heat up while stirring it continuously until the browned bits of food have dissolved. Keep the mixture aside.
- In reserved oxtail fat, cook parsnip, onion, turnip, carrots and mushrooms in a big stock pot for about 10 minutes until the vegetables have softened. Put in the browned oxtails afterwards. Sprinkle in the brandy on top and igniting it.
- Add the reserved water-and-browned bits mixture into the vegetables-and-oxtails mixture. Pour in the remaining 5 cups of water. Put in the barley, savory, pepper, bay leaf and salt and allow the mixture to boil, then lower the heat setting. Cover the pot and let the mixture gently simmer for 2 hours. Adjust the amount of seasonings depending on your taste.

Nutrition Information

- Calories: 588 calories;
- Total Fat: 26.8
- Sodium: 1409
- Total Carbohydrate: 22
- Cholesterol: 214
- Protein: 63.3

762. Oyster And Mushroom Stuffing

Serving: 16 | Prep: 20mins | Cook: 1hours | Ready in:

Ingredients

- 1/2 cup margarine
- 1 large onion, chopped
- 2 cups chopped celery
- 1 (12 ounce) package fresh mushrooms, sliced
- 8 cups dry bread crumbs
- 1 egg, beaten
- 1 pint shucked oysters, chopped
- 1/2 cup chicken broth
- 1 teaspoon poultry seasoning
- 1 teaspoon dried sage
- 1/2 teaspoon salt
- 1/2 teaspoon ground black pepper

Direction

- Preheat an oven to 165°C/325°F.
- Melt margarine in big skillet on medium heat; mix and cook celery and onion for about 10 minutes till celery is tender. Mix mushrooms in; mix and cook for 5-8 minutes till they release their juice and tender.
- Mix oysters, egg and breadcrumbs in bowl; mix cooked veggies with margarine and juices, black pepper, salt, sage, poultry seasoning and chicken broth in till combined well. Put stuffing in 2-qt. casserole dish.
- In preheated oven, bake for about 45 minutes till top is browned, oysters are cooked and stuffing is hot.

Nutrition Information

- Calories: 309 calories;
- Cholesterol: 30
- Protein: 12
- Total Fat: 9.7
- Sodium: 619
- Total Carbohydrate: 42.9

763. PHILLY Slow Cooker Beef Stroganoff

Serving: 4 | Prep: 15mins | Cook: 8hours | Ready in:

Ingredients

- 1 pound cubed stewing beef
- 1 cup chopped onions
- 1 cup chopped mushrooms
- 1/2 cup beef broth
- 1/2 cup PHILADELPHIA Herb & Garlic Cream Cheese Spread
- 1 tablespoon flour
- 225 grams fettuccine, cooked, drained

Direction

- In a slow cooker, combine the onions, mushrooms and meat together.
- Mix in the broth. Put the lid onto the slow cooker. Let the mixture cook on low setting for 6-8 hours or on high setting for 3-4 hours.
- Mix the flour and cream cheese spread together. Put the cream cheese mixture into the meat mixture right before serving time; mix the 2 mixtures until well-combined and the cream cheese has fully melted. Put it on top of the newly cooked pasta and mix until well-coated.

Nutrition Information

- Calories: 532 calories;

- Cholesterol: 90
- Protein: 29
- Total Fat: 25.1
- Sodium: 287
- Total Carbohydrate: 48.5

764. Paleo Chicken Marsala

Serving: 5 | Prep: 15mins | Cook: 14mins | Ready in:

Ingredients

- 4 skinless, boneless chicken breast halves
- sea salt and ground black pepper to taste
- 1 tablespoon extra-virgin olive oil, or more as needed
- 2 tablespoons unsalted butter, divided
- 6 (1 ounce) slices prosciutto, cut into thirds
- 1 small shallot, minced
- 8 ounces crimini mushrooms, stemmed and halved
- 1/2 cup sweet Marsala wine
- 1/2 cup chicken stock
- 1/4 cup chopped flat-leaf parsley

Direction

- On a hard, level surface, put chicken cutlets between 2 plastic wrap sheets. Firmly pound a meat mallet's smooth side onto the meat until the thickness is 1/4-inch. Use pepper and salt to season both sides.
- In a big frying pan, heat 1 tablespoon butter and 1 tablespoon olive oil over medium-high heat until the butter melts. In the frying pan, put the chicken cutlets; cook for 5 minutes per side until turning golden brown on both sides.
- Lower the heat to medium, pour olive oil into the frying pan if necessary. In the frying pan, put shallots and prosciutto; stir and cook for 1 minute until warmed. Mix in mushrooms and cook for 5 minutes until turning brown. Use pepper and salt to season. Add wine to the frying pan; simmer for 1 minute until the flavors blend. Pour in chicken stock; stir and simmer for 1 minute until the sauce partially decreases.
- Mix into the frying pan with 1 tablespoon of butter. Put the chicken back into the pan; simmer for 1 minute until the chicken has fully heated. Use pepper, salt, and parsley to garnish.

Nutrition Information

- Calories: 357 calories;
- Total Carbohydrate: 5.8
- Cholesterol: 97
- Protein: 28.9
- Total Fat: 20.5
- Sodium: 811

765. Pan Fried Fingerling Potatoes With Wild Mushroom Sauce

Serving: 6 | Prep: 20mins | Cook: 50mins | Ready in:

Ingredients

- 2 tablespoons butter
- 1 1/2 pounds fingerling potatoes, halved lengthwise
- 2 cups sliced mixed wild mushrooms (small portobella, crimini, shiitake)
- 2 cloves garlic, minced
- 1 large shallot, thinly sliced
- 1 cup chicken broth
- 1/4 cup dried mixed wild mushrooms
- 2 teaspoons Dijon mustard
- 3/4 teaspoon herbes de Provence
- 1/2 cup creme fraiche or heavy cream
- Freshly ground black pepper to taste
- Chopped fresh thyme

Direction

- In a large skillet over medium heat, put butter to melt. Put in potatoes; cook for 30 minutes,

stirring occasionally, or until potatoes are tender. (Use foil to tent it will fasten the cooking).
- Mix in shallot, garlic, and fresh mushrooms; cook for 10 more minutes. Add herbs, mustard, dried mushrooms, and broth; cook for 5 minutes over high heat or until most of the broth has cooked off. Mix in crème fraiche and cook for 5 more minutes. Add fresh thyme and pepper to taste.

Nutrition Information

- Calories: 240 calories;
- Protein: 5.2
- Total Fat: 11.6
- Sodium: 256
- Total Carbohydrate: 30.5
- Cholesterol: 38

766. Pan Roasted Halibut With Clamshell Mushrooms And Lemon Butter Sauce

Serving: 2 | Prep: 15mins | Cook: 15mins | Ready in:

Ingredients

- 1 tablespoon olive oil
- 1 tablespoon butter
- 1/4 cup clamshell mushrooms, or more to taste
- salt and freshly ground black pepper to taste
- 2 (7 ounce) halibut fillets
- 1 pinch cayenne pepper, or to taste
- 1/4 cup water
- 1/2 lemon, juiced
- 1 1/2 tablespoons butter, room temperature but not soft
- 1 tablespoon chopped flat-leaf Italian parsley

Direction

- On medium-high heat, place a tablespoon butter and oil in a heavy pan; heat until the butter begins to foam and melts. Add a pinch of salt and mushrooms in the pan with oil and melted butter. Sauté for about 5 minutes until golden brown. Move the mushrooms to the edges to make a space in the middle of the pan.
- Sprinkle cayenne pepper and salt on each side of the halibut to season; put fish in the middle of the pan. Cook fillets for 3-4 minutes on each side until flaky. Move the halibut fillets in a warm serving dish.
- In the same pan, pour in water; boil. While boiling, use a wooden spoon to scrape off the accumulated browned bits at the bottom. Continue boiling for 1-2 minutes until the water reduces by half. Stir in lemon juice.
- Mix in parsley and butter in the mushroom mixture. Form sauce by continuously stirring until the butter melts. Take off from heat; season with black pepper and salt. Ladle mushroom and sauce over the halibut fillets.

Nutrition Information

- Calories: 407 calories;
- Total Fat: 25.8
- Sodium: 212
- Total Carbohydrate: 0.6
- Cholesterol: 102
- Protein: 41.8

767. Pan Seared Cod, Broccoli, And Mushrooms With Creamy Alfredo Sauce

Serving: 4 | Prep: 25mins | Cook: 15mins | Ready in:

Ingredients

- Seasoning Mix:
- 2 tablespoons cornstarch
- 1/2 teaspoon paprika

- 1/2 teaspoon kosher salt
- 1/4 teaspoon white pepper
- 1 pinch cayenne pepper (optional)
- 4 (4 ounce) cod fillets
- 1 tablespoon olive oil
- 1 tablespoon butter
- 1 large clove garlic, minced
- 1 (8 ounce) package fresh mushrooms, quartered
- Salt to taste
- 4 green onions, diced
- 1 (15 ounce) jar Classico® Fresh Creamy Alfredo Sauce
- For the broccoli:
- 1 tablespoon olive oil
- 1 large clove garlic, minced
- 1 1/2 pounds broccoli crowns, trimmed into individual florets
- 1 pinch white sugar
- 1/8 teaspoon kosher salt
- 1/4 cup water
- 1 lemon, cut into wedges
- 2 tablespoons pecan halves, toasted

Direction

- In a dish, mix cayenne (if using), white pepper, kosher salt, paprika and cornstarch. Pat fish dry using paper towels. Use the seasoning mix to coat fish on every sides.
- On medium heat, heat oil and butter in one 12 in. skillet. Put in minced garlic and cook for about half a minute till garlic becomes fragrant yet not brown. Put in a salt pinch and quartered mushrooms; cook for 3 minutes till mushrooms become browned a bit. Take mushrooms out of skillet. Put in 1 tbsp. of extra olive oil if the pan is dry.
- Raise heat to medium high. Add fish lightly into skillet in a single layer. Sear for about 5 minutes till forms crusty on the bottom. Flip the fish and sear the other side for roughly 4 minutes. Take fish out of pan.
- Lower heat to medium low. Bring back the mushrooms to the skillet along with the chopped green onions; mix. Pour in the Classico Creamy Alfredo Sauce and heat for 4 minutes but don't let it boil. Add the fish to the sauce. Lower heat to low to keep warm.
- On medium heat, heat 1 tbsp. of olive oil in another lidded skillet. Put in minced garlic and cook for roughly half a minute. Add broccoli into the pan and use a big kosher salt pinch and white sugar to season. Pour in water, cover up; steam on medium heat for roughly 8-10 minutes till stalks are soft and broccoli turns bright green.
- Along the platter's rim, arrange broccoli in a circle with the crowns facing outward. Gently add fish into the center. Squeeze two lemon wedges on top of broccoli and fish. Add mushrooms and sauce on top of the fish. Use toasted pecans to decorate.
- Serve alongside extra lemon wedges if you want.

Nutrition Information

- Calories: 480 calories;
- Total Fat: 29.9
- Sodium: 1221
- Total Carbohydrate: 28
- Cholesterol: 137
- Protein: 31.1

768. Parchment Cooked Fish With Morels, Spring Garlic, And Thyme

Serving: 4 | Prep: 30mins | Cook: 30mins | Ready in:

Ingredients

- 1 pound fresh morel mushrooms
- salt and ground black pepper to taste
- 4 (6 ounce) Pacific halibut fillets
- 1 1/2 teaspoons butter
- 1/2 cup chopped garlic scapes
- 5 sprigs fresh thyme, leaves stripped and chopped
- 1 tablespoon canola oil, or as needed

- 4 12x20-inch pieces of parchment paper

Direction

- Preheat an oven to 175°C/350°F.
- In a dry skillet, put morel mushrooms on medium heat. Sprinkle black pepper and salt. Cook, mixing often, for 5 minutes till juice evaporates and mushrooms release their juice.
- Sprinkle both sides of halibut fillets with black pepper and salt.
- In a big skillet, heat butter on medium low heat. Cook halibut fillets, 2 minutes per side, till golden brown on the outside. Take fish out of skillet; put aside.
- Stir and cook garlic scapes in same skillet to cook fish for 1 minute till fragrant. Take pan off heat. Mix thyme and morel mushrooms with garlic scapes till combined.
- Fold a parchment paper piece crosswise in half. Cut a very big valentine-like heart shape with scissors out of folded paper as big as you can. Repeat with leftover parchment to create 4 big heart shapes.
- Open heart shapes. Brush canola oil to brush right sides of hearts.
- In unoiled/left half of every heart, put 1/4 morel mushroom mixture. On mushroom mixture, put halibut fillet. Sprinkle black pepper and salt on fish.
- Over fish, fold oiled right half of heart. Fold 1/4-in. parchment paper over, beginning with rounded end, working your way down towards the point, folding while you go. Fold edge over again to enclose mushrooms and fish in a bundle using a double-folded, sealed edge.
- Allow 1/4-in. bottom point unfolded.
- Use an inserted straw in open bottom to blow air in the bundle to puff it up as if it were a small balloon. Enclose air by twisting bottom closed.
- On 2 baking sheets, put parchment bundles. Don't allow bundles to touch each other.
- In preheated oven, bake for 15 minutes till fish isn't translucent in the middle.
- Serving: Put every portion on a plate. Cut open parchment carefully to reveal juices, mushrooms and fish. When you open the bundle, it will release hot steam.

Nutrition Information

- Calories: 280 calories;
- Total Fat: 9
- Sodium: 104
- Total Carbohydrate: 11.1
- Cholesterol: 58
- Protein: 38.8

769. Pasta Salad I

Serving: 6 | Prep: | Cook: | Ready in:

Ingredients

- 3 cups fusilli pasta
- 3/4 cup broccoli florets
- 3/4 cup cauliflower florets
- 1/2 cup red onion, sliced
- 1/2 cup thinly sliced carrots
- 1/2 cup red bell pepper, chopped
- 1/2 cup chopped green bell pepper
- 1/2 cup chopped mushrooms
- 1/2 cup chopped celery
- 3/4 cup light mayonnaise
- 1/4 cup distilled white vinegar
- 1/4 cup white sugar
- salt and pepper to taste

Direction

- Follow the package directions to cook pasta. Drain the pasta and rinse under cold water.
- In a large serving bowl, place pasta and toss in all of the vegetables till combined.
- Combine sugar, vinegar and mayonnaise; whisk till smooth. Top the salad with dressing; mix well. Add pepper and salt to taste. Serve.

Nutrition Information

- Calories: 472 calories;
- Sodium: 31
- Total Carbohydrate: 97.1
- Cholesterol: 0
- Protein: 15.8
- Total Fat: 1.9

770. Pasta Shells With Portobello Mushrooms And Asparagus In Boursin Sauce

Serving: 6 | Prep: 15mins | Cook: 25mins | Ready in:

Ingredients

- 1 tablespoon butter
- 1 tablespoon olive oil
- 1 pound portobello mushrooms, stems removed
- 1/2 teaspoon salt
- 1 1/4 cups low-sodium chicken broth
- 1 (5.2 ounce) package pepper Boursin cheese
- 3/4 pound uncooked pasta shells
- 1 pound fresh asparagus, trimmed

Direction

- Put a big pan over medium heat, heat the olive oil and melt the butter in it. Slice the mushrooms in half and 1/4 inch thick. Cook the mushrooms until they are tender and lightly browned, about 8 minutes then add salt for seasoning. Add the Boursin cheese and chicken broth, stirring it in. Lower the heat and let the sauce simmer with constant stirring until it has blended well.
- Boil lightly salted water in a big pot then add shell pasta and cook for 5 minutes. Add the asparagus and continue cooking for 5 more minutes until the asparagus is tender and the pasta is al dente, then drain the water. Mix with the mushroom sauce then serve.

Nutrition Information

- Calories: 400 calories;
- Sodium: 388
- Total Carbohydrate: 51.6
- Cholesterol: 35
- Protein: 14.1
- Total Fat: 16.6

771. Pasta With Sugar Snap Peas, Parmesan And Mushrooms

Serving: 4 | Prep: 10mins | Cook: 11mins | Ready in:

Ingredients

- 8 ounces penne pasta
- 1 (6 ounce) package sugar snap peas, or as desired
- 2 tablespoons olive oil, or more to taste
- 1 tablespoon margarine
- 8 white mushrooms, sliced
- 2 green onions, minced
- 1 clove garlic, minced
- 1 lemon, zested
- 1 tablespoon lemon juice
- salt and ground black pepper to taste
- 1/4 cup grated Parmesan cheese
- 2 tablespoons chopped fresh mint (optional)

Direction

- Boil lightly salted water in a big pot; add penne and cook for 6 minutes, tossing sometimes. Add sugar snap peas to the pasta and cook for another 3 minutes until the pasta is soft but still firm to bite. Strain.
- Replace the pot onto the stove and heat margarine and olive oil over medium heat. Add lemon zest, garlic, green onions, and mushrooms; cook while stirring for 2 minutes until aromatic. Mix in lemon juice and use pepper and salt to season. Add sugar snap

peas and cooked pasta, mix to combine. Put mint and Parmesan cheese on top.

Nutrition Information

- Calories: 365 calories;
- Sodium: 152
- Total Carbohydrate: 51.6
- Cholesterol: 4
- Protein: 13.1
- Total Fat: 12.3

---

772. Pasta And Fresh Cilantro Crunchy Stuff

Serving: 16 | Prep: 20mins | Cook: 30mins | Ready in:

Ingredients

- 4 bunches cilantro leaves
- 2 bunches fresh basil, stems removed
- 3 cloves garlic
- 24 ounces freshly grated Parmesan cheese
- 1/4 cup olive oil
- salt and pepper, to taste
- 2 tablespoons olive oil
- 2 tablespoons minced garlic
- 2 pounds crimini mushrooms, sliced
- 1 (8 ounce) jar sun-dried tomatoes packed in oil, drained and chopped
- 3 (16 ounce) jars Alfredo pasta sauce
- 2 (16 ounce) packages fusilli pasta

Direction

- Set oven to 375°F (190°C) to preheat.
- Process 3 garlic cloves, basil, and cilantro together in a food processor or blender until very finely minced. In a large mixing bowl, combine herb mixture with 1/4 cup olive oil and Parmesan thoroughly; sprinkle with pepper and salt to season. Press mixture firmly into a medium glass baking dish, about 1 inch thick.
- Bake for about 5 to 7 minutes in the preheated oven until top is crispy and lightly brown. Take out of the oven, mix well, and place back into the oven until golden brown, for 5 to 7 minutes more. Take out of the oven; use a spoon to break apart; let cool.
- Meanwhile, heat olive oil over low heat in a large pan. Brown 2 tablespoons garlic lightly; mix in mushrooms, and cook until tender. Mix in Alfredo sauce and sun-dried tomatoes; cook to warm.
- Bring lightly salted water in a large pot to a boil. Put in pasta and cook until al dente, for 8 to 10 minutes; drain. Combine pasta with sauce, and scatter with crunchy stuff. Serve.

Nutrition Information

- Calories: 733 calories;
- Cholesterol: 72
- Protein: 31.9
- Total Fat: 45.4
- Sodium: 1617
- Total Carbohydrate: 53.1

---

773. Pasta With Clam Sauce

Serving: 6 | Prep: 15mins | Cook: 45mins | Ready in:

Ingredients

- 1 pound fresh mushrooms, sliced
- 1 green bell pepper, diced
- 2 tablespoons butter
- 1 pound fettuccini pasta
- 1/2 large head broccoli, cut into florets
- 3/4 cup butter, divided
- 1/4 cup grated Parmesan cheese
- 1/2 teaspoon dried oregano
- 1/2 teaspoon dried parsley
- 1/4 teaspoon garlic powder
- 1/4 teaspoon ground black pepper
- 1/4 cup all-purpose flour
- 1 pint heavy cream

- 1 (14.5 ounce) can chicken broth
- 2 (6.5 ounce) cans minced clams, drained

Direction

- Cook bell pepper and mushrooms in 2 tbsp. butter till tender in big skillet on medium heat. Take off heat; put aside.
- Boil big pot of lightly salted water. Add pasta; cook till al dente for 8-10 minutes. Drain. Steam broccoli for 5-10 minutes till bright green in steamer/in colander above pasta water.
- Toss 1/4 cup butter, black pepper, garlic powder, parsley, oregano, Parmesan and cooked pasta. Put a cover on. To keep warm, put aside.
- Melt 1/2 cup butter in medium saucepan on medium heat. Add flour all at once, whisking till smooth. Whisk chicken broth and cream a little at a time, then cook till mixture is thick. Mix bell pepper, mushrooms, clams and reserved broccoli in; heat through. Toss with pasta and serve immediately.

Nutrition Information

- Calories: 938 calories;
- Protein: 32
- Total Fat: 60.6
- Sodium: 358
- Total Carbohydrate: 70.8
- Cholesterol: 224

774. Pasta With Tomato Sauce, Sausage, And Mushrooms

Serving: 4 | Prep: 10mins | Cook: 25mins | Ready in:

Ingredients

- 2 tablespoons extra-virgin olive oil
- 1 onion, chopped
- 2 pounds sweet Italian pork sausage, cut into 3/4-inch pieces
- 5 cups sliced fresh mushrooms
- 1/3 cup dry white wine
- 2 1/2 cups passata (crushed tomatoes)
- salt
- 1 pinch red pepper flakes
- 1 (16 ounce) package penne pasta

Direction

- In large saucepan, heat oil over medium heat. Cook the onion for 5 minutes or until translucent and soft. Mix in the sausage. Cook while stirring for 5 minutes or until brown. Put in wine and mushrooms; simmer. Mix in the passata; simmer. Cook for 8-10 minutes, until the sauce begins to thicken. Season with red pepper flakes and salt.
- In the meantime, boil the lightly salted water in large pot. Put in penne. Cook for 11 minutes, until tender but still firm to bite, stirring occasionally. Drain. Put into sauce. Mix to blend. Enjoy!

Nutrition Information

- Calories: 1104 calories;
- Total Fat: 54.6
- Sodium: 2279
- Total Carbohydrate: 101.4
- Cholesterol: 130
- Protein: 52.2

775. Pasta, Chicken And Artichokes

Serving: 4 | Prep: 25mins | Cook: 15mins | Ready in:

Ingredients

- 4 ounces uncooked pasta
- 1 teaspoon olive oil
- 1 teaspoon minced garlic

- 3 skinless, boneless chicken breast halves - cut into strips
- 1/4 cup chicken broth
- 1/4 cup fresh chopped broccoli
- 1/4 cup chopped tomatoes
- 1/4 (14 ounce) can artichoke hearts, drained and sliced
- 1/4 cup fresh sliced mushrooms
- 1/4 cup chopped red bell pepper
- salt and pepper to taste
- 4 tablespoons grated Parmesan cheese
- 1 tablespoon chopped fresh parsley

Direction

- Bring a large pot of water to a boil. Cook pasta in boiling water until done. Drain, and put aside.
- Heat olive oil in a large sauté pan over medium high heat. In oil, brown garlic and chicken for about 5 mins. Discard from pan. Put aside.
- In the pan, pour the chicken broth. Put in tomato and broccoli. Cook for about 5 mins. Mix in pasta, cooked chicken, red bell pepper, mushrooms and artichoke hearts. Cook until hot or for 3-5 mins longer. Season with pepper and salt to taste.
- Place into the serving bowl, add parsley and Parmesan cheese on top. Enjoy.

Nutrition Information

- Calories: 267 calories;
- Sodium: 267
- Total Carbohydrate: 25.6
- Cholesterol: 49
- Protein: 23.2
- Total Fat: 7.5

776. Pastachutta

Serving: 8 | Prep: 10mins | Cook: 20mins | Ready in:

Ingredients

- 1 (16 ounce) package spaghetti
- 1/4 cup butter
- 4 cloves garlic, thinly sliced
- 1 (8 ounce) package fresh mushrooms, sliced
- 1 onion, chopped
- salt and pepper to taste

Direction

- Boil the lightly salted water in a large pot. Put in spaghetti. Cook until al dente or for 8-10 mins, then drain, do not rinse.
- In the meantime, in a large pan, melt butter over medium-high heat. Sauté onion, mushrooms and garlic until tender. Toss with the cooked spaghetti. Season to taste with pepper and salt.

Nutrition Information

- Calories: 272 calories;
- Total Fat: 6.7
- Sodium: 46
- Total Carbohydrate: 44.7
- Cholesterol: 15
- Protein: 8.1

777. Pastrami Chicken Bake

Serving: 7 | Prep: 30mins | Cook: 30mins | Ready in:

Ingredients

- 1 cup uncooked long-grain white rice
- 1 1/3 cups chicken broth, divided
- 1 cup water
- 4 ounces sliced pastrami
- 5 skinless, boneless chicken breast halves
- 10 slices bacon
- 1 (10.75 ounce) can condensed cream of mushroom soup
- 1 cup sour cream
- 1 (4.5 ounce) can mushrooms, drained

Direction

- Boil 1 cup water and 1 cup chicken broth in a saucepan. Add rice; mix. Lower heat; cover. Simmer till rice is firm and al dente for 20 minutes. Press cooked rice on bottom of 9x13-in. baking dish.
- Preheat an oven to 165°C/325°F.
- Put small pastrami piece where chicken pieces will be put on rice. Lengthwise halve every chicken breast; use bacon slice to wrap each piece. Put over rice and pastrami. Mix mushrooms, sour cream and soup in a medium bowl; put on all. Put 1/3 cup of chicken broth around dish's circumference.
- In the preheated oven, bake till fork tender for 30-40 minutes, uncovered.

Nutrition Information

- Calories: 514 calories;
- Total Fat: 29.7
- Sodium: 905
- Total Carbohydrate: 27.9
- Cholesterol: 101
- Protein: 31.8

778. Penne With Asparagus And Mushrooms

Serving: 8 | Prep: 15mins | Cook: 45mins | Ready in:

Ingredients

- 1/2 cup olive oil
- 2 cloves garlic, crushed
- 1 (10 ounce) package fresh mushrooms, sliced
- 1 bunch fresh asparagus, trimmed and chopped
- 1 (14.5 ounce) can pureed tomatoes
- salt and pepper to taste
- 1 (16 ounce) package uncooked penne pasta
- 1 cup heavy cream

Direction

- In a skillet, heat olive oil over medium heat. Sauté garlic until browned lightly. In the skillet, put mushrooms. Cook for 5 mins. Mix in asparagus. Cook until tender, about 5 mins. Stir in tomatoes and season with pepper and salt. Lower the heat to low, simmer for 20 mins.
- Boil the lightly salted water in a large pot. Put penne pasta into pot and cook until al dente, about 8-10 mins; then drain.
- Mix heavy cream into skillet. Keep cooking until the sauce thickens, about 10 mins. Place over cooked pasta. Enjoy!

Nutrition Information

- Calories: 472 calories;
- Total Fat: 26.1
- Sodium: 234
- Total Carbohydrate: 49.7
- Cholesterol: 41
- Protein: 11.5

779. Penne With Pancetta And Mushrooms

Serving: 4 | Prep: 15mins | Cook: 20mins | Ready in:

Ingredients

- 1 (12 ounce) package penne pasta
- 1 (3 ounce) package pancetta bacon, diced
- 2 tablespoons butter
- 1 (10 ounce) package sliced mushrooms
- 1 tablespoon minced garlic
- 1/2 cup heavy cream
- 1/4 teaspoon Italian seasoning
- 1/4 cup grated Parmesan cheese, or to taste

Direction

- Boil the lightly salted water in large pot. Put in pasta and cook until al dente, about 8-10 minutes; then drain. Put aside. In the meantime, in large skillet, cook pancetta over medium heat for 5 minutes or until brown but not crispy. Place on a paper towel-lined plate to drain. Put aside.
- Remove the pancetta grease from skillet. Put in butter. Raise the heat to medium-high; mix in the sliced mushrooms. Cook while stirring until mushrooms releases their liquid and soften. Put in minced garlic, cook for 2 minutes more. Lower the heat to medium-low, then stir in Italian seasoning and cream. Simmer until sauce has slightly thicken.
- Toss cooked penne with sauce to serve. Sprinkle Parmesan cheese over.

Nutrition Information

- Calories: 537 calories;
- Total Carbohydrate: 66.2
- Cholesterol: 68
- Protein: 18.8
- Total Fat: 23.4
- Sodium: 299

780. Pita Bread Tofu Sandwiches

Serving: 2 | Prep: 15mins | Cook: 15mins | Ready in:

Ingredients

- 1 tablespoon olive oil
- 1/2 (12 ounce) package tofu, cubed
- 6 mushrooms, sliced, or more to taste
- 1 cup chopped broccoli
- 1/2 cup sliced onion
- 2 stalks celery, chopped
- 3 tablespoons soy sauce
- 1 1/2 teaspoons cornstarch
- 2 pita bread rounds
- 1/2 cup shredded Cheddar cheese

Direction

- On medium-high heat, heat oil in a pan. Sauté celery, tofu, onion, mushrooms, and broccoli for 5 mins until tender.
- In a bowl, combine cornstarch and soy sauce. Pour mixture in the pan with tofu. Cook for 4-5 mins until thick.
- In a toaster, hear pit bread for a minute until warm. Scoop tofu mixture on pita bread. Garnish with Cheddar cheese.

Nutrition Information

- Calories: 473 calories;
- Protein: 24.5
- Total Fat: 21.3
- Sodium: 1908
- Total Carbohydrate: 48.9
- Cholesterol: 30

781. Pita Pizza

Serving: 1 | Prep: 5mins | Cook: 15mins | Ready in:

Ingredients

- 1 pita bread round
- 1 teaspoon olive oil
- 3 tablespoons pizza sauce
- 1/2 cup shredded mozzarella cheese
- 1/4 cup sliced crimini mushrooms
- 1/8 teaspoon garlic salt

Direction

- Turn on the grill to medium-high heat to preheat.
- Use pizza sauce and olive oil to spread over one side of the pita. Add mushrooms and cheese on top; use garlic salt to season.
- Use oil to lightly grease the grill grate. Grill pita pizza for about 5 minutes with cover until the cheese melts completely.

Nutrition Information

- Calories: 405 calories;
- Total Fat: 18
- Sodium: 1156
- Total Carbohydrate: 39.9
- Cholesterol: 44
- Protein: 19.7

782. Plantain Veggie Burgers

Serving: 6 | Prep: 15mins | Cook: 15mins | Ready in:

Ingredients

- 2 plantains, peeled and chopped
- 1/2 cup spinach
- 1/4 cup bread crumbs
- 1/4 cup cornmeal
- 1/4 cup shiitake mushrooms
- 1/4 cup black olives
- 1 clove garlic
- 1 1/2 tablespoons paprika
- 1 tablespoon fresh oregano
- 3 tablespoons butter
- salt and ground black pepper to taste

Direction

- Blend oregano, paprika, garlic, olives, mushrooms, cornmeal, breadcrumbs, spinach and plantains till moldable batter forms in a food processor; shape to patties.
- Melt butter on medium heat in a skillet; pan-fry patties for 6-8 minutes per side till golden brown. Season with pepper and salt.

Nutrition Information

- Calories: 179 calories;
- Protein: 2.4
- Total Fat: 7.2
- Sodium: 132
- Total Carbohydrate: 28.8
- Cholesterol: 15

783. Porcini Mushroom Pasta

Serving: 6 | Prep: | Cook: | Ready in:

Ingredients

- 1 tablespoon olive oil
- 2 cloves garlic, minced
- 1/2 red onion, minced
- 1/2 cup red bell pepper, julienned
- 1/2 cup julienned carrots
- 1/2 cup dry red wine
- 1 cup rehydrated porcini mushrooms
- 1 1/2 cups crushed tomatoes
- 2 teaspoons chopped fresh basil
- 1 teaspoon dried rosemary, crushed
- salt and pepper to taste
- 6 cups tagliatelle (wide noodles)

Direction

- In a big skillet, heat oil over medium heat. Add onions and garlic, sauté for 4 minutes, and then add carrots as well as red bell pepper and sauté for another 4 minutes. Pour in red wine, increase the heat and boil for 1 minute; and then lower the heat to medium-low, add mushrooms and cook for 3 minutes.
- Add basil, rosemary and tomatoes and put in pepper and salt to taste. Simmer for 10 minutes and enjoy the sauce on top of the cooked noodles.

Nutrition Information

- Calories: 335 calories;
- Sodium: 19
- Total Carbohydrate: 56.1
- Cholesterol: 0
- Protein: 13.8
- Total Fat: 4.3

784. Porcini Mushroom Soup

Serving: 6 | Prep: 25mins | Cook: 55mins | Ready in:

Ingredients

- 3 tablespoons butter
- 1 bulb fennel, diced
- 2 leeks, white parts only, trimmed and sliced
- 1 large Spanish onion, diced
- 4 cloves garlic, minced
- 6 cups chicken stock
- 3 large Yukon Gold potatoes, peeled and diced into 3/4-inch pieces
- 2 cups fresh porcini mushrooms
- 1 teaspoon dried thyme
- 2 cups heavy whipping cream
- 1/2 cup cream sherry
- 1/2 teaspoon Worcestershire sauce
- salt and ground black pepper to taste

Direction

- Place a large pot on medium heat; melt butter. Include in garlic, onion, leeks and fennel; cook while stirring for around 10 minutes, till softened. Mix in thyme, porcini mushrooms, potatoes and chicken stock. Allow to boil; turn the heat down to medium-low; simmer for 30-35 minutes, till the potatoes become tender.
- Take pot away from the heat; mix in black pepper, salt, Worcestershire sauce, cream sherry and heavy cream. Using an immersion blender, purée till smooth.
- Take the pot back to the heat. Simmer for around 10 minutes, till warmed through.

Nutrition Information

- Calories: 480 calories;
- Total Carbohydrate: 34.5
- Cholesterol: 125
- Protein: 6.3
- Total Fat: 36.1
- Sodium: 942

785. Porcini Braised Boar With Artichoke And Fennel

Serving: 8 | Prep: 50mins | Cook: 3hours | Ready in:

Ingredients

- 3 cups dry cannellini beans
- 1 quart chicken or pork stock
- 2 cups water
- 4 pounds wild boar (cinghiale) roast, cut into serving-size pieces
- 1/4 cup olive oil
- 8 ounces fresh porcini, chanterelles or stemmed shiitake mushrooms, thickly sliced
- 1/4 cup chopped garlic
- 1/4 cup minced fresh rosemary
- sea salt and ground black pepper to taste
- 8 large artichoke hearts, cut into eighths
- 2 large fennel bulbs, cored and thinly sliced
- 1/4 cup olive oil
- 2 tablespoons minced garlic
- 1/2 teaspoon crushed red pepper flakes
- 1/2 cup white wine
- 1/4 cup freshly squeezed lemon juice
- extra-virgin olive oil for drizzling
- 1/2 cup grated pecorino Toscano (or pecorino Romano) cheese
- 1/2 cup chopped Italian flat leaf parsley
- 1 lemon, zested

Direction

- Place the beans in much of cold water and soak them overnight.
- Drain the cannellini beans and pour them into a large Dutch oven together with water and chicken stock. Bring the mixture to a boil over high heat. Adjust the heat to medium-low. Cover the pot and simmer for 1 hour, skimming off any foam that forms. Remove the boar from the fridge and let it rest at room temperature during this time.

- Add 1/4 cup of olive oil in a large skillet and heat it over high heat until it starts to smoke. Add the boar pieces and sear until browned on every side. Transfer the seared boar into the top of the gently simmering beans in the pot. Heat the skillet until it smokes again. Mix in porcini mushrooms. Let them cook for 2 minutes until softened. Add 1/4 cup of the garlic. Continue cooking until the garlic turns golden brown. Sprinkle the mixture with chopped rosemary. Cook the mixture for 30 seconds longer, and then add the mushrooms into the beans and boar.
- Cover the skillet and keep simmering the boar and beans for approximately 1 1/2 hours, adding more water if necessary until they are all tender. Once they're ready, season them lightly with freshly ground pepper and sea salt to taste.
- Once the beans are nearly ready, add the artichoke hearts and some water into a large skillet. Cover the skillet and steam over high heat for about 2 minutes until just tender. Add the sliced fennel and steam the mixture for 1 minute longer. Drain in a colander. Place the skillet back into the stove.
- Adjust the heat to medium-high. Pour in 2 tbsp. of minced garlic and 1/4 cup of olive oil. Cook the mixture while frequently stirring until the garlic turns golden. Sprinkle the garlic with red pepper flakes. Add the drained vegetables. Cook and stir the vegetables for about 2 minutes until they are golden and tender. Whisk in white wine. Cook the mixture until almost evaporated. Season the mixture with salt, pepper, and lemon juice.
- To serve the dish, mound the vegetables into the middle of a large platter. Arrange the boar pieces on the top. Scoop the beans around the vegetables. Drizzle extra-virgin olive oil liberally over the mixture. Sprinkle parsley, lemon zest strands, and pecorino Toscano cheese.

Nutrition Information

- Calories: 820 calories;
- Sodium: 481
- Total Carbohydrate: 74.2
- Cholesterol: 118
- Protein: 64.7
- Total Fat: 30.3

786. Pork Chop Casserole I

Serving: 6 | Prep: | Cook: | Ready in:

Ingredients

- 2 (1 ounce) packages dry onion soup mix
- 3 cups water
- 2 cups instant rice
- 1 (4.5 ounce) can mushrooms, drained
- salt and pepper to taste
- 6 (3/4 inch) thick pork chops

Direction

- Preheat an oven to 175°C/350°F.
- Mix water and dry onion soup mix till melted in a medium size bowl; put into a 10x15-in. baking dish. Add mushrooms and rice; mix to distribute well. To taste, pepper and salt. In 1 layer, add pork chops on the mixture. Push down pork chops into the mixture to cover them.
- Tightly cover the baking dish with aluminum foil; bake for 1 hour in the preheated oven.

Nutrition Information

- Calories: 295 calories;
- Total Fat: 5.6
- Sodium: 981
- Total Carbohydrate: 33
- Cholesterol: 59
- Protein: 26.6

787. Pork Chop And Potato Casserole

Serving: 5 | Prep: 20mins | Cook: 1hours | Ready in:

Ingredients

- 1 tablespoon vegetable oil
- 6 boneless pork chops
- 1 (10.75 ounce) can condensed cream of mushroom soup
- 1 cup milk
- 4 potatoes, thinly sliced
- 1/2 cup chopped onion
- 1 cup shredded Cheddar cheese

Direction

- Preheat an oven to 200°C/400°F.
- Heat oil in a big skillet on medium high heat. Put pork chops in oil; sear.
- Mix milk and soup in a medium bowl. Put onions and potatoes in a 9x13-in. baking dish. Put browned chops over onions and potato; put soup mixture over everything.
- In the preheated oven, bake for 30 minutes. Put cheese on top; bake for 30 more minutes.

Nutrition Information

- Calories: 705 calories;
- Total Fat: 46.8
- Sodium: 636
- Total Carbohydrate: 37.9
- Cholesterol: 123
- Protein: 32.7

788. Pork Chops In Mushroom Gravy

Serving: 4 | Prep: 15mins | Cook: 25mins | Ready in:

Ingredients

- 1 tablespoon olive oil
- 4 bone-in pork chops
- 1 teaspoon garlic salt
- 1 teaspoon ground black pepper
- 1 tablespoon olive oil
- 1 (6 ounce) package sliced fresh mushrooms
- 1 (10.75 ounce) can golden mushroom soup (such as Campbell's®)
- 2 tablespoons water

Direction

- In a big skillet, heat 1 tbsp. of olive oil on medium heat. Use black pepper and garlic salt to sprinkle pork chops, then fry pork chops in the hot oil about 5-8 minutes each side, until browned. Transfer the chops to a plate.
- In the skillet, heat 1 tbsp. of olive oil, then cook and stir in the hot oil the mushrooms for 5-8 minutes, until softened. As you stir, scrape up and dissolve any browned bits of food into mushrooms. Add to the skillet the water and golden mushroom soup, then stir into mushrooms.
- Add into mushroom sauce the pork chops and accumulated juices while scooping sauce over chops. Simmer for 10-15 minutes, until juices run clear and meat is not pink anymore while scooping additional sauce over chops occasionally as they cook.

Nutrition Information

- Calories: 367 calories;
- Total Fat: 23.9
- Sodium: 1036
- Total Carbohydrate: 8
- Cholesterol: 75
- Protein: 29

789. Pork Chops With Garden Rice

Serving: 6 | Prep: 15mins | Cook: 1hours15mins | Ready in:

Ingredients

- 6 (1 inch thick) pork chops
- 1/2 teaspoon salt
- 1/4 teaspoon ground black pepper
- 1/2 teaspoon paprika
- 2 tablespoons olive oil
- 1 clove garlic, minced
- 1 (14 ounce) can vegetable broth
- 1 cup uncooked long grain white rice
- 1 (14.5 ounce) can Italian-style diced tomatoes, drained
- 1/2 cup chopped green bell pepper
- 1/2 cup chopped orange bell pepper
- 1/3 cup chopped green onions
- 1/2 cup thinly sliced fresh mushrooms

Direction

- Preheat an oven to 175°C/350°F.
- Season pork chops with paprika, pepper and salt. Heat oil in a skillet on medium heat; sauté garlic for 1 minute. Brown pork chops for 2 minutes per side.
- Boil rice and vegetable broth in a pot. Mix mushrooms, green onions, orange and green bell pepper and Italian-style diced tomatoes in; cook till heated through for 5 minutes. Put in a 9x13-in. baking dish; put pork chops over veggies and rice.
- Cover; in the preheated oven, bake for 1 hour till pork's internal temperature is 63°C/145°F and veggies and rice are tender.

Nutrition Information

- Calories: 366 calories;
- Total Carbohydrate: 32.1
- Cholesterol: 69
- Protein: 27
- Total Fat: 13.2
- Sodium: 496

790. Pork Chops With Italian Sausage

Serving: 4 | Prep: 30mins | Cook: 45mins | Ready in:

Ingredients

- 4 thick cut pork chops
- salt and pepper to taste
- 1 tablespoon olive oil
- 1/4 pound sweet Italian sausage
- 1 onion, slivered
- 1/4 pound mushrooms, sliced
- 1 clove garlic, minced
- 1/4 cup dry red wine
- 1 (8 ounce) can tomato sauce
- 1/2 teaspoon Italian seasoning

Direction

- Preheat oven to 375° F (190° C).
- Dredge pork chops with pepper and salt. In a big frying pan, brown properly in olive oil. Take chops away from the pan and leave aside. Pour off and eliminate all but 1 tablespoon of pan drippings.
- Transfer the casing from crumble meat and sausage to the same pan. Stir in mushrooms and onions. Cook while stirring till sausage and onions are lightly browned. Stir in garlic. In casserole dish, position pork chops, spreading sausage mixture over them. Add tomato sauce and wine. Dredge with Italian seasoning.
- Use foil to cover then bake for 45 minutes.

Nutrition Information

- Calories: 260 calories;
- Cholesterol: 48
- Protein: 19.2
- Total Fat: 15.3

- Sodium: 553
- Total Carbohydrate: 8.8

791. Pork Chops With Mushrooms And Grape Tomatoes

Serving: 4 | Prep: 15mins | Cook: 20mins | Ready in:

Ingredients

- 4 (1 1/2 inches thick) boneless pork chops
- 1 pinch seasoned salt, or to taste
- 1 pinch lemon-pepper seasoning, or to taste
- 1 tablespoon olive oil
- 1 cup white wine, divided
- 1/2 cup water
- 1 cup oyster mushrooms, pulled apart but not chopped
- 1/2 green bell pepper, diced
- 1/2 small onion, minced
- 2 cloves garlic, minced
- 1/2 cup grape tomatoes
- 1 tablespoon butter

Direction

- Season pork chops with lemon-pepper seasoning and seasoned salt.
- Over medium-high heat, in a large skillet, heat olive oil. Add seasoned pork chops; cook for 3-5 minutes on each side until golden. Pour water and half cup wine over pork chops; bring to a simmer. Cook for 8-10 minutes until the center of chops is no longer pink and the liquid has mostly evaporated. Place chops on serving plates.
- Stir garlic, onion, green bell pepper and oyster mushrooms into the skillet. Raise heat to high and cook while stirring often for 3-5 minutes until onion softens and all liquid has evaporated. Add the remaining half cup wine, butter and tomatoes. Cook while stirring for 1-2 minutes until heated through.
- Serve tomato and mushroom mixture over pork chops.

Nutrition Information

- Calories: 454 calories;
- Total Fat: 20.3
- Sodium: 213
- Total Carbohydrate: 5.7
- Cholesterol: 126
- Protein: 48.2

792. Pork Stroganoff

Serving: 4 | Prep: | Cook: | Ready in:

Ingredients

- 4 (1 1/4 inch) thick pork chops
- 2 tablespoons vegetable oil
- 1 onion, thinly sliced
- 1/4 pound fresh mushrooms, sliced
- 1/4 cup water
- 2 teaspoons prepared mustard
- 1/2 teaspoon salt
- 1/2 cup sour cream
- 2 tablespoons chopped fresh parsley, for garnish

Direction

- In a big skillet over medium-high heat, heat oil and cook chops on both sides until well browned. Move the chops away from the pan and set aside.
- Insert mushrooms and onion into the skillet and cook until tender, stirring from time to time. Move the chops back into the skillet then stir salt, mustard and water in. Increase the heat to high and bring it to a boil. Adjust the heat to low and cover it up. Let it simmer for 1 hour. Transfer chops to a warm platter.
- Add sour cream into the skillet and heat thoroughly, being careful not to boil. Empty

the sauce over pork chops and garnish with parsley. Serve.

Nutrition Information

- Calories: 299 calories;
- Sodium: 384
- Total Carbohydrate: 4.8
- Cholesterol: 82
- Protein: 26.9
- Total Fat: 19

793. Portabella Mushroom Dressing

Serving: 8 | Prep: | Cook: | Ready in:

Ingredients

- 4 stalks celery
- 1 onion, chopped
- 2 large portobello mushrooms, sliced
- 3 fresh shiitake mushrooms, stemmed and sliced
- 8 crimini mushrooms, sliced
- 2 cloves garlic, minced
- 1 (12 ounce) package dry bread stuffing mix with seasoning packet reserved
- 3 (14.5 ounce) cans chicken broth

Direction

- Preheat the oven to 175°C or 350°F.
- Cook and mix garlic, mushrooms, onion and celery for 3 minutes in a skillet. Mix in 1 can of chicken broth and cook till vegetables are soft. With bread crumb stuffing, mix mushroom mixture. Put packet of seasoning on top of dressing mixture and coat by tossing.
- Heat the rest of chicken broth in a 2-quart saucepan till hot. Put broth on top of mixture. Mix thoroughly.
- Into a 2-quart casserole dish, put the stuffing and allow to bake for 30 to 40 minutes.

Nutrition Information

- Calories: 188 calories;
- Total Fat: 1.5
- Sodium: 694
- Total Carbohydrate: 36.5
- Cholesterol: < 1
- Protein: 6.6

794. Portobello Artichoke Soup

Serving: 4 | Prep: 25mins | Cook: 37mins | Ready in:

Ingredients

- 1/2 cup butter, divided
- 2 carrots, peeled and diced
- 2 stalks celery, sliced
- 1/2 cup chopped green onions
- 2 portobello mushrooms, chopped
- 4 cups chicken broth
- 2 (14 ounce) cans artichoke hearts, drained and sliced
- 3/4 teaspoon dried thyme
- 3/4 teaspoon dried oregano
- 1/4 teaspoon ground cayenne pepper
- 2 bay leaves
- 1/4 cup all-purpose flour
- 1/2 cup milk
- 1 cup heavy whipping cream

Direction

- In a large pot, melt 1/4 cup butter over medium heat. Sauté green onions, celery, and carrots until vegetables begin to brown, for about 10 minutes. Mix in Portobello mushrooms; cook for 3 to 4 minutes until tender.
- Transfer chicken broth to the pot. Add bay leaves, cayenne pepper, oregano, thyme, and

artichoke hearts. Simmer for 15 to 20 minutes until flavors blend.
- In a small skillet, melt remaining 1/4 cup butter over low heat. Stir in flour, cook, stirring for about 1 minute until a paste is formed. Stir in milk. Bring to a simmer; cook and stir continuously for about 5 minutes until thickened.
- Transfer milk mixture into the soup. Gradually mix in heavy cream. Simmer for 3 to 5 minutes until soup is cooked through and slightly thickened. Remove bay leaves, enjoy.

Nutrition Information

- Calories: 560 calories;
- Total Fat: 46.5
- Sodium: 1931
- Total Carbohydrate: 29.1
- Cholesterol: 150
- Protein: 9.7

795. Portobello Bellybuttons

Serving: 4 | Prep: 15mins | Cook: 15mins | Ready in:

Ingredients

- 1 (16 ounce) package cheese tortellini
- 3 tablespoons butter
- 1 clove garlic, minced
- 2 portobello mushrooms, chopped
- 1/2 pound button mushrooms, sliced
- 1/4 cup white wine
- 1/2 tablespoon dried basil
- salt and pepper to taste
- 1/2 cup grated Parmesan cheese

Direction

- Boil lightly salted water in a large pot and add pasta. Cook until tender but still firm to the bite and drain.
- While the water is boiling, in a skillet, melt the butter and cook the garlic until aromatic. Stir in basil, white wine, button mushrooms and Portobello mushrooms. Season with pepper and salt to taste. Continue cooking the mushrooms until tender. Pour the mushroom mixture into drained pasta; stir. Put grated Parmesan cheese on top and serve.

Nutrition Information

- Calories: 512 calories;
- Total Carbohydrate: 57.8
- Cholesterol: 81
- Protein: 22.6
- Total Fat: 21.6
- Sodium: 778

796. Portobello Burgers With Goat Cheese

Serving: 4 | Prep: | Cook: 50mins | Ready in:

Ingredients

- 2 medium beets
- 1/4 cup olive oil
- 2 tablespoons balsamic vinegar
- 1 teaspoon dried rosemary
- 2 cloves garlic, minced and divided
- 4 portobello mushroom caps
- 1/2 cup goat cheese
- 4 sandwich buns, split and toasted
- 1 1/2 cups baby spinach leaves
- 3 tablespoons mayonnaise
- 2 cloves garlic, minced
- 2 limes, juiced

Direction

- Preheat the oven to 400°F (200°C).
- Cut off beets' tops and place them in a baking dish, then cover the bottom of the dish with enough water.

- Roast for 40 to 50 minutes in the preheated oven until they are easily poked with a knife. Refrigerate till cool. Slice and set aside.
- Preheat the broiler of the oven and set the rack to the second level from the heat source.
- In a bowl, whisk together 2 cloves minced garlic, balsamic vinegar, olive oil, and rosemary. Spread the ribbed side of the portobello mushroom caps with about half of the mixture; arrange the mushrooms with the ribbed sides facing upwards on a baking sheet.
- Broil the mushrooms 5 to 7 minutes until tender, avoid burning the garlic. Flip the mushrooms and brush the tops of the caps with the remaining olive oil mixture. Return to the oven and broil for about 5 more minutes until tender.
- Spread the half of each of the sandwich rolls with equal amounts of goat cheese. Top each with the spinach and a portion of the sliced beets. In a bowl, whisk the lime juice, mayonnaise, and garlic together; pour evenly on the remaining sandwich roll halves and top each with one mushroom cap. Bring together the two halves to make sandwiches, then serve.

Nutrition Information

- Calories: 489 calories;
- Sodium: 497
- Total Carbohydrate: 38.5
- Cholesterol: 26
- Protein: 14.1
- Total Fat: 32.8

797. Portobello Mushroom Appetizer

Serving: 6 | Prep: 15mins | Cook: 15mins | Ready in:

Ingredients

- 2 cloves garlic, minced
- 1/4 cup olive oil
- 6 portobello mushrooms
- 1 1/2 cups diced tomato
- 4 ounces blue cheese, crumbled

Direction

- Heat oven to 190°C (375°F) beforehand.
- Stirring olive oil and minced garlic together in a small bowl. Brushing portobello mushrooms using a paper towel to clean them. Cut the stem off and discard. Use olive oil and garlic mixture to brush the mushroom caps. On a baking sheet, lay mushroom caps, gills facing upward. On every mushroom cap, use 1/4 cup of diced tomatoes to dredge on.
- In the preheated oven, allow to bake for 13 minutes. Removing from the oven; use blue cheese to spread on top of the tomatoes. Returning the mushrooms back to the oven; allow to bake till the cheese is bubbly and melted. Before serving, let the mushrooms cool down for a few minutes.

Nutrition Information

- Calories: 185 calories;
- Sodium: 273
- Total Carbohydrate: 8.2
- Cholesterol: 14
- Protein: 7.3
- Total Fat: 14.8

798. Portobello Mushroom Caps And Veggies

Serving: 4 | Prep: 15mins | Cook: 15mins | Ready in:

Ingredients

- 1 tablespoon olive oil
- 1 tablespoon garlic, peeled and minced
- 1 onion, cut into strips
- 1 green bell pepper, cut into strips

- 1/4 teaspoon salt
- 4 large portobello mushroom caps

Direction

- In a medium skillet, heat olive oil on moderate heat. Stir in green bell pepper, onion and garlic, then use salt to season. Cook until vegetables are soft, for 5 minutes.
- Lower heat of skillet to low and put into the skillet with mushroom caps. Cover and cook until soft, for 5 minutes each side.

Nutrition Information

- Calories: 79 calories;
- Total Fat: 3.7
- Sodium: 154
- Total Carbohydrate: 10.3
- Cholesterol: 0
- Protein: 3.5

799. Portobello Mushroom Pasta With Basil

Serving: 4 | Prep: 10mins | Cook: 25mins | Ready in:

Ingredients

- 1 (16 ounce) package farfalle (bow-tie) pasta
- 2 tablespoons olive oil
- 1 pound portobello mushrooms, chopped
- 3 cloves garlic, minced
- 1/4 cup balsamic vinegar
- 1 teaspoon ground black pepper
- 1/2 cup shaved Pecorino Romano cheese
- 1/2 cup chopped fresh basil

Direction

- Bring lightly salted water in a big pot to a boil. Cook at a boil with bow-tie pasta for 12 minutes while stirring sometimes, until cooked through but still firm to the bite. Drain pasta and turn back to the pot.
- While boiling the pasta, in a big nonstick skillet, heat olive oil on moderate heat, then cook and stir in the hot oil with garlic and mushrooms for 10 minutes, until mushrooms are tender. Drizzle into the mushroom mixture with balsamic vinegar while stirring.
- Stir into the pot of pasta with mushroom mixture, and use pepper to season, then stir. Put basil and Pecorino Romano cheese on top.

Nutrition Information

- Calories: 564 calories;
- Protein: 22.9
- Total Fat: 13.7
- Sodium: 196
- Total Carbohydrate: 91.4
- Cholesterol: 15

800. Portobello Mushroom Stroganoff

Serving: 4 | Prep: 10mins | Cook: 20mins | Ready in:

Ingredients

- 3 tablespoons butter
- 1 large onion, chopped
- 3/4 pound portobello mushrooms, sliced
- 1 1/2 cups vegetable broth
- 1 1/2 cups sour cream
- 3 tablespoons all-purpose flour
- 1/4 cup chopped fresh parsley
- 8 ounces dried egg noodles

Direction

- Prepare a large pot of mildly salted and bring it to a boil. Put in egg noodles and cook for 7 minutes until al dente. Take it away from heat, drain, and put aside.
- In the meantime, in a large heavy skillet, melt butter on medium heat. Put in onion, cook and stir until tender. Increase to medium-high heat

and put in sliced mushrooms. Cook until the mushrooms turn brown and limp. Transfer to a bowl and put aside.
- Whisk vegetable broth in the same skillet, stir to make sure no browned bits stays at the bottom of the pan. Boil, cook until mixture has reduced by 1/3. Turn the heat to low and put the onion and mushroom back to the skillet.
- Take the pan away from the heat, stir together flour and sour cream; combine with the mushrooms. Place the skillet back to the heat and continue to cook on low heat, just until the sauce thickens. Mix in parsley and sprinkle with pepper and salt to season. Pour over cooked egg noodles and serve.

Nutrition Information

- Calories: 525 calories;
- Sodium: 295
- Total Carbohydrate: 53.3
- Cholesterol: 101
- Protein: 12.8
- Total Fat: 30.1

801. Portobello Pesto Egg Omelette

Serving: 1 | Prep: 10mins | Cook: 15mins | Ready in:

Ingredients

- 1 teaspoon olive oil
- 1 portobello mushroom cap, sliced
- 1/4 cup chopped red onion
- 4 egg whites
- 1 teaspoon water
- salt and ground black pepper to taste
- 1/4 cup shredded low-fat mozzarella cheese
- 1 teaspoon prepared pesto

Direction

- Over medium heat, heat the olive oil in a skillet. In the heated oil, cook the red onion and portobello mushroom for 3-5 minutes until mushrooms soften.
- Together in a small bowl, whisk water and the egg whites; pour the mixture over the onion and mushroom mix. Add salt and pepper to season the egg whites. Cook and stir occasionally, about 5 minutes, until the egg whites are not runny anymore. Sprinkle the mixture with mozzarella cheese; add the pesto on top. Fold the omelette in half and keep cooking for 2-3 minutes until the cheese melts.

Nutrition Information

- Calories: 259 calories;
- Total Fat: 12
- Sodium: 501
- Total Carbohydrate: 12
- Cholesterol: 19
- Protein: 28

802. Portobello Pot Pie

Serving: 8 | Prep: 30mins | Cook: 1hours | Ready in:

Ingredients

- 2 (9 inch) unbaked pie crusts
- 6 small red potatoes
- 3 tablespoons olive oil
- 1 cup sliced onion
- 1 cup thinly sliced fresh shiitake mushrooms
- 3 1/2 cups water
- 1/4 cup tamari or soy sauce
- 5 tablespoons rice flour
- 2 portobello mushroom caps, cut into bite size pieces
- 1 teaspoon dried thyme
- 2 teaspoons dried sage
- 2 stalks celery, chopped
- 1 carrot, cubed

Direction

- Start preheating oven to 350°F (175°C). Press 1 of pie crusts into and up sides a 9-in. pie plate.
- Boil water in a saucepan. Put in potatoes. Cook for 10-15 mins or until tender. Drain, then cut into cubes. Put aside.
- In large saucepan, heat one tablespoon olive oil over low heat. Put in shiitake mushrooms and onion. Allow mushrooms to sweat with a cover, stirring occasionally, about 7 mins. Add tamari and water. Boil. Then whisk in the rice flour, stirring until no lumps remain. Let simmer.
- In a large skillet, heat the remaining olive oil over medium-high heat. Put in portobello pieces. Briefly sauté until outside of the mushrooms have browned. Put mushrooms into gravy mixture along with potatoes, celery and carrots. Simmer, stirring occasionally, about 10 mins. Season with sage and thyme. Pour into prepared crust. Add other pie crust to cover, then seal by crimping edges. Create a few slits in top of the crust to vent steam.
- Bake in prepared oven for 40 mins or until the crust turns golden brown.

Nutrition Information

- Calories: 418 calories;
- Total Fat: 20.4
- Sodium: 763
- Total Carbohydrate: 51.9
- Cholesterol: 0
- Protein: 8

803. Portobello Stacks

Serving: 4 | Prep: 20mins | Cook: 30mins | Ready in:

Ingredients

- 4 portobello mushrooms
- 1 large onion, sliced 1/4 inch thick
- 1/4 cup balsamic vinegar
- 1 eggplant, sliced into 1/2 inch rounds
- 1 tomato, sliced 1/2 inch thick
- 4 slices provolone cheese

Direction

- In balsamic vinegar, marinate onions and mushrooms for 20 minutes.
- Preheat an oven to 175°C/350°F.
- In 4 stacks, layer cheese, tomato, onion, mushroom and eggplant on a nonstick baking pan.
- In the preheated oven, bake till cheese is golden brown for 30 minutes.

Nutrition Information

- Calories: 195 calories;
- Total Carbohydrate: 21.5
- Cholesterol: 20
- Protein: 12.2
- Total Fat: 8.2
- Sodium: 267

804. Portobello Stuffed Mushroom Burger

Serving: 4 | Prep: 10mins | Cook: 15mins | Ready in:

Ingredients

- vegetable cooking spray
- 4 portobello mushroom caps
- 2 cups fresh spinach leaves
- 1/4 cup shredded aged Cheddar cheese
- 1/4 cup 1% cottage cheese
- 1/8 teaspoon garlic powder
- 1/8 teaspoon salt
- 4 thin, multi-grain hamburger buns

Direction

- Preheat an oven to 200 °C or 400 °F.

- With vegetable spray, coat rounded ends of mushroom caps and put on baking sheet, greased side facing down.
- In microwave-safe bowl, put the spinach, drizzle with several drops of water, and on high, microwave for a minute. Cut cooked spinach; stir with salt, garlic powder, cottage cheese and Cheddar cheese. Onto prepped mushroom caps, spread the spinach mixture.
- In prepped oven, bake for about 12 minutes till mushrooms are soft. Put on hamburger buns and serve.

Nutrition Information

- Calories: 195 calories;
- Sodium: 433
- Total Carbohydrate: 28.4
- Cholesterol: 8
- Protein: 10.4
- Total Fat: 5

805. Portobello, Eggplant, And Roasted Red Pepper Panini

Serving: 4 | Prep: 40mins | Cook: 20mins | Ready in:

Ingredients

- 2 red bell peppers
- 4 portobello mushroom caps
- 1 cup fat-free balsamic vinaigrette
- 4 (1/2 inch thick) slices eggplant, peeled
- 1 teaspoon garlic powder
- 1 teaspoon onion powder
- 2 teaspoons grated Parmesan cheese
- 8 slices focaccia bread
- 1/4 cup fat free ranch dressing
- 4 thin slices Swiss cheese
- 4 thin slices Asiago cheese

Direction

- Set the oven's broiler to preheating. Position the oven rack 6-inches away from the heat source. Use an aluminum foil to line the baking sheet.
- Slice the peppers in half, starting from top to bottom. Remove their seeds, stem, and ribs. Arrange the peppers onto the prepared baking sheet, cut-sides down.
- Cook the peppers under the preheated broiler for 5 minutes until the skin of the peppers turn blistered and blackened. Toss the peppers into the bowl and cover them tightly with a plastic wrap. Let the peppers steam as they cool for 20 minutes. Once the peppers are cool, remove their skins; discard. Refrigerate them overnight.
- In a resealable plastic bag, add the Portobello mushroom caps and drizzle them with the balsamic vinegar. Squeeze any excess air out; seal. Allow them to marinate inside the fridge overnight.
- The next day, follow the manufacturer's instructions on how to preheat the electric double-sided grill, just like the George Foreman® grill. Sprinkle onion powder and garlic powder all over the slices of eggplant.
- Take the Portobello mushrooms out of the marinade. Discard the leftover marinade from the Portobello mushrooms. Cook the mushrooms on the preheated grill for 4-5 minutes until tender. Cook also the slices of eggplant onto the preheated grill for 4-5 minutes until tender. Transfer them onto the plate. Sprinkle them with Parmesan cheese; put aside.
- In assembling the sandwiches, spread the ranch dressing onto each focaccia slice. Set the cheese slice on each bread piece. Distribute the slices of eggplant, a Portobello mushroom, and roasted peppers among the four bread slices. Place the remaining bread on each top.
- Coat the double-sided grill with cooking spray. Cook the sandwiches for 4-5 minutes until they are already hot in the center, the bread turns golden brown, and the cheese has melted.

Nutrition Information

- Calories: 679 calories;
- Total Carbohydrate: 100.5
- Cholesterol: 46
- Protein: 28.1
- Total Fat: 19
- Sodium: 1779

806. Potato Casserole

Serving: 12 | Prep: 15mins | Cook: 1hours10mins | Ready in:

Ingredients

- 1 (30 ounce) package frozen hash brown potatoes
- 2 cups shredded Cheddar cheese
- 1 (16 ounce) container sour cream
- 1 (10.75 ounce) can condensed cream of mushroom soup
- 1 onion, chopped
- 1 cup butter
- 3 cups crushed corn flakes

Direction

- Preheat oven to 425° F (220° C).
- In a lightly greased 9x13 - inch pan, add the hash browns. In a big bowl, whisk the soup, sour cream and cheese.
- In a large frying pan, mix the onion with a stick of butter over medium heat, then sauté for about 5 minutes. Transfer to the soup mixture and scatter on potatoes in the dish.
- In the dish, place the crushed corn flakes all over. Melt the leftover stick of butter and scatter equally over the corn flakes.
- Bake at 425° F (220° C) for 60 minutes.

Nutrition Information

- Calories: 400 calories;
- Total Fat: 35.5
- Sodium: 483
- Total Carbohydrate: 23.1
- Cholesterol: 77
- Protein: 8.5

807. Potato Ginger Soup

Serving: 6 | Prep: 10mins | Cook: 20mins | Ready in:

Ingredients

- 3 large potatoes, sliced
- 4 cups chicken broth
- 1 pound fresh mushrooms, chopped
- 3 tablespoons grated fresh ginger root
- pepper to taste
- 1/4 cup chopped green onion

Direction

- Combine potatoes, mushrooms, chicken broth and ginger in a large pot. Boil, cook for 20 mins. Add pepper to season. Working in batches, puree with a blender or in pan with an immersion blender. Enjoy hot, decorated with the green onions.

Nutrition Information

- Calories: 162 calories;
- Sodium: 16
- Total Carbohydrate: 35.5
- Cholesterol: 0
- Protein: 6.2
- Total Fat: 0.5

808. Potsticker Salad

Serving: 6 | Prep: 15mins | Cook: 20mins | Ready in:

Ingredients

- 1 (10 ounce) package egg noodles
- 12 frozen vegetable potstickers
- 2 tablespoons vegetable oil
- 2 tablespoons water
- 1/2 cup water chestnuts, drained and sliced
- 1/2 cup baby corn
- 1 carrot, shredded
- 1 (15 ounce) can straw mushrooms
- 1/2 cup Thai peanut sauce
- 1/4 cup chopped roasted peanuts

Direction

- Boil water in a large pot and cook egg noodles until al dente or in 5-7 minutes. Drain well and put it aside.
- On medium heat, put on a large frying pan and heat oil. Add potstickers to cook with 1 or 2 turns until they become golden brown. Pour water into the pan; decrease the heat to low and continue cooking with cover until the liquid has evaporated or for another 3 minutes. Put it under cold water to rinse; drain and cut into halves.
- Combine potstickers, noodles, peanut sauce, mushrooms, carrot, baby corn and water chestnuts in a large mixing bowl. Let it chill in 1 hour. Add peanuts on top to serve.

Nutrition Information

- Calories: 408 calories;
- Protein: 15.5
- Total Fat: 13.3
- Sodium: 804
- Total Carbohydrate: 59.9
- Cholesterol: 34

809. Prime Rib With Au Jus

Serving: 20 | Prep: 20mins | Cook: 2hours10mins | Ready in:

Ingredients

- 1 (10 pound) boneless prime rib roast
- 1 cup butter, softened
- 2 1/2 cups coarse kosher salt
- 1 tablespoon chopped fresh tarragon
- 1 teaspoon ground allspice
- 1 teaspoon freshly ground black pepper
- Au Jus:
- 1 tablespoon olive oil
- 1 tablespoon butter
- 2 large onions, chopped
- 2 pounds baby bella mushrooms, chopped
- 4 cups water
- 2 tablespoons beef broth base (such as Orrington Farms®)

Direction

- Preheat an oven to 260°C/500°F. Put a rack on a shallow roasting pan.
- Use 1 cup softened butter to coat the whole roast; put roast on rack, fat-side up.
- Mix black pepper, allspice, tarragon and salt in a bowl; rub roast with salt mixture all over.
- In preheated oven, bake roast for approximately 50 minutes till outside is browned and crisp. Lower oven temperature to 175°C/350°F; keep baking roast for 35-40 minutes till the internal temperature is 65°C/150°F.
- Take roast out of the oven. Scoop juices from the pan into a small bowl. Put aside. Use aluminum foil to cover and allow to rest before cutting for 15 – 20 minutes.
- Heat 1 tbsp. butter and olive oil in a big saucepan on medium heat. Add onions; cook for about 5 minutes till golden brown. Add mushrooms; cook for approximately 10 minutes till tender. Mix in reserved pan juices, beef broth base and water; simmer for 30-45 minutes till flavors merge. Serve au jus alongside the roast.

Nutrition Information

- Calories: 410 calories;
- Total Fat: 32

- Sodium: 11828
- Total Carbohydrate: 3.1
- Cholesterol: 107
- Protein: 27.1

810. Pumpkin Lasagna

Serving: 10 | Prep: 35mins | Cook: 40mins | Ready in:

Ingredients

- 1 tablespoon minced fresh sage, divided
- 2 teaspoons salt, divided
- 1 teaspoon ground black pepper, divided
- 1/2 teaspoon ground nutmeg
- 1/2 teaspoon ground cloves
- 2 tablespoons olive oil
- 1 1/2 pounds sliced baby bella mushrooms
- 1 large onion, diced
- 2 cloves garlic, minced
- 3 cups pumpkin puree, divided
- 1 1/2 cups heavy whipping cream, divided
- 1 1/2 cups grated Parmesan cheese
- cooking spray
- 12 lasagna noodles
- 1 cup ricotta cheese
- 1 cup shredded mozzarella cheese
- 1 dash ground nutmeg
- 1 dash ground cloves
- 2 tablespoons butter, cut in small pieces

Direction

- Heat oven to 200°C (400°F).
- Combine black pepper, sage, salt, 1/2 teaspoon cloves and half tsp. nutmeg in a little bowl to make a spice mixture.
- Warm olive oil on medium-high heat in a big skillet. Cook in oil garlic, mushrooms, half of spice mixture and onion; stir and cook until mushrooms are soft, and all liquid has disappeared, 5 minutes.
- Mix 3/4 cup heavy cream, 2 cups pumpkin puree, remaining spice mixture and half cup Parmesan cheese in a bowl.
- Use cooking spray to grease a 9x 13-in. baking dish. Layer with 4 noodles overlapping slightly, 1/2 of pumpkin mixture, half the mushroom mixture, half cup ricotta, and half cup mozzarella cheese. Repeat layering again. Put the last 4 pasta noodles on the top.
- Mix the left 3/4 cup heavy cream, left one cup pumpkin puree, one dash of cloves and one dash of nutmeg. Pour on top of pasta noodles. Finish with the last one cup of Parmesan on top. Spot with butter and use foil to cover.
- Bake in the oven, 20 minutes. Remove the foil and bake until bubbling, 15 more minutes.

Nutrition Information

- Calories: 401 calories;
- Total Fat: 24.7
- Sodium: 932
- Total Carbohydrate: 33
- Cholesterol: 73
- Protein: 15.1

811. Pumpkin Ravioli With Crispy Margherita® Prosciutto

Serving: 2 | Prep: 8mins | Cook: 25mins | Ready in:

Ingredients

- 1 ounce pignoli (pine nuts)
- 1/2 pound pumpkin or butternut squash ravioli
- 1/2 cup extra virgin olive oil
- 1 clove garlic, sliced thin
- 1/3 cup sliced fresh mushrooms
- 1/4 cup Margherita® Prosciutto
- 1 tablespoon amaretto liqueur
- 3 tablespoons unsalted butter
- 1 1/2 cups chicken stock
- 4 leaves fresh sage

Direction

- Preheat the oven to 350°. On a cookie tray, put the pine nuts, put in the oven for 5 to 8 minutes at 350 till browned lightly.
- Individually, put ravioli in big pot of boiling water, cook following package instruction for 8 to 10 minutes. Sift out with big draining.
- Individually, sauté mushrooms, garlic and olive oil in sauce pan for 1 to 2 minutes. Put in Margherita(R) Prosciutto.
- Sauté till prosciutto and garlic are light brown then put in Amaretto, letting it to burn off/flame, then put in the butter.
- When butter is liquefied, put chicken stock in. Lower heat and allow to simmer for 2 to 3 minutes. Take off heat and put baked pinoli nuts.
- Ladle sauce out onto ravioli in pasta dish, jazz up with fresh sage or fry sage leaves to crispy.

Nutrition Information

- Calories: 4250 calories;
- Total Fat: 131
- Sodium: 2652
- Total Carbohydrate: 584.8
- Cholesterol: 541
- Protein: 173.7

812. Purple Yam Pancakes

Serving: 6 | Prep: 20mins | Cook: 45mins | Ready in:

Ingredients

- Spicy Mushroom Sauce:
- 1 tablespoon vegetable oil
- 12 large mushrooms, finely chopped
- 1/2 large onion, chopped
- 2 tablespoons butter
- 6 large tomatoes
- 1 large bell pepper, cut into chunks
- 1/2 large onion
- 5 large fresh hot chile peppers, stemmed
- 2 pickled jalapeno peppers
- 1 cup chopped fresh parsley
- 1/2 cup chopped fresh cilantro
- 2 cloves garlic
- 1 cube vegetable bouillon (such as Maggi®)
- 1 teaspoon dried thyme
- 1 teaspoon ground cumin
- 1 teaspoon cayenne pepper
- 1 pinch salt and freshly ground black pepper to taste (optional)
- 1 1/4 cups vegetable broth
- 2 tablespoons dark soy sauce
- water as needed
- Pancakes:
- 3 purple yams, cut into wedges
- 2 cups all-purpose flour
- 1 onion
- 2 eggs
- 2 teaspoons salt
- 1 teaspoon garlic powder
- 1 red bell pepper, chopped
- 1 teaspoon paprika
- 1 teaspoon chile powder
- 1 teaspoon ground black pepper
- 1 tablespoon vegetable oil, or to taste
- 1/2 pound ground beef
- 1/2 pound ground chicken

Direction

- In skillet, heat a tablespoon of oil over moderately-low heat. Cook and mix mushrooms and half chopped onion for 5 to 10 minutes till tender and clear. Put the butter.
- In blender, mix garlic, cilantro, parsley, jalapeno peppers, chili peppers, onion, bell pepper chunks and tomatoes; process till nearly smooth.
- To skillet of mushrooms, mix black pepper, salt, cayenne pepper, cumin, thyme, vegetable bouillon cube and blended tomato mixture and mix till thoroughly incorporated. Put sufficient water, soy sauce and vegetable broth to create sauce. Place cover and let simmer for 30 to 35 minutes till sauce has thickens.
- In food processor bowl, mix garlic powder, 2 teaspoons salt, eggs, 1 onion, flour and purple yams; pulse till combined. Into batter, fold the

red bell pepper with spatula and add 1 teaspoon of black pepper, chili powder and paprika to season. Stir till well incorporated.
- In skillet, heat a tablespoon of oil over moderately-high heat. Onto skillet, drop the batter by big spoonfuls. Over every pancake, scoop some ground chicken and some ground beef; top with several additional spoonfuls of batter. Let pancakes cook for 3 to 5 minutes till equally browned. Turn and cook for 2 to 3 minutes till browned on another side. Place cover on skillet and cook pancakes on low heat for 5 minutes till chicken and beef are cooked completely. Redo with the rest of batter. Serve along with mushroom sauce.

Nutrition Information

- Calories: 640 calories;
- Cholesterol: 118
- Protein: 30.6
- Total Fat: 19.1
- Sodium: 1470
- Total Carbohydrate: 91.8

813. Quiche Au Chou Romanesco (Romanesco And Mushroom Quiche)

Serving: 8 | Prep: 15mins | Cook: 48mins | Ready in:

Ingredients

- 1 sheet frozen puff pastry, thawed
- 1 cup Romanesco cauliflower florets
- 1 1/2 tablespoons butter
- 1 1/2 cups sliced fresh mushrooms
- 1 tablespoon fresh oregano leaves
- salt and ground black pepper to taste
- 2 tablespoons water (optional)
- 3 eggs
- 1/2 cup milk
- 2 tablespoons milk
- 1/2 cup heavy whipping cream
- 2 tablespoons heavy whipping cream
- 3/4 cup shredded Swiss cheese
- 1 tablespoon shredded Swiss cheese

Direction

- Set the oven at 4250F (2200C). Line parchment paper on a 9-inch quiche pan.
- In the quiche pan, press puff pastry and trim to fit the pan. Use a folk to prick pastry and refrigerate it.
- Boil water in a pot and add Romanesco florets, cook for 3 minutes or until crisp-tender. Drain.
- In a big pan, melt butter over medium heat. Add mushrooms; cook and stir for 5 minutes or until lightly browned. Mix in pepper, salt, oregano and drained Romanesco florets. Cook for 5 minutes or until florets look tender, if they start to stick, add more water.
- In a large bowl, beat eggs. Whisk in 1/2 cup plus 2 tablespoons heavy cream and 1/2 cup plus 2 tablespoons milk. Mix in mushroom mixture. In the pan, pour over pastry. Top with 3/4 cup plus 1 tablespoon Swiss cheese.
- Bake in the prepared oven for 30 minutes or until pastry is golden and quiche is set.

Nutrition Information

- Calories: 334 calories;
- Protein: 9.2
- Total Fat: 25.9
- Sodium: 176
- Total Carbohydrate: 16.9
- Cholesterol: 113

814. Quick Chick

Serving: 4 | Prep: 10mins | Cook: 25mins | Ready in:

Ingredients

- 1/2 tablespoon vegetable oil

- 2 skinless, boneless chicken breast halves - cut into 1 inch pieces
- 1 cup chopped celery
- 2 onions, sliced, separated into rings
- 1 (4.5 ounce) can mushrooms, with liquid
- 2 tablespoons soy sauce
- 1 teaspoon vegetable oil

Direction

- Heat oil on medium high heat in a medium skillet; sauté chicken till all sides are browned well. Mix in soy sauce, mushrooms with liquid, onions and celery; cover skillet. Boil; lower heat to low. Simmer till chicken is cooked through and celery is tender for 15 minutes.

Nutrition Information

- Calories: 129 calories;
- Protein: 15.5
- Total Fat: 3.8
- Sodium: 649
- Total Carbohydrate: 8.2
- Cholesterol: 34

815. Quick Ground Beef Stroganoff

Serving: 8 | Prep: 15mins | Cook: 24mins | Ready in:

Ingredients

- 1 1/2 pounds ground beef
- 1 (8 ounce) package sliced fresh mushrooms
- 1 small onion, diced
- 4 cloves garlic, minced
- 1 (8 ounce) package wide egg noodles
- 1/4 cup all-purpose flour
- 1 (10.5 ounce) can beef consomme
- 1/2 cup white wine
- 1 tablespoon Dijon mustard
- 2 teaspoons Worcestershire sauce
- 1 cup sour cream

Direction

- In a large skillet over medium heat, combine ground beef with garlic, onion, and mushrooms. Cook for about 7 minutes, stirring, until onions and mushrooms are softened and beef turns brown. Drain and discard drippings from the skillet.
- Bring a big pot of lightly salted water to a rolling boil. Put in egg noodles and bring back to a boil. Cook noodles without covering for about 6 minutes, stirring once in a while, until tender but al dente. Drain off water.
- Mix flour into the skillet with beef until beef is well coated. Add wine and consommé; heat to a boil. Turn heat to medium-low. Add Worcestershire sauce and mustard. Mix in sour cream and cook, about 1 minute longer, until thoroughly heated. Spoon over cooked noodles to serve.

Nutrition Information

- Calories: 399 calories;
- Total Carbohydrate: 28
- Cholesterol: 88
- Protein: 22
- Total Fat: 20.6
- Sodium: 327

816. Quick Mushroom Ceviche

Serving: 6 | Prep: 15mins | Cook: | Ready in:

Ingredients

- 6 (4 ounce) jars sliced mushrooms, drained
- 1 small white onion, chopped
- 1/2 cup chopped cilantro leaves
- 1/2 cup ketchup
- 3 limes, juiced

- salt to taste
- 2 avocados - peeled, pitted, and chopped

Direction

- In a glass bowl, mix together cilantro, onion, and mushrooms. Add lime juice and ketchup, mix thoroughly. Use salt to season. Refrigerate for 30 minutes. Use chopped avocado to drizzle before eating.

Nutrition Information

- Calories: 171 calories;
- Cholesterol: 0
- Protein: 4.3
- Total Fat: 10.3
- Sodium: 739
- Total Carbohydrate: 21.3

817. Quick And Easy Greek Spaghetti

Serving: 4 | Prep: 15mins | Cook: 40mins | Ready in:

Ingredients

- 1 (8 ounce) package spaghetti
- extra-virgin olive oil, or as needed
- 1 (10 ounce) bag fresh spinach
- 1 (8 ounce) package sliced fresh mushrooms
- 1/4 cup red wine vinegar
- 1/4 cup balsamic vinegar
- 2 (14.5 ounce) cans diced tomatoes
- 1/4 cup chopped fresh basil
- 1 tablespoon chopped fresh parsley
- 1 (6 ounce) can sliced black olives, drained (optional)
- 2 ounces crumbled feta cheese, or to taste

Direction

- Allow lightly salted water in a big pot to come to a rolling boil. At a boil, cook spaghetti for 12 minutes until soft yet firm to the bite, tossing sometimes. Strain and put aside.
- In a big saucepan, heat olive oil over medium heat. In the hot oil, stir and cook mushrooms and spinach for 10 minutes until they release their liquid. Add balsamic vinegar and red wine vinegar, boil it. Mix black olives, parsley, basil and tomatoes into the boiling mixture, keep stirring and cooking for another 10 minutes until the flavors combine.
- Stir into the tomato mixture with the cooked spaghetti and lower the heat to medium-low. Simmer the sauce and pasta for 8-10 minutes until the flavors combine, mix feta cheese into the pasta. Sprinkle additional feta cheese over and enjoy.

Nutrition Information

- Calories: 413 calories;
- Total Fat: 11.7
- Sodium: 1095
- Total Carbohydrate: 60.7
- Cholesterol: 13
- Protein: 16.1

818. Quinoa Chard Pilaf

Serving: 8 | Prep: 20mins | Cook: 20mins | Ready in:

Ingredients

- 1 tablespoon olive oil
- 1 onion, diced
- 3 cloves garlic, minced
- 2 cups uncooked quinoa, rinsed
- 1 cup canned lentils, rinsed
- 8 ounces fresh mushrooms, chopped
- 1 quart vegetable broth
- 1 bunch Swiss chard, stems removed

Direction

- On medium heat, heat oil in a big pot; mix in garlic and onion. Sauté for 5mins until the onion is tender. Stir in mushrooms, lentils, and quinoa; add broth then cover. Cook for 20mins.
- Take off from heat. Shred the chard and stir it into the pot gently; cover. Let it stand for 5mins until the chard wilts.

Nutrition Information

- Calories: 224 calories;
- Total Carbohydrate: 36.6
- Cholesterol: 0
- Protein: 9.6
- Total Fat: 4.7
- Sodium: 323

819. Quinoa Mushroom 'Risotto'

Serving: 4 | Prep: 20mins | Cook: 30mins | Ready in:

Ingredients

- 2 cups water
- 1 cup quinoa
- 1 tablespoon coconut oil
- 1 teaspoon chicken bouillon granules
- 2 tablespoons coconut oil
- 4 cups sliced crimini ('baby bella') mushrooms
- 1/2 large yellow onion, thinly sliced
- 1 large red bell pepper, seeded and thinly sliced
- salt to taste
- 1/4 cup red wine
- 2 tablespoons soy sauce
- 1/4 cup grated Parmesan cheese, or to taste (optional)

Direction

- In a saucepan, combine chicken bouillon granules, 1 tablespoon coconut oil, quinoa, and water; boil it. Lower the heat to medium-low, and simmer for 15 minutes until you can see white threads on the quinoa grains.
- In a skillet, heat 2 tablespoons coconut oil over medium-high heat. Sauté red bell pepper, onion, and mushrooms in the hot oil for 5-7 minutes until tender. Use salt to season.
- Mix soy sauce and red wine into the vegetable mixture; simmer it, lower the heat to medium-low, and cook for 10 minutes until the liquid has decreased.
- In a big serving bowl, combine vegetables and quinoa; put Parmesan cheese on top.

Nutrition Information

- Calories: 338 calories;
- Cholesterol: 4
- Protein: 13.4
- Total Fat: 14.7
- Sodium: 705
- Total Carbohydrate: 35.9

820. Rabbit Loin Cigars

Serving: 1 | Prep: 15mins | Cook: 23mins | Ready in:

Ingredients

- 2 teaspoons vegetable oil
- 1 cup morel mushrooms
- 1 teaspoon minced shallot
- salt and pepper to taste
- 1/4 sheet frozen puff pastry, thawed
- 3 spears white asparagus, trimmed
- 1/2 cup beef or veal demiglace
- 1 tablespoon butter
- 6 ounces rabbit loin
- 1 egg yolk, beaten

Direction

- Pre heat oven to 175 degrees C (350 degrees F). Use the parchment paper to line the baking sheet.
- Heat oil on medium high heat in a small-sized skillet. Put in pepper, salt, shallot and mushrooms. Cook and whisk for 5-10 minutes till mushrooms break down into a paste. Take out of the heat and let it cool down slightly.
- Lay sheet of the puff pastry out onto a clean working surface and roll out to fit rabbit loin's length. Spread over the surface with mushroom paste. Add rabbit loin onto middle and arrange asparagus alongside the rabbit. Roll pastry around asparagus and rabbit into one tight-closed cylinder, pinching ends to seal. Add onto prepped baking sheet, and use the egg yolk to brush pastry's top.
- Bake in the preheated oven for 10-13 minutes till pastry turns deep golden-brown. Take out of oven and allow it to stand for 5 minutes. Meat should have the internal temperature of no less than 65 degrees C (145 degrees F).
- When rabbit is cooking, heat demi-glace on medium heat in a small-sized skillet. Once becoming melted and hot, whisk in butter till the butter melts and then take out of the heat.
- To serve, halve the pastry crosswise, and put into middle of a serving plate. Sprinkle sauce around the plate.

Nutrition Information

- Calories: 845 calories;
- Total Fat: 57.1
- Sodium: 335
- Total Carbohydrate: 38.9
- Cholesterol: 323
- Protein: 44.7

821. Rachel's Turkey Loaf

Serving: 6 | Prep: 15mins | Cook: 1hours | Ready in:

Ingredients

- 1 pound ground turkey
- 2 eggs, lightly beaten
- 1/2 cup chopped fresh mushrooms (optional)
- 1 1/2 cups Italian seasoned bread crumbs
- 1 (1 ounce) envelope dry onion soup mix
- 2/3 cup ready-to-serve creamy tomato soup, divided
- 1/4 cup ketchup, divided
- 1/4 cup barbeque sauce, divided
- 2 tablespoons Worcestershire sauce, divided
- chili powder to taste

Direction

- Set the oven to 350°F (175°C) and start preheating.
- Mix a tablespoon Worcestershire sauce, 2 tablespoons barbeque sauce, 2 tablespoons ketchup, 1/3 cup creamy tomato soup, soup mix, bread crumbs, mushrooms, eggs and turkey in a bowl. Mold the mixture into a loaf shape; transfer to a baking dish. Top with chili powder.
- Mix the rest of each of Worcestershire sauce, barbeque sauce, ketchup and creamy tomato soup in another bowl. Put aside.
- Bake loaf in the prepared oven for 45 minutes. Pour sauce on top; keep baking 15 minutes until it reaches a minimum internal temperature of 165°F (74°C).

Nutrition Information

- Calories: 308 calories;
- Total Fat: 9.5
- Sodium: 1282
- Total Carbohydrate: 34
- Cholesterol: 118
- Protein: 22.2

822. Ravioli Soup

Serving: 4 | Prep: 10mins | Cook: 10mins | Ready in:

Ingredients

- 2 cups water
- 1 cube chicken bouillon
- 1 pound prepared fresh cheese ravioli
- 2/3 cup baby spinach leaves
- 2 fresh mushrooms, sliced
- 1/4 cup sliced carrot
- 1/2 cup frozen mixed peas and carrots
- 1 tablespoon olive oil
- 1 dash soy sauce
- salt and black pepper to taste

Direction

- Boil bouillon cube and water in a big saucepan. In the pot, put ravioli and cook for 5 minutes, mixing from time to time. Add in soy sauce, olive oil, frozen peas and carrots, carrot, mushrooms and spinach; allow to cook for 5 minutes till vegetables are soft. Put salt and pepper to season.

Nutrition Information

- Calories: 319 calories;
- Total Fat: 11.9
- Sodium: 517
- Total Carbohydrate: 40
- Cholesterol: 45
- Protein: 14.2

823. Refreshing Salad With Grilled Oyster Mushrooms

Serving: 4 | Prep: 15mins | Cook: 5mins | Ready in:

Ingredients

- 16 ounces fresh oyster mushrooms, stemmed and sliced
- 1/4 cup olive oil, divided
- salt to taste
- 1 cucumber, halved and sliced
- 2 tomatoes, halved and quartered
- 1 onion, sliced and separated into rings
- 1 green bell pepper, seeded and sliced
- 2 carrots, shredded
- 1 avocado, cut into 1/2-inch chunks
- 2 tablespoons fresh lemon juice, or to taste

Direction

- Put the rack of the oven approximately 6-in. from the heat source and turn on the oven's broiler to preheat.
- In a bowl, combine mushrooms with 1 pinch of salt and 2 tablespoons olive oil. Put in an oven-safe pan.
- Put in the preheated oven and broil for 5-10 minutes until crunchy, checking frequently.
- In a big serving bowl, mix together avocado, carrots, green bell pepper, onion, tomatoes, and cucumber; mix lightly.
- Add lemon juice and the leftover olive oil to the salad, then sprinkle salt over to taste. Mix to blend.
- Top the salad with mushrooms; mix again.

Nutrition Information

- Calories: 312 calories;
- Total Fat: 22.2
- Sodium: 80
- Total Carbohydrate: 25.2
- Cholesterol: 0
- Protein: 6.8

824. Restaurant Style Shoyu Miso Ramen

Serving: 4 | Prep: 15mins | Cook: 4hours30mins | Ready in:

Ingredients

- 1/4 cup dried black fungus
- 2 cups mirin

- 1 1/4 cups soy sauce, divided
- 1/2 cup brown sugar
- 6 green onion bulbs, chopped, divided
- 1/2 onion, coarsely chopped
- 6 cloves garlic, peeled
- 2 pounds skin-on, boneless pork belly
- butcher's twine
- 4 eggs
- 2 tablespoons brown sugar
- 1/2 cup miso paste
- 4 (3 ounce) packages ramen noodles, or to taste
- 4 sheets nori (dry seaweed), quartered
- 1 naruto (fish paste stick with a red spiral pattern). sliced

Direction

- Preheat an oven to 135°C/275°F.
- In a big bowl, put black fungus and use water to fill.
- In an oven-safe pot, mix garlic, chopped onion, 3 green onion bulbs, 1/2 cup brown sugar, 1/2 cup soy sauce and mirin on high heat; boil.
- On flat work surface, put pork bell, skin-side down. Lengthwise, roll up. Use butcher's twine to wrap. In pot, put pork belly with the mirin mixture. Use a lid to partially cover.
- In preheated oven, bake for about 4 hours till an inserted instant-read thermometer in the middle reads 63°C/145°F and pork is tender.
- Boil another pot of water on high heat. Put eggs into pot gently. Cook for 8-10 minutes till yolks are barely set. Put eggs into bowl with ice water. Let eggs sit for about 1 minute. Take out of water; peel eggs.
- In a container, put 2 tbsp. brown sugar, 1/2 cup soy sauce, 1 cup water and eggs. Dampen a paper towel in mixture. Cover container with damp paper towel. Refrigerate for 4 hours up to overnight.
- Drain fungus. Put into liquid in pot with pork belly. Put lid on. Refrigerate for 4 hours to overnight.
- From top of pork belly mixture, skim fungus. Put into pot that has 8 cups water. The fungus has to be covered in pork belly fat. Put in miso paste and 1/4 cup soy sauce; boil.
- Use a knife to remove pork belly skin. Chop meat to pieces to your preferred thickness. Lengthwise, slice eggs in half.
- Boil another pot of water. In boiling water, cook ramen, occasionally mixing, for about 3 minutes till noodles are tender but firm to chew; drain.
- Diagonally in each bowl's corner, put 4 slices of nori. Put noodles on the top. In separate corners, put several pork belly slices and 2 egg halves. Use black fungus to cover. Put green onions on top. Put broth in. Put several naruto slices in every bowl. Before serving, let sit for about 3 minutes.

Nutrition Information

- Calories: 1104 calories;
- Protein: 47.1
- Total Fat: 43.5
- Sodium: 7959
- Total Carbohydrate: 103.1
- Cholesterol: 283

825. Rice So Nice

Serving: 4 | Prep: 5mins | Cook: 1hours | Ready in:

Ingredients

- 1 cup long grain white rice
- 1/2 cup butter
- 1 (10.5 ounce) can beef broth
- 1 (10.5 ounce) can condensed French onion soup
- 1 (4 ounce) can sliced mushrooms

Direction

- Heat an oven to 190°C or 375°F.
- Place the rice in an oven-safe, medium bowl. Add in French onion soup and beef broth.

- Transfer the mushrooms can contents into bowl, and put in butter stick without mixing. Use an oven-safe plate, lid or foil as bowl cover.
- Bake in prepped oven, about an hour. Take bowl out of oven and mix. Rest for several minutes prior to serving.

Nutrition Information

- Calories: 437 calories;
- Cholesterol: 64
- Protein: 7.1
- Total Fat: 24.8
- Sodium: 1170
- Total Carbohydrate: 47

826. Rich Viennese Potato Soup

Serving: 8 | Prep: 15mins | Cook: 45mins | Ready in:

Ingredients

- 7 cups plus 3 tablespoons beef broth OR chicken broth, divided
- 2 cups onion, sliced
- 2 1/2 cups sliced leeks
- 1 1/2 teaspoons dried marjoram
- 8 cups russet potatoes, peeled and cubed
- 3/4 cup heavy cream
- 1/2 teaspoon ground black pepper
- 1 pinch ground cardamom
- 1/2 pound fresh mushrooms, sliced
- salt and pepper to taste
- 1/2 cup chopped and precooked carrots
- 1 cup cooked and diced potatoes

Direction

- In a big, non-stick pot, put 2 tablespoons of broth and 1 tablespoon of oil over medium heat. Add marjoram, leeks, and onions and sauté until the vegetables are soft, or for about 15 minutes.
- Add 7 cups of broth and potatoes, lower the heat to low, put a cover on and bring to a simmer for 25 minutes. Add cardamom, ground black pepper, and heavy cream. Working in small batches, puree the soup in a food processor or a blender.
- In a big frying pan, sauté the leftover 1 tablespoon of broth and mushrooms over medium heat until the mushrooms turn golden and the liquid has evaporated. Use pepper and salt to season to taste. Add the pre-cooked potatoes, pre-cooked carrots, and mushrooms to the pureed soup. Mix together and enjoy.

Nutrition Information

- Calories: 265 calories;
- Total Carbohydrate: 39.7
- Cholesterol: 31
- Protein: 8.1
- Total Fat: 9.1
- Sodium: 723

827. Risotto Ai Funghi Porcini In Pentola A Pressione (Porcini Mushroom Risotto)

Serving: 4 | Prep: 15mins | Cook: 30mins | Ready in:

Ingredients

- 4 ounces fresh porcini mushrooms
- 3 cups beef stock
- 1/4 cup extra-virgin olive oil, divided
- 1 clove garlic, crushed
- 1 cup white wine, divided
- 1 bunch fresh parsley, chopped, divided
- salt to taste
- 1 spring onion, finely sliced
- 1 1/2 cups Arborio rice

- 3/4 cup grated Parmesan cheese
- 2 tablespoons butter

Direction

- Use a vegetable brush or a clean cloth to remove dirt from the porcini mushrooms. Cut into bite sized pieces.
- In a saucepan, heat beef stock on low power; cover and keep warm.
- In a skillet, heat 2 tbsp. olive oil on medium heat. Sauté garlic for a minute until lightly golden. Add the mushrooms and cook for 2-3 minutes until soft. Add half cup wine and cook for 3-5 minutes until the alcohol evaporates. Keep cooking for another 10 minutes until the mushrooms are soft but firm; pour a little beef stock if it becomes too dry.
- Turn off heat; add salt and half of the parsley over the mushroom. Season with salt. Put a lid on and keep warm.
- In a stovetop pressure cooker, heat the remaining 2 tbsp. olive oil. Sauté spring onion for a minute until soft. Add and cook Arborio rice for 2-3 minutes until coated in oil and toasted; stir. Turn the heat up and add the remaining half cup wine. Let it simmer for 2 minutes until the rice absorbs most of the wine and the alcohol evaporates.
- Pour the beef stock in the pressure cooker. Secure lid following the cooker's manual and turn heat to high. Cook for about 5 minutes until it whistles. Lower heat to low and cook for 4 minutes.
- Remove cooker off heat and relieve pressure in accordance with the cooker's manual; uncover. Mix 1-2 tbsp. cooking liquid to mushroom mixture, butter and Parmesan cheese with the rice. Set aside for 2-3 minutes. Top with the remaining parsley.

Nutrition Information

- Calories: 644 calories;
- Total Fat: 25
- Sodium: 389
- Total Carbohydrate: 75.8
- Cholesterol: 28
- Protein: 15.9

828. Roast Beef Tenderloin

Serving: 6 | Prep: 15mins | Cook: 1hours5mins | Ready in:

Ingredients

- 1/3 cup dried porcini mushrooms
- 1 cup warm water
- 2 1/2 pounds trimmed beef tenderloin roast, tied
- salt and ground black pepper to taste
- 1 tablespoon vegetable oil
- 1 tablespoon unsalted butter
- 1/2 cup sliced shallots
- 1 pinch salt
- 1/4 cup tarragon vinegar
- 1 cup veal stock
- 1/4 cup heavy cream
- 1 tablespoon unsalted butter
- 1 tablespoon chopped fresh tarragon
- salt and ground black pepper to taste

Direction

- Mix water and porcini mushrooms in a bowl and let it soak for an hour until soft. Drain and keep the liquid. Dice and set the mushrooms and put the reserved liquid aside.
- Preheat the oven to 165 degrees Celsius or 325 degrees Fahrenheit.
- Generously season the beef with pepper and salt. In a big ovenproof skillet, heat vegetable oil on high heat. Put the beef in the skillet and cook for 5-8 minutes on each side, until all sides are brown.
- Bring the heat down to medium and mix in a tablespoon of butter, a pinch of salt, and shallots and cook for 5-7 minutes until shallots become translucent and soft.
- Place tarragon vinegar in the skillet and bring it to a boil and scrape browned bits off the

bottom. Mix until the liquid reduces to half for 2-4 minutes.
- Place in 1/2 cup of reserved mushroom liquid, pepper, salt, mushrooms, cream, and veal stock then mix. Bring the beef back into the skillet.
- Roast it in the heated oven for around 45 minutes until the meat becomes medium rare. An instant-read thermometer inserted in the center should read 54 degrees Celsius or 130 degrees Fahrenheit. Move the meat to a plate and loosely tent it with foil. Put the skillet on high heat and let the pan juices boil.
- Mix in tarragon and a tablespoon of butter and use pepper and salt to season. Bring the tenderloin back with any built-up juices to the skillet and serve.

Nutrition Information

- Calories: 489 calories;
- Cholesterol: 173
- Protein: 56.8
- Total Fat: 25
- Sodium: 149
- Total Carbohydrate: 5.8

829. Roasted Eggplant And Mushrooms

Serving: 2 | Prep: 10mins | Cook: 45mins | Ready in:

Ingredients

- 1 medium eggplant, peeled and cubed
- 2 small zucchini, cubed
- 1/2 small yellow onion, chopped
- 1 (8 ounce) package mushrooms, sliced
- 1 1/2 tablespoons tomato paste
- 1/2 cup water
- 1 clove garlic, minced
- 1/2 teaspoon dried basil
- salt and pepper to taste

Direction

- Set the oven to 230°C or 450°F.
- In a 2-qt. casserole dish, add mushrooms, onion, zucchini and eggplant. Mix together water and tomato paste in a small bowl, then stir in pepper, salt, basil and garlic. Drizzle over the vegetables and blend well.
- In the preheated oven, bake until eggplant is softened while stirring from time to time, or for 45 minutes. If the vegetables start to stick, put in additional water as needed, however, vegetables should be fairly dry, with lightly browned edges.

Nutrition Information

- Calories: 118 calories;
- Total Fat: 1.1
- Sodium: 111
- Total Carbohydrate: 25.8
- Cholesterol: 0
- Protein: 6.6

830. Roasted Mushroom And Sunchoke Bisque

Serving: 6 | Prep: 20mins | Cook: 1hours20mins | Ready in:

Ingredients

- 2 pounds Jerusalem artichokes, scrubbed and sliced 1/3-inch thick
- 1 large Yukon Gold potato, diced
- 6 large cloves garlic
- 2 tablespoons olive oil, divided
- sea salt and freshly ground black pepper to taste
- 8 ounces mushrooms, sliced
- 2 tablespoons vegan margarine
- 1 large onion, diced
- 1 teaspoon sea salt
- 2 cups water

- 6 cups mushroom broth
- 1 tablespoon chopped fresh sage
- 1/2 cup soy milk (optional)

Direction

- Preheat the oven to 220°C or 425°Fahrenheit.
- In a big bowl, mix a tablespoon of olive oil, Jerusalem artichokes, garlic, and potatoes together; sprinkle black pepper and sea salt to season. Transfer the mixture to a baking dish. In another bowl, mix a tablespoon of olive oil and the mushrooms together; place in another baking dish.
- Bake the potato mixture for 20mins in the preheated oven. Put the mushrooms in the oven then bake for another 25mins until the potatoes are a bit brown and soft. Take both of the baking sheets out of the oven; set aside.
- On medium-low heat, melt vegan margarine in a big stockpot; add onion. Cook for 7-10mins until the onion in the margarine is fully soft. Mix in mushrooms and roasted potato mixture into the onions, water, and a teaspoon of sea salt; simmer mixture for 4-5mins while mixing from time to time. Mix in sage and mushroom broth into the mixture; cover. Cook for 20mins on the stockpot and cook to let the flavors meld.
- Cool the soup for a bit then transfer into a blender in batches until not more than halfway full filling the pitcher. Press the lid down firmly using a folded kitchen towel then start the blender carefully. Use a few fast pulses to move the soup then leave the blender on puree. Move the blended batches to a clean pot. You can also use a stick blender to puree the soup in the pot. If using, mix soy milk into the finished bisque then serve.

Nutrition Information

- Calories: 273 calories;
- Total Fat: 9.1
- Sodium: 872
- Total Carbohydrate: 43.5
- Cholesterol: 0

- Protein: 7.1

831. Roasted Portobello, Red Pepper, And Arugula Salad For One

Serving: 1 | Prep: 15mins | Cook: 30mins | Ready in:

Ingredients

- 1 portobello mushroom, stem removed
- 1 tablespoon olive oil
- 1 teaspoon red wine vinegar
- 1 clove garlic, thinly sliced
- 1/4 shallot, thinly sliced
- salt and pepper to taste
- 1/2 roasted red pepper, cut into strips
- 3 cups arugula leaves
- 1 ounce grated Romano cheese
- 1 tablespoon Greek salad dressing

Direction

- Set oven to 425 °F (220 °C) to preheat. Line an aluminium foil on a baking sheet.
- Brush olive oil on both sides of the mushroom and lay them onto the baking sheet. Remember to put Gill-side up. Sprinkle with red wine vinegar and the remaining olive oil on top. Sprinkle with shallot and slices of garlic; use salt and pepper to season to taste. Lastly put the piece of roasted red pepper on top then wrap the mushroom tightly in the foil.
- Place the baking sheet into the preheated oven and let the mushroom bake for about half an hour till the mushroom gets tender.
- Put salad dressing and Romano cheese on the arugula and toss to coat. Lay the mixture on a plate. Place the pepper and hot mushroom on top. The dish is ready to be served!

Nutrition Information

- Calories: 352 calories;
- Sodium: 644
- Total Carbohydrate: 15.2
- Cholesterol: 29
- Protein: 14.5
- Total Fat: 27.5

832. Roasted Vegetables With Walnuts, Basil And Balsamic Vinaigrette

Serving: 5 | Prep: 15mins | Cook: 10mins | Ready in:

Ingredients

- 1/2 small red bell pepper, cut into 1-inch cubes
- 1/2 small orange bell pepper, cut into 1-inch cubes
- 1/4 medium red onion, cut into 1-inch cubes, separated
- 4 ounces baby portabella mushrooms, halved
- 1 tablespoon extra virgin olive oil
- 1/4 teaspoon sea salt
- 3/4 cup sugar snap peas
- 1 small zucchini, sliced 1/4-inch thick
- 1 small yellow summer squash, sliced 1/4-inch thick
- 2 cloves garlic, minced
- 2 teaspoons balsamic vinegar
- 2 tablespoons fresh snipped basil
- 1/2 cup California walnuts, coarsely chopped

Direction

- Preheat an oven to 400°F. Put mushrooms, onion and bell peppers in big bowl; toss with salt and olive oil. In 1 layer, put on big baking sheet, don't crowd veggies. Cook them for 10 minutes.
- Add garlic, yellow squash, zucchini and snap peas; lightly mix. Put walnuts on top; cook till all veggies are crisp-tender and the walnuts are toasted for 5-10 minutes.
- Drizzle balsamic; toss well then sprinkle basil over.

Nutrition Information

- Calories: 137 calories;
- Sodium: 94
- Total Carbohydrate: 8.8
- Cholesterol: 0
- Protein: 3.9
- Total Fat: 10.5

833. Roasted Wild Mushrooms And Potatoes

Serving: 4 | Prep: | Cook: 1hours5mins | Ready in:

Ingredients

- 2 pounds new potatoes (such as Yukon Gold), halved
- 2 tablespoons olive oil, or more if needed
- salt to taste
- 1 teaspoon olive oil
- 2 ounces pancetta, chopped
- 1/4 pound king trumpet mushrooms, cut into chunks
- 1/4 pound chanterelle mushrooms, cut into chunks
- 1/4 pound nameko mushrooms, trimmed
- 1/4 pound clamshell (shimeji) mushrooms, trimmed
- 3 tablespoons sherry vinegar
- 2 tablespoons chopped fresh tarragon
- 2 cloves garlic, minced
- 1 tablespoon olive oil (optional)

Direction

- Preheat the oven to 200°C or 400°F.
- Into a big roasting pan, put the potatoes and sprinkle 2 tablespoons of olive oil on top. Scatter salt over and stir to cover potatoes in olive oil and salt. Flip, cut sides facing up.

- In the prepped oven, roast for half an hour.
- Meanwhile, into a big skillet, put a teaspoon of olive oil over medium heat and let pancetta cook in the hot oil for 5 minutes, mixing frequently, till pancetta releases some fat and resembles a cooked ham. Mix in clamshell mushrooms, nameko, chanterelle and king trumpet, putting a pinch of salt as it cooks.
- Raise the heat to high and let mushrooms cook for 10 minutes till mushrooms start to brown and most of the juices steams off.
- Raise the oven heat up to 220°C or 425°F.
- In the baking dish, mix the potatoes; add pancetta and mushrooms to potatoes. Put back to the oven and let bake for 10 minutes; mix and keep baking for 10 minutes longer till potatoes are tender, soft and browned. Allow to slightly cool for 10 minutes.
- Sprinkle sherry vinegar on top of mushrooms and potatoes, scatter 1 tablespoon of olive oil, garlic and tarragon on top, and combine by tossing. Taste and alter the seasoning. Put to serving platter.

Nutrition Information

- Calories: 335 calories;
- Sodium: 168
- Total Carbohydrate: 44.9
- Cholesterol: 5
- Protein: 9.7
- Total Fat: 13.7

834. Rolled Flank Steak

Serving: 6 | Prep: 45mins | Cook: 1hours | Ready in:

Ingredients

- 1 (2 pound) beef flank steak
- 1/4 cup soy sauce
- 1/2 cup olive oil
- 2 teaspoons steak seasoning
- 8 ounces thinly sliced provolone cheese
- 4 slices thick cut bacon
- 1/2 cup fresh spinach leaves
- 1/2 cup sliced crimini mushrooms
- 1/2 red bell pepper, seeded and cut into strips

Direction

- Arrange the flank steak onto a cutting board with the short end closest to you. Beginning from one of long sides, slice through meat horizontally to within half an in. of opposite edge. You could also tell the butcher to butterfly flank steak for you instead of chopping it on your own.
- Combine steak seasoning, olive oil and soy sauce in a gallon-size resealable plastic bag. Let the flank steak marinate in fridge for 4 hours to overnight.
- Preheat the oven to 175 degrees C (350 degrees F). Grease a glass baking plate.
- Lay out flank steak flat in front of you along with grain of meat running from the left side to right side. Layer provolone across steak, leaving a one-in. border. Arrange mushrooms, red pepper, spinach and bacon across cheese which covered the steak in stripes running with same direction as meat's grain. Roll flank steak up and away from you, so that once the roll is sliced into pinwheel-shape, each filling ingredients is visible. Roll them firmly, but be careful not to squeeze fillings out of ends. When rolled, tie every 2 in. with the kitchen twine.
- Add into the prepped baking dish, and bake in the preheated oven till the internal temperature reads 65 degrees C (145 degrees F) or for 60 minutes. Take out of oven and allow it to stand for 5-10 minutes prior to slicing into one-in. slices. Ensure to take out the twine prior to serving!

Nutrition Information

- Calories: 472 calories;
- Protein: 31.4
- Total Fat: 36.9
- Sodium: 1422

- Total Carbohydrate: 3
- Cholesterol: 67

835. Romantic Chicken With Artichokes And Mushrooms

Serving: 4 | Prep: 10mins | Cook: 35mins | Ready in:

Ingredients

- 4 skinless, boneless chicken breast halves
- salt and pepper to taste
- 1 tablespoon olive oil
- 1 tablespoon butter
- 1 (14 ounce) can marinated quartered artichoke hearts, drained, liquid reserved
- 1 cup sliced fresh mushrooms
- 1 cup white wine
- 1 tablespoon capers

Direction

- Add pepper and salt to season the chicken. In a large skillet, heat butter and oil over medium heat. Brown the chicken in butter and oil for 5-7 mins on each side. Discard from the skillet, then put aside.
- Put the mushrooms and artichoke hearts in the pan. Sauté until the mushrooms are tender and brown. Put the chicken back to the skillet. Add wine and reserved artichoke liquid. Lower the heat, simmer until the juices run clear and the chicken is no longer pink, about 10-15 mins.
- Mix in the capers, simmer for 5 more mins. Discard from the heat and enjoy right away.

Nutrition Information

- Calories: 312 calories;
- Sodium: 426
- Total Carbohydrate: 9.6
- Cholesterol: 75
- Protein: 25

- Total Fat: 16.2

836. Rosemary Chicken Stew

Serving: 8 | Prep: 25mins | Cook: 2hours30mins | Ready in:

Ingredients

- 2 pounds boneless skinless chicken breasts, cut into bite-size pieces
- 1 (10 ounce) package fresh mushrooms, sliced
- 3 medium onions, sliced
- 1 (16 ounce) can diced tomatoes with juice
- 1 pound carrots, sliced
- 4 celery ribs, sliced
- 1 pound dried great Northern beans, soaked overnight
- 6 cloves garlic, chopped
- 1 1/2 teaspoons dried rosemary
- water
- salt and pepper to taste
- cornstarch

Direction

- Over medium heat, place onions, mushrooms and chicken in a big stock pot. Mix in celery, carrots and tomatoes. Stir in rosemary, garlic, beans, and just enough water not to fully cover. Bring mixture to a low simmer, cook about 2-3 hours until chicken is soft. Add salt and pepper to taste. If required to thicken, stir in cornstarch.

Nutrition Information

- Calories: 365 calories;
- Total Fat: 6.6
- Sodium: 216
- Total Carbohydrate: 42.3
- Cholesterol: 57
- Protein: 34.7

837. Russian Mushroom Salad

Serving: 8 | Prep: 30mins | Cook: 25mins | Ready in:

Ingredients

- 2 potatoes
- 1 tablespoon butter
- 4 cups chopped mushrooms
- 4 hard-boiled eggs, peeled and diced
- 2 red onions, finely chopped
- 1 cup mayonnaise, or to taste
- 1 cup finely chopped pickles
- 1 cup finely chopped cornichons

Direction

- Cover unpeeled potatoes with salted water in a pot then boil. Lower heat to medium-low then simmer for 20 minutes till tender. Drain and let cool till it's easy to handle. Peel the potatoes then dice.
- In a big skillet, melt butter over medium heat. Place in mushrooms and cook while stirring for 8-10 minutes till browned. Take away from the heat and cool.
- Use 2 diced eggs to cover a mold's bottom. Layer on top with 1 onion, 1/4 cup of mayonnaise, 1/2 of the mushrooms and all of the potatoes. Spread another 3 1/2 tablespoons of mayonnaise, the leftover eggs, all of the cornichons and 1/4 cup of mayonnaise on top. Add mayonnaise, mushrooms and the leftover onion to finish layers.
- Store in the fridge for 1-2 hours till firm. Onto a serving plate, invert and lift off the mold.

Nutrition Information

- Calories: 314 calories;
- Protein: 6.2
- Total Fat: 26.2
- Sodium: 609
- Total Carbohydrate: 15.1
- Cholesterol: 120

838. Salisbury Steak Slow Cooker Style

Serving: 10 | Prep: 20mins | Cook: 3hours45mins | Ready in:

Ingredients

- 2 1/2 pounds extra lean ground beef
- 3/4 cup finely chopped onion
- 3/4 cup finely chopped celery
- 1/2 cup milk
- 1/2 cup finely chopped mushrooms
- 1/2 cup Italian-seasoned panko (Japanese bread crumbs)
- 2 tablespoons all-purpose flour
- 2 tablespoons whole wheat flour
- 3 tablespoons vegetable oil, divided
- 1 (4 ounce) package sliced fresh mushrooms
- 1/2 onion, thinly sliced
- 2 (10.75 ounce) cans reduced-fat, reduced-sodium cream of mushroom soup (such as Campbell's® Healthy Request)
- 3/4 cup low-sodium beef broth
- 2 tablespoons low-sodium Worcestershire sauce
- 1 (1 ounce) packet dry onion gravy mix
- 1 teaspoon ground black pepper

Direction

- In a big bowl, mix together panko, chopped mushrooms, milk, celery, chopped onion and ground beef. Form mixture into 10 patties.
- In a wide and shallow bowl, mix whole wheat flour and all-purpose flour. Put patties in the flour mixture and coat. Transfer coated patties on a platter but do not stack them.
- Use a big skillet to heat 2 tablespoons of oil on medium high heat. Put in patties and cook for 3-5 minutes per side until browned. Transfer browned patties in a slow cooker crock.
- In a small skillet, heat the remaining oil on medium heat and cook while stirring sliced

mushrooms and sliced onion for about 5 minutes until they are tender.
- In a bowl, mix together cream of mushroom soup with cooked mushroom and onion mixture, black pepper, onion gravy mix, Worcestershire sauce and beef broth until smooth. Pour the mixture on top of beef patties in the slow cooker.
- Let it cook for 3-3 1/2 hours on High until patties are very firm, hot and grey in the middle. You may also cook for 4-5 hours on Low. An instant-read thermometer should read 160°F or 70°C when inserted in the middle.

Nutrition Information

- Calories: 369 calories;
- Sodium: 472
- Total Carbohydrate: 16.7
- Cholesterol: 93
- Protein: 29.7
- Total Fat: 20.2

839. Salmon With Green Fettuccine

Serving: 3 | Prep: 15mins | Cook: 35mins | Ready in:

Ingredients

- 12 ounces spinach fettuccine pasta
- 1 (14.75 ounce) can canned salmon, drained, liquid reserved
- 1 1/2 cups milk
- 1/4 cup finely diced onion
- 1 1/2 cups fresh sliced mushrooms
- 3 tablespoons butter
- 1/4 cup all-purpose flour
- 1/4 cup dry white wine
- 1/4 cup grated Parmesan cheese
- 2 tablespoons chopped fresh parsley
- 1/4 teaspoon dried dill weed
- salt and pepper to taste

Direction

- Boil pasta in salted water until tender. Drain the pasta. Drain the can of salmon over 2 cups measure. Pour enough milk to make 1 3/4 cups.
- Meanwhile, to prepare sauce, in a large sauté pan, melt butter over medium heat. Put the onion and mushrooms; stir until onion is tender. Lower the heat to low, and add in flour. Take out from the heat.
- Add the milk mixture and wine into cooked vegetables. Heat the again, and let it boil, stirring from time to time. Lower the heat, and simmer for 2 minutes. Break salmon until flaky; add into the sauce. Add in parsley, dill and Parmesan cheese. Season with pepper and salt to taste and cook thoroughly. Serve over hot pasta.

Nutrition Information

- Calories: 817 calories;
- Total Carbohydrate: 77.1
- Cholesterol: 136
- Protein: 52.5
- Total Fat: 31.3
- Sodium: 562

840. Sauceless Garden Lasagna

Serving: 6 | Prep: 20mins | Cook: 45mins | Ready in:

Ingredients

- 1 medium zucchini, halved lengthwise and sliced
- 1/3 cup chopped red onion
- 1 cup shredded mozzarella cheese, divided
- 1/2 cup crumbled feta cheese
- 2 portobello mushrooms, sliced
- 4 cups fresh baby spinach
- 1/4 cup chopped fresh basil

- 1 tablespoon chopped fresh oregano
- 3 cloves garlic, minced
- 3 tablespoons olive oil
- 1/4 cup balsamic vinegar
- 1 teaspoon sugar
- 1/2 teaspoon salt
- 1/4 teaspoon freshly ground black pepper
- 1 (8 ounce) package no-boil lasagna noodles
- 9 roma (plum) tomatoes, thinly sliced

Direction

- Preheat the oven at 350°F (175°C). Use a cooking spray to slightly grease a 9x9 inch baking dish.
- Mix spinach, zucchini, garlic, red onion, feta cheese, 1/2 cup of mozzarella cheese and mushrooms together in a big bowl. Put in balsamic vinegar and olive oil then mix in with salt, pepper, sugar, basil and oregano. Mix the mixture thoroughly.
- In the greased baking dish, put lasagna noodles at the bottom. Put a layer of tomato slices on top of the lasagna noodles. Put a good amount of spinach mixture evenly on top. It's normal for this dish to shrink in size while cooking. Put slices of tomatoes on top of the spinach mixture then put a layer of lasagna noodles again. Put another layer of tomatoes on top and do whole layering process again until the baking dish is filled to the top, finish off the layers with the spinach mixture. Top with the remaining cheese.
- Put in the preheated oven and bake for 35-45 minutes or until the vegetables and noodles are soft. Let the lasagna set and cool down a bit before slicing then serve warm.

Nutrition Information

- Calories: 286 calories;
- Protein: 12.9
- Total Fat: 15.5
- Sodium: 576
- Total Carbohydrate: 25.3
- Cholesterol: 32

841. Saucy Chicken Cordon Bleu

Serving: 5 | Prep: | Cook: | Ready in:

Ingredients

- 4 skinless, boneless chicken breast halves
- 4 slices ham
- 4 slices Swiss cheese
- 1 cup all-purpose flour
- 1 teaspoon salt
- 1/2 teaspoon ground black pepper
- 1/2 teaspoon paprika
- 2 eggs, beaten
- 1/3 cup milk
- 1 cup dry bread crumbs
- 1/4 cup olive oil
- 1 (10.75 ounce) can condensed cream of mushroom soup
- 1/2 pound fresh mushrooms, sliced
- 1/4 teaspoon garlic powder
- 1/8 teaspoon curry powder
- 1/4 cup white wine
- 1/2 cup sour cream
- 2 sprigs fresh parsley, for garnish

Direction

- Set the oven to 350°F or 175°C for preheating.
- Flatten the chicken breasts, making sure you do not break the meat through. Roll each slice of ham in a cheese slice, and then roll them up in chicken breasts. Put flour in a bowl or shallow dish, and then season it with paprika, pepper, and salt. In another bowl or dish, whisk milk and eggs together. Dredge the chicken rolls into the seasoned flour, and then into the egg mixture. Dredge them lastly into the bread crumbs. Put oil into a large skillet and heat it. Add the chicken and fry until golden brown; put aside.
- For the sauce, mix garlic powder, wine, sour cream, soup, curry powder, and mushrooms in a large bowl. Mix them all together. Arrange

the browned chicken into a 9x13-inches baking dish. Pour sauce mixture all over the chicken. Let it bake inside the preheated oven for 15-20 minutes. Garnish this dish with fresh parsley sprigs.

Nutrition Information

- Calories: 667 calories;
- Sodium: 1480
- Total Carbohydrate: 45.7
- Cholesterol: 175
- Protein: 43.7
- Total Fat: 33

842. Sauerkraut Pierogi Filling

Serving: 24 | Prep: 5mins | Cook: 22mins | Ready in:

Ingredients

- 16 ounces sauerkraut
- 1/2 cup butter
- 1 onion, chopped
- 1 cup chopped mushrooms (optional)
- salt and ground black pepper to taste

Direction

- In a food processor, grind the sauerkraut, then move it into a pan. Cook and stir for about 10 minutes on medium heat until it becomes soft; use a colander to drain.
- In a pan, heat the butter on medium heat. Mix in the mushrooms and onions. Cook and stir for about 10 minutes until the onion becomes translucent and soft.
- Mix the onion mixture with the sauerkraut and put pepper and salt; cook for 2 minutes. Spread it on a plate to fully cool.

Nutrition Information

- Calories: 42 calories;

- Cholesterol: 10
- Protein: 0.4
- Total Fat: 3.9
- Sodium: 158
- Total Carbohydrate: 1.8

843. Sausage Mushroom Pizza

Serving: 8 | Prep: 30mins | Cook: 12mins | Ready in:

Ingredients

- Reynolds Wrap® Heavy Duty Aluminum Foil
- 2 tablespoons cornmeal
- 2 pounds frozen pizza dough, thawed or Whole Wheat Sesame Dough (below)
- 1/2 cup pizza sauce
- 1/8 teaspoon crushed red pepper
- 8 ounces bulk Italian sausage, cooked and drained
- 1 cup thinly sliced fresh mushrooms
- 8 ounces shredded Italian cheese blend
- Grated Parmesan cheese (optional)
- Snipped fresh basil (optional)

Direction

- Set the oven to 450°F for preheating. Use the Reynolds Wrap® Heavy Duty Aluminum Foil to cover the two large baking sheets. Sprinkle the sheets with cornmeal.
- Split the thawed pizza dough or whole wheat sesame seed dough into 8 equal portions. Cover the dough and allow it to rest for 10 minutes.
- On a lightly floured surface, unroll each of the dough into a 6-inch circle. Place the rolled dough onto the prepared baking sheets. Use a fork to prick the crusts. Make sure you won't let them rise.
- Let them bake for 7 minutes until browned slightly. Mix the crushed red pepper and pizza sauce in a small bowl. Spread the pizza sauce on top of each crust. Then place the sausage and mushrooms on top. Drizzle with Italian

blend cheese. Let them bake for 5 more minutes until the cheese has melted. Sprinkle with fresh basil and/or Parmesan cheese if desired.
- For the grilling, use Reynolds Wrap® Heavy Duty Aluminum Foil to line the grill rack. Preheat the grill and then lower the heat to medium-hot. Coat each top of the dough with 1 tbsp. of olive oil using a brush. Arrange the dough circles onto the foil-lined grill rack, oiled-sides down. Cover the grill and cook the dough for 1 minute until the bottom is firm and browned. Place the dough circles onto the clean surface, positioning them grilled-side up. Place the pizza toppings on top following the directions above. Place the assembled pizzas back into the foil-lined grill rack. Cover the grill and cook for 2-3 minutes until the cheese has melted and the bottom is browned. To ensure even browning, rearrange the pizzas as needed.

Nutrition Information

- Calories: 477 calories;
- Total Fat: 16.7
- Sodium: 1304
- Total Carbohydrate: 59.3
- Cholesterol: 32
- Protein: 20.6

844. Sausage Mushroom Quiche

Serving: 6 | Prep: 20mins | Cook: 30mins | Ready in:

Ingredients

- 1 pound small fresh button mushrooms
- 1 pound ground pork breakfast sausage
- 1/2 cup chopped fresh parsley
- 3 eggs
- 1 cup half-and-half cream
- 1/2 cup grated Parmesan cheese

- 1/4 teaspoon salt
- 1 (9 inch) unbaked 9 inch pie crust

Direction

- Preheat oven to 400°F or 200°C. Snip off the stems of the mushroom and cut any large pieces in half.
- In a big pan, crush the sausage and add the mushrooms. Cook on medium-high heat until all the liquid from the mushrooms has evaporated and both mushrooms and meat have lightly browned. Remove the grease then add parsley.
- In a big bowl, whisk the eggs then add the cheese, cream and salt. Pour egg mixture into the pan with the sausage and mushroom. Blend well. Scoop mixture into the pie shell.
- Bake for 25-30 minutes until the filling is firm and crust is well browned. Set aside for 10 minutes before serving.

Nutrition Information

- Calories: 612 calories;
- Sodium: 1101
- Total Carbohydrate: 20.6
- Cholesterol: 167
- Protein: 19.9
- Total Fat: 50.3

845. Sausage Stuffed Mushrooms

Serving: 48 | Prep: 40mins | Cook: 16mins | Ready in:

Ingredients

- 1 (16 ounce) package Johnsonville® Ground Italian Sausage
- 48 large fresh mushrooms
- 1/2 cup dry bread crumbs
- 1 (8 ounce) package cream cheese, softened
- 3 garlic cloves, minced

- 2 tablespoons finely chopped fresh parsley
- 1 tablespoon lemon juice
- 1/4 cup grated Parmesan cheese

Direction

- In a skillet over medium heat, cook and crumble sausage until lightly browned and no longer pink; allow to drain.
- Eliminate and discard stems from mushrooms. Place the mushroom caps on baking sheets lined with foil.
- In a bowl, combine bread crumbs, cooked sausage, garlic, cream cheese, lemon juice and parsley. Stir until blended.
- In mushroom caps, spoon sausage mixture carefully. Scatter with cheese. Bake with no cover at 400 °F until mushrooms are lightly browned and soften. Serve while still hot.

Nutrition Information

- Calories: 60 calories;
- Total Fat: 4.7
- Sodium: 119
- Total Carbohydrate: 1.9
- Cholesterol: 13
- Protein: 2.9

846. Sausage And Kale Soup

Serving: 8 | Prep: 20mins | Cook: 30mins | Ready in:

Ingredients

- 1 pound Italian sausage links, halved lengthwise
- 2 large carrots, chopped
- 1 small onion, chopped
- 2 cloves garlic, minced
- 6 cups chicken broth
- 1 cup chopped portobello mushroom caps
- 1 cup chopped cauliflower
- 2 cups coarsely chopped kale
- 1 bay leaf
- 1/2 teaspoon oregano

Direction

- Heat a big pot on medium heat; cook sausages in pot, 3-5 minutes per side, till browned. Put sausages on cutting board for cooling. Keep sausage drippings in the pot.
- Cook and mix onion and carrots in the reserved sausage drippings for 5-7 minutes till onion is translucent. Mix garlic into onion and carrot mixture; mix and cook for 10-15 seconds. Put chicken broth into pot; boil while scraping browned food bits off from the bottom of pan using a wooden spoon.
- Put sausage back in broth with oregano, bay leaf, kale, cauliflower and mushrooms; mix. Lower heat to low; simmer for 15 minutes till veggies are tender but still firm enough to keep their shape. Put sausages on cutting board; slice into 1-in. half-moons. Put back into the soup; simmer for 5 more minutes.

Nutrition Information

- Calories: 173 calories;
- Total Carbohydrate: 8.2
- Cholesterol: 26
- Protein: 9.7
- Total Fat: 11.3
- Sodium: 1217

847. Sausage And Mushroom Mini Pizzas

Serving: 8 | Prep: 20mins | Cook: 12mins | Ready in:

Ingredients

- 2 tablespoons cornmeal
- 1 (.25 ounce) package active dry yeast
- 1 cup warm water
- 1 3/4 cups whole wheat flour, divided

- 1 1/4 cups all-purpose flour
- 2 tablespoons sesame seeds
- 1/2 teaspoon salt
- 2 tablespoons olive oil
- 1/2 cup pizza sauce
- 1/8 teaspoon crushed red pepper flakes
- 8 ounces bulk Italian sausage, cooked and drained
- 1 cup thinly sliced fresh mushrooms
- 8 ounces shredded Italian blend cheese
- Grated Parmesan cheese (optional)
- Snipped fresh basil (optional)
- Reynolds Wrap® Heavy Duty Foil

Direction

- Start preheating the oven to 450°F. Cover Reynolds Wrap(R) Heavy Duty Foil over 2 large baking sheets. Sprinkle cornmeal over.
- Stir yeast into one cup of warm water. Allow to stand until puffy, or about 5 mins. Combine salt, sesame seeds, 1 1/4 cups of whole-wheat flour and all-purpose flour in a large bowl. Put in olive oil and yeast mixture. Stir the dough together with a wooden spoon. Turn the dough out onto a lightly floured surface. Knead in enough of additional whole-wheat flour (1/4-1/2 cup) to create the moderately stiff dough that is elastic and smooth (3-4 mins total).
- Separate the dough into eight equal parts. Allow to rest 10 mins with a cover. On a lightly floured surface, roll to shape each dough portion into a 6-in. circle. Place onto the prepared baking sheets. Use a fork to prick the crusts. Do not allow to rise.
- Bake until light brown, or about 7 mins. Combine crushed red pepper and pizza sauce in a small bowl. Add pizza sauce, followed by the sausage and the mushrooms on top of each crust. Sprinkle Italian blend cheese over. Bake until cheese melts, or about 5 more mins. Sprinkle fresh basil (optional) and Parmesan cheese over, if desired.
- To Grill: Line Reynolds Wrap(R) Heavy Duty Foil on the grill rack. Start preheating the grill; lower the heat to medium-hot. Brush one tablespoon of the olive oil over tops of the dough circles. Put the dough circles on the foil-lined grill rack, the oiled sides facing down. Grill, covered, until bottom is firm and browned, or about one minute. Place the dough circles grilled side up onto a clean surface. Assemble the pizzas, put back to the foil-lined grill rack. Grill, covered until cheese is melted and the bottom is browned, or about 2-3 mins, if necessary, rearranging the pizzas to assure even browning.

Nutrition Information

- Calories: 383 calories;
- Total Fat: 17.9
- Sodium: 694
- Total Carbohydrate: 40.3
- Cholesterol: 32
- Protein: 17.1

848. Sausage And Mushroom Stuffing

Serving: 8 | Prep: 20mins | Cook: 15mins | Ready in:

Ingredients

- 1 3/4 cups Swanson® Chicken Broth
- Generous dash ground black pepper
- 1 stalk celery, coarsely chopped
- 1 small onion, coarsely chopped
- 3 ounces mushrooms, sliced
- 4 cups Pepperidge Farm® Herb Seasoned Stuffing
- 1/2 pound bulk sausage, cooked and crumbled

Direction

- In a 2-qt saucepan, heat the onion, broth, celery, and black pepper over medium-high heat. Bring the mixture to a boil. Adjust the heat to low. Mix in mushrooms. Cover the pan

and cook for 5 minutes until all of the vegetables are tender.
- Lightly mix the sausage and stuffing into the pan.

Nutrition Information

- Calories: 194 calories;
- Cholesterol: 17
- Protein: 7.9
- Total Fat: 7.6
- Sodium: 867
- Total Carbohydrate: 23.8

849. Sauteed Mushrooms

Serving: 6 | Prep: 5mins | Cook: 30mins | Ready in:

Ingredients

- 1/2 cup butter
- 1 pound sliced mushrooms
- 1 (1 ounce) package dry ranch salad dressing mix

Direction

- Melt butter over low heat. Mix in dry ranch salad dressing mix. Add mushrooms and stir to coat. Cook for at least a half hour while stirring frequently, until the mushrooms are very tender.

Nutrition Information

- Calories: 164 calories;
- Total Fat: 15.6
- Sodium: 439
- Total Carbohydrate: 4.8
- Cholesterol: 41
- Protein: 2.5

850. Sauteed Sugar Snap Peas With Mushrooms

Serving: 2 | Prep: 5mins | Cook: 10mins | Ready in:

Ingredients

- 2 tablespoons olive oil
- 4 fresh mushrooms, or more to taste, sliced
- salt to taste
- 20 sugar snap peas, or more to taste

Direction

- Prepare a sauté pan, heat over medium heat. Add olive oil. Use salt for seasoning mushrooms and sauté with olive oil for approximately 5 minutes till tender.
- During the time mushrooms are cooking, add water into a small pot and bring to a boil. Put sugar snap peas in; allow to cook for 1-2 minutes till bright green. Using a slotted spoon, remove sugar snap peas out of water and toss snap peas with mushrooms for 1-2 minutes in the pan. Use salt for seasoning and serve right away.

Nutrition Information

- Calories: 537 calories;
- Sodium: 80
- Total Carbohydrate: 72.9
- Cholesterol: 0
- Protein: 21.6
- Total Fat: 13.6

851. Savory Crab Stuffed Mushrooms

Serving: 8 | Prep: 25mins | Cook: 20mins | Ready in:

Ingredients

- 3 tablespoons butter, melted

- 24 fresh mushrooms
- 2 tablespoons butter
- 2 tablespoons minced green onions
- 1 teaspoon lemon juice
- 1 cup diced cooked crabmeat
- 1/2 cup soft bread crumbs
- 1 egg, beaten
- 1/2 teaspoon dried dill weed
- 3/4 cup shredded Monterey Jack cheese, divided
- 1/4 cup dry white wine

Direction

- Preheat oven to 400 °F (200 °C). Prepare a baking dish of 9x13 inch with 3 tablespoons butter.
- Eliminate stems from mushrooms. Leave the caps aside. Chop stems finely.
- Melt 2 tablespoons butter on moderate heat in a medium saucepan. Mix in the chopped stems and green onions and cook for around 3 minutes until soft. Take away saucepan from heat. Mix in crabmeat, lemon juice, dill weed, soft bread crumbs, egg and 1/4 cup Monterey Jack cheese. Blend the mixture thoroughly.
- In the buttered pan, place mushroom caps, and stir until caps are coated with the butter. Place caps cavity side up, and stuff green onion and crabmeat mixture generously into cavities. Put the rest of Monterey Jack cheese on top. In the pan, pour wine around the mushrooms.
- In the preheated oven, bake for approximately 15 to 20 minutes with no cover, until cheese is melted and lightly browned. Serve while still warm.

Nutrition Information

- Calories: 176 calories;
- Sodium: 233
- Total Carbohydrate: 7.3
- Cholesterol: 65
- Protein: 9.8
- Total Fat: 11.8

852. Savory French Crepes

Serving: 4 | Prep: 30mins | Cook: 15mins | Ready in:

Ingredients

- 2 eggs
- 1 1/2 cups milk
- 2 tablespoons butter
- 1/4 cup buckwheat flour
- 3/4 cup all-purpose flour
- 1 pinch salt
- 3 tablespoons butter
- 1/2 cup cremini mushrooms, sliced
- 1/2 cup oyster mushrooms, sliced
- 1 cup diced tomatoes
- 2 cups baby spinach leaves
- 4 teaspoons butter, divided
- 1 cup shredded Gruyere cheese, divided

Direction

- In a blender, mix milk, eggs, and 2 tablespoons of butter. Add all-purpose flour, buckwheat flour, and a dash of salt. Puree until the mixture becomes smooth. Let batter rest overnight in the refrigerator.
- In a big skillet melt 3 tablespoons of butter on medium-high heat. Stir cremini mushrooms in and cook for 10 minutes until they turn golden brown. Add the spinach and tomatoes; stir and cook for 3-4 minutes until spinach wilts. Set aside.
- In a large skillet, melt 1 teaspoon of butter on medium heat. Depending on pan size, put about 1/4 cup of batter in the hot pan and make sure to distribute the batter evenly by immediately tilting and swirling the skillet. Cook for 3-4 minutes until edges start to turn brown and center becomes set. In the center of each crepe, sprinkle 1/4 of filling and sprinkle on 3 tablespoons Gruyere cheese on each. Set aside remaining cheese. Over the filling, fold the crepes in thirds to form triangles. With the

remaining Gruyere cheese on top, serve crepes.

Nutrition Information

- Calories: 507 calories;
- Sodium: 369
- Total Carbohydrate: 30.7
- Cholesterol: 186
- Protein: 20.9
- Total Fat: 34.1

853. Scim's Fettucine Alfredo With Shrimp

Serving: 4 | Prep: 20mins | Cook: 30mins | Ready in:

Ingredients

- 1/2 cup butter
- 1 pint heavy cream
- 1/2 pound fresh mushrooms, sliced
- 15 medium shrimp - peeled, deveined and cooked
- 3/4 cup grated Parmesan cheese
- 8 ounces dry fettuccine pasta

Direction

- Mix cream and butter in big saucepan on low heat, occasionally mixing till butter melts. Add parmesan, cooked shrimp and mushrooms; mix. Cover; simmer till sauce starts to thicken for 15 minutes.
- Boil big pot of lightly salted water as sauce simmers. Add pasta; cook till al dente for 8-10 minutes. Drain. Toss hot pasta with sauce; serve.

Nutrition Information

- Calories: 909 calories;
- Cholesterol: 272
- Protein: 20.6
- Total Fat: 73
- Sodium: 482
- Total Carbohydrate: 47.1

854. Scrumptious Salisbury Steak In Mushroom Gravy

Serving: 6 | Prep: 10mins | Cook: 25mins | Ready in:

Ingredients

- 1 pound ground beef
- 1 egg
- 3 tablespoons crushed buttery round cracker crumbs
- 2 tablespoons finely chopped onion
- 1/2 teaspoon salt
- 1/2 teaspoon pepper
- 1/4 teaspoon poultry seasoning
- 2 (4 ounce) cans sliced mushrooms with juice
- 3 tablespoons butter
- 3 tablespoons all-purpose flour
- 3 cups milk
- 3 cubes beef bouillon

Direction

- Use your hands to mix poultry seasoning, pepper, salt, onion, cracker crumbs, egg and ground beef in a medium bowl; form to 6 1-in. thick patties.
- Fry patties in a big skillet on medium high heat till brown for 3-4 minutes per side. Drain off grease. Transfer patties onto a platter to keep warm.
- In the same skillet, melt butter. Add mushrooms; mix and cook for 2 minutes. Sprinkle with flour; mix in till blended. Mix in beef bouillon and milk; mix and cook on medium heat till it begins to thicken and is smooth. Put patties back into gravy; cook on low heat, occasionally mixing, with no cover, for about 10 minutes.

Nutrition Information

- Calories: 296 calories;
- Cholesterol: 102
- Protein: 19.4
- Total Fat: 18.6
- Sodium: 950
- Total Carbohydrate: 12.6

855. Seafood Lasagna II

Serving: 8 | Prep: 30mins | Cook: 1hours | Ready in:

Ingredients

- 9 lasagna noodles
- 1 tablespoon butter
- 1 cup minced onion
- 1 (8 ounce) package cream cheese, softened
- 1 1/2 cups cottage cheese
- 1 egg, beaten
- 2 teaspoons dried basil leaves
- 1/2 teaspoon salt
- 1/8 teaspoon freshly ground black pepper
- 2 (10.75 ounce) cans condensed cream of mushroom soup
- 1/3 cup milk
- 1/3 cup dry white wine
- 1 (6 ounce) can crabmeat, drained and flaked
- 1 pound cooked small shrimp
- 1/4 cup grated Parmesan cheese
- 1/2 cup shredded sharp Cheddar cheese

Direction

- Boil pot with lightly salted water. Cook pasta till al dente for 8-10 minutes; drain. Rinse under cold water. Preheat an oven to 175°C/350°F.
- Cook onion in butter in a skillet on medium heat till tender; take off heat. Mix pepper, salt, basil, egg, cottage cheese and cream cheese in.
- Mix shrimp, crabmeat, wine, milk and soup in medium bowl.
- On bottom of a 9x13-in. baking dish, lay 3 cooked lasagna noodles. Spread 1/3 onion mixture on noodles. Spread 1/3 soup mixture on onion layer. Repeat soup, onion and noodle layers 2 times. Put Parmesan and Cheddar cheese on top.
- In preheated oven, bake till bubbly and heated through for 45 minutes.

Nutrition Information

- Calories: 471 calories;
- Sodium: 1205
- Total Carbohydrate: 29.9
- Cholesterol: 206
- Protein: 33
- Total Fat: 23.5

856. Sensational Sirloin Kabobs

Serving: 8 | Prep: 15mins | Cook: 15mins | Ready in:

Ingredients

- 1/4 cup soy sauce
- 3 tablespoons light brown sugar
- 3 tablespoons distilled white vinegar
- 1/2 teaspoon garlic powder
- 1/2 teaspoon seasoned salt
- 1/2 teaspoon garlic pepper seasoning
- 4 fluid ounces lemon-lime flavored carbonated beverage
- 2 pounds beef sirloin steak, cut into 1 1/2 inch cubes
- 2 green bell peppers, cut into 2 inch pieces
- skewers
- 1/2 pound fresh mushrooms, stems removed
- 1 pint cherry tomatoes
- 1 fresh pineapple - peeled, cored and cubed

Direction

- Stir together distilled white vinegar, soy sauce, light brown sugar, seasoned salt, garlic powder, garlic pepper seasoning, and lemon-lime soda. Keep half of the mixture for basting later. Drop steak in a large zip-top plastic bag and pour the remaining marinade over the meat. Close the bag and marinate in the fridge for 8 hours or even overnight.
- Boil water in a saucepan and blanch green peppers for a minute. Drain and set aside.
- Pre-heat grill on high. Alternately cue the mushrooms, green peppers, steak, tomatoes, and pineapples onto skewers. Dispose of the marinade.
- Grease the grates lightly. Grill the kabobs for 10 minutes or until cooked to liking. Turn and baste often at the last five minutes of grilling.

Nutrition Information

- Calories: 326 calories;
- Total Fat: 17.4
- Sodium: 608
- Total Carbohydrate: 19.2
- Cholesterol: 76
- Protein: 24

857. Sensational Steak Sandwich

Serving: 4 | Prep: 30mins | Cook: 4hours20mins | Ready in:

Ingredients

- 2 tablespoons olive oil
- 1 pound thinly sliced sirloin steak strips
- 8 ounces sliced fresh mushrooms
- 1 green bell pepper, seeded and cut into strips
- 1 medium onion, sliced
- 10 slices provolone cheese
- 1 loaf French bread
- 1 (14 ounce) can beef broth
- 1/2 teaspoon salt
- 1/2 teaspoon ground black pepper
- 1/2 teaspoon garlic powder
- 2 tablespoons Worcestershire sauce
- 1/8 teaspoon red pepper flakes
- 1/4 cup Pinot Noir or other dry red wine
- 1/2 cup prepared horseradish (optional)
- 1/2 cup brown mustard (optional)

Direction

- In a large skillet, heat the oil over medium heat. Put in the beef, then cook until browned. Put in the onion, bell pepper and mushrooms; cook and mix for around 5 minutes, until beginning to turn tender.
- In a slow cooker, blend the red wine, red pepper flakes, Worcestershire sauce, pepper, salt, and beef broth. Move the vegetables and beef to the slow cooker, then stir to combine. Cook while covered on High for 3 - 4 hours, till the beef becomes extremely softened.
- Preheat the oven to 425° F (220° C). Drain the liquid from the slow cooker, reserve for dipping. Cut lengthwise the French bread loaf like a submarine sandwich. Mix the mustard and horseradish together; spread onto the inner of the loaf. On both sides of the loaf, position slices of provolone cheese, fill with vegetables and beef. Seal the loaf, then wrap aluminum foil around the entire sandwich.
- In the preheated oven, bake for 10 - 15 minutes. Bake without the aluminum foil for crunchier bread. Cut into servings. Serve with the juices reserved from the slow cooker as dipping.

Nutrition Information

- Calories: 908 calories;
- Total Fat: 40.6
- Sodium: 2586
- Total Carbohydrate: 78.8
- Cholesterol: 109
- Protein: 55.7

858. Sesame Cabbage And Mushrooms

Serving: 4 | Prep: 15mins | Cook: 6mins | Ready in:

Ingredients

- 2 1/2 tablespoons dark sesame oil, divided
- 6 ounces shiitake mushroom caps, sliced
- 4 cups thinly sliced napa cabbage
- 1 tablespoon reduced-sodium soy sauce
- 1/4 teaspoon freshly ground black pepper
- 1/4 cup cilantro leaves
- 2 tablespoons toasted sesame seeds

Direction

- Set a large skillet over high heat. Put in 2 tablespoons sesame oil; whirl to coat. Stir-fry mushrooms for about 4 minutes, until browned. Put in cabbage; stir-fry for 2 minutes.
- Take the skillet away from heat. Stir in black pepper, soy sauce, and 1 1/2 teaspoon sesame oil until well mixed. Place sesame seeds and cilantro on top.

Nutrition Information

- Calories: 133 calories;
- Total Fat: 10.9
- Sodium: 151
- Total Carbohydrate: 6.4
- Cholesterol: 0
- Protein: 2.9

859. Sherry Chicken And Mushrooms

Serving: 4 | Prep: 15mins | Cook: 35mins | Ready in:

Ingredients

- 4 skinless, boneless chicken breast halves
- salt and ground black pepper to taste
- garlic powder, or to taste
- 2 tablespoons butter
- 1 small onion, chopped
- 1 (8 ounce) package sliced fresh mushrooms
- 1 tablespoon olive oil (optional)
- 1/4 cup cream sherry
- 1/4 cup chicken broth, or as needed (optional)
- 4 slices provolone cheese

Direction

- Season chicken with garlic powder, pepper, and salt.
- Put butter and heat over medium heat in a skillet; add chicken and cook each side in the melted butter for 3-4 minutes until juices run clear and not pink in the center. Take the chicken from the skillet.
- Stir and cook mushrooms and onions in the same skillet; put in olive oil. Cook for 5-10 minutes until mushrooms and onions are slightly tender. Add chicken broth and sherry into the skillet, bring to a boil for about 2 minutes, while using a wooden spoon to drag the browned bits of food off the bottom of the pan.
- Place the chicken back to the skillet, simmer onion mixture and chicken for about 15 minutes, covered, until liquid is slightly reduced. Scoop mushrooms and onion on top of each chicken breast and place a slice of provolone cheese on each top. Take the skillet away from the heat; cover the skillet for about 5 minutes until cheese melts.

Nutrition Information

- Calories: 334 calories;
- Total Carbohydrate: 6.6
- Cholesterol: 96
- Protein: 32.2
- Total Fat: 19.3
- Sodium: 432

860. Shiitake Angel Hair Pasta

Serving: 4 | Prep: | Cook: |Ready in:

Ingredients

- 6 ounces angel hair pasta
- 6 ounces fresh sliced shiitake mushrooms
- 1 clove garlic, minced
- 1/2 onion, chopped
- 1/4 cup white wine
- 1 tablespoon olive oil
- 1/4 cup chicken broth
- 1/2 cup heavy whipping cream
- salt to taste
- ground black pepper to taste
- 2 tablespoons grated Parmesan cheese
- 2 tablespoons chopped fresh parsley

Direction

- Sauté onion and garlic with olive oil on a medium heat, then add the mushrooms until fragrant. Add in wine and chicken stock, cooking until reduced by 1/2 volume. Blend in the cream, reducing until the thickness you want, and season to taste with pepper and salt.
- At the same time, cook the pasta in a boiling large pot of salted water until cooked through but still firm to the bite.
- Drain the pasta and coat with the sauce. Serve the dish on warmed plates, topping with parsley and grated Parmesan cheese.

Nutrition Information

- Calories: 301 calories;
- Sodium: 194
- Total Carbohydrate: 28.4
- Cholesterol: 43
- Protein: 7.5
- Total Fat: 16.3

861. Shiitake Mushroom, Sun Dried Tomato Pesto, And Shrimp Pasta

Serving: 4 | Prep: 10mins | Cook: 30mins |Ready in:

Ingredients

- 1 (16 ounce) package farfalle (bow-tie) pasta
- 1/4 cup butter
- 1/4 cup olive oil
- 2 tablespoons minced garlic
- 1 cup sliced shiitake mushrooms
- 1/2 cup sliced yellow onion
- 1 pound cooked shrimp, peeled and deveined
- 1 (14 ounce) can diced tomatoes
- 1/2 cup sun-dried tomato pesto
- 1/2 cup white wine
- 2 tablespoons lemon juice
- 1/2 cup half-and-half
- 1/2 cup shredded Parmesan cheese, plus more for topping
- 1/4 cup chopped flat-leaf parsley
- 1 teaspoon red pepper flakes
- 1 teaspoon freshly ground black pepper
- 1 teaspoon sea salt

Direction

- In a large pot, boil lightly salted water. Cook bow-tie pasta at a boil for approximately 12 minutes, stirring occasionally, till cooked through yet still firm to the bite; drain.
- Over medium heat, heat a skillet; add olive oil and butter. Cook and stir garlic in the hot butter-oil for around 1 minute till fragrant. Put in onion and mushrooms; cook and stir for approximately 5 minutes till softened.
- Mix diced tomatoes, shrimp, lemon juice, wine, and pesto into mushroom-onion mixture; simmer for 10 minutes. Take away skillet from heat; add Parmesan cheese, half-and-half, red pepper flakes, parsley, salt, and black pepper and mix till sauce is combined well.

- In a serving bowl, place pasta. Spoon sauce over pasta and add extra Parmesan cheese on top.

Nutrition Information

- Calories: 959 calories;
- Total Fat: 40.6
- Sodium: 1152
- Total Carbohydrate: 96.8
- Cholesterol: 272
- Protein: 46.7

862. Shiitake Scallopine

Serving: 8 | Prep: 10mins | Cook: 20mins | Ready in:

Ingredients

- 1 pound angel hair pasta
- 1/4 cup extra virgin olive oil
- 2 cloves garlic, minced
- 2 bulbs shallots, minced
- 1 pound shiitake mushrooms, thinly sliced
- 1/2 teaspoon dried thyme
- 1/2 cup white wine
- 4 (6 ounce) cans marinated artichoke hearts, drained and chopped
- 1/4 cup small capers

Direction

- In a big pot, let lightly salted water boil. Put pasta and cook until al dente or for 8 to 10 minutes. Drain it.
- Over low heat, heat oil in a big heavy skillet. Sweat shallots and garlic until they start to become fragrant. Turn heat to medium. Put thyme and mushrooms. Sauté for about 3 minutes until mushrooms begin to soften. Use wine to deglaze the pan and let simmer for 2 minutes. Stir in capers and artichokes and let simmer for 2 to 3 minutes more.
- Put mushroom mixture over the pasta. Serve.

Nutrition Information

- Calories: 354 calories;
- Total Fat: 13.2
- Sodium: 562
- Total Carbohydrate: 51.2
- Cholesterol: 0
- Protein: 10.4

863. Shredded Roast Spaghetti Sauce

Serving: 28 | Prep: | Cook: | Ready in:

Ingredients

- 4 pounds bone-in pork roast
- 3 teaspoons salt
- 1/4 cup all-purpose flour
- 1/4 cup olive oil
- 2 cups hot water
- 3 cloves crushed garlic
- 1 onion, chopped
- 2 bay leaves
- 1 teaspoon celery salt
- 1 teaspoon ground black pepper
- 2 teaspoons white sugar
- 1/2 teaspoon crushed red pepper flakes
- 1 teaspoon Italian-style seasoning
- 1/4 teaspoon monosodium glutamate (MSG)
- 1/2 teaspoon dried oregano
- 1/2 teaspoon dried basil
- 1/2 teaspoon dried parsley
- 1/2 teaspoon dried rosemary, crushed
- 1/8 teaspoon ground nutmeg
- 4 (6 ounce) cans tomato paste
- 1 quart water
- 1 cup red wine
- 1/2 cup sliced black olives
- 1 cup fresh sliced mushrooms
- 8 anchovy fillets, mashed (optional)

Direction

- Add salt to pork roast to taste, dip in flour. In a big pot, heat the oil. Slowly brown roast on all sides of the pork in hot oil. Put in hot water, cook slowly while covered until the meat is almost falls apart for about 3 hours. Use a folk to tear meat into small pieces.
- In the same pot, put in the anchovy fillets (if you want), mushrooms, olives, wine, water, tomato paste, nutmeg, rosemary, parsley, basil, oregano, monosodium glutamate, seasoning, chile pepper, sugar, black pepper, celery salt, bay leaves, onion, and garlic. Mix the ingredients together, set the heat to low, cover the pot tightly and simmer the mixture for two hours, stir occasionally. Uncover, then keep cooking until the thickness reaches the consistency you want.

Nutrition Information

- Calories: 243 calories;
- Total Fat: 18.1
- Sodium: 599
- Total Carbohydrate: 6.9
- Cholesterol: 48
- Protein: 11.9

864. Shrimp & Scallop Stroganoff

Serving: 6 | Prep: 20mins | Cook: 20mins | Ready in:

Ingredients

- 2 tablespoons butter, divided
- 1 (8 ounce) package fresh mushrooms, sliced
- 1 pound shrimp, peeled and deveined
- 1 pound sea scallops, rinsed and drained
- 2 tablespoons all-purpose flour
- 1/2 teaspoon ground black pepper
- 1 (8 ounce) bottle clam juice
- 1 cup sour cream
- 2 tablespoons dry sherry
- 1 tablespoon chopped fresh parsley

Direction

- In a large skillet, heat a tablespoon of butter over medium-high heat. Mix in the mushrooms and cook until they turn golden. Take the mushrooms out using a slotted spoon and put aside.
- In the skillet, melt the remaining 1 tablespoon of butter, stir in scallops and shrimp; cook and turn for 3 minutes until the shrimp turn pink. Take scallops and shrimp using a slotted spoon, then put aside.
- Combine clam juice, black pepper, and flour together in a medium bowl.
- Pour the clam juice mixture into the skillet, then boil. Turn down the heat to medium-low and simmer until the mixture is thickened. Turn down the heat to low, mix in the sour cream. Place the scallops, shrimp, and mushrooms back into the skillet; stir in sherry and cook till heated through. Dust with parsley.

Nutrition Information

- Calories: 287 calories;
- Total Fat: 13.9
- Sodium: 395
- Total Carbohydrate: 8.3
- Cholesterol: 168
- Protein: 30.9

865. Shrimp Cognac And Baked Cheese Grits

Serving: 12 | Prep: 30mins | Cook: 1hours30mins | Ready in:

Ingredients

- 6 cups water

- 3/4 teaspoon salt
- 2 cups yellow grits
- 1 3/4 teaspoons salt
- 1/2 teaspoon ground black pepper
- 1/2 cup unsalted butter
- 2 tablespoons minced garlic
- 1 (8 ounce) package shredded Cheddar cheese
- 3 eggs
- 1 cup whole milk
- 1/4 cup clarified butter
- 2 tablespoons minced garlic
- 1 leek, halved and cut into 1/4-inch pieces
- 2 ounces fresh morel mushrooms, chopped
- 3 ounces fresh oyster mushrooms, chopped
- 3 ounces fresh chanterelle mushrooms, chopped
- 2 tomatoes, peeled, seeded, and chopped
- 1 tablespoon Creole seasoning
- 1/2 cup cognac
- 1/2 cup shrimp stock
- 1/3 cup veal stock
- 1 pound peeled and deveined gulf shrimp
- 2 tablespoons chopped fresh thyme
- 3 tablespoons unsalted butter
- salt and black pepper to taste

Direction

- Start preheating the oven to 350°F (175°C). Oil a 9x13-in. baking dish.
- In a big pot, boil 3/4 teaspoon of salt and water. Stir in grits and boil again. Lower the heat to low; cook for 30 minutes until the grits are very thick and soft, whisking often. Take away from heat, then mix in Cheddar cheese, 2 tablespoons garlic, 1/2 cup butter, 1/2 teaspoon of pepper, and 1 3/4 teaspoons of salt until the cheese melts. In a bowl, whisk milk with eggs until smooth; mix into the grits until evenly blended. Add to the prepared baking dish.
- Put in the preheated oven and bake for 1 hour until the top turns golden brown and the middle of the grits are hot.
- In the meantime, in a skillet, heat clarified butter over medium heat. Mix in 2 tablespoons of garlic and cook for 2 minutes until turning golden. Add leeks, and cook for another 1 minute. Mix in Creole seasoning, tomatoes, chanterelle mushrooms, oyster mushrooms, and morel mushrooms; stir and cook for 3 minutes until the mushrooms start to render their liquid. Add cognac and simmer for 2 minutes, then add veal stock and shrimp stock. Simmer again and cook until the liquid has decreased by 1/2. Mix in 3 tablespoons of butter, thyme, and the shrimp. Stir and cook over low heat for 4 minutes until the shrimp is not opaque anymore; use pepper and salt to season.
- Enjoy the mushroom sauce and shrimp with the baked grits.

Nutrition Information

- Calories: 425 calories;
- Total Carbohydrate: 26.9
- Cholesterol: 165
- Protein: 18.4
- Total Fat: 24.1
- Sodium: 846

866. Shrimp Piccata

Serving: 4 | Prep: 10mins | Cook: 22mins | Ready in:

Ingredients

- 1 (16 ounce) package linguine pasta
- 1/4 cup olive oil
- 1/4 cup butter
- 1 pound uncooked medium shrimp, peeled and deveined
- 10 baby bella mushrooms, sliced
- 2 cloves garlic, chopped
- 1 (6 ounce) jar marinated artichoke hearts, chopped, with juice
- 1/2 lemon, juiced
- 3 tablespoons capers with juice
- 1 splash dry white wine (optional)
- salt and ground black pepper to taste

Direction

- Bring lightly salted water in a big pot to a boil. In boiling water, cooking linguine for 11 minutes until it is tender yet still firm to the bite, then drain.
- In a saucepan, heat butter and olive oil on medium heat. Put in garlic, mushrooms and shrimp, then cook and stir for 1 to 2 minutes until fragrant. Put in white wine, capers, lemon juice and artichokes, then cook and stir for 10 minutes, until shrimp is soft and all contents bubble. Scoop over individual beds of pasta with shrimp piccata, then add pepper and salt to taste.

Nutrition Information

- Calories: 769 calories;
- Total Fat: 30.7
- Sodium: 651
- Total Carbohydrate: 89.4
- Cholesterol: 203
- Protein: 36.6

867. Shrimp Stuffed Mushrooms

Serving: 10 | Prep: 15mins | Cook: 10mins | Ready in:

Ingredients

- 2 pounds large mushrooms
- 3/4 pound cooked baby shrimp
- 1 cup crushed bacon flavored crackers
- 1 cup cream cheese, softened
- 1/2 cup shredded sharp Cheddar cheese

Direction

- Heat oven to 220°C (425°F) beforehand. Grease a medium baking dish lightly.
- Cut stems from mushrooms. Chop stems finely, and put aside. In the baking dish, place caps cavity side up.
- Mix together cream cheese, crushed bacon flavored crackers, cooked baby shrimp, and mushroom stems in a medium bowl.
- Generously stuff mushroom stem mixture into mushroom caps. Place sharp Cheddar cheese on top.
- In the preheated oven, allow to bake till cheese browned lightly and melted for 8-10 minutes.

Nutrition Information

- Calories: 191 calories;
- Sodium: 214
- Total Carbohydrate: 7.5
- Cholesterol: 83
- Protein: 13.2
- Total Fat: 12.5

868. Shrimp Tetrazzini

Serving: 4 | Prep: 10mins | Cook: 55mins | Ready in:

Ingredients

- 2 tablespoons butter
- 1 onion, chopped
- 8 ounces shrimp, shelled and deveined
- 8 ounces fresh mushrooms, sliced
- 1/4 cup all-purpose flour
- 1/4 cup mayonnaise
- 1 teaspoon salt
- 2 cups milk
- 1/4 cup sherry
- 1 (8 ounce) package spaghetti
- 1/4 cup grated Parmesan cheese

Direction

- Cook the spaghetti in the big pot of the boiling salted water till al dente. Drain off well.
- On medium-low heat, melt the butter in the medium-sized saucepan. Put the onion into the melted butter and whisk till the onion softens. Put in the mushrooms and shrimp,

- cook for 5 minutes, whisk frequently. Take the shrimp mixture out of the saucepan, add into a medium bowl and put aside.
- Take the saucepan out of the heat. Mix the sherry, milk, salt, mayonnaise and flour in saucepan. Stir them well. Bring saucepan back to heat and cook till the sauce is thickened.
- Add the sauce to the bowl of shrimp mixture. Put spaghetti into the bowl and stir them well.
- Add all of the ingredients into the 1.5 qt. casserole plate or the baking pan. Drizzle parmesan cheese over the mixture. Bake at 175 degrees C (350 degrees F) for half an hour.

Nutrition Information

- Calories: 565 calories;
- Sodium: 1007
- Total Carbohydrate: 61.4
- Cholesterol: 120
- Protein: 27.6
- Total Fat: 22.6

869. Shrimp And Mushroom Linguini With Creamy Cheese Herb Sauce

Serving: 4 | Prep: 15mins | Cook: 15mins | Ready in:

Ingredients

- 1 (8 ounce) package linguini pasta
- 2 tablespoons butter
- 1/2 pound fresh mushrooms, sliced
- 1/2 cup butter
- 2 cloves garlic, minced
- 1 (3 ounce) package cream cheese
- 2 tablespoons chopped fresh parsley
- 3/4 teaspoon dried basil
- 2/3 cup boiling water
- 1/2 pound cooked shrimp

Direction

- Boil a large pot with mildly salted water. Put in linguini and cook for 7 minutes until tender. Drain.
- In the meantime, heat 2 tablespoons butter in a large skillet on medium-high heat. Put in mushrooms; cook while stirring until soft. Place onto a plate.
- Melt half cup of butter with the minced garlic in the same pan. Pour in the cream cheese, use a spoon to break it up as it melts. Mix in the basil and parsley. Simmer for 5 minutes. Stir in boiling water until sauce is smooth. Mix in cooked mushrooms and shrimp; heat sauce through.
- Mix linguini with shrimp sauce, serve right away.

Nutrition Information

- Calories: 601 calories;
- Total Fat: 38.3
- Sodium: 403
- Total Carbohydrate: 44
- Cholesterol: 210
- Protein: 23.2

870. Simple Hot And Sour Soup

Serving: 4 | Prep: 10mins | Cook: 20mins | Ready in:

Ingredients

- 1 3/4 ounces dried shiitake mushrooms
- 1 ounce dried cloud ear mushrooms
- 1/2 (12 ounce) package silken tofu, cut into 1/2-inch cubes
- 1 (8 ounce) can bamboo shoots, cut into thin matchstick-size pieces
- 2 teaspoons vinegar
- 1 teaspoon ground white pepper
- 10 fluid ounces chicken stock
- 2 ounces cooked ham, thinly sliced
- 1 teaspoon soy sauce

- 1 teaspoon Shaoxing cooking wine
- salt to taste
- 2 teaspoons corn flour
- 2 teaspoons water
- 2 eggs, beaten
- 1 teaspoon sesame oil

Direction

- Soak cloud ear mushrooms and shiitake mushrooms in a bowl of water for 30 minutes until tender. Let it drain and slice the mushrooms into smaller pieces.
- Boil water in a pot and stir in tofu to cook for 60 seconds. Remove the tofu using a slotted spoon and transfer it to a bowl. Bring the water to boil again, add bamboo shoots and cook for another 60 seconds. Let it drain and set the bamboo shoots aside.
- In a bowl, combine white pepper and vinegar.
- In a large saucepan, boil the chicken stock and stir in mushrooms, bamboo shoots, and ham. Bring it back to boil and add the salt, soy sauce, Shaoxing wine, and the tofu. Return to boil.
- Whisk water and corn flour in a bowl until completely dissolved. Pour it into the chicken stock mixture and stir until the soup starts to get thick. Pour the beaten eggs into the soup and cook for 2-3 minutes, stirring it slowly to form cooked egg clumps.
- Put in vinegar-pepper mixture and stir and drizzle sesame oil over the soup.

Nutrition Information

- Calories: 185 calories;
- Protein: 11.8
- Total Fat: 8
- Sodium: 574
- Total Carbohydrate: 19.4
- Cholesterol: 101

871. Simply Marinated Mushrooms

Serving: 6 | Prep: 15mins | Cook: 10mins | Ready in:

Ingredients

- 1 cup water
- 1 1/2 pounds fresh mushrooms, stems removed
- 1/4 cup olive oil
- 1 teaspoon dried thyme
- 1 teaspoon salt
- 3 tablespoons fresh lemon juice
- 3 teaspoons minced garlic
- 1/2 teaspoon ground black pepper
- 3 tablespoons dried parsley
- 1/8 teaspoon onion powder

Direction

- In a large pot, boil water. Stir in mushrooms and simmer for about 10 minutes. Take away from heat and drain.
- In a large bowl, whisk the thyme, olive oil, lemon juice, salt, pepper, garlic, onion powder and parsley together. Add mushrooms and toss to coat. Refrigerate to marinade overnight, and rewarm when serving.

Nutrition Information

- Calories: 115 calories;
- Total Fat: 9.5
- Sodium: 393
- Total Carbohydrate: 7.2
- Cholesterol: 0
- Protein: 2.5

872. Sirloin Tips And Mushrooms

Serving: 6 | Prep: 15mins | Cook: 45mins | Ready in:

Ingredients

- 3 tablespoons olive oil
- 3 cloves garlic, minced
- 1 1/2 pounds beef sirloin
- 1 (16 ounce) can mushrooms, with liquid
- 1 (8 ounce) can tomato sauce
- salt to taste
- freshly ground pepper, to taste
- 3/4 cup red wine

Direction

- Slice the beef into cubes. Heat olive oil in a large skillet over medium/high heat and brown the beef cubes together with garlic.
- Put in red wine, pepper, salt, tomato sauce, mushrooms with liquid. Cook until the beef cubes become tender, half an hour. If desired, while cooking, pour in a bit more wine.

Nutrition Information

- Calories: 257 calories;
- Total Fat: 13.5
- Sodium: 556
- Total Carbohydrate: 7.1
- Cholesterol: 49
- Protein: 21.7

873. Slovak Sauerkraut Christmas Soup

Serving: 10 | Prep: 15mins | Cook: 2hours | Ready in:

Ingredients

- 1 (32 ounce) package sauerkraut, chopped
- 2 1/2 quarts chicken broth
- 6 black peppercorns
- 4 bay leaves
- salt to taste
- 2 cups dried forest mushroom blend
- 3/4 pound Hungarian style dry paprika sausage
- 3/4 pound smoked ham
- 3/4 cup chopped pitted prunes
- 2 tablespoons vegetable oil
- 1 large onion, finely chopped
- 2 tablespoons all-purpose flour
- 2 teaspoons sweet Hungarian paprika
- 1 cup water
- 1 cup sour cream

Direction

- In a large pot, put the mushrooms, salt, bay leaves, peppercorns, chicken broth, and sauerkraut; allow to boil. Add the entire piece of ham and the sausage. Allow to simmer on medium heat for 1 1/2 hours. After the first hour, put in the prunes.
- Take the meat out from the soup and put aside. Discard the bay leaves.
- In a large skillet, heat the oil on medium. Add in the onion and fry until translucent. Use paprika and flour to dust on the onion; stir and cook for 1 minute. Use a fork to stir in water slowly to avoid forming lumps. Allow to boil and thicken. Add into the soup pot. Cube the ham and sausage and put into the soup, stir. Allow to boil and cook for 10 more minutes.
- Transfer into bowls and place a dollop of sour cream on top to serve.

Nutrition Information

- Calories: 386 calories;
- Total Carbohydrate: 21.4
- Cholesterol: 53
- Protein: 15.5
- Total Fat: 26.5
- Sodium: 1326

874. Slow Cooked Beef Stew

Serving: 6 | Prep: 25mins | Cook: 8hours5mins | Ready in:

Ingredients

- 2 pints water
- 3 carrots, cut into chunks
- 3 cups mushrooms, halved or quartered
- 1/2 rutabaga, peeled and cut into small chunks
- 1 1/2 pounds cubed beef stew meat
- 2 tablespoons vegetable oil, or more if needed
- 3/4 cup all-purpose flour
- 2 teaspoons dried parsley
- 2 teaspoons dried thyme
- 3 cubes beef bouillon, crumbled
- 5 grinds freshly ground black pepper
- 1 teaspoon yeast extract spread (such as Marmite®)
- 2 teaspoons tomato paste (optional)
- 2 dashes Worcestershire sauce

Direction

- Put kettle on in order to have the boiled water ready. Into the slow cooker, mix rutabaga, mushrooms and carrots.
- In the big bowl, mix vegetable oil and beef. Turn beef in oil till well-coated with your hands or wooden spoon.
- In the second big bowl, stir pepper, beef bouillon cubes, thyme, parsley and flour together. Put in beef, reserving oil for another use, and coat using seasoned flour.
- Heat reserved oil to the big skillet or wok and heat on medium low heat. Put in beef, shaking off the excess flour and saving for later use. If meat sticks to pan, put in additional oil; stir in Worcestershire sauce, tomato paste, and yeast extract spread. Cook 5-10 minutes or till beef is not pink in the middle anymore.
- Drizzle the reserved flour on top of vegetables in slow cooker. Add the boiling water, small amount at a time, onto the vegetables and whisk to mix in the flour. Put in beef along with the cooking juices.
- Cook on Low setting for 8-10 hours or till meat becomes soft and flavors become well-combined.

Nutrition Information

- Calories: 471 calories;
- Cholesterol: 99
- Protein: 34.5
- Total Fat: 27.5
- Sodium: 586
- Total Carbohydrate: 20.7

875. Slow Cooked Goose

Serving: 6 | Prep: 20mins | Cook: 6hours | Ready in:

Ingredients

- 1 bunch celery, chopped
- 1 (12 ounce) package baby carrots, chopped
- 1 cup cream of celery soup
- 1 cup cream of chicken soup
- 1 cup cream of mushroom soup
- 1 cup cut-up mushrooms
- 8 fresh sage leaves
- 3 tablespoons fresh rosemary
- 2 tablespoons fresh thyme
- 2 (10 pound) goose, cut up

Direction

- In a bowl, mix thyme, rosemary, sage, mushrooms, cream of the mushroom soup, cream of the chicken soup, cream of the celery soup, carrots and celery.
- Place the goose pieces into a slow cooker. Add vegetable mixture and soup over goose.
- Cook on High for 6-8 hours or until the goose is tender.

Nutrition Information

- Calories: 1362 calories;
- Total Fat: 72
- Sodium: 1367
- Total Carbohydrate: 16.9
- Cholesterol: 500
- Protein: 152

876. Slow Cooker Chicken Cacciatore

Serving: 6 | Prep: 15mins | Cook: 9hours | Ready in:

Ingredients

- 6 skinless, boneless chicken breast halves
- 1 (28 ounce) jar spaghetti sauce
- 2 green bell pepper, seeded and cubed
- 8 ounces fresh mushrooms, sliced
- 1 onion, finely diced
- 2 tablespoons minced garlic

Direction

- Place chicken into a slow cooker. Add garlic, onion, mushrooms, green bell peppers and spaghetti sauce on top.
- Cook, covered, for 7-9 hours on Low.

Nutrition Information

- Calories: 261 calories;
- Total Fat: 6.1
- Sodium: 590
- Total Carbohydrate: 23.7
- Cholesterol: 63
- Protein: 27.1

877. Slow Cooker Chicken Creole

Serving: 4 | Prep: 10mins | Cook: 12hours | Ready in:

Ingredients

- 4 skinless, boneless chicken breast halves
- salt and pepper to taste
- Creole-style seasoning to taste
- 1 (14.5 ounce) can stewed tomatoes, with liquid
- 1 stalk celery, diced
- 1 green bell pepper, diced
- 3 cloves garlic, minced
- 1 onion, diced
- 1 (4 ounce) can mushrooms, drained
- 1 fresh jalapeno pepper, seeded and chopped

Direction

- In a slow cooker, place chicken breasts. Sprinkle with Creole-style seasoning, pepper, and salt to season for taste. Mix in jalapeno pepper, mushroom, onion, garlic, bell pepper, celery, and tomatoes with liquid.
- Cook on High for 5 to 6 hours or on Low for 10 to 12 hours.

Nutrition Information

- Calories: 189 calories;
- Sodium: 431
- Total Carbohydrate: 13.8
- Cholesterol: 68
- Protein: 29.6
- Total Fat: 1.9

878. Slow Cooker Chicken And Mushroom Stew

Serving: 6 | Prep: 20mins | Cook: 6hours15mins | Ready in:

Ingredients

- 1/2 cup all-purpose flour
- 1 teaspoon dried basil
- 1 teaspoon dried thyme
- 1 teaspoon dried rubbed sage
- 1 teaspoon ground black pepper
- 5 chicken thighs, quartered
- 1 tablespoon olive oil, or as needed
- 1 large yellow onion, diced
- 1 large bell pepper, diced
- 8 ounces chorizo sausage, thinly sliced
- 2 cloves garlic, crushed
- 1 (8 ounce) package sliced fresh mushrooms
- 1 cup chicken stock
- 1 (10.75 ounce) can cream of mushroom soup
- 1 (10.75 ounce) can cream of celery soup
- 1 cup sour cream
- 2 teaspoons Cajun seasoning
- 1 teaspoon cayenne pepper

Direction

- In a large resealable bag, combine black pepper, sage, thyme, basil, and flour; put chicken in bag and seal, shake to evenly coat the chicken.
- In a large skillet placed over medium heat, heat olive oil. Cook and stir onion and bell pepper for 5 to 10 minutes until lightly soft. Add garlic and chorizo sausage; cook and stir until sausage is done, approximately 5 minutes. Remove mixture to a slow cooker and throw mushrooms on top.
- In the same skillet, cook and stir coated chicken (with all the flour included), adding more oil if required, 5 to 10 minutes until chicken is browned. Transfer to the slow cooker.
- In the same skillet, pour chicken stock and heat to a boil, while scraping with a wooden spoon to remove the browned bits of food from the bottom of the skillet. Pour all brown bits and liquid into slow cooker.
- In a bowl, combine cayenne pepper, Cajun seasoning, sour cream, cream of celery soup and cream of mushroom soup; scoop into slow cooker.
- Cook on High for 2 hours; lower setting to Low and continue to cook for 4 more hours.

Nutrition Information

- Calories: 554 calories;
- Total Fat: 37.3
- Sodium: 1577
- Total Carbohydrate: 23.7
- Cholesterol: 115
- Protein: 31

879. Slow Cooker Chicken With Mushroom Wine Sauce

Serving: 4 | Prep: 10mins | Cook: 6hours | Ready in:

Ingredients

- 1 (10.75 ounce) can condensed cream of mushroom soup
- 1 teaspoon dried minced onion
- 1 teaspoon dried parsley
- 1/4 cup white wine
- 1/4 teaspoon garlic powder
- 1 tablespoon milk
- 1 (4 ounce) can mushroom pieces, drained
- salt and pepper to taste
- 4 boneless, skinless chicken breast halves

Direction

- Combine mushroom pieces, milk, garlic powder, wine, parsley, onion and soup in a slow cooker. Season with pepper and salt. Transfer chicken to the slow cooker, covering with the soup mixture.
- Cook for 5-6 hours on low setting or 3-4 hours on High setting.

Nutrition Information

- Calories: 208 calories;
- Total Fat: 7.1
- Sodium: 956
- Total Carbohydrate: 7.6
- Cholesterol: 61
- Protein: 24.9

880. Slow Cooker Pork With Mushrooms And Barley

Serving: 6 | Prep: 20mins | Cook: 8hours | Ready in:

Ingredients

- 3 cloves garlic, finely chopped
- 1 teaspoon salt
- 6 pork chops
- 1/2 cup barley
- 8 ounces white mushrooms, sliced
- 1/2 onion, chopped
- 2 (14 ounce) cans chicken broth
- 1/2 cup water
- 2 teaspoons Worcestershire sauce
- 1 bay leaf
- 1 pinch salt and ground black pepper to taste

Direction

- Rub 1 tsp. salt and chopped garlic into porkchops.
- Put barley in slow cooker; top using porkchops. Cover using chopped onion and white mushrooms. Add few grinds of fresh black pepper, salt, bay leaf, Worcestershire sauce, water and chicken broth.
- Put slow cooker on low; cover. Cook for 8 hours.

Nutrition Information

- Calories: 236 calories;
- Cholesterol: 68
- Protein: 28.8
- Total Fat: 6.3

- Sodium: 1077
- Total Carbohydrate: 14.9

881. Slow Cooker Stuffing

Serving: 16 | Prep: 25mins | Cook: 8hours55mins | Ready in:

Ingredients

- 1 cup butter or margarine
- 2 cups chopped onion
- 2 cups chopped celery
- 1/4 cup chopped fresh parsley
- 12 ounces sliced mushrooms
- 12 cups dry bread cubes
- 1 teaspoon poultry seasoning
- 1 1/2 teaspoons dried sage
- 1 teaspoon dried thyme
- 1/2 teaspoon dried marjoram
- 1 1/2 teaspoons salt
- 1/2 teaspoon ground black pepper
- 4 1/2 cups chicken broth, or as needed
- 2 eggs, beaten

Direction

- Put margarine or butter in a skillet and melt it over medium heat. Add mushroom, parsley, onion, and celery and cook while stirring them frequently in melted butter.
- Spoon the cooked vegetables over the bread cubes in a huge mixing bowl. Season the mixture with sage, salt and pepper, marjoram, poultry seasoning, and thyme. Pour in broth, just enough to moisten the mixture. Stir in eggs. Pour the mixture into the slow cooker. Cover the slow cooker.
- Let the mixture cook on a high setting for 45 minutes. Adjust the heat to low. Cook the mixture for 4-8 more hours.

Nutrition Information

- Calories: 197 calories;
- Total Fat: 13.1
- Sodium: 502
- Total Carbohydrate: 16.6
- Cholesterol: 54
- Protein: 3.9

882. Smothered Pork Chops With Bourbon And Mushrooms

Serving: 4 | Prep: 10mins | Cook: 1hours | Ready in:

Ingredients

- 4 (8 ounce) center-cut pork chops
- salt and ground black pepper to taste
- 2 tablespoons vegetable oil
- For the Sauce:
- 2 tablespoons butter
- 2 cups thinly sliced onion
- 1 (8 ounce) package thinly sliced baby bella mushrooms
- 1 teaspoon white sugar
- 1/4 cup bourbon
- 1 1/2 cups beef broth
- 1/2 cup heavy cream
- salt and ground black pepper to taste

Direction

- Start preheating oven to 375°F (190°C).
- Add pepper and salt to season the pork chops. In a frying pan, heat oil over medium-high heat. Put in pork chops; then cook for 3-4 mins on each side or until browned. In a baking dish (about 9x13-inch), put the browned chops. Wipe out all the residual oil from pan.
- In the same pan, melt butter over medium heat. Put in sugar, mushrooms, and onion. Cook while stirring for one minute. Turn the heat to medium-low and cover pan. Simmer the mixture for 10 mins or until the onions have softened. Uncover the pan; stir mixture, scraping up any browned bits from bottom. Keep cooking the onions for 3 more mins.
- Add bourbon to onion mixture and cook for 3-4 mins or until mostly evaporated. Put in cream and broth; then simmer. Cook about 10 mins; transfer over browned chops in baking dish. Wrap in aluminum foil.
- Bake in prepared oven for 25 to 30 mins or until an instant-read thermometer registers 145°F (63°C) when inserted into pork.

Nutrition Information

- Calories: 509 calories;
- Protein: 32.4
- Total Fat: 33.4
- Sodium: 472
- Total Carbohydrate: 11.2
- Cholesterol: 126

883. Snapper In Black Sauce

Serving: 6 | Prep: 20mins | Cook: 30mins | Ready in:

Ingredients

- 1/2 cup dried porcini mushrooms
- 1 cup boiling water
- 2 tablespoons olive oil
- 2 onions, chopped
- 3 cloves garlic, minced
- 1/2 teaspoon ground nutmeg
- 1/2 cup ground walnuts
- 1 bay leaf
- salt and pepper to taste
- 2 pounds red snapper fillets
- 1/2 cup all-purpose flour
- 2 tablespoons chopped fresh parsley

Direction

- Let the porcini mushrooms soak in water for 30 seconds. Drain the soaked mushrooms and keep the drained liquid, then cut the porcini mushrooms into smaller pieces.
- Preheat the oven to 350°F (175°C).

- In a big oven-safe skillet, put in the olive oil and heat up over medium heat setting; put in the garlic and onion and sauté it in hot oil for about 5 minutes until the onion is translucent and soft. Put in the bay leaf, nutmeg, reserved mushroom liquid, walnuts and mushrooms and allow the mixture to simmer; cook for 5-10 minutes until the mixture turns dark in color and has reduced in volume. Coat the snapper fillets with flour then shake it to remove any excess flour. Add the floured snapper fillets into the skillet and coat it with the sauce mixture.
- Put the skillet inside the preheated oven and let the fish mixture bake for about 20 minutes until you could flake the fish meat apart with ease using a fork. Top it off with parsley then serve.

Nutrition Information

- Calories: 320 calories;
- Total Carbohydrate: 16.9
- Cholesterol: 56
- Protein: 36.2
- Total Fat: 11.4
- Sodium: 75

884. So Divine Stuffed Mushrooms

Serving: 12 | Prep: 15mins | Cook: 1hours | Ready in:

Ingredients

- 24 white mushrooms, stems removed
- 1 tablespoon olive oil
- 1 (12 ounce) package bulk pork sausage
- 1/4 cup crumbled blue cheese
- 1 tablespoon Worcestershire sauce
- 1 tablespoon balsamic vinegar
- 1 clove garlic, minced
- 1 dash lemon juice
- salt and ground black pepper to taste

Direction

- Set the oven to 325°F (165°C), and start preheating.
- On a baking sheet, place the mushroom caps with the cavity-side facing upwards. Give the mushroom caps a drizzle of olive oil. In a bowl, combine pepper, salt, lemon juice, garlic, balsamic vinegar, Worcestershire sauce, blue cheese and sausage. Fill the sausage mixture into the mushroom caps.
- Bake in the oven for about 1 hour until the sausage is no longer pink.

Nutrition Information

- Calories: 101 calories;
- Total Carbohydrate: 2
- Cholesterol: 18
- Protein: 5.5
- Total Fat: 8.1
- Sodium: 304

885. So Shiitake Wontons

Serving: 10 | Prep: 45mins | Cook: 10mins | Ready in:

Ingredients

- 2 large eggs, divided
- 1 tablespoon water
- 1 1/4 pounds ground pork
- 1 (8 ounce) package shiitake mushrooms, stemmed and diced
- 1 tablespoon soy sauce
- 1/2 teaspoon sesame oil
- 1 1/2 teaspoons cornstarch
- 1 teaspoon onion powder
- waxed paper
- 4 cups chicken broth
- 1 (16 ounce) package wonton wrappers

Direction

- Into a small bowl, separate an egg white; stir in water. Set egg yolk aside.
- In a bowl, mix sesame oil, soy sauce, shiitake mushrooms, pork, the leftover a whole egg and an egg yolk. Combine using hand till just incorporated. Put in the onion powder and cornstarch; combine filling evenly.
- Line waxed paper on a baking sheet.
- Separate and put the wonton wrappers onto the work area. Onto the middle of one wrapper, put a rounded dollop of filling. Moisten edges slightly with mixture of egg white. Fold a corner over filling towards the opposing corner to make a triangle; press to seal. Moisten edges once more and gather in corners to make a little purse-like pouch. On the prepped baking sheet, put the wonton. Repeat with the rest of wrappers and filling.
- In a big pot, let chicken broth come to boil. Carefully drop in the wontons; cook for approximately 5 minutes till clear.

Nutrition Information

- Calories: 281 calories;
- Total Fat: 10.2
- Sodium: 778
- Total Carbohydrate: 28.3
- Cholesterol: 80
- Protein: 16.7

886. Sour Cream Mushroom Chicken

Serving: 6 | Prep: | Cook: | Ready in:

Ingredients

- 1 (10.75 ounce) can condensed cream of chicken soup
- 1 (10.75 ounce) can condensed cream of mushroom soup
- 2 cups sour cream
- 3/4 cup dry white wine
- 1/2 onion, chopped
- 1 cup fresh sliced mushrooms
- 1/2 teaspoon garlic powder
- 1/2 teaspoon salt
- 1/2 teaspoon ground black pepper
- 6 skinless, boneless chicken breast halves
- 1 tablespoon chopped fresh parsley, for garnish

Direction

- Set an oven to preheat to 175°C (350°F).
- Mix together the pepper, salt, garlic powder, mushrooms, onion, wine or broth, sour cream, cream of mushroom soup and cream of chicken soup in a 9x13-inch baking dish, then stir all together. Lay out the chicken breasts over the mixture. Let it bake for an hour in the preheated oven without cover or until the juices run clear and the chicken becomes tender.

Nutrition Information

- Calories: 416 calories;
- Total Fat: 23.5
- Sodium: 975
- Total Carbohydrate: 12.7
- Cholesterol: 106
- Protein: 32.3

887. Southern Fried Cabbage With Bacon, Mushrooms, And Onions

Serving: 10 | Prep: 15mins | Cook: 30mins | Ready in:

Ingredients

- 1 pound bacon
- 1 large head cabbage, chopped
- 1 large onion, chopped
- 1 (8 ounce) package sliced fresh mushrooms
- salt and ground black pepper to taste

Direction

- In a big skillet, add bacon and cook on medium high heat for approximately 10 minutes, while turning from time to time, until browned evenly. Drain the bacon slices on paper towels then crumble once cooled. Save only 3 tbsp. bacon drippings in the skillet, drain off the rest.
- In the reserved bacon drippings, cook and stir mushrooms, onion and bacon for around 20 minutes, until softened and browned slightly. Fold bacon into cabbage mixture, then season with black pepper and salt.

Nutrition Information

- Calories: 123 calories;
- Protein: 8
- Total Fat: 6.4
- Sodium: 368
- Total Carbohydrate: 9.6
- Cholesterol: 16

888. Southern Style Fried Mushrooms

Serving: 2 | Prep: 15mins | Cook: 5mins | Ready in:

Ingredients

- 2 cups vegetable oil for frying
- 1/4 cup red cooking wine
- 2 teaspoons water
- 1/2 cup all-purpose flour
- 1 teaspoon chopped fresh parsley
- 3/4 teaspoon minced garlic
- 1/2 teaspoon kosher salt
- ground black pepper to taste
- 10 button mushrooms
- 2 tablespoons grated Parmesan cheese

Direction

- In a large saucepan or deep-fryer, heat oil to 350 °F (175 °C).
- Whisk water, wine, parsley, flour, garlic, pepper, and salt together in one bowl until no lumps are visible and well combined. Plunge every mushroom one by one into the mixture to coat. Put the coated mushrooms carefully into the hot oil, prevent mushrooms from touching and sticking together while cooking. Cook for around 5 to 6 minutes until golden brown. Take away from oil and place on a plate lined with paper towels to drain. Scatter Parmesan cheese over and serve.

Nutrition Information

- Calories: 382 calories;
- Total Fat: 24.1
- Sodium: 741
- Total Carbohydrate: 33.2
- Cholesterol: 4
- Protein: 7

889. Spaghetti With Broccoli And Mushrooms

Serving: 5 | Prep: 20mins | Cook: 20mins | Ready in:

Ingredients

- 1 pound uncooked spaghetti
- 2 (10 ounce) packages frozen chopped broccoli
- 2 (4.5 ounce) cans sliced mushrooms, drained
- 1/2 cup butter
- 1 tablespoon salt
- 2 teaspoons ground black pepper
- 1 cup grated Parmesan cheese
- 2 teaspoons lemon juice
- 1 teaspoon garlic powder
- 1 teaspoon dried basil

Direction

- Bring a large pot of salted water to boil. Put in spaghetti. Return water to a rolling boil. Cook the pasta until al dente and drain well.
- In a large saucepan, combine basil, garlic powder, lemon juice, Parmesan cheese, pepper, salt, butter, mushrooms and broccoli. Heat mixture on low heat until broccoli and mushrooms are hot, stirring often.
- In a large serving dish, put hot mixture and spaghetti, and toss lightly then serve.

Nutrition Information

- Calories: 633 calories;
- Total Fat: 26
- Sodium: 2079
- Total Carbohydrate: 77.9
- Cholesterol: 66
- Protein: 24.1

890. Spaghetti With Tomato And Sausage Sauce

Serving: 16 | Prep: 15mins | Cook: 3hours30mins | Ready in:

Ingredients

- 1 pound beef sausage
- 1 onion, minced
- 2 cups fresh sliced mushrooms
- 1/4 cup olive oil
- 2 (6 ounce) cans tomato paste
- 1 (46 fluid ounce) can tomato juice
- 1 (16 ounce) can crushed tomatoes
- 1 cup Burgundy wine
- 1 1/2 tablespoons dried oregano
- 1 tablespoon dried basil
- 2 tablespoons dried parsley
- 1 tablespoon minced garlic
- 2 tablespoons garlic salt
- 1/2 cup white sugar
- 2 pounds spaghetti

Direction

- Start preheating the oven at 350°F (175°C). Cook sausage about 30 minutes. Slice into bite-sized pieces, and put aside.
- In a Dutch oven, sauté mushrooms and onion in olive oil until soft. Use a slotted spoon to transfer, and put aside. Blend wine, Italian tomatoes, tomato juice, tomato paste into Dutch oven. Stir until become smooth. Combine in sugar, garlic salt, garlic, parsley, basil and oregano. Bring mushroom and onion with sausage back to the sauce. Heat to a boil. Lower the heat, and simmer for a minimum of 3 hours. Cover the pot if the sauce looks too thick.
- Based on the package directions, cook pasta. Drain. Pour sauce over pasta and then enjoy.

Nutrition Information

- Calories: 415 calories;
- Total Fat: 12.2
- Sodium: 1428
- Total Carbohydrate: 61.1
- Cholesterol: 19
- Protein: 14

891. Special Vegan Chili

Serving: 4 | Prep: 20mins | Cook: 44mins | Ready in:

Ingredients

- 1 tablespoon canola oil
- 1/2 cup chopped red bell pepper
- 1/3 cup chopped yellow onion
- 1/3 cup minced carrot
- 2 cloves garlic, minced
- 1/3 cup minced cremini mushrooms
- 1 (19 ounce) can mixed beans, drained
- 1 1/2 cups canned diced tomatoes, with juices
- 1 tablespoon chili powder
- 1 1/2 teaspoons ground flax seeds

- 1/2 teaspoon ground cumin
- 1/2 teaspoon dried oregano
- 2 pinches ground black pepper

Direction

- In a big skillet, heat oil on medium-heat. Sauté garlic, carrot, onion, and red bell pepper for 8-10 minutes until lightly toasted. Add mushrooms and cook for a minute.
- Put red bell pepper mixture in a pot. Stir in black pepper, oregano, cumin, flax seeds, chili powder, diced tomatoes with juice, and mixed beans; mix well. Let it boil. Simmer, uncovered, for 30 minutes while stirring occasionally until flavors have blended.

Nutrition Information

- Calories: 198 calories;
- Cholesterol: 0
- Protein: 9.4
- Total Fat: 4.4
- Sodium: 693
- Total Carbohydrate: 28.6

892. Spicy Basil Chicken

Serving: 4 | Prep: 15mins | Cook: 15mins | Ready in:

Ingredients

- 2 tablespoons chili oil
- 2 cloves garlic
- 3 hot chile peppers
- 1 pound skinless, boneless chicken breast halves - cut into bite-size pieces
- 1 1/2 teaspoons white sugar
- 1 teaspoon garlic salt
- 1 teaspoon black pepper
- 5 tablespoons oyster sauce
- 1 cup fresh mushrooms
- 1 cup chopped onions
- 1 bunch fresh basil leaves

Direction

- Over medium-high heat, heat oil in a skillet, then add chile peppers and garlic and cook until turned golden brown. Stir in sugar and chicken and then season with pepper and garlic salt. Let cook until the chicken is no longer pink but not done.
- Mix the oyster sauce into skillet. Stir in onions and mushrooms and continue to cook until chicken juices run clear and onions are tender. Transfer from heat and stir in basil. Leave to stand for two minutes prior to serving.

Nutrition Information

- Calories: 244 calories;
- Total Carbohydrate: 11.9
- Cholesterol: 69
- Protein: 28.2
- Total Fat: 9.4
- Sodium: 656

893. Spicy Harissa Chicken Kebabs

Serving: 4 | Prep: 25mins | Cook: 35mins | Ready in:

Ingredients

- 4 tablespoons mild harissa paste or sauce
- 2 tablespoons honey
- 1/2 lemon, juiced
- 4 boneless, skinless chicken breasts, cut into 1-inch cubes
- 2 yellow squash, thickly sliced
- 2 green zucchini, thickly sliced
- 1 red onion, thickly sliced
- 2 cups thickly sliced button mushrooms
- 3 tablespoons olive oil
- 1 tablespoon ground cumin
- 1/2 teaspoon salt and pepper
- Reynolds Wrap® Aluminum Foil

Direction

- Start preheating oven to 425°F.
- In a bowl, whisk lemon juice, honey and harissa together. Put in chicken; mix until coated.
- Evenly skewer chicken among eight wooden skewers. Put aside.
- Mix pepper and salt, cumin, olive oil, mushrooms, onion, zucchini and squash together until combined completely.
- On a table, place the Reynolds Wrap(R) Aluminum Foil sheet, about 1 1/2-2 feet long and put a quarter of vegetables in the middle of foil. Top the vegetables with two chicken skewers. Fold up ends, then outside of foil to make the foil packet.
- Repeat this process three times more. Put foil packets onto a cookie sheet.
- Bake for 20 mins in the oven at 425°F; then open foil packets. Cook until the chicken is cooked throughout and browned lightly, about 15 more mins.
- Optional Serving: Enjoy individual foil packets alongside the warm pita.

Nutrition Information

- Calories: 321 calories;
- Sodium: 446
- Total Carbohydrate: 23.1
- Cholesterol: 65
- Protein: 27.9
- Total Fat: 14.3

894. Spicy Italian Sausage Blended Burger

Serving: 4 | Prep: 20mins | Cook: 26mins | Ready in:

Ingredients

- 1 (8 ounce) package cremini mushrooms
- 3 tablespoons olive oil, divided
- 1 teaspoon sea salt
- 2 cups chopped kale
- 1 pound bulk Italian sausage
- 1 teaspoon harissa (optional)
- 4 slices smoked mozzarella cheese
- 4 hamburger buns, split and toasted
- 1/2 cup marinara sauce, warmed

Direction

- Preheat the oven to 175°C or 350°Fahrenheit.
- In a food processor, pulse mushrooms until chopped finely; move to a roasting pan. Mix in 2tbsp olive oil then spread salt.
- Bake for 10mins in the 350°F oven until tender; cool for 15mins to room temperature.
- On medium heat, heat the remaining tablespoon of olive oil in a big pan. Cook and stir kale in hot oil for 2-4mins until just wilted. Slightly cool for 5mins.
- In a food processor, pulse kale until chopped finely.
- In a bowl, mix harissa, mushrooms, Italian sausage, and kale together using your hands; shape into four patties. Avoid packing the patties too firmly.
- On medium-high heat, heat a cast iron pan or oven-safe grill pan. Cook patties in the pan for 5mins until brown; turn.
- Place the grill pan in the oven. Cook for another 8mins until the other side is brown. Add a slice of mozzarella cheese over each patty; broil for a minute more until the cheese melts.
- Serve with marinara sauce on toasted buns.

Nutrition Information

- Calories: 599 calories;
- Total Fat: 39.5
- Sodium: 1856
- Total Carbohydrate: 35.3
- Cholesterol: 56
- Protein: 25.8

895. Spicy Korean Chicken And Ramen Noodle Packets

Serving: 4 | Prep: 20mins | Cook: 25mins | Ready in:

Ingredients

- 3 tablespoons gochujang (Korean chile paste)
- 3 tablespoons soy sauce
- 1/3 cup water
- 2 tablespoons sesame oil
- 1 1/2 teaspoons sugar
- 2 boneless, skinless chicken breasts, thinly sliced
- 1 cup (1-inch) slices green onions
- 1 cup thinly sliced red cabbage
- 2 cups thinly sliced button mushrooms
- 1 zucchini, thinly sliced
- 2 (3 ounce) packages ramen noodles, cooked al dente
- Reynolds Wrap® Aluminum Foil

Direction

- Preheat an oven to 425°F.
- In a big bowl, mix sugar, sesame oil, water, soy sauce and gochujang till combined.
- Add cooked ramen noodles, zucchini, mushrooms, cabbage, green onions and sliced chicken into big bowl with gochujang mixture; toss to coat.
- On a table, put 1 1/2-2 feet Reynolds wrap aluminum long sheet of foil. In middle of foil, put 1/4 ramen noodle mixture. Fold ends up then outside to make a foil packet.
- Repeat it thrice. On cookie sheet tray, put foil packets.
- Bake for 25 minutes in the oven till chicken is cooked through.

Nutrition Information

- Calories: 193 calories;
- Sodium: 1341
- Total Carbohydrate: 13.3
- Cholesterol: 29
- Protein: 14.8
- Total Fat: 9.4

896. Spinach Mushroom Omelet

Serving: 2 | Prep: 15mins | Cook: 15mins | Ready in:

Ingredients

- 1 egg
- 3 egg whites
- 1 tablespoon grated Parmesan cheese
- 1 tablespoon shredded reduced-fat Cheddar cheese
- 1/4 teaspoon salt
- 1/8 teaspoon red pepper flakes
- 1/8 teaspoon garlic powder
- 1/8 teaspoon ground nutmeg
- 1/8 teaspoon ground black pepper
- 1/2 teaspoon olive oil
- 1/2 cup sliced fresh mushrooms
- 1/4 cup diced green onion
- 2 tablespoons finely chopped red bell pepper
- 1 cup torn fresh spinach
- 1/2 cup diced fresh tomato

Direction

- In a small bowl, beat egg and egg whites. Add in pepper, nutmeg, garlic powder, red pepper flakes, salt, cheddar cheese and parmesan cheese.
- In a big frying pan, heat oil over medium heat. Stir fry bell pepper, green onion and mushrooms for about 5 minutes until they become tender. Put in spinach and cook until just wilted. Add in egg mixture and diced tomato. Lift the edges as the eggs set so that the uncooked part flows underneath. Cook for 10-15 minutes until egg mixture sets. Slice into wedges before serving right away.

Nutrition Information

- Calories: 114 calories;
- Total Fat: 5.1
- Sodium: 490
- Total Carbohydrate: 5.7
- Cholesterol: 96
- Protein: 12.5

897. Spinach Mushroom Quiche

Serving: 6 | Prep: 25mins | Cook: 30mins | Ready in:

Ingredients

- 2 tablespoons butter
- 2 cups fresh sliced mushrooms
- 2 cups torn spinach leaves
- 6 green onions, chopped
- 1 (8 ounce) package refrigerated crescent rolls
- 1 (1 ounce) package herb and lemon soup mix
- 1/2 cup half-and-half
- 4 eggs, beaten
- 1 cup shredded Monterey Jack cheese

Direction

- Set oven to 375°F (190°C) to preheat.
- In a skillet, melt margarine over medium heat; cook, stirring continuously, onions, spinach, and mushrooms until tender, for 5 minutes. Take skillet away from the heat.
- Coat a round pan or pie plate of 9-inch with nonstick cooking spray. Arrange crescent roll triangles in a circle with narrow tips hanging about 2 inches beyond the rim of the pie plate. Press dough down the side and bottom of the pie plate until all gaps are filled.
- Whisk eggs, half-and-half cream, and soup mix together in a medium bowl. Mix the cooked vegetables and cheese into the egg mixture until incorporated. Pour filling into the prepared pie crust. Fold the dough points that are hanging over the edge back in over the filling.
- Bake in the preheated oven for half an hour or until a knife comes out clean from the center of the quiche.

Nutrition Information

- Calories: 343 calories;
- Sodium: 705
- Total Carbohydrate: 22.8
- Cholesterol: 177
- Protein: 15
- Total Fat: 21.5

898. Spinach Mushroom And Ricotta Fettuccine

Serving: 4 | Prep: 10mins | Cook: 20mins | Ready in:

Ingredients

- 1 (16 ounce) package spinach fettuccine pasta
- 1 teaspoon butter
- 3 cups mushrooms
- 1 (10 ounce) package frozen chopped spinach
- 1 (15 ounce) container ricotta cheese
- 1 lemon, juiced

Direction

- Boil a big pot of lightly salted water, then add the pasta and let it cook for 8-10 minutes or until it becomes al dente, then drain.
- Melt the butter in a big saucepan on medium heat. Mix in the mushrooms and let it cook until it becomes tender. Mix in spinach and let it cook until it becomes tender and thawed. Take out of the heat and mix in ricotta cheese, then stir well.
- Add the lemon juice into the spinach mixture and pour on top of the cooked pasta. Stir well then serve.

Nutrition Information

- Calories: 502 calories;
- Protein: 29.2
- Total Fat: 12.6
- Sodium: 452
- Total Carbohydrate: 75.2
- Cholesterol: 36

899. Spinach Salad With Curry Vinaigrette

Serving: 6 | Prep: 45mins | Cook: |Ready in:

Ingredients

- 1/4 pound slab bacon
- 1 tablespoon curry powder
- 3 tablespoons red wine vinegar
- 1 tablespoon prepared Dijon-style mustard
- 9 tablespoons vegetable oil
- salt and pepper to taste
- 12 cups flat leaf spinach - rinsed, dried and stems removed
- 12 fresh mushrooms, sliced

Direction

- Cut the rind off the bacon and dice into 1" cubes. In a big, deep skillet, add bacon and cook on medium high heat until bacon is crispy and browned. Cover and lower heat to the lowest setting to keep warm the bacon.
- Toast curry powder in a small and dry skillet on medium heat for a half minute, while stirring frequently, until tangy, then take away from the heat.
- Whisk mustard and vinegar together in a medium sized bowl. Pour oil into the bowl in a thin stream until oil is totally blended while whisking continuously. Put in curry powder, stir till smooth. Use salt and pepper to taste.
- Toss vinaigrette, mushrooms, spinach and bacon together in a big bowl until coated equally. Adjust pepper and salt to taste and serve promptly.

Nutrition Information

- Calories: 297 calories;
- Total Carbohydrate: 5.2
- Cholesterol: 13
- Protein: 5.2
- Total Fat: 29.5
- Sodium: 270

900. Spinach And Mushroom Casserole

Serving: 6 | Prep: 20mins | Cook: 20mins |Ready in:

Ingredients

- 2 tablespoons butter
- 1 pound fresh mushrooms, sliced
- 2 (10 ounce) packages fresh spinach, rinsed and stems removed
- 1 teaspoon salt
- 4 tablespoons butter, melted
- 1/4 cup finely chopped onion
- 1 1/2 cups shredded Cheddar cheese, divided

Direction

- Turn oven to 350°F (175°C) to preheat. Lightly oil a 2-quart casserole dish.
- In a large skillet, melt 2 tablespoons butter over medium heat. Sauté mushrooms in melted butter for about 8 to 10 minutes until softened.
- In the meantime, put spinach into a large pot. Cook over medium heat until wilted; drain, pressing or squeezing to remove excess liquid. Transfer spinach to the prepared baking dish; top with 1/2 of the cheese, onion, 4 tablespoons melted butter, and salt. Place mushrooms in a layer on top of spinach and scatter with the remaining cheese.

- Bake for 20 minutes in the preheated oven.

Nutrition Information

- Calories: 257 calories;
- Total Carbohydrate: 7.5
- Cholesterol: 60
- Protein: 11.3
- Total Fat: 21.5
- Sodium: 721

901. Spinach And Mushroom Frittata

Serving: 6 | Prep: | Cook: | Ready in:

Ingredients

- 1 (10 ounce) package frozen chopped spinach, thawed and squeezed thoroughly to remove liquid
- 4 eggs or equivalent egg substitute
- 1 cup part-skim ricotta cheese
- 3/4 cup freshly grated Parmesan cheese
- 3/4 cup chopped portobello mushrooms
- 1/2 cup finely chopped scallions with some green tops
- 1/4 teaspoon dried Italian seasonings
- 1 pinch Salt and pepper, to taste

Direction

- Preheat oven to 375°.
- Mix all ingredients together in a big bowl till well mixed. Use cooking spray to spray one 9-in. pie dish and fill with the spinach mixture.
- Bake till becoming set and browned, about half an hour. Allow it to cool down for 20 minutes, chop into wedges and serve.

Nutrition Information

- Calories: 167 calories;
- Cholesterol: 146
- Protein: 14.9
- Total Fat: 9.7
- Sodium: 288
- Total Carbohydrate: 6.1

902. Spinach And Mushroom Quesadillas

Serving: 16 | Prep: 10mins | Cook: 25mins | Ready in:

Ingredients

- 1 (10 ounce) package chopped spinach
- 2 cups shredded Cheddar cheese
- 2 tablespoons butter
- 2 cloves garlic, sliced
- 2 portobello mushroom caps, sliced
- 4 (10 inch) flour tortillas
- 1 tablespoon vegetable oil

Direction

- Following directions on package, prepare spinach. Drain and dry by patting.
- Set oven to 3500F (1750C) and preheat. On one side of each tortilla, sprinkle half cup of cheese. On baking sheets, put tortillas cheese side up, and bake until cheese is melted, about 5 minutes.
- In a skillet, melt the butter over medium heat. Mix in mushrooms and garlic, and cook for about 5 minutes. Stir in spinach, and continue cooking for 5 minutes. On the cheese side of each tortilla, pour an equal amount of the mixture. Fold the tortillas in half over the filling.
- In a separate skillet, heat oil on medium heat. Put quesadillas one by one into the skillet, and cook each side for 3 minutes, until golden brown. Cut each quesadilla into 4 wedges and serve.

Nutrition Information

- Calories: 154 calories;
- Total Fat: 9.5
- Sodium: 247
- Total Carbohydrate: 10.9
- Cholesterol: 22
- Protein: 6.7

903. Spinach And Mushroom Quiche With Shiitake Mushrooms

Serving: 6 | Prep: 20mins | Cook: 35mins | Ready in:

Ingredients

- 1 prepared 9-inch single pie crust
- 1/4 cup butter
- 1 bunch green onions, chopped
- 3 cloves garlic, chopped
- 1 slice turkey bacon, cut into 1/2-inch pieces
- 1 (9 ounce) bag fresh spinach
- 1 (3.5 ounce) package shiitake mushrooms, sliced
- 1/2 cup chopped broccoli florets
- 1/4 cup shredded sharp Cheddar cheese
- 4 eggs, beaten
- 3/4 cup milk
- 1/2 teaspoon sea salt
- 1/2 teaspoon black pepper
- 1/2 cup shredded sharp Cheddar cheese

Direction

- Set the oven at 1900C (3750F) and start to preheat.
- Put pie peel into a 9-inch pie dish.
- In a large skillet, melt butter over medium heat; cook and stir garlic and green onions for 5 minutes, or until softened. Cook and mix turkey bacon in the onion mixture until it is aromatic.
- Mix broccoli, shiitake mushroom and spinach into green onion mixture; cook while stirring vegetables for 5 to 7 minutes, or until softened. Add 1/4 cup Cheddar cheese and mix.
- Use spoon to transfer vegetable mixture into pie crust.
- In a bowl, beat eggs, black pepper, sea salt and milk together; pour this mixture gently over vegetable filling, slightly mix eggs into the filling.
- Bake for 15 minutes in the prepared oven; top the quiche with half a cup of Cheddar cheese and bake 10 more minutes. Use alumium oil to cover quiche and bake for 10 more minutes, or until quiche has set and insert a toothpick into the quiche then takes it out clean.
- Let quiche cool for 5 minutes and then serve.

Nutrition Information

- Calories: 381 calories;
- Total Fat: 27.2
- Sodium: 575
- Total Carbohydrate: 21.9
- Cholesterol: 164
- Protein: 13.7

904. Spinach And Mushroom Salad

Serving: 4 | Prep: 15mins | Cook: 30mins | Ready in:

Ingredients

- 4 slices bacon
- 2 eggs
- 2 teaspoons white sugar
- 2 tablespoons cider vinegar
- 2 tablespoons water
- 1/2 teaspoon salt
- 1 pound spinach
- 1/4 pound fresh mushrooms, sliced

Direction

- Put bacon in a big, deep skillet. Cook over moderately high heat until equally browned. Crumble and set aside, save 2 tbsp. bacon fat.
- In a saucepan, add eggs, and pour in cold water to cover totally. Bring water to a boil. Cover, take away from heat, and allow eggs to stand in hot water for about 10 to 12 minutes. Take the eggs out of hot water, cool, peel and slice into wedges.
- Bring 2 tbsp. bacon fat back to the skillet, then stir in salt, water, vinegar and sugar, keep it warm.
- Rinse and remove stems from spinach, dry completely and crumble into pieces in a salad bowl. Drizzle the warm dressing over and toss well to coat.
- Place bacon and mushrooms on top of the salad, decorate with egg.

Nutrition Information

- Calories: 126 calories;
- Total Carbohydrate: 7.5
- Cholesterol: 103
- Protein: 10.6
- Total Fat: 6.8
- Sodium: 625

905. Spinach, Turkey, And Mushroom Lasagna

Serving: 12 | Prep: 30mins | Cook: 1hours | Ready in:

Ingredients

- 12 lasagna noodles
- 1 Vidalia onion, diced
- 2 cloves garlic, minced
- 1 pound ground turkey
- 1 (8 ounce) package sliced white mushrooms
- salt and ground black pepper to taste
- 2 (9 ounce) packages frozen spinach, thawed
- 2 cups whole milk ricotta cheese
- 1/4 cup heavy whipping cream
- zest of 2 lemons
- 1/2 teaspoon Italian seasoning
- 1/4 teaspoon ground nutmeg
- 1 (28 ounce) jar spaghetti sauce
- 2 cups grated Asiago cheese
- 2 cups shredded Cheddar cheese

Direction

- Boil a big pot with lightly salted water; cook lasagna noodles, occasionally mixing, in boiling water for 8 minutes till tender but firm to chew. Drain.
- Mix garlic and onion on medium high heat in big skillet; mix and cook for 5 minutes till onion is translucent. Add turkey; cook for 5-7 minutes till not pink. Add mushrooms; season with pepper and salt. Cook for 6 minutes till soft; take off heat. Cool.
- In clean dish towel, wrap thawed spinach; wring spinach to extract as much water as you can above bowl. Mix nutmeg, Italian seasoning, lemon zest, heavy cream, ricotta cheese and spinach in another bowl.
- Preheat an oven to 190°C/375°F.
- Use 3 tbsp. spaghetti sauce to coat bottom of 9x13-in. baking dish; layer with 4 cooked lasagna noodles, 1/2 spinach mixture, 1/2 turkey mixture, 1/3 Asiago cheese, 1/3 cheddar cheese then 3/4 cup spaghetti sauce over. Layer 4 extra noodles, leftover turkey and spinach mixtures, extra 1/3 Asiago cheese, 1/3 extra cheddar cheese then 3/4 cup extra spaghetti sauce. Put leftover 4 lasagna noodles, the spaghetti sauce, the Asiago cheese then cheddar cheese over; use aluminum foil to cover.
- In preheated oven, bake for 35 minutes then remove aluminum foil; put oven temperature on 220°C/425°F. Bake for 15 minutes till crust is golden.

Nutrition Information

- Calories: 453 calories;
- Protein: 28.1
- Total Fat: 24.1

- Sodium: 709
- Total Carbohydrate: 32.7
- Cholesterol: 93

906. Steak N Gravy

Serving: 4 | Prep: 30mins | Cook: 1hours | Ready in:

Ingredients

- 4 (4 ounce) venison steaks
- 1 cup all-purpose flour
- 2 tablespoons ground bay leaves
- 1 pinch salt and pepper
- 4 tablespoons olive oil, divided
- 1/2 onion, chopped
- 6 fresh mushrooms, sliced
- 1 tablespoon minced garlic
- 1 (10.5 ounce) can beef gravy
- 1/4 cup milk

Direction

- Cut all gristle and fat off meat. Use a meat tenderizer to pound each steak out till thin yet not tearing. Mix pepper, salt, bay leaf and flour in a shallow bowl. Dredge steaks in flour mixture till coated evenly.
- In a big heavy skillet, heat 1 tbsp. olive oil on medium heat. Sauté onions till translucent and soft. Mix garlic and mushrooms in. Cook till tender. Take out of skillet; put aside. Heat leftover oil. Fry every steak, 2 minutes per side till golden brown. Put onion mixture into skillet. Mix milk and gravy in; lower heat and cover. Simmer for 30-40 minutes. Occasionally mix to avoid sticking.

Nutrition Information

- Calories: 424 calories;
- Total Carbohydrate: 32.2
- Cholesterol: 101
- Protein: 32.1

- Total Fat: 18
- Sodium: 498

907. Steak Salad (Ranen Salad)

Serving: 4 | Prep: 30mins | Cook: 5mins | Ready in:

Ingredients

- 1 1/2 pounds beef sirloin steak
- 8 cups romaine lettuce, torn into bite-size pieces
- 6 roma (plum) tomatoes, sliced
- 1/2 cup sliced fresh mushrooms
- 3/4 cup crumbled blue cheese
- 1/4 cup walnuts
- 1/3 cup vegetable oil
- 3 tablespoons red wine vinegar
- 2 tablespoons lemon juice
- 1/2 teaspoon salt
- 1/8 teaspoon ground black pepper
- 3 teaspoons Worcestershire sauce
- 1/8 teaspoon liquid smoke flavoring

Direction

- Set the oven to broiler setting and start preheating. Broil steak for 3 to 5 minutes each side or until steak reaches desired doneness. Cool then cut into bite-size slices.
- Lay out mushrooms, tomatoes and lettuce on chilled platters. Sprinkle with walnuts and blue cheese. Add steak slices on top.
- Whisk together smoke flavoring, Worcestershire sauce, pepper, salt, lemon juice, vinegar and oil in a small bowl. Pour over salad.

Nutrition Information

- Calories: 586 calories;
- Protein: 36.3
- Total Fat: 45.6
- Sodium: 760

- Total Carbohydrate: 8.6
- Cholesterol: 110

908. Steak Tips With Mushroom Sauce

Serving: 6 | Prep: 10mins | Cook: 40mins | Ready in:

Ingredients

- 2 1/2 pounds sirloin tips, uncut
- 1/2 (750 milliliter) bottle Burgundy wine
- 2 (14.5 ounce) cans beef broth
- 4 portobello mushroom caps, sliced
- 1/4 cup butter
- 1 clove garlic, chopped
- 1/2 teaspoon dried thyme
- 1/4 teaspoon salt, or to taste
- 1/2 teaspoon ground black pepper, or to taste
- 1 shallot, finely chopped
- 2 tablespoons all-purpose flour

Direction

- Preheat an outdoor grill for medium-high heat. In a large skillet, melt butter over medium-high heat. Sauté the shallot until transparent, then put in mushrooms, cook while covered for around 5 minutes until darkened. Take the mushrooms away from pan, and leave aside. Deglaze the pan with one can of beef broth, and burgundy wine. Raise the heat, then boil. Let the mixture boil till it lessens by 1/3.
- Grill the sirloin tips to the wanted doneness. Spice with pepper if wanted and salt. Transfer to a plate, and leave aside.
- Once the sauce is reduced, mix in the remaining can of beef broth and garlic. Set to a boil again, then keep cooking for another 5 - 10 minutes. Sauce will become thin like au jus. Fold in flour, then cook till the sauce reaches the desired thickness. Taste and modify seasoning if needed. Mix in the mushrooms. Spoon mushroom sauce over the tips to serve.

Nutrition Information

- Calories: 455 calories;
- Protein: 35.2
- Total Fat: 25.4
- Sodium: 672
- Total Carbohydrate: 9.3
- Cholesterol: 121

909. Steak And Ale Pie With Mushrooms

Serving: 8 | Prep: 45mins | Cook: 40mins | Ready in:

Ingredients

- 1 1/4 pounds cubed beef stew meat
- 1 onion, diced
- 1 (12 fluid ounce) can pale ale or lager beer
- 2 cloves garlic, minced
- 1/2 teaspoon dried thyme
- 1 1/2 teaspoons chopped fresh parsley
- 2 tablespoons Worcestershire sauce
- salt and pepper to taste
- 2 cups peeled and cubed potatoes
- 1 1/2 cups quartered fresh mushrooms
- 1 tablespoon all-purpose flour
- 1 pastry for double-crust pie

Direction

- In a large saucepan, add the ale, onion, and beef stew meat. Simmer over low heat for around 30 minutes, till the meat becomes softened.
- Preheat the oven to 400° F (200° C).
- Season the beef with pepper, salt, Worcestershire sauce, parsley, thyme, and garlic. Blend in the mushrooms and potatoes. Simmer, covered, over medium heat for 10 - 15 minutes, till potatoes become softened enough to pierce with a fork. In a small bowl, whip a small amount of the sauce and flour together,

then mix into the beef. Simmer till partially thickened.
- Press one pie crust into the bottom and up the sides of a 9-inch pie plate. Fill the crust with hot beef mixture then top with the leftover pie crust. To vent steam, cut slits in the top crust then crimp the edges to seal altogether.
- In the preheated oven, bake for 35 - 40 minutes till the gravy is bubbling and the crust becomes golden brown.

Nutrition Information

- Calories: 473 calories;
- Total Fat: 28.7
- Sodium: 319
- Total Carbohydrate: 32.4
- Cholesterol: 47
- Protein: 17.5

910. Steak And Kidney Pie With Bacon And Mushrooms

Serving: 8 | Prep: 50mins | Cook: 3hours | Ready in:

Ingredients

- 1/2 pound beef kidney
- 1 tablespoon vegetable oil
- 1/4 cup all-purpose flour
- salt and pepper to taste
- 1 pound beef for stew, cut in 1 inch pieces
- 4 slices thick sliced bacon, cut into 1 inch pieces
- 1 medium onion, chopped
- 1 (6 ounce) package sliced mushrooms
- 1/2 cup beef stock
- 1/2 cup red wine
- 4 large potatoes, peeled, cut into 1-inch chunks
- 2 tablespoons butter
- 1/2 cup milk
- 1 (17.25 ounce) package frozen puff pastry, thawed
- 1 egg, beaten with 2 teaspoons water

Direction

- Split the kidney in half then take the skins and tubes off. Rinse using cold water then pat to dry. Dice the kidney into 1/2 cubes. Use a big and heavy pot and pour in the vegetable oil, set the heat to medium high. Season the flour with salt and pepper using a bowl. Mix the kidney and stew meat in the flour then shake the excess off. Sear the meat in the hot oil until it becomes brown then remove. Add the bacon to the pot. Cook the bacon until it becomes crisp. Add in the mushroom and onion and cook for 2 minutes to soften. Pour the beef stock in, browned meat and the wine. Let it boil while stirring constantly for about 5 to 10 minutes. When it start thickens, lower the heat and simmer for one and a half to two hours or until the meat becomes tender. Take it away from the heat and let it cool to room temperature.
- Put the potatoes in a sauce pan then fill it with water just enough to cover the potatoes. Heat over high heat until it boils. Lower the heat to medium low and let it simmer for 20 minutes until it tenders. Drain the water out then mash with milk and butter. Add salt and pepper to taste. Set aside to cool.
- Prepare the oven and preheat to 375°F or 190°C.
- Place one sheet of puff pastry into a 9-inch pie dish and press it. Trim the edges to make it fit. Fill with cooled meat mixture. Top it with the mashed potatoes about an inch thick then take the remaining sheet of puff pastry and place it on top. Trim the excess pastry around the edges then flute the edges using a fork. Apply the top with beaten egg.
- Let it bake in the preheated oven between 20 to 25 minutes or until crust becomes golden brown.

Nutrition Information

- Calories: 767 calories;
- Total Fat: 42.6
- Sodium: 539

- Total Carbohydrate: 65.9
- Cholesterol: 190
- Protein: 27.9

911. Strip Steak With Red Wine Cream Sauce

Serving: 6 | Prep: 15mins | Cook: 30mins | Ready in:

Ingredients

- 1 tablespoon vegetable oil
- 2 red onions, sliced
- 1 (8 ounce) package button mushrooms, sliced
- 1 tablespoon vegetable oil
- 6 New York strip steaks
- salt and ground black pepper to taste
- 1 cup red Zinfandel wine
- 1 cup beef broth
- 2 tablespoons Dijon mustard
- 1 cup heavy whipping cream

Direction

- Set the heat to medium-high, then heat a tablespoon of vegetable oil in a skillet. Cook the red onions by stirring in with the mushrooms for 10 minutes until they soften. Take a bowl and place the mixture in it.
- Use a tablespoon of vegetable oil to coat a skillet that's set on medium-high heat. Use paper towels to pat the steaks dry, then add a pinch of salt and black pepper to taste. Add each steak onto the skillet and cook, making sure the outsides turn brown while the insides depend on your preferred doneness. If you want medium, you would opt to cook each side for 5 minutes. Transfer the steaks from the skillet.
- In the same skillet, add red Zinfandel wine and remove any leftover browned bits of steak. Add some Dijon mustard and beef broth while whisking them into the wine. Then, let it boil. Cook and occasionally stir the mixture for 5 minutes until it looks slightly reduced. Carefully pour in the cream by whisking, and let the sauce stand for another 5 minutes to thicken. Combine the meat and mushrooms with the sauce. Serve with sauce on top of the steaks.

Nutrition Information

- Calories: 649 calories;
- Protein: 69.3
- Total Fat: 33.9
- Sodium: 413
- Total Carbohydrate: 7.5
- Cholesterol: 200

912. Stroganoff Casserole

Serving: 8 | Prep: 10mins | Cook: 43mins | Ready in:

Ingredients

- 1/4 cup butter, divided
- 1 (8 ounce) package egg noodles (such as Inn Maid® Fine Egg Noodles)
- 2 (4 ounce) cans mushroom pieces and stems, drained
- 1 small onion, finely chopped
- 2 pounds ground turkey
- salt and ground black pepper to taste
- 2 (10.75 ounce) cans condensed cream of mushroom soup
- 1 (8 ounce) container sour cream
- 1 packet Swedish meatballs seasoning and sauce mixes (such as McCormick®)
- 2 meatball seasoning packets
- 1/4 cup milk, or more to taste

Direction

- Set the oven at 350°F (175°C) and start preheating. In a 9x13-in. casserole dish, place 2 tablespoons of butter.
- Insert the casserole dish into the preheating oven to melt butter. Take away from the oven,

leaving the heat on; spread the melted butter around the dish to evenly coat the bottom.
- Fill lightly salted water into a large pot; bring to a rolling boil. Mix in egg noodles; turn back to boil. Cook while stirring occasionally the noodles, uncovered, around 6 minutes, or till tender yet firm to bite. Strain.
- Place a large skillet on medium heat; melt the remaining 2 tablespoons of butter. Include in onion and mushrooms; cook while stirring for around 5 minutes, or till the onions turn soft. Include in ground turkey. Cook while breaking the meat up, 5-7 minutes, or till crumbled and browned. Season with pepper and salt. Include in meatball seasoning packets, sour cream and mushroom soup. Stir properly, including in milk, 3-5 minutes longer, or till the sauce is thickened to your desired consistency.
- Mix sauce and the egg noodles, place into the casserole dish. Use aluminum foil to cover.
- Bake for around 30 minutes in the preheated oven, or till the top is bubbling.

Nutrition Information

- Calories: 491 calories;
- Total Fat: 27
- Sodium: 1100
- Total Carbohydrate: 33.3
- Cholesterol: 136
- Protein: 30.2

913. Stroganoff Casserole With A Twist

Serving: 6 | Prep: 15mins | Cook: 40mins | Ready in:

Ingredients

- 1 tablespoon butter
- 1 pound ground beef
- 3/4 teaspoon ground black pepper
- 1/2 teaspoon onion powder
- 1/2 teaspoon salt
- 1 (10.75 ounce) can condensed cream of mushroom soup
- 1/2 cup sour cream
- 12 saltine crackers
- 1 (10 ounce) box frozen chopped spinach, thawed and squeezed dry
- 1 (4 ounce) package sliced button mushrooms, or more to taste
- 4 slices Muenster cheese

Direction

- Pre-heat the oven to 175 degrees C (350 degrees F). Rub the butter all over the 2-qt. baking plate.
- Heat the big skillet on medium heat. Put in the salt, onion powder, pepper and ground beef and cook and whisk for 5-8 minutes or till brown.
- Combine together sour cream and cream of the mushroom soup in the bowl.
- Lay the 6 saltine crackers in bottom of prepped baking plate. Add half of ground beef on top. Dollop a third of mushroom soup mixture on top of the beef. Lay the leftover saltines over the top. Use extra a third of mushroom soup mixture and spinach to cover. Spread mushroom soup mixture and the leftover ground beef over the top. Cover with the mushrooms.
- Bake in preheated oven for roughly half an hour or till bubbling. Add the Muenster cheese on top and keep baking for roughly 5 minutes longer or till the cheese melts.

Nutrition Information

- Calories: 365 calories;
- Total Carbohydrate: 11.6
- Cholesterol: 77
- Protein: 20.8
- Total Fat: 26.6
- Sodium: 796

914. Stuffed Chicken With Margherita® Capicola

Serving: 4 | Prep: 20mins | Cook: 20mins | Ready in:

Ingredients

- 8 skinless, boneless chicken breast halves
- 16 slices Margherita® Capicola
- 16 slices fontina cheese
- 4 portobello mushrooms, sliced
- 8 toothpicks (to hold chicken cutlets together)
- 1 cup all-purpose flour for dredging
- 1/2 cup vegetable oil for frying
- 1 tablespoon unsalted butter
- 1/4 cup white wine
- 1 cup chicken broth
- 2 tablespoons parsley
- Salt and pepper to taste

Direction

- Butterfly chicken breast to make a pocket.
- Put 2 portobello mushrooms slices, fontina cheese, and 2 capicola slices. Secure with a toothpick. Put into all-purpose flour to roll.
- In a big sauté pan, heat oil over medium to high. Sear the flour-coated chicken breasts until all sides are brown.
- In a roasting pan or a Dutch oven, put the browned chicken breasts; add pepper, salt, parsley, chicken stock, white wine, and butter.
- Bake at 425° for 7 minutes, baste and cook for another 7 minutes. On a dish, put the chicken breasts in the middle, drizzle with pan juices and use parsley to garnish and enjoy.

Nutrition Information

- Calories: 1207 calories;
- Sodium: 1610
- Total Carbohydrate: 33.8
- Cholesterol: 287
- Protein: 89.3
- Total Fat: 77.9

915. Stuffed Cod Wrapped In Bacon

Serving: 8 | Prep: 15mins | Cook: 10mins | Ready in:

Ingredients

- 8 (6 ounce) fillets cod
- 2 tablespoons sesame oil
- 2 tablespoons chili sauce
- 8 slices bacon
- 1 leek, chopped
- 1 ounce enoki mushrooms

Direction

- Preheat an outdoor grill to high heat. While the grill is heating up, steep some toothpicks inside the water.
- On each fish fillet, spread a thin layer of chili sauce and sesame oil on 1 side. At one end, add in a couple of mushrooms and some leeks. Roll towards the other end. Use a bacon slice to wrap each roll, and secure using 2 toothpicks.
- Put on the preheated grill, and cook while covered for 5 minutes. Pay attention to the bacon grease flare-ups. Flip over, and cook for 5 minutes longer, till fish could be simply flaked and bacon is crisp.

Nutrition Information

- Calories: 231 calories;
- Total Fat: 8.4
- Sodium: 393
- Total Carbohydrate: 3
- Cholesterol: 72
- Protein: 33.9

916. Stuffed Mega 'Shrooms

Serving: 6 | Prep: 20mins | Cook: 20mins | Ready in:

Ingredients

- 1 pound large, white mushrooms, stems removed and minced
- 1 tablespoon minced garlic
- 2 tablespoons dried parsley
- 1/2 cup shredded Monterey Jack cheese
- 1/2 cup softened butter
- 1/2 cup dry bread crumbs
- 1 (16 ounce) jar Alfredo pasta sauce (optional)

Direction

- Turn oven to 350°F (175°C) to preheat. Line aluminum foil over a baking sheet.
- Combine minced mushroom stems with butter, cheese, parsley, and garlic. Fill the mixture into mushroom caps; thickly coat the stuffing-side with bread crumbs. Arrange stuffed mushroom on the prepared baking sheet, stuffing-side up.
- Bake for 20 to 30 minutes in the preheated oven until the stuffing is bubbly and the bread crumbs turn golden brown. In the meantime, heat Alfredo sauce over medium heat in a saucepan. Drizzle Alfredo sauce over baked stuffed mushrooms to serve.

Nutrition Information

- Calories: 446 calories;
- Sodium: 964
- Total Carbohydrate: 13.4
- Cholesterol: 80
- Protein: 9.9
- Total Fat: 40.9

917. Stuffed Morel Mushrooms

Serving: 12 | Prep: 20mins | Cook: 5mins | Ready in:

Ingredients

- 6 large fresh morel mushrooms
- 1 (8 ounce) package cream cheese at room temperature
- 1/2 (8 ounce) package imitation crabmeat, minced
- 1 teaspoon finely chopped green onion, or to taste
- 1/4 cup dry breading mix (such as Drake's Crispy Frymix®)
- 2 cups vegetable oil for frying, or as needed

Direction

- Clean whole morel mushrooms of dirt and grit gently; in a colander, place mushrooms, stem sides down and allow about 5 minutes to drain.
- Cut bottoms of hollow stems to have enough room for filling.
- Stir green onion, crabmeat, and cream cheese till combined evenly in bowl.
- Scoop the mixture in a resealable, heavy plastic bag. Force the cream cheese mixture into a corner of the bag. Cut a small snip off the bag's corner.
- Insert the trimmed end of the plastic bag into each mushroom's hollow stem and fill the mushroom with the blend of cream cheese.
- In a shallow bowl, place dry breading mix. Roll in the dry mix the stuffed mushrooms; tap off excess breading.
- In a large saucepan or deep-fryer, heat vegetable oil to 350 °F (175 °C).
- Deep-fry the stuffed mushrooms for around 3 to 4 minutes until the mushrooms are soften and the breading is golden brown. Place on paper towels to drain.

Nutrition Information

- Calories: 117 calories;
- Sodium: 193
- Total Carbohydrate: 4.1
- Cholesterol: 22
- Protein: 2.5
- Total Fat: 10.2

918. Stuffed Mushrooms I

Serving: 9 | Prep: 20mins | Cook: 20mins | Ready in:

Ingredients

- 36 fresh mushrooms
- 1 (8 ounce) package cream cheese, softened
- 1 (6 ounce) can crab meat, drained
- 1/2 teaspoon garlic salt

Direction

- Prepare the oven by preheating to 350°F (175°C). Use a nonstick cooking spray to lightly grease a baking sheet.
- Stem mushrooms. Set aside 1/3 to 1/2 of the stems and mince them.
- Beat cream cheese until smooth.
- Mix crab meat and minced mushroom stems in a small bowl. Whisk the cream cheese into the stem and clam mixture. Put in garlic salt and combine well. Fill the mushroom caps with the cheese mixture. On the prepared baking sheet, arrange the caps.
- Then bake mushrooms for 20 minutes at 350°F (175°C), or until the mushrooms and crab mixture are hot, and most of the liquid from the mushrooms has collected in the pan.

Nutrition Information

- Calories: 121 calories;
- Cholesterol: 44
- Protein: 7.9
- Total Fat: 9.2
- Sodium: 240

- Total Carbohydrate: 3.1

919. Stuffed Mushrooms II

Serving: 24 | Prep: | Cook: | Ready in:

Ingredients

- 1 pound fresh mushrooms, stems removed
- 1 (12 ounce) package chicken-flavor stuffing mix
- 1 (10.75 ounce) can condensed cream of mushroom soup
- 10 3/4 fluid ounces milk

Direction

- Prepare the oven by preheating to 350°F (175°C). Prepare one 9x13-inch baking dish that is greased.
- Ready stuffing based on package directions.
- Stuff mushrooms with stuffing and layer in baking dish.
- Use one can of milk to dilute can of soup. Place over the mushrooms, cover, and bake for 25 minutes.

Nutrition Information

- Calories: 75 calories;
- Total Carbohydrate: 12.2
- Cholesterol: 1
- Protein: 3.2
- Total Fat: 1.6
- Sodium: 348

920. Stuffed Mushrooms With Sour Cream

Serving: 24 | Prep: 30mins | Cook: 15mins | Ready in:

Ingredients

- 24 mushrooms, caps and stems diced
- 1/2 orange bell pepper, diced
- 1/2 onion, diced
- 1 small carrot, diced
- 2 slices bacon, diced
- 1 cup shredded Cheddar cheese
- 1/2 cup sour cream
- 1 1/2 tablespoons shredded Cheddar cheese, or to taste

Direction

- In a skillet, put bacon, carrot, onion, orange bell pepper and mushroom stems over medium heat. Stir and cook until softened, about 5 minutes. Mix in sour cream and 1 cup of Cheddar cheese; cook for about 2 minutes until the cheese is melted and stuffing is well combined.
- Set the air fryer to 350°F (175°C), and start preheating.
- On the baking tray, place mushroom caps. Add a heaped amount of stuffing to each mushroom cap. Sprinkle 1 1/2 tablespoons of Cheddar cheese over the mushroom caps.
- Put the mushrooms tray into the basket of the air fryer. Cook for about 8 minutes until cheese melts.

Nutrition Information

- Calories: 43 calories;
- Protein: 2.4
- Total Fat: 3.1
- Sodium: 55
- Total Carbohydrate: 1.7
- Cholesterol: 8

921. Stuffed Mushrooms With Spinach

Serving: 12 | Prep: 15mins | Cook: 30mins | Ready in:

Ingredients

- 2 tablespoons butter
- 5 slices bacon
- 1 (10 ounce) package frozen chopped spinach
- 12 large mushrooms
- 3 tablespoons butter
- 2 tablespoons finely chopped onion
- 2 cloves garlic, peeled and minced
- 3/8 cup heavy cream
- 1/4 cup grated Parmesan cheese
- salt and pepper to taste
- 2 tablespoons butter, melted

Direction

- Set the oven to 400°F (200°C), and start preheating. Coat a 9x13 inch baking dish with 2 tablespoons of butter.
- In a large, deep skillet, arrange bacon and heat over medium high heat until evenly brown. Drain, crumble and put aside.
- In a medium saucepan, put frozen spinach with 1/4 cup water. Let it come to a boil, then lower the heat to medium, cover up and cook spinach for 10 minutes. Uncover and stir. Take out of the heat and drain.
- Cut off the stems from mushrooms. In the baking dish, place mushroom caps. Chop the stems finely.
- In a medium saucepan, melt 3 tablespoons of butter over medium heat, and stir in garlic and onion. Cook for 5 minutes, or until tender, then stir in heavy cream, chopped mushroom stems, spinach and bacon. Let the cream come to a boil. Take out of the heat and stir in pepper, salt and Parmesan cheese.
- Generously stuff the mixture with mushroom caps. Give it a drizzle of 2 tablespoons melted butter. Bake in the oven for half an hour until lightly browned.

Nutrition Information

- Calories: 163 calories;
- Total Fat: 15.7
- Sodium: 199
- Total Carbohydrate: 2.5

- Cholesterol: 38
- Protein: 4

922. Stuffed Mushrooms, Leeks, White Beans And Pecans

Serving: 8 | Prep: 10mins | Cook: 20mins | Ready in:

Ingredients

- 16 ounces button or cremini mushrooms
- Salt to taste
- 2 ribs chopped celery
- 1 leek, white and light green parts only, cleaned
- 1 large clove garlic
- 2 tablespoons extra virgin olive oil, divided
- 1/2 teaspoon sea salt
- 1/3 cup toasted chopped pecans
- 1/3 cup panko bread crumbs
- 1/2 cup grated Parmesan cheese, plus additional for garnish
- 1/2 cup canned cannellini beans, rinsed and drained
- 1/2 teaspoon red pepper flakes
- 1/2 teaspoon fresh ground black pepper
- 1/3 cup grated fontina cheese, for garnish
- finely chopped flat-leaf parsley, for garnish
- Reynolds Wrap® Aluminum Foil

Direction

- Set the oven to 350°F, and start preheating. Line Reynolds Wrap(R) Aluminum Foil on a baking sheet. Grease or spray the foil. Wipe clean the mushrooms with a damp paper towel and cut the stems. Arrange the mushrooms upside down on the baking sheet and scatter a pinch of salt. Bake for 10 minutes, until just soften.
- Finely chop the garlic, leeks and celery. In a saucepan, heat 1 tablespoon of the olive oil over medium heat. Once warmed, add in sea salt and leek mixture. Sauté for about 5-6 minutes until softened.
- Mix black pepper, pepper flakes, beans, Parmesan, panko breadcrumbs and pecans together in another bowl. Stir to blend, use the back of a spoon to slightly mash the beans. Add in the remaining tablespoon oil and leek mixture, stir again. The filling mixture can be made an hour in advance.
- Generously stuff the mushroom caps with vegetable mix. Sprinkle the grated fontina and a bit of extra Parmesan on top. Bake for 10 more minutes or until the top is just golden. Garnish with parsley and serve warm.

Nutrition Information

- Calories: 148 calories;
- Total Carbohydrate: 10.6
- Cholesterol: 10
- Protein: 6.7
- Total Fat: 10
- Sodium: 316

923. Stuffed Pork Loin

Serving: 8 | Prep: 20mins | Cook: 2hours45mins | Ready in:

Ingredients

- 3 tablespoons margarine
- 1/2 cup chopped onion
- 1/2 cup chopped mushrooms
- 2 stalks celery, chopped
- 3 cups torn day-old bread
- salt and ground black pepper to taste
- 1 (4 pound) boneless pork loin roast
- 3 tablespoons water, or as needed
- 1 tablespoon ground thyme
- 1 tablespoon herbes de Provence
- 1 pinch garlic powder, or to taste

Direction

- Start preheating the oven at 300°F (150°C).

- Heat margarine over medium heat in a skillet; cook and stir celery, mushrooms, and onion in the heated margarine for about 12 minutes until vegetables are softened. Move vegetables to a bowl. Mix bread into vegetables until moist; flavor with black pepper and salt.
- Slice the pork loin nearly in half lengthwise, slicing to about 1-inch from the bottom; open pork loin like a book. Use plastic wrap to cover and lightly pound using a meat mallet to flatten the meat. Ladle the stuffing onto the pork loin, roll the meat over the stuffing, and use kitchen twine to bind the pork loin together in 3 places.
- Put the bound loin in a roasting pan and spread about 3 tablespoons of water around the roast. Flavor the roast with garlic powder, herbes de Provence, thyme, black pepper, and salt.
- Roast the stuffed pork loin for 2 1/2 to 3 hours until an instant-read meat thermometer shows 160°F (70°C) when inserted into the center of the stuffing. Let the meat rest for 15 minutes before untying and cutting.

Nutrition Information

- Calories: 360 calories;
- Protein: 39.9
- Total Fat: 17.4
- Sodium: 223
- Total Carbohydrate: 8.5
- Cholesterol: 109

924. Stuffed Pork Tenderloin

Serving: 5 | Prep: 25mins | Cook: 35mins | Ready in:

Ingredients

- 1 tablespoon extra-virgin olive oil, or as needed
- 10 white mushrooms, minced
- 1 shallot, minced
- 1/2 teaspoon dried thyme
- 1/2 teaspoon garlic powder
- 1/2 teaspoon dried sage
- 1/2 teaspoon ground black pepper
- 1/4 teaspoon salt
- 1/4 cup chopped fresh parsley
- 2 cups fresh spinach
- 1 teaspoon Dijon mustard
- 1 (2 pound) pork tenderloin, butterflied and pounded flat
- 4 slices prosciutto
- 2 tablespoons extra-virgin olive oil

Direction

- Start preheating the oven at 350°F (175°C).
- In a skillet, heat 1 teaspoon of olive oil over medium heat; cook and stir salt, black pepper, sage, garlic powder, thyme, shallot, and mushrooms in the hot oil for 5 to 10 minutes until the liquid has reduced and mushrooms and shallots are tender. Put in parsley; cook and stir for 1 minute. Stir in spinach; cook and stir for about 5 minutes until wilted. Blend in mustard. Take away from the heat.
- Put the pork tenderloin on a work surface; arrange prosciutto atop the tenderloin. Spread prosciutto with the mushroom-spinach mixture, except for 1/2-inch border on all sides. Tightly roll the tenderloin around the filling and bind together using kitchen string to keep closed.
- In a large skillet, heat 2 tablespoons of olive oil over medium heat; put the rolled tenderloin in the heated oil. Sear for about 10 minutes until all sides turn golden brown. Place the seared tenderloin into a 9x13-inch casserole dish.
- Bake in the prepared oven for 25 to 30 minutes until the center of pork is no longer pink. An instant-read thermometer should show at least 160°F (71°C) when inserted into the center.

Nutrition Information

- Calories: 296 calories;
- Total Carbohydrate: 4.2
- Cholesterol: 89

- Protein: 32.1
- Total Fat: 16.2
- Sodium: 440

925. Stuffed Red Peppers With Quinoa, Mushrooms, And Turkey

Serving: 8 | Prep: 30mins | Cook: 1hours30mins | Ready in:

Ingredients

- 2 cups water
- 1 cup uncooked quinoa
- 1 tablespoon olive oil
- 1 onion, diced
- 1 pound ground turkey
- salt and ground black pepper to taste
- 12 mushrooms, chopped, or more to taste
- 1 (24 ounce) jar tomato sauce, or more to taste
- 1 (6 ounce) can tomato paste
- 8 large red bell peppers - tops, seeds, and membranes removed
- 1 (8 ounce) package shredded Cheddar cheese, or to taste

Direction

- Boil quinoa and water in a saucepan. Lower heat to medium low and cover; simmer for 15-20 minutes till quinoa is tender.
- Heat olive oil on medium heat in a big skillet. Add onion; cook for 5 minutes till soft. Add turkey; season with pepper and salt. Mix and cook for 5-7 minutes till turkey isn't pink. Add mushrooms; cook for 5 minutes till soft.
- Preheat an oven to 175°C/350°F.
- Put cooked turkey mixture into big bowl. Add tomato paste, tomato sauce and cooked quinoa. Mix well; as needed, add extra tomato sauce till filling has a casserole-consistency.
- Put red bell peppers into baking dish; in each, put even filling amount.
- In preheated oven, bake for 45 minutes then remove from oven. Put cheddar cheese over each stuffed pepper. Bake for 10 minutes till cheese melts.

Nutrition Information

- Calories: 389 calories;
- Cholesterol: 71
- Protein: 25.8
- Total Fat: 17.4
- Sodium: 850
- Total Carbohydrate: 34.6

926. Stuffing Recipe

Serving: 12 | Prep: 1hours | Cook: 30mins | Ready in:

Ingredients

- 1 cup water
- 2 1/2 cups uncooked wild rice
- 1/2 cup butter
- 1 pound ground pork sausage
- 2 1/2 cups chopped onions
- 2 cups chopped celery
- 2 1/2 cups chopped mushrooms
- 1 1/2 teaspoons dried thyme
- 1 1/2 teaspoons dried rosemary
- 2 teaspoons salt
- 1 1/2 teaspoons pepper
- 6 cups cubed whole wheat bread
- 2 large Rome beauty apples - peeled, cored, and chopped
- 1 cup raisins
- 1 (14.5 ounce) can chicken broth

Direction

- Boil water in a medium saucepan. Mix in wild rice. Lower the heat. Cover the pan and simmer the mixture for 45 minutes until the rice is tender and the water is absorbed.
- Set the oven to 350°F (175°C) for preheating.

- Put butter in a large and heavy skillet and melt it over medium heat. Mix in celery, sausage, and onions. Cook for 10-12 minutes until browned all over; drain. Mix in rosemary, thyme, and mushrooms. Cook the mixture for 2 minutes until the mushrooms are browned lightly. Remove it from the heat. Season the mixture with salt and pepper.
- Combine the sausage mixture and cooked rice in a large bowl together with apples, raisins, and whole wheat bread. Whisk in chicken broth gradually until the mixture is moistened.
- Transfer the mixture into the large baking dish. Bake inside the preheated oven for 30 minutes until browned lightly.

Nutrition Information

- Calories: 453 calories;
- Total Carbohydrate: 50.3
- Cholesterol: 46
- Protein: 11.4
- Total Fat: 24.4
- Sodium: 846

927. Suki's Spinach And Feta Pasta

Serving: 4 | Prep: 25mins | Cook: 15mins |Ready in:

Ingredients

- 1 (8 ounce) package penne pasta
- 2 tablespoons olive oil
- 1/2 cup chopped onion
- 1 clove garlic, minced
- 3 cups chopped tomatoes
- 1 cup sliced fresh mushrooms
- 2 cups spinach leaves, packed
- salt and pepper to taste
- 1 pinch red pepper flakes
- 8 ounces feta cheese, crumbled

Direction

- Boil a large pot of lightly salted water. In boiling water, cook pasta till al dente; let drain.
- In the meantime, in a large skillet, heat olive oil over medium-high heat; add in garlic and onion, and cook until they have the color of golden brown. Stir in spinach, mushrooms, and tomatoes. Add red pepper flakes, pepper, and salt to season. Cook for an addition of 2 minutes, till spinach is wilted and tomatoes are heated through. Lessen heat to medium, stir in pasta and feta cheese, and cook till heated through.

Nutrition Information

- Calories: 451 calories;
- Sodium: 656
- Total Carbohydrate: 51.8
- Cholesterol: 50
- Protein: 17.8
- Total Fat: 20.6

928. Summer Lamb Kabobs

Serving: 20 | Prep: 20mins | Cook: 12mins |Ready in:

Ingredients

- 5 pounds boneless lamb shoulder, cut into 1 inch pieces
- 6 tablespoons Dijon mustard
- 4 tablespoons white wine vinegar
- 4 tablespoons olive oil
- 1/2 teaspoon salt
- 1/2 teaspoon black pepper
- 1/2 teaspoon chopped fresh rosemary
- 1/2 teaspoon crumbled dried sage
- 4 cloves garlic, chopped
- 4 green bell peppers, cut into large chunks
- 1 (10 ounce) package whole fresh mushrooms
- 1 (16 ounce) can pineapple chunks, drained with juice reserved
- 1 pint cherry tomatoes
- 4 onions, quartered

- 1 (10 ounce) jar maraschino cherries, drained and juice reserved
- 1/3 cup melted butter or margarine

Direction

- Put lamb in a big bowl.
- Take another bowl and mix together olive oil, vinegar, mustard, salt, pepper, garlic, sage, and rosemary. Spoon the mixture over the lamb and mix well to coat. Cover the bowl and marinate in the refrigerator overnight.
- Set outdoor grill for direct heat.
- Thread lamb, vegetables, and fruit onto bamboo or stainless steel skewers. Keep some of the liquid from the cherries and the pineapple chunks.
- Put melted butter in a small bowl and stir in a few splashes of the pineapple and the cherry juices. Use this for basting.
- Arrange the skewers on the grill. Turn and baste with butter mixture during the 12-minute grilling time.

Nutrition Information

- Calories: 406 calories;
- Cholesterol: 90
- Protein: 20
- Total Fat: 30.3
- Sodium: 266
- Total Carbohydrate: 13.2

929. Summer Vegetarian Chili

Serving: 6 | Prep: | Cook: |Ready in:

Ingredients

- 2 tablespoons extra-virgin olive oil
- 1 cup chopped red onion
- 5 large cloves garlic, crushed or minced
- 2 tablespoons chili powder, or more to taste
- 2 teaspoons ground cumin
- 2 cups juicy chopped fresh tomatoes
- 1 (15 ounce) can no-salt-added black beans, drained
- 1 cup water (or red wine)
- 1 cup chopped bell pepper (any color)
- 1 cup chopped zucchini
- 1 cup corn kernels
- 1 cup chopped white or portobello mushrooms
- 1 cup chopped fresh cilantro, packed
- 1/8 teaspoon cayenne pepper, or more to taste
- Salt and freshly ground black pepper, to taste

Direction

- In a medium pot, heat oil. Sauté cumin, chili powder, garlic, and onion on medium heat for 5 minutes until onion is soft. Add all the other ingredients except garnishes and mix. Boil then reduce heat once it boils; simmer until veggies are soft, about 20 minutes. Add extra liquid if necessary.
- Serve with rice, preferably brown, or as is. Top with any of these ingredients if you want: fresh cilantro, guacamole, fat-free sour cream, onion, or reduced-fat cheddar cheese.

Nutrition Information

- Calories: 178 calories;
- Total Fat: 5.8
- Sodium: 640
- Total Carbohydrate: 27.8
- Cholesterol: 0
- Protein: 7.1

930. Sunday Brunch Bake

Serving: 12 | Prep: 15mins | Cook: |Ready in:

Ingredients

- 12 eggs

- 1/3 cup BREAKSTONE'S or KNUDSEN Sour Cream
- 1 (16 ounce) package breakfast pork sausage
- 1 cup sliced fresh mushrooms
- 1 onion, chopped
- 2 tomatoes, chopped
- 1 (8 ounce) package KRAFT Finely Shredded Triple Cheddar Cheese

Direction

- Heat the oven to 400 °F.
- Using a whisk, mix sour cream and eggs till well incorporated. Put into a 13x9-inch baking dish coated with cooking spray. Bake till egg mixture is softly set, about 10 minutes. In the meantime, in big skillet over moderate heat, cook the onions, mushrooms and sausage for 6 to 8 minutes or till sausage is cooked, mixing from time to time. Drain.
- Lower oven heat to 325 °F. Scoop tomatoes on top of egg layer; top with cheese and sausage mixture.
- Bake till middle is firm, about 30 minutes.

Nutrition Information

- Calories: 249 calories;
- Total Fat: 20.2
- Sodium: 529
- Total Carbohydrate: 3.2
- Cholesterol: 180
- Protein: 14.4

931. Super Easy Slow Cooker Chicken

Serving: 4 | Prep: 15mins | Cook: 3hours | Ready in:

Ingredients

- 1 (10.75 ounce) can condensed low fat cream of chicken and herbs soup
- 1 (4 ounce) can mushroom pieces, drained
- 1/2 red onion, chopped
- 1 1/2 pounds skinless, boneless chicken breast halves - cut into strips
- 1 dash Marsala wine

Direction

- In a slow cooker, combine wine, chicken, onion, mushroom pieces, and soup.
- Cook on Low setting for 2 and a half hours to 3 hours.

Nutrition Information

- Calories: 234 calories;
- Total Fat: 5.7
- Sodium: 684
- Total Carbohydrate: 8.2
- Cholesterol: 91
- Protein: 34.9

932. Suz's Vegetable Manicotti

Serving: 4 | Prep: 30mins | Cook: 20mins | Ready in:

Ingredients

- 6 manicotti shells
- 2 red bell pepper, cut into 1 inch pieces
- 2 large portobello mushrooms
- 1 (32 ounce) container part-skim ricotta cheese
- 2 cups shredded mozzarella cheese
- 1 egg
- salt and pepper to taste
- 1/2 teaspoon Italian seasoning
- 1/2 teaspoon garlic powder
- 2 cups spaghetti sauce

Direction

- Bring lightly salted water in a large pot to a boil. Cook pasta in boiling water until al dente, about 8 to 10 minutes; drain off water. Remove manicotti to a sheet of aluminum foil or waxed paper to cool.

- Grill red bell pepper until tender and dark spots appear on its skin; lay on a plate and allow to cool. Grill mushrooms until most of the moisture runs out and mushrooms are softened; remove to a cool plate. Mix 1 1/2 cups mozzarella cheese, egg, ricotta cheese, garlic powder, Italian seasonings, pepper and salt to taste together in a medium mixing bowl until well combined.
- Turn oven to 350°F (175°C) to preheat.
- Once mushrooms are cooled, chop and put into cheese mixture. Once peppers are cooled, peel off skin, dice, and put into cheese mixture.
- Spoon spaghetti sauce into 1 thin layer on the bottom of a 9x13-inch baking dish. Fill cheese mixture into manicotti; arrange stuffed manicotti in the baking dish. Stream spaghetti sauce over the stuffed pasta and scatter with 1/2 cup of mozzarella cheese. Bake pasta for 20 minutes in the preheated oven.

Nutrition Information

- Calories: 728 calories;
- Total Fat: 35.7
- Sodium: 1168
- Total Carbohydrate: 55
- Cholesterol: 163
- Protein: 47.1

933. Swedish Chanterelle Mushroom Pate

Serving: 8 | Prep: 25mins | Cook: 1hours10mins | Ready in:

Ingredients

- 1 tablespoon butter
- 2 cloves garlic, minced
- 2 shallots, finely chopped
- 1 tablespoon butter
- 1 pound fresh or frozen chanterelle mushrooms, torn
- 1/4 cup chopped fresh parsley
- 3/4 pound ground pork
- 2 egg whites
- 1 1/2 teaspoons salt
- 1/2 teaspoon ground black pepper
- 1/2 cup whipping cream
- 10 thin slices smoked ham

Direction

- Prepare the oven by preheating to 300 degrees F (150 degrees C). Get an 8 1/2 x4 1/2 inch loaf pan and line with aluminum foil.
- Place a skillet on the stove and turn on to medium heat then melt 1 tablespoon butter. Mix in the shallots and garlic; stir and cook for about 5 minutes until shallots is soft and translucent. Then place it into a mixing bowl, and reserve to cool. Put the left tablespoon of butter using the same skillet over medium-high heat. Mix in the chanterelles, and let cook for 5 minutes until soft and edges are golden. Mix in the parsley and cook for 30 seconds more, and then transfer into the mixing bowl, and let it cool for 5 minutes.
- Add in the pepper, salt, egg whites and ground pork into the mushroom mixture using your hands to blend equally. Mix in the cream until absorbed well by pork mixture. Line with smoked ham the sides and bottom of the loaf pan. Put the meat mixture into the loaf pan and compress the top to flatten.
- Place inside the preheated oven for about 1 hour until no more pink color in the middle, and achieved the internal temperature of 160 degree F (72 degrees C). You can present it chilled or warm in slices.

Nutrition Information

- Calories: 229 calories;
- Protein: 13.4
- Total Fat: 16
- Sodium: 744
- Total Carbohydrate: 6.8

- Cholesterol: 66

934. Sweet Maple Pork Chops

Serving: 6 | Prep: 20mins | Cook: 25mins | Ready in:

Ingredients

- 1 egg, lightly beaten
- 1 quart heavy cream, divided
- salt to taste
- ground black pepper to taste
- 6 boneless pork chops
- 1/2 cup quick cooking oats
- 1 quart vegetable oil for frying
- 1 tablespoon butter
- 1 large onion, cut into 1 inch chunks
- 1 clove garlic, diced
- 3/4 cup maple syrup
- 6 ounces sliced fresh mushrooms
- 2 tablespoons chopped fresh basil leaves

Direction

- In a shallow bowl, mix pepper, salt, 3 cups of the heavy cream and egg. Season pork chops with pepper and salt, then dip in cream mixture. Coat by dredging in oats. Repeat to completely coat the chops.
- In a skillet, heat oil over medium-high heat. Place coated chops in hot oil with tongs. Fry until both sides are browned. Discard from the heat. Put aside.
- In a skillet, melt butter over medium heat (if oil has been drained, use the same pan). Cook garlic, onion, and pork chops until the onion becomes tender. Add maple syrup. Mix in basil and mushrooms. Season with pepper and salt. Lower the heat, cover and cook until the pork chops are done, about 10 mins. Discard the chops from the skillet, saving the sauce.
- Mix remaining cream with the reserved sauce into skillet. Boil. Cook while stirring until thickened. Place over pork chops to serve.

Nutrition Information

- Calories: 943 calories;
- Total Carbohydrate: 39
- Cholesterol: 285
- Protein: 18.8
- Total Fat: 81
- Sodium: 115

935. Sweet Potato And Mushroom Croquettes

Serving: 16 | Prep: 40mins | Cook: 48mins | Ready in:

Ingredients

- 3 large red potatoes, peeled and diced
- 2 sweet potatoes, peeled and diced
- 1 1/2 cups cooked rice
- 1/4 cup milk
- 1/4 cup butter, divided
- 1 teaspoon salt, divided
- 1 tablespoon olive oil
- 1 cup finely chopped cremini mushrooms
- 1 tablespoon minced garlic
- 1 teaspoon chopped fresh thyme
- 1 teaspoon chopped fresh marjoram
- 2 tablespoons Madeira wine
- 1 1/2 cups bread crumbs
- 1/2 cup grated Parmesan cheese
- 1/2 teaspoon ground black pepper
- 1/2 teaspoon dried marjoram
- 1/2 teaspoon dried thyme
- 1/4 cup canola oil

Direction

- In a large pot, cover sweet potatoes and red potatoes with salted water; heat to a boil. Turn heat to medium-low; simmer for about 20 minutes until potatoes are tender. Drain off water. Add 1/2 teaspoon salt, 2 tablespoons butter, milk and rice into the pot of potatoes; mash until incorporated.

- Chill potato mixture, covered, for about 15 minutes, until cool.
- In a large skillet, heat olive oil and the remaining 2 tablespoons butter. Put in fresh marjoram, fresh thyme, garlic and mushrooms, cook while mixing for about 15 minutes until mushrooms are soft and release the moisture. Add Madeira wine, scrape up to loosen browned bits from the pan bottom using a wooden spoon.
- Take 1/4 cup of cooled potato mixture, holding in the palm of one hand; flatten slightly. Put 1 tablespoon of mushroom mixture into the center, shaping potato mixture into a ball around mushroom mixture with the back of a spoon. Do the same with the rest of mushroom and potato mixtures.
- In a shallow dish, combine dried thyme, dried marjoram, pepper, Parmesan cheese, bread crumbs and 1/2 teaspoon salt. Drop potato ball in bread crumb mixture gently then roll around until well coated. Flatten the potato balls into patties by pressing them down.
- Heat canola oil over medium heat in a large skillet. Cook the patties, 4 pieces at a time, about 4 minutes on each side, until crispy and golden.

Nutrition Information

- Calories: 214 calories;
- Cholesterol: 10
- Protein: 4.8
- Total Fat: 8.7
- Sodium: 300
- Total Carbohydrate: 29.1

936. Sweet And Sour Tofu Veggies

Serving: 4 | Prep: | Cook: | Ready in:

Ingredients

- 3 cups water
- 1 1/2 cups long-grain brown rice
- 1 pound firm tofu
- 1/4 cup unsweetened pineapple juice
- 2 tablespoons fresh lemon juice
- 2 tablespoons ketchup
- 2 tablespoons real maple syrup
- 2 tablespoons tamari
- 1 tablespoon dark sesame oil
- 2 1/4 teaspoons arrowroot powder
- 2 1/2 teaspoons grated fresh ginger root
- 2 tablespoons vegetable oil
- 1 onion, thinly sliced
- 1 carrots, sliced diagonally
- 4 ounces fresh green beans, cut into 1-inch lengths
- 1 large chopped red bell pepper
- 8 ounces fresh mushrooms, sliced
- 1 zucchini, cut into 1/2-inch slices
- 1 cup pineapple chunks

Direction

- In a medium-sized saucepan, boil 2 cups of water on high heat. Put in rice, lower the heat, and let it simmer for 30-40 minutes till the water has been absorbed and rice softens. Move into a serving platter and keep them warm.
- Get rid of the excess water from tofu, and then chop it into half-an-inch cubes.
- In a small-sized bowl, stir together ginger, arrowroot, sesame oil, tamari, maple syrup, ketchup, lemon juice and pineapple juice.
- In a big skillet or wok, heat vegetable oil on medium high heat. Put in zucchini, mushrooms, bell pepper, green beans, carrot and onion and stir-fry for 3-5 minutes till becoming soft.
- Put in the pineapple, tofu and pineapple juice mixture. Cook, whisk frequently, for roughly 2 minutes till sauce becomes thick. Scoop sauce and veggies onto the brown rice and serve.

Nutrition Information

- Calories: 666 calories;
- Sodium: 632
- Total Carbohydrate: 94
- Cholesterol: 0
- Protein: 28.6
- Total Fat: 22.8

- Calories: 471 calories;
- Total Fat: 13.7
- Sodium: 630
- Total Carbohydrate: 58.2
- Cholesterol: 84
- Protein: 29.8

937. Swiss Steak Quick And Easy

Serving: 6 | Prep: 20mins | Cook: 1hours | Ready in:

Ingredients

- 1 tablespoon vegetable oil
- 2 pounds cube steaks, pounded thin and cut into bite-size pieces
- 1 1/2 tablespoons all-purpose flour
- 1 medium onion, chopped
- 1 pound mushrooms, sliced
- salt and pepper to taste
- 1 (1.2 ounce) package brown gravy mix
- 2 (14.5 ounce) cans stewed tomatoes
- 1 (12 ounce) package egg noodles

Direction

- In a Dutch oven, heat oil over medium heat. Coat the steak strips by dredging it in flour and place them into the hot oil, one batch at a time. Fry the strips on both sides until they turn brown then transfer it onto a warm platter. Repeat the process until all strips are browned. Move the meat back into the oven and mix in stewed tomatoes, gravy mix, pepper, salt, mushrooms and onions, then bring it to a boil. Let it simmer for about 30 to 45 minutes. When there's about 20 minutes left until the steak is done, boil a big pot of water then add the pasta. Cook until al dente for about 8 to 10 minutes then drain.
- Place the Swiss steak over the noodles. Serve.

Nutrition Information

938. Tarte Flambee

Serving: 4 | Prep: 20mins | Cook: 20mins | Ready in:

Ingredients

- 2 tablespoons butter
- 2 onions, sliced
- 1 cup mushrooms, sliced
- 1/2 cup creme fraiche
- 1/2 cup fromage blanc (French-style fresh cheese)
- salt and ground black pepper to taste
- 1 (11 ounce) package thin-crust pizza dough, at room temperature
- 8 strips cooked bacon
- 1/2 cup shredded mozzarella cheese (optional)

Direction

- Set an oven to 200°C (400°F) to preheat, then grease a baking tray lightly.
- In a big frying pan, melt the butter on medium heat. Add the mushrooms and onions then cook and stir for around 5 minutes, until tender. Take away from the heat and allow to cool a bit.
- In a small bowl, mix together the fromage blanc and creme fraiche, then sprinkle with pepper and salt to season.
- On the prepped baking tray, spread the pizza dough, then scoop the creme fraiche mixture on top. Evenly cover with bacon strips, mushrooms and onions and leave a 1-inch border. Scatter the mozzarella cheese over.

- Let it bake for about 15 minutes in the preheated oven, until the crust turns deep golden brown in color.

Nutrition Information

- Calories: 714 calories;
- Sodium: 1718
- Total Carbohydrate: 50.3
- Cholesterol: 122
- Protein: 31.6
- Total Fat: 42.8

939. Tava Or Turkish Stew

Serving: 6 | Prep: 15mins | Cook: 40mins | Ready in:

Ingredients

- 2 tablespoons olive oil, divided
- 1 1/2 pounds skinless, boneless chicken breast halves - cut into 1 inch cubes
- 1/2 (12 ounce) jar roasted red bell peppers, drained
- 1 (14.5 ounce) can diced tomatoes with juice
- 1 (6 ounce) jar mushrooms, drained
- 1 onion, diced
- 1 tablespoon minced garlic
- salt and pepper to taste
- 1 (16 ounce) package shredded mozzarella cheese

Direction

- Set the oven to 350°F (175°C) for preheating. Grease the medium casserole dish lightly.
- Put 1 tablespoon of oil in a skillet and heat it over medium heat. Cook the chicken until all of its juices run clear.
- In a blender or food processor, blend the roasted red peppers until smooth. Combine the cooked chicken, garlic, onion, tomatoes, roasted red peppers, and mushrooms into the prepared dish. Season the mixture with pepper and salt. Drizzle 1 tablespoon of olive oil over the mixture and top it with mozzarella cheese.
- Let it bake inside the preheated oven for 30 minutes until the cheese is bubbly and melted.

Nutrition Information

- Calories: 397 calories;
- Total Carbohydrate: 9.4
- Cholesterol: 113
- Protein: 43.7
- Total Fat: 19.5
- Sodium: 854

940. Teresa's Hearty Chicken Cacciatore

Serving: 6 | Prep: 25mins | Cook: 50mins | Ready in:

Ingredients

- extra virgin olive oil
- 1/4 pound pancetta (Italian bacon), thickly sliced
- 1/2 cup all-purpose flour
- 1 tablespoon dried Italian herb seasoning
- 1 tablespoon red pepper flakes
- 6 chicken thighs with skin and bone
- 1 small green bell pepper, chopped
- 1 small sweet onion, diced
- 1 pound baby portobello mushrooms, sliced
- 1/2 cup chopped fresh basil
- 3 cloves garlic, chopped
- 3 tablespoons tomato paste
- 1 (28 ounce) can diced tomatoes with juice
- 1/2 cup dry red wine, or more to taste
- 1 tablespoon cornstarch (optional)
- 2 tablespoons water (optional)
- 1 (16 ounce) package rigatoni pasta
- freshly shredded Parmesan cheese to taste
- salt and ground black pepper to taste

Direction

- In a large nonstick skillet, heat olive oil on medium heat and cook while stirring the pancetta for 5 -8 minutes until they start to turn dark brown. Remove the pancetta pieces with a slotted spoon and put aside.
- In a shallow bowl, mix together red pepper flakes, Italian seasoning, and flour.
- Press chicken thighs into flour mixture and tap off any excess flour.
- Brown the dredged chicken thighs in the skillet with oil and the pancetta drippings for 8 - 10 minutes on each side. Move the cooked thighs onto a platter and keep warm.
- Using the same skillet, cook while stirring the portobello mushrooms, sweet onion, and green bell pepper for about 8 minutes until the onion turn translucent.
- Stir in red wine, diced tomatoes and their juices, tomato paste, garlic and basil into the sauce.
- Allow the sauce to boil and place back the chicken and pancetta. If the sauce doesn't come up to almost covering the chicken pieces, add in more dry red wine.
- Turn the heat down to low and simmer for 35 - 50 minutes until chicken thighs are soft and are no longer pink inside.
- You can mix together water, cornstarch, and 1 tablespoon of the sauce and stir this into the skillet to make it thicker if you want.
- About 15 minutes before serving, boil a big pot of lightly salted water.
- Stir in rigatoni and bring back to a boil. Cook while uncovered on medium heat, occasionally stirring, for about 13 minutes until pasta is thoroughly cook but still slightly firm, then drain.
- In a big platter, place the cooked rigatoni and use chicken thighs as topping to serve.
- Ladle the sauce generously over the pasta and the chicken, and sprinkle with black pepper, salt, and Parmesan cheese. Serve with any extra sauce on the side.

Nutrition Information

- Calories: 654 calories;
- Sodium: 505
- Total Carbohydrate: 77.1
- Cholesterol: 72
- Protein: 35.6
- Total Fat: 21.1

941. Terrific Turkey Tetrazzini

Serving: 8 | Prep: | Cook: | Ready in:

Ingredients

- 3 pounds turkey, cooked
- 1 pound sliced mushrooms
- 6 tablespoons butter or margarine
- 6 tablespoons flour
- 1 cup chicken broth
- 2 cups Kikkoman PEARL Original Soymilk
- 1 pound spaghetti
- 1 cup Parmesan cheese
- Salt and pepper to taste

Direction

- Slice the turkey into bite-sized portions. In a saucepan, liquify the butter, then mix in flour; let cook till it begins to bubble. Slowly put the chicken stock, mixing till sauce thickens, then put the soymilk, cheese, pepper and salt. Put the mushrooms and turkey and gently simmer.
- Meantime, let the pasta cook following packaging directions, allow to drain and mix into turkey mixture. Put into a baking dish that is non-stick. Let bake at 450°F till heated completely and the cheese has melted.

Nutrition Information

- Calories: 680 calories;
- Total Carbohydrate: 52.1
- Cholesterol: 161
- Protein: 65.3

- Total Fat: 21.9
- Sodium: 340

942. Thai Hot And Sour Soup

Serving: 6 | Prep: 10mins | Cook: 15mins |Ready in:

Ingredients

- 3 cups chicken stock
- 1 tablespoon tom yum paste
- 1/2 clove garlic, finely chopped
- 3 stalks lemon grass, chopped
- 2 kaffir lime leaves
- 2 skinless, boneless chicken breast halves - shredded
- 4 ounces fresh mushrooms, thinly sliced
- 1 tablespoon fish sauce
- 1 tablespoon lime juice
- 1 teaspoon chopped green chile pepper
- 1 bunch fresh coriander, chopped
- 1 sprig fresh basil, chopped

Direction

- Boil the chicken stock in a big saucepan. Mix in the garlic and tom yum paste, cook for approximately 2 minutes. Mix in the kaffir lime leaves and lemon grass. In the saucepan, put the chicken, and cook for 5 minutes till juices run clear and the chicken is not pink anymore.
- Stir in the mushrooms. Put in the green chile pepper, lime juice and fish sauce. Keep on cooking till well incorporated. Take away from heat, put the basil and coriander, serve warm.

Nutrition Information

- Calories: 71 calories;
- Total Fat: 1.8
- Sodium: 639
- Total Carbohydrate: 4.9
- Cholesterol: 21

- Protein: 9.1

943. Thai Noodles

Serving: 4 | Prep: | Cook: |Ready in:

Ingredients

- 1/2 pound dried rice noodles
- 1 pound skinless, boneless chicken breast halves
- 1 dash soy sauce
- 1 green bell pepper, sliced
- 1 red bell pepper, sliced
- 1 cucumber, coarsely chopped
- 1 carrot, grated
- 10 mushrooms, halved
- 1 onion, chopped
- 2 cloves garlic, minced
- 1 tablespoon minced fresh ginger root
- 1 1/2 tablespoons red chile sauce
- 3/4 cup peanut sauce
- 2 tablespoons oyster sauce
- 1 tablespoon sesame oil
- 1 tablespoon sesame seeds

Direction

- Cook the rice noodles following the package directions.
- Cut chicken breasts to strips. Marinate chicken in soy sauce for half an hour.
- In a wok or big saucepan, heat sesame oil on medium heat. Cook the chicken until it's not pink. Add onions, ginger, and garlic. Cook until the onions become tender. Add cucumbers and mushrooms. Cook until the mushrooms become tender. Add hot chili pepper sauce, oyster sauce, peanut sauce, carrot, and peppers. Cook until heated.
- Toss sauté with cooked rice noodles. Top with sesame seeds.

Nutrition Information

- Calories: 571 calories;
- Total Fat: 18.5
- Sodium: 372
- Total Carbohydrate: 65.4
- Cholesterol: 66
- Protein: 36.9

944. Thai Shrimp Curry With A Kick

Serving: 4 | Prep: 15mins | Cook: 15mins | Ready in:

Ingredients

- 24 uncooked large shrimp, peeled and deveined
- 1/4 teaspoon salt
- 1/8 teaspoon cayenne pepper
- 2 tablespoons extra-virgin olive oil
- 1/2 cup finely diced red onion
- 3 cloves garlic, minced
- 2 teaspoons freshly grated gingerroot
- 1 lime, juiced
- 1 (8 ounce) package sliced fresh mushrooms
- 1 (14.5 ounce) can Hunt's® Diced Tomatoes, drained
- 1 cup chicken broth
- 1/4 teaspoon crushed red pepper flakes
- 1 (14 ounce) can coconut milk
- 1 tablespoon fish sauce
- 8 leaves Thai basil, chopped
- 1 teaspoon curry powder
- 1/4 cup chopped fresh cilantro (optional)
- 1 lime, quartered (optional)

Direction

- Sprinkle cayenne pepper and salt on shrimp.
- Heat olive oil in big pan on medium heat. Add red onion; cook for a minute. Add ginger and garlic; cook for 30 seconds. Add shrimp and lime juice; cook for 1 minute per side till shrimp is pink. Put shrimp in small bowl.
- Put crushed red pepper, chicken broth, mushrooms and diced tomatoes into pan; cook for 5 minutes till mushrooms start to soften. Add Thai basil, fish sauce, curry powder and coconut milk; cook till heated through. Put shrimp back into pan; cook for 1 minute more.
- Serve with lime wedge; if desired, garnish with cilantro.

Nutrition Information

- Calories: 406 calories;
- Protein: 26.2
- Total Fat: 29.2
- Sodium: 1221
- Total Carbohydrate: 14.4
- Cholesterol: 193

945. Thai Stuffed Tofu

Serving: 4 | Prep: 30mins | Cook: 15mins | Ready in:

Ingredients

- 2 (12 ounce) packages extra firm tofu
- 1/4 cup dried shiitake mushrooms
- 1 zucchini, coarsely chopped
- 1 onion, halved
- 3 cloves garlic
- 1 jalapeno pepper, seeded and coarsely chopped
- 1 egg
- 2 tablespoons soy sauce
- 2 tablespoons minced fresh ginger, or to taste
- 1 tablespoon cornstarch
- 1 tablespoon hoisin sauce
- 1/4 cup shredded cabbage
- 1/4 cup vegetable oil, divided

Direction

- Strain tofu; cut each piece into 4 squares; then, cut each square into 2 triangles diagonally. Set triangles aside.

- In a bowl of hot water, put shiitake mushrooms; let rehydrate for around 20 minutes, or till plump and moist. Cut out the woody stems; chop finely.
- In a food processor, put jalapeno pepper, garlic, onion and zucchini; process till a paste forms and transfer into a bowl, then mix in hoisin sauce, cornstarch, ginger, soy sauce, egg and the shiitake mushrooms. Fold in shredded cabbage.
- Place a large skillet with 2 tablespoons of vegetable oil on medium heat. Using paper towels, pat the tofu triangles dry; pan-fry in hot oil for 2-3 minutes per side, or till browned on all sides except from 1 narrow side for the stuffing. Take the tofu triangles away; allow to cool till easy to handle.
- Cut a slit into the unbrowned side of a tofu triangle, using a sharp paring knife; scoop out the center of the tofu, using a grapefruit spoon, keeping the walls of the triangle around 1/4-in. thick. Fill the stuffing generously into each triangle, using a spoon, allowing the stuffing to mound out of the tofu piece.
- Place the skillet with remaining 2 tablespoons of vegetable oil on medium heat; place the tofu triangles into the hot oil, stuffing sides down, and pan-fry for around 5 minutes, or till the stuffing is hot and set inside and the stuffing edge is browned. Turn the triangles on their sides; refry in the hot oil to rewarm, 1-2 minutes.

Nutrition Information

- Calories: 374 calories;
- Cholesterol: 47
- Protein: 21
- Total Fat: 25.1
- Sodium: 555
- Total Carbohydrate: 22.5

946. The Best Seafood Stuffed Mushrooms

Serving: 6 | Prep: 30mins | Cook: 15mins | Ready in:

Ingredients

- 1 (8 ounce) package softened cream cheese
- 1 egg yolk
- 1 tablespoon Italian bread crumbs
- 1 green onion, chopped
- 1 tablespoon lemon juice
- 1 teaspoon Worcestershire sauce
- 1 teaspoon garlic powder
- 1 pinch salt and ground black pepper to taste
- 1 (6 ounce) can snow crab, drained
- 1 (4 ounce) can small shrimp, drained
- 12 large white mushrooms, stems removed
- 1 cup Italian bread crumbs

Direction

- Prepare the oven by preheating to 400°F (200°C). Use aluminum foil to line a baking sheet.
- In the bowl of a mixer, put pepper, salt, garlic powder, Worcestershire sauce, lemon juice, green onion, 1 tablespoon bread crumbs, egg yolk, and cream cheese. Stir until smooth and equally combined. Add in the shrimp and snow crab then fold. Fill the mushrooms with this mixture, then press into the rest of bread crumbs to cover. Transfer onto baking sheet stuffing-side-up once coated.
- Place in the preheated oven then bake for 12 to 14 minutes until the mushrooms have softened slightly. Then set the oven to broil, and place the mushrooms to broil for a few minutes until the tops are bubbly and golden.

Nutrition Information

- Calories: 278 calories;
- Total Fat: 15.6
- Sodium: 389
- Total Carbohydrate: 17.5
- Cholesterol: 132

- Protein: 17.4

---

947. The Mushroom Steak Stuff

Serving: 4 | Prep: 25mins | Cook: 35mins | Ready in:

Ingredients

- 4 slices bacon
- 2 tablespoons olive oil
- 1 (16 ounce) package rigatoni pasta
- 1/2 cup butter
- 1 pound beef top sirloin, thinly sliced
- 1 (6 ounce) package sliced fresh mushrooms
- 1 teaspoon prepared yellow mustard
- 1/4 teaspoon minced fresh ginger root
- 1 pinch salt and pepper to taste
- 2 tablespoons red wine
- 1 tablespoon Marsala wine
- 1 cup crumbled feta cheese
- 2/3 cup heavy cream

Direction

- Preheat the oven to 190°C (375°F).
- Put the bacon in a big, deep skillet. Cook on medium - high heat until brown evenly. Drain on a paper towel-lined plate, then put aside. On high heat, boil a big pot of lightly salted water with 2 tablespoons of olive oil. Put in the rigatoni pasta, then cook for 8 to 10 minutes until al dente; drain.
- In the meantime, melt the butter over medium heat in a big skillet. Put in the sirloin strips, then cook for 6 minutes, until it is no longer pink. Transform the sirloin to a casserole dish and mix mushrooms into the hot skillet. Cook and mix for 2 minutes, season with pepper, salt, ginger and mustard, and cook for another 3 minutes. Pour in the Marsala wine and red wine, then simmer over medium - high heat. Put in 1/2 the crumbled feta cheese and cream, lower heat to medium-low, then simmer for 5 minutes, occasionally mixing. The feta lets the cream thicken. The cream sauce is not a gravy, so it won't thicken like gravy. When finished, pour the mushroom mixture atop the sirloin strips, then dust with the leftover feta cheese.
- Bake in the preheated oven until bubbly and hot, about 10 minutes. Crumble the bacon over, then serve atop rigatoni pasta.

Nutrition Information

- Calories: 1331 calories;
- Sodium: 1170
- Total Carbohydrate: 87.5
- Cholesterol: 283
- Protein: 61.1
- Total Fat: 81.8

---

948. The Very Best Spaghetti Sauce

Serving: 12 | Prep: 30mins | Cook: 6hours30mins | Ready in:

Ingredients

- 18 roma (plum) tomatoes
- 2 (6 ounce) cans tomato paste
- 1/2 cup butter
- 4 cloves garlic, minced
- 5 bay leaves
- 1 large white onion, chopped
- 1 large zucchini, chopped
- 1 green bell pepper, chopped
- 1 red bell pepper, chopped
- 1 (8 ounce) package fresh mushrooms, sliced
- 2 tablespoons dried oregano
- 1 tablespoon Italian seasoning
- 2 teaspoons chili powder
- 1/4 cup brown sugar
- 1 (15 ounce) container ricotta cheese

Direction

- Boil a big pot of lightly salted water. Put in tomatoes and cook for 10 minutes. Drain and use cold water to rinse. Skin the tomatoes, put back into the pot then mash them. Mix in 2 cups of water and tomato paste. Cover and allow it to simmer on low heat.
- Meanwhile, in a big skillet, melt butter over medium heat. Sauté bay leaves and garlic for a minute. Mix in onions then sauté until translucent. Mix in mushrooms, red and green bell peppers and zucchini. Cook slowly and stir for 5 to 7 minutes.
- Mix the vegetables into the tomato sauce. Put in brown sugar, chili powder, Italian seasoning and oregano. Simmer for 6 to 8 hours over low heat. Ten minutes before serving, mix in the ricotta cheese.

Nutrition Information

- Calories: 193 calories;
- Total Fat: 11.2
- Sodium: 335
- Total Carbohydrate: 19.1
- Cholesterol: 31
- Protein: 7.4

949. Three Pepper Pilaf

Serving: 4 | Prep: | Cook: | Ready in:

Ingredients

- 4 skinless chicken thighs
- 3 cups chicken stock
- 1 onion, chopped
- 3 cloves garlic, chopped
- 1 teaspoon ground turmeric
- 4 ounces fresh mushrooms, sliced
- 12 ounces uncooked white rice
- 3 tomatoes, sliced
- 1 red bell pepper, sliced
- 1 green bell pepper, sliced
- 1 yellow bell pepper, thinly sliced

Direction

- Boil chicken pieces with chicken stock in a big pot, putting garlic and onion into stock prior to boiling. Once chicken is cooked through, take out of stock and reserve. Put in turmeric and mix, then reserve stock.
- Heat oil in a big skillet. Put in mushrooms and sauté for a minute. Put in rice, mix for 2 minutes, then put in stock. Simmer gently for 20 minutes. Meanwhile, peel and cut tomatoes and put into the pilaf mixture. Slice the cooked chicken into bite size portions, and put into skillet, together with the yellow, green and red bell peppers. Mix everything together and simmer over low heat, mixing, till all liquid is soaked up and rice is fluffy and separate.

Nutrition Information

- Calories: 467 calories;
- Total Fat: 4.4
- Sodium: 551
- Total Carbohydrate: 83.1
- Cholesterol: 58
- Protein: 23.3

950. Tofu Egg Noodles In Coconut Sauce

Serving: 6 | Prep: 30mins | Cook: 35mins | Ready in:

Ingredients

- 4 eggs
- 1 tablespoon soy sauce, or to taste
- 1 tablespoon sesame oil, or as needed
- canola oil, or as needed
- 1 (12 ounce) package extra-firm tofu, cubed
- 2 cups sliced fresh mushrooms
- 2 cups broccoli florets
- 1/4 cup chopped cashews
- 1 (10 ounce) package frozen shelled edamame (green soybeans)

- 1 (16 ounce) package egg noodles
- 1/2 cup unsweetened soy milk
- 1/2 cup peanut butter
- 1/4 cup reduced-fat coconut milk
- 1 teaspoon tahini

Direction

- Preheat the oven to 175 °C or 350 °F.
- In a bowl, mix soy sauce and eggs together. Over medium heat, heat a non-stick skillet; add in the egg mixture and let cook for 3 to 5 minutes till set. Onto work area, slip the eggs and slice into bite-size squares.
- In a big skillet, heat canola oil and sesame oil over medium heat. Put the tofu; let cook for 8 to 10 minutes till golden brown on every side. Turn tofu onto a plate. To skillet, put the broccoli and mushrooms; let cook for 5 to 7 minutes till broccoli is soft.
- In a baking dish, put the cashews; in prepped oven, let cook for 8 to 12 minutes, tossing from time to time to prevent burning, till toasted.
- In a microwave-safe bowl, put the edamame, place cover and allow to cook in microwave for 1 to 2 minutes till hot.
- With slightly salted water, fill a big pot and bring to a rolling boil. Mix in the egg noodles for 8 minutes, return to a boil, and allow to cook over medium heat till soft yet firm to the bite. Let drain.
- In a big saucepan, mix tahini, coconut milk, peanut butter and soy milk together over medium heat. Mix for 2 to 4 minutes till tahini and peanut butter have dissolved. Put the egg noodles, edamame, mushroom and broccoli mixture, tofu and egg; mix by tossing. Put toasted cashews on top to serve.

Nutrition Information

- Calories: 695 calories;
- Sodium: 383
- Total Carbohydrate: 70.5
- Cholesterol: 187
- Protein: 35.3
- Total Fat: 32.9

951. Tofu Mushroom Ramen Soup

Serving: 3 | Prep: 20mins | Cook: 20mins | Ready in:

Ingredients

- 3 tablespoons cooking oil, divided
- 10 ounces bok choy, stems and greens chopped and separated
- 3 green onions, chopped and divided
- 4 cloves garlic, minced
- 1 (32 ounce) carton beef stock
- 3 1/2 ounces shiitake mushrooms, stemmed and sliced
- 2 (1.12 ounce) packages miso soup mix
- 2 tablespoons soy sauce
- 1 pound tofu, drained and cubed
- 2 tablespoons hoisin sauce
- 3 (3 ounce) packages ramen noodles
- 2 hard-boiled egg, sliced

Direction

- In a big saucepan, heat 2 tbsp. oil on medium heat. Add garlic, white parts of green onions and bok choy stems. Cook for about 3 minutes till soft. Mix soy sauce, miso soup mix, mushrooms and beef stock in; boil. Simmer on low heat.
- As broth simmers, in a skillet heat leftover 1 tbsp. oil on high heat. Add tofu. Cook for about 5 minutes till golden brown. Put hoisin sauce in. Toss till coated. Take off from heat.
- Mix ramen noodles and bok choy leaves into broth mixture. Put heat on high. Boil for 3-5 minutes till noodles are cooked. Put eggs and tofu on top; serve.

Nutrition Information

- Calories: 508 calories;
- Total Carbohydrate: 32.6

- Cholesterol: 142
- Protein: 29.2
- Total Fat: 30.1
- Sodium: 2098

952. Tofu With Ground Pork Stir Fry

Serving: 4 | Prep: 15mins | Cook: 30mins | Ready in:

Ingredients

- 1 cup uncooked long grain white rice
- 2 cups water
- 2 tablespoons vegetable oil
- 2 cloves garlic, minced
- 1/2 pound ground pork
- 6 fresh shiitake mushrooms, diced
- 1 (14 ounce) package cubed firm tofu
- 1 green onion, thinly sliced
- 1 tablespoon Asian chile pepper sauce
- 1 tablespoon ketchup
- 2 tablespoons tamari

Direction

- Boil the rice and water in a pot then lower the heat to low, cover the pot and allow to simmer for 20 minutes.
- In a wok, heat the oil on high heat and cook the garlic in the oil for a minute. Add the pork then cook it for 5 minutes until it's browns evenly.
- Add the tofu, green onions, and mushrooms in the wok and mix them. Add the chili pepper sauce, tamari, and ketchup while stirring. Continue to cook until it's heated through then serve on top of cooked rice.

Nutrition Information

- Calories: 524 calories;
- Total Fat: 24
- Sodium: 599

- Total Carbohydrate: 47.1
- Cholesterol: 37
- Protein: 31.2

953. Tom Yum Koong Soup

Serving: 5 | Prep: 10mins | Cook: 40mins | Ready in:

Ingredients

- 1/2 pound medium shrimp - peeled and deveined
- 12 mushrooms, halved
- 1 (4.5 ounce) can mushrooms, drained
- 4 cups water
- 2 lemon grass
- 4 kaffir lime leaves
- 4 slices galangal
- 4 chile padi (bird's eye chiles)
- 1 1/2 tablespoons fish sauce
- 1 1/2 limes, juiced
- 1 teaspoon white sugar
- 1 teaspoon hot chile paste
- 1 tablespoon tom yum soup paste (optional)

Direction

- Trim the lemongrass and chop into pieces similar to size of matchstick.
- To prepare the stock: Transfer shrimp shells and heads into water and cook for about 20 minutes. Switch off the fire. Let the heads and shells to soak for 20 more minutes prior to discarding.
- Trim the lemongrass and then chop into pieces that resemble size of matchstick.
- Add chili paste, sugar, lime juice, fish sauce, chili padi, galangal, kaffir lime leaves, lemon grass and stock into a pot and heat to boil. After boiling for five minutes, place in both mushrooms and shrimps. Then cook for 10 more minutes. Stud with coriander leaves.

954. True Italian Porcini Mushroom Risotto

Serving: 4 | Prep: 15mins | Cook: 39mins | Ready in:

Ingredients

- 1 ounce dried porcini mushrooms
- 1 cup hot water
- 1 (32 ounce) carton beef stock
- 1/4 cup olive oil, divided
- 3 cloves garlic
- 1 teaspoon dried rosemary
- salt and ground black pepper to taste
- 1 cup white wine, divided
- 1/4 cup butter, divided
- 1 shallot, chopped
- 1 3/4 cups Arborio rice
- 1/3 cup grated Parmesan cheese

Direction

- In a bowl, put porcini mushrooms and cover with hot water. Soak for an hour till tender. Drain, setting soaking water aside. Squeeze the mushrooms to get rid of the extra water, then coarsely chop.
- In a saucepan, boil beef stock. Lower the heat to low and put a cover on to keep warm.
- In skillet, heat 3 tablespoons of oil on moderate heat. Put in the garlic cloves; cook for 2 minutes till aromatic. Put in the mushrooms; cook and mix for 5 to 6 minutes till tender. Add pepper, salt and rosemary to season. Throw the garlic cloves; add half cup of wine. Raise the heat to moderately-high and let simmer for 3 to 5 minutes till wine is reduced.
- In saucepan on moderately-low heat, heat 2 tablespoons of butter and leftover 1 tablespoon of oil. Cook and mix the shallot for 3 minutes till tender. Cook and mix Arborio rice for 3 minutes till aromatic and toasted. Add leftover half cup of wine. Let simmer for 3 minutes till wine is soaked in.
- Into saucepan, scoop 1/3 of the warm stock; cook and mix till soaked in. Scoop in the rest of the stock and the reserved soaking water in small amounts and cook for 15 to 18 minutes, mixing continuously, till risotto is creamy and soft.
- Take risotto off the heat; mix in Parmesan cheese and leftover 2 tablespoons of butter. Let rest for 3 to 5 minutes prior to serving.

Nutrition Information

- Calories: 737 calories;
- Total Fat: 28.3
- Sodium: 319
- Total Carbohydrate: 91.6
- Cholesterol: 36
- Protein: 16

955. Turkey Mushroom Tetrazzini

Serving: 6 | Prep: 20mins | Cook: 45mins | Ready in:

Ingredients

- 8 ounces uncooked linguine pasta
- 2 tablespoons butter
- 2 cups fresh mushrooms, quartered
- 1/2 cup sliced green onion
- 1/4 cup chopped red bell pepper
- 1/4 cup all-purpose flour
- 1/8 teaspoon black pepper
- 2 tablespoons garlic spread seasoning (such as Johnny's® Great Caesar! Garlic Spread & Seasoning)
- 1 1/4 cups chicken broth
- 1 1/4 cups heavy cream
- 2 cups chopped cooked turkey
- 3/4 cup grated Parmesan cheese, divided
- 1/4 cup sliced almonds
- 2 tablespoons chopped fresh parsley (optional)

Direction

- Preheat the oven to 175°C or 350°F. Oil a rectangular baking dish, 2 quarts in size.
- Fill slightly salted water into a big pot and bring to a rolling boil. When boiling, mix in linguine, and bring back to a boil. Let the pasta cook without a cover for 11 minutes, mixing from time to time, till pasta has cooked completely yet still firm to the bite. Drain thoroughly in a colander placed in sink.
- In a big skillet, heat the butter; cook and mix bell pepper, green onion and mushrooms for 5 minutes till vegetables are softened and onion is translucent. Mix in garlic spread seasoning, black pepper and flour. Add cream and chicken broth, beating the mixture till thickened and smooth, 5 to 8 minutes longer. Mix in cooked linguine, 1/2 the Parmesan cheese and turkey, and gently mix to coat every ingredient in sauce.
- Into the prepped baking dish, scatter the mixture, and scatter the rest of the Parmesan cheese and almonds on top. In the prepped oven, bake for 20 minutes till mixture is bubbling and surface has started to brown, and scatter parsley on top prior to serving.

Nutrition Information

- Calories: 515 calories;
- Protein: 25.6
- Total Fat: 30.3
- Sodium: 676
- Total Carbohydrate: 37
- Cholesterol: 123

956. Turkey Tetrazzini

Serving: 6 | Prep: 25mins | Cook: 25mins | Ready in:

Ingredients

- 2 (8 ounce) packages angel hair pasta
- 1/4 cup butter
- 2/3 cup sliced onion
- 1/4 cup all-purpose flour
- 2 cups milk
- 1 teaspoon salt
- 1/4 teaspoon ground white pepper
- 1/2 teaspoon poultry seasoning
- 1/4 teaspoon ground mustard
- 1 cup shredded sharp Cheddar cheese, divided
- 2 tablespoons chopped pimento peppers (optional)
- 1 (4.5 ounce) can sliced mushrooms
- 1 pound cooked turkey, sliced

Direction

- Preheat oven to 200 °C or 400 °F. In a big pot, let lightly salted water boil. Put pasta and cook until almost tender or for 4 minutes. Drain it.
- Over medium heat, melt butter in a saucepan. Put onion, then cook and stir until tender. Mix the flour in until blended. Stir milk in gradually to avoid lumps from forming. Use mustard, poultry seasoning, pepper and salt to season. Over medium heat, cook it until the mixture thickens, stirring constantly. Move it away from heat and add pimento and 2/3 cup of cheese. Keep on stirring until cheese melts. In cheese sauce, put undrained mushrooms.
- At the bottom of 9x13 inch baking dish, put a layer of pasta. Put a layer of turkey to cover and put a layer of cheese sauce. Repeat the layers. Over top, sprinkle remaining 1/3 cup of cheese.
- In the preheated oven, bake for about 25 minutes until cheese on top is toasted and until sauce is bubbly.

Nutrition Information

- Calories: 604 calories;
- Cholesterol: 113
- Protein: 38.9
- Total Fat: 26.4
- Sodium: 914
- Total Carbohydrate: 52.1

957. Turkey A La King

Serving: 4 | Prep: 10mins | Cook: 15mins | Ready in:

Ingredients

- 2 tablespoons butter
- 3 fresh mushrooms, sliced
- 1 tablespoon all-purpose flour
- 1 cup chicken broth
- 1/2 cup heavy cream
- 1 cup chopped cooked turkey
- 1/3 cup frozen peas, thawed
- salt and pepper to taste

Direction

- Cook butter in a big skillet over moderately low heat till golden brown. Sauté the mushrooms till soft. Mix in flour till smooth. Gradually mix in chicken broth, and cook till thickened slightly. Mix in peas, turkey and cream. Turn the heat to low, and let cook till thickened. Add pepper and salt to season.

Nutrition Information

- Calories: 233 calories;
- Sodium: 92
- Total Carbohydrate: 4.5
- Cholesterol: 83
- Protein: 12.2
- Total Fat: 18.6

958. Twenty Minute Chicken

Serving: 6 | Prep: 5mins | Cook: 15mins | Ready in:

Ingredients

- 3 boneless, skinless chicken breast halves
- 1/2 large onion, chopped
- 2 (10 ounce) packages sliced fresh button mushrooms
- 1/4 cup olive oil
- salt and freshly ground black pepper to taste
- 1 clove garlic, chopped (optional)
- 1 cup shredded mozzarella cheese

Direction

- Turn the oven to 400°F (200°C) to preheat. Rinse the chicken breasts, use paper towels to pat dry, and halve each breast.
- In a big frying pan, heat 2 tablespoons oil over medium-high heat. Quickly sear the chicken, turn, for 5 minutes, or until no sign of pink remains.
- In the meantime, heat 2 tablespoons oil in a separate big frying pan over medium-high heat. Mix in garlic (if using), onions, and mushrooms; cook for 5 minutes, or until they are tender and nice.
- Add the contents of the 2 frying pans to a baking dish, sprinkle over the top with cheese, and bake for approximately 5 minutes.

Nutrition Information

- Calories: 219 calories;
- Total Fat: 13.1
- Sodium: 160
- Total Carbohydrate: 4.9
- Cholesterol: 46
- Protein: 21.2

959. Uszka Do Barszczu (Mushroom Dumplings For Borscht)

Serving: 10 | Prep: 25mins | Cook: 43mins | Ready in:

Ingredients

- Filling:
- 3 1/2 ounces dried wild mushrooms

- 2 tablespoons butter
- 1 large onion, chopped
- salt and ground black pepper to taste
- 2 tablespoons bread crumbs, or as needed (optional)
- Dough:
- 8 cups all-purpose flour
- 1 cup hot milk
- 1 egg yolk

Direction

- In a small pan, put the dried mushrooms and pour hot water to cover, then boil. Cook for about 20 minutes until it becomes soft. Drain it and cut it into little pieces.
- In a pan, melt the butter on medium heat. Stir in onion, then cook and stir for about 3 minutes until beginning to soften. Mix in the mushrooms and keep on cooking for about 5 minutes until the onion becomes soft. Put black pepper and salt to season. If the filling appears too wet, add breadcrumbs.
- In a big bowl, mix the egg yolk, hot milk and flour. Using a fork, stir it quickly until a smooth and soft dough forms.
- On a lightly-floured surface, roll out the dough. Slice it into 1 1/2 inch squares then put a teaspoon of filling on its center. Fold the dough over the filling to create a triangle and secure by pinching the edges. Bring together the bottom corners and pinch together.
- Boil a big pot of lightly salted water. Cook dumplings for about 10 minutes, in batches, until it floats to the water's surface. Using a slotted spoon, move the dumplings onto a serving plate.

Nutrition Information

- Calories: 439 calories;
- Total Fat: 4.6
- Sodium: 70
- Total Carbohydrate: 84.8
- Cholesterol: 29
- Protein: 13.6

960. Vareniky

Serving: 6 | Prep: 30mins | Cook: 40mins | Ready in:

Ingredients

- For the Dough:
- 1 1/2 cups milk
- 2 tablespoons sunflower seed oil
- 1 egg yolk
- 3 1/2 cups all-purpose flour
- 1/2 teaspoon salt
- For the Filling:
- 3 1/2 ounces dried porcini mushrooms
- 1/2 cup hot water
- 1 pound potatoes, peeled
- 2 onions, chopped
- 3 tablespoons vegetable oil
- salt and pepper to taste
- To Cook Vareniky:
- 1 gallon water
- 1 tablespoon salt

Direction

- To combine dough, in a bowl, mix 1/2 teaspoon salt, flour, egg yolk, sunflower oil, and milk. Knead the dough with your hand or use an electric mixer until it forms a smooth and stiff dough. Form dough into a log, encase in plastic wrap and reserve.
- Soak dried porcini for 45 minutes in 1/2 cup of hot water. In the meantime, cook potatoes for about 20 minutes in boiling salted water to cover until tender. Drain the potatoes and let to steam dry for 1 or 2 minutes.
- Cut rehydrated mushrooms and save the soaking liquid. Then mash the potatoes while adding mushroom-soaking liquid in order to moisten.
- Over medium heat, heat vegetable oil in a skillet and then mix in chopped onions. Cook while stirring for about 5 minutes until onion has turned translucent and softened. Mix in chopped mushrooms.

- Combine mushrooms, onions and mashed potatoes. Season with pepper and salt to taste. Reserve the filling as you roll out vareniky dough.
- Chop dough into discs of approximately 3/8 inch thick and two inches wide (one cm thick and five cm in diameter). Roll or flatten each disc on a surface that is lightly floured to form a thin circle. Transfer filling by tablespoonfuls into the middle of each vareniky. Then fold dough in half and pinch the edges to seal. Repeat this until all dumplings are filled.
- Heat tablespoon of salt and gallon of water to boil in a large pot and then add vareniky. Gently stir once. Let to simmer about 10 to 15 minutes until all dumplings float to the top. Drain thoroughly prior to serving.

Nutrition Information

- Calories: 553 calories;
- Sodium: 1444
- Total Carbohydrate: 87
- Cholesterol: 39
- Protein: 17.4
- Total Fat: 14.9

961. Veal Chop With Portabello Mushrooms

Serving: 2 | Prep: 15mins | Cook: 25mins | Ready in:

Ingredients

- 5 tablespoons olive oil, divided
- 1 tablespoon butter
- 2 veal chops
- 1 portobello mushroom, sliced
- 1 1/2 cups chicken broth
- 1 1/2 teaspoons fresh rosemary, chopped
- 1/2 cup red wine

Direction

- Heat butter and 4 tablespoons olive oil in skillet on medium high heat then cook chops for 2-3 minutes per side till browned.
- Mix mushrooms in when browned; cook for 1 minute. Add rosemary and chicken broth; cover. Simmer for 10 minutes. Mix red wine in and increase heat; cook till sauce reduces by half, with no cover. To avoid over-cooking, you can remove veal chops at any time and put back into pan at final minute.
- Drizzle leftover 1 tablespoon olive oil; serve.

Nutrition Information

- Calories: 555 calories;
- Total Carbohydrate: 5.2
- Cholesterol: 97
- Protein: 21.7
- Total Fat: 45.2
- Sodium: 838

962. Veal Forestiere

Serving: 6 | Prep: 15mins | Cook: 15mins | Ready in:

Ingredients

- 1 1/2 pounds thin veal cutlets
- 1/4 cup all-purpose flour for coating
- 3 tablespoons butter
- 1 tablespoon minced garlic
- 1 tablespoon minced shallot
- 1/2 pound crimini mushrooms, sliced
- 1/2 cup Marsala wine
- 1/2 cup veal stock
- 1 (10 ounce) can artichoke hearts, drained and sliced
- salt and pepper to taste

Direction

- Slightly flour veal cutlets and shake the excess off. Warm butter over medium-high heat on a big skillet until melted. Cook cutlets in pan for

1-2 minutes on each side until browned and almost cooked through. Take out veal from the pan and reserve.
- Sauté shallots and garlic in skillet until shallots become soft. Add in mushrooms, continue cooking until mushrooms start to moist. Add in the wine; cook 2-3 minutes longer, stirring with a spoon to scrape the bottom of the pan. Add in stock and letting it simmer for 5-10 minutes or until liquid starts to reduce.
- Put back the veal into the pan with artichokes, cooking until heated thoroughly. Sprinkle with pepper and salt. Serve on plates and scoop sauce all over the veal.

Nutrition Information

- Calories: 261 calories;
- Cholesterol: 71
- Protein: 18
- Total Fat: 10.5
- Sodium: 578
- Total Carbohydrate: 19

963. Veal Meat Loaf

Serving: 8 | Prep: 15mins | Cook: 1hours | Ready in:

Ingredients

- 2 pounds ground veal
- 2 eggs, lightly beaten
- 1 cup dry bread crumbs
- 1/2 cup warm water
- 1 (1 ounce) envelope dry onion soup mix
- 2 large carrots, grated
- 1 pint shiitake mushrooms, sliced

Direction

- Preheat an oven to 175°C/350°F.
- Mix shiitake mushrooms, carrots, soup mix, water, dry breadcrumbs, eggs and ground vela in bowl; put in 9x5-inch loaf pan.
- In preheated oven, bake for 1 hour till internal temperature is 70°C/160°F.

Nutrition Information

- Calories: 237 calories;
- Total Fat: 8
- Sodium: 512
- Total Carbohydrate: 15.8
- Cholesterol: 127
- Protein: 23.7

964. Veal Or Chicken Marsala

Serving: 4 | Prep: 30mins | Cook: | Ready in:

Ingredients

- 4 boneless, skinless chicken breasts or veal cutlets
- 2 tablespoons flour
- 4 tablespoons butter, divided
- 2 cups mushrooms, sliced
- 3/4 cup Holland House® Marsala Cooking Wine
- 1/4 cup water (optional)
- 2 tablespoons fresh parsley, chopped
- 1/4 teaspoon rosemary (optional)

Direction

- Pound the chicken (or the veal) until thin. Lightly dredge with flour on both sides. In a large skillet, put 2 tablespoons butter to melt and put in mushrooms then sauté for about 10 minutes over medium heat until browned. Remove mushrooms and put it aside.
- Put the rest 2 tablespoons butter in the skillet and melt it. Put in chicken and cook through for 4 minutes per side. Transfer to a serving platter. Put the mushrooms back to the pan, mix in the rosemary, parsley, water, and cooking wine. Heat and pour the mixture over chicken.

Nutrition Information

- Calories: 301 calories;
- Protein: 21
- Total Fat: 14.4
- Sodium: 131
- Total Carbohydrate: 11
- Cholesterol: 82

965. Vegan Lettuce Wraps

Serving: 4 | Prep: 40mins | Cook: 7mins | Ready in:

Ingredients

- Dipping Sauce:
- 1/3 cup vegetarian hoisin sauce
- 1 teaspoon water, or more to taste
- 1/2 teaspoon sambal oelek (chile paste), or more to taste
- Seasoning Sauce:
- 1 tablespoon vegetarian oyster sauce
- 1 tablespoon water
- 1/2 teaspoon sambal oelek (chile paste) (optional)
- 1/2 teaspoon mushroom seasoning
- 1/4 teaspoon sesame oil
- 1/4 teaspoon white sugar
- 1/4 teaspoon salt
- Wraps:
- 1 tablespoon vegetable oil
- 2 slices ginger
- 5 ounces fried tofu, diced
- 4 ounces jicama, peeled and diced
- 3 fresh shiitake mushrooms, diced
- 1/4 teaspoon salt
- ground black pepper to taste
- 1/2 red bell pepper, diced
- 8 large butterhead lettuce leaves
- 1 tablespoon toasted sesame seeds, or to taste

Direction

- To prepare dipping sauce, combine 1/2 teaspoon sambal oelek, 1 teaspoon water and hoisin sauce together.
- In a bowl, combine 1/4 teaspoon salt, sugar, sesame oil, mushroom seasoning, 1/2 teaspoon sambal oelek, 1 tablespoon water and oyster sauce together to prepare seasoning sauce.
- In a big skillet, heat the oil over medium heat. Cook and mix the ginger for 30 seconds till aromatic. Put the pepper, 1/4 teaspoon salt, shiitake mushrooms, jicama and tofu; cook and mix for 5 minutes till mushrooms turn golden brown. Put seasoning sauce and red bell pepper; cook and mix for a minute till heated completely. Take off heat.
- In the middle of every lettuce leaf, put 1 or 2 tablespoons tofu mixture. Scatter sesame seeds over. Put a teaspoon of dipping sauce; roll up the lettuce to seal tofu mixture. Redo with the rest of lettuce leaves and tofu mixture. Serve with the rest of dipping sauce on the side.

Nutrition Information

- Calories: 225 calories;
- Protein: 8.4
- Total Fat: 13
- Sodium: 730
- Total Carbohydrate: 20.9
- Cholesterol: < 1

966. Vegan Mushroom Bolognese

Serving: 4 | Prep: 20mins | Cook: 35mins | Ready in:

Ingredients

- 2 tablespoons olive oil
- 1 onion, chopped
- 1 medium carrot, diced
- 1 celery stalk, diced
- 2 cloves garlic, minced

- 2 cups button mushrooms, quartered
- 1 cup red wine
- 1 (14.5 ounce) can whole peeled tomatoes
- 1 tablespoon salt
- 1 teaspoon ground black pepper
- 1/2 teaspoon dried sage
- 3 bay leaves
- 1/2 teaspoon basil

Direction

- Start by heating some olive oil over medium heat on a skillet. Add some onion and let it cook for about 5 minutes until the onion becomes soft and translucent, stirring often. Take garlic, celery, carrot, and add to the skillet to soften it by cooking for about 3 minutes. Place in mushrooms and cook for about 3 minutes until tender. Add your selected red wine then leave it to cook for about 3 minutes until the wine has mostly evaporated.
- To continue, add tomatoes to the skillet then season with bay leaves, sage, black pepper, and salt. Let this cook over heat that is set to medium-high and allow it to boil. When that's done, lower down the heat to low, cover the skillet, and let it simmer for about 20 minutes. After it's simmered, take out the bay leaves and add basil.

Nutrition Information

- Calories: 162 calories;
- Sodium: 1923
- Total Carbohydrate: 12.8
- Cholesterol: 0
- Protein: 3.1
- Total Fat: 7.2

967. Vegan Mushroom Ceviche

Serving: 6 | Prep: 25mins | Cook: 10mins | Ready in:

Ingredients

- 3 tablespoons olive oil
- 2 cloves garlic, chopped
- 3 (8 ounce) packages fresh white mushrooms, chopped
- salt to taste
- 6 tomatoes, chopped
- 2 carrots, grated
- 1 white onion, chopped
- 2 tablespoons chopped fresh cilantro
- 1 fresh serrano pepper, seeded and chopped
- 1 pickled jalapeno pepper, seeded and chopped
- 1/2 cup lime juice
- 1/2 cup tomato juice
- 1/2 cup ketchup
- 2 tablespoons pickled jalapeno pepper juice
- 2 avocados - peeled, pitted, and sliced

Direction

- In a big skillet, heat olive oil over medium heat. Cook garlic in the hot oil for 10 seconds. Mix in mushrooms and use salt to season; cook for 8 minutes until tender. Take away from heat.
- In a big bowl, put mushrooms and add jalapeno pepper, serrano pepper, cilantro, onion, carrots, and tomatoes.
- In another bowl, mix together pickle juice, ketchup, tomato juice, and lime juice. Add to the mushroom mixture and allow to sit, about 20 minutes. Use avocado slices to garnish and enjoy.

Nutrition Information

- Calories: 253 calories;
- Total Fat: 17.4
- Sodium: 389
- Total Carbohydrate: 24.2
- Cholesterol: 0
- Protein: 6.9

968. Vegan Pasta With Spinach, Mushrooms, And Garlic

Serving: 2 | Prep: 15mins | Cook: 15mins | Ready in:

Ingredients

- 1/2 (16 ounce) box penne pasta
- 3 tablespoons olive oil, divided
- 1 (8 ounce) package sliced fresh mushrooms
- 1 bunch spinach, roughly chopped
- 2 cloves garlic, chopped
- 2 tablespoons balsamic vinegar
- salt and ground black pepper to taste

Direction

- Boil a big pot of lightly salted water, then add penne and cook for about 11 minutes, stirring from time to time, until it becomes tender yet firm to the bite; drain.
- In a skillet, heat 1 tbsp. of olive oil on medium heat and cook the mushrooms for 3-5 minutes, until light brown. Mix in garlic and spinach. Cook for about 3 minutes until the spinach becomes wilted. Add the drained pasta and mix to blend. Stir in balsamic vinegar and leftover 2 tbsp. of olive oil, then add pepper and salt to season.

Nutrition Information

- Calories: 658 calories;
- Total Carbohydrate: 94.7
- Cholesterol: 0
- Protein: 23.5
- Total Fat: 23.9
- Sodium: 228

969. Vegan Shepherd's Pie

Serving: 4 | Prep: 10mins | Cook: 48mins | Ready in:

Ingredients

- olive oil cooking spray
- 1 (10 ounce) package sliced fresh mushrooms
- 1 yellow onion, chopped
- 2 (14 ounce) cans Italian-style diced tomatoes
- 1 (12 ounce) jar mushroom gravy, or to taste
- 1 (12 ounce) package frozen mixed vegetables
- 2 tablespoons vegan margarine (such as Earth Balance®)
- 1 3/4 cups water
- 1/4 teaspoon garlic powder
- 1/2 cup rice milk
- 2 1/4 cups instant mashed potatoes (such as Betty Crocker® Potato Buds®)
- 1 tablespoon egg substitute

Direction

- Preheat the oven to 375° F (190° C).
- Heat a large frying pan over medium-high heat; use olive oil spray to grease. Put in onion and mushrooms; sauté for around 5 minutes until soft. Put in frozen vegetables, gravy, and diced tomatoes. Boil. Lower heat to low, then cook for 8-10 minutes until flavors blend.
- In a saucepan, melt vegan margarine over medium heat. Add garlic powder and water; heat to a boil. Take away from heat. Pour in rice milk and mix in egg substitute and mashed potatoes.
- Spoon the mushroom mixture in an unoiled 8-inch glass baking dish. Pour potato mixture over.
- In the preheated oven, bake for around 20 minutes until top becomes golden brown.

Nutrition Information

- Calories: 305 calories;
- Cholesterol: < 1
- Protein: 10.3
- Total Fat: 8.1
- Sodium: 714
- Total Carbohydrate: 51.1

970. Vegan Spaghetti

Serving: 1 | Prep: 20mins | Cook: 20mins | Ready in:

Ingredients

- 1 large zucchini
- 1/2 cup vegetable broth, or as needed, divided
- 1 small onion, diced
- 1 1/2 tablespoons tomato paste
- 1 small tomato, diced
- 1 small portobello mushroom, cubed
- 1 tablespoon minced garlic
- 2 teaspoons dried oregano
- 1 teaspoon dried thyme
- 1/2 teaspoon dried tarragon
- 1/2 teaspoon dried marjoram
- 1/2 (12 ounce) package veggie meat substitute (such as Yves® Ground Round)
- 2 cups fresh spinach, roughly chopped

Direction

- Use a spiralizer with the large shredder blade to make zucchini into noodles. Set them aside.
- In a big pot, mix and cook tomato paste, 1/4 cup broth, and onion on medium heat. Cook for 3 minutes or until onion begins to tenderize. Add mushroom, tarragon, garlic, marjoram, tomato, thyme, and oregano. Cook for 3 more minutes or until mushroom starts to soften.
- To the pan with the mushroom mixture, add the spinach, remaining 1/4 cup broth, and veggie meat. If mixture seems dry add another 1/4 cup broth. Stir and cook until sauce starts to thicken, and veggies are tender, 10 minutes.
- Mix in the zucchini noodles with the sauce in the pan and cook for 3-5 minutes or until desired firmness is achieved.

Nutrition Information

- Calories: 442 calories;
- Total Carbohydrate: 53
- Cholesterol: 0
- Protein: 43.1
- Total Fat: 9.9
- Sodium: 1189

971. Vegan Stir Fry Noodles

Serving: 2 | Prep: 20mins | Cook: 15mins | Ready in:

Ingredients

- 1/2 (8 ounce) package dried soba noodles
- 1 tablespoon oil, or as needed
- 1/4 cup onion
- 2 cloves garlic, finely chopped
- 1 cup assorted mushrooms
- 1/4 cup chopped eggplant
- 6 leaves bok choy, chopped
- 2 tablespoons soy sauce
- 1 teaspoon teriyaki sauce
- ground black pepper to taste
- 1 teaspoon sesame oil
- 1 green onion, finely chopped

Direction

- Put a big pot of water that's lightly salted to a boil. Cook the soba noodles in the boiling hot water and mix it occasionally until the noodles are tender but still are firm to chew about 5-6 minutes and then drain the noodles.
- In a big skillet on medium heat, heat up the oil and put the garlic and onions in, stir fry for about a minute. Add in the eggplant and mushrooms and cook those for 2 minutes. Put in prepared soba noodles, soy sauce, pepper, teriyaki sauce, and bok choy. For two minutes, cook it until the bok choy gets tender.
- Drizzle some sesame oil and top green onions over the vegetables; serve.

Nutrition Information

- Calories: 326 calories;

- Total Fat: 10
- Sodium: 1500
- Total Carbohydrate: 53
- Cholesterol: 0
- Protein: 12.2

972. Vegan Stroganoff

Serving: 4 | Prep: 15mins | Cook: 20mins | Ready in:

Ingredients

- 1 (12 ounce) box whole wheat rigatoni
- 1 tablespoon vegan margarine
- 1 small onion, chopped
- 1 tablespoon minced garlic
- 1 (12 ounce) package vegetarian beef crumbles (such as Boca®)
- 1 (12 ounce) package sliced fresh mushrooms
- 6 ounces vegan sour cream
- 1 (1 ounce) package dry onion and mushroom soup mix (such as Lipton®)
- 1 cup boiling water
- 1 cube vegetable bouillon
- 1/4 cup soy milk
- 2 tablespoons nutritional yeast
- salt and ground black pepper to taste

Direction

- Boil a large pot of lightly salted water. Cook rigatoni while stirring from time to time in the boiling water for around 12 minutes until tender yet firm to the bite.
- Meanwhile, in a large deep skillet, melt margarine over medium-high heat. Put in garlic and onion; lower heat to medium, then sauté for 3-5 minutes till onion is translucent. Put in mushrooms and vegetarian crumbles; sauté for around 5 minutes till mushrooms become tender.
- In a small bowl, mix soup mix and vegan sour cream together.
- Drizzle bouillon cube with boiling water, then stir thoroughly until dissolved. Mix into the frying pan, then heat to a simmer. Stir in nutritional yeast, soy milk, and sour cream mixture. Cook for 3-4 minutes until heated through. Flavor with pepper and salt. Drain rigatoni, then enjoy with sauce.

Nutrition Information

- Calories: 666 calories;
- Total Fat: 17.6
- Sodium: 1099
- Total Carbohydrate: 94.8
- Cholesterol: 0
- Protein: 33.4

973. Vegan Stuffing

Serving: 10 | Prep: 30mins | Cook: 1hours15mins | Ready in:

Ingredients

- 1 loaf vegan, gluten-free, brown rice bread (such as Food for Life®), cubed
- 2 tablespoons vegan margarine (such as Earth Balance®)
- 1 1/2 cups mixed forest mushrooms, diced
- 1 1/4 cups sweet onion, chopped
- 2 1/2 teaspoons dried sage
- 1 1/2 teaspoons dried rosemary
- 1/2 teaspoon dried thyme
- sea salt and freshly ground black pepper to taste
- 6 tablespoons vegan margarine (such as Earth Balance®), melted
- 1 1/2 cups low-sodium vegan broth
- 8 ounces fresh cranberries
- 1 cup Granny Smith apple, peeled and chopped
- 1/3 cup minced fresh parsley

Direction

- Preheat the oven to 175°C or 175°Fahrenheit. Use aluminum foil to line a baking sheet.
- Transfer the bread cubes onto the foil-lined baking sheet. Toast for 10mins in the preheated oven until aromatic and pale golden. Take it out of the oven but keep the oven on. Cool the bread cubes then move to a big bowl.
- While toasting the bread, melt 2tbsp margarine on medium heat in a big pot. Put the onions and mushrooms in melted margarine and cook for 5mins until the onions are a bit translucent. If needed more moisture, add a bit of vegetable broth. Cook and stir in black pepper, sage, salt, thyme, and rosemary for another 2mins using a wooden spoon until well incorporated.
- Move the mushroom mixture with the toasted bread in a bowl then toss to distribute the mixture evenly. Add 6tbsp melted margarine and vegan broth onto the mixture. Gently but thoroughly mix in parsley, apple, and cranberries. In a casserole dish, spread the stuffing then use aluminum foil to cover.
- Bake for 45mins in the preheated oven; checking at the 25mins mark to avoid burning. Remove the cover then gently mix. Bake for another 15mins until brown on top. Slightly cool to serve.

Nutrition Information

- Calories: 337 calories;
- Total Fat: 19.8
- Sodium: 154
- Total Carbohydrate: 37.9
- Cholesterol: 0
- Protein: 2.4

974. Vegan Tacos With Mushrooms And Tomatillos

Serving: 3 | Prep: 20mins | Cook: 30mins | Ready in:

Ingredients

- 15 tomatillos, husked and halved
- 2 dried chile de arbol peppers
- 2 tablespoons vegetable oil
- 18 ounces cremini mushrooms, sliced
- salt to taste
- 9 (6 inch) corn tortillas
- Garnish:
- 1/2 onion, chopped
- 1/2 cup chopped fresh cilantro

Direction

- Put oven rack 6-in. away from heat source; preheat oven broiler. Line aluminum foil on baking sheet; put, cut side up, tomatillos over.
- In preheated oven, broil for 20 minutes till tomatillos caramelize and are dark brown. Remove from oven; slightly cool.
- In small skillet, toast chile de arbol peppers on medium heat, flipping once, for 3 minutes till beginning to lightly brown in spots, don't char; put on plate.
- Heat oil in big skillet on medium heat as tomatillos cool. Add mushrooms; cook, frequently mixing, for 5 minutes till soft.
- Blend arbol chiles and 3 tomatillos till smooth in blender; put on mushrooms in skillet. Add leftover tomatillos and roasting juices from baking sheet; stir well. Cook on low heat for 5-8 minutes till mushrooms are soft; use salt to season.
- In skillet, warm corn tortillas; divide mushroom mixture among tortillas. Put cilantro and chopped onion on.

Nutrition Information

- Calories: 425 calories;
- Protein: 14.5
- Total Fat: 13.7
- Sodium: 109
- Total Carbohydrate: 64.7
- Cholesterol: 0

975. Vegan Tofu Quiche

Serving: 8 | Prep: 30mins | Cook: 55mins | Ready in:

Ingredients

- 1/8 cup vegetable oil
- 1 medium sweet onion (such as Vidalia®), chopped
- 1 (8 ounce) package sliced fresh mushrooms
- 1 clove garlic, minced
- 1 (8 ounce) package fresh spinach, cut into strips
- 1/4 cup red wine
- 2 tablespoons balsamic vinegar
- 1 teaspoon liquid smoke
- 1 (9 inch) vegan pie crust
- 1 1/2 pounds extra-firm tofu, cubed, or more to taste
- 1/4 cup arrowroot
- 1/4 cup nutritional yeast
- 1/4 cup olive oil
- 1/4 cup Dijon mustard
- 2 teaspoons agar-agar powder

Direction

- In a big pot at medium heat, heat vegetable oil then fry onion for 5 minutes. Put in garlic and mushrooms, cook for 5 more minutes, stirring regularly. Between stirs, cover the pot. Add in balsamic vinegar, red wine, spinach and liquid smoke. Briefly stir then close the lid, take away from the heat. Let it cool down.
- Preheat the oven at 175°C (or 350°F). Place pie crust in a 9 or 10 inch pie plate.
- In a food processor, add tofu, arrowroot, nutritional yeast, olive oil, mustard and agar powder then mix until the mixture form a thick paste. Transfer to mushroom mixture to make a more liquid paste. Pour then scrape them into the pie crust.
- Bake for about 45 minutes in the prepared oven, until the center is set and the crust is golden. Allow the quiche to completely cool before cutting

Nutrition Information

- Calories: 349 calories;
- Total Carbohydrate: 22.7
- Cholesterol: 0
- Protein: 13.7
- Total Fat: 23.5
- Sodium: 338

976. Vegan Tofu Spinach Lasagna

Serving: 8 | Prep: 15mins | Cook: 1hours40mins | Ready in:

Ingredients

- 1 (12 ounce) package fresh mushrooms, sliced
- 1 onion, chopped
- 1 (28 ounce) can tomato sauce
- 1 (28 ounce) can diced tomatoes
- 1 tablespoon Italian seasoning
- 1 (8 ounce) package whole wheat lasagna noodles, dry
- 1 (16 ounce) package frozen chopped spinach, thawed and drained
- 1 (16 ounce) package soft tofu
- 1 (16 ounce) package firm tofu
- 1/4 cup unsweetened almond milk
- 1/4 cup lemon juice, or to taste
- 1/2 teaspoon garlic powder

Direction

- Put a frying pan over medium-high heat. Cook the onion and mushrooms until tender. Mix in the Italian seasoning, tomato sauce and diced tomatoes into the sautéed onion and mushrooms. Simmer the mixture for at least an hour or until the sauce is thick and all the flavors have combined.
- Put water in a big pot with a little bit of salt and boil. Put in the lasagna noodles and cook

- for about 8 minutes while occasionally stirring until pasta firm to chew but tender. Drain the noodles.
- Preheat oven at 350°F (175°C).
- Remove excess liquid from the spinach by squeezing it.
- In a food processor or blender, put the almond milk, lemon juice, garlic powder, firm tofu and soft tofu. Blend the mixture until the texture resembles ricotta cheese. In a big bowl, put the tofu mixture and mix in the spinach.
- In a 9x13-inch pan, put in a thin layer of sauce evenly on bottom and add a layer of lasagna noodles and 1/2 of tofu mixture on top. Do the whole layering process again with the remaining ingredients finishing with left sauce, lasagna noodles, tofu, more noodles, and a little sauce on top. Use aluminum foil to cover the baking pan.
- Put in heated oven and bake for 40-50 minutes or until the top is bubbling and hot.

Nutrition Information

- Calories: 289 calories;
- Sodium: 692
- Total Carbohydrate: 37.3
- Cholesterol: 0
- Protein: 21.5
- Total Fat: 8.6

977. Vegan Vegetable Double Tortilla Pizza

Serving: 4 | Prep: 15mins | Cook: 20mins | Ready in:

Ingredients

- 1 tablespoon vegetable oil
- 2 (12 inch) flour tortillas
- 1/2 cup tomato sauce, or more to taste
- 5 mushrooms, sliced
- 1/2 green bell pepper, chopped
- 1/2 red onion, chopped
- 1/2 white onion, chopped
- 5 black olives, sliced
- 3 pieces sun-dried tomatoes, chopped
- 1/2 jalapeno pepper, chopped

Direction

- Set the oven to 400°F (200°C) and start preheating. Use parchment paper to line a baking sheet; brush olive oil over.
- Place a tortilla on the lined baking sheet; add 1/4 cup tomato sauce. Place another tortilla on top; spread 1/4 cup tomato sauce more on top of tortilla. Garnish the pizza with jalapeno pepper, sun-dried tomatoes, black olives, white onion, red onion, green bell pepper and mushrooms.
- Bake in the prepared oven for about 20 minutes until toppings become softened.

Nutrition Information

- Calories: 245 calories;
- Protein: 6.5
- Total Fat: 8.8
- Sodium: 621
- Total Carbohydrate: 35.7
- Cholesterol: 0

978. Vegetable Cashew Saute

Serving: 8 | Prep: 30mins | Cook: 15mins | Ready in:

Ingredients

- 1 (16 ounce) package whole wheat rotini pasta
- 2 tablespoons dark sesame oil
- 1/4 cup soy sauce
- 1/4 cup balsamic vinegar
- 2 tablespoons white sugar
- 1/4 cup dark sesame oil
- 3 cups chopped broccoli
- 1 cup chopped carrots
- 1 cup chopped red bell pepper

- 2 cups chopped fresh shiitake mushrooms
- 1 cup shelled edamame (green soybeans)
- 3/4 cup chopped unsalted cashew nuts

Direction

- Prepare a large pot of lightly salted water and bring to a boil. Cook the rotini until al dente, about 10-12 minutes, and drain.
- Combine sugar, vinegar, soy sauce, and 2 tablespoons sesame oil in a small bowl.
- In a skillet, heat the one quarter cup of sesame oil over medium heat. Mix in cashews, shelled edamame, mushrooms, red bell pepper, carrots, and broccoli. Stir in the sesame oil sauce. Cook with a cover until vegetables are tender but crisp, about 5 minutes. Pour over the cooked pasta and serve.

Nutrition Information

- Calories: 446 calories;
- Sodium: 494
- Total Carbohydrate: 57.2
- Cholesterol: 0
- Protein: 16.3
- Total Fat: 19.3

979. Vegetable Lo Mein Delight

Serving: 4 | Prep: 15mins | Cook: 15mins | Ready in:

Ingredients

- 8 ounces angel hair pasta
- 3/4 cup chicken broth
- 1/4 cup soy sauce
- 1 tablespoon cornstarch
- 2 tablespoons canola oil
- 1 3/4 cups chopped celery
- 1 3/4 cups sliced fresh mushrooms
- 1 3/4 cups sliced red bell peppers
- 1/2 cup sliced onion
- 2 cups bean sprouts
- 2 cups snow peas
- 1 cup chow mein noodles

Direction

- In a pot, let lightly salted water boil. Put angel hair pasta and cook until al dente or for 3 to 5 minutes. Drain it.
- Whisk cornstarch, soy sauce and chicken broth together in a small bowl.
- Over medium-high heat, heat oil in a wok. Stir in onion, peppers, mushrooms and celery. Cook for about 3 minutes. Put snow peas, bean sprouts and broth mixture. Continue to cook and stir until vegetables are tender but crisp for about 5 minutes.
- Toss the vegetable mixture and the cooked pasta together in a big bowl. Put chow mein noodles on top and serve.

Nutrition Information

- Calories: 397 calories;
- Sodium: 1115
- Total Carbohydrate: 61.6
- Cholesterol: 0
- Protein: 14.6
- Total Fat: 12.6

980. Vegetable Medley II

Serving: 4 | Prep: 20mins | Cook: 15mins | Ready in:

Ingredients

- cooking spray
- 1 tomato, diced
- 1 pinch garlic pepper seasoning
- 2 cups fresh mushrooms, sliced
- 2 yellow squash, cubed
- 2 zucchini, cubed

Direction

- Use cooking spray to spray a big skillet, then add the tomatoes. Let it cook for 5 minutes on medium heat and add the garlic pepper. Stir in the zucchini, squash and mushrooms and let it simmer for 10-15 minutes, until the vegetables become tender-crisp.

Nutrition Information

- Calories: 66 calories;
- Total Fat: 1.5
- Sodium: 202
- Total Carbohydrate: 12.6
- Cholesterol: 0
- Protein: 3.3

981. Vegetable Stuffed Cannelloni

Serving: 8 | Prep: 45mins | Cook: 1hours5mins | Ready in:

Ingredients

- 8 cannelloni noodles
- 5 cloves garlic, minced
- 5 shallots, chopped
- 2 tablespoons olive oil
- 1 cup dry sherry
- 2 cups heavy whipping cream
- salt and pepper to taste
- 1 onion, chopped
- 1 cup fresh sliced mushrooms
- 1 zucchini, chopped
- 1 small eggplant, diced
- 2 roasted red bell peppers, diced
- 1 teaspoon dried basil
- 1 teaspoon dried oregano
- 3/4 cup ricotta cheese
- 1 cup grated Parmesan cheese

Direction

- Parboil the cannelloni in a large pot filled with salted water. (Parboiling is when you cook the noodles partially in boiling water and finish cooking them when inside the oven.)
- In the meantime, cook 2 shallots and 2 garlic cloves in a medium saucepan with 1 tbsp. of olive oil over medium heat for half a minute. Add the sherry. Adjust the heat to high. Cook and reduce the liquid by half. Mix in cream. Reduce the liquid until they turned 1 1/2 cups. Remove it from the heat and season it with salt and pepper to taste. Put aside.
- Put 1 tbsp. of olive oil in a large skillet that is set over medium heat. Cook the 3 garlic cloves, 3 shallots, onion, eggplant, mushrooms, and zucchini in hot oil until they turn tender. Pour the mixture into the large bowl and mix in Parmesan cheese, ricotta, red peppers, oregano, and basil. Season the mixture with salt and pepper to taste; put aside.
- Set the oven to 350°F or 175°C for preheating. Grease the 9x13-inches baking dish lightly. Stuff the cannelloni with the vegetable and cheese filling. Arrange the cannelloni into the prepared baking dish. Drizzle it with cream sauce.
- Let it bake inside the preheated oven for 25 minutes.

Nutrition Information

- Calories: 424 calories;
- Sodium: 290
- Total Carbohydrate: 28.8
- Cholesterol: 90
- Protein: 10
- Total Fat: 28.9

982. Vegetable And Tofu Stir Fry

Serving: 4 | Prep: 30mins | Cook: 15mins | Ready in:

Ingredients

- 1 tablespoon vegetable oil
- 1/2 medium onion, sliced
- 2 cloves garlic, finely chopped
- 1 tablespoon fresh ginger root, finely chopped
- 1 (16 ounce) package tofu, drained and cut into cubes
- 1/2 cup water
- 4 tablespoons rice wine vinegar
- 2 tablespoons honey
- 2 tablespoons soy sauce
- 2 teaspoons cornstarch dissolved in
- 2 tablespoons water
- 1 carrot, peeled and sliced
- 1 green bell pepper, seeded and cut into strips
- 1 cup baby corn, drained and cut into pieces
- 1 small head bok choy, chopped
- 2 cups fresh mushrooms, chopped
- 1 1/4 cups bean sprouts
- 1 cup bamboo shoots, drained and chopped
- 1/2 teaspoon crushed red pepper
- 2 medium green onions, thinly sliced diagonally

Direction

- Place a large skillet with oil on medium-high heat. Stir in onions; cook for 1 minute. Mix in ginger and garlic; cook for 30 seconds. Mix in tofu; cook till golden brown.
- Mix in baby corn, bell pepper and carrots; cook for 2 minutes. Mix in crushed red pepper, bamboo shoots, bean sprouts, mushrooms and bok choy; heat through. Take away from the heat.
- Mix soy sauce, honey, rice wine vinegar and water in a small saucepan; simmer the mixture. Cook for 2 minutes, then mix in the water and cornstarch mixture. Simmer till the sauce is thickened. Transfer the sauce over the tofu and vegetables. Garnish with scallions.

Nutrition Information

- Calories: 215 calories;
- Cholesterol: 0
- Protein: 13.6
- Total Fat: 9.4
- Sodium: 507
- Total Carbohydrate: 24

983.   Vegetarian Sloppy Joe

Serving: 4 | Prep: 15mins | Cook: 30mins | Ready in:

Ingredients

- 1 tablespoon olive oil
- 1 small onion, chopped
- 1 (15 ounce) can brown lentils
- 1 (15 ounce) can stewed tomatoes, cut small
- 1/4 cup barbeque sauce
- 1/4 cup ketchup
- 2 tablespoons mild miso paste
- 1 ounce dried shiitake mushrooms, cut small
- 2 tablespoons ground allspice
- 2 cloves garlic, minced, or more to taste

Direction

- In a big frying pan, heat oil over medium heat. Add onion, stir and cook for 10 minutes the onion is brown and soft. Add garlic, allspice, shiitake mushrooms, miso paste, ketchup, barbeque sauce, tomatoes, and lentils; stir and cook for 20-25 minutes until the mixture is thick and the flavors blend.

Nutrition Information

- Calories: 232 calories;
- Cholesterol: 0
- Protein: 9.9
- Total Fat: 4.5
- Sodium: 1024
- Total Carbohydrate: 41.7

984. Veggie Quinoa Burgers

Serving: 8 | Prep: 30mins | Cook: 15mins | Ready in:

Ingredients

- 1/2 cup quinoa
- 1 cup water
- 2 teaspoons olive oil
- 4 carrots, peeled and minced
- 2 stalks celery, minced
- 1/2 red bell pepper, minced
- 1 onion, minced
- 4 cloves garlic, minced
- 2 tablespoons minced fresh ginger root
- 2 cups minced fresh mushrooms
- 1 (19 ounce) can kidney beans, rinsed and drained
- 1/2 bunch fresh dill, chopped
- 2 cups chopped fresh spinach
- 1 egg (optional)
- 1/2 cup dry bread crumbs
- 2 tablespoons sesame oil
- 4 slices shredded mozzarella cheese
- salt and ground black pepper to taste
- 1 tablespoon olive oil

Direction

- Preheat outdoor grill to high heat; oil grate lightly.
- Boil water and quinoa in saucepan; lower heat to low. Put lid on saucepan; cook for 15 minutes till water is absorbed completely. Take off heat; put aside and let cool.
- Heat 2 tsp. olive oil in skillet on medium high heat; mix and cook mushrooms, ginger, garlic, onion, red bell pepper, celery and carrots in hot oil for 10 minutes till soft. Put aside; cool.
- Use fork to mash kidney beans in a big bowl; add carrot mixture and quinoa to means. Mix.
- Mix pepper, salt, mozzarella cheese, sesame oil, breadcrumbs, egg, spinach and dill into kidney bean mixture; form to 8 patties.
- On each side of each patty, brush 1 tbsp. olive oil.
- Put patties in big baking dish.
- On preheated grill, grill for 7-8 minutes per side till hot in the middle.

Nutrition Information

- Calories: 263 calories;
- Total Fat: 10.7
- Sodium: 336
- Total Carbohydrate: 31.1
- Cholesterol: 32
- Protein: 12

985. Veggie Tacos

Serving: 6 | Prep: 15mins | Cook: 25mins | Ready in:

Ingredients

- 1 tablespoon olive oil
- 1 1/2 pounds cremini mushrooms, coarsely chopped
- 1 red bell pepper, diced
- 1 (15 ounce) can pinto beans, rinsed and drained
- 1 (1 ounce) packet taco seasoning mix
- 2 green onions, sliced thinly
- 1/4 cup water
- 6 (8 inch) whole wheat tortillas

Direction

- In a skillet, heat the olive oil on moderately-high heat. Put in the red bell peppers and mushrooms; sauté for 20 minutes till mushrooms are meaty and soft. Put in the water, green onions, taco seasoning mix and pinto beans. Mix thoroughly; keep cooking for 5 minutes longer till the entire liquid is evaporated.
- Distribute mushroom filling equally among tortillas. Top with your desire taco toppings.

Nutrition Information

- Calories: 220 calories;
- Cholesterol: 0
- Protein: 11.6
- Total Fat: 3.3
- Sodium: 761
- Total Carbohydrate: 42.4

986. Veneto Chicken

Serving: 8 | Prep: 15mins | Cook: 50mins | Ready in:

Ingredients

- 3 large tomatoes - peeled, seeded and chopped
- 1 (3 pound) whole chicken, cut into pieces
- 4 tablespoons olive oil
- 1 onion, chopped
- 1 stalk celery, chopped
- 1/2 cup dry white wine
- 1/4 teaspoon dried oregano
- 1 pinch salt
- 1 pinch ground black pepper
- 2 tablespoons balsamic vinegar
- 1/4 pound fresh mushrooms, sliced

Direction

- Coat chicken lightly in flour. Over medium-high heat, heat oil. Briefly fry chicken pieces; turn to brown evenly. Add celery and onion; cook for 1-2 minutes. Stir in chopped tomatoes and wine. Season with ground pepper, salt and oregano as preferred. Cover, lower the heat; simmer gently for half an hour, turn pieces once.
- Pour in mushrooms and balsamic vinegar; cook for 5-10 more minutes.

Nutrition Information

- Calories: 463 calories;
- Total Fat: 32.6
- Sodium: 130
- Total Carbohydrate: 5.7

- Cholesterol: 128
- Protein: 32.9

987. Vietnamese Kabocha Squash Soup

Serving: 8 | Prep: 30mins | Cook: 25mins | Ready in:

Ingredients

- 12 dried shiitake mushrooms
- 1 (10.5 ounce) package bean-thread noodles, or to taste
- 1 kabocha squash, quartered and seeded
- 1 pound ground turkey
- 1 1/2 teaspoons fish sauce, or more to taste
- 1 pinch ground white pepper
- 3 quarts water
- 1 quart chicken stock
- 1 pound shrimp
- 2 scallions, chopped
- 3 tablespoons chopped cilantro, or to taste
- cracked black pepper to taste

Direction

- Set the oven for preheating to 425°F (220°C).
- Slice 4 of the shiitakes into smaller cubes and 8 of them into halves. Submerge in hot water and soak for half an hour to rehydrate. Meanwhile, soak noodles in cold water for 15 minutes.
- Place the kabocha squash on a baking pan and add some water to the pan.
- Roast the squash inside the preheated oven for about 15 minutes until softened.
- Drain the noodles and cut into small pieces. Stir together diced shiitakes, noodles, turkey, white pepper and fish sauce well with a fork. Mixing the mixture well makes a delicious and chewy meatballs.
- Bring the chicken stock and water to a boil in a big stockpot. Form the turkey mixture into a quenelles or shape of an egg balls with 2, wet and hot spoons. Put the meatballs and cook for

10 to 30 seconds into the boiling broth until they floats.
- Peel the squash if preferred and cut into cubes measuring 1 1/2-inch per each. Put into the soup with shrimp and the halved shiitakes. Cook for 5 minutes more until shrimp is opaque.
- Taste and add more fish sauce if preferred. Place cilantro, black pepper and scallions on top.

Nutrition Information

- Calories: 411 calories;
- Total Fat: 5.5
- Sodium: 561
- Total Carbohydrate: 69.7
- Cholesterol: 128
- Protein: 25.7

988. West Coast Cod And Shrimp

Serving: 4 | Prep: 20mins | Cook: 1hours | Ready in:

Ingredients

- 2 cups water
- 1 cup uncooked long-grain white rice
- 1 teaspoon olive oil
- 2 tablespoons butter
- 1/4 cup minced onion
- 1 tablespoon minced garlic
- 1 1/2 cups heavy cream
- 1/4 cup milk
- 1 1/2 tablespoons cornstarch
- 1/2 pound fresh shrimp, peeled and deveined
- 1 cup sliced fresh mushrooms
- 1 tablespoon chopped fresh dill
- seasoning salt to taste
- pepper to taste
- 1 pound cod fillets
- 1 tablespoon grated Parmesan cheese
- 1 tablespoon chopped fresh parsley

Direction

- Boil water in a medium-sized saucepan. Mix in the rice, lower heat, and put the cover on. Let it simmer till water is absorbed for 20 minutes.
- Preheat oven to 175 degrees C (350 degrees F). Use olive oil to coat a medium-sized baking dish.
- On medium heat, melt the butter in a medium-sized saucepan and sauté the garlic and onion till soft. Whisk in the heavy cream. Whisk cornstarch and milk in a small-sized bowl, and mix into the saucepan to thicken the heavy cream mixture. Take away from heat, mix in the mushrooms and shrimp and use pepper, seasoning salt, and dill to season.
- In the prepared baking dish, arrange the cod. Add the heavy cream mixture on top of the cod. Drizzle with parsley and Parmesan cheese.
- Keep it covered, and bake for half an hour in the preheated oven till the fish could be flaked easily using a fork and the sauce turns bubbly. Serve on the rice.

Nutrition Information

- Calories: 730 calories;
- Sodium: 309
- Total Carbohydrate: 46.3
- Cholesterol: 275
- Protein: 39
- Total Fat: 42.8

989. White Pizza With Porcinis

Serving: 12 | Prep: 20mins | Cook: 40mins | Ready in:

Ingredients

- 2 1/2 pounds bread flour

- 1 ounce salt
- 1/2 ounce honey
- 2 1/2 cups warm water
- 1 (.25 ounce) package active dry yeast
- 3 tablespoons olive oil
- 1 clove garlic, minced
- 8 ounces rehydrated porcini mushrooms
- salt and pepper to taste
- 1/8 cup cornmeal
- 1 cup shredded fontina cheese
- 1/2 cup grated Parmesan cheese
- 2 tablespoons chopped fresh parsley

Direction

- In an electric mixer with a dough hook, mix together warm water, honey, salt and flour. Process for 2 minutes over low heat. Add in yeast; mix over medium speed for 6 minutes more. Drizzle with oil and combine for an additional 2 minutes. The dough will be a little firm. Form into 6-ounce balls. The pizza will be rounder if the balls are rolled rounder. Settle in a warm area covered with a moist towel until doubled in volume.
- Set oven to 230°C (or 450°F) and start preheating, then place the pizza stone in prepared oven. Make sure to bring in pizza stone prior to preheating to make it warm in advance.
- In a large skillet, heat olive oil to medium heat. Mix in garlic and sauté for 30 seconds. Add in mushrooms; sauté for another 2 minutes. Season with pepper and salt to taste.
- Unroll or pat pizza dough out to 1/4" thick on a surface dusted with a little flour. Place on a cornmeal-coated wooden plank; brush a little olive oil onto the crust. Sprinkle Parmesan and Fontina cheeses onto the crust, then add sautéed mushrooms. Gently place pizza onto pizza stone.
- Bake at 450°F (230°C) for about 10-15 minutes until crust turn golden brown and cheese has bubbled and melted. Add parsley to decorate.

Nutrition Information

- Calories: 498 calories;
- Protein: 21.1
- Total Fat: 9.5
- Sodium: 1038
- Total Carbohydrate: 80.5
- Cholesterol: 13

990. White Wine Almond Chicken

Serving: 6 | Prep: 20mins | Cook: 1hours30mins | Ready in:

Ingredients

- 3/4 cup white wine
- 1 cup chicken broth
- 1 cup heavy cream
- 3 tablespoons all-purpose flour
- 1 pound fresh mushrooms, sliced
- 1 white onion, finely chopped
- 1 cup sliced almonds
- salt and pepper to taste
- 6 skinless, boneless chicken breast halves

Direction

- In a medium saucepan, heat most of the cream (reserve a little), broth and wine over medium low heat. Thicken the flour with enough reserved cream to create a thin paste. Put this into saucepan, stirring frequently until thickened. Mix in onions and mushrooms.
- Preheat the oven to 325°F (165°C).
- Add chicken in a baking dish of 9x13 inches. Pour the sauce over chicken and add almonds on top. Bake in the preheated oven for 90 minutes.

Nutrition Information

- Calories: 438 calories;
- Total Fat: 24.9
- Sodium: 360

- Total Carbohydrate: 12.4
- Cholesterol: 123
- Protein: 36.1

991. White Wine And Mushroom Sauce

Serving: 4 | Prep: 15mins | Cook: 30mins | Ready in:

Ingredients

- 2 tablespoons unsalted butter
- 5 cloves garlic
- 1 green bell pepper, diced
- 1 small onion, chopped
- 1 (8 ounce) package sliced fresh mushrooms
- 1 cup white wine
- 1 cup chicken broth
- 2 tablespoons cornstarch
- 1/4 cup cold water
- 1/4 cup heavy cream
- 1/4 cup grated Romano cheese
- 1/4 cup grated Parmesan cheese

Direction

- In a heavy skillet over medium heat, melt butter. Put in garlic and cook for about 5 minutes in hot butter until it is browned.
- In the skillet, mash the garlic and add to butter, stir well. Put in onion and green bell pepper; cook for 5-7 minutes for the onion to turn translucent.
- Add mushrooms into the onion and pepper mixture, stir; cook for about 5 minutes with stirs until the mushrooms are browned slightly. While stirring, stream in heavy cream. Put in Parmesan cheese and Romano cheese. Keep on cooking for another 5-10 minutes until the cheese is melted and the mixture is hot.
- In the skillet, add wine and let it cook for 5-10 minutes for the liquid to reduce by half. Put in chicken broth; cook until it simmers. Let it cook for about 5 minutes until it is reduced slightly.
- In a small bowl, combine cornstarch and water to dissolve the cornstarch completely. Stir the mixture into the liquid in skillet and cook for 5-10 minutes with regular stirs to thicken the liquid.

Nutrition Information

- Calories: 254 calories;
- Sodium: 421
- Total Carbohydrate: 12.5
- Cholesterol: 49
- Protein: 7.4
- Total Fat: 15.1

992. Wild Mushroom Balls

Serving: 20 | Prep: 25mins | Cook: 1hours5mins | Ready in:

Ingredients

- 3 tablespoons dried morel mushrooms
- 2 tablespoons dried porcini mushrooms
- 1/4 cup salted butter, divided
- 1 large leek, finely chopped
- 1 (9 ounce) package mixed mushrooms, sliced (shiitake, chanterelle, portobello, oyster)
- salt and ground black pepper to taste
- 4 1/4 cups vegetable stock, or to taste
- 2 onions, finely chopped
- 1 teaspoon chopped fresh thyme
- 1 bay leaf
- 1 (16 ounce) package Arborio rice
- 3/4 cup mascarpone cheese
- 1 (6 ounce) package grated Parmesan cheese, divided
- 2 teaspoons jerk seasoning, or more to taste
- 1 tablespoon all-purpose flour, or as needed
- salt and ground black pepper to taste
- 2 eggs
- 1/2 (8 ounce) package panko bread crumbs

- oil for frying

Direction

- In a mixing bowl, steep porcini mushrooms and dried morel with 2 cups water.
- Melt 2 tablespoon butter over medium heat in a large skillet. Sauté leek in heated butter for 2 to 3 minutes until tender. Stir in mixed sliced mushrooms; sauté for 2 to 3 minutes longer until softened. Season with pepper and salt. Pour leek mixture into a mixing bowl.
- In a saucepan, bring vegetable stock to a low simmer.
- Wipe the skillet used for mixture of leek, and bring it back to medium heat. Put in and sauté bay leaf, thyme, and onions in the remaining butter for about 5 minutes until tender. Add rice; cook for 2 to 3 minutes, mixing, until all the grains are coated.
- Transfer the re-hydrated mushroom from the bowl and add the liquid into the rice. Let come to boil; stir for 3 to 5 minutes until all liquid has been absorbed. Cut mushrooms into small pieces and add to rice. Add a ladle of heated stock into rice at a time; stirring until liquid is almost absorbed fully after each adding; approximately 20 minutes in total.
- Mix jerk seasoning, 3/4 of the Parmesan cheese, mascarpone cheese, and leek mixture into the rice until, mix till incorporated. Turn off the heat and allow to cool for at least 30 minutes until handleable.
- Add salt and pepper to flour to season; distribute flour mixture over a plate.
- In a mixing bowl, beat eggs together with pepper and salt.
- Combine panko and the remaining Parmesan cheese in a dish.
- Use your hand or small ice cream scoop to shape small balls of risotto. Dust the ball with flour, coat with beaten eggs, and turn into panko mixture. Transfer ball to a baking sheet and cover the balls with plastic wrap. Chill for 8 hours to overnight in the fridge.
- Heat oil in a saucepan. Working in batches, fry mushroom ball until golden brown, turning halfway through cooking, about 4 minutes for each batch.

Nutrition Information

- Calories: 242 calories;
- Protein: 8.1
- Total Fat: 11.9
- Sodium: 309
- Total Carbohydrate: 27.8
- Cholesterol: 43

993. Wild Mushroom Sauce

Serving: 4 | Prep: 5mins | Cook: 15mins | Ready in:

Ingredients

- 4 tablespoons butter
- 1/4 cup finely chopped shallots
- 2 ounces portobello mushrooms, sliced
- 2 ounces crimini mushrooms, sliced
- 2 ounces shiitake mushrooms, sliced
- 2 ounces morel mushrooms, sliced
- 2 ounces chanterelle mushrooms, sliced
- 1/2 cup red wine
- 6 fluid ounces beef demi glace
- salt and freshly ground black pepper to taste

Direction

- Melt the butter on medium heat in a saucepan. Sauté the shallots briefly, then whisk in all mushrooms. Sauté for roughly 3 minutes till becoming soft and translucent. Add the red wine, and let it simmer for 3 minutes. Whisk in the demi-glace, and let it simmer till the sauce becomes thick or for 6 minutes.

Nutrition Information

- Calories: 389 calories;
- Protein: 4.5
- Total Fat: 30.4

- Sodium: 1923
- Total Carbohydrate: 21.1
- Cholesterol: 32

994. Wild Mushroom Stuffing

Serving: 5 | Prep: | Cook: | Ready in:

Ingredients

- 2 cups hot water
- 1 ounce dried porcini mushrooms
- 1 3/4 pounds egg bread, crust trimmed
- 6 tablespoons unsalted butter
- 4 cups coarsely chopped leeks
- 1 cup shallots, chopped
- 1 1/4 pounds crimini mushrooms, sliced
- 1/2 pound fresh sliced shiitake mushrooms
- 2 cups chopped celery
- 1 cup chopped fresh parsley
- 1 cup chopped toasted hazelnuts
- 3 tablespoons chopped fresh thyme
- 2 tablespoons chopped fresh sage
- 2 eggs
- 3/4 cup chicken stock
- salt to taste
- ground black pepper to taste
- 1 cup dried porcini mushrooms

Direction

- Mix porcini mushrooms and 2 cups of hot water, let sit till mushrooms are tender. Approximately half an hour. Allow to drain, setting aside soaking water. Press porcini to dry and roughly chop.
- Preheat the oven to 165°C or 325°F. Among 2 baking sheets, distribute cubed bread. Bake till starting to brown. Approximately 15 minutes. Let cool then put to a huge bowl.
- In a heavy Dutch oven, liquify butter over medium-high heat. Put shiitake mushrooms, crimini or button, shallots and leeks. Sauté for 15 minutes till soft and golden. Add in porcini mushrooms and celery and sauté for 5 minutes more. To the bowl with the bread crumbs, put the mixture. Add in sage, thyme, hazelnuts and parsley. Put pepper and salt to season and mix in the beaten eggs.
- To bake stuffing in a turkey: with the stuffing, stuff the primary cavity. In a big glass measuring cup, mix half cup of the saved porcini soaking liquid and broth. To the leftover stuffing, put sufficient broth mixture to moisten. Into a buttered baking dish, scoop the leftover stuffing. Cover using a buttered foil. Let stuffing bake in a dish together with turkey for half an hour till heated through. Remove the cover and let bake for 15 minutes till top is crisp.
- To bake every stuffing in pan: preheat an oven to 325°F. Grease a baking dish, 15x10x2-inch in size with butter. Add 3/4 cup of broth and 3/4 cup of saved porcini soaking liquid into the stuffing. Put into the prepped dish. Cover using a buttered foil and let bake for an hour till heated through. Remove the cover and bake for 15 minutes till top is crisp.

Nutrition Information

- Calories: 969 calories;
- Sodium: 938
- Total Carbohydrate: 116.5
- Cholesterol: 192
- Protein: 37.5
- Total Fat: 40.8

995. Wild Rice Pilaf

Serving: 5 | Prep: 5mins | Cook: 25mins | Ready in:

Ingredients

- 1/2 pound sausage
- 1 (6 ounce) package uncooked long grain and wild rice
- 1 (4.5 ounce) can sliced mushrooms

Direction

- In a medium skillet over medium high heat, cook sausage until evenly brown. Drain and put aside.
- In the meantime, in a saucepan, bring water to a boil. Add rice and mix in sausage and mushrooms. Lower heat, cover and simmer for 20 minutes.

Nutrition Information

- Calories: 307 calories;
- Total Carbohydrate: 28.8
- Cholesterol: 32
- Protein: 9.9
- Total Fat: 16.8
- Sodium: 971

996. Ziti With Italian Sausage

Serving: 8 | Prep: 15mins | Cook: 1hours15mins | Ready in:

Ingredients

- 1 pound Italian sausage, casings removed
- 1/2 cup diced celery
- 1/2 cup diced onion
- 1 (14.5 ounce) can peeled and diced tomatoes
- 1 (15 ounce) can tomato sauce
- 1/4 teaspoon garlic powder
- 1 1/2 teaspoons salt
- 1 teaspoon dried oregano
- 1 pound dry ziti pasta
- 2 (4.5 ounce) cans sliced mushrooms, drained
- 8 ounces shredded mozzarella cheese
- 1/4 cup grated Parmesan cheese

Direction

- In a skillet, cook the sausage with onion and celery over medium heat for 5-10 minutes or until the sausage is brown evenly. Drain the excess grease. Put aside.
- In another skillet, combine oregano, salt, garlic powder, tomato sauce and tomatoes over medium-low heat. Simmer while you prep the pasta.
- Boil the lightly salted water in a large pot. Cook pasta until al dente, about 8-10 minutes; then drain.
- Start preheating the oven to 350°F (175°C). Layer the ziti, the mushrooms and the sausage, followed by the mozzarella cheese, then the sauce in a 3-quart baking dish. Repeat these layers, and place grated Parmesan on top.
- Bake in prepared oven for 45 minutes or until bubbly and brown.

Nutrition Information

- Calories: 465 calories;
- Total Fat: 17
- Sodium: 1620
- Total Carbohydrate: 52.3
- Cholesterol: 43
- Protein: 24.6

997. Zucchilattas

Serving: 10 | Prep: 15mins | Cook: 20mins | Ready in:

Ingredients

- 2 tablespoons butter
- 1 1/2 pounds sliced zucchini
- 1 pound mushrooms, sliced
- 1 onion, sliced
- 1 1/2 pounds tomatoes, chopped
- salt and pepper to taste
- 1 1/2 pounds Monterey Jack cheese, shredded
- 10 (10 inch) flour tortillas

Direction

- Start preheating the oven to 350°F (175°C). Lightly grease a 9x13-in. baking dish with oil.

- In a large skillet, melt butter over medium heat. Mix pepper, salt, tomatoes, onion, mushrooms and zucchini together. Then put them into skillet. Cook while stirring until vegetables become soft.
- Warm tortillas in prepared oven until soft, about 2 to 3 mins. Stuff Monterey Jack cheese and zucchini mixture into warmed tortillas, saving some both for toppings. Then roll filled tortillas then place in baking dish, seam side facing down. Add remaining zucchini mixture to cover. Place the remaining cheese on top.
- Bake for 15 mins in prepared oven, until cheese is bubbly.

Nutrition Information

- Calories: 537 calories;
- Total Fat: 28.9
- Sodium: 852
- Total Carbohydrate: 44.9
- Cholesterol: 67
- Protein: 25.6

998. Zucchini Boats With Ground Turkey

Serving: 8 | Prep: 35mins | Cook: 34mins | Ready in:

Ingredients

- 4 zucchini
- 1 pound ground turkey
- 1/2 cup chopped green bell pepper
- 1/2 cup chopped sweet red pepper
- 1 small onion, chopped
- 1/2 cup chopped fresh mushrooms
- 1/2 cup chopped fresh spinach leaves
- 1 cup shredded Cheddar cheese
- 1 (6 ounce) can tomato paste
- 1 pinch garlic powder, or to taste
- salt and ground black pepper to taste

Direction

- Trim zucchini ends; cut in 1/2 lengthwise. Spoon out and set pulp aside, leaving a half inch shell.
- Set the oven to 350°F (175°C) and start preheating. Grease a 9x13-inch baking dish.
- Over medium heat, in a skillet, mix spinach, mushrooms, onion, sweet red pepper, green bell pepper, turkey and reserved zucchini pulp. Cook for 8-10 minutes until the turkey is no longer pink. Drain. Take out of the heat; add pepper, salt, garlic powder, tomato paste and half cup Cheddar cheese; combine well. Scoop mixture into zucchini shells; put in the greased baking dish. Top with the rest of Cheddar cheese.
- Bake in the prepared oven for 25-30 minutes, uncovered, until zucchini becomes tender.

Nutrition Information

- Calories: 184 calories;
- Total Fat: 9.3
- Sodium: 320
- Total Carbohydrate: 9.6
- Cholesterol: 57
- Protein: 17.4

999. Zucchini Saute

Serving: 6 | Prep: 20mins | Cook: 25mins | Ready in:

Ingredients

- 1 tablespoon vegetable oil
- 1 onion, sliced
- 2 tomatoes, chopped
- 2 pounds zucchini, peeled and cut into 1 inch thick slices
- 1 green bell pepper, chopped
- salt to taste
- ground black pepper to taste
- 1/4 cup uncooked white rice
- 1/2 cup water

Direction

- In a sauté pan, heat oil over medium heat. Put in onion then cook and stir for 3mins. Put in green pepper, zucchini and tomatoes then mix. Use black pepper and salt to season. Decrease heat then cover. Allow it to simmer for 5 minutes.
- Mix in water and rice then cover. Cook for 20 minutes over low heat.

Nutrition Information

- Calories: 94 calories;
- Protein: 3.2
- Total Fat: 2.8
- Sodium: 19
- Total Carbohydrate: 16.1
- Cholesterol: 0

1000. Zucchini And Mushroom Salad With Ricotta Salata

Serving: 4 | Prep: 20mins | Cook: | Ready in:

Ingredients

- 4 large yellow zucchini, sliced into long, thin strips
- 1 pound crimini mushrooms, cleaned and trimmed
- 8 sprigs fresh chervil, chopped
- 1/2 pound ricotta salata cheese, coarsely grated
- 3 tablespoons lemon juice
- salt and black pepper to taste

Direction

- In a salad bowl, add in lemon juice, ricotta salata cheese, chervil, mushrooms, zucchini strips, and toss gently. Add salt and pepper to taste.

Nutrition Information

- Calories: 263 calories;
- Total Fat: 12.9
- Sodium: 704
- Total Carbohydrate: 22.4
- Cholesterol: 50
- Protein: 18.3

1001. Zucchini With Chickpea And Mushroom Stuffing

Serving: 8 | Prep: 30mins | Cook: 30mins | Ready in:

Ingredients

- 4 zucchini, halved
- 1 tablespoon olive oil
- 1 onion, chopped
- 2 cloves garlic, crushed
- 1/2 (8 ounce) package button mushrooms, sliced
- 1 teaspoon ground coriander
- 1 1/2 teaspoons ground cumin, or to taste
- 1 (15.5 ounce) can chickpeas, rinsed and drained
- 1/2 lemon, juiced
- 2 tablespoons chopped fresh parsley
- sea salt to taste
- ground black pepper to taste

Direction

- Set an oven to preheat to 175°C (350°F), then grease a shallow baking dish.
- Scoop out the flesh from the zucchini and chop the flesh, then put it aside. Put the shells in the prepped dish.
- In a big skillet, heat the oil on medium heat. Sauté the onions for 5 minutes, then add the garlic and sauté for another 2 minutes. Stir in the mushrooms and chopped zucchini and sauté for 5 minutes. Stir in the pepper, salt, parsley, lemon juice, chickpeas, cumin and

coriander. Scoop the mixture into the zucchini shells.
- Let it bake for 30-40 minutes in the preheated oven or until the zucchini becomes tender.

Nutrition Information

- Calories: 107 calories;
- Total Fat: 2.7
- Sodium: 170
- Total Carbohydrate: 18.4
- Cholesterol: 0
- Protein: 4.5

Index

A

Ale 14,375,518

Almond 15,565

Apple 3,9,21,316

Arborio rice 230,310,472,545,566

Artichoke 5,6,7,8,11,12,13,111,138,170,182,185,201,231,271,284,405,417,444,449,454,478

Asparagus 5,6,7,10,11,12,139,140,182,183,229,230,231,237,332,359,378,418,442,446

Avocado 3,9,10,25,297,348

B

Bacon 3,4,5,7,8,9,11,12,14,25,26,88,140,143,234,235,236,245,259,286,315,383,419,506,519,522

Baguette 7,242

Barley 3,4,5,6,7,10,11,14,21,85,96,97,99,100,101,105,107,108,115,127,158,205,215,243,244,247,347,359,376,389,405,412,503

Basil 6,7,13,14,184,217,245,457,476,509

Beans 5,6,12,14,150,151,177,419,526

Beef 3,4,5,7,8,9,10,11,12,13,28,31,32,36,37,64,69,74,83,111,112,113,114,115,116,120,122,123,124,125,126,127,130,131,134,135,136,137,138,246,247,269,298,312,321,330,334,347,351,355,371,376,379,380,383,415,432,437,466,473,500

Beer 11,251,375

Biscuits 9,292

Blueberry 4,75

Boar 12,449

Bratwurst 8,251

Bread 5,6,11,12,152,164,183,186,304,401,447

Brie 4,7,8,85,95,96,237,238,253,356,459,557,563

Brisket 10,346

Broccoli 4,5,6,8,9,11,12,14,85,141,142,185,191,254,298,331,384,439,507

Broth 7,21,240,334,485

Brussels sprouts 163,236

Burger 3,4,5,8,9,10,11,12,13,14,15,25,26,27,29,35,37,39,41,47,51,52,54,55,56,58,59,61,63,69,70,71,72,75,78,81,126,248,297,340,353,390,407,421,448,455,459,510,562

Butter 5,6,11,12,40,140,151,167,196,264,313,385,416,439,522

C

Cabbage 6,13,14,176,491,506

Caramel 8,260

Carrot 8,254

Cashew 15,558

Cauliflower 5,8,11,144,258,377

Celery 9,316,317

Champ 8,259

Chard 3,13,22,467

Cheddar 3,7,23,30,78,206,219,220,231,232,235,238,239,240,241,247,248,252,262,263,264,273,274,281,292,319,342,344,345,350,356,377,391,408,410,426,427,429,430,447,451,459,460,461,489,495,496,511,513,514,515,516,525,528,531,546,570

Cheese 3,4,6,7,8,9,10,11,12,13,26,38,39,44,47,53,55,59,67,80,86,182,185,193,205,208,240,249,261,264,292,298,301,306,320,

331,339,348,356,359,377,398,408,422,423,426,437,455,494,497,531

Cherry 5,145

Chicken
3,4,5,7,8,9,10,11,12,13,14,15,16,21,30,31,45,49,57,83,84,91,94,108,110,118,127,132,133,226,233,238,241,244,248,252,255,256,262,264,266,267,268,271,272,273,274,275,276,277,278,279,280,281,282,283,284,285,286,287,288,289,290,291,292,293,294,295,296,306,307,308,314,318,319,320,321,322,331,332,337,339,341,343,350,351,352,357,358,363,364,366,373,378,391,395,396,402,403,404,408,409,421,424,435,438,444,445,478,481,485,491,501,502,506,509,511,522,531,536,547,550,563,565

Chickpea 15,571

Chipotle 9,297

Chorizo 11,12,377,407,419

Clams 11,12,386,439

Coconut 3,14,17,542

Cod 12,14,15,439,522,564

Cognac 13,494

Crab 4,8,9,13,87,257,302,303,304,305,486

Cream
3,4,5,6,7,8,9,10,11,12,13,14,16,17,18,21,24,32,87,88,89,103,104,147,187,188,236,245,287,291,306,307,308,309,310,311,312,313,317,320,322,333,345,359,410,415,431,437,439,440,497,506,520,524,531

Croissant 3,4,49,68,76

Crostini 3,57

Crumble
10,27,37,51,54,56,57,71,73,86,131,159,259,348,433,516,541

Curry 11,14,411,513,539

D

Dal 12,413

Dijon mustard
26,27,38,50,74,75,76,152,200,212,217,248,282,299,304,306,307,308,312,355,376,383,425,438,466,520,527,529,557

Duck 10,355

Dumplings 5,15,136,547

E

Egg
3,4,6,7,9,12,13,14,32,33,34,67,68,187,194,210,221,238,326,327,328,329,430,433,458,460,474,520,542

English muffin 35,81

F

Fat
16,17,18,19,20,21,22,23,24,25,26,27,28,29,30,31,32,33,34,35,36,37,38,39,40,41,42,43,44,45,46,47,48,49,50,51,52,53,54,55,56,57,58,59,60,61,62,63,64,65,66,67,68,69,70,71,72,73,74,75,76,77,78,79,80,81,82,83,85,86,87,88,89,90,91,92,93,94,95,96,97,98,99,100,101,102,103,104,105,106,107,108,109,110,111,112,113,114,115,116,117,118,119,120,121,122,123,124,125,126,127,128,129,130,131,132,133,134,135,136,137,138,139,140,141,142,143,144,145,146,147,148,149,150,151,152,153,154,155,156,157,158,159,160,161,162,163,164,165,166,167,168,169,170,171,172,173,174,175,176,177,178,179,180,181,182,183,184,185,186,187,188,189,190,191,192,193,194,195,196,197,198,199,200,201,202,203,204,205,206,207,208,209,210,211,212,213,214,215,216,217,218,219,220,221,222,223,224,225,226,227,228,229,230,231,232,233,234,235,236,237,238,239,240,241,242,243,244,245,246,247,248,249,250,251,252,253,254,255,256,257,258,259,260,261,262,263,264,265,266,267,268,269,270,271,272,273,274,275,276,277,278,279,280,281,282,283,284,285,286,287,288,289,290,291,292,293,294,295,296,297,298,299,300,301,302,303,304,305,306,307,308,309,310,311,312,313,314,315,316,317,318,319,320,321,322,323,324,325,326,327,328,329,330,331,332,333,334,335,336,337,338,339,340,341,342,343,344,345,346,347,348,349,350,351,352,353,354,355,356,357,358,359,360,361,362,363,364,365,366,367,368,369,370,371,372,373,374,375,376,377,378,379,380,381,

382,383,384,385,386,387,388,389,390,391,392,393,394,395,396,397,398,399,400,401,402,403,404,405,406,407,408,409,410,411,412,413,414,415,416,417,418,419,420,421,422,423,424,425,426,427,428,429,430,431,432,433,434,435,436,437,438,439,440,441,442,443,444,445,446,447,448,449,450,451,452,453,454,455,456,457,458,459,460,461,462,463,464,465,466,467,468,469,470,471,472,473,474,475,476,477,478,479,480,481,482,483,484,485,486,487,488,489,490,491,492,493,494,495,496,497,498,499,500,501,502,503,504,505,506,507,508,509,510,511,512,513,514,515,516,517,518,519,520,521,522,523,524,525,526,527,528,529,530,531,532,533,534,535,536,537,538,539,540,541,542,543,544,545,546,547,548,549,550,551,552,553,554,555,556,557,558,559,560,561,562,563,564,565,566,567,568,569,570,571,572

Fennel 9,12,293,449

Feta 3,9,14,35,323,529

Fettuccine 6,9,10,13,14,182,307,332,333,480,512

Fish 4,12,93,440

Flank 10,13,334,367,477

Flour 283

Focaccia 6,192

Fontina cheese 565

French bread 28,38,57,67,87,96,121,132,155,186,192,205,212,222,242,490

G

Galangal 11,411

Garlic 3,4,5,6,7,10,12,15,32,36,88,89,103,120,151,157,165,192,236,339,340,341,342,437,440,545,553

Gin 3,13,18,461

Gnocchi 4,6,10,91,193,344

Goose 13,375,500

Gorgonzola 8,62,275,365

Gouda 4,7,67,68,213,316,353

Grapes 9,292

Gratin 6,8,187,270

Gravy 8,10,11,12,13,14,22,269,341,346,365,393,394,411,451,488,517

H

Haddock 12,423

Halibut 12,439

Ham 3,7,9,10,11,44,227,297,342,359,365,383

Harissa 14,509

Hazelnut 10,360

Heart 3,5,6,10,14,44,122,196,361,536

Herbs 8,287

Honey 10,363,364

Horseradish 3,39

I

Irish stout 124

J

Jerusalem artichoke 474,475

Jus 13,197,462

K

Kale 7,11,12,13,228,375,424,484

Kidney 14,519

L

Lamb 5,14,115,529

Leek 4,6,8,12,14,95,162,203,282,424,425,526

Lemon 5,7,11,12,140,217,384,439

Lettuce 15,49,79,224,551

Lime 6,186

Ling 6,7,11,13,196,236,385,386,387,497

Lobster 9,11,302,389

M

Macaroni 10,356

Madeira 109,533,534

Mandarin 10,11,342,395

Marjoram 4,97

Marsala wine 205,206,267,268,276,277,307,308,320,366,393,394,403,438,531,541,549

Mascarpone 12,47,420

Mayonnaise 4,61

Meat 3,4,6,8,9,10,11,12,15,45,48,68,98,199,233,276,299,361,368,379,400,421,469,550

Milk 3,17,320

Mince 10,89,92,115,175,193,361

Mint 12,412

Miso 11,13,402,470

Molasses 3,50

Morel 4,7,9,12,14,99,230,309,440,523

Mozzarella 11,329,403,404

Mushroom 1,3,4,5,6,7,8,9,10,11,12,13,14,15,16,18,19,21,22,24,25,27,32,35,40,47,50,51,52,53,54,55,57,63,69,82,85,87,88,89,91,92,97,98,99,100,101,102,103,104,105,106,109,110,111,118,120,125,126,131,132,138,139,140,142,146,147,150,151,153,155,158,159,160,162,164,165,167,172,178,180,182,183,186,187,189,190,192,193,201,202,203,204,205,206,207,208,211,216,217,218,224,225,230,235,236,237,239,241,244,245,247,248,249,250,253,254,257,258,259,261,264,269,277,281,282,284,288,289,291,292,293,294,301,302,303,304,305,307,308,309,310,311,313,315,317,322,323,328,331,332,333,334,335,337,339,340,341,342,343,345,346,347,350,353,357,359,360,364,366,370,372,373,375,376,377,378,379,384,385,386,387,389,392,394,396,397,398,399,400,401,402,404,405,406,407,408,409,410,411,412,413,414,415,416,417,418,419,420,421,422,423,424,425,426,427,428,429,431,433,437,438,439,442,444,446,448,449,451,453,454,456,457,459,464,465,466,468,470,472,474,476,478,479,482,483,484,485,486,488,491,492,496,497,498,501,502,503,504,505,506,507,511,512,513,514,515,516,518,519,523,524,525,526,528,532,533,540,541,543,545,547,549,551,552,553,556,566,567,568,571

Mustard 351

N

Noodles 12,14,15,433,520,538,542,554

Nut 7,12,16,17,18,19,20,21,22,23,24,25,26,27,28,29,30,31,32,33,34,35,36,37,38,39,40,41,42,43,44,45,46,47,48,49,50,51,52,53,54,55,56,57,58,59,60,61,62,63,64,65,66,67,68,69,70,71,72,73,74,75,76,77,78,79,80,81,82,83,84,85,86,87,88,89,90,91,92,93,94,95,96,97,98,99,100,101,102,103,104,105,106,107,108,109,110,111,112,113,114,115,116,117,118,119,120,121,122,123,124,125,126,127,128,129,130,131,132,133,134,135,136,137,138,139,140,141,142,143,144,145,146,147,148,149,150,151,152,153,154,155,156,157,158,159,160,161,162,163,164,165,166,167,168,169,170,171,172,173,174,175,176,177,178,179,180,181,182,183,184,185,186,187,188,189,190,191,192,193,194,195,196,197,198,199,200,201,202,203,204,205,206,207,208,209,210,211,212,213,214,215,216,217,218,219,220,221,222,223,224,225,226,227,228,229,230,231,232,233,234,235,236,237,238,239,240,241,242,243,244,245,246,247,248,249,250,251,252,253,254,255,256,257,258,259,260,261,262,263,264,265,266,267,268,269,270,271,272,273,274,275,276,277,278,279,280,281,282,283,284,285,286,287,288,289,290,291,292,293,294,295,296,297,298,299,300,301,302,303,304,305,306,307,308,309,310,311,312,313,314,315,316,317,318,319,320,321,322,323,324,325,326,327,328,329,330,331,332,333,334,335,336,337,338,339,340,341,342,343,344,345,346,347,348,349,350,351,352,353,354,355,356,357,358,359,360,361,362,363,364,365,366,367,368,369,370,371,372,373,374,375,376,377,378,379,380,381,382,383,384,385,386,387,388,389,390,391,392,393,394,395,396,397,398,399,400,401,402,403,404,405,406,407,408,409,410,411,412,413,414,415,416,417,418,419,420,421,422,423,424,425,426,427,428,429,430,431,432,433,434,

435,436,437,438,439,440,441,442,443,444,445,446,447,448,449,450,451,452,453,454,455,456,457,458,459,460,461,462,463,464,465,466,467,468,469,470,471,472,473,474,475,476,477,478,479,480,481,482,483,484,485,486,487,488,489,490,491,492,493,494,495,496,497,498,499,500,501,502,503,504,505,506,507,508,509,510,511,512,513,514,515,516,517,518,519,520,521,522,523,524,525,526,527,528,529,530,531,532,533,534,535,536,537,538,539,540,541,542,543,544,545,546,547,548,549,550,551,552,553,554,555,556,557,558,559,560,561,562,563,564,565,566,567,568,569,570,571,572

O

Oil 56,233,257,273,295,328,371,376,412,495,546

Olive 8,10,249,350

Onion 3,4,5,7,8,9,10,11,12,14,37,99,102,126,155,209,249,254,260,300,336,337,359,371,392,433,506

Orange 5,6,10,127,161,162,342

Oxtail 12,436

Oyster 3,10,11,12,13,16,19,337,379,437,470

P

Paella 5,117

Pancakes 6,13,179,464

Pancetta 12,446

Paprika 139

Parmesan 12,18,20,23,30,43,45,46,48,53,54,59,65,66,69,70,77,85,86,94,98,102,107,141,148,156,163,167,168,169,170,171,177,178,185,186,188,190,192,193,197,198,199,203,206,209,213,216,217,222,225,226,229,230,232,236,237,238,240,241,245,250,251,254,255,256,262,263,271,272,276,277,278,279,280,281,290,294,295,302,308,309,310,311,313,314,325,328,329,332,334,339,340,343,344,345,352,361,362,369,377,403,405,407,409,416,417,426,432,435,442,443,444,445,446,447,455,460,463,468,473,480,482,483,484,485,488,489,492,493,496,507,508,511,514,525,526,533,534,536,537,545,546,560,564,565,566,567,569

Pasta 3,5,6,7,8,9,10,12,13,14,15,19,128,140,144,174,185,188,197,221,229,243,250,254,278,287,310,311,326,328,340,348,412,441,442,443,444,445,448,457,492,529,553

Pastrami 3,12,53,445

Pastry 4,89,213

Pear 3,4,54,61

Peas 5,6,8,12,13,144,150,162,172,203,250,258,427,442,486

Pecan 6,14,157,526

Pecorino 457

Peel 348,389,479,564

Penne 7,8,10,11,12,211,271,343,373,446

Pepper 3,4,6,7,9,10,11,13,14,59,74,150,169,193,210,211,303,344,370,378,399,460,475,485,528,542

Pesto 3,13,20,458,492

Pickle 7,10,211,357

Pie 6,8,10,12,13,14,15,170,239,251,361,368,419,425,458,482,518,519,553

Pizza 3,4,6,7,8,9,10,11,12,13,15,54,59,60,63,71,72,82,86,103,191,199,223,257,271,331,365,366,373,447,482,484,558,564

Plantain 12,448

Polenta 3,8,18,275

Porcini 8,9,11,12,13,14,15,258,301,386,394,448,449,472,545,564

Pork 3,4,5,7,9,10,11,12,14,21,66,67,72,128,129,133,164,165,169,232,309,341,346,357,370,401,419,431,450,451,452,453,503,504,526,527,533,544

Port 3,4,5,6,7,8,10,11,12,13,15,17,24,34,41,42,58,61,62,63,64,6

5,71,130,145,196,197,209,211,212,213,218,220,225,229,237,248,258,263,277,284,289,311,346,350,351,375,385,387,442,454,455,456,457,458,459,460,475,549

Potato 4,5,7,8,9,10,11,12,13,14,98,99,102,114,122,143,147,239,264,270,293,318,321,364,370,371,387,438,451,461,472,476,533,553

Poultry 366

Prawn 3,20

Prosciutto 9,13,291,463,464

Pulse 272,295,317,421

Pumpkin 13,463

Q

Quail 11,376

Quinoa 13,14,15,467,468,528,562

R

Rabbit 13,468

Rice 4,5,6,7,8,9,11,12,13,15,79,81,108,109,142,147,148,149,160,165,167,171,173,175,176,178,179,203,223,238,240,256,283,291,296,313,316,323,384,400,414,420,427,431,434,435,452,471,568

Ricotta 9,14,15,331,512,571

Rigatoni 6,177

Risotto 6,7,8,9,13,14,167,230,258,310,313,468,472,545

Rosemary 4,7,8,13,104,212,281,478

S

Sage 10,333

Salad 3,6,7,9,10,11,12,13,14,15,24,48,49,182,184,191,194,195,198,210,213,215,216,217,220,224,241,296,318,335,342,345,354,359,389,412,414,441,461,470,475,479,513,515,517,571

Salmon 9,13,319,324,480

Salsa 9,42,65,263,297,429

Salt 77,81,85,87,97,118,126,151,190,252,268,294,343,373,440,514,522,526,530,537

Sausage 3,4,5,6,7,8,10,12,13,14,15,44,66,67,83,94,102,105,132,157,164,165,169,228,249,250,332,343,369,420,424,425,444,452,482,483,484,485,508,510,569

Savory 4,5,6,7,13,105,132,133,166,216,486,487

Scallop 6,13,166,493,494

Seafood 7,13,14,225,232,489,540

Seasoning 439,545,551

Sesame seeds 243

Shallot 11,410

Sherry 9,10,13,295,359,370,491

Sirloin 10,13,351,489,498

Snapper 14,504

Soup 3,4,5,6,7,8,9,10,11,12,13,14,15,16,21,24,82,83,84,85,86,87,88,89,90,91,92,93,94,95,96,97,98,99,100,101,102,103,104,105,106,107,108,109,110,172,183,190,229,244,247,283,293,298,311,313,316,317,338,343,345,347,359,362,371,374,375,376,389,402,405,406,415,417,424,436,449,454,461,469,472,484,497,499,538,543,544,563

Spaghetti 6,7,9,10,11,13,14,15,168,169,170,198,240,243,325,336,382,403,467,493,507,508,541,554

Spinach 3,4,5,6,7,8,9,10,12,14,15,22,66,68,69,100,106,138,170,171,185,206,207,216,231,247,264,290,313,315,335,342,368,415,426,427,511,512,513,514,515,516,525,529,553,557

Squash 5,6,7,15,129,152,168,169,170,198,223,563

Steak 3,4,9,10,11,13,14,42,47,50,69,74,301,316,334,335,354,367,385,477,479,488,490,517,518,519,520,535,541

Stew 3,5,6,7,8,9,10,11,12,13,14,23,110,111,113,114,115,116,118,119,120,121,122,124,126,127,128,129,130,131,132,133,13

4,135,136,137,138,200,218,233,265,293,297,357,379,399,412,416,432,478,500,501,536

Stock 107

Stuffing 5,6,8,9,11,12,13,14,15,143,157,176,181,249,305,384,416,437,485,503,528,555,568,571

Sugar 12,13,66,67,153,157,164,165,169,442,486

Swiss chard 22,23,467

T

Tabasco 225,425

Taco 6,15,186,556,562

Tea 293,421

Teriyaki 4,7,73,232

Thai basil 16,242,539

Thyme 5,6,7,12,140,173,208,237,239,351,440

Tilapia 10,337

Tofu 3,8,9,11,12,14,15,23,251,315,381,447,534,539,542,543,544,557,560

Tomatillo 15,556

Tomato 4,6,9,10,12,13,14,30,79,106,166,174,182,194,315,325,338,422,444,453,492,508,539

Tortellini 7,9,12,225,227,313,424

Trout 7,226

Truffle 8,270

Turkey 3,4,5,9,11,13,14,15,27,41,51,75,76,77,107,108,325,393,394,469,516,528,537,545,546,547,570

V

Veal 15,549,550

Vegan 11,14,15,375,390,508,551,552,553,554,555,556,557,558

Vegetables 5,6,7,10,13,114,132,154,173,197,201,240,348,359,476

Vegetarian 4,6,7,9,11,14,15,77,78,176,180,221,326,388,530,561

Venison 7,236

W

Walnut 4,7,12,13,61,208,422,426,476

Watercress 7,229

Wine 7,8,10,11,12,14,15,239,287,341,394,428,502,520,550,565,566

Worcestershire sauce 29,30,35,37,38,39,41,42,58,59,68,71,72,75,82,90,91,97,98,113,114,122,127,149,189,226,273,279,297,299,300,316,321,352,356,358,367,368,385,390,400,419,421,449,466,469,480,490,500,503,505,517,518,540

Wraps 3,4,9,15,30,43,50,60,65,73,79,315,323,551

Y

Yam 13,464

Z

Zest 5,6,109,179

L

lasagna 20,181,199,232,254,255,290,329,344,345,351,352,362,432,463,481,489,516,557,558

Conclusion

Thank you again for downloading this book!

I hope you enjoyed reading about my book!

If you enjoyed this book, please take the time to share your thoughts and post a review on Amazon. It'd be greatly appreciated!

Write me an honest review about the book – I truly value your opinion and thoughts and I will incorporate them into my next book, which is already underway.

Thank you!

If you have any questions, **feel free to contact at:** author@pennsylvaniarecipes.com

Mary Grace

pennsylvaniarecipes.com

Made in United States
Troutdale, OR
11/19/2024